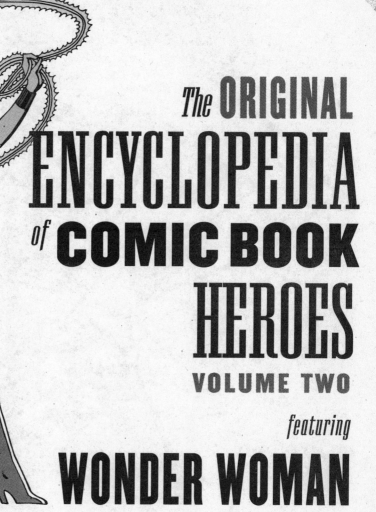

The *ORIGINAL*
ENCYCLOPEDIA
of COMIC BOOK
HEROES
VOLUME TWO

featuring

WONDER WOMAN

The ORIGINAL ENCYCLOPEDIA of COMIC BOOK HEROES

VOLUME TWO

featuring

WONDER WOMAN

by **Michael L. Fleisher**

assisted by Janet E. Lincoln

**WONDER WOMAN created by
William Moulton Marston**

To **PREAM**

DAN DIDIO Senior VP-Executive Editor BOB HARRAS Editor-collected edition ROBBIN BROSTERMAN Senior Art Director
PAUL LEVITZ President & Publisher GEORG BREWER VP-Design & DC Direct Creative RICHARD BRUNING Senior VP-Creative Director
PATRICK CALDON Executive VP-Finance & Operations CHRIS CARAMALIS VP-Finance JOHN CUNNINGHAM VP-Marketing
TERRI CUNNINGHAM VP-Managing Editor ALISON GILL VP-Manufacturing HANK KANALZ VP-General Manager, WildStorm
JIM LEE Editorial Director-WildStorm PAULA LOWITT Senior VP-Business & Legal Affairs
MARYELLEN MCLAUGHLIN VP-Advertising & Custom Publishing JOHN NEE VP-Business Development
GREGORY NOVECK Senior VP-Creative Affairs SUE POHJA VP-Book Trade Sales CHERYL RUBIN Senior VP-Brand Management
JEFF TROJAN VP-Business Development, DC Direct BOB WAYNE VP-Sales

THE ORIGINAL ENCYCLOPEDIA OF COMIC BOOK HEROES Volume Two—Featuring WONDER WOMAN
Published by DC Comics. Cover, introduction and compilation © 2007 DC Comics. All Rights Reserved.
Originally published as The Encyclopedia of Comic Book Heroes. Volume Two—Wonder Woman.
Copyright © 1976 Michael L. Fleisher. All Rights Reserved. All illustrations copyright © DC Comics.
All characters, their distinctive likenesses and related elements featured in this publication are trademarks of DC Comics.
The stories, characters and incidents featured in this publication are entirely fictional. DC Comics does not read
or accept unsolicited submissions of ideas, stories or artwork.

DC Comics, 1700 Broadway, New York, NY 10019 A Warner Bros. Entertainment Company.
Printed in Canada. First Printing. ISBN: 1-4012-1365-0 ISBN 13: 978-1-4012-1365-7

INTRODUCTION

THIRTY-EIGHT YEARS HAVE PASSED since that historic day in 1969 when Gerda Gattel, DC Comics' dedicated archivist and librarian, ushered me and my research assistant, Janet Lincoln, into the medium-sized, one-room library, lined with floor-to-ceiling bookshelves, that served as the repository for bound volumes of the company's carefully preserved back issues, thousands upon thousands of them—two copies each of every single DC comic book ever published.

Janet and I spent five years in that library, taking painstakingly detailed notes on every single Wonder Woman comic book story produced in the character's first twenty-seven years of publication — from the Alluring Amazon's debut in *All-Star Comics* No. 8, in December 1941-January 1942, to a January-February 1969 story in *Wonder Woman* No. 180, in which Diana Prince, having renounced and relinquished her Amazon powers, invades what she suspects to be the lair of the treacherous Doctor Cyber and ends up cradling the dying Steve Trevor in her arms.

The end result of our efforts was *The Encyclopedia of Comic Book Heroes Vol 2: Wonder Woman,* which was published by Collier Books, a division of Macmillan Publishing Co., Inc., in 1976.

As all of us who haven't spent our lives huddling in caves now know, of course, Wonder Woman's comic book stock has skyrocketed over the course of the last 31 years. Whereas, in the mid-1970s you could have purchased a mint-condition *All-Star Comics* No. 8 for a paltry $150 or so, today you'd have to pony up about $44,000 for a mint-condition copy—although a cheapie in merely very fine condition can be had for a bargain-basement $32,500 (better buy several while supplies last)!

I wish I could report that copies of this Wonder Woman encyclopedia have appreciated in value that much in the past 31 years. They haven't. But they have become a lot scarcer and pricier than they used to be, with brand-new copies long since unavailable and used copies going for as high as $190 a pop on Amazon.com, fueled by ecstatically positive reader reviews in the 93% to 100% range. Let's face it! Even if you were as lovely as Aphrodite, as wise as Athena, with the speed of Mercury and the strength of Hercules, you'd still have to put your magic lasso and bracelets of submission up for sale on eBay to afford one!

But—whew!—not anymore! The spankin' new DC Comics collectors' reprint edition you've just purchased has set you back a mere fraction of that—which is cause for celebration, don't you think, fellow Maid from Paradise Isle fans?

MICHAEL L. FLEISHER, September 2007

PREFACE

The Encyclopedia of Comic Book Heroes began as something of a lark, and ended as a labor of love.

In early 1969, I was working as a writer/editor for the Encyclopaedia Britannica, writing entries for an encyclopedia that the company intended to market overseas. One afternoon, as a humorous way of relieving the office tedium, one of the other writers composed a short biography of Clark Kent written in the same stuffy, pedantic style that characterized the biographies of real people in the encyclopedia we were working on. "KENT, CLARK," it began. "United States journalist who is secretly Superman. . . ."

As the bogus entry made its way around the room, the editorial office exploded with laughter. People laughed because, by using a serious, pseudo-scholarly style in connection with subject matter generally regarded as frivolous, the author had successfully satirized the pomposity of our encyclopedia.

But I saw the Clark Kent entry in a different light. Already keenly interested in popular culture, I saw it as treating the comic book mythos as other, more "respectable" bodies of mythic literature have traditionally been treated, i.e., as a serious intellectual subject. I also saw that entry as a means of escape from my deadly dull job at the Britannica.

"Hey! This is a terrific idea," I exclaimed aloud in the midst of the merriment. "Somebody should do a whole book of these."

That idea seemed so ridiculous seven years ago that everyone started laughing all over again, but I was already out of the room, down the corridor, slamming that Clark Kent article onto the office copy machine, beginning to dream up the thousands of other articles I would write to go along with it.

I should say here and now that I was neither a comic book fan nor a comic book collector. I had not so much as glanced sideways at a comic book since the wise old age of fourteen, when, in what seemed at the time a decision born of maturity and sound judgment, I had sold my entire collection to a junk lady on Third Avenue for a penny a magazine.

Nevertheless, that night in 1969, using the xeroxed Clark Kent article as my inspiration and the classic comic book stories reprinted in Jules Feiffer's The Great Comic Book Heroes as source material, I hammered out a half dozen sample entries and a two-page proposal for a one-volume encyclopedia of the comics. The following afternoon, I showed it all to an acquaintance in publishing, and within four hours he had called me on the telephone to say that his people loved the idea and that we had ourselves a deal.

Only then, after the commitment to write the book had actually been made, did I even begin to ponder the problem of how I was going to gain access to the many old comics that would be necessary to my research. Fortunately for me, the major comic book publishers were all willing to give me access to their extensive files of back issues. Later, a network of fans and collectors would help me acquire the various issues published by companies now defunct.

So it is that, one morning in March 1969, I walked into the offices of National Periodical Publications, Inc., publishers of DC Comics, and was introduced to Gerda Gattel, then National's librarian, now retired. Her ring of keys jangling, Mrs. Gattel led me down a carpeted executive corridor to the locked door of the DC Comics Library. She knew that I intended to write a serious reference guide to the literature of the great comic book heroes, and she was proud that her precious library was at last to be used for serious research, rather than merely by client businessmen seeking out action pictures of super-heroes to laminate onto T-shirts and beach blankets.

As she swung open the library door and flicked on the light, I remember that I gasped a little. The library was only a medium-sized room, but its walls were lined with floor-to-ceiling bookshelves packed with neatly bound volumes of back-issue comic books, thousands upon thousands of them, two copies each of every single comic book National Periodicals had ever published. I had never imagined there would be so many.

Mrs. Gattel noticed my surprise, and her eyes twinkled with the slightly mischievous pleasure of a fabulously wealthy connoisseur showing an amazed visitor through the exquisitely stocked wine cellar. "You said you wanted to study all the heroes," she smiled benignly, taking in the entire room with a sweeping gesture of her arm. "We have dozens of them. Where would you like to begin?"

I began with Batman, whose exploits are chronicled in Volume 1 of this encyclopedia, and after Batman I went on to Wonder Woman, transported, despite my adulthood and education, into an eerily garish world of magic and enchantment which I thought I had left behind forever at age fourteen.

Few fictional characters of any kind have enjoyed the kind of hold over their readers that the great heroes and heroines of comic books have exerted for nearly four decades. Their adventures are read by millions of young people in every state of the United States and in dozens of foreign countries. And among the heroines, Wonder Woman is without peer. Only two other characters in the history of comic books — Batman and Superman — have been published continuously for so long a period. More people have thrilled to the exploits of Wonder Woman than have ever heard of Juliet or seen a play by Shakespeare. She is probably the most famous fighting heroine since Joan of Arc.

Yet the adventures of Wonder Woman, and the vast popular literature of which they are a part, are already all but lost to us. Destroyed on a massive scale during the paper drives of the 1940s — "Save your scrap to beat the Jap!" admonished one of the popular patriotic slogans appearing in the margins of many comics — and hysterically assailed during the 1950s as a root cause of juvenile delinquency, comic books have been almost universally derided as trash by adults and cherished only by their children.

In the entire world, not one library, university, or public or private institution of any kind has taken the trouble to acquire and preserve a complete set of Wonder Woman's adventures for posterity. Nowhere in the world is there a single research facility where the complete adventures of even one major comic book hero or heroine have been safely preserved and made available for study. Reasonable people may debate the value of the comics as art or literature, but no one can deny that they constitute the most widely read body of children's literature in the history of the world. Perhaps one day, there will be sufficient serious interest in the comics to warrant their widespread distribution on microfilm to libraries and universities, but as of this writing that day seems a long way off.

The writing of this volume required that Janet Lincoln and I have access to a complete file of Wonder Woman's adventures. Such a file is available in only one place, the corporate library at National Periodical Publications, Inc., and it has been preserved there, along with complete files of the adventures of National's other comic book characters, partially through the foresight of the company's management, but mainly through the efforts of one determined woman.

At the time this project began, Gerda Gattel had been the guardian of the DC Comics archives for twelve years, and involved in comics for more than twenty. During the long years when the comics were regarded as garbage even by most of their creators, when comic books and comic book artwork were routinely destroyed and discarded by their publishers to eliminate the expense of storing them, she fought, and agitated, and cajoled to be allowed to maintain a real library at National, to be provided with bookshelves and storage space, and to be permitted to take occasional time off from her full-time job as the company proofreader in order to keep and maintain the library on her own.

Janet Lincoln and I spent seven full years working on *The Encyclopedia of Comic Book Heroes*. In that time, we examined more than 10,000 comic book stories and filled approximately 20,000 5" x 8" index cards with detailed notes on what we had read.

As the years passed, my original one-volume project expanded to encompass eight volumes, consuming in the process thirty-one reams of typing paper and producing, in the end, a completed typewritten manuscript of more than two million words. As the project grew in scope, my original publisher lost interest and eventually withdrew, and I am deeply grateful that the Macmillan Publishing Company has taken an interest in what, from a commercial standpoint, can only be regarded as a costly and risky project.

The *Wonder Woman* encyclopedia that you hold in your hands is the second volume of the eight-volume "labor of love" that I spoke of in my opening sentence. Other encyclopedias dealing with literary material, such as encyclopedias of Greek mythology or English literature, are able to refer their readers to the literature itself, but, with the exception of the occasional Wonder Woman stories reprinted in hardcover volumes, or the Wonder Woman comics still surviving in valuable private collections — a copy of All Star Comics No. 8, for example, the first comic book in which Wonder Woman ever appeared, currently brings a price of upwards of $150 on the collectors' market — the stories referred to in this volume are not available for examination.

For that reason, the material dealt with in this book has been covered in excruciating detail, retaining generous portions of the original dialogue and textual narrative and employing a style designed to present the material clearly while evoking what Jules Feiffer has termed the "florid preliteracy" of the comics.

As you browse through the pages of this volume, renewing your acquaintance with such diabolical masters and mistresses of villainy as the Cheetah, Dr. Psycho, and the Duke of Deception — and perhaps meeting for the first time such crafty lesser lights as the Snow Man (". . . the bravest men quiver at the mere mention of the insidious villain's name, fearing his brutality") — I hope you too find yourself transported into that world of magic and enchantment I spoke of earlier. And whether you're a serious student of sociology or popular culture — or just a stone comics fanatic with the smell of four-color ink in your nostrils and bits of cheap pulp paper floating like flotsam in your blood — I hope you have a real good time there.

MICHAEL L. FLEISHER

New York City, 1976

ACKNOWLEDGMENTS

The author would like to extend his heartfelt thanks to the management and staff of National Periodical Publications, Inc., publishers of DC Comics, without whose generous cooperation this volume could not have been written. In particular, the author would like to thank:

Carmine Infantino, Publisher, for generously extending the hospitality of his organization to the author and his assistant throughout the seven-year-long period during which *The Encyclopedia of Comic Book Heroes* was being researched and written.

Sol Harrison, Vice President-Director of Operations, for his generous advice, assistance, and support throughout the project, particularly in connection with the accumulation and reproduction of illustrative material.

Bernard Kashdan, Vice President-Business Manager, for generously granting permission for the use of the comic book illustrations reproduced in this volume.

Gerda Gattel, Librarian (ret.), whose devotion to the DC Comics Library, for sixteen years, made possible the research on which this encyclopedia is based. For this devotion, and for many personal kindnesses extended to the author and his assistant during the period of their research, the author would like to extend his special thanks.

Joe Kubert, Editor, for his advice and encouragement.

Joe Orlando, Editor, for his advice and encouragement, and for his generosity in sharing many insights born of a lifetime in comics.

Denny O'Neil, Editor, for his advice and encouragement.

Julius Schwartz, Editor, for generously sharing his many insights and anecdotes.

E. Nelson Bridwell, Associate Editor, for sharing with the author the broad reach of his knowledge.

Milton Snapinn, Head, Export Department, for his assistance in assembling the back-issue negatives used to produce many of the illustrations in this volume.

Lois Barker, Export Department, for her ready, affectionate wit, and for her assistance in assembling the back-issue negatives used to produce many of the illustrations in this volume.

Jack Adler, Production Manager, for generously using his technical expertise to review the illustrations in this volume to ensure their suitability for reproduction.

Wayne Seelal, Photographer, for giving generously of his time and technical knowhow to help photograph the comic book illustrations reproduced in this volume.

Joe Letterese, Debra Ulrich, and Morris Waldinger, of the Production Department, for advising the author in connection with the retouching of the comic book illustrations reproduced in this volume.

The author would also like to extend his thanks to the following individuals, each of whom, in one way or another, made a significant contribution toward the preparation of this volume:

Neal Adams, Dick Giordano, and Frank McLaughlin, artists, and Mike Nolan, comic book fan, collector, and compiler of comic book indexes, for their encouragement and support, and for their help in putting the author in contact with other individuals who have made contributions toward the preparation of this volume.

Murphy Anderson, artist, for his encouragement and support, for giving generously of his time to retouch some of the comic book illustrations reproduced in this volume, and for his generous loan of rare comic books from his personal collection.

Jerry and Jean Bails, scholars, comic book collectors, and publishers of *The Who's Who of American Comic Books* and other publications; Otto Binder, writer; and Mike Friedrich, writer and comic book publisher, for their encouragement and support.

Linda Brown, for her generous help in preparing for publication many of the comic book illustrations reproduced in this volume.

Carol Fein, formerly secretary to the publisher of National Periodical Publications, Inc., for the numerous kindnesses extended to the author and his assistant during the period of their research.

Mark Hanerfeld, comic book collector and former publisher of *The Comic Reader;* Don and Margaret Thompson, authors, comic book collectors, and publishers of *Newfangles* and other publications; and Marvin Wolfman, Editor, Magazine Management Company, Inc., Marvel Comics Group, for their encouragement and support, and for their generous loan of rare comic books from their personal collections.

Earl Hokens, photographer, for giving generously of his time and technical knowhow to help photograph the comic book illustrations reproduced in this volume.

Mrs. Everett Larson, Acting Head, Reference Section, the Library of Congress, for giving unstintingly of her time to help the author and his assistant locate rare comic books in the library's archives.

Alan Light, publisher of *The Buyer's Guide for Comic Fandom* and other publications, for generously making space in *The Buyer's Guide* available to the author to help him in locating the owners of rare comic book materials necessary to his research.

Robert Porfirio, Department of American Studies, California State University, Fullerton, for sharing with the author the broad reach of his knowledge.

Byron Preiss, Byron Preiss Visual Publications, Inc., for his help in acquiring space in comic book fan publications in order to help the author locate owners of rare comic book materials.

Phil Seuling, chairman of the New York Comic Art Convention and proprietor of Phil Seuling's Comic Sales, for his generous loan of rare comic books from his personal collection and inventory.

Roy Thomas, Editor, Magazine Management Company, Inc., Marvel Comics Group, and Jean Thomas, for their advice, encouragement, and numerous personal kindnesses, including the generous loan of rare comic books from their personal collection.

Glynis Wein, Head, Coloring Department, Magazine Management Company, Inc., Marvel Comics Group, for advising the author in connection with the retouching of the comic book illustrations reproduced in this volume.

Len Wein, Editor, Magazine Management Company, Inc., Marvel Comics Group, and Dagne Crowley, for their generous loan of rare comic books from their personal collections.

Marc Weinberger, for his friendship, encouragement, advice, and unstinting support.

In addition, the author would like to acknowledge all of the gifted men and women who, by their work in the comics, have enriched the lives of all of us.

HOW TO USE THIS BOOK

The Encyclopedia of Comic Book Heroes: Volume 2 — Wonder Woman is a comprehensive encyclopedic chronicle of the comic book adventures of Wonder Woman for the first twenty-seven years of her ongoing career. Comprised of approximately 510 entries — ranging in length from a few short lines to more than fifty printed pages, and assembled in a convenient A-Z format — it contains detailed accounts of more than 600 separate adventures. In addition, this volume contains 180 illustrations culled directly from the comics, including pictures of Wonder Woman, her friends, adversaries, and Amazon equipment, as well as scenes of Paradise Island, its pantheon of deities, and other aspects of Amazon life and culture.

The entries in this volume are based on detailed notes taken by the author and his assistant on each of the comic books containing Wonder Woman's adventures. The entries contain a wealth of detail on the plot of each adventure, the powers and equipment employed by Wonder Woman and her adversaries, the major themes and relationships that emerge from Wonder Woman's collected adventures, and on every other topic of interest to followers of Wonder Woman. No reference work can serve as a substitute for its subject, but a conscientious effort has been made to organize and record within this volume data pertaining to every aspect of Wonder Woman's life and adventures.

In studying the comic books containing Wonder Woman's adventures and in writing the entries in this encyclopedia, the author and his assistant made use of no outside sources whatever. Only the direct, firsthand evidence of the comic books themselves was used. Accordingly, The Encyclopedia of Comic Book Heroes: Volume 2 — Wonder Woman is a detailed reference guide only to Wonder Woman's comic book adventures. It contains no information concerning either the literary and artistic genesis of the character or the various writers and artists who have, since 1941, been creatively responsible for shaping her destiny.

Definitions:

Throughout this encyclopedia, the word "text" is used to designate a single comic book story, and the word "texts" is used to designate two or more comic book stories, or, occasionally, as a synonym for "chronicles." The word "chronicles" is used to designate all of the many texts which, taken together, comprise the Wonder Woman legend. The word "chroniclers" is used to designate the artists and writers who have been collectively responsible for "recording" Wonder Woman's adventures for posterity.

In comic books, the thoughts and dialogue of the characters appear printed inside roughly ovular shapes called "word balloons." Other writing, usually narrative and frequently in the third person, appears at the opening of each story and above or below some of the pictures. Throughout this encyclopedia, these fragments of narrative writing, known as captions, are referred to as the "narrative text" or "textual narrative."

Treatment of Events:

In the writing of this encyclopedia, certain conventions were employed. Wonder Woman and all the other characters appearing in the chronicles were treated as though they were real people, and the adventures were treated as though they were actual historical events. The comic books containing the accounts of Wonder Woman's exploits were studied as though they were historical documents chronicling the lives and adventures of actual persons.

The legend of Wonder Woman is elaborate and complex. Individual comic book sources sometimes differ in recounting a given set of events, and sources can often be found to support conflicting sets of "facts." In cases where comic book sources were discrepant with regard to particular details of Wonder Woman's life and career, an effort was made to reconcile the discrepancies in light of the total data available. A fact attested to in several comic books was accorded more weight than a contradictory fact stated in only one comic book. A statement made in a comic book concerning a contemporary event in Wonder Woman's life was accorded more weight than a contradictory statement concerning that same event made years later in the form of a recollection or flashback. Wherever strong support exists in the texts for opposing sets of facts, the evidence for both is examined in detail in this encyclopedia.

Dating:

The events described in any given comic book were assumed to have taken place on the issue date of that comic book, except in those cases where the events were clearly described as past events or where internal textual evidence argued persuasively for a different dating, such as in the case of an adventure taking place at Christmastime in an issue dated February.

Most comic books bear issue dates of either a single month or a single season. In the case of a comic book issued on a bimonthly basis, the issue is given a bimonthly dating, e.g., November–December 1945. When events are described in the encyclopedia as having occurred in a two-month period, e.g., in November–December 1945, it is because those events were recorded in a bimonthly comic book.

When an event is described as having taken place "in" a given month or season, it means that the event is described in the texts as taking place in the present, i.e., during the period of the issue date. When an event is described as having taken place "by" a particular month or season, it means that the event is described in the texts as having taken place in the past, prior to the period of the issue date.

If, for example, the Cheetah is described as escaping from Transformation Island, the Amazon prison facility, *in* Summer 1945, it means that the Cheetah is shown or described as escaping from Transformation Island in a comic book dated Summer 1945. If, on the other hand, the Cheetah is described as having escaped from Transformation Island *by* Summer 1945, it means that the Cheetah is shown or described, in a comic book dated Summer 1945, as having escaped from Transformation Island sometime in the recent past.

Characters with Dual Identities:

In the case of characters with dual identities — e.g., Diana Prince and Wonder Woman, or Priscilla Rich and the Cheetah — actions and quotations are attributed in this encyclopedia to one identity or the other depending on which role the character is playing at the time he or she performs the action being described or recites the speech being quoted. Wonder Woman dressed in her heroine's costume is referred to as Wonder Woman. Wonder Woman dressed in her everyday attire is referred to as Diana Prince. Similarly, the Cheetah dressed in her Cheetah costume is referred to as the Cheetah. The Cheetah dressed in her everyday attire is referred to as Priscilla Rich.

The distinction is important. In the world of the chronicles, the fact that Diana Prince is Wonder Woman is a closely guarded secret. To their contemporaries, the U.S. Army nurse-turned-intelligence operative and the super-heroine are two different persons. Accordingly, they are often referred to in this encyclopedia as though they were two different people.

Entries:

The vast majority of the entries in this volume are articles about persons, but there are also numerous entries on gods and goddesses, extraterrestrial and extradimensional aliens, mythical lands, distant planets and alien dimensions, aliases, and a host of other subjects.

At approximately 45,000 words, the article on Wonder Woman is the longest and most exhaustive entry in the entire encyclopedia. It contains a complete account of Wonder Woman's origin, an exhaustive inventory of her Amazon powers and equipment, a complete month-by-month chronology of the first twenty-seven years of her crime-fighting career, a comprehensive analysis of the major themes and relationships of the chronicles, and many other features.

As such, the Wonder Woman entry is the hub of this encyclopedia. By reading the month-by-month chronology (*see* WONDER WOMAN [section I 2, Developments]) and then following up the various cross-references, the reader will eventually come upon every entry in this volume. Any character appearing in two or more Wonder Woman stories has automatically been accorded an entry of his own, as have all the famous legendary and historical personages — men and women such as Julius Gaius Caesar, King Arthur, Leonardo da Vinci, and Queen Boadicea — whom Wonder Woman has encountered in the course of her numerous journeys into the past.

Characters appearing in only one Wonder Woman story have sometimes been accorded entries of their own and sometimes not, depending on their importance within the single story in which they appear, their significance within the overall Wonder Woman legend, and other factors.

In general, one character from each story — usually the villain, but not always — has been chosen to serve as the vehicle for summarizing the plot of the story. The roles played by such subsidiary characters as Etta Candy and the Holliday Girls are summarized in their individual entries.

Titles:

The titles of individuals — e.g., Dr., Prof., Dean, Count — are given in parentheses in the entry title after the individual's name, as indicated in the following examples:

PSYCHO (Dr.)
CHEMICO (Prof.)
MERRILY, MEG (Dean)
GASTON (Count)

Whether a title is spelled out (e.g., Doctor) or abbreviated (e.g., Dr.) depends on which form is employed most often in the actual text or texts in which the character appears.

In cases where a title reflects actual rank or status, or academic or professional standing, the entries have been inserted in alphabetical order in the encyclopedia under the last name of the individual, as in the four examples listed above.

Often, however, particularly in the case of villains, what would be a title in the case of an ordinary person is, in comic books, actually part of an individual's name. Here are two examples:

DOCTOR POISON
MASTER DE STROYER

In cases such as these, the entries have been inserted in alphabetical order in the encyclopedia under the individual's name *including* the title, as in the two examples listed above.

Doctor Poison is not referrred to as Doctor, after all, because she is a doctor of philosophy or a doctor of medicine. Doctor Poison is merely a pseudonym employed by Princess Maru.

Similarly, in the case of Master De Stroyer, Master is not a title, but part of the villain's name.

Quotations:

The Encyclopedia of Comic Book Heroes: Volume 2 — Wonder Woman contains numerous quotations from the comic book literature, some of them quite lengthy. With rare exceptions, the words in comic books are all lettered by hand, and all the lettering is done in capitals. Hand lettering makes possible a wide variety of letter sizes and styles not readily duplicated in mechanically set type. Because all-capital lettering is jarring and confusing outside the comic book context, the quotations in this volume have all been translated into the more familiar form of small letters and capitals. Great care has been taken, however, and a wide range of type styles employed, to ensure capturing the flavor of the original hand-lettering as well as the essence and spirit of the comic book style. In every case, the quotations in this volume were carefully transcribed by hand from the original comic books and then set into type in a manner calculated to re-create as closely as possible the style of the original.

Cross-References:

Cross-references are indicated by capitals and small capitals, as in the following example:

VILLAINY INCORPORATED. Eight villainesses, led by the sadistic Saturnian slave driver EVILESS, who escape from TRANSFORMATION ISLAND in March–April 1948 and set out to "conquer the Amazons on Paradise Island and use it for a base to raid Earth countries." Besides Eviless, the group includes the CHEETAH, QUEEN CLEA, DOCTOR POISON, GIGANTA, HYPNOTA THE GREAT, the SNOW MAN, and ZARA. Villainy Incorporated is ultimately defeated by WONDER WOMAN

The cross-references in the above example, from the first paragraph of the entry on Villainy Incorporated, indicate the existence of separate articles elsewhere in the encyclopedia, on Eviless, Transformation Island, the Cheetah, Queen Clea, Doctor Poison, Giganta, Hypnota the Great, the Snow Man, Zara, and of course Wonder Woman. Since the duplication of information in the various articles of this encyclopedia has been kept to a minimum, the articles indicated by the cross-references invariably contain new information not available in the entry in which the cross-reference appears.

Textual References:

In order to relate the innumerable statements and quotations in this encyclopedia to their precise sources in the chronicles, a system of textual references was devised relating every single fact in this volume to its source in the collected comic book adventures of Wonder Woman.

A textual reference consists of the title of a comic book series (e.g., Comic Cavalcade, Sensation Comics, Wonder Woman); the issue number of a particular comic book in that series and the story number of the specific story being cited; the issue date, as stated on the comic book's indicia; the title of the story being cited, if it has a title; and, in cases where a story has been divided into parts or chapters, the titles of the individual parts or chapters where part or chapter titles exist.

For a complete listing of the abbreviations used in the textual references, consult the Table of Abbreviations at the end of this essay.

Textual references appear in the encyclopedia in parentheses, directly following the fact or group of facts which they are intended to substantiate. The shorter entries in the encyclopedia generally contain only one textual reference apiece, indicating that all of the information in any one such entry derives from a single textual source. In the case of entries containing two or more textual references, however, each textual reference applies to the information in that article following the textual reference that directly precedes it.

The following is a typical textual reference:

(WW No. 70/2, Nov '54: "The Invisible Trail!")

The textual reference given above informs the reader that whatever quotation(s) or statement(s) preceded the reference can be found or substantiated in the Wonder Woman comic book series; issue number 70; the second Wonder Woman story in the issue; issue date November 1954; story title "The Invisible Trail!"

Here is another example:

(WW No. 44, Nov/Dec '50: "The Monarch of the Sargasso Sea!" chs. I–III — no title; "Wonder Woman's Decision"; "The Final Battle of the Sargasso Sea")

The textual reference given above informs the reader that whatever quotation(s) or statement(s) preceded the reference can be found or substantiated in the Wonder Woman comic book series; issue number 44; the only story in the issue featuring Wonder Woman (indicated by the lack of story number); issue date November-December 1950; story title "The Monarch of the Sargasso Sea!"; the story is divided into three separate chapters, the first of which has no title, the second of which is entitled "Wonder Woman's Decision," and the third of which is entitled "The Final Battle of the Sargasso Sea."

In cases where a story lacks an overall title, the textual reference simply appears without one, as in the following examples:

(WW No. 1/3, Sum '42)
(WW No. 15, Win '45: chs. 1–3 — "The First Battle of Neptunia"; "The Masters of the Water"; "In the Killer's Cage")

In the cases of textual references pertaining to comic books containing more than one Wonder Woman story, a story number has been inserted in each textual reference — directly following the issue number and separated from it by a slash mark — to indicate the precise position in the comic book of the story being referred to.

This system of story numbering applies only to fully illustrated Wonder Woman stories. It does not apply to stories without illustrations or to those featuring the logo of a major character other than Wonder Woman. Where a textual reference refers to a comic book containing only one Wonder Woman story, a story number would be

superfluous and has therefore not been included.

A typical issue in the Sensation Comics series, for example, contains one story about Wonder Woman followed by one or more stories featuring other heroes or heroines. Textual references pertaining to comic books in the Sensation Comics series therefore contain no story number, for no issue of Sensation Comics has ever contained more than one story about Wonder Woman. Here is a typical textual reference to a comic book in the Sensation Comics series:

(Sen No. 39, Mar '45: "In the Clutches of Nero")

Wherever a textual reference fails to contain a story number, the comic book which it cites may be understood to contain only one Wonder Woman story.

In the case of the Wonder Woman series, however, a single issue may contain as many as four illustrated Wonder Woman stories. Wonder Woman No. 3, for example, contains four illustrated Wonder Woman stories. They are therefore numbered consecutively from one to four, from the front of the comic book to the back. Here is a textual reference to one of the four Wonder Woman stories in Wonder Woman No. 3:

(WW No. 3/4, Feb/Mar '43: "Ordeal of Fire!")

This textual reference informs the reader that whatever quotation(s) or statement(s) preceded the reference can be found or substantiated in the Wonder Woman comic book series; issue number 3; the fourth Wonder Woman story in the issue; issue date February–March 1943; story title "Ordeal of Fire!"

Frequently, a comic book in the Wonder Woman series contains three or four consecutive stories which, taken together, form one long story. In cases where a statement in the encyclopedia refers to the entire sequence of stories in such a comic book, and not just to any one of them, a special type of textual reference has been employed, as in the following example:

(WW No. 11/1–3, Win '44: "The Slaves of the Evil Eye"; "The Unseen Menace"; "The Slave Smugglers")

This textual reference informs the reader that whatever statement(s) preceded the reference can be substantiated in the Wonder Woman comic book series; issue number 11; the entire sequence of stories one through three, inclusive; issue date

Winter 1944; story titles "The Slaves of the Evil Eye," "The Unseen Menace," and "The Slave Smugglers."

Whenever information normally included in a textual reference is stated beforehand in the body of an entry, that information is omitted from the textual reference, as in the following two examples:

The Crimson Centipede is defeated by Wonder Woman in April 1967 (WW No. 169/1: "Wonder Woman Battles the Crimson Centipede!").

Sensation Comics No. 81 describes Wonder Woman as a "disciple of peace and love" (Sep '48: "When Treachery Wore a Green Shirt!").

The following example, the first paragraph of the entry on Dr. Psycho, illustrates the extensive use of textual references in the major entries of the encyclopedia:

PSYCHO (Dr.). A "psychopathic madman" (WW No. 18/3, Jul/Aug '46: "Ectoplasmic Death") whose all-consuming passion is "to enslave the women of the world" (WW No. 18/2, Jul/Aug '46: "The Drugged WAC"). A "noted occultist" who uses "ectoplasmic energy" drawn from the spirit world to achieve his evil ends, Dr. Psycho is the husband of MARVA PSYCHO (WW No. 5/1, Jun/Jul '43: "Battle for Womanhood") and the brother of the villainous KING IRONSIDES (CC No. 23, Oct/Nov '47: "Siege of the Iron Giants").

Occasionally, a textual reference will be followed, within the parentheses, by the words "and others," as in the following example:

(Sen No. 68, Aug '47: "Secret of the Menacing Octopus!"; and others)

These added words indicate that evidence to substantiate whatever statement(s) preceded the reference can be found in the specific comic book issue cited, in this case Sensation Comics No. 68, and in at least two other comic books as well. When such a textual reference follows a direct quotation, it means that the quotation itself was taken from the comic book issue cited, but that data supporting the substance of the quotation is available in at least two other Wonder Woman texts as well.

Using this Encyclopedia:

If you already have in mind the title of an entry you wish to look up, simply turn to that entry in the appropriate alphabetical listing. If more than one listing is possible and you are uncertain which listing has been employed — if you are uncertain, for example, whether Doctor Cyber has been listed under Doctor Cyber or under Cyber (Doctor) — it is suggested that you try both.

If you have no specific entry title in mind but would like to consult a month-by-month chronology of Wonder Woman's crime-fighting career, such a chronology is available in the Wonder Woman article (see WONDER WOMAN [section I 2, Developments]).

Similarly, if you would like to learn what Wonder Woman was doing during a particular time period — during March–April 1947, for example — merely consult the career chronology for that particular time period and follow the cross-references to the various articles dealing with Wonder Woman's adventures during the time period that interests you. Here is what the career chronology has to say about Wonder Woman's activities in March–April 1947:

In March–April 1947 Wonder Woman battles "COSMETIC" KOSMET (WW No. 22/1: "The Color Thief"), matches wits with DUKE MEPHISTO SATURNO (WW No. 22/2: "The Island of Evil"), and journeys to Venus to thwart the sinister machinations of GELL OSEY (WW No. 22/3: "Jealousy Visits the Winged Women of Venus!").

Separate entries may be found in this volume for all three of the names cross-referenced.

In Conclusion:

The Encyclopedia of Comic Book Heroes: Volume 2 — Wonder Woman has been designed for both the browser and the researcher, the casual fan and the serious collector. Great care has been taken to make it enjoyable as well as functional, entertaining as well as definitive. Whether you are engaged in scholarly research or reading for pleasure, writing a thesis or preparing a trivia quiz, The Encyclopedia of Comic Book Heroes: Volume 2 — Wonder Woman will provide you with the information you seek, and with many hours of pleasure as well.

ABBREVIATIONS

Titles of comic book series:

AS   *All Star Comics*
CC   *Comic Cavalcade*
Sen   *Sensation Comics*
WW   *Wonder Woman*

Months and seasons:

Jan   January
Feb   February
Mar   March
Apr   April
May   May
Jun   June
Jul   July

Aug   August
Sep   September
Oct   October
Nov   November
Dec   December

Spr   Spring
Sum   Summer
Fall   Fall
Win   Winter

Other abbreviations:

chs.   chapters
pts.   parts
No.   issue number

A

ACHILLES. The greatest, strongest, bravest, and most beautiful of the heroes of Greek mythology, and one of the most renowned heroes of all time. While he was an infant, his mother, the sea nymph Thetis, dipped him in the river Styx to render him invulnerable, but he remained vulnerable in that part of the heel by which she held him, the proverbial "Achilles heel." WONDER WOMAN fights and defeats Achilles during a time-journey to ancient AMAZONIA that she makes in Summer 1944 (WW No. 9/3). (*See* GIGANTA.)

AGENT X. An Axis spy, apparently a Caucasian female, who is in reality none other than COLONEL TOGO KU, "chief of Japanese spies in America," in disguise. At first, Agent X appears to be merely a cohort of the mysterious Dr. Cue, but WONDER WOMAN learns ultimately that Agent X, Dr. Cue, and Colonel Togo Ku are all one and the same person. Colonel Togo Ku is defeated by Wonder Woman in September 1942 (Sen No. 9). (*See* TOGO KU [COLONEL].)

AH-WA-NE. An American Indian "woodcarver and scientist [who] died one hundred and fifty years ago!" WONDER WOMAN journeys into the past to authenticate one of his totem poles in May–June 1951.

Museum curator Nora Lester is about to lose her job for insisting that a totem pole she recently purchased for the museum is the work of the famous Ah-Wa-Ne. The totem pole appears to commemorate the exploits of Wonder Woman, and since Ah-Wa-Ne died before Wonder Woman was born, the museum officials feel certain that the totem pole is inauthentic.

To solve the mystery and protect Nora Lester's reputation, Wonder Woman journeys into the past—accompanied by curator Lester and museum head Dane Benton—to the year 1775, where Wonder Woman and her two companions endure a series of harrowing frontier experiences and Wonder Woman performs numerous heroic feats. Ultimately, they come upon Ah-Wa-Ne executing a totem-pole memorial to these very feats, which explains how Wonder Woman's exploits came to be commemorated in a totem pole carved a century and a half before her birth (WW No. 47/2: "Mystery of the Indian Totem Pole").

AIR PIRATES. A gang of "ruthless female pi-

rates," led by the beautiful blond Nifty and her unnamed red-haired husband, who kidnap PROF. CHEMICO in November–December 1946 with the intention of torturing him into revealing the secret of "how to safely generate atomic power" (WW No. 20/1: "Terrors of the Air"). (*See* CHEMICO [PROF.].)

AKNATEN. An ancient pharaoh who ruled the land of Egypt "more than 4000 years ago," and who has survived into the 20th century by means of "rare spices." His attempts to "wipe out . . . modern civilization" with a deadly "aeropyramic gas" are thwarted by WONDER WOMAN in May–June 1947. Aknaten is not to be confused with Akhenaten (or Ikhnaton), the young pharaoh who ruled Egypt from 1379–1362 B.C.

In May–June 1947 PROF. CHEMICO—Holliday College's "brilliant chemist and authority on ancient Egyptian history"—is in Egypt, exploring the tomb of "King Aknaten, pharoah [sic] of Egypt more than 4000 years ago."

Suddenly, Prof. Chemico is seized by a strange, overpowering compulsion to leave Aknaten's tomb and return to his laboratory to begin work on a deadly "aeropyramic gas" which, if released in the Earth's atmosphere, would swiftly burn up all its oxygen, resulting in the immediate annihilation of all Earthly life.

Traveling to Egypt to investigate Prof. Chemico's mysterious disappearance, Wonder Woman and the HOLLIDAY GIRLS are soon taken captive by the supposedly long-dead pharaoh and dragged into the depths of his "subterrestrial temple."

"Thou art astounded that I, Aknaten, ancient Egyptian pharoah [sic] still live," intones the pharaoh. "But I and my slaves are immortalized by rare spices for as long as I **will** to live!"

Moments later, the pharaoh's monologue continues:

I, with the wisdom of the ages use this super-radio sending machine to project thought waves which hit the brains of modern scientists!

Thus I inspire them to invent deadly weapons capable of destroying modern civilization during its frequent wars. Even now my final and most deadly weapon, **aeropyramic gas,** is implanted in the brain of your Prof. Chemico!

Once the **aeropyramic** gas explosively contacts air,

1

it ignites and can **never** be extinguished! A continuous aeropyramic flame will encompass the world, consuming all the atmospheric oxygen.

When Wonder Woman asks Aknaten why he is unleashing his deadly aeropyramic gas upon the world, the pharaoh replies: "To wipe out your modern civilization and to restore my ancient Egyptian civilization to the world with **me** its ruler!"

With some eleventh-hour assistance from STEVE TREVOR, however, Wonder Woman turns the tables on Aknaten and his slaves, frees the Holliday Girls, and smashes the diabolical "super-radio sending machine" which is controlling the mind of Prof. Chemico and forcing him to work on the deadly aeropyramic gas. Rather than allow themselves to be captured, however, Aknaten and his slaves "weirdly dematerialize," vanishing into nothingness (WW No. 23/2: "The Vanishing Mummy!").

ALAIN (Prince). An 11th-century prince who is aided by WONDER WOMAN during one of her journeys into the past. In the year 1086, Wonder Woman rescues Prince Alain from the clutches of the evil Black Baron and restores him to his rightful place on the throne (WW No. 72/1, Feb '55: "S.O.S. from the Past!").

ALDEN, FAITH. A student at the HOLLIDAY COLLEGE FOR WOMEN who wanders into Paula's secret laboratory (see GUNTHER, PAULA VON [BARONESS]) and impetuously throws the switch which activates the Amazon "space transformer," only to find herself miraculously transported into the past, to the Puritan America of 1692. There, Faith is tried and sentenced to death for witchcraft, and when WONDER WOMAN, STEVE TREVOR, ETTA CANDY, and the HOLLIDAY GIRLS journey into the past to rescue her, they are similarly tried and sentenced for the crime of being "the witch's friends." Ultimately, however, Wonder Woman—aided by Steve Trevor—engineers their escape from the superstitious Puritans, and soon, through the magic of the space transformer, they are all safely back home in the 20th century (Sen No. 73, Jan '48: "The Witches' Trials").

ALPHA (Prof.). An Amazon scientist who lives and works on PARADISE ISLAND.

In April 1958 Prof. Alpha unveils her "SOS Carrier," a fantastic machine which "picks up the vibrations of people in extraordinary distress—anywhere in the world—and instantly transports you there!"

When the SOS Carrier's special distress alarm sounds, indicating that someone, somewhere, is in desperate trouble, WONDER WOMAN steps inside the Carrier's cabinetlike compartment, only to emerge moments later, through some malfun tioning of the apparatus, in the prehistoric pa where some cave people are being menaced by giant tyrannosaurus.

"Something's wrong with the **SOS** Carrier!" e claims Wonder Woman. "It responded to vibr tions of help **not** from people in the present—b from **these** cave people—thousands of years in th past!"

After taming the wild tyrannosaurus so that will no longer endanger the lives of the cave pe ple, Wonder Woman steps back inside the SO Carrier and returns to Prof. Alpha's laboratory the 20th century.

She has no sooner emerged from the Carrie however, than its distress alarm rings once mor This time, through another mechanical malfunc tion, the SOS Carrier transports Wonder Woma hundreds of years into the future, to a time whe Earth is being subjected to continual attacks b invaders from the planet JUPITER. The earthme have survived a recent Jovian attack by retreatin underground, but the invaders' super-scientifi weapons have caused nature on the surface of th planet to run amok: plants and insects, grow suddenly to many times their normal size, nov threaten the Earth's very existence.

Wonder Woman defeats the Jovian invaders then annihilates the gigantic mutant insects b leading them into the sea to drown. With her work in the future completed, Wonder Woman step back inside the SOS Carrier and returns to her own time.

The next alarm from the SOS Carrier carries Wonder Woman "to an **identical** world—but in **another** dimension—whose physical laws are entirely different" from those prevailing on Earth. Here, Wonder Woman defeats the villainous dictator Blunt, who has seized control of the country after forcibly ousting its democratically elected government. After imparting to the populace the courage it needs to revolt against Blunt and bring an end to his tyrannical rule, Wonder Woman returns to Paradise Island in Prof. Alpha's SOS Carrier just in time to thwart an invasion of the island by a Martian space armada (WW No. 97: "The Runaway Time Express!" pts. 1–3–"Stone Age Rodeo!"; "The Day Nature Ran Wild!"; "The Menace of Earth's Twin!"). (See also MARS [THE PLANET].)

In August 1958 Prof. Alpha unveils a new invention, the "X-Dimension machine," designed to "transport the user to a dimension beyond any yet known to us!" It is this invention which transports Wonder Woman to the strange world known as DIMENSION X (WW No. 100/1: "The Forest of Giants!" pts. 1–2–"The Challenge of Dimension X!"; "The Forest of Giants!").

ALTHEA (Princess). The lovely blond ruler of the SARGASSO SEA KINGDOM. Forced into servitude by the power-mad MASTER DE STROYER, Althea and her subjects are liberated in November–December 1950 through the heroic efforts of WONDER WOMAN (WW No. 44: "The Monarch of the Sargasso Sea!" chs. I–III–no title; "Wonder Woman's Decision"; "The Final Battle of the Sargasso Sea"). (*See* MASTER DE STROYER.)

Princess Althea

AMAZONIA. In the WONDER WOMAN chronicles, the "magnificent city" of ancient Greece which was the stronghold of the AMAZONS prior to their migration–under the guidance of the goddess APHRODITE–to a "promised haven of peace and protection" on PARADISE ISLAND (WW No. 1/1, Sum '42).

AMAZONIUM. A metal developed by the AMAZONS which is described as "the hardest metal known." WONDER WOMAN's bracelets of submission are fashioned from it (WW No. 52/1, Mar/Apr '52: "Her Majesty–Queen Wonder Woman!"; and others), and, according to some texts, her tiara is also (WW No. 53/3, May–Jun '52: "The Secret Treasure at Rainbow's End!"; and others). Some texts assert that the magic lasso is made of amazonium (WW No. 70/1, Nov '54: "The Volcano Maker!"; and others), but this is not correct: the magic lasso is fashioned from golden links of fine chain from QUEEN HIPPOLYTE's magic girdle (Sen No. 6, Jun '42; and others). According to Wonder Woman No. 125, Wonder Woman's Amazon plane is made of "elastic amazonium" (Oct '61: "Wonder Woman–Battle Prize!"), but this claim is disputed by Sensation Comics No. 45, which asserts that the Ama-

zon plane is fashioned from "amazsilikon" (Sep '45: "In the Enemy's Hands"). (*See* WONDER WOMAN [section C 2, the bracelets of submission; C 3, the magic lasso; C 4, the robot plane; and C 5, the tiara]; *see also* AMAZONS [section F 1, the magic girdle].)

AMAZONS. In Greek mythology, a race of female warriors who inhabited the northern coast of Asia Minor. They were ruled by a queen, and were rigorously schooled in the arts of hunting and warfare. Men were rigidly excluded from their civilization.

In the WONDER WOMAN chronicles, the Amazons are a race of immortal women–shaped by the hands of the goddess APHRODITE–who inhabit a secret island haven known as PARADISE ISLAND. As its name implies, Paradise Island is a worldly paradise, a "land of love and beauty" (CC No. 19, Feb/Mar '47: "The Battle for Eternal Youth") where "women rule supreme in harmony and happiness" (CC No. 1, Win '42: "The Mystery of the House of the Seven Gables"). It is, however, "a paradise for women only," a place "which no man may enter" (WW No. 1/1, Sum '42), for it is Aphrodite's law that if ever a man sets foot on Paradise Island, the Amazons must relinquish their priceless birthright of eternal life and everlasting happiness.

On Paradise Island, aloof from the hatreds and the antagonisms of the "man's world," the Amazons have constructed a mighty city "that for all the world seems to be born of ancient Greece" (AS No. 8, Dec/Jan '41–'42: "Introducing Wonder Woman"). Their patron goddesses are ATHENA, goddess of wisdom, and Aphrodite, goddess of love and beauty.

Queen Hippolyte and Wonder Woman, 1953

Paradise Island

The Amazons are ruled by QUEEN HIPPOLYTE, the mother of Princess Diana, the Amazon princess known to the world as Wonder Woman. Ancient Greek is the regularly spoken language, but the Amazons frequently speak English to accommodate female visitors from the outside world. Amazon dress is reminiscent of that of ancient Greece, but modern dress has made substantial inroads into the island by January 1959 (WW No. 103/1: "The Wonder Woman Album!"). On their wrists, Amazons wear heavy metal bracelets which serve to symbolize their eternal submission to the goddess Aphrodite and as reminders of their ancient enslavement at the hands of HERCULES, and therefore of the folly of submitting to male domination. (*See also* WONDER WOMAN [section C 2, the bracelets of submission].)

It is this complex Amazon culture which has produced the mighty Wonder Woman. In order to make the accumulated data concerning the Amazons as accessible as possible, this article has been divided into the following sections:

A. History
B. Aphrodite's Law
C. The Amazon Code
D. Amazon training
E. Amazon culture
   1. Sports
   2. Festivals and holidays
   3. Transportation
   4. Communication
F. Amazon magic
   1. The magic girdle
   2. The magic sphere
   3. The magic Venus girdles
G. Amazon science

A. History. Virtually all of that which has been preserved concerning the history of the Amazons is recorded in Wonder Woman No. 1/1.

"The planet Earth," explains the text, "is ruled by rival gods — Ares, god of war, and Aphrodite, goddess of love and beauty." Ares is determined that "men shall rule [the Earth] with the sword," but Aphrodite has vowed that "women shall conquer men with love!"

In ancient times, "the swordsmen of Ares, (now called Mars) slew their weaker brothers and plundered them." In these dark and bloody times "women were sold as slaves—they were cheaper than cattle"—and were nothing more than pieces of property to be owned and traded by men.

"But Aphrodite shaped with her own hands a race of super women, stronger than men."

"I will breathe life into these women," said the goddess as she put the final touches on her beautiful creations, "and also the power of love! They shall be called 'Amazons.'"

Then Aphrodite "gave her own magic girdle to the Amazon queen" and told the Amazons that "so long as your leader wears this magic girdle you Amazons shall be unconquerable!"

Somewhere in ancient Greece, "the Amazons built a magnificent city, Amazonia, and easily defeated all armies which attacked them."

MARS was "furiously angry at Aphrodite" for having created a race of women stronger than men: "You cheated me!" cried the bloodthirsty war god. "You made Amazon women stronger than men! But I will conquer your Amazons and punish them!"

But Aphrodite only laughed at Mars. "That for your threats!" she cried derisively, snapping her fingers in the war god's face.

In anger, "Mars inspired Hercules, strongest man in the world, to make war on the Amazons!"

"I'll take this magic girdle from Hippolyte, the Amazon queen," bragged Hercules, "and bring her women back in chains!"

At the head of a "mighty army," the boastful

"The planet Earth is ruled by rival gods . . . ."

Hercules marched to Amazonia and "challenged the queen to personal combat!"

"Come forth, Hippolyte," taunted Hercules, "if thou dare to fight the strongest man in the world!"

"I dare fight any man!" cried Hippolyte, and the battle was joined.

As the battle began, "Hercules's club snapped the queen's puny sword like a dry stick, leaving her unarmed," whereupon the mighty Hercules called on Hippolyte to "Surrender or die!"

Hippolyte, however, would not admit defeat. "No mere man can conquer an Amazon!" she cried, and leaped back into the battle. As Aphrodite had promised, ". . . the magic girdle gave her strength," and soon the powerful Hercules went down in defeat.

Stung by his defeat at the hands of the Amazon queen, Hercules resolved to win through treachery that which he had been unable to win on the battlefield. "I will make love to her," he thought to himself, "and steal the magic girdle!"

"Hercules used woman's own weapon
against Queen Hippolyte . . . ."

"I invite you beautiful Amazons to a banquet tonight in our tents," announced Hercules to the assembled Amazons, "to seal our pact of eternal friendship!" Disarmed by Hercules's seeming act of friendship, the Amazons agreed to attend.

That night, at the banquet, "Hercules used woman's own weapon against Queen Hippolyte. He made love to her!"

"Thou art as beautiful as Aphrodite!" flattered Hercules, as he touched his goblet to Hippolyte's.

"And thou art strong as Ares," replied Hippolyte graciously, "—without this magic girdle I could never have conquered thee!"

"Let me hold thy girdle, O queen—" beseeched Hercules deceitfully. "Just to touch it will send my spirits soaring since thou hast worn it!"

"I ought not—" replied Hippolyte, "but I cannot resist thee!"

No sooner had Hercules laid hands on the magic girdle, however, than he immediately showed his true colors: rallying his warriors to arms, he called on them to attack the Amazons and take them prisoner.

"The Amazons . . . were defeated."

"The Amazons fought furiously but without the magic girdle they were defeated."

"Bind the prisoners," cried Hercules when the battle had been won. "We will loot the city!"

"Hola!" cried his joyous troops. "Amazonia is ours!"

Now ignominiously defeated, the once-valiant Amazons were pressed into slavery. "The Greeks, fearing the strength of their captives, put the Amazons in heavy chains" and paraded them through the streets of Amazonia. "Loaded with fetters, beaten and tormented by their captors, the Amazons were in despair."

In desperation, a tearful Queen Hippolyte "prayed to Aphrodite for help."

"O divine goddess," beseeched Hippolyte, clasping her manacled hands together in fervent prayer, "forgive my sin! Give us strength to break our chains and recover the magic girdle!"

Aphrodite took pity on Hippolyte and came to her in a vision: "You may break your chains," promised the goddess. "But you must wear these wrist bands always to teach you the folly of submitting to men's domination!"

"We will obey, goddess!" promised Hippolyte.

Soon, with Aphrodite's help, the Amazons turned on their captors and defeated them. Queen Hippolyte felled Hercules with a mighty blow and recovered the magic girdle. Then, "quickly arming themselves, the Amazons boarded the Greek

"Hippolyte recovered the magic girdle."

ships" and sailed away from their ancient strong-hold of Amazonia.

"Guided by Aphrodite, the Amazons sailed far seas to their promised haven of peace and protection." There, "on Paradise Isle they built a splendid city which no man may enter—a paradise for women only!" (Sum '42).

B. Aphrodite's Law. Throughout the chronicles, the terms "Aphrodite's law" and "Amazon code" are invoked to signify the set of carefully defined moral, ethical, and religious principles which govern the behavior of Wonder Woman and her sister Amazons. Often these phrases are used interchangeably, but more often Aphrodite's law is used to designate the special code of restrictions which the goddess Aphrodite has imposed upon her Amazon worshippers, while Amazon code is used to designate a more general moral and ethical code, such as might profitably serve as a guide to humane behavior by people everywhere. It is this distinction which is employed throughout the remainder of this article. (*See also* section C, the Amazon Code.)

Of all the majestic classical architectural creations which dot the city of the Amazons on Paradise Island, perhaps the grandest is the sacred temple to the goddess Aphrodite (WW No. 3/4, Feb/Mar '43: "Ordeal of Fire!"; and others). Inside the temple (CC No. 19, Feb/Mar '47: "The Battle for Eternal Youth"), or nearby (WW No. 1/1, Sum '42), is "a spring of eternal youth . . . where fair Amazons for centuries have renewed their lovely youth . . . !" (CC No. 19, Feb/Mar '47: "The Battle for Eternal Youth").

Indeed, the blessings of eternal youth, eternal beauty, and everlasting happiness are the birth-right of every Amazon so long as she remains in the safety and seclusion of Paradise Island. If an Amazon were to leave Paradise Island, however, and journey to the world of men—known among the Amazons as "man's world"—she would immediately relinquish that birthright, though the question of precisely how Aphrodite's law is actually applied in cases of this kind is treated ambiguously in the chronicles.

In May 1944, for example, MALA's airplane is hijacked, and Mala, hurled out of the plane into the waters off New York City, is compelled to spend some time in New York City. Wonder Woman indicates, however, that Mala will not lose her birthright because she did not go to New York voluntarily (Sen No. 29: "Adventure of the Escaped Prisoner").

The best example of an Amazon who has left Paradise Island to dwell in "man's world" is, of course, Wonder Woman herself, but the texts are inconsistent regarding exactly how Aphrodite's law has affected Wonder Woman's status as an Amazon. In June 1942, for example, when Wonder Woman returns to Paradise Island—for the first time since her initial departure—to receive the special "magic lasso" (*see* WONDER WOMAN [section C 3, the magic lasso]) made for her at the command of Athena and Aphrodite, Wonder Woman expresses surprise that she has been allowed to return to Paradise Island at all, even for a visit. Queen Hippolyte replies that this has been a special case, granted through the specific charity of the goddesses (Sen No. 6), but the fact remains that, in the years that follow, Wonder Woman makes frequent visits to Paradise Island without ever arousing the wrath of the goddesses.

The texts are also inconsistent regarding the extent to which Wonder Woman has relinquished her Amazon birthright of eternal youth and beauty. Several texts assert that Wonder Woman has been made the sole exception to Aphrodite's otherwise inviolable rule (WW No. 168/2, Feb '67: "Never in a Million Years!"; and others), but Wonder Woman No. 173/1 asserts that "the terrible price **Wonder Woman** had to pay to remain on man's world was to lose her immortality!" (Nov/Dec '67: "Wonder Woman's Daring Deception!"), and other texts seem to support this view: "Were you to set foot on man's world," says Queen Hippolyte to the Amazon Luria in January–February 1952, "--it would mean the loss of your Amazon heritage of immortality! This is the terrible price **Wonder Woman** has had to pay for her mission on man's world!" (WW No. 51/2: "Wonder Woman's Strange Substitute!").

There are a number of other inconsistencies as well. Many texts, for example, indicate that an Amazon who leaves Paradise Island for "man's world" will, by relinquishing her right to immortality, merely grow old and die in the customary way. At least one text, however, states that an Amazon who leaves Paradise Island will "grow old immediately and die—by Aphrodite's law," within the space of only a few seconds (WW No. 168/2, Feb '67: "Never in a Million Years!").

Another tenet of Aphrodite's law is that "If any but an Amazon drinks of its water without Aphrodite's permission, the spring [of eternal youth] will dry up and all Amazons will grow old and die!" Indeed, when AMBROSE VENTURE's accomplice, Roba Jewel, drinks of its magic water in February–March 1947, the spring dries up instantly. Aphrodite finally agrees to allow the spring to flow once again, but only on the condition that Roba remain on Paradise Island forever, "learning to worship love and beauty!" (CC No. 19: "The Battle for Eternal Youth").

Another tenet of Aphrodite's law states that no Amazon may ever marry, upon penalty of losing her rights and privileges as an Amazon. It is therefore Aphrodite's law which prohibits Wonder Woman from marrying STEVE TREVOR, for so long as Wonder Woman needs her Amazon powers to help others, she cannot relinquish them in order to marry Trevor.

"I know that Steve loves **Wonder Woman,** the **glamorous** Amazon princess," remarks Queen Hippolyte to her daughter in March–April 1950. "But if you marry, you will no longer be an Amazon. You will be **plain** Lt. Diana Prince forever. Do you think Steve will love you then, in **that** identity?" (Sen No. 96: "Wonder Woman's Romantic Rival!").

In May–June 1950, Wonder Woman states the consequences of marriage for an Amazon even more explicitly: "By Aphrodite's law, no Amazon may marry and still remain an Amazon. If I marry Steve, I shall cease being an Amazon and forfeit the magic lasso, plane, and bracelets with which I have fought crime and injustice!

"Have I the right to become Mrs. Steve Trevor, and think only of my own happiness? Or should my first thoughts be of the people whom only I can help?" (Sen No. 97: "Wonder Woman, Romance Editor").

Perhaps the most vital tenet of Aphrodite's law is the one which holds that no man must ever set foot on Paradise Island. The texts are extremely inconsistent regarding the precise nature of—and penalties for—violation of this stricture against male presence, but the chronicles are unanimous in asserting that the appearance of a man on Paradise Island would violate the most fundamental precept of Aphrodite's law.

In actuality, however, Steve Trevor spends some time recuperating on Paradise Island in December

1941–January 1942, and despite the fact that Queen Hippolyte displays a great deal of anxiety regarding his presence there, nothing very dire seems to happen as a result (AS No. 8: "Introducing Wonder Woman"). Some later texts attempt to mitigate this obvious violation of Aphrodite's law by suggesting either that Trevor was housed outside the Amazons' city during his sojourn on Paradise Island (WW No. 1/1, Sum '42) and was therefore exempt from the traditional restrictions, or that he was nursed back to health in a special "island laboratory" situated somewhere off the Paradise Island coast (WW No. 159, Jan '66: "The Golden Age Secret Origin of Wonder Woman"). One text states that Wonder Woman—then known only as Princess Diana — took steps to "prevent [Trevor] from actually touching the ground with his feet" during his stay on Paradise Island, and that this precaution was sufficient to forestall a violation of Aphrodite's taboo (WW No. 45/1, Jan/Feb '51: "The Wonder Woman Story!").

On another occasion, the crew of a Nazi submarine comes ashore on Paradise Island and attempts to conquer it. The raiders are beaten back by Wonder Woman and Mala, and the Amazons suffer no apparent ill effects from this brief male incursion (Sen No. 37, Jan '45: "The Invasion of Paradise Island").

Nevertheless, numerous texts contain the statement that Aphrodite's law prohibits the presence of men on Paradise Island, and the Amazons go to extreme lengths to prevent men from ever setting foot there.

Wonder Woman No. 30/1 observes that "If men land on Paradise Island, all the Amazons lose their birthright, the gift of eternal youth!" (Jul/Aug '48: "The Secret of the Limestone Caves"), and Wonder Woman No. 33/1 states that the Amazons will "lose [their] eternal youth and beauty if a man sets foot on Paradise Island" (Jan/Feb '49: "The Four Dooms" pts. 1–2—"Paradise Island Condemned!"; "The Titanic Trials!").

Sensation No. 89 observes that, "by Aphrodite's law," if a man sets foot on Paradise Island, the Amazons "lose [their] powers" (May '49: "Amazon Queen for a Day!"), and Wonder Woman No. 35/2 says that if a man "sets foot on Paradise Island, **Aphrodite's law** will be broken--[the Amazons'] fountain of youth and beauty will dry up and [the Amazons will] no longer be immortal!" (May/Jun '49: "Jaxo, Master of Thought!").

Wonder Woman No. 118 states that if a man were to land on Paradise Island, "the special power of Amazons to help anyone in distress--[would] be lost!" (Nov '60: "Wonder Woman's Impossible Decision!") and, in August 1961,

Queen Hippolyte says that "By the law of our patron goddess--no man is allowed to set foot on our island! Under penalty of our losing both our unique Amazon powers--and possession of our island-home!" (WW No. 124: "The Impossible Day!").

A tenet of Aphrodite's law that receives widespread—and varied—treatment in the chronicles is the principle that if an Amazon allows her metal bracelets to be welded together by shackles affixed to them by a man, she loses her Amazon strength and "becomes weak as other women in a man-ruled world!" (WW No. 2/4, Fall '42). (*See* WONDER WOMAN [section C 2, the bracelets of submission].)

C. The Amazon Code. Unlike Aphrodite's law, the Amazon code involves no special ritualized behavior or carefully preserved taboos. Rather, it is a thoughtful, carefully articulated moral and ethical code which "stresses love and service to humanity . . . !" (WW No. 40/1: "Hollywood Goes to Paradise Island" pts. 1–2–"The Mile High Menace!"; "The Undersea Invasion!").

"Govern yourselves with love, kindness, and service to others!" says Wonder Woman to the people of NEW METROPOLO in May–June 1951. "That is the Amazon code!" (Sen No. 103: "100 Year Duel!").

The texts refer repeatedly to "the Amazon way of peace and loving kindness" (Sen No. 102, Mar/Apr '51: "The Queen of the South Seas!") and to the "Amazon code of justice and mercy" (WW No. 43/1, Sep/Oct '50: "The Amazing Spy Ring Mystery").

Specifically, the Amazon code compels Amazons to obey all lawful authority, even when it appears capricious (Sen No. 75, Mar '48: "The Return of 'Shaggy,' the Leprechaun!"); "to help everyone in distress--no matter who!" (Sen No. 104, Jul/Aug '51: "The End of Paradise Island"); "to save lives always--enemies or not!" (WW No. 28/2, Mar/Apr '48: "Trap of Crimson Flame"); and to be concerned always with the welfare of others (Sen No. 99, Sep/Oct '50: "The Man Who Couldn't Make a Mistake!").

"We Amazons have discovered," Wonder Woman tells Steve Trevor in January–February 1950, "that the greatest happiness in life is to help others!" (WW No. 39/3: "A Day in the Life of Wonder Woman!").

D. Amazon Training. By the standards that prevail on "man's world," all Amazons are fantastically powerful, and gifted with what can only be described as superhuman powers and abilities. Though Wonder Woman is a champion among the Amazons, and the frequent victor in Amazon athletic and other competitions, the powers of her

Amazon girls undergo Amazon training, 1945

sister Amazons are on the same order as her own. These superhuman powers and abilities are the result of intensive and highly specialized Amazon training, a phenomenon that is referred to in the chronicles repeatedly.

Briefly stated, Amazon training involves learning to use, and to harness toward constructive ends, the virtually unlimited potential of the human mind. By training their minds and bodies until they are able to control the flow of mental energy into their muscles and limbs, Amazons develop superhuman strength and extraordinarily acute senses. "Amazon girls get their strength," explains Wonder Woman in Fall 1944, "from brain energy given by Aphrodite!" (WW No. 10/3: "Wonder Woman's Boots!"). In February 1966, Wonder Woman is more specific: "Amazons," she tells Steve Trevor, "can release brain energy into their muscles at will--giving them super-strength! Anyone can do it--with will power and training!" (WW No. 160/1: "The Amazon of Terror!").

Repeatedly in the chronicles, Wonder Woman expresses her conviction that anyone could duplicate her amazing Amazon feats, "if she went through the rigorous training that I did!" (WW No. 39/3, Jan/Feb '50: "A Day in the Life of Wonder Woman!"). On one occasion, Wonder Woman states that "I can prove that Amazon training makes any girl powerful" (WW No. 6/3, Fall '43: "The Conquest of Paradise"), and, indeed, as the years wear on, several "man's world" girls become super-strong by undergoing Amazon training on Paradise Island under Wonder Woman's careful guidance, among them BARONESS PAULA VON GUNTHER, OLIVE NORTON, and WANTA WYNN.

Nowhere in the chronicles are the precise techniques of Amazon training described in detail, but occasional texts provide valuable insights into the abilities and attributes which are inculcated by such training: Amazons must "learn all human languages," past, present, and future (WW No. 1/2, Sum '42: "Wonder Woman Goes to the Circus!"). Amazons "practice enduring heat by repulsing it with [their] body electricity!" (Sen No. 18, Jun '43). All Amazons "practice yogi [sic]" (WW No. 5/3, Jun/Jul '43). Every Amazon has the "ability to hold her breath underwater for long periods" (CC No. 9, Win '44: "The Subsea Pirates"), and Amazon training endows Amazons with supersensitive hearing (Sen No. 63, Mar '47: "The Wail of DOOM!"). According to Wonder Woman No. 29/1, ". . . Amazons are trained to withstand both heat and cold!" (May/Jun '48: "Ice World's Conquest!"), and according to Wonder Woman No. 32/1, "an Amazon's brain has been trained to remember the talk of a hundred people!" (Nov/Dec '48: "Uvo of Uranus!").

". . . [W]e Amazons have been trained to have photographic vision!" explains Wonder Woman in January 1949. "We can memorize whole pages at a single glance!" (Sen No. 85: "The Girl Who Wanted to Be an Amazon!"). In March–April 1949, after she has miraculously survived the effects of a devastating bomb explosion, Wonder Woman explains that "Amazons are taught how to roll outside the area of a bomb blast!" (WW No. 34: "The Mystery of the Rhyming Riddle!" chs. 1–3–"Deception Strikes Again"; "The Phantasms of Deception!"; "The Mystery of the Rhyming Riddle!"). (*See also* WONDER WOMAN [section C 1, the benefits of Amazon training].)

E. Amazon Culture. 1. Sports. In Amazon life, very few activities are more important than sports, for it is through participation in sports that Amazons learn to control the forces of "dominance" and rebellion which, destructively unleashed, have produced so much horror and misery in "man's world."

Amazon sports, at least insofar as they are portrayed in the chronicles, are rough, and although jealousy and hostility are virtually nonexistent, at least on the surface, the contestants are fiercely competitive and eager to win.

In the "girl-roping contest," played from atop giant kangaroos called "kangas," Amazon contestants attempt to lasso their opponents off their mounts and pull them to the ground. "This contest is a **free-for-all!**" explains an Amazon referee in June 1942. "You will lasso an opponent, pull her to the ground, and tie her up. Attendants will furnish fresh lariats and carry defeated contestants off the field!" (Sen No. 6).

In "bullets and bracelets," Amazon contestants shoot at one another with pistols and attempt to parry the bullets with their Amazon bracelets. It is Princess Diana's skill at this sport that enables her to win the right to come to America—where she becomes known as Wonder Woman—in December 1941–January 1942, as well as to deflect the countless bullets and other missiles fired at her by uncounted villains throughout her career. Queen Hippolyte explains the rules of bullets and bracelets as follows: "Each of you will shoot five times. Your opponent must catch the bullets on her bracelet—or else expect to be wounded!" (AS No. 8: "Introducing Wonder Woman"). (*See also* WONDER WOMAN [section A, Origin].)

Although Amazon games seem violent, even

An Amazon girl-roping contest, 1942

brutal, by contemporary American standards, Amazons recoil in horror at the violence and brutality of "man's world" sports. In April 1948, for example, when Wonder Woman visits Paradise Island with some slides of man's world activities, she shows one depicting a boxing match, with one contender knocking his opponent from the ring with a mighty punch. "What a strange sport!" exclaims one Amazon. "Looks as if the one who hurt [sic] the other most wins!" (Sen No. 76: "Murder Referees the Round!").

2. *Festivals and holidays.* The chronicles deal specifically with only two major Amazon feast days. To hail the arrival of the Winter solstice, the Amazons celebrate Diana's Day, a holiday given over to feasting, gaming, and the giving of gifts (WW No. 3/1, Feb/Mar '43). (*See also* DIANA.)

In January, the Amazons celebrate the annual harvest with a huge harvest festival (Sen No. 37, Jan '45: "The Invasion of Paradise Island").

3. *Transportation.* The Amazons have two means of transportation worthy of special note: they have a space fleet, consisting of swan-shaped aircraft capable of interplanetary travel (WW No. 32/1, Nov/Dec '48: "Uvo of Uranus!" pts. 1–2–"The Amazing Global Theft!"; "Thunder in Space!"), and they have "sky kangas." Sky kangas are gigantic kangaroos, specially "bred by the Amazons for short space trips," which journey through space by making long, nimble leaps "from meteorite to planetoid" (WW No. 5/2, Jun/Jul '43). The sky kangas were first introduced to the Amazons by masked invaders from outer space who rode their sky kangas onto Paradise Island and attempted to conquer it. The Amazons defeated the

space raiders, but kept the sky kangas (WW No. 23/3, May/Jun '47: "Wonder Woman and the Coming of the Kangas!").

4. *Communication.* The principal Amazon communications device is the mental radio. (*See* WONDER WOMAN [section C 7, the mental radio].)

Wonder Woman receives a mental radio message from Queen Hippolyte, 1946

F. Amazon Magic. 1. *The magic girdle.* When the goddess Aphrodite created the Amazons (*see* section A, History), she entrusted Queen Hippolyte with a wide belt — the so-called "magic girdle" — which had been forged from tiny golden links of a "very special metal." "So long as we Amazons keep it," explains Hippolyte in Fall 1943, "we cannot be conquered!" (WW No. 6/3: "The Conquest

Baroness Paula von Gunther and Wonder Woman leap through outer space astride an Amazon sky kanga

of Paradise"). Whenever the magic girdle falls into the hands of an evildoer, however, Hippolyte and her Amazons weaken, temporarily forfeiting their unique invulnerability to conquest until such time as they are able to recover it. Wonder Woman's magic lasso is fashioned from golden links of metal taken from the magic girdle at the behest of Aphrodite and Athena. (*See also* WONDER WOMAN [section C 3, the magic lasso].)

2. *The magic sphere.* This device, which resembles a round television screen, was given to Queen Hippolyte by Athena, goddess of wisdom. "When tuned to any time or place in the world's history its viewplate shows everything that happened there!" (Sen No. 24, Dec '43: "Adventure of the Pilotless Plane"). According to Sensation No. 26, the magic sphere "records all past events and also foretells the future" (Feb '44: "The Masquerader"). Its principal limitation is that it reveals events taking place only "within the Earth's atmosphere" (WW No. 33/2, Jan/Feb '49: "The Menace of Murkton!"), and not, for example, events taking place on distant planets.

Amazon prisoners wearing their magic Venus girdles, 1948. In the foreground (left to right) are: Queen Clea, Priscilla Rich (alias the Cheetah), Giganta, Zara, Eviless (arm raised), Byrna Brilyant (alias the Snow Man), Princess Maru (alias Doctor Poison), and Hypnota the Great

Aphrodite appears to Wonder Woman and Queen Hippolyte in the magic sphere, 1945

3. *The magic Venus girdles.* Strictly speaking, the magic Venus girdles are not Amazon artifacts, but Venusian ones. However, following Wonder Woman's trip to the planet VENUS—where she first encounters the Venus girdles—in October–November 1942, the girdles come into general Amazon usage, particularly on TRANSFORMATION ISLAND, where they are used to control potentially rebellious prisoners (AS No. 13: "Shanghaied into Space!").

Magic Venus girdles are wide belts fashioned from "Aphrodite's magnetized gold" (WW No. 12/2, Spr '45: "The Ordeal of Fire"). Each is un-

breakable, even by Wonder Woman, and locks around the wearer's waist by means of a special keylock situated at the front. The girdles compel their wearers to obey any commands made of them, and banish from their minds all thoughts of evil deeds.

QUEEN DESIRA of Venus explains that ". . . girdles of magnetic gold charge every body cell with vitalizing currents and harmonize the brain. When [the] brains [of those imprisoned in them] become normal . . . [they] will lose their desire for conflict and will **enjoy** serving others and submitting to loving authority!" (WW No. 12/3, Spr '45: "The Conquest of Venus").

When a prisoner is locked into a Venus girdle, he or she becomes overwhelmed by "a feeling of peace" and contentment (WW No. 12/2, Spr '45: "The Ordeal of Fire") and eager to live "by . . . peaceful principles" (CC No. 19, Feb/Mar '47: "The Battle for Eternal Youth").

When the Saturnian slave driver EVILESS arrives on Transformation Island as a prisoner in March–April 1948, she asks Mala about the Venus girdle in which she is about to be imprisoned.

"It [the girdle] is magic metal from Venus," replies Mala, "--it removes all desires to do evil and compels complete obedience to loving authority" (WW No. 28/1: "Villainy Incorporated!").

Unfortunately, however, the Venus girdles can also be used to compel obedience to villainous authority if they fall into the wrong hands. On one occasion, for example, the Cheetah imprisons Wonder Woman in a Venus girdle and compels her to commit acts which almost result in the deaths of Steve Trevor and Claudia (CC No. 11, Sum '45: "The Cheetah Returns!"). (*See* CHEETAH, THE.)

G. Amazon Science. The Amazons are the custodians of an incredible super-science which continually produces new, wondrous mechanical and electronic devices. A complete catalogue of Amazon inventions would be vast, but some of the more spectacular ones deserve mention:

In December 1941–January 1942 Wonder Woman develops the amazing "purple healing ray" with which she saves the life of the sorely wounded Steve Trevor (AS No. 8: "Introducing Wonder Woman"). Later, she concentrates the properties of the purple healing ray into tablets so that Trevor can carry them with him on a dangerous mission and take them if he becomes wounded (WW No. 2/1, Fall '42). Over the years, the miraculous healing powers of the purple ray are frequently employed to heal severely injured persons within a matter of moments. On one occasion, Wonder Woman even uses it to bring Steve Trevor back to life after he has been murdered (Sen No. 66, Jun '47: "Prisoners of Cops and Robbers").

In Spring 1945, "with the advice of Desira, Queen of Venus," Wonder Woman and Baroness Paula von Gunther construct an "electro-chemical **space transformer**" which changes Earth bodies to Venus bodies in the flash of a spark! This apparatus," Wonder Woman explains, "breaks down the human body's atomic structure and rearranges its spatial relativity in the universe, as explained by Professor Einstein. Our machine transfers a living body from Earth to the planet Venus!" (WW No. 12/1).

By May–June 1946 Baroness Paula von Gunther has developed the "space transformation machine"—apparently based on the principles of the "space transformer"—which, when properly adjusted, "will rearrange your body atoms in time as

THE AMAZON PRINCESS AND PAULA EXPLAIN THEIR INVENTION.

WITH THE ADVICE OF DESIRA, QUEEN OF VENUS, WE HAVE BUILT THIS ELECTRO-CHEMICAL **SPACE TRANSFORMER** WHICH CHANGES EARTH BODIES TO VENUS BODIES IN THE FLASH OF A SPARK!

© NPP 1945

Wonder Woman and Baroness Paula von Gunther demonstrate the electrochemical space transformer, 1945

well as space," thus enabling one to make journeys into the past (WW No. 17/1: "The Winds of Time"). On one occasion, Wonder Woman refers to "our Amazon trans-materialization machine . . . [which] dematerializes a person and materializes him again in any time or place selected" (Sen No. 60, Dec '46: "The Ordeal of Queen Boadicea"), but "trans-materialization machine" is undoubtedly just another name for the space transformer. The DUKE OF DECEPTION uses the Amazon "trans-materialization machine," spelled without the hyphen, to steal Holliday College in March–April 1949 (WW No. 34: "The Mystery of the Rhyming Riddle!" chs. 1–3–"Deception Strikes Again"; "The Phantasms of Deception!"; "The Mystery of the Rhyming Riddle!").

In May–June 1951 Amazon scientists peer into the future with a device called a "futuro-scope" (Sen No. 103: "100 Year Duel!").

In her Amazon airplane, Wonder Woman carries an "Amazon omni-wave transmitter" which enables her to receive distress calls on every existing wavelength (WW No. 55/2, Sep/Oct '52: "The Chessmen of Doom!"). (See WONDER WOMAN [section C 4, the robot plane].)

In March–April 1953 Wonder Woman and Steve Trevor reduce themselves to the size of insects with an Amazon "minimizer" in order to thwart a "termite invasion" menacing the Earth (WW No. 58/3: "Terror of the Termites").

Wonder Woman No. 60/1 refers to the Amazon "futuray" with which one can peer into the future, and the Amazon "time-and-space projector" with which one can observe the past (Jul/Aug '53: "The War That Never Happened!").

In January 1957 an "Amazon video-scope" enables Diana Prince–the girl who is secretly Wonder Woman–to track Steve Trevor through the heavens as he makes a test flight in a new aircraft (WW No. 87/2: "Island of the Giants!").

In April 1958 Wonder Woman unveils an ingenious new video-communications device known as an Amazon "uni-televisor" (WW No. 97: "The Runaway Time Express!" pts. 1–3–"Stone Age Rodeo!"; "The Day Nature Ran Wild!"; "The Menace of Earth's Twin!").

By August 1958 Wonder Woman has installed a video-communications apparatus in one of her Amazon bracelets which Queen Hippolyte uses to summon her to Paradise Island (WW No. 100/1: "The Forest of Giants!" pts. 1–2 — "The Challenge of Dimension X!"; "The Forest of Giants!"). (See WONDER WOMAN [section C 2, the bracelets of submission].)

By October 1958 Wonder Woman and Steve Trevor have begun wearing special rings containing miniature radios to enable them to communicate over long distances (WW No. 101/2: "The Fun House of Time!").

By October 1965 Queen Hippolyte and the Amazons have invented the "AS-R beam"—for "atomic structure reassembly beam"—which enables them to reassemble the atoms of either a person or a thing that has been totally destroyed and restore it to its original undamaged form. They use the new invention to bring Wonder Woman and Steve Trevor back to life again after the famous couple has been obliterated in an atomic explosion (WW No. 157: "I--the Bomb!").

AMAZSILIKON. The material from which, according to Sensation Comics No. 45, WONDER WOMAN's Amazon plane is made (Sep '45: "In the Enemy's Hands"). According to Wonder Woman No. 125, however, the plane is "fashioned out of elastic amazonium, hardest substance known . . ." (Oct. '61: "Wonder Woman--Battle Prize!"). (See also AMAZONIUM; WONDER WOMAN [section C 4, the robot plane].)

AMERICAN ADOLF. The pen name of a master criminal — the self-styled "supreme crime leader"—whose diabolical book, *My War Against Society*, describes in meticulous detail "the great crime empire" he intends to found in the United States.

American Adolf's book contains a four-step blueprint for the conquest of the United States by its criminal element: (1) Kill or conquer all rival crime leaders; (2) Organize a national crime army; (3) Murder important U.S. Army officers, break Federal prisons; and (4) Take over the national government.

Wonder Woman foils American Adolf's scheme to overthrow the United States Government in September 1943. When she seizes the airplane from which the villain has been spraying poison gas onto American troops and hurls it to the ground, American Adolf allows himself to die in the wreckage rather than submit to capture (Sen No. 21: "War Against Society").

ANDREWS, ANGLES. A ruthless underworld chieftain who tries unsuccessfully to learn Wonder Woman's secret identity. He and his henchmen are apprehended by Wonder Woman in November–December 1953 (WW No. 62/1: "Wonder Woman's Triple Identity!").

ANDRO (Prof.). The pseudonym employed by a diabolical extraterrestrial alien with extraordinary mental powers—a "crystal creature" from a distant planet who can "travel through time or space by **mentotravel!** Or cause volcanoes, earthquakes, fire or flood by **mentoforce!**"—who, in August 1960, poses as an earthling as part of his scheme to

"produce the greatest catastrophe since . . . time began": the destruction of the Earth by means of a titanic "S-time bomb." The fiendish plot is foiled by WONDER WOMAN, who annihilates the evil "crystal being" by luring him into the path of a lightning bolt, which shatters him into tiny fragments (WW No. 116: "The Time Traveler of Terror!").

ANGLE MAN, THE. A treacherous criminal mastermind—the man with a million angles—who makes repeated attempts to destroy WONDER WOMAN between 1954 and 1968.

In November 1954, at a secret conference of underworld gang chiefs, the Angle Man unveils his scheme to capture Wonder Woman by first uncovering the secret of her dual identity. The assembled gang chiefs approve the plan and agree to pay the villain $1 million if he can deliver Wonder Woman into their clutches.

Not long afterward, when Wonder Woman makes a public appearance at "Celebrity Corner" to have her footprints immortalized in wet cement alongside those of other notables, she does not realize that one of the Angle Man's henchmen has secretly mixed a special phosphorescent dye into the gray cement.

Following the conclusion of the footprint ceremony, the Angle Man's accomplices are able to follow Wonder Woman wherever she goes by observing her phosphorescent footprints through special glasses. Keeping Wonder Woman constantly in sight, the henchmen see the Amazon princess change into her Diana Prince identity, and they promptly take Diana prisoner. They shove her into a rowboat and row her toward a roaring waterfall, intending to throw her over the watery precipice, but Diana escapes from the rowboat

I'VE GOT A MILLION ANGLES! THAT'S WHY THEY CALL ME *ANGLE MAN*! WATCH THE PAPERS! YOU'LL SOON SEE WHAT'LL HAPPEN TO *WONDER WOMAN*!

© NPP 1962

The Angle Man, 1962

and, through a ruse, tricks the criminals into believing that Diana Prince and Wonder Woman are two different persons. Moments later, Wonder Woman apprehends the Angle Man and his entire gang (WW No. 70/2: "The Invisible Trail!").

In November 1955 a mysterious crate arrives at the offices of the *DAILY GLOBE* in care of Wonder Woman. Inside the crate is $1 million in one-dollar bills and an explanatory note from an anonymous donor offering to let Wonder Woman donate the $1 million to charity if only she will "shoot a movie," starring herself, according to the enclosed script.

Wonder Woman searches through the crate in vain for the movie script until she realizes that the dollar bills themselves have been stacked in such a way as to form a code, which, once deciphered, spells out a script for an action-packed movie.

In order to win the $1 million for charity, Wonder Woman sets out to shoot the scenes described in the coded script, but as she progresses from one scene to another, she finds that each of the required scenes leads her into a diabolical deathtrap from which it takes all of her Amazon skill and endurance to escape. Slowly she comes to realize that the $1 million and the strangely coded movie script are all part of a gangland plot to destroy her, but, for the sake of charity, she pushes on with her movie-making mission nonetheless.

Finally, the coded movie script brings Wonder Woman to an amusement park's hall of mirrors, where the Angle Man and his cohorts fell her with knockout gas and then emerge from the shadows to finish her off. They are about to fire a fusillade of bullets into the apparently unconscious Amazon, when Wonder Woman, who has come prepared for a trap like this one, leaps to her feet, wards off the gangsters' bullets with her Amazon bracelets, and apprehends the plotters (WW No. 78/3: "The Million Dollar Mystery!").

In April 1956, on a crowded street corner, STEVE TREVOR asks Wonder Woman to marry him, and Wonder Woman responds as she always does when Trevor proposes. "I give you my Amazon word of honor!" she replies. "The moment I'm convinced there's no more crime—we'll marry—and I'll retire from public life!"

On this occasion, however, Trevor's proposal and Wonder Woman's reply are recorded by a newsreel camera crew, and before long, the intimate conversation is being played for newsreel audiences in movie theaters throughout the country.

The newsreel inspires the Angle Man with the idea of forcing Wonder Woman into marriage, and therefore into retirement, by bringing a temporary halt to all crime. Before long, at the Angle Man's direction, all crime in the city has come to a standstill.

The unprecedented lull in criminal activity makes Steve Trevor eager to foreclose on Wonder Woman's marriage promise, but Wonder Woman suspects that the lull has been orchestrated for her benefit and comes up with a plan for ferreting out the truth.

Soon, television audiences throughout the land witness what at first glance appears to be the wedding of Wonder Woman and Steve Trevor. The Angle Man and his henchmen, who assume that Wonder Woman is now married and that their criminal activities can therefore resume, promptly attempt a bank robbery, but Wonder Woman is on the scene to apprehend them all and to explain that the television wedding was not a real wedding at all, but merely a rehearsal—with a bridesmaid standing in for Wonder Woman—intended to draw the underworld out into the open again (WW No. 81/3: "The Vanishing Criminal!").

In August 1956 the Angle Man unveils yet another plot to destroy Wonder Woman. This time he has created a lifelike "humanoid," a "mechanical woman" designed and dressed to look exactly like Wonder Woman. His humanoid, explains the Angle Man, is literally capable of destroying Wonder Woman.

Ultimately, Wonder Woman—who does not know that her look-alike adversary is only a mechanical woman—finds herself locked in deadly battle with her evil double inside "the central switch room which controls the power supply of the whole city!"

As they grapple, however, an iron railing gives way, and the humanoid Wonder Woman topples over the side and plummets lifeless to the ground, its delicate mechanism shattered by the fall. Lying on the ground nearby is the Angle Man, who had been hiding in the switch room in hopes of witnessing Wonder Woman's defeat, only to be struck by his creation as it toppled toward the floor. Now aware for the first time that her deadly opponent was not a real human being at all, Wonder Woman swiftly takes the dazed Angle Man into custody (WW No. 84/1: "The Secret Wonder Woman!").

In August 1957 Wonder Woman gives a lecture over network radio about the famous Amazon plane (*see* WONDER WOMAN [section C 4, the robot plane]) which obeys her spoken commands by responding to the unique vibrations of her voice. She does not suspect, however, that the Angle Man and his henchmen are tape-recording the lecture so that, with the help of some minor editing, they can use it to issue commands to the robot plane.

Soon afterward, while Wonder Woman is flying over the city in her plane, the Angle Man and his cohorts use their recording of Wonder Woman's voice, broadcast over a loudspeaker, to countermand her verbal instructions to the aircraft. The result is mechanical chaos, with the robot plane torn between Wonder Woman's verbal commands on the one hand, and the opposing commands of the tape recording on the other. Hurled out of the plane by its wild gyrations, Wonder Woman manages to survive the fall and, by seizing a chimney in her bare hands and using it as a giant megaphone, regains control of her plane by drowning out the gangsters' tape recording. With her Amazon plane once again under her control, Wonder Woman easily apprehends the Angle Man and his cohorts (WW No. 92/2: "The Revolt of the Winged Robot!").

In February 1958 the Angle Man unveils yet another plot to destroy Wonder Woman. The scheme involves stealing a supply of radium from a local hospital and then leaving behind a trail of easily discernible footprints for Wonder Woman to follow. The footprint trail leads Wonder Woman to a science exhibition where a newly invented time machine is on display. When Wonder Woman enters the time machine to retrieve the stolen radium, the door slams shut and Wonder Woman is transported into the future to the year 4457 A.D.

In the world of the future, Wonder Woman battles and defeats a towering giant—the Angle Man's 45th-century descendant—who threatens the Earth. Then, stepping into the time machine and returning to her own time, Wonder Woman swiftly apprehends the Angle Man and his cohorts (WW No. 96/3: "Prisoner of the Time Capsule!").

In July 1960 the Angle Man makes yet another attempt to destroy Wonder Woman. In this text, the villain wears an elaborate costume—consisting of a purple dress suit with a high silk hat and a red cape ornamented with gold astrological symbols—as contrasted with the simple business suit he has traditionally worn.

This time, the Angle Man has invented Animox, a diabolical "mechanical brain" with the power to "animate any inanimate object" and to obey any command punched into its complex master control panel. Upon learning that Wonder Woman is scheduled to explore a graveyard of ancient ships, the Angle Man flies over the area where Wonder Woman will be swimming and drops Animox into the water. Programmed into Animox are instructions to animate the figureheads decorating the various sunken ships and use them to destroy Wonder Woman.

When Wonder Woman and Steve Trevor arrive at the ancient "graveyard of ships," they are seized by animated figureheads which have sprung miraculously to life. On the ocean floor, however, Wonder Woman discovers Animox and realizes that it is responsible for the diabolical animation of the figureheads. After making several fruitless attempts to destroy Animox, Wonder Woman uses its master control panel to order it to transform itself, and all the figureheads it has animated, into guided missiles and to shoot itself and the figureheads into outer space.

As Animox and the animated figureheads soar through the sky toward interstellar oblivion, they crash into the Angle Man's airplane circling overhead, sending the Angle Man plummeting out of his disabled plane toward the sea below. Realizing now that it must have been the Angle Man who masterminded the Animox plot, Wonder Woman catches the villain in midair and apprehends him (WW No. 115: "Graveyard of Monster Ships!").

In February 1962, at a meeting of underworld czars, the Angle Man unveils yet another scheme to defeat Wonder Woman and receives a commitment from the assembled crime chiefs to pay him $1 million if his plan succeeds.

Soon afterward, when Wonder Woman appears on the sidewalk in front of Celebrity Theatre to immortalize her footprints in wet cement alongside those of other notables, she becomes imprisoned in the special rock-hard, quick-drying cement which the Angle Man has substituted for the sidewalk's regular cement.

With Wonder Woman helplessly stuck in the special cement, the Angle Man and his henchmen emerge from hiding to mock her futile efforts to escape, and to steal the ticket receipts of the lavish $1,000-per-seat party that had been scheduled to take place immediately following the footprint ceremony.

Unable to pry herself loose from the special cement, Wonder Woman breaks free of the sidewalk by making a mighty leap into the air with her feet still encased in a solid block of cement.

As the adventure proceeds, the Angle Man and his cohorts pursue Wonder Woman relentlessly—by car and helicopter—determined to kill her before she can break free of the imprisoning cement. For her part, Wonder Woman is faced with the twofold challenge of escaping from her gangland pursuers and rescuing the numerous people in distress who cross her path.

Ultimately, however, a bolt of lightning shatters the block of cement into a thousand fragments, freeing Wonder Woman and enabling her to apprehend the Angle Man and his henchmen (WW No. 128/2: "Vengeance of the Angle Man!").

In May 1962 the Angle Man and his gang attempt to rob the proceeds of a charity carnival, but Wonder Woman—who is visiting the carnival with Steve Trevor—swiftly apprehends them (WW No. 130: "The Mirage Mirrors!").

In October 1963 the underworld unveils a golden statuette—the so-called "Golden WW"—which it intends to award, like a filmland Oscar, to the criminal who either captures or destroys Wonder Woman during the week the underworld "academy" is in session. Of the three famous criminals who make separate bids to win the Golden WW, the first is the Angle Man.

When the underworld academy first unveils its award, however, the Angle Man is in prison. After sending Wonder Woman a message asking her to pay him a visit, the Angle Man begs her to help him obtain a parole and give him the opportunity to prove that he has given up his evil ways.

Moved by Angle Man's plea, Wonder Woman uses her influence with the parole board to win the Angle Man a parole, and then sets out to help him find an honest job. Because of the Angle Man's prison record and long-standing reputation as a criminal mastermind, however, no one will hire him. When finally a movie producer offers to shoot a movie about Wonder Woman and the Angle Man if both of them will consent to act in it, Wonder Woman agrees in order to help the Angle Man get a new start in life.

After shooting on the film has begun, the Angle Man proposes a scene in which he rescues Wonder Woman after she has been bound with her own magic lasso (see WONDER WOMAN [section C 3, the magic lasso]) and hurled into the ocean.

Once Wonder Woman is underwater, however, helplessly bound with the magic lasso, the Angle Man seizes the free end of the lasso, makes Wonder Woman his prisoner, and attempts to kill her. Suddenly, however, the villain is attacked by a giant octopus, and in the ensuing confusion Wonder Woman turns the tables on her captor, breaks free of her bonds, and rescues the Angle Man from the giant octopus. The villain is returned to prison with his parole revoked, his attempt to win the Golden WW having ended in ignominious failure (WW No. 141: "The Academy of Arch-Villains!"). (See also MOUSE MAN; FIREWORKS MAN, THE.)

A Wonder Woman text for April 1966 describes an encounter between Wonder Woman and the Angle Man which, judging from a number of textual details, can have taken place no later than 1942. In it, the Angle Man and his henchmen use a special "micro-reducing ray" to reduce themselves to the size of molecules so that they can travel inside the brain of Steve Trevor—whom they have captured—and probe his memory cells for valuable military secrets to sell to the highest bidder. Wonder Woman reduces herself in size and pursues the criminals, and, in a battle inside Trevor's brain, ultimately apprehends them all. After she and her captives have reached the outside world by way of Trevor's bloodstream, Wonder Woman uses the Angle Man's "enlargo-ray" to restore them all to their normal size (WW No. 161/2: "Battle Inside of a Brain!").

A Wonder Woman text for August 1966 describes an encounter between Wonder Woman and the Angle Man which, judging from a number of textual details, can have taken place no later than 1942. In it, Wonder Woman is captured by the Angle Man and forced, under the compulsion of her magic lasso, to steal "America's secret defense weapons" and bring them to the villain's secret headquarters aboard a submerged submarine. Ultimately, however, with the help of Steve Trevor, Wonder Woman turns the tables on her captors and flees the Angle Man's submarine hideout. As Wonder Woman and Trevor streak toward the surface, the villains aboard the submarine attempt to destroy them with a torpedo, but Wonder Woman destroys the submarine—and apparently everyone aboard it, though that is never actually stated—by kicking the live torpedo back into the submarine, where it explodes with a titanic roar (WW No. 164: "Wonder Woman--Traitor!").

In January–February 1968 the Angle Man attempts to end Wonder Woman's crime-fighting career by having one of his henchmen take her picture with a diabolical "protocamera," a device that strips Wonder Woman of all her superhuman powers. Next, the Angle Man delivers a supply of special "super-power pills" to Steve Trevor, promising that the new pills will endow Trevor with superhuman powers.

The new super-power pills perform exactly as the Angle Man has promised, and Trevor soon finds himself miraculously transformed into a mighty super-hero. In celebration of his newly acquired powers, Trevor designs himself a red, white, and blue costume and assumes the name the Patriot. Unwittingly, however, Trevor is playing directly into the Angle Man's hands, for the villain reasons that with Wonder Woman deprived of her Amazon powers, and Trevor on the scene to replace her as the Patriot, Wonder Woman will marry Trevor and retire from crime-fighting. Once Trevor exhausts his supply of super-power pills, he will lose his powers also, leaving the Angle Man and his fellow criminals free to plunder the city.

Ultimately, however, Wonder Woman and the Patriot invade the Angle Man's secret hideout, capture the villain and his cohorts, and destroy the film from the fiendish protocamera, thus restoring Wonder Woman's superhuman powers (WW No. 174/1: "Steve Trevor—Alias the Patriot!").

ANGLER, THE. A gangland chieftain who concocts an elaborate scheme to learn WONDER WOMAN's secret identity. He and his henchmen are apprehended by Wonder Woman in July 1955.

Posing as an "eccentric millionaire" and employing the alias Albert Smith, the Angler deposits $1 million in a local bank and then publicly announces his intention to donate the money to a children's charity if Wonder Woman will "privately reveal her secret identity only to him!"

Reluctant to disclose her secret identity to anyone, but at the same time feeling that it would be wrong of her to deny the children's charity the $1 million, Wonder Woman visits the bank to assure herself that the proffered $1 million is actually on deposit there and then goes to the home of "Albert Smith" and reveals to him that she is secretly Diana Prince.

Suddenly the villain's henchmen leap from their hiding places and make Wonder Woman—now dressed in her Diana Prince clothing—their prisoner. They are taking her to an out-of-the-way spot for a gangland-style execution when she races away from them, changes back into her Wonder Woman identity, and then returns to apprehend the Angler and his henchmen. Through a ruse, she manages to dupe the criminals into believing that they have seen Diana Prince and Wonder Woman simultaneously, thereby safeguarding the secret of her dual identity (WW No. 75/2: "$1,000,000 Secret!").

ANGLONIA. A strange country, situated "somewhere near Palestine" not far from "an unmapped desert," whose inhabitants still live as their "knightly ancestors" did in the 13th century. Anglonia is the home of Hubert, rightful heir to the throne, and of BLACK ROBERT OF DOGWOOD, a villainous usurper (Sen No. 62, Feb '47: "The Mysterious Prisoners of Anglonia").

ANTI ELECTRIC. A mysterious villain who uses terroristic methods in his attempt to seize control of some of America's most powerful corporations. He is secretly Mr. Keen, president of a giant railroad. As Anti Electric, Keen wears a bizarre green costume featuring a green cowl and a yellow lightning bolt emblazoned across his chest. Anti Electric is defeated and apprehended by WONDER WOMAN.

In June–July 1948 a mysterious villain known as Anti Electric interrupts regular television broadcasting to announce that he has invented "a **de-activating electronic generator** which broadcasts

an interfering electronic wave that will stop any electric current in the world!" To demonstrate his power over electricity, Anti Electric focuses his "de-activating current at the railroad's electric power lines," then declares that the railroads will not run again until 90 percent of its stock has been transferred over to him. Then, turning his devastating new weapon on the telephone power lines, the villain announces that "My de-activator current will keep all lines dead until I control the National Telephone Co.!"

Soon afterward, Anti Electric makes yet another announcement: "My de-activating current is blanketing National Airport--it will stop ignition on all planes. I demand stock ownership of National Airways!"

Next, Anti Electric issues an ultimatum to the electric company: "I have de-activated the electric light current--your city shall remain dark until I am given a majority of the **Power and Light Company's** stock."

With the city virtually paralyzed, Wonder Woman sets out to learn the true identity of Anti Electric and bring the villain to justice. She manages to locate Anti Electric's hideout, only to be taken prisoner by the villain and his gang of female accomplices.

With Wonder Woman a hostage, the chief executives of the major corporations and utilities decide that they have no choice but to meet Anti Electric's demands. After signing over their firms' stock to Anti Electric, they hand it over to STEVE TREVOR for delivery to the villain. When Trevor arrives at the agreed-upon rendezvous point, he too is taken prisoner by Anti Electric and his cohorts. Ultimately, however, Wonder Woman turns the tables on her captors, frees Steve Trevor, and apprehends Anti Electric and his gang (CC No. 27: "Anti Electric").

APHRODITE. In Greek mythology, the goddess of love and beauty.

In the WONDER WOMAN chronicles, she is—along with ATHENA—one of the patron goddesses of the AMAZONS. Her temple is among the most prominent buildings on PARADISE ISLAND, and she is the island's chief benefactress and protectress.

It was Aphrodite who created the Amazons, endowed QUEEN HIPPOLYTE with the "magic girdle," delivered the Amazons from their enslavement at the hands of HERCULES, and led them to "their promised haven of peace and protection" on Paradise Island (WW No. 1/1, Sum '42). (See AMAZONS.)

Later, after Queen Hippolyte had learned to mold the human form under the guidance of Athena, it was Aphrodite who bestowed upon

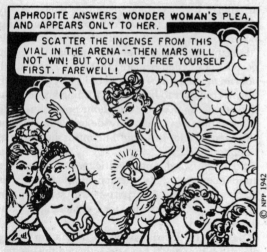

APHRODITE ANSWERS WONDER WOMAN'S PLEA, AND APPEARS ONLY TO HER.

SCATTER THE INCENSE FROM THIS VIAL IN THE ARENA--THEN MARS WILL NOT WIN! BUT YOU MUST FREE YOURSELF FIRST. FAREWELL!

© NPP 1942

Aphrodite answers a plea from Wonder Woman, 1942

Hippolyte's statue the divine gift of life which transformed it into the child Diana, princess of the Amazons (WW No. 1/1, Sum '42), later to become known to the world at large as Wonder Woman.

The metal bracelets which all Amazons wear symbolize their submission to the goddess Aphrodite and serve as reminders of their enslavement by Hercules and of the folly of submitting to male domination. It is Aphrodite who provides and protects the fountain of eternal youth from which the Amazons draw their birthright of eternal beauty and everlasting happiness. Indeed, the code of mystical lore and taboo which governs so much of Amazon behavior is known as "Aphrodite's law." Wonder Woman No. 2/1 describes Wonder Woman as "Aphrodite's agent" to the "man's world" (Fall '42).

When Queen Hippolyte creates new facial features out of clay for BARONESS PAULA VON GUNTHER, who has been horribly scarred in a raging fire, Aphrodite uses "golden rays of light" to give the new face life (WW No. 3/4, Feb/Mar '43: "Ordeal of Fire!").

In April–May 1943 Aphrodite informs Paula that she must perform "three labors of love" if she hopes to become initiated into Aphrodite's service (WW No. 4/1). Later, after Paula has successfully performed the three arduous labors, Aphrodite accepts her "as initiate in the service of love and beauty!" (WW No. 4/4). (*See* GUNTHER, PAULA VON [BARONESS].)

In December 1943 Aphrodite provides Wonder Woman with "an idea for controlling [her] airplane by mental radio," an inspiration that leads to the creation of the famous robot plane (Sen No. 24: "Adventure of the Pilotless Plane"). (*See* WONDER WOMAN [section C 4, the robot plane].)

In January–February 1947, after QUEEN ATOMIA has escaped from her imprisoning Venus girdle and returned to a life of evil, Aphrodite welds the Venus girdle onto Atomia permanently "with the rays of eternal love! No power can remove it," proclaims Aphrodite. "Forever thy heart shall overflow with kindness. Thou shalt ever be devoted to the worship of love, beauty and humanity!" (WW No. 21/3: "Ruler of the Atom World").

In May–June 1947, after Wonder Woman and the HOLLIDAY GIRLS have been transformed into VALKYRIES by GUNDRA and her followers, it is Aphrodite who restores them to their proper human forms (WW No. 23/1: "Siege of the Savage War Maidens"). (*See* ODIN.)

In April–May 1976, seven years after STEVE TREVOR'S death at the hands of DOCTOR CYBER'S henchmen, Aphrodite uses her divine powers to bring Trevor back to life again (WW No. 223: "Welcome Back to Life . . . Steve Trevor!").

ARTHUR (King). A British chieftain of the 5th–6th century A.D., and the central figure of a large body of pseudo-historical and romantic literature. In legend he is the ruler of Camelot, the seat of his court and of the Round Table. The wizard MERLIN is his seer and counselor. His wife, QUEEN GUINEVERE, betrays him by having an amour with SIR LANCELOT, his dearest knight.

In Wonder Woman No. 54/1, Merlin is portrayed as a villain who has stolen Arthur's enchanted sword, Excalibur, kidnapped the queen, and locked them both away in his impregnable stronghold, Castle Sinister.

By July–August 1952 bizarre fireballs have begun raining down from the sky, wreaking havoc throughout the earth. When Wonder Woman retrieves two of the fireballs, extinguishes their flames, and then splits open their hollow inner cores, she finds King Arthur and Sir Lancelot imprisoned inside.

King Arthur explains that Merlin stole Excalibur, and that when he and his knights marched on Castle Sinister to retrieve it, a rain of blazing fireballs came hurtling out of the sky, engulfing him and his knights and carrying them off.

"These fireballs must really be time machine missiles with which Merlin trapped you," muses WONDER WOMAN aloud, "--sending you and your knights into our time--rendering you powerless against him!"

Transported through the time barrier to Arthur's Camelot—along with King Arthur, Sir Lancelot, and STEVE TREVOR—by means of the Amazon "time-and-space transformer" (*see* AMAZONS [section G, Amazon science]), Wonder Woman singlehandedly defeats the evil Merlin, recovers

Excalibur, and rescues the kidnapped Guinevere from the villain's clutches ("The Wizard of Castle Sinister!").

ASTRA (Queen). The infant queen of the planet INFANTA, one of a number of young girls, abandoned to the elements by the ancient Spartans as "weaklings," who were rescued from certain death by QUEEN HIPPOLYTE and the AMAZONS. In honor of her great courage, Hippolyte named her Astra, "after the stars." After the Amazons had resettled Astra and her peers on the planet Infanta, Astra's "remarkable prowess and devotion to others" had earned her the right to become Infanta's queen. Twice in the past, Astra has come to the aid of WONDER WOMAN and the Amazons: once when Astra and her fellow Infantas helped defeat a combined force of Martian men and DUXO boys who had invaded PARADISE ISLAND (WW No. 36/1, Jul/Aug '49: "The Girl Who Saved Paradise Island!"), and once when Astra accompanied Wonder Woman into outer space to battle the DUKE OF DECEPTION and his Martian space fleet (Sen No. 92, Aug '49: "The Pebble That Saved the World!").

Queen Astra

ASTRONIMO (Professor). Professor of astronomy at the HOLLIDAY COLLEGE FOR WOMEN in Washington, D.C. His name is alternately rendered as Astronomo.

In March–April 1947, with the help of the HOLLIDAY GIRLS, Professor Astronimo constructs an instrument-carrying rocket designed to gather useful scientific data on the planet VENUS. It is by stowing away aboard this rocket that GELL OSEY journeys to Venus, creating a crisis for both QUEEN DESIRA and WONDER WOMAN (WW No. 22/3: "Jealousy Visits the Winged Women of Venus!"). (*See* OSEY, GELL.)

Professor Astronimo, March-April 1947

In November 1947, after a series of "robot super-stratosphere" aircraft being tested by the U.S. Army have crashed in flames for no apparent reason, it is Professor Astronimo who provides the sorely needed explanation: "Your robot stratosphere planes must have torn through the cosmic dust curtain!" he explains. "Now there is nothing to prevent the rays of the sun from scorching the Earth to a cinder!" Soon, continues the professor, "every living thing--**every** substance in the path of the rays will melt like butter! What's worse--any stratospheric disturbance will increase the rip in the cosmic curtain!"

Professor Astronimo's alarming revelation leads ultimately to Wonder Woman's battle with the ruthless QUEEN FLAMINA (Sen No. 71: "The Invasion of the Sun Warriors").

Professor Astronimo, November 1947

In October 1948 Professor Astronimo warns of an impending invasion by aliens inhabiting a planet beneath the surface of the MOON:

My calculations show that the moon is **hollow**! It contains a planet and a sun of its own.

There is no life or atmosphere on the **outside** of the moon, but there **is** a highly developed civilization **inside**!

Now my calculations prove that the men of the inner moon are planning to invade. . . .

To silence Professor Astronimo and prevent him from providing Earth people with further information concerning their impending invasion, the moon aliens temporarily steal his mind away with their diabolical "mental drainage" machine, but Earth is ultimately saved—and the moon aliens defeated—through the heroic efforts of Wonder Woman (Sen No. 82: "Brain Pirates from the Inner Moon-World!"). (*See* LUNAR [KING].)

ATHENA. In Greek mythology, the goddess of wisdom.

In the WONDER WOMAN chronicles, she is—along with APHRODITE—one of the patron goddesses of the AMAZONS. It was Athena who taught QUEEN HIPPOLYTE "the secret art of moulding a human form" which enabled her to sculpt the lifelike statue which, once Aphrodite had granted it the gift of life, became the Amazon princess Diana, later to become known to the world at large as Wonder Woman (WW No. 1/1, Sum '42).

Athena bestowed upon Queen Hippolyte the divine gift of the "magic sphere" (Sen No. 24, Dec '43: "Adventure of the Pilotless Plane"). Together with Aphrodite, she instructed Hippolyte to fashion the "magic lasso" for Wonder Woman, and endowed it with the power to control the behavior of others (Sen No. 6, Jun '42). (*See also* AMAZONS [section F 2, the magic sphere]; WONDER WOMAN [section C 3, the magic lasso].)

ATLANTIS. A legendary island in the Atlantic Ocean which, according to Plato, was the site of a powerful kingdom more than 11,000 years ago before it sank to the bottom of the sea. According to Wonder Woman No. 8/1, Atlantis sank beneath the waves one million years ago (Spr '44: "Queen Clea's Tournament of Death") and survives to this day as a "subsea realm," on dry land, "beneath the bottom of the Atlantic Ocean" (CC No. 18, Dec/Jan '46-'47: "The Menace of the Rebel Manlings").

Although Atlantis lies far beneath the ocean surface, it is not covered with water, for "When Atlantis sank beneath the sea, the earth folded over it, sealing it in a vast air pocket under the ocean floor." Two extinct volcano craters link At-

lantis with the surface world, one providing an entranceway, the other an exit (WW No. 8/1, Spr '44: "Queen Clea's Tournament of Death").

Throughout Atlantis, women reign supreme. They are tall, statuesque—much larger than girls from the surface world—and beautiful, but they are also arrogant, vain, and inclined to cruelty. Like the ancient Romans, they delight in violent sports and fierce gladiatorial combats.

The men of Atlantis—called "manlings"—are weak, undersized, unintelligent, and generally fit for only the most menial tasks. "Manlings are dull and stupid," remarks a lovely Atlantean warrior in Spring 1944, "—they **never** escape from us **Atlantean** girls! We keep them working constantly as slaves or soldiers--that is all a **manling** desires!" (WW No. 8/1: "Queen Clea's Tournament of Death").

Despite this contemptuous pronouncement, however, Atlantis experiences two manling revolts between Spring 1944 and December 1946–January 1947 (WW No. 8/3, Spr '44: "The Captive Queen"; CC No. 18, Dec/Jan '46-'47: "The Menace of the Rebel Manlings").

The elite corps of an Atlantean army consists of phalanxes of women shock troops who soar through the air on the backs of giant pterodactyls (WW No. 8/2, Spr '44: "The Girl with the Iron Mask"; and others).

The two leading nations of Atlantis are AURANIA and VENTURIA. Aurania is ruled by the lovely QUEEN EERAS. Venturia is ruled by QUEEN CLEA until Spring 1944, when she is deposed through the efforts of WONDER WOMAN (WW No. 8/1-3: "Queen Clea's Tournament of Death"; "The Girl with the Iron Mask"; "The Captive Queen"). Thereafter, Queen Eeras's daughter OCTAVIA rules Venturia, first as its queen (WW No. 8/3, Spr '44: "The Captive Queen"), and later as its democratically elected president (Sen No. 35, Nov '44: "Girls Under the Sea").

In Spring 1944 Wonder Woman visits Atlantis for the first time and has a series of adventures there (WW No. 8/1-3: "Queen Clea's Tournament of Death"; "The Girl with the Iron Mask"; "The Captive Queen"). (*See* EERAS [QUEEN].)

In November 1944 Wonder Woman journeys to Atlantis to battle the evil SONTAG HENYA (Sen No. 35: "Girls Under the Sea").

In December 1946–January 1947 Wonder Woman returns to Atlantis to thwart the sinister machinations of the evil MANLIUS (CC No. 18: "The Menace of the Rebel Manlings").

In January–February 1953, shortly after the *Swordfish*, the world's first atomic-powered submarine, has vanished without a trace in the midst of its maiden voyage, Earth's plant life begins growing at a ferocious pace, transforming the city where Wonder Woman lives, almost overnight, into an impenetrable jungle. On the hunch that the disappearance of the *Swordfish* and the spectacular acceleration of the city's plant growth may somehow be related, Wonder Woman sets out in search of the missing submarine, but as her Amazon plane (*see* WONDER WOMAN [section C 4, the robot plane]) plows through the ocean depths, it is attacked by a strange saucerlike craft—a so-called "submarine saucer"—which scoops up the plane with Wonder Woman inside it and carries it off to the "strange world" of Atlantis located beneath the ocean floor.

Eons ago, Wonder Woman soon learns, Atlantis's scientists formulated and carried out a plan to "detach Atlantis from Earth and move it beneath the bed of the sea" in order to safeguard it against attack by hostile nations. Ever since, Atlantis and its super-scientific civilization have prospered beneath the ocean floor, periodically sending out scouting parties to reconnoiter the surface world in order to monitor its level of scientific achievement. Fearful that, with the advent of their first atomic-powered submarine, the people of the surface world have finally developed their technology to the point of being capable of launching a devastating attack against Atlantis, the Atlanteans captured the new submarine and, as a form of preventive warfare, unleashed a special "pollen" against the surface world with the intention of rapidly accelerating its plant growth and transforming the entire planet into an impenetrable, uninhabitable jungle.

Ultimately, however, Wonder Woman persuades the Atlanteans that preventive warfare against the surface world is unnecessary, and even promises to defend Atlantis herself in the event the subsea realm is ever attacked.

"From now on," promises the Atlantean leader, as Wonder Woman prepares to depart for home with the kidnapped submarine, "--we shall not seek to avenge ourselves against Earth—as long as people like you live on it!" (WW No. 57/2: "Vengeance of the Undersea Empire!"). The Atlantis described in this adventure is clearly not the Atlantis portrayed in Wonder Woman's earlier Atlantean adventures.

ATOMIA (Queen). The red-haired, green-eyed monarch of Atomic Kingdom U-235, the "ruling planet" of a vast "atomic universe." After her treacherous dictatorial ambitions have been repeatedly thwarted by WONDER WOMAN—and after the goddess APHRODITE has welded a "magic Venus girdle" around her waist "with the rays of

eternal love"—Atomia resolves henceforth to use the power of the atom to help humanity.

In January–February 1947 a mysterious "sphere of uranium atoms"—released by the detonation of an atomic bomb at a test site somewhere in the Pacific—grows rapidly in size and complexity by "capturing neutrons from the fragments of the [exploded] atom bomb." As the "hurtling ball of atomic radioactivity" propels itself through the air, Paula (*see* GUNTHER, PAULA VON [BARONESS]), acting under Wonder Woman's instructions, snares it with a "magnetic Amazon sky trap" and takes it to her secret laboratory for study.

Queen Atomia and three of her neutron slaves

From the captured sphere of uranium atoms—called an "atomic universe"—Paula carefully isolates one uranium atom so that she and Wonder Woman can examine it under the "Amazon mass spectrometor." After ETTA CANDY and the HOLLIDAY GIRLS have been summoned to Paula's laboratory to observe the forthcoming atomic experiments, Wonder Woman and her friends gaze at the isolated uranium atom through a special "Amazon microscope," watching it resolve before their very eyes into a tiny atomic world populated by protons and neutrons.

"But . . ." cries Wonder Woman in amazement, "those **protons** on the atom planet are really **women**! And the **neutrons**--see, they're turning into creatures like **robots**!"

Indeed, the mysterious atom world is ruled by the beautiful but treacherous Queen Atomia, attended by a bevy of lovely blond "proton girls" and served by an army of blue "neutron slaves" or "neutron robots."

Furious with Wonder Woman and Paula for "capturing the [atomic] universe I was building," Atomia resolves to wreak vengeance on the unsuspecting humans. By ordering her neutron slaves to "turn on more electronic force," she causes her entire atom planet to leap from the stage of the

Amazon microscope into a beaker of water in a nearby section of the laboratory.

The chemical reaction which results when Atomia's U-235 kingdom comes into contact with the water in the beaker produces "hydroxo gas," a "strange vapor" which renders Wonder Woman and her companions unconscious, shrinks them to microscopic size, and transports them into Atomia's atomic world in the form of proton girls. "The radioactive vapor has turned the mortals into protons," gloats Atomia. "Ha ha!"

Atomia's scheme involves transforming Wonder Woman, Paula, Etta Candy, and the Holliday Girls into mindless neutron slaves, but the captives manage ultimately to escape and make their way back to their own full-sized world (WW No. 21/1: "The Mystery of the Atom World").

Atomia has by no means been defeated, however, for now she plots to increase the size of her atom universe a millionfold and destroy the entire Earth. "We uranium atoms are the **largest,** most **powerful** of all," she gloats. "Enough of us working together can destroy the atoms of all other matter—blow the Earth into a million pieces and reduce it to our size. Ha-haa!"

By ordering her neutron slaves to "turn on the electronic force," Atomia can propel her atomic kingdom through the air like a meteor, guiding it as if it were an aircraft. By crashing her atom planet against the Amazon "spectrometor cylinder" in which Wonder Woman and Paula had enclosed it, Atomia succeeds in blowing up the spectrometer and escaping from Paula's laboratory.

Guided by Atomia, the atomic universe streaks through the air to a uranium mine, where the arrival of Atomia's kingdom produces "a tremendous explosion," causing "trillions of uranium atoms" to be "drawn into Queen Atomia's kingdom," thus greatly increasing its size.

Expanded by the explosion at the uranium mine, the atomic universe is now a threat to the entire world: a while ago, one could examine it only under a special microscope, but now it has grown so large that it dwarfs great buildings.

While attempting to combat the new atomic menace, Wonder Woman and STEVE TREVOR are overcome by hydroxo gas, reduced in size, and transported into Atomia's atomic world. After a brief struggle with Atomia's neutron slaves, however, Wonder Woman captures Atomia with her magic lasso (see WONDER WOMAN [section C 3, the magic lasso]). Climbing atop two of the neutron robots, Wonder Woman, Atomia, and Trevor travel piggy-back to Paula's laboratory in the full-sized world, where Paula uses her daughter Gerta's "en-

larging machine" (see GUNTHER, GERTA VON) to transform Wonder Woman, Trevor, and Queen Atomia to full human size. Atomia will be taken to Reform Island (see TRANSFORMATION ISLAND) to receive Amazon rehabilitative therapy, and the atomic universe, "no longer ruled by the power of the evil queen . . . shoots aimlessly into the stratosphere, no longer bent on destruction" (WW No. 21/2, Jan/Feb '47: "Tide of Atomic Fire").

While Wonder Woman is flying toward Reform Island with the captive Queen Atomia, however, the queen executes a spectacular escape with the aid of the two neutron robots Wonder Woman and Trevor had used earlier as transportation to the outer world. In an effort to wreak vengeance on Wonder Woman for her past defeats, Atomia kidnaps Etta Candy and the Holliday Girls, but Wonder Woman races to the scene, smashes the two neutron robots, and recaptures Atomia.

On Reform Island, Atomia is locked into a magic Venus girdle to make her loving and submissive (see AMAZONS [section F, the magic Venus girdles]), but the Venus girdle loosens in the midst of an Amazon athletic contest, then falls off entirely, and Atomia once again becomes her former, treacherous self.

Because the other Amazon prisoners on Reform Island are still wearing their Venus girdles, they are compelled to obey anyone who chooses to command them, a fact Atomia uses to her advantage in launching a spectacular prisoner revolt. Havoc reigns until Wonder Woman appears on the scene, captures Atomia with her magic lasso, and compels her to end the inmate rebellion.

To prevent a recurrence of the difficulties posed by the loosened Venus girdle and Atomia's subsequent rebellion, the goddess Aphrodite welds a Venus girdle around Atomia's waist "with the rays of eternal love," assuring that it will remain fixed there for all time.

"No power can remove it," explains Aphrodite. "Forever thy heart shall overflow with kindness. Thou shalt ever be devoted to the worship of love, beauty and humanity!"

Then Wonder Woman gives Atomia a draft of "liquid hydroxo gas." "It will shrink you again to your normal proton size," she explains. "You are now ready to return to your [atom] planet!"

With Atomia a proton once again, Wonder Woman uses an Amazon "telescopic gun" to shoot her "into the stratosphere and onto [her] atomic world!"

On Kingdom U-235, Atomia is welcomed joyously by her subjects. Fortified with Aphrodite's power of eternal love, Atomia resolves henceforth to use the mighty powers of the atom to further mankind's greatest goals (WW No. 21/3, Jan/Feb '47: "Ruler of the Atom World").

AURANIA. One of the two leading nations of AT-LANTIS, a continent which, according to the WON-DER WOMAN chronicles, sank beneath the Atlantic Ocean one million years ago. Atlantis's other leading nation is VENTURIA.

Though Atlantis lies far beneath the surface of the Atlantic, it is not covered with water, for "When Atlantis sank beneath the sea, the earth folded over it, sealing it in a vast air pocket under the ocean floor."

Throughout Atlantis, women reign supreme. They are tall, statuesque—much larger than girls from the surface world—and beautiful, but they are also arrogant, vain, and inclined to cruelty. Like the ancient Romans, they delight in violent sports and fierce gladiatorial combats.

The men of Atlantis—called "manlings"—are weak, undersized, unintelligent, and generally fit for only the most menial tasks. "Manlings are dull and stupid," remarks a lovely Venturian warrior in Spring 1944, "—they **never** escape from us **Atlantean** girls! We keep them working constantly as slaves or soldiers--that is all a **manling** desires!" (WW No. 8/1: "Queen Clea's Tournament of Death").

Despite this contemptuous pronouncement, however, Atlantis experiences two manling revolts between Spring 1944 and December 1946–January 1947 (WW No. 8/3, Spr '44: "The Captive Queen"; CC No. 18, Dec/Jan '46–'47: "The Menace of the Rebel Manlings").

The elite corps of an Atlantean army consists of phalanxes of women shock troops who soar through the air on the backs of giant pterodactyls (WW No. 8/2, Spr '44: "The Girl with the Iron Mask"; and others).

QUEEN EERAS, the ruler of Aurania and a close friend of Wonder Woman, is the mother of OCTAVIA, who becomes the ruler of Venturia following the final overthrow of QUEEN CLEA in Spring 1944 (WW No. 8/3: "The Captive Queen").

AUTOMATO. A far-distant planet inhabited by "robot people" who invade the planet JUPITER in September–October 1951.

In September–October 1951 WONDER WOMAN encounters a group of Jovian children who have fled to Earth with their nurse to escape an invasion of their home planet by the robot people of Automato. Journeying to Jupiter in her Amazon plane (see WONDER WOMAN [section C 4, the robot plane]), Wonder Woman turns back the robot invasion and helps the warring parties resolve their differences. Jupiter is rich in duranium, a metal desperately needed by Automato's robot people. When Wonder Woman locates a hitherto undiscovered supply of the precious metal, the conflict is resolved and peace comes to both planets (Sen No. 105: "The Secret of the Giant Forest").

BADRA. An evil alien from the planet Hator who is endowed with incredible superhuman powers. She and her gang of ruthless female criminals are apprehended by WONDER WOMAN in February–March 1948.

The beautiful raven-haired Badra is the sole survivor of the terrible war which destroyed Hator and annihilated its entire "loveless, lawless population," for whom hatred, duplicity, and continual warfare had been the accepted way of life.

When the final battle had broken out, young Badra — next in line to the planet's throne — had hidden in a secret room, and the cataclysmic explosion that destroyed the entire planet had somehow catapulted her safely to Earth, where she had grown to maturity.

Endowed with phenomenal, unearthly powers, Badra "moves faster than the speed of light" and "is not susceptible to the laws of gravity," enabling her to fly through the air without either aircraft or special equipment. A cunning thief endowed with superhuman strength, she "crashes through walls and ceilings — takes what [she] wants — and disappears!"

Wonder Woman apprehends Badra and her gang and, since no Earth prison could possibly hold her, takes Badra to TRANSFORMATION ISLAND, where she will be taught "to love instead of hate!" (CC No. 25: "Hatred of Badra!").

Badra

BALE (Duke). A tyrannical moon-man who is responsible for the cruel oppression of the MOON's inhabitants. Acting on a plea for aid from the moon's exploited population, WONDER WOMAN journeys to the moon in October 1956, defeats Duke Bale, and, by her example, inspires the moon people to fight for their freedom against the forces of tyranny (WW No. 85/1: "The Sword in the Sky!").

BAMKO, JOE "the Gyp." The leader of a gang of criminals, "wanted for hijacking Army supplies," who attempt to steal $1 billion in gold bullion from the vault of the U.S. Treasury Building, only to be apprehended by WONDER WOMAN (Sen No. 38, Feb '45: "Racketeers Kidnap Miss Santa Claus").

BARANIA. The medieval kingdom which is the scene of a power struggle between the young King Philippe and his "villainous uncle," COUNT GASTON (WW No. 27/3, Jan/Feb '48: "The Mystical Power of Idea-Forms!").

BAR-L RANCH. The Texas ranch owned by HARD CANDY, the father of ETTA CANDY (Sen No. 67, Jul '47: "The Secret of the Bar-L Ranch!").

BARNACLE (Captain). The modern-day pirate chieftain who is the leader of the Barnacle Gang. He and his henchmen are apprehended by WONDER WOMAN.

In July–August 1951 Captain Barnacle and his gang find the map to a long-lost treasure buried "three centuries ago" by the pirate CAPT. STORM. The land it is buried on, however, is now part of the campus of the HOLLIDAY COLLEGE FOR WOMEN in Washington, D.C.

Disguised as workmen, Captain Barnacle and his henchmen invade the Holliday College grounds and make off with the treasure, but they are ultimately outwitted by Wonder Woman, who apprehends the Barnacle Gang and turns the treasure over to Holliday College, which was threatened with closing unless it could come up with $200,000 by the end of the month (WW No. 48/2: "The Treasure of Capt. Storm").

BEETA LAMDA. The Holliday College sorority of which ETTA CANDY is president.

BELLARA ISLAND. An uncharted island kingdom, ruled by King Terro and his wife Queen Yilla, which is the scene of WONDER WOMAN's battle with the evil PRIME MINISTER ZAGO (WW No. 52/1, Mar/Apr '52: "Her Majesty — Queen Wonder Woman!").

BIG REXO GANG, THE. "A group of ruthless

criminals specializing in holdups of military posts." They are apprehended by WONDER WOMAN in November–December 1949 after STEVE TREVOR has accidentally stumbled upon their hideout (Sen No. 94: "S O S Wonder Woman!").

BITTERLAND. The icy domain of the Seal Men, lying far beneath the South Polar ice cap, separated from EVELAND by the River of Destruction. Bitterland is ruled by KING RIGOR, aided and abetted by his treacherous son, Prince Pagli. WONDER WOMAN defeats the Seal Men in Summer 1945 and compels them to sign a peace treaty with the lovely maidens of Eveland ((WW No. 13/1–3: "The Icebound Maidens"; "The Mystery Maid"; "Slaves in the Electric Gardens"). (*See* RIGOR [KING].)

BLACK ROBERT (of Dogwood). A "vile traitor" who, by February 1947, has usurped the throne of Anglonia and cast Hubert, the country's rightful ruler, into a dungeon. Black Robert is defeated, and Hubert restored to the throne, through the heroic efforts of WONDER WOMAN and STEVE TREVOR.

In February 1947 Steve Trevor and Wonder Woman, "flying over Asia, are blown off their course across an unmapped desert" and forced to crash-land "somewhere near Palestine," in the tiny nation of Anglonia.

Emerging from the wreckage of their plane, Trevor and Wonder Woman find themselves standing in the middle of a 13th-century jousting field, where they are taken prisoner by knights clad in medieval armor, henchmen of the evil Black Robert of Dogwood.

". . . King Richard of Briton led a crusade through here to free Jerusalem centuries ago!" observes Wonder Woman. "Some knights became lost in these mountains. Their descendants, our captors, still live as did their knightly ancestors!"

Confusion arises immediately over the fact that Steve Trevor is an exact double for Hubert, rightful heir to Anglonia's throne. Sometime in the recent past, Black Robert had overthrown the lawful government of King Richard and cast his son Hubert into a dungeon. Now Black Robert believes that Hubert somehow escaped the dungeon and returned to claim the throne, and Hubert's Anglonian partisans believe that their man has returned to lead them against Black Robert. They rescue Trevor just as he is about to be beheaded by Black Robert's executioners, and he agrees to lead them in an assault on Black Robert's castle fortress.

The partisans fight bravely, but they are poorly equipped and no match for Black Robert's well-armed henchmen. Just as the battle appears lost, however, Wonder Woman arrives on the scene to turn the tide in favor of Trevor and his allies. Before long, Black Robert has been defeated and Hubert restored to the throne.

Disdainful of pomp, ceremony, and power, Hubert invites Wonder Woman and Trevor to remain in Anglonia and rule the country in his stead, but they persuade him to institute a democracy in place of the traditional monarchy and let the people elect a president (Sen No. 62: "The Mysterious Prisoners of Anglonia.").

BLAKFU. The blackhearted king of the MOLE MEN. He is defeated and reformed in April–May 1943 through the heroic efforts of WONDER WOMAN and BARONESS PAULA VON GUNTHER.

Far beneath the surface of the earth, the treacherous Blakfu rules over the Mole Men with an iron hand. Life far underground has rendered the Mole Men almost totally blind, making it necessary for them to use slaves — girls kidnapped from the "upper world," called "eyes" — to perform the seeing function for them.

By April–May 1943 Blakfu has decided to invade the upper world:

> We must conquer America **now** and rule the world! For centuries we've waited for upper world men to weaken. The First World War seemed our opportunity, but it ended too quickly — too many nations survived!
>
> Today 2 billion people are fighting on every continent! Every nation in the world has seen chaos and bloodshed within its own boundaries, except the United States — taking over the rest of the battle-scarred world will be **simple**. . . .
>
> We'll undermine the American capitol, drop all important buildings to the underworld, and capture government officials. Our excavations [to the upper world] are nearly complete!

Soon a huge hole in the ground appears on the campus of the HOLLIDAY COLLEGE FOR WOMEN, and ETTA CANDY and the HOLLIDAY GIRLS fall into it and hurtle to the underworld, where they are taken prisoner by the ruthless Mole Men. When Paula and Wonder Woman descend into the Mole Men's subterranean domain soon afterward, they too are taken captive. Weighted with shackles and fitted with special iron shoes, Wonder Woman is forced to dance before the Mole Men atop an electrified metal grid.

"When this girl's [Wonder Woman's] chains are removed," cackles Blakfu, "she must dance to save herself from electrocution! Her slave sandals and the electrified floor plate neutralize each other if contacts are brief. But when she stops dancing, she will die!"

After dancing for hours, Wonder Woman breaks

free of the electrical grid and, with Paula's help, organizes a successful revolt of the Mole Men's female slaves. Before long, every single Mole Man has been taken prisoner.

Calla, the chief slave, is in love with Blakfu, but, being almost totally blind, the mole monarch is unaware of Calla's great beauty. Using her Amazon surgical skill, Wonder Woman performs a series of operations that restore the eyesight of Blakfu and the Mole Men. Gazing upon Calla for the first time, Blakfu becomes aware of the true "beauty of women" and no longer feels the need to enslave or mistreat them. He promptly announces his intentions to make Calla his queen and to rule his subterranean kingdom in peace and justice (WW No. 4/2).

In December 1944 Blakfu is one of the six infamous villains and villainesses impersonated by actors in BEDWIN FOOTH's "underworld crime [theatrical] company" (Sen No. 36: "Battle Against Revenge").

BLITZ (Supreme Leader). The leader of a ruthless band of Nazi "war criminals" who have eluded the Allies and set up a new headquarters deep in the African jungle. Their attempt to conquer the world with their diabolical "brain wave of death" is thwarted by WONDER WOMAN.

In September–October 1946 America's military establishment is in turmoil, with "scores of high military officials . . . dropping dead," apparently struck down by some mysterious, invisible weapon.

One sunny afternoon at Happytime Beach, MARYA THE MOUNTAIN GIRL — who has been "earning money to go through college by working as a lifeguard" — dives into the surf to rescue Admiral Seagoer, who is calling for help and seems in imminent danger of drowning. When other swimmers finally reach the stricken admiral, however, they find Seagoer dead and Marya inexplicably vanished.

Certain that a relationship exists between Marya's disappearance and the deaths of America's military leaders, Wonder Woman decides to search for Marya in hopes of locating the "invisible ray" responsible for the rash of mysterious deaths.

Indeed, Wonder Woman's hunch is correct, for Marya has been kidnapped by Nazi war criminals who plan to use her brain to provide power for their sinister new super-weapon.

"Ve Nazis vere defeated by physical weapons," gloats one of the Nazis, "— but zere is **no** vay to combat our **mental brain vave** of **death!**

"Ve escaped der Allies und stole dis submarine," continues the Nazi, as he and his cohorts speed away with the captive Marya aboard their "rocket-like submarine." "Now ve make your brain destroy America! Ve few escaped Nazis und our supreme leader [Supreme Leader Blitz] vill rule der vorld!"

Pursuing the Nazis to darkest Africa, Wonder Woman rescues Marya from the villains' clutches. The war criminals, however, are still at large, determined to conquer America with their brain wave of death (WW No. 19/1: "Invisible Terror!").

While Marya and Wonder Woman set out in search of the Nazis once again, Supreme Leader Blitz and his henchmen ponder the problem of obtaining new slaves to power their diabolical death ray: ". . . ve must haff slaves for our machine!" exclaims Blitz. "Many of der slaves making der death ray haf died because der brains und body energy iss used up--already der oomvolts of der machine haf fallen off so ve cannot reach America! Ve mus haf more slaves if ve are to control America!"

Blitz and his Nazis have cowed the chief of the local Meanug tribe into capturing members of the Zoogoo tribe to use as slaves for the brain wave machine. When Wonder Woman and Marya intervene in a valiant attempt to prevent the Meanugs from capturing and enslaving the Zoogoos, they are taken prisoner by the Meanugs and are about to be decapitated when STEVE TREVOR, who has flown to Africa in response to an urgent "mental radio" message (see WONDER WOMAN [section C 7, the mental radio]) from Wonder Woman, appears on the scene and rescues them. Freed from the clutches of the Meanugs, Wonder Woman, Marya, and Trevor set out in search of the war criminals' secret jungle headquarters (WW No. 19/2, Sep/Oct '46: "The Witchdoctor's Cauldron").

Realizing that locating and storming the secret headquarters is a hopeless proposition — since Supreme Leader Blitz can destroy them at any time with the brain wave of death merely by knowing their whereabouts and forming a mental image of them in his mind — Wonder Woman decides that the safest course for herself and her friends is for her to surrender to the enemy in hopes of being taken into the very heart of the "terrible death ray fortress."

After surrendering to Blitz's Meanug allies, Wonder Woman is taken through the jungle to the "death ray headquarters," but because her bracelets have been chained together by her male captors, she no longer possesses the superhuman strength necessary to defeat the war criminals. (See WONDER WOMAN [section C 2, the bracelets of submission].)

Realizing that Wonder Woman has been deprived of her Amazon powers, Marya bravely assults the death ray fortress, only to be taken prisoner also, but together the two women manage to break free of their shackles and to capture Supreme Leader Blitz and his entire Nazi "death ray gang" (WW No. 19/3, Sep/Oct '46: "In the Lair of the Death Ray Criminals").

BLIZZARD (Prime Minister). The ruthless prime minister of ICEBERG-LAND. His scheme to conquer New York City, and then the world, is thwarted by WONDER WOMAN.

In May–June 1948 PROF. CHEMICO of Holliday College unveils his latest invention, the "climate-changer--a machine which will heat the ice-bound regions of the frozen North! With this machine, man can reclaim the coldest portions of the globe and grow tropical flowers at the North Pole!"

With his fabulous climate-changer, Prof. Chemico can make the surrounding environment either hotter or colder. "I hope it'll help relieve the food shortage in the world by enabling crops to be grown in the unproductive frigid regions," he explains. "I start for the North Pole tomorrow to experiment--"

News of Prof. Chemico's climate-changer is hardly welcome at the North Pole, however, where its use to heat up the environment would spell disaster for the "icicle men" and "snow maidens" of Iceberg-Land.

Having learned by radio of Prof. Chemico's forthcoming expedition to the North Pole, Prime Minister Blizzard persuades lovely Princess Snowina, Iceberg-Land's ruler, that they must steal the machine to prevent it from melting away their entire civilization. In addition, however, Blizzard hopes to use the climate-changer to make himself master of the world.

Aided by Princess Snowina's soldiers, Blizzard steals the climate-changer from Prof. Chemico's expeditionary vessel and uses it to create a huge glacier, which he equips with a "powerful propeller motor" to provide it with speed and mobility. When Princess Snowina attempts to intervene, Blizzard makes her his prisoner. Blizzard's scheme involves ramming his colossal glacier into New York Harbor and wrecking the entire city with it. "When the world discovers what I've done to the largest city in the world," thinks Blizzard, "they'll meet my terms."

After making prisoners of Wonder Woman, Prof. Chemico, the HOLLIDAY GIRLS, and the crew of Prof. Chemico's ship, Blizzard crashes his glacier into New York Harbor. Crowds panic and huge skyscrapers teeter and totter on the brink of collapse. "It seems certain," notes the narrative text, "that New York City will be destroyed."

Wonder Woman, however, turns the tables on her captor and, "with super-herculean strength . . . pulls the giant ice mass out to sea," where it will melt harmlessly. Returning Iceberg-Land to the control of the lovely Princess Snowina, Wonder Woman explains that Americans were unaware of Iceberg-Land's existence. Now that they know Princess Snowina's people are dependent upon the North Pole's frozen climate for their very survival, they will see to it that Prof. Chemico's climate-changer is never used there (WW No. 29/1: "Ice World's Conquest!").

BLUE SEAL GANG, THE. A gang of ruthless criminals — secretly led by Mr. Leeder, owner of *Fearless Men Magazine* — who are apprehended in December 1947 through the heroic efforts of WONDER WOMAN and lovely Chic Novelle.

In December 1947 the Blue Seal Gang makes an unsuccessful attempt to assassinate Chic Novelle's sister, Mayor Rita Novelle of Triboro City, in retaliation for her refusal to accept their backing in the recent election and her unwillingness to help them loot the Triboro City treasury. Rescued from death by Wonder Woman — who applies some "Amazon healing salve" to her gunshot wounds — the mayor is kidnapped from her hospital bed soon afterward by members of the same gang. The gang also kidnaps SELLDOM WRIGHT, Chic Novelle's boyfriend, in the hope that his sudden disappearance will convince the police that Wright is the criminals' secret leader.

Selldom Wright and Rita Novelle are rescued from the villains' clutches by Wonder Woman and Chic Novelle, who invade their hideout, capture the criminals, and expose Mr. Leeder as their leader (Sen No. 72: "The Menace of the Blue Seal Gang").

BOADICEA (Queen). A British queen who, in 60 A.D., led a short-lived revolt against Roman rule, burning several towns and military posts, killing 70,000 Romans and collaborationist Britons, and annihilating the 9th Roman legion marching to their rescue. Her forces finally crushed in a desperate battle in which thousands of Britons fell, Boadicea either died of shock or committed suicide by taking poison.

In Sensation Comics No. 60 — which contains numerous historical inaccuracies, most notably the unmistakable inference that Boadicea and her followers succeeded in driving the Romans from Britain — WONDER WOMAN and young BIFTON JONES journey into the past, to ancient Britain in the year 60 A.D., to rescue Boadicea and her two daughters from a Roman dungeon so that they may be free to launch their famous revolt.

"In a tremendous battle near London," notes

the textual narrative, "Queen Boadicea wipes out the 9th legion, killing 70,000 Romans!" The statement is highly inaccurate, in that it confuses the 70,000 Romans and friendly Britons massacred by Boadicea and her followers (according to the Roman historian Tacitus [*ca.* 56–*ca.* 120 A.D.]) with the vastly smaller Roman 9th legion cut to pieces on the battlefield.

"With the help of the Amazon princess and you, my son," remarks Boadicea gratefully to Bifton Jones, "we have driven Nero's vicious legions from England!" (Dec '46: "The Ordeal of Queen Boadicea").

BOSS, THE. The leader of a gang of criminals who are apprehended by WONDER WOMAN.

In September–October 1951 leprechaun MOON O'DAY sends Diana Prince (*see* PRINCE, DIANA [WONDER WOMAN]) a magic typewriter, to be forwarded as a gift to Wonder Woman, which possesses the magical power to make happen whatever is typed on it. If, for example, one were to type "Rain, rain go away . . ." while it was raining outside, the rainfall would immediately cease.

While it sits on Diana Prince's desk at Military Intelligence, the miraculous typewriter is stolen by a night watchman in cahoots with an underworld chieftain known as the Boss. Aided by the powers of the magic typewriter, the Boss and his henchmen commit a series of spectacular crimes. Wonder Woman finally apprehends the criminals, but the magic typewriter is destroyed in the encounter (WW No. 49/3: "The Mystery of the Magic Typewriter!").

BOURABIA. The "flat sandy island" kingdom, ruled by the good Princess Aranee, which is the scene of WONDER WOMAN's battle with the evil genii ZOXAB. The location of Bourabia is uncertain, for the text states only that it is far from PARADISE ISLAND and that Wonder Woman must race "across uncharted seas" to get there (WW No. 61/2, Sep/Oct '53: "Prisoners of the Ruby Ring!").

BRAIN. The leader of a gang of ruthless spies who are known both as the Green Hat Spy Gang and as the Black Hat Spies. They are apprehended by WONDER WOMAN in March–April 1953.

In March–April 1953 Brain concocts an elaborate scheme to destroy Wonder Woman psychologically by faking her death so that the world believes she has perished, and then by making it impossible for her to prove that she is actually alive. In this way, Brain and his henchmen hope to completely demoralize Wonder Woman, causing her to doubt her own identity and rendering her ineffective as a force against the underworld. Ultimately, hope the criminals, Wonder Woman will become careless and change into her secret civil-ian identity while they are watching, thus enabling them to eliminate her at will, without worrying about the advantage of surprise her secret identity gives her.

As Brain's scheme proceeds, Wonder Woman begins to doubt her own identity, and even her sanity. She begins to question whether she is really Wonder Woman at all, or only an impostor. Ultimately, however, she realizes she has been duped and swiftly apprehends Brain and his gang (WW No. 58/1: "Seven Days to Doom!").

BRAIN PIRATE, THE. The leader of a band of ghostly extradimensional pirates who inhabit DM-X, an alien dimension also referred to as "the inner world."

In August 1965 WONDER WOMAN visits a bookstore specializing in old comic books and begins nostalgically browsing through an old Wonder Woman comic containing accounts of some of her past adventures. Suddenly she finds herself embroiled in a furious battle with the Brain Pirate, an extradimensional villain who takes her prisoner — along with STEVE TREVOR, ETTA CANDY, and the HOLLIDAY GIRLS — and carries his captives to his sanctuary in the inner world, where he robs Trevor and the Holliday Girls of their brains and transforms them into mindless automatons, powerless to do anything but obey his commands. Wonder Woman ultimately defeats the Brain Pirate and his cohorts, however, and restores her friends to normal (WW No. 156: "The Brain Pirate of the Inner World!").

The text is ambiguous on the question of whether Wonder Woman's battle with the Brain Pirate is merely a daydream prompted by her reading of the old comic book, or whether she is actually time-teleported into the past to fight a villain she had defeated previously during her early days as a crime-fighter. The text is explicit, however, in its assertion that the Brain Pirate and his crew are villains out of Wonder Woman's recorded past, enemies she vanquished years ago and is now compelled to battle again, either in fact or in fantasy.

In actuality, however, the early texts contain no record of a Brain Pirate, or of a dimension DM-X or "inner world." The texts do record an early battle with KING LUNAR, the evil ruler of the "inner moon-planet," a world beneath the surface of the MOON (Sen No. 82, Oct '48: "Brain Pirates from the Inner Moon-World!"). King Lunar and his cohorts use "mental drainage" machinery to transform their enemies into mindless zombies, and there are some superficial similarities between King Lunar's world and that of the Brain Pirate. So many meaningful dissimilarities also exist, however, that King

Lunar and the Brain Pirate cannot possibly be regarded as identical villains.

BRAND, LEWIS. A museum visitor-counter who is dissatisfied with his job because he feels that it is useless, trivial, and unimportant. His job takes on new meaning for him in January–February 1950, however, when WONDER WOMAN proves to him that his job is actually "vital and exciting! No one is unimportant in a democracy," insists Wonder Woman, "--and that goes for his job!" (WW No. 39/1: "The Trail of Thrills!").

BRAVO (Col.). A daredevil circus parachutist who is an exact double for STEVE TREVOR (Sen No. 98, Jul/Aug '50: "Wonder Woman's Strange Mission!"). (*See also* BROWN, JANET.)

BREKEL (Boss). A vicious racketeer and master of impersonation (Sen No. 51, Mar '46: "The Crime of Boss Brekel!") who is described as "the slickest counterfeiter in the world" and "one of the underworld's most notorious criminals" (Sen No. 77, May '48: "Tress's Terrible Mistake!").

Boss Brekel, 1946

In March 1946 WONDER WOMAN smashes Boss Brekel's counterfeiting ring and rescues ETTA CANDY and the HOLLIDAY GIRLS from seemingly certain death at its hands. Wonder Woman's efforts to apprehend the Brekel gang are complicated by the fact that Brekel has murdered and impersonated Secret Service Agent Speed Ferrett, so that he now occupies Ferrett's post within the Secret Service. It is only as the adventure draws to a close that Wonder Woman unmasks the bogus Speed Ferrett as the fugitive Brekel (Sen No. 51: "The Crime of Boss Brekel!").

Within two years, Boss Brekel has escaped from prison and returned to the counterfeiting racket, and before long ". . . the country [has been]

flooded with counterfeit government savings bonds."

". . . [O]ur whole national economy is in grave jeopardy!" exclaims the Secretary of the Treasury. "If they get away with this our nation would be in danger of bankruptcy!"

After locating the counterfeiters' hideout and being briefly held captive there, Wonder Woman finally apprehends the Boss Brekel gang in May 1948 (Sen No. 77: "Tress's Terrible Mistake!").

BRIAN, VINCENT. An artist who, in November 1956, becomes convinced that Diana Prince and WONDER WOMAN are one and the same person. By means of an elaborate ruse, however, Wonder Woman persuades Brian that he has made an error in judgment, thereby preserving the secret of her dual identity (WW No. 86/1: "The Painting That Betrayed Wonder Woman!").

BRILYANT, BYRNA. The schoolteacher from Fair Weather Valley, U.S.A., who is secretly the SNOW MAN (Sen No. 59, Nov '46: "Reign of Blue Terror").

BROWN, EVE. The sister of LILA BROWN.

In March 1942 Eve Brown is working as an "errand girl" in the Washington, D.C., office of United States Military Intelligence when it becomes apparent that someone has been leaking secret information to the Nazis. Suspicion focuses on Diana Prince, recently hired as secretary to Colonel Darnell (*see* DARNELL [GENERAL]), and as a result Diana is ordered confined to her quarters pending an investigation.

Probing the security leaks as WONDER WOMAN, however, Diana discovers that the real culprit is Eve Brown. Although Eve is not really a bad person, the Nazis have succeeded in making her their dupe. Ultimately, Wonder Woman succeeds in

Eve Brown and Steve Trevor, 1942

smashing a Nazi spy ring (*see* GROSS) and in exonerating Diana Prince of any complicity in the spying. Eve Brown is apprehended by ETTA CANDY and the HOLLIDAY GIRLS, but Diana requests that instead of being imprisoned for what she has done, Eve be released from custody and permitted to enroll as a student at the HOLLIDAY COLLEGE FOR WOMEN (Sen No. 3).

In April 1942, while Eve is attending classes at Holliday College, she is approached by Gestapo agents who attempt to recruit her for the "school of espionage" operated by BARONESS PAULA VON GUNTHER in "an abandoned coal mine in West Virginia." Eve, however, promptly notifies the authorities, and soon STEVE TREVOR and Wonder Woman find themselves embroiled in a battle of wits with the treacherous baroness (Sen No. 4). (*See* GUNTHER, PAULA VON [BARONESS].)

In February–March 1943 Eve Brown is arrested as a spy when she is falsely implicated in a spy plot by Baroness Paula von Gunther, but she is exonerated soon afterward through the efforts of Wonder Woman (WW No. 3/1). (*See* GUNTHER, PAULA VON [BARONESS].)

BROWN, JANET. A young blonde, desperately in love with STEVE TREVOR despite the fact that she has never met him, who asks WONDER WOMAN, in her capacity as romance editor of the DAILY GLOBE, to help her meet Trevor and win his love. Although in love with Trevor herself, Wonder Woman regards it as her "duty as an Amazon" to help Janet win the heart of the handsome military intelligence officer, but despite her best efforts to play Cupid on Janet's behalf, Trevor has eyes only for Wonder Woman. Janet is heartbroken at Trevor's lack of interest in her, and Wonder Woman must fight back her own tears at the thought that Trevor may decide to abandon her for this newcomer. The dilemma is happily resolved, however, when Janet meets and falls in love with Col. Bravo, a daredevil circus parachutist who is Trevor's exact double (Sen No. 98, Jul/Aug '50: "Wonder Woman's Strange Mission!").

BROWN, JESSE. A high school student, heartbroken at his failure to obtain action photographs of WONDER WOMAN for a high school project, whose problem is solved when Wonder Woman helps him accumulate the pictures he needs (WW No. 89/2, Apr '57: "The Amazon Album!").

BROWN, LILA. The sister of EVE BROWN. Lila serves as STEVE TREVOR's secretary from March 1942 (Sen No. 3) until June–July 1943, when she is killed by a fountain-pen bomb placed on Trevor's desk by the villainous DR. PSYCHO (WW No. 5/3).

BRUTEX. The would-be tyrant, inadvertently responsible for the creation of the PACIFIC OCEAN,

whose attempt to conquer Mount Surana and destroy the Earth is thwarted by WONDER WOMAN in November–December 1949.

Long ago, Mount Surana sat atop the Plain of Plenty, a fertile plain which occupied that portion of the planet Earth now known as the Pacific Ocean. In the days when the Pacific Ocean was a large land mass, it was inhabited by the subjects of the lovely Queen Bravura, who lived there "in ways of peace and love."

One of their number, however, a would-be dictator named Brutex, was determined to marry Queen Bravura and "rule the world with fear and might!" Rebuffed by the peace-loving queen, Brutex had decided to seize power by force. While the nation's women were all gathered atop Mount Surana for an annual feast day celebration, Brutex had set off a titanic explosion in the plain, but had miscalculated its effect. The explosion tore the entire plain free of the planet Earth and hurled it into outer space. Mount Surana became a tiny planetoid, inhabited by Queen Bravura and her country's women, while Brutex and his fellow males — including Bravura's lover Nestor — soared safely into outer space atop another massive land chunk.

"And thus it was," explains Queen Bravura to Wonder Woman, "that a vast hole was left in the Earth when the entire Plain of Plenty was hurled into space--a gigantic cavity which was filled by the torrential rains caused by the effects of the explosion on the atmosphere--and it is this which you now call the Pacific Ocean!"

In November–December 1949 Queen Bravura's desperate plea for help brings Wonder Woman racing into outer space, where Brutex has developed a fleet of spacecraft with the intention of subjugating Mount Surana and then destroying the Earth. When Brutex's space fleet attacks Mount Surana, Wonder Woman battles the invaders valiantly, only to be taken prisoner by Brutex and his followers. Ultimately, however, she turns the tables on her captors, rescues the peace-loving males — including Nestor — from imprisonment on Brutex's planetoid, and thwarts Brutex's scheme to destroy the Earth.

Queen Bravura and Nestor are happily reunited at long last, and Brutex and his cohorts will remain incarcerated on Mount Surana until they have learned to mend their evil ways (WW No. 38/2: "Wonder Woman Captures the Moon!").

BUGHUMANS. The inhabitants of a highly-advanced civilization of "gigantic, poisonous viruses" whose attempt to conquer the Earth is thwarted by WONDER WOMAN.

In July 1946 Wonder Woman is summoned to

Paula's secret laboratory (*see* GUNTHER, PAULA VON [BARONESS]), where she learns that GERTA VON GUNTHER has "recently . . . discovered a new form of microscopic life — and has invented a means of **enlarging** it to any size! Then she cages these horrible things which seem part human and part monster. She named them 'Bughumans.' Th-They even wear **clothes**!"

Gerta describes her discovery to Wonder Woman:

One day, looking through my microscope, I saw this peculiar virus which I call a "**Bughuman**." It was multicellular and had certain characteristics belonging both to insects and humans.

This machine enlarges the **Bughumans** to whatever size I want to study them. My machine generates two kinds of rays — one enlarges a virus — the other shrinks it. After studying a **Bughuman** I shrink it down again.

. . . **Bughumans** are fascinating! I bet they can talk — I've discovered they have vocal chords. Somewhere they must have a civilization — equal to ours — maybe superior!

Despite a stern warning from Wonder Woman, Gerta refuses to abandon her potentially-dangerous Bughuman research, and one day a group of enlarged Bughumans seize Gerta's enlarging machine and flee the laboratory with Gerta as their captive.

". . . [T]he **Bughumans** carry Gerta and her machine higher and higher into the stratosphere," to a strange green "cloud-mold" which is the home of the entire Bughuman civilization, and, using Gerta's enlarging machine, enlarge their entire cloud-mold world from microscopic to human size.

Wonder Woman and Paula race to Gerta's rescue, only to be captured by the Bughumans and dragged to the laboratory of the Bughuman scientist Prof. Buggo, who uses Gerta's machine to reduce all three women to microscopic size.

"If the reducing machine works on you," gloats Prof. Buggo, "we'll turn it on Earth people and make all humans small and helpless — our slaves!'

As "the powerful electric rays shrink the beautiful Amazon and her friends into tiny midgets," Prof. Buggo goes wild with excitement. "Now we **BUGHUMANS** can rule the world!" he cries ecstatically.

Ultimately, however, with some eleventh-hour assistance from STEVE TREVOR and the HOLLIDAY GIRLS, Wonder Woman escapes with Gerta's machine and turns it on the Bughumans.

"I'll make these creatures so small," remarks Wonder Woman, "[that] they [will] never again . . . reach Earth, feed on humans and pass on their horrible diseases!"

Gerta, for her part, has learned a much-needed lesson. "I've learned being a rebel only leads to disaster . . ." she explains. "I promise always to submit to loving authority" (Sen No. 55: "The Bughuman Plague").

BULLFINCH, GLORIA. The wealthy owner of the Bullfinch's Department Store chain. In August 1942 WONDER WOMAN foils a plot by Gloria's fiancé, Prince Guigli del Slimo, and his henchmen to loot the Bullfinch store in Washington, D.C., and persuades Gloria Bullfinch to raise the wages of her sales clerks from an oppressive $11 per week to a generous $22 per week (Sen No. 8).

CADMEA. The island home of the villainess IN-VENTA (WW No. 33/1, Jan/Feb '49: "The Four Dooms" pts. 1–2 — "Paradise Island Condemned!"; "The Titanic Trials!").

CAESAR, GAIUS JULIUS (100–44 B.C.). A Roman general, dictator, and statesman, whose career shaped the destiny of the Greco-Roman world and who remains, to this day, one of the great figures of world history. WONDER WOMAN meets Julius Caesar — who pays "homage to her bravery and beauty" — during a time-journey to ancient Rome that she makes in November–December 1946 (WW No. 20/3: "The Pirates' Galley Slave").

CALCULUS (Prof.). The "famed mathematician of Holliday College" who, with WONDER WOMAN's help, creates a fantastic "thinking machine" capable of solving in seconds problems that would take a human being years. The thinking machine is stolen, and Prof. Calculus kidnapped, by "CRIME-BRAIN" DOONE, but Doone and his cohorts are ultimately apprehended by Wonder Woman (CC No. 29, Oct/Nov '48: "Machine of Schemes").

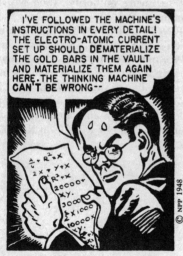

Prof. Calculus

CANDY, ETTA. The daughter of HARD CANDY, the sister of Mint Candy, and the undisputed leader of the HOLLIDAY GIRLS. Etta, a chubby redhead with an insatiable sweet tooth, is a student at the HOL-LIDAY COLLEGE FOR WOMEN in Washington, D.C., where she serves as president of the Beeta Lamda

sorority. Her favorite candies are caramels, and "Woo woo!" is her favorite exclamation. Nothing makes Etta more enthusiastic than the prospect of a rough-and-tumble battle with evil men. She is slightly scatterbrained, but she is also generous, good-hearted, and fiercely loyal to WONDER WOMAN. Her boyfriend, OSCAR SWEETGULPER, is a student at STARVARD COLLEGE.

Etta Candy, 1946

In February 1942, in the midst of her first battle with the treacherous DOCTOR POISON, Wonder Woman visits Holliday College and seeks out Etta Candy, whom she met as nurse Diana Prince when Etta was in the hospital having her appendix removed. ". . . [W]e need a hundred pretty girls," Wonder Woman tells Etta, "brave enough to capture dangerous men!"

When word spreads through the college that Wonder Woman is recruiting girls to help fight the Nazis, "hundreds of girls volunteer and **Wonder Woman** picks the prettiest and strongest." Led by Etta, this loyal group of student allies — the so-called Holliday Girls — helps Wonder Woman defeat Doctor Poison, capture a gang of Nazi spies, and rescue STEVE TREVOR from their clutches (Sen No. 2). (*See* DOCTOR POISON.)

From February 1942 onward, the Holliday Girls appear as the frequent allies of Wonder Woman in her unceasing crusade against crime and injustice. With the exception of Etta Candy, however, the

Holliday Girls are an ever-changing group: frequently the texts provide no names for them, or only first names, and these names invariably change from text to text. As used in this article and throughout this encyclopedia, the term Holliday Girls designates whichever students of Holliday College happen to be helping Wonder Woman in the particular adventure being described; it may refer to only two or three girls, or to a group of as many as a hundred. Usually, fewer than half a dozen Holliday Girls participate in any one adventure, but whenever the Holliday Girls appear, Etta Candy is always among them. Wherever it is necessary to distinguish between Etta Candy's actions and those of the other Holliday Girls, such distinctions will be made.

By March 1942 Wonder Woman has provided Etta Candy with her own "mental radio" receiver (see WONDER WOMAN [section C 7, the mental radio], and in March 1942 she transmits a mental radio message to Etta which represents the first use of the mental radio outside of PARADISE ISLAND. Etta and the Holliday Girls also participate in this month's adventure, in which Wonder Woman captures the Nazi spy GROSS and exonerates her alter ego, Diana Prince, of responsibility for a series of security leaks (Sen No. 3). (See also BROWN, EVE.)

In April 1942, when Wonder Woman smashes BARONESS PAULA VON GUNTHER's "school of espionage," Etta Candy and the Holliday Girls help Wonder Woman and Steve Trevor capture the Nazis and rescue the baroness's slave girls from her clutches (Sen No. 4).

In May 1942, when German spies attempt to sabotage *The Octopus*, the "Navy's new mystery submarine," Wonder Woman defeats the Axis agents with the help of Steve Trevor and the Holliday Girls (Sen No. 5).

In Summer 1942 Etta Candy and Wonder Woman are taken prisoner by the Japanese spy SAN YAN, but Wonder Woman ultimately turns the tables on her captors and apprehends San Yan and his Axis henchmen (WW No. 1/2: "Wonder Woman Goes to the Circus!").

In Fall 1942 Etta Candy and the Holliday Girls journey to the planet MARS in response to an urgent mental radio summons from Wonder Woman. In a Martian dungeon, Etta gives Wonder Woman a vial of acid to pour on her shackles, enabling her to escape (WW No. 2/4). (See CRAFTI [COUNT].)

In November 1942 Etta Candy travels to the planet EROS with Wonder Woman and Steve Trevor to help them crush the insurrection led by the villainess REBLA (Sen No. 11).

In December 1942 Etta Candy and the Holliday Girls help Wonder Woman defeat BARONESS PAULA VON GUNTHER and her slaves and rescue Steve Trevor from their clutches (Sen No. 12).

In Winter 1943 Etta Candy and the Holliday Girls help Wonder Woman and Steve Trevor defeat "the flame forces" of the sinister ZARA (CC No. 5: "Mystery of the Crimson Flame").

In February–March 1943 Etta is invited to Paradise Island to participate in the annual Diana's Day celebration. While she is there, Wonder Woman battles KEELA and her sinister mistress, BARONESS PAULA VON GUNTHER (WW No. 3/1). Etta is instrumental in rescuing Wonder Woman from the baroness's clutches (WW No. 3/2, Feb/Mar '43), and later helps Wonder Woman rescue GERTA VON GUNTHER and other captive children from a Nazi concentration camp near Vienna (WW No. 3/3, Feb/Mar '43).

In March 1943 Wonder Woman rescues Etta Candy and the Holliday Girls from a band of Nazis who have taken them prisoner aboard SIMON SLIKERY's yacht (Sen No. 15).

In April 1943 Diana Prince (see PRINCE, DIANA [WONDER WOMAN]) travels to HARD CANDY's Bar-L Ranch, in Texas, to attend the wedding of Etta Candy and Prince Hylo Goulash. The wedding is called off, however, when Wonder Woman exposes Goulash as KARL SCHULTZ, a "Gestapo agent working for the Japs." Throughout the adventure, Wonder Woman is aided by the Holliday Girls, but without Etta, who is busy preparing herself for the wedding (Sen No. 16).

In April–May 1943 Etta Candy and the Holliday Girls are captured by the MOLE MEN, but regain their freedom soon afterward by participating in the subterranean slave revolt organized by Wonder Woman (WW No. 4/2). (See BLAKFU.)

Etta Candy and the Holliday Girls

In May 1943 Etta Candy and the Holliday Girls, responding to an urgent mental radio message from Wonder Woman in Egypt, travel to Cape Cod to smash a "secret broadcasting station" and rescue two kidnapped children from the clutches of Axis agents (Sen No. 17: "The Talking Lion!"). (*See* YASMINI [PRINCESS].)

In June 1943 Etta Candy and the Holliday Girls are abducted — along with Steve Trevor — by the villainous QUITO and imprisoned in "the secret city of gold." They are rescued soon afterward, however, through the heroic efforts of Wonder Woman (Sen No. 18).

In June–July 1943 Etta Candy and the Holliday Girls are taken prisoner by the war god MARS. Ultimately, however, they help Wonder Woman, Steve Trevor, and Baroness Paula von Gunther defeat Mars's forces and restore control of the MOON to the goddess DIANA (WW No. 5/2).

In September 1943 Wonder Woman is drugged into senselessness during her battle with AMERICAN ADOLF, but Baroness Paula von Gunther and the Holliday Girls restore her to normal by administering a special antidote (Sen No. 21: "War Against Society").

In October 1943 Etta Candy is captured by the CHEETAH and rescued by Wonder Woman (Sen No. 22: "The Secret Submarine").

In November 1943 Etta Candy and the Holliday Girls obtain employment at the General Aircraft Company in an effort to solve the mystery of the "war laugh mania." It is Etta who first discovers that the mysterious disease is somehow related to the regulation overalls distributed to the plant's workers (Sen No. 23). (*See* WAR LAUGH MANIA.)

In Spring 1944 Etta Candy and the Holliday Girls are instrumental in the defeat of QUEEN CLEA, evil ruler of the Atlantean nation of VENTURIA (WW No. 8/2: "The Girl with the Iron Mask"). (*See* CLEA [QUEEN].)

In May 1944 Etta Candy, the Holliday Girls, and Steve Trevor help Wonder Woman and MALA escape from the clutches of the evil MIMI MENDEZ (Sen No. 29: "Adventure of the Escaped Prisoner"). (*See* MENDEZ, MIMI.)

In June 1944 Wonder Woman journeys into the fourth dimension with several of the Holliday Girls — not including Etta — to rescue Steve Trevor (Sen No. 30: "The 4th Dimension Kidnapers"). (*See* UNREAL, ANTON.)

In Summer 1944 Etta Candy and the Holliday Girls become embroiled in the bizarre events surrounding PROF. ZOOL and his "electronic evolutionizer" (WW No. 9/1–3: "Evolution Goes Haywire!"; "The Freed Captive"; no title). (*See* GIGANTA.)

In Summer 1944 a group of Holliday Girls are carried off by giant vultures to the lair of the VULTURE KING (CC No. 7: "The Vulture's Nest!").

In Fall 1944 Etta Candy and the Holliday Girls are taken captive when they sneak aboard the Saturnian "submo-space ship" commanded by DUKE MEPHISTO SATURNO. They are rescued soon afterward, however, through the heroic efforts of Wonder Woman (WW No. 10/1: "Spies from Saturn"). Wonder Woman and Etta Candy are subsequently imprisoned aboard a Saturnian spacecraft, but Wonder Woman turns the tables on her captors, captures Duke Mephisto Saturno, and assumes command of the spacecraft (WW No. 10/3: "Wonder Woman's Boots!").

*Etta Candy receives a mental radio
message from Wonder Woman, 1946*

In December 1944 Etta Candy and the Holliday Girls help Wonder Woman apprehend the members of BEDWIN FOOTH's "underworld crime [theatrical] company" (Sen No. 36: "Battle Against Revenge").

In Winter 1944 Etta Candy and the Holliday Girls are hypnotized and kidnapped by Hypnota disguised as SERVA. They are rescued soon afterward, however, through the heroic efforts of Wonder Woman (WW No. 11/2: "The Unseen Menace"). (*See* HYPNOTA [THE GREAT].)

In March 1945 Etta Candy and two of the Holliday Girls join PROFESSOR HOMOS on his daring expedition to NEW DISCOVERY ISLAND, where they are taken prisoner by the brutal NERO (Sen No. 39: "In the Clutches of Nero"). (*See* NERO.)

In Spring 1945 Etta Candy and the Holliday Girls help Wonder Woman apprehend the Third World War Promoters (WW No. 12/1). (*See* DESIRA [QUEEN].)

In May 1945 Etta Candy and the Holliday Girls are ensnared by "CREEPER" JACKSON's terrifying "octopus plants" when they attempt to investigate the mysterious disappearance of Lyra Lang (Sen No. 41: "The Octopus Plants").

In Summer 1945 Etta Candy helps Wonder Woman, Steve Trevor, and Claudia escape from the fiendish deathtrap prepared for them by the CHEETAH (CC No. 11: "The Cheetah Returns!").

In September 1945 Etta Candy, the Holliday Girls, and Steve Trevor fly to the jungles of Mexico to rescue Wonder Woman from the clutches of "GENERAL" JOSÉ PIEREZ and his brutal Mexican bandidos (Sen No. 45: "In the Enemy's Hands").

In October 1945 Etta Candy and the Holliday Girls are taken captive by the LAWBREAKERS' PROTECTIVE LEAGUE and are rescued by Steve Trevor (Sen No. 46: "The Lawbreakers' League").

Etta Candy and the Holliday Girls are tortured by the Lawbreakers' Protective League, 1945

In December 1945 Etta Candy and the Holliday Girls are taken prisoner — along with Wonder Woman — by TOPSO AND TEENA, but they are rescued when Steve Trevor arrives on the scene and frees Wonder Woman from her magic lasso (see WONDER WOMAN [section C 3, the magic lasso]), with which the villains had bound her (Sen No. 48).

In Winter 1945 Etta Candy and the Holliday Girls help Wonder Woman defeat the ruthless PALTRO DEBUM (CC No. 13: "The Underwater Follies") and become embroiled in the events surrounding Wonder Woman's battles with the evil SOLO (WW No. 15: chs. 1–3 — "The First Battle of Neptunia"; "The Masters of the Water"; "In the Killer's Cage").

In January 1946, when Etta Candy and the Holliday Girls travel to Lake Iceberg to participate in an intercollegiate skiing competition, they are taken captive by the villainess ZAVIA. They are rescued soon afterward by Wonder Woman, how-

ever, with the help of Steve Trevor (Sen No. 49: "The Mystery of Lake Iceberg").

In February 1946 Etta Candy and the Holliday Girls help Wonder Woman apprehend the "EARS" FELLOCK gang (Sen No. 50: "The Case of the Girl in Braces").

In March 1946 Etta Candy and the Holliday Girls are taken captive by members of the BOSS BREKEL gang and sent hurtling off a bridge in a locked car. They are rescued in the nick of time by Wonder Woman (Sen No. 51: "The Crime of Boss Brekel!").

In March–April 1946 Etta Candy and the Holliday Girls become embroiled in Wonder Woman's battles with KING PLUTO, "vicious ruler of the dark planet" (WW No. 16/1–3: "The Secret of the Dark Planet!"; "The River of Liquid Fire"; "King Pluto's Revenge").

In April 1946 Wonder Woman rescues Etta Candy and the Holliday Girls from a fire set by PROF. CHEMICO, who has been driven temporarily insane by one of the "rare poisonous flies" bred by PROF. TOXINO (Sen No. 52: "The Brand of Madness"). (See TOXINO [PROF.].)

In April–May 1946, when Etta Candy and the Holliday Girls discover that WANTA WYNN is wearing anklets and bracelets made of plastic instead of genuine bracelets of submission to the goddess APHRODITE, they are taken prisoner by the villainess and hurled into a river, anchored to a heavy metal safe. They are rescued from seemingly certain death by Wonder Woman (CC No. 14: "The Severed Bracelets"). (See WYNN, WANTA.)

In May–June 1946 Etta Candy and the Holliday Girls journey through the time barrier to ancient Rome, and Wonder Woman joins them soon afterward, summoned by an urgent mental radio message from Etta. In ancient Rome, Wonder Woman battles and defeats the evil dictator SULLA (WW No. 17: "The Winds of Time").

In June 1946, when DR. FIENDO seizes control of the U.S. Government, Etta Candy and the Holliday Girls are arrested on charges of having engaged in "subversive activities" — along with Wonder Woman, Steve Trevor, and GENERAL DARNELL — and sentenced to death by firing squad. They are all rescued from seemingly certain death by Wonder Woman (Sen No. 54: "The Treachery of Fiendo"). (See FIENDO [DR.].)

In June–July 1946 Etta Candy and the Holliday Girls help Wonder Woman defeat the evil URIAH SKINFLINT (CC No. 15: "Flaming Fury").

In July–August 1946 Etta Candy and the Holliday Girls are trapped by DR. PSYCHO, who plans to kill them by exposing them to "an overdose of the somnatic rays" emanating from the "war-prevento

*Wonder Woman rescues Etta Candy
from a sniper's bullet, 1946*

machine." They are rescued from seemingly certain death by Wonder Woman (WW No. 18/1: "The Return from the Dead").

Soon afterward, Dr. Psycho lures Etta Candy and the Holliday Girls into a deathtrap along with Steve Trevor and General Darnell, but Wonder Woman rescues them before they can come to any harm (WW No. 18/2, Jul/Aug '46: "The Drugged WAC").

Not long afterward, with Dr. Psycho presumed dead in a titanic explosion, Etta Candy throws a party at Holliday College to celebrate the villain's demise. Dr. Psycho is alive and well, however, and when he invades the festivities disguised as an innocent guest, Etta is saved from a ghastly death only by the heroic intervention of Wonder Woman (WW No. 18/3, Jul/Aug '46: "Ectoplasmic Death").

In August 1946 DR. NOVEL captures Wonder Woman and a group of Holliday Girls and is about to kill them all with electrically-detonated bombs when Etta Candy throws the master electrical switch, plunging Dr. Novel's factory headquarters into darkness and making it impossible for the bomb detonators to function. Under cover of the darkness, Wonder Woman escapes her bonds and takes Dr. Novel into custody (Sen No. 56: "Anti-Atomic Metal").

In September 1946 Etta Candy and the Holliday Girls are taken captive by SYONIDE and rescued by Wonder Woman (Sen No. 57: "Hatchet of Death").

In November–December 1946 Etta Candy, the Holliday Girls, Steve Trevor, and Prof. Chemico are kidnapped by NIFTY and her gang of "ruthless female pirates," but Wonder Woman follows Steve Trevor's "brain wave length" to the pirates' hideaway, rescues her friends, and captures the criminals (WW No. 20/1: "Terrors of the Air"). (*See* CHEMICO [PROF.].)

In January–February 1947 Wonder Woman, Etta Candy, the Holliday Girls, and Baroness Paula von Gunther are knocked unconscious by "hydroxe gas" and taken as prisoners to the bizarre "aton world" of QUEEN ATOMIA. Ultimately, howevex they escape and return to their own world (WV No. 21/1: "The Mystery of the Atom World". Sometime later, Etta Candy and the Holliday Girl again become the prisoners of Queen Atomia, bu Wonder Woman rescues them soon afterwar (WW No. 21/3, Jan/Feb '47: "Ruler of the Aton World").

In March–April 1947 "COSMETIC" KOSMET cap tures Etta Candy and the Holliday Girls and take Wonder Woman prisoner soon afterward. They ar all rescued by Steve Trevor (WW No. 22/1: "Th Color Thief").

In March–April 1947 Etta Candy and the Holli day Girls are taken captive – along with Wonde Woman and Steve Trevor – by Saturnian invader under the command of DUKE MEPHISTO SATURNC but Wonder Woman turns the tables on her cap tors and rescues her friends from the villains clutches (WW No. 22/2: "The Island of Evil").

In April–May 1947 Etta Candy travels to ZAN ISLAND to help PRINCE SLEEKO start a school there only to become embroiled in a native uprisin instigated by Sleeko's evil half-brother, PRINC SLAMBO (CC No. 20: "The Buddha Wishing Ring") (*See* SLAMBO [PRINCE].)

In May–June 1947 Etta Candy and the Holliday Girls are carried off to VALHALLA by GUNDRA an her bloodthirsty VALKYRIES, but they are rescue and returned to Earth through the heroic efforts o Wonder Woman (WW No. 23/1: "Siege of the Sav age War Maidens"). (*See* ODIN.)

In May–June 1947 Wonder Woman, Etta Candy and the Holliday Girls are taken captive by the evi AKNATEN, but, with some assistance from Stev Trevor, Wonder Woman turns the tables on he captors and rescues the Holliday Girls (WW No 23/2: "The Vanishing Mummy!").

In July–August 1947 Etta Candy and the Holli day Girls are taken captive by the MASK and ar rescued by Wonder Woman (WW No. 24/2: "Th Challenge of the Mask").

In September–October 1947 Etta Candy make an unexpected landing on the planetoid RYKORNL and unintentionally sets in motion a bizarre chair of events culminating in an attempt by th Rykornians to invade the Earth (WW No. 25/1 "Siege of the Rykornians"). (*See* TASSEL [KING].

In September–October 1947, in far-off ZARIKAN Etta Candy and the Holliday Girls become cap tives of the PURPLE PRIESTESS, only to be rescue soon afterward by Wonder Woman (WW No. 25/3 "The Judgment of Goddess Vultura"). (*See* PURPLE PRIESTESS, THE.)

WHERE DID YOU GET IT?

SOME MAN SAID HE'D BUY MY LAST TWO TICKETS. HE HAD ONLY A $100 BILL, SO I GAVE HIM $95 IN SMALL BILLS FOR CHANGE.

© NPP 1946

Diana Prince (Wonder Woman) and Etta Candy, 1946

In October–November 1947, on remote WOOLOO ISLAND, Etta Candy and the Holliday girls become the prisoners of KING IRONSIDES. They are ultimately rescued by Steve Trevor and Wonder Woman (CC No. 23: "Siege of the Iron Giants"). (*See* IRONSIDES [KING].)

In November 1947 Etta Candy and the Holliday Girls are taken captive by the "sun warriors" of QUEEN FLAMINA. They are rescued soon afterward by Wonder Woman (Sen No. 71: "The Invasion of the Sun Warriors").

In November–December 1947 Wonder Woman, Etta Candy, and the Holliday Girls are taken captive by QUEEN CELERITA and the "flying giantesses" of MERCURY. About to be cold-bloodedly murdered, they are rescued in the nick of time by QUEEN DESIRA and the winged women of VENUS (WW No. 26/1: "Speed Maniacs from Mercury!"). (*See* CELERITA [QUEEN].)

In November–December 1947 Etta Candy and the Holliday Girls become embroiled in the war between the "genii people" of the White Star and the "golden women" of the Red Planet (WW No. 26/3: "The Golden Women and the White Star!"). (*See* CRYSTALLAR [KING].)

In January 1948 Wonder Woman, Steve Trevor, Etta Candy, and the Holliday Girls journey into the past to the year 1692 to rescue their friend FAITH ALDEN, who has been sentenced to death by the Puritans for practicing witchcraft (Sen No. 73: "The Witches' Trials").

In March–April 1948 Etta Candy and the Holliday Girls become embroiled in Wonder Woman's battle with VILLAINY INCORPORATED (WW No. 28/1–3: "Villainy Incorporated!"; "Trap of Crimson Flame"; "In the Hands of the Merciless!").

In April 1948 Etta Candy and the Holliday Girls

are kidnapped by KING DIAMOND and Nina and are rescued by Wonder Woman (Sen No. 76: "Murder Referees the Round!").

In May–June 1948 Etta Candy and the Holliday Girls accompany Prof. Chemico's expedition to the North Pole, where they are taken captive by the "icicle men" (WW No. 29/1: "Ice World's Conquest!"). (*See* BLIZZARD [PRIME MINISTER].)

In July 1948 Etta Candy stows away aboard Steve Trevor's aircraft and accompanies him to the exotic SUN COUNTRY (Sen No. 79: "Land of Mirrors!"). (*See* LEILA.)

In August–September 1948 Etta Candy and the Holliday Girls take part in Wonder Woman's adventure on the island kingdom of POGOLANA (CC No. 28: "The Sinister Countess Hatra!"). (*See* HATRA [COUNTESS].)

In September 1948 Etta Candy and the Holliday Girls are taken captive by DR. FRENZI's henchmen and are rescued by Wonder Woman (Sen No. 81: "When Treachery Wore a Green Shirt!").

In October 1948 Etta Candy and the Holliday Girls are transformed into mindless automatons by KING LUNAR, only to be rescued soon afterward through the heroic efforts of Wonder Woman (Sen No. 82: "Brain Pirates from the Inner Moon-World!").

In October–November 1948 Etta Candy and the Holliday Girls are kidnapped by "CRIME BRAIN" DOONE's henchmen and are rescued by Wonder Woman (CC No. 29: "Machine of Schemes").

In January–February 1949 Etta Candy and the Holliday Girls are kidnapped by aliens from the planet Murkton, but Wonder Woman wins their release by persuading the aliens that their resentment toward Earth is unfounded (WW No. 33/2: "The Menace of Murkton!"). (*See* PALLIDA [QUEEN].)

In March–April 1949 Etta Candy and the Holliday Girls are temporarily imprisoned on LIMBO when Holliday College is stolen by the DUKE OF DECEPTION. Etta and her friends are ultimately rescued, however, through the heroic efforts of Wonder Woman (WW No. 34: "The Mystery of the Rhyming Riddle!" chs. 1–3 — "Deception Strikes Again"; "The Phantasms of Deception!"; "The Mystery of the Rhyming Riddle!"). (*See* DECEPTION, DUKE OF.)

In November–December 1949 Etta Candy and the Holliday Girls play a crucial role in Wonder Woman's wager with the woman-hating THOMAS TIGHE (WW No. 38/3: "The Five Tasks of Thomas Tighe!").

In July–August 1950 Etta Candy and the Holliday Girls take up the dangerous sport of midget auto racing, only to find themselves embroiled in the conflict between Art Fairdeal and the unscrupulous JOSH SLICKER (WW No. 42/1: "Danger on the Speedway!").

In November–December 1950 Etta Candy and the Holliday Girls accompany CAPT. SEADUNK's expedition to the Sargasso Sea, where they become embroiled in a hair-raising adventure with the villainous MASTER DE STROYER (WW No. 44: "The Monarch of the Sargasso Sea!" chs. I–III — no title; "Wonder Woman's Decision"; "The Final Battle of the Sargasso Sea"). (See MASTER DE STROYER.)

This episode marks the last textual appearance of Etta Candy and the Holliday Girls for almost exactly a decade, until October 1960, when Wonder Woman visits the campus of Holliday College and narrates two short stories to Etta Candy and three other Holliday Girls: TINA TOY, LITA LITTLE, and THELMA TALL (WW No. 117: "Fantastic Fishermen of the Forbidden Sea!").

In January 1962 aliens from PLANET K attempt to capture Etta Candy, Tina Toy, Lita Little, Thelma Tall, and several other Holliday Girls as "specimens" of Earth life. Repeatedly thwarted by Wonder Woman, however, they are forced to flee Earth empty-handed (WW No. 127/1: "Invaders of the Topsy-Turvy Planet"). (See also KUU-KUU.)

Wonder Woman No. 156 contains an account of Wonder Woman's battle with the BRAIN PIRATE. In the course of the adventure, Etta Candy and the Holliday Girls are taken captive by the Brain Pirate but ultimately are rescued by Wonder Woman (Aug '65: "The Brain Pirate of the Inner World!").

CANDY, HARD. The hard-bitten, warm-hearted Texas rancher who is the father of ETTA CANDY and

YEP AN' LAST YEAR WHEN RUSTLERS TRIED TO ROB US OF ALL OUR THOROUGH-BREDS, RAINBOW AND STAR-DUST LED THEIR PACK O' WILD HOSSES AGIN 'EM AN' DROVE 'EM OFF SCARED STIFF!

© NPP 1948

Hard Candy

her brother Mint Candy and the owner of the Bar-L Ranch.

Diana Prince, the girl who is secretly WONDER WOMAN, visits the Bar-L Ranch in April 1943 to attend the wedding of Etta Candy and Prince Hylo Goulash, but the wedding is cancelled when Wonder Woman exposes the groom-to-be as Gestapo agent KARL SCHULTZ (Sen No. 16).

In July 1947, a seemingly harmless bet between Hard Candy and rancher DAREDEVIL DIX leads to a crisis requiring the intervention of Wonder Woman (Sen No. 67: "The Secret of the Bar-L Ranch!"). (See DIX, DAREDEVIL.)

In January–February 1948, with the aid of a pair of wild horses, Wonder Woman apprehends a gang of rustlers who have been plaguing the Bar-L Ranch (WW No. 27/2: "The Legend of Rainbow and Stardust!").

CANDY, MINT. The son of HARD CANDY and the brother of ETTA CANDY (WW No. 1/4, Sum '42).

CAPITAL CITY. The name given to the resident city of WONDER WOMAN in Wonder Woman No. 174/1 (Jan/Feb '68: "Steve Trevor — Alias the Patriot!"). Appearing as it does in only one text, the name Capital City may be presumed to be a thinly disguised reference to Washington, D.C., or else the result of a chronicler's error. (See WONDER WOMAN [section I 1, Locales].)

CAPTIVE HAVEN. A utopian prison on the planet VENUS where voluntarily submissive prisoners lead lives of happiness and contentment. The THIRD WORLD WAR PROMOTERS are incarcerated there in Spring 1945 (WW No. 12/2: "The Ordeal of Fire").

CARLTON, MARY. A magazine writer who, while researching an article on WONDER WOMAN, correctly deduces that Wonder Woman and Diana Prince are the same person. Through the skillful use of Amazon ventriloquism, however, Wonder Woman persuades Mary that she has made a mistake, thereby safeguarding the secret of her dual identity (WW No. 53/2, May/Jun '52: "The Wonder Woman Nobody Knows!").

CARY, HELEN. A lovely blond girl who has deliberately allowed herself to be convicted of a murder she did not commit, that of "military intelligence operative" Capt. Jack Lane. WONDER WOMAN rescues her from being wrongfully executed in June 1949.

In June 1949 a girl giving her name only as Mary Smith is about to be executed, having confessed the murder of Capt. Jack Lane. Wonder Woman learns, however, that the condemned girl is really Helen Cary, the sister of Phil Cary, and that she has confessed murdering Capt. Lane only because she believes that her brother committed the murder. Helen is therefore determined to protect him and thus shield her family from disgrace. Helen further believes that her brother is a member of the Rogo Spy Gang, "a gang of desperate spies," and that he murdered Capt. Lane to prevent him from exposing them.

Wonder Woman discovers, however, that Phil Cary is a military intelligence operative who has infiltrated the Rogo Spy Gang for the government. When Wonder Woman apprehends the spies and exposes their leader as the real murderer of Capt. Lane, Helen Cary is exonerated and released (Sen No. 90: "The Secret of the Modern Sphinx!").

CASE, JANE. An alias employed by WONDER WOMAN in January–February 1952 when she assumes the role of a librarian as part of her plan to trap the GARO gang (WW No. 51/1: "The Amazing Impersonation!").

CASINO. A ruthless "munitions racketeer" who is apprehended by WONDER WOMAN in Fall 1944. Casino and his cohorts have taken STEVE TREVOR prisoner and are about to execute him when Wonder Woman invades their nightclub headquarters — ". . . the invincible Amazon surprises a gangster council of death passing sentence on Steve" — captures the criminals, and rescues Trevor from their clutches (CC No. 8: "The Amazon Bride").

CELERITA (Queen). The beautiful red-haired giantess who is the ruler of the planet MERCURY. She and her followers are transformed from tyrannical villainesses into humane, peace-loving people through the heroic efforts of WONDER WOMAN and QUEEN DESIRA of VENUS.

In November–December 1947 Wonder Woman and the HOLLIDAY GIRLS climb aboard Wonder Woman's Amazon plane (see WONDER WOMAN [section C 4, the robot plane]) for a journey to PARADISE ISLAND, but the plane's "delicate direction finder" has been damaged in a recent thunderstorm and the plane hurtles off course, completely out of control, soaring through interstellar space to Mercury, nearest planet to the SUN.

Upon landing, Wonder Woman and her friends encounter Mercury's beautiful "flying giantesses" — tall, statuesque women whose winged sandals and helmets endow them with the power of flight — and are ushered into the presence of Mercury's ruler, the lovely but ruthless Queen Celerita.

At one time, explains the queen, the men and women of Mercury lived side by side in equality and tranquility. One day, however, the Mercurian women had tuned in a radio program from the planet Earth. "The broadcast," continues Queen Celerita, "told a story of what it called the typical

© NPP 1947

Queen Celerita, 1947

family. All the women did was flit about playing cards, gossiping, and spending money while the men slaved to support them and a maid did the housework!"

The "easy life" described in the radio broadcast sounded so "luxurious" that Celerita and her followers promptly set about enslaving the men of their planet and establishing themselves as Mercury's rulers. Before long, the traditional equality of Mercurian men and women had given way to a system in which the flying giantesses were indolent tyrants and the Mercurian men were slaves forced to perform the most menial chores on the planets.

Taken captive by Queen Celerita and her sister giantesses for expressing opposition to the totalitarian regime, Wonder Woman is made a Mercurian slave and is put to work digging a huge pit in which the Holliday Girls are to be buried alive.

In desperation, Wonder Woman dispatches an urgent mental radio message (see WONDER WOMAN [section C 7, the mental radio]) to Queen Desira of Venus. Just as things have begun to appear hopeless for Wonder Woman and her friends, Queen Desira and an army of her winged women swoop down on Queen Celerita and her giantesses and imprison them in magic Venus girdles to make them kind, loving, and humane (*see* AMAZONS [section F 3, the magic Venus girdles]).

Wonder Woman and the Holliday Girls are promptly set free, and the Mercurian giantesses, under the beneficent influence of the magic girdles, promise to live in harmonious equality with their men from now on (WW No. 26/1: "Speed Maniacs from Mercury!").

CEREBRUM (Dr.). The idealistic inventor of the "war-prevento machine," a device designed to make war-making obsolete by using "somnatic rays [to] render warmakers unconscious long enough for us to capture and imprison them and their armies."

In July–August 1946, however, DR. PSYCHO escapes from prison and steals the war-prevento machine, intending to use it "to enslave and kill the innocent people of the world!"

WONDER WOMAN ultimately recovers the machine, but the dreadful encounter with Dr. Psycho has convinced Dr. Cerebrum that his machine must be destroyed for the good of humanity.

"No **machine** can prevent wars!" explains Wonder Woman. "Unscrupulous people can turn the most humanitarian instrument into a deadly weapon. Men must develop deep, lasting love" (WW No. 18/1: "The Return from the Dead").

CHANG. A "savage Tartar chief" who is defeated by WONDER WOMAN.

In September–October 1949, archaeologists digging near the GREAT WALL OF CHINA unearth an ancient Chinese mummy case believed to be 2,000 years old, containing a statue of a Chinese warrior princess. Wonder Woman and the archaeologists are perplexed to discover that the princess appears to be carrying an Amazon shield and wearing the trousers and sandals of the ancient AMAZONS.

To solve the mystery, Wonder Woman travels to ancient China by means of the Amazon "space transformer" (*see* AMAZONS [section G, Amazon science]), where she helps Princess Mei, the model for the mysterious statue, defeat an army of barbarians led by the Tartar chieftain Chang.

"You will recall," explains Princess Mei, ". . . that the ancient Amazons conquered Asia Minor. My own ancestors journeyed here and founded this land. For centuries, we ruled China but now this province alone remains a matriarchy--and for this the barbarians would destroy us!"

"You have saved us from the barbarians, Amazon!" remarks one of Princess Mei's followers gratefully. "But who knows when or where they will strike again?"

"The Amazon was a wall of strength to us!" exclaims another.

"And I will leave a great wall to protect you!" replies Wonder Woman.

"And so it was," observes the textual narrative, "that the amazing Amazon races across the land, erecting **the Great Wall** of China to keep out the northern barbarians." (WW No. 37/1: "The Riddle of the Chinese Mummy Case!").

CHEETAH, THE. A cruel and treacherous archvillainess whose diabolical cunning and cold-blooded brutality have made her one of WONDER WOMAN's most terrifying adversaries. Like the predatory cat that has inspired her costume and whose name she has adopted, the Cheetah is a "treacherous, relentless huntress" who stalks her prey with the grace and ferocity of an exotic feline. In everyday life, she is Priscilla Rich, a "beautiful and clever debutante" whose "terrible [inner] feeling of inferiority" periodically causes "her Cheetah self" to seize control of her personality.

Priscilla Rich, 1943

In Fall 1943 Wonder Woman agrees to put on an exhibition of Amazon feats at a war relief fund charity benefit, unaware that Priscilla Rich, the pretty blond debutante who heads the committee which organized the benefit, is insanely envious of her and furious with a man named Courtley Darling for paying more attention to Wonder Woman than to herself. When Wonder Woman performs an escape trick as part of her act, Priscilla surreptitiously attempts to transform the stunt into an inescapable deathtrap. Wonder Woman survives the attempt on her life, but she remains unaware that it was Priscilla who tried to kill her.

REMOVING THE BAG OF MONEY, THE CHEETAH CLOSES THE SAFE AGAIN.

The Cheetah, 1943

Later that night, as Priscilla sits alone in her room, her "pent up passions burst forth!"

"As Priscilla seats herself before her mirror," explains the textual narrative, "a curious thing happens. The girl's evil self, long repressed, takes control of her body. Psychologists use mirrors in this way to discover people's real selves. The mirror creates in Priscilla a dual personality, like Dr. Jekyll and Mr. Hyde."

"Horrors!" cries Priscilla, as she gazes upon her evil inner self — her Cheetah self — in the mirror for the very first time. "That's not me — or is it?"

"Don't you know me?" replies the evil reflection. "I am the **real** you — the Cheetah — a treacherous, relentless huntress!"

As Priscilla gazes into the mirror, hypnotized by the hidden part of her personality now revealed there, the image of the Cheetah commands her to fashion a special cheetah costume. "From now

AS PRISCILLA SEATS HERSELF BEFORE HER MIRROR A CURIOUS THING HAPPENS. THE GIRL'S EVIL SELF, LONG REPRESSED, TAKES CONTROL OF HER BODY. PSYCHOLOGISTS USE MIRRORS IN THIS WAY TO DISCOVER PEOPLE'S REAL SELVES. THE MIRROR CREATES IN PRISCILLA A DUAL PERSONALITY, LIKE DR. JEKYLL AND MR. HYDE.

HORRORS! THAT'S NOT ME — OR IS IT?

DON'T YOU KNOW ME? I AM THE REAL YOU — THE CHEETAH — A TREACHEROUS, RELENTLESS HUNTRESS!

Seated before her mirror, Priscilla Rich discovers her Cheetah self, 1943

on," intones the reflection, "when I command, you shall go forth dressed like your **true** self and do as I command you---"

When Priscilla has finally completed and donned her Cheetah costume, the Cheetah image in the mirror speaks to her again. "Quick now," it urges hatefully, "the night passes! While darkness hides your villainy take your revenge on Courtley Darling and **Wonder Woman!**"

Now completely under the baleful control of her Cheetah self, Priscilla steals the proceeds from her own war relief benefit and frames Wonder Woman and Courtley Darling for the crime. After Wonder Woman has been arrested and charged with the theft, the Cheetah anonymously bails her out and then lures her to a lonely warehouse, where she hurls both Wonder Woman and Courtley Darling into a huge storage bin piled with loosely packed wheat. Wonder Woman and Darling sink into the wheat like stones into quicksand, but with the help of STEVE TREVOR and ETTA CANDY they manage to escape.

Wonder Woman senses that the Cheetah is really Priscilla Rich, but she is not certain, knowing only that the Cheetah must be "some girl's evil self, the incarnation of jealousy and hate."

Outside the warehouse, Wonder Woman, Courtley Darling, Steve Trevor, and Etta Candy look up to see the Cheetah, perched atop the warehouse roof, setting the building afire. Stunned to see that Wonder Woman and Courtley Darling have survived her deathtrap, the Cheetah hurls herself into the flames.

"The Amazon defeated me . . . !" she cries. "If she lives, I die! Arr-rr-rgh!"

To Wonder Woman, the Cheetah's true identity remains a mystery. All she knows for certain is that the Cheetah "must have been someone whom I made feel inferior in some way . . ." (WW No. 6/1: "Wonder Woman and the Cheetah").

It soon becomes apparent that the Cheetah managed to survive the warehouse fire, although the text offers no explanation beyond her observation that ". . . the skin I wear preserves me from fire." Since her previous encounter with Wonder Woman, the Cheetah has become the secret owner of a lavish beauty salon and has acquired a group of slave girls, who are kept in shackles and dressed in zebra-striped costumes because "zebras are the cheetah's favorite prey." The beauty salon is operated by Brenda West, one of the Cheetah's slaves, and is patronized by the wives of U.S. Army officers, who do not realize that while they relax at the salon their minds are being silently probed for top-secret intelligence information by psychic Gail Young, another of the Cheetah's slave girls, and that the information she gleans is ultimately passed on to the Japanese.

Brenda West and Gail Young are not willing allies of the Cheetah, but the Cheetah has discovered that Major Jerry Young — Gail's brother and Brenda's fiancé — commands a secret U.S. air base in China, and she has threatened to disgrace him by revealing the location of the secret base to the Japanese — and then informing the Army that Major Young was responsible for the security leak — unless both Gail and Brenda agree to do her bidding.

Acting on Wonder Woman's instructions, however, Etta Candy visits the beauty salon and rescues Gail and Brenda from the Cheetah's clutches. Wonder Woman, meanwhile, flies to China, where she thwarts an attempt by the Japanese to capitalize on the Cheetah's secret information by attacking Major Young's air base. The Cheetah, however, remains at large, and Wonder Woman is still not certain of her true identity (WW No. 6/2, Fall '43: "The Adventure of the Beauty Club").

The Cheetah, 1943

Soon afterward, when a team of women athletes visits PARADISE ISLAND to compete with some young women who have been the recipients of special Amazon training (see WONDER WOMAN [section C 1, the benefits of Amazon training]), the Cheetah sneaks onto the island disguised as one of the guest athletes and sets out to wreak vengeance on Wonder Woman.

Cautiously awaiting her opportunity, the Cheetah steals QUEEN HIPPOLYTE's magic girdle (see AMAZONS [section F 1, the magic girdle]) — thereby rendering Wonder Woman, Hippolyte, and all the other AMAZONS vulnerable to defeat — and makes Hippolyte her prisoner. Wonder Woman bravely hurls herself at the villainess, but the loss of the magic girdle has weakened the Amazons and endowed the Cheetah with great strength and endurance. The battle seesaws back and forth, with "the unconquerable power of the magic girdle evenly matched by **Wonder Woman's** superb strength," but Wonder Woman finally manages to wrench away the stolen girdle and defeat the Cheetah, whom the Amazons then unmask as Priscilla Rich.

"My Cheetah personality is compelled to confess!" exclaims Priscilla, under the influence of Wonder Woman's magic lasso (see WONDER WOMAN [section C 3, the magic lasso]). "I've lived a double life. Beneath my house is a secret room, my Cheetah's den, with underground passages. . . .

"My two personalities were enemies--Priscilla wanted to be good but the Cheetah wouldn't let her! Your magic lasso binds the Cheetah for the first time--oh, **keep** me a prisoner here and train my Cheetah self!"

Wonder Woman agrees. The Cheetah will be sent to Reform Island (see TRANSFORMATION ISLAND) to undergo rehabilitative training under the guidance of the Amazons (WW No. 6/3, Fall '43: "The Conquest of Paradise").

In October 1943, however, the Cheetah returns to plague Wonder Woman. According to Sensation No. 22, the Cheetah had begged Wonder Woman to allow her to remain on Reform Island as a prisoner following her previous defeat:

"Oh, **Wonder Woman**," cried the vanquished Cheetah, "you've conquered the Cheetah personality — these bonds feel wonderful! Keep me here in Amazon prison and train me to control my evil self!"

"You shall become an Amazon prisoner," Wonder Woman had replied, "but first you must return to the world of men, free the girls you've enslaved and make restitution to everyone you've injured!"

"I'll do anything **you** command!" promised the Cheetah.

Wonder Woman had returned Priscilla Rich to the United States and set her free. ". . . [I]t was a risk!" remarks Wonder Woman's alter ego, Diana Prince, in October 1943. "But no one could restore the Cheetah's victims except Priscilla, and **Wonder Woman** believed her evil self was under control!"

Now, however, a new top-secret Navy submarine, the *Wonder Woman*, has disappeared from its berth, and soon afterward Steve Trevor is attacked in his office by a girl dressed in a Cheetah costume. As Diana Prince, Wonder Woman succeeds in warding off Trevor's assailant, but the villainess escapes. Fearful that Priscilla Rich has returned to crime as the Cheetah, Wonder Woman trails

Trevor's assailant to the Rich estate, where she finds a girl in a Cheetah costume fighting with Priscilla Rich.

This new Cheetah, explains Priscilla, "is Sandra, one of my former slaves — when I freed the girls, she impersonated the Cheetah to get revenge on me," presumably by dressing as the Cheetah and framing Priscilla for her crimes.

Satisfied with this explanation, Wonder Woman departs, but in fact Priscilla has not reformed at all. She stole the Navy submarine and attacked Trevor, and, seeing that she was being followed by Wonder Woman, ordered her slave Sandra to don a Cheetah costume so that she could divert suspicion from herself. Far from having freed her zebra-clad slave girls, the Cheetah keeps them in cages and whips them brutally for even the most minor infractions of her sadistic discipline.

Soon afterward, Priscilla offers to help Wonder Woman recover the missing submarine by leading her to the place where, she claims, her slave Sandra has hidden it. Once aboard the submarine, however, Priscilla transforms herself into the Cheetah, takes Wonder Woman captive, and attempts to torture and humiliate her by forcing her to dance before her while laden down with shackles and heavy chains. Wonder Woman disarms her tormentor, however, with a clever psychological ploy, goading the Cheetah into performing a dance of her own in full view of her assembled slave girls. The Cheetah is such a graceful, talented dancer that, as she dances, her feelings of inferiority vanish, along with her need to strike out at others.

"It's superb!" exclaims Wonder Woman as the Cheetah dances on and on. "You're a born dancer — your dancing could attract **millions** of admirers! Oh, Cheetah, why don't you dance and make people **love** you?"

Wonder Woman's therapeutic ploy works. "Under **Wonder Woman's** influence, the Cheetah feels her personality changing!"

"Oh — oh — what's happening to me?" thinks the Cheetah. "I'm no longer jealous of **Wonder Woman!** I don't hate pretty girls — I — I —

"I-I'm Priscilla," she exclaims finally, "— I'll **never** let the Cheetah personality control me again! I'll take the submarine back and make restitution!"

After the stolen submarine has been returned to the Navy, Priscilla attempts to explain why, in spite of her promise to Wonder Woman that she would reform, she had been overcome by the Cheetah side of her personality: "When **Wonder Woman** captured me on Paradise Island," she explains, "I was happy. But when I returned I felt **inferior** again and my evil self controlled me!" ("The Secret Submarine").

In December 1944 the Cheetah is one of the six infamous villains and villainesses impersonated by actors in BEDWIN FOOTH's "underworld crime [theatrical] company" (Sen No. 36: "Battle Against Revenge").

In Summer 1945 a distraught MALA summons Wonder Woman to Reform Island to inform her that Priscilla Rich has escaped. A search is begun, but when a Cheetah costume is found abandoned on the beach, the Amazons assume that Priscilla has committed suicide and stop looking for her.

Unbeknownst to Wonder Woman and the other Amazons, however, the Cheetah has stowed away aboard Wonder Woman's robot plane (*see* WONDER WOMAN [section C 4, the robot plane]) after leaving a Cheetah costume on the beach to throw the Amazons off her trail. While Wonder Woman is en route back to the United States, the Cheetah emerges from hiding and attacks her, but Wonder Woman gains the upper hand and takes the Cheetah prisoner.

Arriving in the United States, Wonder Woman leaves the Cheetah locked in a local jail for safekeeping until she can find time to return her to Reform Island, but the wily villainess seduces a guard into approaching her cell for a kiss, steals his keys, and escapes. At large once again, the Cheetah sets out to fulfill the mission that had prompted her escape from Reform Island — vengeance on her cousin Claudia, who, in her eyes, has usurped both her fame as a dancer and her place in the Rich household.

Priscilla Rich and her cousin Claudia are exact look-alikes, except for the fact that Priscilla's eyes

THE CHEETAH, IN HER MOMENT OF IMAGINED TRIUMPH, SEES **WONDER WOMAN** ESCAPING FROM HER CLUTCHES AND FALLS, DEFEATED, INTO THE FIRE SHE KINDLED.

THE AMAZON DEFEATED ME BY MAGIC — SHE IS NOT HUMAN! IF SHE LIVES, I DIE! ARR-RR-RGH!

15A

© NPP 1943

The Cheetah, 1943

are green, while Claudia's are brown. Following Priscilla's departure for Reform Island, Priscilla's parents had adopted Claudia and taken her into their home. A graceful, talented dancer like Priscilla, Claudia has established herself as a successful dancer in Priscilla's absence.

Furious with her cousin for robbing her of her "home and dancing fame," Priscilla invades the Rich home as the Cheetah and imprisons Claudia in a secret hideaway beneath the house, donning brown contact lenses so that no one will be able to tell that she has taken Claudia's place.

Not long afterward, the Cheetah uses a clever ruse to trap Wonder Woman in a magic Venus girdle, thus forcing Wonder Woman to obey her every command (see AMAZONS [section F 3, the magic Venus girdles]), and soon afterward she takes Steve Trevor prisoner also.

Forcing Wonder Woman to balance herself atop a thin high wire in her secret underground dungeon, with Trevor in one arm and Claudia in the other, the Cheetah lights a raging oil fire directly beneath her, dooming Wonder Woman either to lose her balance and fall into the blaze or to remain on the wire until the heat of the fire melts it, toppling her into the flames.

After the Cheetah has left, however, Wonder Woman dispatches an urgent mental radio message (see WONDER WOMAN [section C 7, the mental radio]) to Etta Candy, who tosses the key to Wonder Woman's magic Venus girdle through the barred window of the Cheetah's dungeon. Catching the key in her mouth, Wonder Woman unlocks the girdle and thus frees herself from the compulsion to obey the Cheetah's command to remain perched on the wire. Just as the fragile wire breaks in two from the heat of the fire below, Wonder Woman springs to safety with Trevor and Claudia in her arms. Soon afterward, she recaptures the Cheetah.

"Wonder Woman, I just can't reform!" says Priscilla Rich despondently.

"Yes, you can!" replies Wonder Woman. "You just have to learn that destroying other people doesn't make you any bigger. Loving people and helping them could make you a powerful, happy girl if you'd learn it!" (CC No. 11: "The Cheetah Returns!").

In March–April 1948 the Cheetah escapes from Transformation Island along with seven other villainesses and joins them in forming VILLAINY INCORPORATED (WW No. 28/1–3: "Villainy Incorporated!"; "Trap of Crimson Flame"; "In the Hands of the Merciless!").

Wonder Woman also battles and defeats the Cheetah in adventures recorded in Wonder Woman No. 160/1 (Feb '66: "The Amazon of Terror!") and Wonder Woman No. 166/2 (Nov '66: "Once a Wonder Woman--!"). Both are marred, however, by numerous inconsistencies and factual errors.

CHEMICO (Prof.). A distinguished member of the faculty of the HOLLIDAY COLLEGE FOR WOMEN in Washington, D.C. He is "the inventor of atomic power" (WW No. 20/1, Nov/Dec '46: "Terrors of the Air"), a "brilliant chemist and authority on ancient Egyptian history" (WW No. 23/2, May/Jun '47: "The Vanishing Mummy!"), and the inventor of the "climate-changer," a machine that will enable man to "reclaim the coldest portions of the globe and grow tropical flowers at the North Pole!" (WW No. 29/1, May/Jun '48: "Ice World's Conquest!").

WHAT'S THIS? STOP--YOU'VE NO RIGHT IN HERE!

© NPP 1946

Prof. Chemico, 1946

In April 1946 Prof. Chemico goes temporarily insane after being bitten by one of the "rare poisonous flies" bred by PROF. TOXINO, but he is cured when WONDER WOMAN forces the villain to administer an antidote (Sen No. 52: "The Brand of Madness").

In November–December 1946 Prof. Chemico announces his creation of the revolutionary new "atom pill," a tiny capsule housing all the awesome energy of the mighty atom. "Up to now," he explains, "scientists only knew how to explode the atom, [but] I've discovered how to harness its energy!"

"Now," observes Diana Prince, the girl who is secretly Wonder Woman, "we can use atomic power to run all our machinery, light our cities-- one little atom pill will run a car for the life of its engine!"

Soon afterward, Prof. Chemico, STEVE TREVOR, and the HOLLIDAY GIRLS are kidnapped by the Air

Pirates, a gang of "ruthless female pirates" — led by the beautiful blond Nifty and her redheaded husband — who intend to torture Prof. Chemico into revealing the secret of "how to safely generate atomic power." After receiving a frantic mental radio message (*see* WONDER WOMAN [section C 7, the mental radio]) from Trevor, however, Wonder Woman follows his "brain wave length" to the pirates' hideaway, rescues her friends, and captures the Air Pirates (WW No. 20/1: "Terrors of the Air").

SPECIAL OPERATOR "N" CALLING HEADQUARTERS--EVERY-THING SET-- WILL JOIN YOU IN FLIGHT--THAT IS ALL--

© NPP 1946

Nifty, co-leader of the Air Pirates

In May–June 1947, while Prof. Chemico is exploring a tomb in Egypt, the evil pharaoh AKNATEN seizes control of his mind and forces him to begin work on a deadly "aeropyramic gas" which, if released into the atmosphere, would swiftly bring an end to all life on Earth. Aknaten is ultimately defeated, however, through the heroic efforts of Wonder Woman (WW No. 23/2: "The Vanishing Mummy!").

In May–June 1948 Prof. Chemico leads an expedition to the North Pole to test his newly developed "climate-changer," a device which, at the touch of a lever, can transform the surrounding environment to any desired temperature. "I hope it'll help relieve the food shortage in the world," he explains, "by enabling crops to be grown in the unproductive frigid regions."

At the North Pole, Prof. Chemico beomes the prisoner of the ruthless PRIME MINISTER BLIZZARD, who steals the professor's climate-changer and attempts to turn it against mankind. Prime Minister Blizzard is ultimately defeated, however, through the heroic efforts of Wonder Woman (WW No. 29/1: "Ice World's Conquest!").

CHEQUERANA. A barren, desolate planet inhabited only by King and Knight, two bizarre creatures whose fantastic cosmic chess game threatens to destroy the Earth. King and Knight are defeated by WONDER WOMAN in a battle which brings about the total destruction of Chequerana.

The barren planet Chequerana sits far out in space, inhabited by only two creatures, King and Knight, the sole survivors of an awesome chess tournament that devastated their entire planet. King and Knight, who closely resemble the chess pieces after which they have been named, are engaged in an incredible cosmic chess game utilizing the various heavenly bodies as "pieces." When a piece is "taken," a colossal interstellar collision obliterates the captured piece. Indeed, by September–October 1952 Knight has sent the planet Earth hurtling toward the SUN, and STEVE TREVOR and Wonder Woman rocket into outer space aboard Wonder Woman's robot plane (*see* WONDER WOMAN [section C 4, the robot plane]), determined to put an end to the inhuman chess game. On Chequerana, King tells them the story of his planet:

> Once, **Chequerana** was a populated planet! We settled all our disputes by playing chess---
> After a while money lost its value and we played for the highest stakes of all [with the winner of each chess game earning the right to slay the loser]!
> Winner played against winner until, in this tournament of death, only we two remained---
> If either of us won against the other, it would have meant death, and the end of our planet! So I got the idea of a chess game of space, using heavenly bodies as pieces! We moved them by means of cosmic energy! Whenever they touched, they exploded! Whatever the result of the game, we remained unharmed!

Taken prisoner by the Chequerians, Wonder Woman and Trevor escape into outer space, only to have King and Knight attempt to blast them out of existence with the same "cosmic ray beams" they use to move their cosmic chess pieces through space.

Landing her plane atop a giant meteor, Wonder Woman rubs its surface with her magic lasso (*see* WONDER WOMAN [section C 3, the magic lasso]), transforming it through super-friction into a gigantic mirror. Then, towing the mirror-surfaced meteor through space behind her plane, she makes one of the cosmic ray beams fired at her by the Chequerians to bounce off it and streak back toward Chequerana, obliterating the barren planet with a titanic roar.

"That ends the chess game of space," comments Trevor grimly, "— and the threat to our universe!" (WW No. 55/2: "The Chessmen of Doom!").

CIRCE. In Greek mythology, a moon goddess,

sorceress, and enchantress. Exiled to the island of Aiaie for murdering her husband, she surrounded herself with wild beasts which were actually men she had transformed. When the warrior hero ODYSSEUS and his crew were cast up on her island, she changed the sailors into swine, but Odysseus escaped and ultimately forced the enchantress to restore his men to normal. Sometime in the past, according to Wonder Woman No. 37/3, QUEEN HIPPOLYTE and her AMAZONS "banished Circe to an island planet in space," called Sorca, "where she could do no harm." WONDER WOMAN defeats Circe during a visit to Sorca in September–October 1949 ("The Secrets of Circe!"). (See OWLER [PROF.].)

CLEA (Queen). The cruel blond monarch who is the ruler of the Atlantean nation of VENTURIA — a "subsea realm" situated somewhere "beneath the bottom of the Atlantic Ocean" (CC No. 18, Dec/Jan '46–47: "The Menace of the Rebel Manlings") — until she is deposed by WONDER WOMAN in Spring 1944. Clea is the mother of the lovely Princess Ptra.

Queen Clea overpowers Wonder Woman, 1944

In Spring 1944 the arrogant and tyrannical Clea makes repeated attempts to overthrow QUEEN EERAS of AURANIA and establish her dominion over all of ATLANTIS, only to be repeatedly thwarted by Wonder Woman (WW No. 8/1–3: "Queen Clea's Tournament of Death"; "The Girl with the Iron Mask"; "The Captive Queen"). (See EERAS [QUEEN].)

In December 1944 Queen Clea is one of the six infamous villains and villainesses impersonated by actors in BEDWIN FOOTH's "underworld crime [theatrical] company" (Sen No. 36: "Battle Against Revenge").

In March–April 1948 Queen Clea escapes from TRANSFORMATION ISLAND along with seven other

villainesses and joins them in forming VILLAINY INCORPORATED (WW No. 28/1–3: "Villainy Incorporated!"; "Trap of Crimson Flame"; "In the Hands of the Merciless!"). (See VILLAINY INCORPORATED.)

Queen Clea and Steve Trevor, 1944

CLOSE, ELY. An unscrupulous businessman whose attempt to steal a priceless automobile fuel formula is thwarted by WONDER WOMAN and the AMAZONS in March 1944.

In order to raise money for the Fun Clinic (see FUN FOUNDATION), Wonder Woman uses chemicals obtained from PARADISE ISLAND to manufacture special fuel tablets which, added to water, produce a miraculous "high octane fuel for automobile engines." Determined to steal the secret fuel formula for themselves, Ely Close and his henchmen invade the laboratory where Paula (see GUNTHER, PAULA VON [BARONESS]) and her Amazon co-workers are busy manufacturing the fuel tablets, and attempt to force them to hand over the formula. Paula outwits Close by concealing the fuel formula inside her cigarette holder, and Wonder Woman and the Amazons ultimately take Close and his henchmen into custody (Sen No. 27: "The Fun Foundation").

CLOSE, NINA. The bespectacled, nondescript wife of Brutus Close. Nina Close is secretly the MASK (WW No. 24/2, Jul/Aug '47: "The Challenge of the Mask").

CLOUDMEN, THE. The inhabitants of a bizarre civilization occupying a mysterious "cloud land" high above the highest clouds. Their ruler is the pompous King Blotto.

In April 1947, when U.S. Army airmen flying jet planes over a certain route begin mysteriously disappearing, STEVE TREVOR decides to fly the oute to see if he can discover what has become of he missing fliers, and WONDER WOMAN follows im secretly in her Amazon plane (*see* WONDER WOMAN [section C 4, the robot plane]).

When Trevor's plane disappears inside a fleecy loud, Wonder Woman "lands on the edge of the loud" and is taken captive by "strange strato- pheric creatures," who take her before King Blotto, ruler of the mysterious cloud land. Inform- ng her that Trevor has already been taken pris- ner, King Blotto satisfies Wonder Woman's curi- osity concerning the missing fliers:

> Only once every 100 years does a star burst over our fields, ladening them with the precious stardust, without which we cannot exist! . . . . But our very existence was threatened when your planes invaded the stratosphere--they swooped over our land too fast to distinguish us but low enough to whisk the stardust off our fields--
>
> We had to find some way of stopping the Earth menace before we were faced with complete famine which would result in our extinction. Finally my chief scientist . . . concocted **stardust gas**--
>
> Now we can shoot rockets filled with stardust gas and extinguish the flame which drives the planes--
>
> The planes are forced to land--we capture the Earth fliers and use them to haul our new stardust reapers . . . .

Set to work pulling a stardust reaper, one of the tractorlike machines used by the Cloudmen to harvest their stardust crop, Wonder Woman es- capes, frees Steve Trevor and the other captive fliers, and then sets to work solving the Cloud- men's jet-plane problem.

"When I slice these moorings," observes Won- der Woman, indicating the special moorings which anchor the cloud land in space, "the clouds will rise far into the super-stratosphere where Earth aviators will never reach their stardust fields."

In the words of the textual narrative, "Wonder Woman is right--immediately the cloud land shoots miles into the stratosphere out of reach of even the most modern rocket ships--." The Cloud- men need never again worry about jet planes ravaging their stardust crop, and Earth pilots need never again fear capture by the Cloudmen (Sen No. 64: "The Adventure of the Little Cloud Peo- ple").

COLUMBUS, CHRISTOPHER (1451–1506). The discoverer of the New World.

In Wonder Woman No. 69/2, after having been transported through the time barrier to the mid- Atlantic Ocean in the year 1492, WONDER WOMAN rescues Columbus's three ships — the *Niña*, *Pinta*, and *Santa Maria* — from being swamped and de- stroyed by a monstrous "kronosaurus," a "giant prehistoric aquatic reptile" (Oct '54: "The Secret Hall of Fame!").

Four years later, in a time-journey recounted in Wonder Woman No. 101/2, Wonder Woman res- cues Columbus's flagship *Santa Maria* from being sucked into the vortex of a giant whirlpool (Oct '58: "The Fun House of Time!").

COMAS SOLA. The gigantic meteor which is the home of the Meteor Men (AS No. 13, Oct/Nov '42: "Shanghaied into Space!"). (*See* DESIRA [QUEEN].)

CONQUEST (Lord). The treacherous Martian conqueror who is — along with the DUKE OF DE- CEPTION and the EARL OF GREED — one of the prin- cipal "three commanders" in the service of the war god MARS. Wonder Woman No. 2/4 describes him as ". . . that cold and cruel conqueror who inspired Mussolini to resurrect the Roman Empire by enslaving helpless Ethiopians, who urged Hitler to weld his iron yoke on the bowed necks of Eu- rope's imprisoned peoples and who persuaded Hirohito to torture into submission the uncounted millions of Asia . . . !" (Fall '42). Conquest bears only hatred for WONDER WOMAN and her sister AMAZONS, whom he contemptuously describes as "those believers in love and peace, who thwart our [Martian] attempts to turn the Earth into a per- manent battlefield" (WW No. 36/1, Jul/Aug '49: "The Girl Who Saved Paradise Island!").

Lord Conquest and a Martian slave girl, 1942

In Fall 1942 the war god Mars concocts an elab- orate scheme to capture Wonder Woman — whose "defense of America and democracy has incensed him" — by taking STEVE TREVOR prisoner and using him as bait to lure Wonder Woman to the planet MARS, but Wonder Woman triumphs over the Martian schemers and rescues Trevor from their clutches. Furious over his humiliation, the war god vows to send his top three commanders to Earth to take her captive (WW No. 2/1). (*See* MARS [THE GOD OF WAR].)

The first of Mars's agents to be dispatched to Earth is the Earl of Greed (WW No. 2/2, Fall '42), but Greed ultimately returns to Mars beaten and humiliated by Wonder Woman. (*See* GREED, EARL OF; DEACON, HEZEKIAH [DR.].)

Incensed, Mars casts Greed into a dungeon and then dispatches the Duke of Deception to Earth with instructions to capture Wonder Woman and return her to Mars as a prisoner (WW No. 2/3, Fall '42). (*See* DECEPTION, DUKE OF.)

Like Greed, however, the Duke of Deception fails in his attempt to capture Wonder Woman, and when he returns to Mars he is forced to join Greed in the dungeons.

Mars's third emissary to Earth is Lord Conquest. Conquest's elaborate scheme to capture Wonder Woman succeeds, and Conquest returns to Mars in triumph. Wonder Woman eventually escapes, however, and returns to Earth, so that once again the war god has been thwarted (WW No. 2/4, Fall '42). (*See* CRAFTI [COUNT].)

In June–July 1943 the Duke of Deception overthrows the war god Mars and establishes himself as ruler of the Martian planet. Mars and Lord Conquest are imprisoned, but the Earl of Greed bribes some guards to let them escape, and Mars and Conquest flee into outer space aboard a Martian space cruiser accompanied by some loyal Martian warriors. (*See* DECEPTION, DUKE OF.)

Fugitives from their own planet, Mars and Conquest hope ultimately to capture Wonder Woman and to force her to help them topple Deception from the throne of Mars. Invading the lunar domain of the goddess DIANA, they take the goddess prisoner and destroy the "moon mirrors" which provide the MOON with its light, but Wonder Woman — aided by Steve Trevor, BARONESS PAULA VON GUNTHER, ETTA CANDY, and the HOLLIDAY GIRLS — defeats the Martians and rescues the goddess from their clutches, thus enabling Diana to restore the moon's light (WW No. 5/2).

In March–April 1949 Lord Conquest is allied with the war god Mars in an elaborate scheme to destroy Wonder Woman (WW No. 34: "The Mystery of the Rhyming Riddle!" chs. 1–3 — "Deception Strikes Again"; "The Phantasms of Deception!"; "The Mystery of the Rhyming Riddle!"). (*See* DECEPTION, DUKE OF.)

According to Wonder Woman No. 36/1, Lord Conquest participated, sometime in the past, in a Martian plot to invade PARADISE ISLAND with the aid of boy allies from the planet DUXO, but the invasion was repelled by Wonder Woman with the aid of QUEEN ASTRA and the girl warriors of INFANTA (Jul/Aug '49: "The Girl Who Saved Paradise Island!").

According to Sensation No. 92, Lord Conquest also participated in a Martian plot to destroy the Earth by bombarding it with "titanic solar rays," but the scheme was thwarted by Wonder Woman with the aid of Queen Astra of the planet Infanta (Aug '49: "The Pebble That Saved the World!") (*See* DECEPTION, DUKE OF.)

In July–August 1951 Lord Conquest leads a Martian space armada in a surprise attack on Paradise Island, but the invasion is quickly repelled by Wonder Woman. Back on Mars, the war god Mars demands an accounting: "If it weren't for America's attempts to preserve peace," he bellows, "we could set all Earth battling, and the planet would fall easy prey to us! Destroy America and Earth is ours! Why did you fail?"

"Y-Y-You know the Amazons protect America, sire!" stammers Conquest. "I-I sought to crush them first--b-b-but **Wonder Woman** tricked me!"

It is then that the Duke of Deception comes forward with a new plot to destroy the Amazons, this time through trickery instead of brute force (Sen No. 104: "The End of Paradise Island"). (*See* DECEPTION, DUKE OF.)

CORINE. The attractive accomplice of blackmailer "EARS" FELLOCK. She is an exact double for wealthy widow Margo Vandergilt.

In February 1946 WONDER WOMAN and STEVE TREVOR set out to smash the "Ears" Fellock blackmail gang. At one point, however, while they are standing together on a dance floor, Trevor insists, somewhat rudely, that Wonder Woman dance with him, and then attempts to put his arms around her.

"You'll never get an Amazon **that** way," snaps Wonder Woman. "Try your cave man style on **man's** world girls!"

Wounded by the rejection, Trevor embarks on a whirlwind romance with wealthy widow Margo Vandergilt and asks her to marry him, unaware that his new girlfriend is really "Ears" Fellock's accomplice Corine, who has kidnapped the real Margo Vandergilt and taken her place. Ultimately, however, Wonder Woman exposes Trevor's fiancée as an impostor, rescues the real Margo Vandergilt from the villains' clutches, and apprehends "Ears" Fellock and his cohorts with some last-minute assistance from the HOLLIDAY GIRLS.

Trevor, chastened by his experience, confesses that he was never really in love with the phony argo Vandergilt, but had merely played up to her hopes of making Wonder Woman jealous (Sen o. 50: "The Case of the Girl in Braces").

RAFTI (Count). A wily Italian count who visits merica in Fall 1942 — accompanied by the giant ammotha — as part of a scheme by LORD CONUEST to capture STEVE TREVOR and WONDER OMAN.

In Fall 1942 the war god MARS dispatches Lord onquest to Earth with instructions to capture onder Woman and Steve Trevor. Assuming "asal" form, Conquest whispers the details of his an into the ear of Italian dictator BENITO MUSSONI, who, believing the idea his own, orders two of is collaborators to America to carry it out: ammotha, a hulking giant of a man who poses as prizefighter, and Count Crafti, a handsome Italn nobleman who poses as his manager. Lord onquest enters the body of Mammotha to control is every move.

Through treachery and guile, Count Crafti capures Wonder Woman and Trevor and turns them ver to Conquest, who takes them to the planet MARS in chains. Dispatching an urgent mental adio message (see WONDER WOMAN [section C 7, he mental radio]) to ETTA CANDY, however, Wonler Woman summons Etta and the HOLLIDAY GIRLS to her rescue. Before long she has defeated he war god Mars, rescued Trevor, and escaped to Earth with her friends (WW No. 2/4).

CRIME CHIEF, THE. A ruthless criminal who, in August 1944, organizes all of America's criminals nto a colossal "crime combine" dedicated to the annihilation of WONDER WOMAN. He is in reality Ely Duel, the Chief of County Detectives. Having aken Wonder Woman captive, the Crime Chief is about to kill her by sending "a 10,000 volt current hrough ... electrodes on Wonder Woman's arms," when Paula (see GUNTHER, PAULA VON BARONESS]) arrives on the scene and helps her escape her bonds, thus enabling Wonder Woman to apprehend the Crime Chief (Sen No. 32: "The Crime Combine").

CRIME MASTER OF TIME, THE. A ruthless criminal from the future who is described as "Public Enemy No. 1 of the year 2300" A.D. He is defeated by WONDER WOMAN in May–June 1952.

Tibro — the villain soon to become known as the Crime Master of Time — escapes from the authorities in his own time and journeys to the 20th century, determined to steal a "portable hydrogen bomb" developed in 1952 and then return with it to his own time "to rule the world of the future."

The villain's special futuristic abilities enable him to assume the identity of anyone he chooses, but because "a person cannot occupy two places simultaneously in the same time," anyone the Crime Master impersonates is instantly transported into some other "time zone." For example, when the villain assumes the identity of STEVE TREVOR — who, as a military intelligence officer, is privy to secret information about the portable H-bomb — the real Trevor is instantaneously transported "thousands of years" into the past, where he and Wonder Woman — who happened to be standing beside Trevor when Tibro's "time beam" struck him, and was therefore similarly affected — "become slaves in an ancient Persian galley!"

Wonder Woman escapes from the Persian galley, however, and returns to the 20th century, where she manages ultimately to apprehend the Crime Master and force him to return Trevor and his other victims to the present. When Trevor and the others arrive in the present, the villain is automatically time-teleported back to the world of 2300 A.D., where he will presumably be taken into custody by the police (WW No. 53/1: "The Crime Master of Time!").

CRIMSON CENTIPEDE, THE. A spectacular green-skinned villain — with sixteen pairs of arms and legs and two red antennae protruding from the top of his head — who is created by the war god MARS to destroy WONDER WOMAN and "spread crime and chaos everywhere!" The Crimson Centipede is defeated by Wonder Woman in April 1967 (WW No. 169/1: "Wonder Woman Battles the Crimson Centipede!").

CRUELO (Lord). An evil nobleman of Moltonia, an exotic world lit by a strange blue sun lying far beneath the North Polar ice. His attempt to conquer the "outside world" is thwarted by WONDER WOMAN.

In July–August 1949 ETTA CANDY and the HOLLIDAY GIRLS are taken captive by Maligno, Lord Cruelo's second-in-command, and taken to Moltonia, where Cruelo's forces have imprisoned the good Princess Lura and driven her fiancé Prince Ardent — Moltonia's rightful ruler — into exile with his followers in the forested region known as "the dark country." By testing the physical endurance of his "outer world" captives, Cruelo hopes to calculate his chances of invading and conquering the outside world.

Flying to Moltonia with Steve Trevor, however, Wonder Woman defeats Lord Cruelo and his henchmen, rescues the captives from his clutches, and restores the exiled Prince Ardent to his throne. Cruelo is killed during a battle with Ardent when he accidentally falls beneath the ray of his own "paralyzing machine" (WW No. 36/3: "The Return of the Flying Saucers!").

CRYSTALLAR (King). The ruler of the evil "genii people" who inhabit the White Star. King Crystallar is defeated by WONDER WOMAN.

In November–December 1947, in response to a desperate call for help from King Crystallar — "He's sending thought waves," thinks Wonder Woman, "in hope that someone'll come to the aid of the White Star people who are being captured by the dreaded **golden women** of the **Red Planet**" — Wonder Woman and the HOLLIDAY GIRLS rocket into outer space to battle the golden women and rescue the genii people. Taken captive by the golden women, they escape and turn their energies to helping King Crystallar's genii people, only to discover that they have been fighting on the wrong side — that the golden women are good and the genii people evil.

"All the planets and stars in our universe, except the White Star," explains Queen Supreema, ruler of the golden women, "formed an organization outlawing wars. We are the policewomen of the league whose job is to stop any universal aggressors!"

Having discovered her grievous error, Wonder Woman rescues the golden women from imminent defeat and captures King Crystallar, thereby restoring peace to the White Star and the Red Planet (WW No. 26/3: "The Golden Women and the White Star!").

CUE (Dr.). "A fiend" who, under the guise of being a legitimate medical practitioner, is secretly "developing disease germs to attack America" and testing them on his unsuspecting patients. He is defeated by WONDER WOMAN, who unmasks him as COLONEL TOGO KU, "chief of Japanese spies in America!" (Sen No. 9, Sep '42).

CYBER (Doctor). *See* DOCTOR CYBER.

D

DAILY GLOBE. A metropolitan daily newspaper which employs WONDER WOMAN as its "romance editor" from May–June 1950 (Sen No. 97: "Wonder Woman, Romance Editor") onward, in which capacity she edits the newspaper's "advice to the lovelorn column" and uses her Amazon powers to solve the romantic problems of her readers.

It is in her capacity as the *Daily Globe*'s romance editor that Wonder Woman meets JANET BROWN, whose problem is that she is desperately in love with STEVE TREVOR (Sen No. 98, Jul/Aug '50: "Wonder Woman's Strange Mission!"). (*See* BROWN, JANET.)

In January–February 1952, in an effort to boost its lagging circulation, the *Daily Globe* offers a prize of $5,000 to whoever can uncover Wonder Woman's secret identity (WW No. 51/1: "The Amazing Impersonation!"). (*See* GARO.)

November 1955 finds Wonder Woman still performing her duties as romance editor (WW No. 78/3: "The Million Dollar Mystery!"), but this is the last time her role as romance editor is mentioned in the chronicles.

DALMA. A rebellious blond Amazon who is intensely jealous of WONDER WOMAN. In Fall 1945 she instigates a revolt among the AMAZONS and then flees to America. Finally recaptured through the efforts of Wonder Woman and STEVE TREVOR, Dalma is sent to Reform Island (*see* TRANSFORMATION ISLAND) for rehabilitative training (CC No. 12: "Rebellion on Paradise Island!").

DANIELS (Prof.). An eminent scientist who dies mysteriously while engaged in "top secret research vital to the future welfare of America!" It is while investigating his death that WONDER WOMAN learns of "a diabolical scheme" by Venusians to invade the Earth concealed inside ordinary raindrops.

By September–October 1952, "invaders, from Venus, the 'water planet,' have devised a diabolical scheme to conquer the Earth--entering unsuspected--as **raindrops!**"

". . . With the next rainfall," announces the Venusian commander, "— Earth will be ours! The foolish Earthlings can't guess that we are invading their planet by a means completely beyond suspicion — H_2O! Water! Instead of **space ships,** we use **raindrops!**"

"Aye!" replies another Venusian. ". . . The next rainfall will bring our armies — to drown Earth — and prepare it for our rule! For **we** control **water** as **earthlings** control **steel!**"

While investigating Prof. Daniels's mysterious death, Wonder Woman learns of the Venusian plot. Daniels had discovered the plot and had been killed by the Venusian invaders to ensure his silence.

Wonder Woman thwarts the Venusian invasion by creating a powerful air current which draws the rainfall carrying the Venusian troops over the North Pole, where it freezes into ice, trapping the would-be conquerors inside the raindrops forever (WW No. 55/3: "Invasion of the Raindrops!"). (*See also* VENUS.)

DARNELL (General). The Chief of United States Military Intelligence. As such, he is STEVE TREVOR's immediate superior within the military. Diana Prince — the girl who is secretly WONDER WOMAN — is his secretary, although she functions more as an intelligence operative than as a clerical worker.

General Darnell

While Steve Trevor is in love with Wonder Woman, Darnell has eyes only for Diana Prince. Both men are completely unaware that the valiant Amazon and the resourceful military intelligence operative are the same person.

Darnell's affection for Diana Prince is less openly expressed than Trevor's for Wonder

Woman, but whenever a tragedy occurs, Darnell's first fears are for Diana; whenever there is danger, his concern is for her safety; whenever she is absent, he wishes she were near him (CC No. 4, Fall '43: "The Purloined Pressure Coordinator"; WW No. 11/3, Win '44: "The Slave Smugglers"; CC No. 7, Sum '44: "The Vulture's Nest!"; and others).

Only once does Darnell openly reveal the true extent of his feelings — in December 1945, when he asks Diana to meet him at a local jewelry store and, when she arrives, presents her with a diamond clip.

"Gen. Darnell," insists Diana, "you mustn't —"

"Nonsense," replies Darnell, "— only wish you'd accept a diamond **ring**!"

Later, when he is alone, Darnell ponders his romantic situation aloud: "Looks like Trevor and myself are confirmed bachelors," he muses, "through no fault of our own" (Sen No. 48).

The later chronicles tend to be confusing and inconsistent regarding Darnell's feelings for Diana Prince. Wonder Woman No. 50/1, for example, portrays him as a married man with a young son named Lee (Nov/Dec '51: "Menace of the Master Spy!"), suggesting that his past intentions toward Diana Prince may not have been entirely honorable. However, since Wonder Woman No. 50/1 is the only text which portrays Darnell as anything but a bachelor, it is perhaps best to regard it as inaccurate.

At least two texts portray Darnell as hopelessly in love with Wonder Woman — Wonder Woman No. 164 goes so far as to place them on the verge of matrimony — but these texts are marred by factual errors and chronological distortions (WW No. 164, Aug '66: "Wonder Woman--Traitor!"; WW No. 169/2, Apr '67: "The Cage of Doom!").

In March 1942, after Steve Trevor has been released from the Walter Reed Army Hospital and returned to his duties at the office of Military Intelligence in Washington, D.C., Diana Prince obtains employment there as Colonel Darnell's secretary (Sen No. 3).

In June 1942 Colonel Darnell is en route to England on a secret government mission when he is taken captive by Germans aided by BARONESS PAULA VON GUNTHER. He is rescued soon afterward by Wonder Woman (Sen No. 6).

In Winter 1945 Darnell is referred to as General Darnell for the first time in the chronicles, indicating a recent promotion from colonel to brigadier general (WW No. 15: chs. 1–3 — "The First Battle of Neptunia"; "The Masters of the Water"; "In the Killer's Cage").

In April 1946 Darnell goes temporarily insane after being bitten by one of the "rare poisonous flies" bred by PROF. TOXINO, but he is cured whe Wonder Woman forces the villain to supply th antidote (Sen No. 52: "The Brand of Madness"

In June 1946, when DR. FIENDO seizes control the U.S. Government, Darnell is arrested as "subversive" — along with Wonder Woman, Stev Trevor, and the HOLLIDAY GIRLS — and is ser tenced to death by firing squad for "treason." The are all rescued from seemingly certain death b Wonder Woman (Sen No. 54: "The Treachery o Fiendo"). (*See* FIENDO [DR.].)

In July–August 1946 Darnell is lured into deathtrap — along with Steve Trevor, ETTA CANDY and the Holliday Girls — by DR. PSYCHO, only to b rescued from death by Wonder Woman (WW No 18/2: "The Drugged WAC"). (*See* PSYCHO [DR.].

Soon afterward, with Dr. Psycho presumed dea in a titanic explosion, Darnell attends the party which Etta Candy gives at Holliday College t celebrate the villain's demise. Dr. Psycho is alive and well, however, and when he invades the party being held in his "honor," Darnell is again rescued from death by the intervention of Wonder Woman (WW No. 18/3, Jul/Aug '46: "Ectoplasmic Death") (*See* PSYCHO [DR.].)

In January–February 1948, when it appears that Diana Prince has been murdered by PIK SOCKET and his henchmen, General Darnell becomes visibly heartbroken (WW No. 27/1: "The Secret of the Kidnapped Dummy!").

In November–December 1951 Darnell courageously allows himself to be branded a traitor so that he can attempt to infiltrate the espionage apparatus of the sinister GENERAL VORO, "the man of a thousand faces" (WW No. 50/1: "Menace of the Master Spy!").

DARNELL, LEE. The young son of GENERAL DARNELL and his wife (WW No. 50/1, Nov/Dec '51: "Menace of the Master Spy!"). Because Lee Darnell appears in only one text, while numerous texts portray General Darnell as a bachelor, Wonder Woman No. 50/1 should probably be dismissed as inaccurate.

DAXO (Duke). The evil usurper of the throne of Humming Bird Isle. He is toppled from power by WONDER WOMAN.

In December 1948, while spending a day at the beach, the HOLLIDAY GIRLS come upon a huge glass bottle with a lovely blond girl unconscious inside it. Unable to open the sealed bottle themselves, they summon WONDER WOMAN, who opens the bottle and then revives the unconscious girl at Paula's secret laboratory (*see* GUNTHER, PAULA VON [BARONESS]).

Introducing herself as Princess Turula of Humming Bird Isle, the girl proceeds to tell her story:

My mother, Queen Sala, ruled Humming Bird Isle after my father, dying in a hunting accident, entrusted it into her wise and gentle hands--

For years, Hummingbird Islanders lived in peace and happiness--but there was someone who plotted an end to our happiness! My uncle, Duke Daxo!--

After raising an army in secret and invading the oyal castle, Daxo had seized power and imprisned Queen Sala, but not before she had sealed er daughter inside a huge bottle and cast it into he sea, hoping that somehow Princess Turula ight one day return with help.

Flying to Humming Bird Isle, named for its ummingbird shape, Wonder Woman, STEVE TREVOR, and Princess Turula are captured by the orces of the evil Daxo, but Wonder Woman escapes a fiendish deathtrap prepared for her by the duke, rescues Trevor, Princess Turula, and Queen Sala from Daxo's clutches, topples Daxo from power, and restores Queen Sala to her throne (Sen No. 84: "The Bottle Cast up by the Sea!").

DAZAM (Duke). An evil duke who inhabits Earth's "twin world," a world "existing simultaneously alongside" Earth, but in an earlier time era. ". . . Everyone on it, is a double of everyone on Earth!" Hurled across a mysterious "time warp" into the parallel world by a freak electrical storm in May–June 1953, WONDER WOMAN helps Tara Terruna — a Wonder Woman counterpart and look-alike whose name, translated into English, means Wonder Woman — defeat the forces of the evil Duke Dazam before returning home safely across the time warp (WW No. 59/1: "Wonder Woman's Invisible Twin!").

DAZZLE, BELLE. A name assumed by WONDER WOMAN during a period of temporary amnesia resulting from a blow on the head she receives while rescuing STEVE TREVOR from a plummeting aircraft in May–June 1950. Dropping to the ground far from Trevor, Wonder Woman, her memory temporarily lost, wanders into a lazy mountain town — so isolated from civilization that no one there has ever heard of her — and hastily responds to a request for her name with the brand name of a local tobacco, Belle Dazzle.

While striving to regain her memory, Wonder Woman works as the town blacksmith — becoming something of a local heroine through her stupendous feats of superhuman strength — until one day a traveling salesman, who has heard the local people bragging about their heroine but not actually seen her, offers to bet them large sums of money that Wonder Woman could defeat Belle Dazzle in an athletic contest.

Before long, Wonder Woman finds herself committed to an athletic contest with herself, but a second accidental blow on the head has restored her memory in the interim, and she is determined to prevent the unscrupulous salesman from taking unfair advantage of her mountain friends. She resolves the dilemma of the athletic contest by using a lifelike Wonder Woman robot as a Wonder Woman stand-in and by seeing to it that the contest ends in a tie, thus thwarting the salesman's attempt to cheat the townspeople and vindicating their faith in her (WW No. 41/2: "Wonder Woman vs. Wonder Woman!").

DEACON, HEZEKIAH (Dr.). The president of the HOLLIDAY COLLEGE FOR WOMEN until Fall 1942, when he is apprehended by WONDER WOMAN for conspiring with the Nazis to rob the United States Treasury.

In Fall 1942 the Nazis attempt to loot the U.S. Treasury by digging an underground tunnel from Holliday College to the Treasury Building, securing Dr. Deacon's cooperation through the efforts of the EARL OF GREED, a lackey of the war god MARS, who visits the college president in "astral" form and tempts him with visions of the riches that will be his for collaborating. Wonder Woman thwarts the scheme to rob the Treasury, however, and unmasks Dr. Deacon as a Nazi conspirator (WW No. 2/2).

DEAN, MARY (Dr.). The brilliant scientist who is the discoverer of "reduso liquid," a chemical formula designed to "reduce germs to such a minute size that they will be unable to harm humans!" Dr. Dean is also the fiancée of the unscrupulous DR. DIRKE, who steals the priceless formula with the intention of using it for evil (WW No. 31/1, Sep/Oct '48: "The Shrinking Formula!").

DEARFIELD, ALTON (Dr.). A "famous atomic scientist" whose discovery of an "atom-neutralizing formula" holds out the promise of "protection against atomic radiation." In September–October 1947 Dr. Dearfield's wife Myrna is kidnapped by the "YELLOW MASK" GANG, "international racketeers" who hope to force her to disclose the hiding place of her husband's priceless formula (WW No. 25/2: "Who'll Adopt Teasy?").

DE BOAR (Baron). A long-dead medieval baron whose suits of armor begin mysteriously disappearing from the nation's museums in November–December 1951. The villain responsible, "the last descendant of Baron De Boar," is apprehended by WONDER WOMAN.

In November–December 1951 the nation is rocked by a series of seemingly inexplicable museum robberies, but in each case the only things stolen are "suits [of armor] which were worn by the villainous Baron De Boar!" The thief is a modern-day descendant of the medieval baron who has found a way to transform the seemingly use-less armor into "looting robots [that] no one will be able to stop!" Indeed, in the days that follow, the miraculous armor robots begin staging one spectacular robbery after another.

Wonder Woman finally captures the villain by advertising the display of a newly-discovered suit of Baron De Boar's armor, concealing herself in-side it, and then surprising the villain after he has stolen the armor and transported it to his hideout (Sen No. 106: "The Knights of Terror!").

DEBUM, PALTRO. A vicious gambler and racket-eer who attempts first to fix a championship water-polo match so that he can profit by betting on the outcome, and later to force a captive WON-DER WOMAN to win money for him by competing in championship athletic events. Debum's criminal career is brought to an end by Wonder Woman, who apprehends the racketeer and his henchmen in Winter 1945 with the help of STEVE TREVOR, ETTA CANDY, and the HOLLIDAY GIRLS (CC No. 13: "The Underwater Follies").

DECEPTION, DUKE OF. A treacherous Martian who is — along with LORD CONQUEST and the EARL OF GREED — one of the principal "three command-ers" in the service of the war god MARS. By using his "astral body" to animate the numerous "false forms" — or ectoplasmic "phantasms" — which he houses in a special storeroom on the planet MARS, Deception can assume the form of anyone he chooses. The war god Mars refers to him as the Lord of Liars (WW No. 2/3, Fall '42), and the chronicles call him "the imperator of illusions," "the master of matter," "the master of illusion" (WW No. 148, Aug '64: "The Olympics of the Doomed"), and the "Martian master of treachery" (Sen No. 104, Jul/Aug '51: "The End of Paradise Island"). In the chronicles, he is referred to both as the Duke of Deception and Duke Deception. The ruthless LYA is his daughter.

The Duke of Deception

In Fall 1942 the war god Mars concocts an elab-orate scheme to capture WONDER WOMAN — whose "defense of America and democracy has incensed him"— by taking STEVE TREVOR prisoner and using him as bait to lure Wonder Woman to the planet Mars, but Wonder Woman triumphs over the Mar-tian schemers and rescues Trevor from their clutches. Furious over his humiliation, the war god vows to send his top three commanders to Earth to take her captive (WW No. 2/1). (*See* MARS [THE GOD OF WAR].)

The first of Mars's agents to be dispatched to Earth is the Earl of Greed (WW No. 2/2, Fall '42) but Greed ultimately returns to Mars beaten and humiliated by Wonder Woman. (*See* GREED, EARL OF; DEACON, HEZEKIAH [DR.].)

Incensed, Mars casts Greed into a dungeon, and then dispatches the Duke of Deception to Earth with instructions to capture Wonder Woman and return her to Mars as a prisoner.

On Earth, Deception instigates a Japanese aerial attack on Hawaii as part of his scheme to capture Wonder Woman, but the valiant Amazon quickly turns the sneak attack on Hawaii into a humilia-ting disaster for the "sly little men from Nippon" and turns Deception's plot into a shambles (WW No. 2/3, Fall '42).

When Deception returns to Mars, beaten and humiliated by Wonder Woman, Mars orders him thrown into the same dungeon with the Earl of Greed.

Mars's third emissary to Earth, however, Lord Conquest, succeeds in making Wonder Woman his prisoner, and when he returns to Mars in triumph, the overjoyed war god orders Deception and Greed released from the dungeons. Wonder Woman ultimately escapes and returns to Earth, so that once again the war god has been thwarted (WW No. 2/4, Fall '42). (*See* CRAFTI [COUNT].)

In June–July 1943 the war god Mars, concerned that the women of Earth have begun displaying too much independence, orders Deception to come up with "an evil inspiration" for putting Earth's "upstart women in their place." The wily Deception promptly pays a call on "an Earth agent who hates women," the diabolical DR. PSYCHO (WW No. 5/1: "Battle for Womanhood").

When Dr. Psycho fails to achieve a victory over Wonder Woman, Mars orders Deception incarcer-ated in the Martian women's prison, where he is put to work scrubbing floors and peeling huge mounds of potatoes. After using his treacherous wiles to persuade the women prisoners that he is their champion and ally, however, Deception launches a prisoner insurrection and seizes control of the prison, then tricks Mars and Lord Conquest

AND SO, ON EARTH, THE DEVIOUS DR. PSYCHO RECEIVES AN EVIL INSPIRATION.

Z-Z-ZUT! A SPIRIT TELLS ME MY HOUR OF VENGEANCE IS AT HAND! WOMEN SHALL SUF- FER WHILE I LAUGH— HA! HO! HA!

© NPP 1943

In spirit form, the Duke of Deception provides Dr. Psycho with "an evil inspiration," 1943

into visiting the prison, takes them captive, and seizes control of the entire planet. The women prisoners, grateful to Deception for his part in winning them their freedom, place Deception on the throne of Mars.

The Earl of Greed, however, bribes some prison guards to let Mars and Conquest escape, and they flee into outer space aboard a Martian space cruiser (WW No. 5/2, Jun/Jul '43). (*See* CONQUEST [LORD].)

In December 1944 the Duke of Deception is one of the six infamous villains and villainesses imper-sonated by actors in BEDWIN FOOTH's "underworld crime [theatrical] company" (Sen No. 36: "Battle Against Revenge").

By April–May 1948 the Duke of Deception has managed to thwart an attempt by his ruthless daughter Lya to topple him from the throne of

Mars and banish him to exile on Earth (CC No. 26: "Deception's Daughter"). (*See* LYA.)

By March–April 1949 the war god Mars has ap-parently regained power on Mars, though how or when this came about is never explained in the chronicles. "Irked by [the] lack of war on Earth," the war god "fumes with rage" at those about him: "**Wonder Woman** is stirring everybody up for peace!" he cries. ". . . My plans for a new world war will be ruined!"

To assuage the war god's anger, the Duke of Deception and a crew of Martians journey to Earth, where they set in motion a scheme to steal Holliday College and lure Wonder Woman to her doom. After the Martians have overpowered Paula (*see* GUNTHER, PAULA VON [BARONESS]) in her se-cret laboratory and locked her inside a torpedo case in the corner of the room, Deception dis-guises himself in a "phantasm" of Paula, takes her place in the laboratory, and uses the Amazon "transmaterialization machine" (*see* AMAZONS [section G, Amazon science]) to make the HOLLI-DAY COLLEGE FOR WOMEN — including its buildings, student body, and staff — vanish from the face of the Earth.

When Wonder Woman discovers that Holliday College has disappeared and that she is unable to contact ETTA CANDY via mental radio (*see* WONDER WOMAN [section C 7, the mental radio]), she races to Paula's laboratory with Steve Trevor in hopes of finding some means of locating Etta and the HOL-LIDAY GIRLS, unaware that the scientist on hand to greet them there is not Paula, but a phantasm look-alike animated by the astral form of Decep-tion.

Hoping to rid himself of Wonder Woman by marooning her in the Ice Age, Deception — speak-ing through his Paula disguise — suggests that Etta Candy and the Holliday Girls may have been transported into the prehistoric past. To test "Paula's" hunch, Wonder Woman and Trevor use the Amazon "space-transformer" (*see* AMAZONS [section G, Amazon science]) to send themselves into the past, while, in the present, Deception jams the machine's controls in an effort to trap them in the prehistoric past forever. Fortunately, however, the space-transformer is equipped with a "mental robot" control mechanism which enables Wonder Woman to activate it mentally from the past — and thus return Trevor and herself to the present — without actually having access to the space-trans-former's controls.

After overcoming a series of prehistoric per-ils — without, however, locating the missing Holli-day Girls — Wonder Woman and Trevor return to the present, where they discover that Deception had tricked them and fled, and find the real Paula locked in the torpedo case. Wonder Woman decides that she must pursue Deception to Mars, where she feels certain Etta Candy and the Holliday Girls are being held captive.

"But Mars takes as prisoners only the astral beings of the dead!" exclaims Paula.

"I will drink Aphrodite's 'elixir of living death,'" replies Wonder Woman, "then surrender to Mars' slave collectors and enter, unknown, into the realm of the war-lord."

And so Wonder Woman "leaves her [physical] body in Paula's care" and, in astral form, begins the long journey to Mars.

"**Wonder Woman's** astral figure, freed from her body by the elixir of living death, travels with the speed of light to a demolished corner of the globe, where Mars's soldiers are collecting prisoners from those who have lost their lives to conquest, greed, and deception!" In astral form, she surrenders to Mars's slave collectors and is taken in shackles to the grim domain of the war god Mars. There the Duke of Deception disguises himself as Etta Candy in order to lure her into Mars's "war games arena," where she is forced to battle the war god's deadliest weapons: a "jet-propelled, robot-controlled flying flame-thrower" and "mechanical paratroopers riding jet-controlled V bombs."

Despite the terrifying odds against her, however, Wonder Woman overcomes every obstacle hurled at her by Mars and his minions. At one point, she is duped into rescuing what is in reality only a phantasm of her sweetheart Steve Trevor.

"In another moment," chortles Deception, as Wonder Woman cradles in her arms what she believes to be the unconscious form of Steve Trevor, "**Wonder Woman** will discover that the phantasm which she thought her Steve--is not just a phantasm--but a **bomb!** Ha ha!"

Seconds later, a titanic explosion splits the air, but Wonder Woman miraculously survives because, in her words, "Amazons are taught how to roll outside the area of a bomb blast!"

Ultimately, with some help from the goddess APHRODITE, Wonder Woman defeats Mars and his lieutenants and forces him to reveal that he has hidden Holliday College on Limbo, his "secret jail . . . in outer space."

Racing to Limbo, Wonder Woman rescues Etta Candy and the Holliday Girls from the Martian troops on guard there and then flies Holliday College back to Earth, strapped to the roof of a Martian spacecraft (WW No. 34: "The Mystery of the Rhyming Riddle!" chs. 1–3 — "Deception Strikes Again"; "The Phantasms of Deception!"; "The Mystery of the Rhyming Riddle!").

The Wonder Woman text for August 1949 recounts an adventure, purported to have taken place sometime in the past, in which the war god Mars, Lord Conquest, and the Duke of Deception plot to destroy the Earth by means of a diabolical new super-weapon in the form of a huge lens, mounted atop a special "attack station" floating in outer space, which is capable of reflecting "titanic solar rays" at the Earth.

Realizing that "once [the Martians] turn its full force on the Earth--all will be lost," Wonder Woman streaks into outer space to battle the would-be conquerors, accompanied by QUEEN ASTRA of the planet INFANTA.

Taken captive by the Martian space fleet and bound by Deception with her own magic lasso (see WONDER WOMAN [section C 3, the magic lasso]), Wonder Woman is commanded to ready the Martian super-weapon for the fatal attack on Earth, but at the last possible moment she flings a tiny pebble at Deception's hand, forcing him to drop his end of the magic lasso, thereby freeing Wonder Woman from his mental control. Smashing the terrible solar lens beyond repair, Wonder Woman assures that it will never again be used against the Earth (Sen No. 92: "The Pebble That Saved the World!").

By May–June 1951 "a strange barrier" has completely enveloped the city of Washington, D.C. It is "invisible--but impenetrable! Composed of an unknown substance!" As a result, "Washington is completely isolated . . .! **Nothing** can pass through the invisible curtain which surrounds [it]!"

Soaring into the stratosphere aboard her Amazon plane (see WONDER WOMAN [section C 4, the robot plane]), Wonder Woman discovers the true nature of the bizarre barrier:

"Imagine a gigantic funnel, with the wide end completely covering Washington, D.C., and the spout extending into space--that's the shape of the invisible trap which holds America's capital as if it were a ship in a bottle!"

And so: "Through the vast reaches of space, **Wonder Woman** trails the origin of the invisible barrier which threatens the peace and security of America."

The trail leads to Mars, where a Martian space fleet commanded by the Duke of Deception has already begun the journey down the invisible funnel toward America so that it can "bomb Washington and destroy the strongest arsenal of democracy on Earth!"

Taken prisoner by the Martians, Wonder Woman escapes, overtakes the Martian space fleet inside the funnel, and destroys it before it can reach Earth. "With the . . . attacking [Martian] fleet destroyed," notes the narrative text, "Deception is defeated," and the nation's capital is "freed from the threat of invasion" (WW No. 47/3: "The Bridge from Mars!").

In July–August 1951 Lord Conquest leads a Martian space armada in a surprise attack on PAR-ADISE ISLAND, but the invasion is quickly repelled by Wonder Woman. Back on Mars, the war god Mars demands an accounting: "If it weren't for America's attempts to preserve peace," he bellows, "we could set all Earth battling, and the planet would fall easy prey to us! Destroy America and Earth is ours! Why did you fail?"

"Y-Y-You know the Amazons protect America, sire!" stammers Conquest. "I-I sought to crush them first--b-b-but **Wonder Woman** tricked me!"

It is then that the Duke of Deception comes forward with a new plot to destroy the AMAZONS, this time through trickery instead of brute force. First the Martians locate Steve Trevor and take him prisoner. When Wonder Woman responds to his frantic calls for help, she comes upon what she believes to be the unconscious form of Steve Trevor floating atop the wreckage of his downed airplane in the middle of the ocean and carries him aboard her Amazon plane, unaware that the real Trevor is a prisoner of the Martians and that the man aboard her plane is the Duke of Decep-tion in disguise.

Ensnaring Wonder Woman with her own magic lasso, Deception commands her to take him to Paradise Island, home of the Amazons, knowing that once he sets foot on Paradise Island, the Am-azons will lose their powers by Aphrodite's law (see AMAZONS [section B, Aphrodite's Law]). Won-der Woman, however, turns the tables on her cap-tor, prevents Deception from landing on Paradise Island, and, while her sister Amazons beat back an invasion of their island by Deception's Martian space fleet, rescues Trevor from the Martians' clutches (Sen No. 104: "The End of Paradise Is-land").

In January 1954 the Duke of Deception imper-sonates "world-famous scientist" Professor Dekon as part of a new scheme to conquer the Earth. Posing as Dekon, Deception warns Wonder Woman of an impending invasion from outer space and, by misleading her as to the true nature of the coming invasion, sends her off on a wild goose chase into space to ensure that she will be far from Earth when his Martian space fleet strikes. Wonder Woman ultimately discovers that she has been tricked, however, and intercepts and demolishes Deception's invasion armada (WW No. 63/2: "The Secret Invasion!").

In April 1954 Wonder Woman awakes from a

night of sleep punctuated by nightmares to find herself locked in a display case on the planet JUPI-TER. A label on the case identifies her as "the last Amazon." Looking around her, Wonder Woman spies other, similar, display cases, containing the "last policeman," the "last clown," and other "last" examples of Earth life. Steve Trevor is the "last soldier."

After smashing her way out of her display case, Wonder Woman asks to be taken to the Jovian leader, who expresses surprise that she is still alive and informs her that she is the sole survivor of a devastated Earth. The Duke of Deception and his Martian followers, he explains, invaded Paradise Island, overwhelmed the Amazons, and went on to conquer the Earth, reducing it in the process to "a desolate desert."

The Jovians meant her no harm, he continues, having merely collected her and a few other Earth specimens for their "planetary museum" now that Earth is a dead planet.

Through astronomical observation, the Jovians know that the Martians landed on Paradise Island by means of some trick, but they do not know what the trick was. Once the Martians had landed, however, the Amazons had lost their invincibility by Aphrodite's law and had been defeated.

Wonder Woman asks the Jovian leader to send her back in time to the period directly preceding the Martian invasion, hoping that if she can dis-cover the strategem that enabled the Martians to land on Paradise Island, she might be able to fore-stall the dreadful chain of events leading to the conquest of the Amazons and the devastation of Earth.

Dispatched into the recent past, Wonder Woman successfully reverses history by discovering the Martian ruse and turning back the Martian inva-sion. The Martians, she learns, had reduced them-selves to the size of bracelet charms, concealed themselves inside an ornate jewelry box, and had themselves dropped on Paradise Island. Once QUEEN HIPPOLYTE had opened the innocent-look-ing box, the invaders had "expanded to life-size" and conquered the Amazons.

Owing to her advance knowledge of what the immediate future will bring, however, Wonder Woman suspects that the mysterious jewelry box may represent the trick described by the Jovians. By opening the box underwater a safe distance from Paradise Island, and luring the Martian space fleet into the path of an erupting underwater volcano, Wonder Woman destroys Deception's in-vasion armada and rescues Earth from destruc-tion (WW No. 65/3: "The Last Amazon!").

By May 1954 the Duke of Deception has used a

special "magnetic ray" to kidnap Earth's greatest athletes and draw them through space to Mars. Deception is trying to convince the other planets in the Solar System to help him invade Earth, but the representatives of the other planets are reluctant, fearing possible defeat. By kidnapping Earth's finest athletes and forcing them to compete against the champions of other planets, Deception hopes to convince his fellow aliens that earthlings can be easily beaten and that they have nothing to fear from invading Earth. The aliens have agreed to become Deception's allies if Earth's finest athletes can be beaten in his tournament.

While investigating the mysterious disappearance of the vanished athletes, Wonder Woman too is drawn to Mars by Deception's magnetic ray and is swiftly taken prisoner. In order to save Earth from a combined invasion by all the planets, Wonder Woman volunteers to represent Earth in the upcoming athletic tournament by competing against every alien athlete in that athlete's best sport. Deception rigs every event in an effort to prevent Wonder Woman from winning, but the valiant Amazon triumphs nevertheless. Consequently, the aliens decline to participate in Deception's invasion scheme, and Wonder Woman and the kidnapped athletes are permitted to return to Earth (WW No. 66/1: "The Olympics of Terror!").

In April 1956 the Duke of Deception uses a "brain-wave deceiver" device to "scramble" Wonder Woman's "brain waves" so that she cannot distinguish between sleeping and waking, nightmare and reality, or fantasy and truth. When Wonder Woman finally realizes what Deception is doing, however, she tricks him into destroying the brain-wave deceiver by creating the mental image of a fearsome dragon in Deception's laboratory. When the panic-stricken Deception fires his raygun at the horrifying "dragon," he inadvertently destroys his own brain-wave device (WW No. 81/1: "The Dream Dooms!").

In August 1956, when a gigantic statue of Wonder Woman appears from out of nowhere in the heart of the city, Wonder Woman discovers a secret passageway into the statue and steps inside it, only to have the entire statue take off like a rocket ship with her imprisoned inside it.

When the huge statue finally comes to a landing, Wonder Woman finds herself in "the land of illusion," a strange planet where the Duke of Deception — who masterminded her abduction — is waiting to defeat her. Wonder Woman's every move, he explains, is being carefully observed by "pirates of outer planets . . . who will invade your planet Earth as soon as I show them that you can

be defeated — and won't be the threat to them — that you have been to other invaders!"

To forestall this new threat to Earth, continues Deception, Wonder Woman must "find the **one single thing** in this land of illusion which is **real** and **prove** it — before an hour elapses! Succeed — and Earth is safe! Your failure — will be the signal to attack!"

Again and again, Wonder Woman attempts to pinpoint the one real thing in the land of illusion, but everything she guesses turns out to be merely a mirage. Finally, however, she realizes that the one real thing in the land of illusion is herself, and once she has proven this to Deception and his alien allies, the projected invasion of Earth is cancelled (WW No. 84/2: "The Planet of Illusion!").

In February 1957 the Duke of Deception concocts an elaborate scheme to lure Wonder Woman far away from the place where he and his Martian space armada intend to launch their latest invasion of Earth. However, Wonder Woman sees through Deception's ruse, intercepts his space fleet, and destroys it (WW No. 88/1: "Mystery of the Vanishing Box!").

By October 1957 the Duke of Deception has devised yet another scheme to conquer Earth, this time by using "shrinking rays" to reduce the entire planet "to the size of a toy." To test the effectiveness of the shrinking rays, Deception and his space fleet launch a surprise attack on Skyscraper City, "one of Earth's biggest cities," reasoning that if they work on Skyscraper City they will work on the rest of the globe as well. Deception and his cohorts succeed in reducing Skyscraper City to the size of a doll's house, but Wonder Woman streaks into space in her Amazon plane, intercepts the Martian space fleet, and destroys it, demolishing the Martian shrinking device and restoring Skyscraper City and its inhabitants to their normal size (WW No. 93/2: "The Shrinking City!").

By November 1957 the Duke of Deception has constructed a "gigantic inter-stellar cannon" with which he plans to destroy Wonder Woman as soon as she steps aboard her Amazon plane. Wonder Woman is completely unaware of Deception's treacherous plot against her, but repeated coincidences prevent her from boarding her plane and thus exposing herself to Deception's cannon. As the text draws to a close, Deception still has not had the opportunity to blast Wonder Woman with his diabolical new weapon (WW No. 94/2: "Target: Wonder Woman!").

In February 1959 the Duke of Deception sets in motion an elaborate scheme to compel Wonder Woman to lead a combined armada of Martian,

Saturnian, and Plutonian space ships in a surprise invasion of Earth. Deception succeeds in capturing Wonder Woman and Steve Trevor, but Wonder Woman escapes and demolishes the three allied invasion fleets before they can mass for their joint Earth invasion (WW No. 104/2: "Key of Deception!").

In August 1964 the Duke of Deception uses his spectacular powers to animate inanimate objects and create complex illusions in an elaborate campaign to drive Wonder Woman into a state of nervous exhaustion by destroying her ability to distinguish between illusion and reality. As Deception's scheme proceeds, Wonder Woman is beset by one bewildering event after another: she answers the telephone, only to discover that the ringing of the phone took place only in her imagination; she answers the doorbell, only to learn that no one has rung it; attacked by a ferocious lion in the hallway of her apartment, she hurls it to the floor, only to discover that the lion was a figment of her imagination and that it is Steve Trevor she has manhandled; sighting a heavy water tower toppling from its foundation, she streaks into the air to catch it, only to find the water tower secure and in no danger of falling; she sees Paradise Island crumbling into the sea and all the Amazons dead, but this too turns out to be merely an illusion.

Now teetering on the verge of nervous collapse, Wonder Woman is seized by a gigantic prehistoric serpent — actually only a small toy animated and enlarged by the Duke of Deception — which soars into space with her at rocket speed, until, moments later, she finds herself aboard Deception's spacecraft, hovering above the Earth.

Deception takes Wonder Woman to Mars, where he forces her to participate in "the Olympics of the doomed," a terrifying tournament in which she must win every single event or forfeit her life, and during which she remains confined in a cage while her opponents remain free. Despite the seemingly overwhelming odds against her, however, Wonder Woman wins every event in the diabolical tournament, tricks Deception into becoming trapped inside the very cage in which he had imprisoned her, and then returns to Earth (WW No. 148: "The Olympics of the Doomed").

In November–December 1967, Wonder Woman No. 173/2 contains the story of an encounter between Wonder Woman and the Martians which is almost identical to a story contained in a much earlier text (i.e., WW No. 65/3, Apr '54: "The Last Amazon!").

DESIRA (Queen). The lovely winged queen of the planet VENUS. It is Queen Desira who bestows upon WONDER WOMAN the miraculous "gift of magnetic hearing," enabling Wonder Woman to receive "thought messages" from Desira across the interstellar void. Desira is the mother of QUEEN EVE, ruler of EVELAND.

THE GOLDEN FIGURE BECOMES DISTINCT — BUT ONLY TO DIANA'S MENTAL VISION.

LISTEN, EARTH PRINCESS OF THE AMAZONS! I HAVE IMPORTANT INFORMATION TO GIVE YOU!

© NPP 1945

Queen Desira, 1945

The women of Venus are lovely creatures — courageous but peace-loving — whose graceful translucent wings enable them to swoop and soar like huge butterflies. The men of Venus are wingless, and, though generally well-meaning, are also somewhat craven, being totally dependent upon the winged women for moral support, guidance, and protection. Wonder Woman No. 12/3 describes them as "defenseless" (Spr '45: "The Conquest of Venus"). On Venus, theirs is indisputably the submissive role.

In October–November 1942, after being locked inside a rocket by Axis agents and launched into outer space, Wonder Woman finds herself on the planet Venus, where she meets Queen Desira and her subjects for the first time.

"Wonder Woman!" cries Desira joyfully. "The oracle of Aphrodite, whom we worship, foretold your coming! . . . We need [you] desperately!"

"I'll bet you're having **man** trouble!" replies Wonder Woman.

"No, our men love us dearly," answers Desira. "They obey us because if they did not, we would fly away from them and they have no wings to follow."

"That's a wonderful way to keep men in their place!" laughs Wonder Woman.

Despite the domestic harmony which prevails on their planet, however, the people of Venus are in desperate straits, for the meteor Comas Sola has crashed into their planet, unleashing the terrible Meteor Men. The invaders are everywhere, killing many Venusians and taking others prisoner.

In the battle that follows, however, Wonder Woman is instrumental in the Venusians' ultimate triumph over their would-be conquerors. In gratitude, "Venus men carry Wonder Woman triumphantly through the streets amid the cheers of happy crowds, while winged women scatter golden flowers in her path."

"Aphrodite has taught us how to make men loving and peaceful," comments Queen Desira happily. "Already these Meteor Men are eating out of our hands!"

"If only we could make Earth men peaceful!" sighs Wonder Woman.

"You can!" replies Desira. "I will direct your efforts. I give you now the gift of **magnetic hearing.** My lips magnetize your earrings, and always you can hear my voice!"

The gift of magnetic hearing will enable Queen Desira to transmit instantaneous thought messages to Wonder Woman from Venus to Earth.

"Goodbye," cries Wonder Woman, as she prepares to return to Earth to resume her battle with the Axis agents who dispatched her to Venus in the first place, "--and thanks for your wonderful gift!" (AS No. 13: "Shanghaied into Space!").

In November 1942, at Queen Desira's request, Wonder Woman, STEVE TREVOR, and ETTA CANDY journey to the distant planet EROS, where they help Marya, the "planetary mother and supreme judge of Eros," crush a revolt led by Rebla, the ruler of a portion of Eros known as Trans Mountania (Sen No. 11).

By Spring 1945, with the aid of information supplied by Queen Desira, Wonder Woman and Paula (*see* GUNTHER, PAULA VON [BARONESS]) have developed a machine capable of providing them with instantaneous transportation to and from Venus:

> With the advice of Desira, queen of Venus, [Wonder Woman and Paula] have built this electro-chemical **space transformer** which changes Earth bodies to Venus bodies in the flash of a spark!
> This apparatus breaks down the human body's atomic structure and rearranges its spatial relativity in the universe, as explained by Professor Einstein. [Their] machine transfers a living body from Earth to the planet Venus!

It is during this period that Queen Desira sends a mental image of herself to Earth to warn Diana Prince — the girl who is secretly Wonder Woman — that a group of evil European munitions manufacturers called the Third World War Promoters are plotting to bring about World War III, an orgy of death and destruction certain to become "the worst war of all time!"

Acting on Desira's dire warning, Diana prepares to set out after the ruthless warmongers, but she is taken captive by the spy NERVA and soon finds herself a prisoner in the "cleverly concealed hideaway" which serves as the stronghold of the "amazing group of world famous European munitions manufacturers and . . . glamorous women spies" who comprise the Third World War Promoters.

"We **must** plan another war, **greater** than ever before!" rants Pierre Fenati, the organization's president. "Our countries are doomed unless we can provoke **all** nations to fight again! Permanent peace talk is nonsense!"

Diana finally escapes from the plotters and changes into her Wonder Woman identity. Before long, with the aid of Steve Trevor and the HOLLIDAY GIRLS, she has successfully apprehended all of the Third World War Promoters.

Then Queen Desira transmits another thought message to Wonder Woman. "Bring these Earth prisoners to Venus, princess," suggests Desira, "—we will show you how to change their warlike nature and make them peace-loving!"

Using the newly constructed "electro-chemical space transformer," Wonder Woman transports herself and the captured Third World War Promoters to Venus. When Pierre Fenati tries to kill Queen Desira with a bomb, Wonder Woman saves her by smothering the bomb in her bare hands. Desira is nevertheless confident that she can reform the criminals. And so, with the Third World War Promoters safely in the hands of Desira and her winged women, Wonder Woman departs for Earth (WW No. 12/1).

On Venus, each of the Third World War Promoters is forced to wear a magic Venus girdle spun from "Aphrodite's magnetized gold" (*see* AMAZONS [section F 3, the magic Venus girdles]). According to Queen Desira, the "girdles of magnetic gold charge every body cell with vitalizing currents and harmonize the brain. When their brains become normal . . . people . . . lose their desire for conflict and . . . enjoy serving others and submitting to loving authority!"

One of the Third World War Promoters, a beautiful redhead named Velma, loosens her girdle and finally succeeds in removing it entirely, thus making her psyche once again vulnerable to evil emotions. When Wonder Woman returns to Venus, Velma imprisons her in a Venus girdle, lassoes Queen Desira with Wonder Woman's magic lasso and ties her two prisoners to a tree, and lights a fire under them, intending to burn them alive. Bound with her own magic lasso, Wonder Woman is unable to break her bonds, but she is able to use her superhuman strength to snap the tree trunk to which she and Desira are tied and to leap safely out of the fire (WW No. 12/2, Spr '45: "The Ordeal of Fire").

Wonder Woman captures Velma soon afterward and leaves her chained to a bed for safekeeping in her Diana Prince apartment, but Velma escapes from her temporary prison with the aid of "Killer" Dogan, a gangland friend. At large once again, Velma decides to return to Venus to loot the planet. "Venus is the richest world in the Solar System," she tells Dogan, "— gold, jewels, wealth untold and no cops, no guns to guard it! We'll take your mob to Venus and the **whole planet** is ours!"

Soon afterward, Velma and the Dogan gang sneak into Paula's secret laboratory, capture Paula and Wonder Woman, and use the space transformer to transport themselves and their captives to Venus, where Velma frees Pierre Fenati and the Third World War Promoters from their magic Venus girdles. All the criminals join forces, intending to bomb Desira's palace and conquer the entire planet, but Wonder Woman escapes from her captors and apprehends them all with the aid of Paula, Queen Desira, and the winged women of Venus. The villains will remain imprisoned on Venus until, in Desira's words, "thou learn to love peace and obedience!"

With Venus secure once more, Wonder Woman and Queen Desira sign a lasting treaty of friendship between Earth and Venus. "Here's the treaty between Earth and Venus," remarks Wonder Woman when the document is finally complete. "You'll make our rebellious prisoners peaceloving — we'll supply inventions requiring Earth force

and strength to construct!" (WW No. 12/3, Spr '45: "The Conquest of Venus").

In March–April 1947 GELL OSEY travels to Venus aboard PROFESSOR ASTRONIMO's new Venus-probe instrument rocket and instigates a revolt among the Venusian prisoners. For a time, Queen Desira herself is a prisoner of the ruthless Gell, but Wonder Woman ultimately quashes the revolt and restores order to Venus (WW No. 22/3: "Jealousy Visits the Winged Women of Venus!"). (*See* OSEY, GELL.)

In November–December 1947, when Wonder Woman and the Holliday Girls are imprisoned by QUEEN CELERITA and the tyrannical "flying giantesses" of MERCURY, Queen Desira and her winged women fly to Mercury to rescue them from seemingly certain death (WW No. 26/1: "Speed Maniacs from Mercury!"). (*See* CELERITA [Queen].)

DESTRUCTION (General). A ruthless Martian general who is described as an "aide-de-camp" to the war god MARS. Within the war god's inner circle, he ranks below Mars's principal "three commanders"— LORD CONQUEST, the EARL OF GREED, and the DUKE OF DECEPTION (WW No. 2/1, Fall '42).

DEXTER, JABEZ. An unscrupulous and powerful rancher in the western United States town of Twin Peaks in the year 1849. WONDER WOMAN battles Dexter and his henchmen during one of her journeys into the past.

Browsing through an old bookstore in March 1949, Wonder Woman comes upon a century-old diary with her own name inscribed on one of its pages. Out of curiosity, she journeys into the past to learn how her name came to be recorded there.

In the town of Twin Peaks in the year 1849, Wonder Woman rescues schoolteacher Julia Ernest from a schoolhouse fire started by the henchmen of rancher Jabez Dexter. Dexter, she learns, is trying to drive Julia out of town in order to prevent the local people from becoming more educated, and hence more likely to dispute his autocratic hold over the town and surrounding territory. When Dexter and his henchmen set the whole town of Twin Peaks ablaze, Wonder Woman apprehends them and rescues the townspeople from the flames. Then, her work in the past completed, she returns to the 20th century, but a permanent record of her exploits remains in the form of an entry in Julia Ernest's diary (Sen No. 87: "Wonder Woman Tames the Wild West!").

DIANA. In mythology, an ancient Italian sylvan goddess whom the Romans regarded as identical to the Greek Artemis, the daughter of Zeus by Leto and the twin of Apollo. She is a goddess of nature and the MOON, virgin of the hunt, and protectress of maidens. Animals, particularly those of the chase — such as the fawn, the stag, and the boar — are sacred to her.

In the WONDER WOMAN chronicles, she is a goddess sacred to the AMAZONS — though her position in the Amazon pantheon is not so exalted as that of APHRODITE and ATHENA — and is the godmother of Princess Diana (AS No. 8, Dec/Jan '41–'42: "Introducing Wonder Woman"), who was named after the moon goddess at birth (WW No. 1/1, Sum '42) and is now known to the world at large as Wonder Woman.

The Amazons hail the arrival of the winter solstice with Diana's Day, a holiday given over to feasting, gaming, and the giving of gifts. Chief among the games is an elaborate hunting ritual, wherein some of the Amazons, dressed as deer, attempt to outrun other Amazons, who are cast in the role of hunters (WW No. 3/1, Feb/Mar '43).

In June–July 1943 a spaceship full of Martian warriors, led by LORD CONQUEST and the war god MARS, invade the lunar domain of the goddess Diana, capture the moon goddess, and destroy the elaborate "moon mirrors" which provide the moon with its light. The Martians are ultimately defeated, however — and the goddess Diana restored to her rightful place of lunar authority — through the heroic efforts of Wonder Woman, STEVE TREVOR, BARONESS PAULA VON GUNTHER, and the HOLLIDAY GIRLS (WW No. 5/2).

DIANA (Princess). The beautiful Amazon princess who battles the forces of crime and injustice as WONDER WOMAN. She is the daughter of QUEEN HIPPOLYTE, ruler of the AMAZONS. Throughout virtually her entire career, Princess Diana works in the office of United States Military Intelligence under the alias of Diana Prince, a name she has borrowed from a nurse at the Walter Reed Army Hospital in Washington, D.C. (See WONDER WOMAN.)

DIMENSION X. An alien dimension visited by WONDER WOMAN in August 1958. It is there that she defeats the fearsome Giants of the Forest.

In August 1958, in the Amazon experimental laboratory on PARADISE ISLAND, PROF. ALPHA unveils her "X-Dimension machine," a device designed to "transport the user to a dimension beyond any yet known to us!"

Wonder Woman offers to test the machine, but when the controls are activated, "**Wonder Woman** not only does **not** vanish . . . into another dimension . . . but [she] is joined . . . by **another** . . . **Wonder Woman**," who steps from the X-Dimension machine and announces that she is "a twin **Wonder Woman!** Champion of **Dimension X**-- from which your machine brought me! **Now** that I

am here," she continues, "--I challenge **Wonder Woman** to a contest to determine **who** is the **greater** of us two!"

Wonder Woman accepts the challenge and soon the contest is under way. After the first part of the contest has ended in a tie, with Wonder Woman winning one event and the challenger from Dimension X winning another, the challenger requests that the third and deciding event be held on her world, Dimension X. And so, by means of Prof. Alpha's X-Dimension machine, the two contestants journey to Dimension X, where, before the third event ever even gets under way, Wonder Woman becomes embroiled in a deadly battle with the Giants of the Forest, brutal giants inhabiting the dense forests of the alien dimension. For defeating the giants, and in the process rescuing her Wonder Woman twin from the giants' clutches, Wonder Woman is declared the winner and champion (WW No. 100/1: "The Forest of Giants!" pts. 1–2 –"The Challenge of Dimension X!"; "The Forest of Giants!").

DIRKE (Dr.). The evil fiancé of Dr. Mary Dean, discoverer of "reduso liquid,"

By September–October 1948 scientist Dr. Mary Dean has created reduso liquid, a chemical she hopes will "reduce germs to such a minute size that they will be unable to harm humans!"

Her ruthless fiancé, however, has other ideas for reduso liquid. "In time of war," remarks Dr. Dirke, "this [formula] would be worth **millions!** It could reduce armies to a size where they would be powerless! **Nations** could be made helpless!"

After seizing the formula and using it to reduce his fiancée to microscopic size to prevent her from interfering with his scheme, Dr. Dirke also uses it on WONDER WOMAN, STEVE TREVOR, and a scientist named Dr. Grey when they attempt to intervene. Dr. Dirke is about to murder his tiny adversaries when Wonder Woman and Dr. Dean restore themselves and their fellow victims to normal size with a hastily created antidote, enabling Wonder Woman to apprehend Dr. Dirke and his henchmen (WW No. 31/1: "The Shrinking Formula!").

DIX, DAREDEVIL. The owner of the Bar-X Ranch in Texas; it adjoins the Bar-L Ranch, owned by ETTA CANDY's father, HARD CANDY.

In July 1947 Dix proposes that in this year's annual rodeo competition the two ranches compete for 100 acres of barren prairie land lying on the boundary between them. Hard Candy agrees, unaware that the land contains valuable uranium deposits. When Dix resorts to criminality to ensure his winning the rodeo, WONDER WOMAN intervenes to rescue ETTA CANDY and the HOLLIDAY GIRLS and expose Dix's villainous attempts to sabotage the

Bar-L Ranch's rodeo effort (Sen No. 67: "The Secret of the Bar-L Ranch!").

DM-X. The alien dimension which is the home of the BRAIN PIRATE (WW No. 156, Aug '65: "The Brain Pirate of the Inner World!").

DOCTOR CYBER. "A strangely beautiful, wholly merciless woman" who is the leader of a vast underworld organization. Her hired assassins murder STEVE TREVOR in January–February 1969 (WW No. 180: "A Death for Diana!").

In November–December 1968 Steve Trevor volunteers for a highly dangerous top-secret mission absolutely vital to the safety and security of the United States: posing as a traitor to his country, Trevor must infiltrate the sprawling underworld apparatus of the mysterious Doctor Cyber. Overnight, the heroic Trevor becomes transformed in the eyes of his countrymen into a spy and a traitor. His name, picture, and description are broadcast nationwide, and citizens are warned that as long as he remains at large, he represents a "grave threat to national security."

Diana Prince is walking the streets of lower Manhattan when a newspaper headline informs her that Trevor is being sought by the authorities on a charge of treason. Unaware of Trevor's top-secret mission, and unwilling to believe that her sweetheart could possibly be guilty of such a heinous crime, Diana is about to change to WONDER WOMAN in hopes of in some way helping him when suddenly she receives an urgent telepathic summons from her mother, QUEEN HIPPOLYTE, informing her that she must return to PARADISE ISLAND at once.

On Paradise Island, home of the AMAZONS, Diana finds her mother in an uncharacteristically solemn mood.

"It is my duty to demand a decision of you, Diana!" begins Hippolyte gravely. "Our time on Earth grows short! For ten thousand years, we have lived here, performing the mission assigned to us . . . helping mankind find maturity! But now, our magic is exhausted!

"We must journey to another dimension, to rest and renew our powers! We are tired, Diana . . . the ages weigh heavily upon us! Will you come--?"

Torn between her desire to remain with her mother and the Amazons and her desire to fly to the aid of Steve Trevor, Diana hesitates and then, after a long pause, announces her decision: "I love you, mother . . ." replies Diana slowly, "you and my sister Amazons! But Steve Trevor desperately **needs** me . . . I must stay!"

"So be it!" answers Hippolyte.

What follows is a mystic "ceremony never before seen on this planet . . . the awesome Amazon rite of renunciation," in which Diana, the royal princess of the mighty Amazons, lays aside the magic lasso, bracelets of submission, and red, white, and blue costume in which she has battled the forces of tyranny and injustice for almost thirty years (see WONDER WOMAN [section C 3, the magic lasso; section C 2, the bracelets of submission]).

"I hereby relinquish all mystic skills!" intones Diana. "I lay upon the sacred altar the glories of the Amazons and willingly condemn myself to the travails of mortals! May the gods be merciful to me!"

After mother and daughter have embraced and said their last, tearful farewells, Diana takes leave of Queen Hippolyte and, clad only in a simple dress, boards her Amazon plane (see WONDER WOMAN [section C 4, the robot plane]) for the return trip to America. As the fantastic robot plane dips its wings and sweeps past Paradise Island, Diana sees the entire island "shimmer, dissolve, [and] vanish [into another dimension] . . . leaving only the azure ocean. . . ." Stoically she sets a course for America, knowing that once she has landed, "the plane will follow the island into oblivion . . . Then I shall be truly alone . . . an orphan . . . without friends, without a home . . . a stranger and alone. . . ."

In the months that follow, Diana Prince — the girl who was once a world-famous superheroine — adjusts gradually to the life of an ordinary human being while pressing her search for Steve Trevor, whom she has been unable to locate since first learning he was being sought as a traitor. One afternoon, however, while she is practicing karate in a local gymnasium, Steve Trevor stumbles weakly through the door and collapses at her feet. Doctor Cyber's agents had seen through his attempts to pose as a traitor, beaten him brutally and shot him several times, and left him for dead in the street. Sped to a hospital, Trevor now lies in a deathlike coma from which he may never recover.

"It's a **miracle** he's alive at all!" explains the attending physician. "We can't tell how extensive the damage is! There could be brain injury! He may spend the rest of his life as he is now!"

Despite having relinquished all of her Amazon powers and equipment (see WONDER WOMAN [section C, the Amazon powers and equipment]), Diana takes up the search for the sinister Doctor Cyber, partly for Trevor's sake, partly because Doctor Cyber represents a dire threat to all mankind (WW No. 179: "Wonder Woman's Last Battle!").

In January–February 1969 Diana Prince and two men who have become her allies invade a "crumbling old house" that they believe may be the sanctuary of the treacherous Doctor Cyber. As they cautiously make their way into the seemingly deserted mansion, Steve Trevor suddenly lurches out of nowhere to warn them back.

"Go **back!**" he cries desperately. **"Get out of here!"**

Trevor begins to explain that Diana and her friends have walked into a trap—that Doctor Cyber's agents kidnapped him from his hospital bed and are now waiting inside the mansion to destroy them—when suddenly staccato bursts of machine-gun fire crackle from inside the mansion and Trevor, mortally wounded, staggers down a flight of stairs, collapsing at Diana's feet and dying moments later in her arms. Doctor Cyber remains at large (WW No. 180: "A Death for Diana!").

DOCTOR POISON. An Axis spy who is described both as Chief of the Nazi Poison Division (Sen No. 2, Feb '42) and as the Chemical Research Chief of the Japanese army (Sen No. 24, Dec '43: "Adventure of the Pilotless Plane"). Doctor Poison—who conceals both her true identity and her gender beneath a hooded smocklike costume and a black mask—is in reality Princess Maru, a beautiful Japanese princess.

In February 1942 STEVE TREVOR and Diana Prince—the girl who is secretly WONDER WOMAN—are kidnapped by Nazi spies posing as Army intelligence agents and taken to Doctor Poison's headquarters, where they are locked in separate cells. Alone in her cell, Diana changes to Wonder Woman and escapes, afterward racing to the campus of the HOLLIDAY COLLEGE FOR WOMEN to seek out ETTA CANDY and recruit the band of loyal student allies henceforth to be known as the HOLLIDAY GIRLS. "Hundreds of girls volunteer" to help Wonder Woman battle Doctor Poison, "and Wonder Woman picks the prettiest and strongest."

Meanwhile, however, Doctor Poison sets in motion a diabolical scheme to cause pandemonium within the ranks of the U.S. Army. "These cylinders," she gloats, "contain **reverso,** the new drug I have invented. **Reverso** confuses the brain centers. It will make soldiers do the exact opposite of what they are told!"

By tapping the water main leading to an Army camp and pouring reverso into the water, Doctor Poison's Nazi henchmen create bedlam in the Army camp, with soldiers countermanding their orders by doing the opposite of what they have been told to do. However, with the help of the Holliday Girls—who seduce the Nazis into a sense of false security with music, dancing, and the promise of romance—Wonder Woman invades Doctor Poison's stronghold, rescues Steve Trevor,

and captures Doctor Poison and her Nazi cohorts, in the process unmasking the villainess as a woman for the first time—"I am the Princess Maru," she shrieks. "My genius shall destroy America!"—and forcing her to provide an antidote to the diabolical reverso drug (Sen No. 2).

Doctor Poison, 1942

In December 1943 QUEEN HIPPOLYTE summons Wonder Woman to PARADISE ISLAND to warn her that a grave danger threatens America. Gazing into Hippolyte's magic sphere (*see* AMAZONS [section F 2, the magic sphere]), Wonder Woman sees "the Japanese army commander reporting to the premier" and hears him gloat that "Her highness, our chemical research chief, has found means to keep all American planes from flying!"

The Japanese chemical research chief, Wonder Woman soon learns, is none other than Princess Maru, alias Doctor Poison, who has escaped from prison and returned to wreak havoc with the American war effort. By means of a diabolical "green gas" of her own invention—one which "enters the carburetor and stops the engine" of any aircraft—Princess Maru succeeds in grounding "all American planes on [the] Chinese front." With America's aircraft thus disabled and unable to provide air support, the Japanese prepare to launch a devastating attack against American ground troops. In addition, Princess Maru captures Steve Trevor and imprisons him in a tiny dungeon in China.

"Princess Maru," exclaims Trevor. "—**now** I remember! You were 'Doctor Poison,' the Jap spy! But we captured you—"

"But you didn't hold me long," replies Princess Maru, "—escaping from your 'democratic' American prison hospitality is very simple for a woman of my talents! Now you and your **Wonder Woman** shall pay for what you did to me!!"

Wonder Woman intervenes, however, to rescue Trevor from Princess Maru's clutches and destroy "the entire Jap air fleet" before it can inflict any casualties on American troops. Taking Princess Maru captive soon afterward, she uses her magic lasso (*see* WONDER WOMAN [section C 3, the magic lasso]) to compel the villainess to reveal how the damage caused by her green gas may best be undone: "If you clean the carburetor with ammonium solution," confesses the princess, "you'll find your [airplane] motors will return to normalcy!" (Sen No. 24: "Adventure of the Pilotless Plane").

In March–April 1948 Doctor Poison escapes from TRANSFORMATION ISLAND along with seven other villainesses and joins them in forming VILLAINY INCORPORATED (WW No. 28/1–3: "Villainy Incorporated!"; "Trap of Crimson Flame"; "In the Hands of the Merciless!"). (*See* VILLAINY INCORPORATED.)

DOCTOR PSYCHO. *See* PSYCHO (DR.).

DOLAN, MARY. A telephone time announcer who is dissatisfied with her job because she feels that it is useless, trivial, and unimportant. Her job takes on new meaning for her in January–February 1950, however, when WONDER WOMAN proves to her that her job is actually "vital and exciting! No one is unimportant in a democracy," insists Wonder Woman, "--and that goes for his job!" (WW No. 39/1: "The Trail of Thrills!").

DOONE, "CRIME BRAIN." The leader of the notorious Sly Fox Mob. Doone is apprehended by WONDER WOMAN in October–November 1948.

In October–November 1948, in an effort to solve "a vital problem in atomic energy" that has been plaguing top-level Army experts, PROF. CALCULUS — "famed mathematician of Holliday College" — develops a phenomenal "thinking machine" capable of solving in seconds problems that would take a human being years. The machine is stolen, however — and the professor himself kidnapped — by "Crime Brain" Doone, who intends to use the vast intellectual powers of the thinking machine to help him plan and execute perfect crimes.

Aided by the machine, Doone commits a series of spectacular robberies, becoming so cocky that he even announces in advance that he is going to loot FORT KNOX, then fulfills his promise despite the U.S. Army's attempts to stop him. By capitalizing on the virtually unlimited problem-solving capacity of the thinking machine, Doone even succeeds in capturing Wonder Woman and in placing her under the machine's absolute control. STEVE

TREVOR, however, trails Wonder Woman to Doone's hideout and disconnects the complex electronic circuits that keep Wonder Woman a prisoner of the machine. Thus freed, Wonder Woman quickly rescues the HOLLIDAY GIRLS — kidnapped by Doone and his henchmen earlier — apprehends Doone and his gangland cohorts, and rescues Prof. Calculus (CC No. 29: "Machine of Schemes").

"Crime Brain" Doone

With "Crime Brain" Doone convicted and sent to prison, leadership of the Sly Fox Mob falls to racketeer SLICK SKEENER. Curiously, however, a text for June 1947 — almost a full year and a half *prior* to the theft of the thinking machine — quotes Skeener as making these remarks to the gang he has just inherited:

> The first job we gotta do is eliminate Major [Steve] Trevor, pardon me! — **Lt. Colonel** Trevor. He got his promotion for jugging "Crime Brain" [Doone] and stopping our thinking machine racket! [Sen No. 66: "Prisoners of Cops and Robbers"].

Since Skeener's remarks clearly refer to events which, judging by the issue dates of the relevant comic books, have not yet taken place, one can only assume that the adventures were published out of sequence and that the issue dates are not accurate indicators of when the events described in them actually took place.

DORMER GANG, THE. A gang of criminals who are apprehended by WONDER WOMAN in July 1954 despite the handicap imposed upon her by the fact that "unique radiations" emanating from a meteor she recently handled have rendered her body temporarily "anti-magnetic," causing it to repel any person or thing with which she comes in contact (WW No. 67/3: "The Runaway Meteor!").

DRASKA (Countess). *See* NISHKI, DRASKA (COUNTESS).

DUEL, ELY. The Chief of County Detectives. Duel is secretly the CRIME CHIEF (Sen No. 32: "The Crime Combine").

DUNCAN, BETH. A young girl who inadvertently learns WONDER WOMAN's secret identity when she sees Diana Prince leap into an empty car on an amusement park caterpillar ride and emerge moments later as Wonder Woman. By creating a Wonder Woman figure from a block of ice, however, and arranging for Beth to see the ice figure and Diana Prince simultaneously, Wonder Woman tricks Beth into believing she has made a mistake, thus preserving the secret of her dual identity (WW No. 54/3, Jul/Aug '52: "Wonder Woman's Triple Threat!").

DUXO. A far-distant planet inhabited by young boys who have been transformed into "followers of hate and force" by the war god MARS.

In ancient Sparta, "it was the cruel custom to leave the infants they thought were weaklings, mostly girls, in the wild hills to perish during the night."

Unbeknownst to the Spartans, however, the AMAZONS under QUEEN HIPPOLYTE made a practice of rescuing the abandoned girls and removing them to a place of safety. The rescued infants would be placed aboard the Amazons' "flying swan planes" and transported to the planet Infanta, where, "because of atmospheric conditions, [the infants] reached [their] full powers at five years and never aged more than that."

Mars's followers would rescue the abandoned Spartan boys and transport them to a similar planet, Duxo, where they would be brought up as cruel warriors in the service of Mars.

According to Wonder Woman No. 36/1, PARADISE ISLAND was invaded sometime in the past by a combined force of Martian men and Duxo boys who subdued the Amazons by means of a special gas. The invaders were routed, however, by a fleet of girl warriors from the planet Infanta — aided by WONDER WOMAN — who raced to the defense of Paradise Island in response to a desperate plea for help from Queen Hippolyte (Jul/Aug '49: "The Girl Who Saved Paradise Island!"). (*See also* ASTRA [QUEEN].)

E

EASEL, ALBERT. An art gallery owner who is secretly in league with the underworld in an elaborate scheme to murder WONDER WOMAN. Easel and his gangland cohorts are apprehended by Wonder Woman.

In July 1954 Wonder Woman pays a visit to the Easel Gallery, owned by Albert Easel, where pictures of her performing various superhuman feats are on display. When Easel offers to donate $10,000 to charity if Wonder Woman can duplicate the seemingly impossible feats depicted in the paintings — such as passing a steel girder through the eye of a sewing needle, or running across the top of a lake without touching the water — Wonder Woman agrees to try.

Wonder Woman successfully performs the feats, but at the scene of each she is forced to battle underworld assassins lying in wait to kill her. It is only after winning the $10,000 for charity and apprehending all the would-be assassins that Wonder Woman realizes that the entire contest was part of a gangland plot to murder her. After paying artists to paint the pictures of Wonder Woman performing the hazardous feats, Easel had given the underworld advance notification of each feat so that they could be on hand to ambush her. Wonder Woman apprehends Easel and uses her magic lasso (*see* WONDER WOMAN [section C 3, the magic lasso]) to compel him to confess (WW No. 67/2: "Portraits of Peril!").

EERAS (Queen). The red-haired ruler of the Atlantean nation of AURANIA, a "subsea realm" situated somewhere "beneath the bottom of the Atlantic Ocean" (CC No. 18, Dec/Jan '46–'47: "The Menace of the Rebel Manlings"). Queen Eeras is the mother of the beautiful OCTAVIA.

In Spring 1944 STEVE TREVOR sets out in search of a top-secret "devitamizer" formula vital to the American war effort. The scientist who developed the formula died after dividing it into three parts and entrusting them to the care of three colleagues, but now the three parts of the formula are scattered throughout the world and Trevor has been assigned to recover them. He has located two of the parts and is searching for the third when he is approached by a tall, statuesque redhead who hands him the missing third part and asks him to reciprocate by flying her home in his Army aircraft.

Following the directions given him by the mysterious redhead, Trevor is soon far out over the Atlantic Ocean, flying over an extinct volcano, when suddenly huge downdrafts of air suck his aircraft down into the volcano's crater and into a strange subsea domain.

Queen Eeras, 1944

"Where the heck **are** we?" gasps Trevor.

"We are **under** the Atlantic Ocean," replies his passenger, "flying above the sunken continent of Atlantis!"

"But Atlantis was lost a million years ago!" exclaims Trevor.

"To us Atlanteans," replies the redhead, "it is the upper world that was lost! Our civilization is far beyond thine — until now we have never desired to find again the world of manlings!

"When Atlantis sank beneath the sea," she continues, "the Earth folded over it, sealing it in a vast air pocket under the ocean floor."

The girl identifies herself as Queen Eeras of AURANIA, the country which, together with neighboring VENTURIA, dominates ATLANTIS. While flying over the surface of Atlantis, however, Trevor's plane runs out of fuel and he and Eeras are forced to land in Venturia, home of Eeras's enemies, where they are swiftly taken prisoner by the warriors of the evil QUEEN CLEA.

Arriving in Venturia soon afterward in response to an urgent mental radio message from Trevor (see WONDER WOMAN [section C 7, the mental radio]), Wonder Woman allows herself to be taken prisoner in hopes of finding him, only to be thrown into a dungeon with the captive Queen Eeras, who recounts her journey to the surface world and her meeting with Trevor:

> The two leading nations of Atlantis are Venturia and Aurania. Ours [i.e., Aurania] is a rich country with many manlings [i.e., diminutive male slaves] — Clea, queen of Venturia, invaded Aurania without warning, seeking gold and slaves!
> Clea caught us unprepared — I and my women officers fought fiercely but were captured. Aurania was conquered! Seeking some means to free my country, I escaped prison and climbed desperately to the lost world above!
> I was fortunate — I found a handsome manling [i.e., Trevor] with a chemical formula that will devitamize Clea and all her army! But again we were captured!

Wonder Woman helps Queen Eeras escape from the dungeon but remains behind herself, fearing retaliation against Trevor if the Venturians find her missing. Pressed into service soon afterward as a slave-attendant to Queen Clea, she is at the ruthless monarch's side at the Venturian gladiatorial arena when Steve Trevor is dragged from his dungeon and forced to battle "two enormous wild boars of prehistoric breed" while armed only with a short sword. He is about to go down under the hooves and tusks of the ferocious boars when Wonder Woman darts into the arena and rescues him, only to have Queen Clea's archers launch a hail of arrows at both of them.

Queen Eeras, meanwhile, arrives at the arena with a small band of Auranian warriors. Releasing chemical devitamizer through the arena's air ducts, Eeras and her followers knock Clea and the Venturians unconscious and take possession of

Venturia. Wonder Woman and Steve Trevor head for home soon afterward, leaving both Aurania and Venturia in the hands of Queen Eeras (WW No. 8/1: "Queen Clea's Tournament of Death").

Not long afterward, when a sailor returns home from a long sea voyage with a fantastic tale of his ship being attacked by giant female pirates and virtually its entire crew taken captive, Wonder Woman flies to Atlantis with the HOLLIDAY GIRLS to investigate, suspecting the Atlantean women may have been responsible for the attack.

In Aurania, Queen Eeras explains that she has locked Venturia's deposed ruler, Queen Clea, in an Auranian dungeon, while allowing Clea's daughter, Princess Ptra, to ascend the throne of Venturia, reasoning that Ptra would never dare attack Aurania with her mother being held captive in Eeras's dungeons. When Wonder Woman and Eeras visit the dungeons, however, they find that Ptra is their prisoner and not Clea, mother and daughter having somehow managed to change places, so that while Ptra was locked away in Eeras's dungeon, Clea was leading a band of Venturian pirates in a raid on an American ship, hoping to capture crewmen as slaves for her army so that she could wage war on Eeras once again.

Indeed, Queen Clea's attack on Aurania is not long in coming, for the American ship she attacked had been carrying large numbers of captured German soldiers who have now been incorporated into Clea's Venturian army. Before long, both Wonder Woman and Queen Eeras — and even ETTA CANDY and the Holliday Girls — have been taken prisoner by Queen Clea and her daughter Ptra.

With the help of the Holliday Girls, however — and with some eleventh-hour assistance from Steve Trevor and the men of United States Military Intelligence — Wonder Woman turns the tables on her captors and captures Queen Clea and her Venturian army, including the German troops who have become her allies. Leaving Atlantis once again in the hands of the good Queen Eeras, Wonder Woman departs for home, announcing her intention to transport Queen Clea and Princess Ptra to Reform Island (see TRANSFORMATION ISLAND), where MALA will endeavor to transform them into useful citizens (WW No. 8/2, Spr '44: "The Girl with the Iron Mask").

It is not long after this that Queen Eeras's daughter Octavia — a tall, beautiful, powerful redhead — journeys to America and seeks out Wonder Woman, explaining that although she never met Wonder Woman in Atlantis, she admires her greatly and hopes that she will consent to share some of her renowned "courage and wisdom" with her. Wonder Woman agrees to take Octavia to

Paradise Island for Amazon training (*see* WONDER WOMAN [section C 1, the benefits of Amazon training]), but Queen Clea, who is a prisoner there, makes Wonder Woman and Octavia her prisoners and flies them to Atlantis aboard Wonder Woman's Amazon plane (*see* WONDER WOMAN [section C 4, the robot plane]).

Regaining consciousness in an Atlantean dungeon, Wonder Woman and Octavia break through the dungeon wall in an attempt to escape, only to find themselves in an adjoining dungeon, where, to their surprise, they find Queen Clea being held prisoner also.

Clea hastily explains that the "manlings" — the undersized men who normally function only as either slaves or soldiers on Atlantis — have revolted and seized power in Atlantis. The American ship she once attacked, she continues, contained a large supply of arms. Clea had hidden them, but the manlings located the arms cache and used them to overpower Atlantis's women and seize control of the continent.

With Octavia's help, Wonder Woman turns the tables on her captors and escapes from the dungeon, but in the interim Queen Clea succeeds in reasserting her dominion over Venturia, and soon Wonder Woman and Octavia find themselves battling Queen Clea and an army of manlings. Ultimately, however, Wonder Woman and Octavia defeat the Venturians, capture Clea, and rescue Queen Eeras, whom the insurrectionists had taken prisoner. Eeras resumes command of Aurania and announces her intention to place Octavia on the throne of Venturia (WW No. 8/3, Spr '44: "The Captive Queen").

In November 1944 Wonder Woman flies to Venturia to protect Octavia from SONTAG HENYA and her band of brutal "anarchists" (Sen No. 35: "Girls Under the Sea").

In December 1946–January 1947 Wonder Woman journeys to Atlantis to rescue both Eeras and Octavia from the tyrannical MANLIUS (CC No. 18: "The Menace of the Rebel Manlings").

EGG FU (the First). A diabolical egg-shaped creature who is an ally and presumably a creation of the Communist Chinese. Wonder Woman No. 157 describes him as possessing "the most baleful brain that [has] ever been steeped in Oriental cunning for the sole purpose of annihilating the free world. . . ." Egg Fu the First is destroyed by WONDER WOMAN in late 1965.

On the Pacific Island of Oolong, Communist China — "a relentless foe . . . who has no more regard for human life--than if it were paper confetti"— has established a sophisticated super-secret military installation commanded by Egg Fu, a gi-

gantic egg-shaped creature who is the inventive mastermind behind the fearsome arsenal of weapons deployed on Oolong, including the awesome "doomsday rocket" with which Egg Fu intends to destroy the entire United States Pacific fleet.

THE AMELICANS **WOULD** BE WARNED IF THE LOCKET WERE FIRED AT RONG RANGE! SO-- WE WILL WAIT UNTIL THEIR FLEET COMES TOO *CLOSE* FOR THEM TO ESCAPE ANNIHILATION ! AND OUR SCOUT PLANES LADAR WARNS US **THAT** WILL BE **VELY** VELY SOON ! HEEEE-HO !

© NPP 1965

Egg Fu (the First)

After eleven American reconnaissance pilots and their aircraft have vanished without a trace while attempting to obtain aerial photographs of the island, U.S. Military Intelligence, concerned that the Communists may be "concealing a top secret weapon" there, assigns the aerial reconnaissance mission to STEVE TREVOR. Flying toward Oolong Island, Trevor ponders the fate of the eleven reconnaissance pilots who preceded him and concludes that their aircraft must have been destroyed by enemy antiaircraft guns "uniquely synchronized to home-in on the vibrations of any aerial camera over the island!"

Determined to avoid the grim fate of his predecessors, Trevor sets the controls of his aircraft on automatic pilot, activates his aerial camera to begin shooting pictures in 60 seconds, and then bails out of his plane and parachutes toward Oolong, snapping pictures of the island and its installations throughout his descent by means of a tiny camera hidden inside a cigarette lighter. Meanwhile, as Trevor had anticipated, his pilotless aircraft explodes in a ball of flame, destroyed by special antiaircraft guns designed to detect the presence of aerial reconnaissance cameras over Oolong.

Landing on the island, Trevor is swiftly taken

prisoner by the Chinese Communists. He is pleased when they fail to notice his tiny cigarette-lighter camera, but he is horrified to learn that mysterious "beams" being fired at him by his captors "are injecting [him] with atomic explosive force! Turning [him] into a human time-bomb! Timed to explode with the force of an erupting volcano! In one hour! Against . . . [the] Pacific fleet!"

Before Trevor can even begin to assimilate what has happened to him, the Communists fire him into the air, a human rocket set to explode as soon as he strikes the Pacific fleet. Also streaking through the air is Egg Fu's doomsday rocket, aimed, like Trevor, at the Pacific fleet.

Realizing that only a final, desperate act of self-sacrifice will save the fleet, Trevor selflessly aims himself toward the doomsday rocket, hoping to detonate both himself and the doomsday rocket before they can keep their deadly rendezvous with the Pacific fleet. Racing to Trevor's rescue, however, and realizing that his plan is suicidal, Wonder Woman climbs out onto the wing of her Amazon plane (see WONDER WOMAN [section C 4, the robot plane]) and leaps into space in a desperate effort to save him. There is a titanic roar as Wonder Woman and Trevor crash head-on into the doomsday rocket. The ships and men of the Pacific fleet remain unharmed, but Wonder Woman and Trevor are blown to atoms by the awesome explosion.

Informed of the terrible explosion and resultant death of her daughter, QUEEN HIPPOLYTE leads the Amazon air fleet in a wide sweep of the blast area, gathering every single atom of matter in the area by means of special Amazon apparatus. Soon afterward, in an Amazon laboratory on PARADISE ISLAND, Hippolyte subjects the accumulated atoms to the newly developed AS-R — for "atomic structure reassembly"— beam developed by Amazon scientists to undo the effects of natural disasters by reassembling the atoms of inanimate objects that have been destroyed. The beam has never been used on a person, but as Queen Hippolyte presses the button which activates it, two human forms begin slowly emerging from the scattered atoms and soon the forms of Wonder Woman and Steve Trevor are clearly discernible. But Hippolyte observes with horror that the famous couple is "glowing like volcanic fire." Indeed, as Wonder Woman and Trevor return miraculously to life, they realize that the action of the AS-R beam has somehow made them both dangerously "explosive . . . a menace to each other--[and to] the whole world" as well (WW No. 157, Oct '65: "I--the Bomb!").

"Shades of Pluto!" cries Hippolyte. "Our AS-R beams reconstructed Wonder Woman and Col. Steve Trevor from the dust of the atomic explosion that destroyed them! But--they've both become human explosives!"

"We have three tasks!" explains Wonder Woman to Trevor. "To avoid people--not to harm them with our detonations! To defeat Egg Fu, the Oriental master mind, before he hurls more weapons of destruction against the free world! And to try to find some way of eliminating the explosive matter he beamed into us!"

Now potentially deadly to anyone they touch, including each other, Wonder Woman and Trevor fly to Oolong Island, where they overcome a series of deathtraps prepared for them by Egg Fu, only to be finally captured by the villain and hurled unconscious into outer space. Revived suddenly by the cold air of the upper atmosphere, however, Wonder Woman and Trevor hurtle by chance into the path of a "fragment of anti-matter from outer space," which destroys the "explosive matter" in their bodies, transforming them into normal human beings once again.

Summoning her Amazon plane and streaking back to Oolong Island for a final confrontation with Egg Fu, Wonder Woman balances herself on a wingtip and lassoes the villain with her magic lasso (see WONDER WOMAN [section C 3, the magic lasso]).

"You cannot resist the power of my lasso!" she cries. "You are compelled to obey my every command! Promise to stop your villainy against the free world! Or suffer the consequences!"

"Nothing can ever stop me from planning the destruction--of you [sic] foolish democracies . . . the first moment I am free!" rages Egg Fu. "Nothing! NOTHING! NOTHING!"

As the diabolical Oriental mastermind strains against the irresistible power of the magic lasso, huge cracks appear in his titanic egglike form and he shatters into a thousand irreparable fragments (WW No. 158/1, Nov '65: "The Fury of Egg Fu!").

EGG FU (the Fifth). A diabolical egg-shaped creature who is an ally and presumably a creation of the Communist Chinese. Egg Fu the Fifth — who is similar in appearance to, but smaller than, EGG FU THE FIRST — is destroyed by WONDER WOMAN in November 1966.

While flying in search of an atomic-powered American submarine which has vanished at sea with its entire crew aboard, Wonder Woman and STEVE TREVOR are fired upon by a freighter and swoop low for a closer look, only to discover that the freighter appears to be empty, with no sign of life on board. When Wonder Woman and Trevor climb aboard the freighter to investigate further, Trevor mysteriously vanishes and Wonder Woman's Amazon plane (*see* WONDER WOMAN [section C 4, the robot plane]) plunges into the ocean depths, completely disregarding her frantic verbal commands.

Leaping into the sea after her rapidly diving airplane, Wonder Woman is taken captive by a horde of Communist Chinese frogmen and soon finds herself, along with Steve Trevor, in the undersea headquarters of the diabolical Egg Fu.

"Egg Fu!" exclaims Wonder Woman. "I thought you had been destroyed!"

"The honorable **Egg Fu, the First,** was destroyed by you, **Wonder Woman!**" replies the villain. "But not before other **Egg Fu's** had been hatched! I am **Egg Fu,** the **Fifth!** My frogmen snatched your comrade [Steve Trevor] from the [freighter] whose [antiaircraft] fire I control automatically from here--that's how I fired on your plane--when it was obviously investigating!"

Held helpless in the grip of her own magic lasso (*see* WONDER WOMAN [section C 3, the magic lasso]), Wonder Woman finally persuades Egg Fu to let her perform a special dance in his honor, and then, in the midst of the dance, clashes her Amazon bracelets (*see* WONDER WOMAN [section C 2, the bracelets of submission]) together with such tremendous power that the resulting vibrations shatter Egg Fu into fragments.

With the kidnapped American submarine safely in tow, Wonder Woman and Steve Trevor head for the surface. When Egg Fu's frogmen attempt to destroy them with a torpedo, Wonder Woman deflects it with one of her bracelets, sending it hurtling back into the villains' undersea hideaway, annihilating the Communists (WW No. 166/1: "The Sinister Scheme of Egg Fu, the Fifth!").

ELAM. A city of the distant future.— the so-called "city of man"— which is inhabited solely by men and ruled by the dictator PROWD (Sen No. 83, Nov '48: "The Sinister Olympics!").

ELLIOT, DON. A youngster who seems destined to become a juvenile delinquent, and ultimately a hardened criminal, until WONDER WOMAN intervenes to help him become a good citizen in August-September 1946. In the secret laboratory of BARONESS PAULA VON GUNTHER, Wonder Woman uses an "introspection machine" to enable Don to peer into the depths of his own personality. As he gazes into the introspection machine, the psychological drama that plays itself out before his eyes makes Don aware, for the first time, that his innermost desire is really to be a good person. So impressed is he by what he has seen, that he vows never again to allow his destructive impulses to

triumph over his creative ones (CC No. 16: "The Battle of Desires").

ENRAGO (Don). The fencing master at the HOLLIDAY COLLEGE FOR WOMEN. In August 1948 he becomes so enraged at having been beaten in a practice match by a female member of his fencing team —"Just like a domineering male," observes Diana Prince, the girl who is secretly WONDER WOMAN, "--a sore loser!"— that he kidnaps and then impersonates her, leading a gang of criminals in a series of spectacular crimes so that the kidnapped co-ed will be blamed for them. The student, Marcia, is ultimately rescued by Wonder Woman, who apprehends the criminals and unmasks Don Enrago as their leader (Sen No. 80: "The Swinging Scimitar!").

EROS. A far-distant planet ruled entirely by women. Joyala is its capital city. Its principal ruler is Marya, Eros's "planetary mother and supreme judge." WONDER WOMAN journeys to Eros to battle the villainess REBLA in November 1942 (Sen No. 11).

EVE (Queen). The daughter of QUEEN DESIRA of VENUS and the ruler of EVELAND, a "tropical country of love and beauty" situated far beneath the South Polar ice cap. Shortly after Eve's arrival in Eveland — where she was sent by Desira on instructions from the goddess APHRODITE — Aphrodite provided her with a "spirit daughter," Princess Eve Lectress, to serve as her successor. In Summer 1945 Eveland is menaced by the Seal Men, the evil inhabitants of BITTERLAND (WW No. 13/1–3: "The Icebound Maidens"; "The Mystery Maid"; "Slaves in the Electric Gardens"). (*See* RIGOR [KING].)

Queen Eve and Wonder Woman, 1945

EVELAND. An earthly paradise —"the tropical country of love and beauty"— which is ruled by the lovely QUEEN EVE, daughter of QUEEN DESIRA of VENUS. According to Wonder Woman No. 13/1, Eveland is identical with the Garden of Eden, which sank beneath the South Polar ice cap sometime after the expulsion of Adam and Eve and remained preserved there, frozen in a state of absolute perfection, throughout the millennia.

Sometime in the past, the goddess APHRODITE journeyed to the planet Venus for an audience with Queen Desira. "Sunken under the South Pole," said the goddess, "is the beautiful Garden of Eden — forbidden to Earth people." Aphrodite instructed Desira to send her daughter Eve to Earth to "replace the Earth girl Eve who was deposed from the garden — she shall rule Eden," continued the goddess, "henceforth to be called Eveland!"

Transported to Eveland from Venus, Desira's daughter found that Aphrodite had taken away her Venusian wings and transformed her into an Earth girl. Today Eveland's entire population consists of lovely "daughters of Venus" who have been spirited to Earth and transformed into Earth girls by Aphrodite (Sum '45: "The Icebound Maidens").

Eveland signs a peace treaty with neighboring BITTERLAND, home of the Seal Men, in Summer 1945, largely through the peacemaking efforts of Wonder Woman (WW No. 13/3: "Slaves in the Electric Gardens"). (See RIGOR [KING].)

EVE LECTRESS (Princess). A "spirit daughter" given to QUEEN EVE by the goddess APHRODITE to succeed her as monarch of EVELAND (WW No. 13/1, Sum '45: "The Icebound Maidens").

EVILESS. The sadistic blond slave driver who, like SATURNETTE, holds the post of Captain (or Commandress) of Women on the planet SATURN, elevating her above the other "Saturnian free girls"

Eviless, 1948

whose function it is to direct the activities of Saturn's vast slave population. Like the other "ruthless woman slave drivers" of Saturn, the stunningly beautiful Eviless wears a tight-fitting bright red leotardlike garment. The chronicles' most notable characterization of the Saturnian people is made by Eviless: ". . . we Saturnians are utterly inhuman," she tells STEVE TREVOR in Fall 1944. "We regard ourselves as machines" (WW No. 10/2: "The Sky Road").

Eviless is actually mentioned by name only in Wonder Woman No. 28, but her resemblance to an unnamed Saturnian villainess appearing in several other texts is so unmistakable that it seems safe to assume that this unnamed villainess is Eviless even if the texts do not actually say so.

In Fall 1944, when Steve Trevor is taken captive by Saturnians under the command of DUKE MEPHISTO SATURNO and imprisoned aboard the Saturnian spacecraft, it is the whip-wielding Eviless who lords it over him with taunts and insults (WW No. 10/2: "The Sky Road"). (See SATURNO, MEPHISTO [DUKE].)

Eviless and Steve Trevor, 1944

In March–April 1947 Duke Mephisto Saturno returns to Earth, determined to avenge his past defeats and plunge Earth into a holocaust of war. When WONDER WOMAN finally foils the Saturnian plot and captures Saturno and a band of Saturnian marauders, Eviless is among the invaders she captures (WW No. 22/2: "The Island of Evil"). (See SATURNO, MEPHISTO [DUKE].)

Wonder Woman No. 28, dated March–April 1948, makes several references to Wonder Woman's battle with the Saturnians of the year before. According to this text, Wonder Woman had "captured every man and woman [Saturnian] marauder" and "had planned to send them back as prisoners to Saturn where they would meet stern justice" for failing in their mission to defeat Wonder Woman and plunge Earth into war.

The female prisoners, however, had begged to be allowed to remain on Earth, explaining that "To be defeated is the worst crime on Saturn," and expressing fears that they would be "put . . . in chains for life" if they were compelled to return to their home planet. Moved by their pleas, Wonder Woman had finally agreed to send only the male Saturnians back to Saturn and to transport the females to TRANSFORMATION ISLAND to undergo rehabilitative training under the guidance of the AMAZONS.

As the Saturnian girls arrive on Transformation Island, they are all locked into magic Venus girdles (*see* AMAZONS [section F 3, the magic Venus gir-

dles]), but Eviless contrives to prevent hers from closing properly, enabling her to remove it whenever she chooses. When the opportunity arises, she overpowers MALA, frees "her Saturnic girls," and instigates a prisoner revolt.

From among the Amazon prisoners undergoing rehabilitation on Transformation Island, Eviless selects seven of the most unrepentant — the CHEETAH, QUEEN CLEA, GIGANTA, HYPNOTA THE GREAT, DOCTOR POISON, the SNOW MAN, and ZARA — and flees the island with them, determined to "conquer the Amazons on Paradise Island and use it for a base to raid Earth countries." Eviless dubs the new group VILLAINY INCORPORATED (WW No. 28/1-3: "Villainy Incorporated!"; "Trap of Crimson Flame"; "In the Hands of the Merciless!"). (*See* VILLAINY INCORPORATED.)

F

FELLOCK, "EARS." The leader of a gang of criminals who blackmail government officials. STEVE TREVOR describes him as "a slimy character . . . [whose] girls vamp important officials into talking too much — then he threatens to expose them for giving away government secrets." With some assistance from the HOLLIDAY GIRLS, WONDER WOMAN apprehends Fellock and his cohorts in February 1946 (Sen No. 50: "The Case of the Girl in Braces"). (*See also* CORINE.)

FENATI, PIERRE. The president of the THIRD WORLD WAR PROMOTERS, a "group of world famous European munitions manufacturers and their glamorous women spies" who are determined to bring about a third world war. Fenati and his Third World War Promoters are defeated by WONDER WOMAN in Spring 1945 (WW No. 12/1–3: no title; "The Ordeal of Fire"; "The Conquest of Venus"). (*See* DESIRA [QUEEN].)

FIENDO (Dr.). A power-mad villain who seizes control of the United States Government and, backed by an army of deputized gangsters whom he dubs the "Peace Police," transforms America into a Fascist police state. Dr. Fiendo is defeated by WONDER WOMAN.

In June 1946 Dr. Fiendo tricks government officials into believing that he has developed an awesome new super-weapon called the "bombardium" or "atom-splitting" machine. When the government offers to buy the machine, Fiendo professes concern that his new super-weapon will be used for terror and destruction instead of peace and refuses to part with the weapon unless the government agrees to create a new cabinet post for him with the title of Premier of Peace. Desperate to obtain the new weapon, the government agrees, unaware that Fiendo's real motive is to use his new cabinet post as a steppingstone to absolute power.

By threatening to use his new super-weapon on anyone who opposes him, Fiendo terrorizes the President and both houses of Congress into granting him total dictatorial power. Before long, his so-called Peace Police have arrested the entire government on trumped-up subversion charges, and even Wonder Woman, GENERAL DARNELL, STEVE TREVOR, and the HOLLIDAY GIRLS find themselves facing trial "for subversive activities against Dr. Fiendo, head of your government!"

With the entire court system — including the Supreme Court — packed with Dr. Fiendo's hirelings, Wonder Woman and her friends are swiftly tried and sentenced to death for treason, but Wonder Woman escapes from the Peace Police, rescues her friends from Fiendo's firing squads, defeats the tyrant and all his henchmen, and restores free government to the United States (Sen No. 54: "The Treachery of Fiendo").

FIREWORKS MAN, THE. A villain, known also as the Human Fireworks, who attempts to murder WONDER WOMAN in October 1963 in order to win a golden statuette — the so-called "Golden WW" — which is being offered by the underworld to the criminal who either captures or destroys Wonder Woman. An ordinary criminal who has transformed himself, by means of complex "chemical experiments," into a human fireworks display with awesome superhuman powers, the Fireworks Man turns himself into "a giant whirling exploding pinwheel," seizes hold of Wonder Woman, and soars into the sky with her, intending to "rocket through space until friction melts her." The villain is destroyed, however, and Wonder Woman is rescued, when the Fireworks Man is accidentally struck by a fragment of a falling meteor (WW No. 141: "The Academy of Arch-Villains!"). (*See also* ANGLE MAN, [THE]; MOUSE MAN.)

FITZ, RED. An alias employed by BEDWIN FOOTH as part of his scheme to lure WONDER WOMAN to Boston, Massachusetts, headquarters of his "underworld crime [theatrical] company" (Sen No. 36, Dec '44: "Battle Against Revenge").

FLAMINA (Queen). The beautiful but ruthless ruler of the Sun People, an all-female civilization that inhabits the SUN. An attempt by Flamina's "sun warriors" — beautiful women who ride through interstellar space astride flame-red horses with golden wings — to invade the Earth is thwarted by WONDER WOMAN.

By November 1947 "robot stratosphere planes" being tested by the United States Army "have torn through the cosmic dust curtain," so that "now there is nothing to prevent the rays of the sun from scorching the Earth to a cinder!"

Realizing that "the cosmic dust curtain must be mended at once," Wonder Woman races to Paula's secret laboratory (*see* GUNTHER, PAULA VON [BARONESS]) to obtain a machine to do the job, unaware that, on the sun, the treacherous Queen Flamina is elated at this latest cosmic development. "Ha haaa!" she gloats. "We have dreamed for centuries of invading the Earth--now at last we shall do it!"

Queen Flamina

Indeed, the Sun People have long wanted to invade the Earth, but Flamina knows that the sun's intense heat is her people's "breath of life" and that "it means death to us if we venture near Earth's cold atmosphere." Now, however, the rent in the cosmic dust curtain caused by the Army's "robot super-stratosphere" aircraft has created an unparalleled opportunity for Queen Flamina and her sun warriors. In Flamina's words:

Because of the rent in the cosmic dust curtain, we can focus superactinic rays on Earth--these rays when connected up with our light receiving sets on Earth will afford us a flaming path to [Earth]!

Earth's atmosphere as it is now is too cold for us and would kill us. But the flaming paths will enable us to safely reach Earth, capture [its] people, and bring them back to the sun as our prisoners.

For a time things look bleak as Wonder Woman and the HOLLIDAY GIRLS become Flamina's prisoners and Flamina's sun warriors begin riding down "the brilliant flaming streams of sunlight [toward Earth] to execute their solar machinations." At the last possible moment, however, Wonder Woman knocks the evil queen unconscious and "smashes the light sending set" in Flamina's castle which is providing her warriors with their sun paths to Earth. "Immediately," notes the textural narrative, "the sun paths disappear and the sun warriors are extinguished," dissolving into nothing before the eyes of astonished onlookers.

". . . [N]ow I can mend the cosmic dust curtain," muses Wonder Woman, "before Queen Flamina revives and gets some new ideas on how to destroy the Earth" (Sen No. 71: "The Invasion of the Sun Warriors").

FOOTH, BEDWIN. The deranged actor who is the mastermind behind the "underworld crime [theatrical] company." He and his accomplices are apprehended by WONDER WOMAN — with some help from STEVE TREVOR and the HOLLIDAY GIRLS — in December 1944.

After putting on an ice skating exhibition at New York's Madison Square Garden for the benefit of disabled war veterans in December 1944, Wonder Woman is approached by a man introducing himself as Red Fitz, manager of the Winter Garden in Boston, Massachusetts, who invites her to perform her ice skating show in Boston. Wonder Woman accepts, unaware that "Red Fitz" is in reality Bedwin Footh, a deranged, egomaniacal actor who is intensely jealous of her fame and determined to destroy her.

"Hah!" grunts Footh to himself. "**She** makes the first page [of the local newspaper] while I, **Bedwin Footh**, greatest actor of all time, must hide in the bowels of the earth, unknown and forgotten! But **she'll** pay me tribute — arrgh!"

Arriving in Boston, Wonder Woman finds herself confronted by six infamous villains from out of her past — the DUKE OF DECEPTION, BLAKFU, DR. PSYCHO, the CHEETAH, GIGANTA, and QUEEN CLEA — only to discover that her diabolical opponents are not her old enemies at all, but rather skillful impersonators in Bedwin Footh's "crime stock company."

"I am Bedwin Footh," gloats the villain, "greatest actor ever ignored by a stupid public! But the

Bedwin Footh

stage's loss is the underworld's gain — my crime stock company is incomparable!"

With some assistance from Steve Trevor and the Holliday Girls, Wonder Woman finally unmasks Red Fitz as Bedwin Footh and apprehends his entire gang of actor-impersonators.

"These 'enemies of **Wonder Woman**,'" confesses Footh, referring to the underworld actors who have been impersonating Wonder Woman's most infamous adversaries, "are actors I control! For 30 years, I've lived in caverns beneath this theatre, capturing successful players and making them join my underworld crime company!" (Sen No. 36: "Battle Against Revenge").

FORT KNOX. A United States Army reservation, located approximately 35 miles south of Louisville, Kentucky, which is the site of the principal gold bullion depository of the U.S. Government. Fort Knox is looted by "CRIME BRAIN" DOONE in October–November 1948, but Doone and his cohorts are ultimately apprehended by WONDER WOMAN (CC No. 29: "Machine of Schemes").

FRENZI (Dr.). The demagogic leader of the Green Shirts, a right-wing vigilante hate organization devoted to expelling "foreigners" from American communities and giving America "back to Americans." Ostensibly a committed ideologue, Dr. Frenzi is in reality a ruthless opportunist capitalizing on the misguided patriotism and xenophobia of his fellow Americans to achieve his own political and financial ends. Exposed as a fraud by WONDER WOMAN, he is apprehended by outraged citizens in September 1948.

In the U.S. town of Oakville — amid red, white, and blue bunting and patriotic paraphernalia — Dr. Frenzi exhorts the townspeople to help him "purify America" by driving the foreign-born from their community. ". . . [I]t is time to give America back to Americans!" he shouts. "Don't let foreigners take your jobs!"

Frenzi's real motive, however, lies in the fat profits to be gleaned from Green Shirt dues and rallies. "America is the land of opportunity," he confides to his henchwoman, "and this is **my** opportunity **to make a fortune!**" In addition, the text suggests that Frenzi is a subversive plotting to launch an insurrection against the government sometime in the future.

When the HOLLIDAY GIRLS are taken prisoner while snooping around Green Shirt headquarters, Wonder Woman attempts to rescue them, only to be forced to surrender in order to prevent the Green Shirts from harming them. Summoned to the scene by a mental radio message (*see* WONDER WOMAN [section C 7, the mental radio]) from Wonder Woman, however, STEVE TREVOR rescues

Dr. Frenzi

*By threatening to murder the Holliday Girls,
Dr. Frenzi and his henchwoman attempt to coerce
Wonder Woman into preaching "doctrines of intol-
erance and prejudice" to the American people . . .*

*. . . but Wonder Woman courageously
defies them, 1948*

Wonder Woman so that she, in turn, can free the
Holliday Girls. When the local townspeople are
made to realize that Dr. Frenzi has been manipulating them for his own selfish purposes, they
swiftly apprehend him so that he may be brought
to trial for his crimes (Sen No. 81: "When Treachery Wore a Green Shirt!").

FUN CLINIC. *See* FUN FOUNDATION.

FUN FOUNDATION. A philanthropic foundation,
"organized by **Wonder Woman,** [which] maintains
1000 Fun Clinics teaching Americans to live, love,
laugh and be happy!" (Sen No. 28, Apr '44: "The
Malice of the Green Imps").

In March 1944 WONDER WOMAN uses chemicals
obtained from PARADISE ISLAND to manufacture
special fuel tablets which, when added to water,
produce a miraculous "high octane fuel for automobile engines," intending to use the money from
the sale of the fuel tablets to support the Fun
Foundation's recreational activities. An attempt by
unscrupulous businessman ELY CLOSE to steal the
secret fuel formula is thwarted by Wonder Woman
with the aid of the AMAZONS and BARONESS PAULA
VON GUNTHER (Sen No. 27: "The Fun Foundation"). (*See* CLOSE, ELY.)

In April 1944 MAYOR PRUDE concocts a scheme
to close down the Fun Clinic in Center City, but the
plot is ultimately thwarted by Wonder Woman
(Sen No. 28: "The Malice of the Green Imps").

FURIOSA. A cunning master spy who is known
also as "the spy queen" and "the mistress of masquerade." In June 1948 Furiosa kidnaps and impersonates STEVE TREVOR as part of a scheme to
capture WONDER WOMAN, but Wonder Woman
sees through the impersonation, apprehends Furiosa and her all-woman spy ring, rescues Steve
Trevor, and recovers "the LE-X formula," a "top-
secret formula for harnessing lunar energy,"
which the spies have stolen (Sen No. 78: "The
Mistress of Masquerade!").

G

GADGET-MAKER, THE. A diabolical maker of lethal gadgets who devises a hideous deathtrap for WONDER WOMAN.

In January 1959 Wonder Woman receives a small ornate box in the mail containing three tiny animals—about the size of trinkets worn on a charm bracelet—only to discover that the seemingly innocuous charms are actually cunningly disguised time bombs which grow miraculously to life-size and pursue her relentlessly with their payloads of destruction. Wonder Woman makes the bombs explode harmlessly, however, and then apprehends the Gadget-Maker (WW No. 103/2: "The Box of Three Dooms!").

GARDEN OF EDEN. An earthly paradise created by God as a home for Adam and Eve, the first man and the first woman.

According to Wonder Woman No. 13/1, the Garden of Eden sank beneath the South Polar ice cap sometime after the expulsion of Adam and Eve and remained preserved there, frozen in a state of absolute perfection, throughout the millennia, until it was repopulated by women from the planet VENUS and renamed EVELAND at the behest of the goddess APHRODITE (Sum '45: "The Icebound Maidens").

GARO. The leader of a gang of criminals who are apprehended by WONDER WOMAN in January–February 1952.

When, in an effort to boost its lagging circulation, the DAILY GLOBE offers a prize of $5,000 to whoever can uncover Wonder Woman's secret identity, gangster Garo reasons that he can eliminate Wonder Woman by systematically killing every woman whose name is put forward by the newspaper's readers. Accordingly, Wonder Woman soon finds herself spending the greater part of her time protecting wholly innocent women from murder attempts by Garo and his henchmen.

"To prevent future murderous attempts which will be made against everyone whom the underworld imagines is **Wonder Woman**," decides Wonder Woman finally, "I must assume an identity criminals will be fooled into thinking **is Wonder Woman**!"

After taking a temporary leave from the office of U.S. Military Intelligence, where she works under the alias of Diana Prince, Wonder Woman assumes a wholly new identity and obtains employment as a librarian under the alias of Jane Case. Soon afterward, she allows passersby to see her, as Jane Case, singlehandedly catching an automobile which has plummeted off a bridge, and when newspaper reporters ask her if she is secretly Wonder Woman, "Jane" admits that she is. The Garo gang barges into the library in an attempt to kill Jane Case as soon as the news of her identity is made public, but Wonder Woman succeeds in apprehending them all.

"You've caught us," sneers Garo, "but now that we know your secret identity--you'll never be safe! Every gang in the land'll be lookin' for Jane Case!"

"They won't find her," replies Wonder Woman, "because--she's going to disappear forever!"

Indeed, with the Garo gang safely behind bars, Jane Case does disappear, as Wonder Woman resumes her customary role as Diana Prince (WW No. 51/1: "The Amazing Impersonation!").

GASTON (Count). The "villainous uncle" of King Philippe, young ruler of the medieval Kingdom of Barania. When Count Gaston enters into a plot with King Ersatz of Skizofrenia to topple Philippe from his throne and impoverish the people of Barania, WONDER WOMAN journeys into the past to vanquish the villains and restore Philippe to his throne.

Determined to seize power in Barania, Count Gaston and his ruthless ally, King Ersatz of nearby Skizofrenia, have kidnapped Philippe's sweetheart, Annette Dubois, and imprisoned her in a dungeon. When Philippe becomes grief-stricken over Annette's disappearance, Gaston deposes him on the pretext that he has become insane, and, as Barania's acting ruler, makes ready to loot the kingdom and divide the booty with King Ersatz.

Meanwhile, in the dungeon where she is being held prisoner, Annette Dubois prays fervently for deliverance. So great is the power of Annette's wish for a savior that Wonder Woman is miraculously catapulted into the past, to medieval Barania, where she frees Annette from the dungeon and, aided by Annette's friends and palace soldiers loyal to Philippe, defeats the forces of Count Gaston and King Ersatz and restores Philippe to his throne (WW No. 27/3, Jan/Feb '48: "The Mystical Power of Idea-Forms!").

GENTLEMAN KILLER, THE. A "vicious spy and killer" who invades SHAMROCK LAND in Fall 1945, where he is repeatedly defeated by WONDER WOMAN. The Gentleman Killer wears a monocle, a top hat, and a full dress suit.

HA THIS LITTLE CANDLE'LL BE MOST USEFUL!

© NPP 1945

The Gentleman Killer

When Wonder Woman, STEVE TREVOR, and ETTA CANDY enter "the redwood forest" in search of the Gentleman Killer in Fall 1945, Etta accidentally tumbles into the opening of a hollow tree and finds herself in the labyrinthine network of underground tunnels which serve as home to the leprechauns, who work all day making tiny shoes for the Irish fairies known as "the little people."

Wonder Woman and her friends befriend the leprechauns, only to be attacked by the Gentleman Killer, who attempts to bury Steve Trevor alive in a rockslide. Wonder Woman rescues Trevor before he can come to any harm, but the Gentleman Killer escapes in the confusion (WW No. 14/1: "Captured by Leprechauns").

Soon afterward, the Gentleman Killer steals the special golden hammers with which the leprechauns fashion shoes for the little people and makes his way through the labyrinthine network of leprechaun tunnels until he emerges in Shamrock Land, a section of the redwood forest ruled by the lovely Princess Elaine and inhabited by kind Irish folk and gentle "little people." Employing the alias Rudolph Hessenpfeffer, the Gentleman Killer charms the naïve Princess Elaine into showing him her collection of priceless jewels and then makes off with them, leaving the princess to die in an explosion he sets to go off in her castle. Wonder Woman rescues Princess Elaine from

the explosion, however, and the Gentleman Killer is apprehended by a citizen of Shamrock Land with the aid of the leprechauns. With the jewels recovered and the leprechauns' golden hammers restored to their rightful owners, Princess Elaine announces that she and her people will work to change the Gentleman Killer into a kind and useful citizen (WW No. 14/2, Fall '45: "The Gentleman Killer Strikes Again!").

Before long, however, the villain has managed to escape, as well as to trick the leprechauns into giving him some of their "magic darts," which have the power to compel anyone struck by them to obey the thrower's every command. Striking Princess Elaine with one of the darts, the Gentleman Killer forces her to appoint him Prime Minister of Shamrock Land and to instruct her subjects to do whatever he commands, but Wonder Woman captures the villain with the aid of Steve Trevor, Etta Candy, the fairy queen of the little people, and the leprechauns Hoppy, Woggle, and SHAGGY (WW No. 14/3, Fall '45).

GERTA. *See* GUNTHER, GERTA VON.

GESTAPO 6 KQZ. The Nazi code name for BARONESS PAULA VON GUNTHER while she was in the employ of the Gestapo (WW No. 4/1, Apr/May '43).

GHU (Prince). The evil brother of the peace-loving Lord Dallu.

Journeying to PARADISE ISLAND in September–October 1951, WONDER WOMAN finds the island in a state of siege, with wounded AMAZONS and demolished buildings everywhere, and a new explosive shell bursting onto the island every ninety minutes to add to the carnage. Impossible though it may seem, however, Amazon "radar tracings" reveal that "the shell[s] could not have been fired from the Earth nor [sic] from any of the planets or stars!" Indeed, the strange markings on the exploded shells indicate that they come from "the land of **Mu**--a continent which vanished 9000 years ago!"

To solve the mystery, Wonder Woman journeys into the past to the lost continent of MU, where she finds the evil Prince Ghu at war with his peace-loving brother Lord Dallu, who is huddled atop a high mountain with his badly outnumbered forces, "firing a shell down [the mountain] every 90 minutes to prevent my brother's forces from coming up here and killing my people!" Unknown to Lord Dallu, however, his shells are never reaching the base of the mountain, but are passing instead through a mysterious "warp in time" and landing on Paradise Island, 9,000 years in the future. Nevertheless, with Wonder Woman's help, Lord Dallu finally triumphs over the evil Prince Ghu, thus bringing the shelling of Paradise Island to an end (WW No. 49/1: "Return of the Phantom Empire").

GHURKOS. The "dread master" of PHOBOS, inner moon of the planet MARS. Ghurkos is defeated by WONDER WOMAN in May–June 1950.

In May–June 1950 Wonder Woman journeys to Phobos to help STEVE TREVOR, who had headed a top-secret expedition to Phobos "to procure fissionable material for peaceful atomic energy use" and now stands accused by the tyrant Ghurkos of having murdered Duke Dorna, a political figure much beloved by the people.

Arriving on Phobos, Wonder Woman establishes Trevor's innocence and rescues Duke Dorna—who is not dead at all, but being secretly held captive by Ghurkos and his henchmen—while thwarting a series of attempts on her life by the tyrant and his cohorts. Liberated from Ghurko's tyranny at last, the people of Phobos promise to cooperate with Earth in developing peaceful uses for atomic energy (WW No. 41/3: "The Trial of Steve Trevor!").

GHURKTON. The capital city of PHOBOS, the inner moon of the planet MARS (WW No. 41/3, May/Jun '50: "The Trial of Steve Trevor!").

GIGANTA. The so-called "gorilla girl," a spectacular redhead with the body of a human and "the mind and savage instincts of a gorilla." Giganta is actually a ferocious female gorilla who has been transformed into a lovely "cave girl" by PROF. ZOOL's "electronic evolutionizer."

In Summer 1944 Prof. Zool of the HOLLIDAY COLLEGE FOR WOMEN unveils his latest invention, the electronic evolutionizer:

> For years I have been experimenting on evolution—at last I have discovered the secret of speeding up the process so that I can turn **apes** into men! My machine—the electronic evolutionizer—will do what it took nature millions of years to do--change apes into humans! After all, monkeys are very close to men. . . .

With his electronic evolutionizer—or "evolution machine"—Prof. Zool evolves a female gorilla named Giganta into a beautiful redheaded cave girl, but despite the fact that she is now a girl, Giganta retains the savage instincts of a female gorilla. When she attacks WONDER WOMAN in Prof. Zool's laboratory, Wonder Woman seizes Giganta in self-defense and hurls her into Zool's complex electronic apparatus. "A violet flame fills the air" as a minor electrical explosion occurs, and "a strange transformation affects those present": Wonder Woman, Prof. Zool, STEVE TREVOR, ETTA CANDY, and the HOLLIDAY GIRLS.

"My evolutionizer," cries Zool, " — it's **reversed**! It's **de**volving us — it'll change us into **apes**!"

AS THE EVOLUTIONARY TRANSFORMATION IS COMPLETED, A BEAUTIFUL GIRL OF AMAZONIAN PROPORTIONS STANDS IN PLACE OF THE GORILLA!

Giganta, 1944

In an effort to halt the devolution process, Wonder Woman hurls the evolutionizer out a window, but she and the others in the laboratory have already become transformed into cave people, and "the devolutionizing machine hurled out the window, hyperatomizes the air for miles around, setting nature back 60 million years to prehistoric times," so that she and her friends are now cave people in the prehistoric world of 60 million B.C.

Largely through the treachery of Giganta—who has remained a savage gorilla girl and who hates and fears Wonder Woman—Wonder Woman and her friends are taken captive by the Tree Men, brutal, tree-dwelling inhabitants of the prehistoric forest. The Tree Men intend to sacrifice them to a huge tyrannosaurus they call "the Tyrant King of the Beast Gods," but Wonder Woman defeats the dinosaur and escapes with her companions. Now she must find and repair Prof. Zool's evolution machine so that it can "take us all back to where we belong!" (WW No. 9/1: "Evolution Goes Haywire!").

Wonder Woman finally locates the evolutionizer and, temporarily at least, manages to repair it. Under its miraculous influence, "millions of years of evolution pass in a moment. Caves and primitive jungles undergo geologic evolution—[and] **Wonder Woman** suddenly finds herself . . . in a world of flowers and beauty."

"Great Aphrodite!" exclaims Wonder Woman. "The evolution machine [has] brought us to the Golden Age when the world was **perfect!**"

But at that very instant, the electronic evolutionizer breaks down, stranding Wonder Woman and her friends in the Golden Age, "when men and women lived in perfect happiness amidst enchanting beauty. . .!"

The Golden Age is an age of absolute innocence, where even the meaning of evil is not yet known. Because perfect contentment and equality exist among the sexes, "Men and women take turns working at home and in the fields . . . !" The rulers of the Golden Age are the handsome King Aros and the lovely Queen Darla.

The naïve people of the Golden Age, however, are easy prey for the treacherous Giganta, who swiftly forms an alliance with the more greedy, brutish faction of Golden Age society, led by the ruthless Jon, and persuades them to join her in overthrowing Aros and Darla and seizing the world for themselves. Before long, King Aros and Queen Darla—and Wonder Woman and her companions—have been taken captive by the insurrectionists, but Wonder Woman turns the tables on her captors and makes Giganta her prisoner.

Still, in Queen Darla's words, "the Golden Age is over--[because] people know now that they **can** be wicked if they choose!"

"But a greater Golden Age will come when humans learn it's more fun to be **good!**" replies Wonder Woman (WW No. 9/2, Sum '44: "The Freed Captive").

Soon afterward, Giganta sets the evolution machine whirring again, but Steve Trevor soon shuts it off again, arguing that there is "no telling where it'll land us!"

Now Wonder Woman and her friends find themselves in ancient AMAZONIA—home of the AMAZONS before their migration to PARADISE ISLAND—where Wonder Woman makes the acquaintance of the Amazons' ruler, QUEEN HIPPOLYTE.

"She's my mother," thinks Wonder Woman, "but I'm not **born** yet! We're back in ancient times long before the Amazons went to Paradise Island!"

Wonder Woman and her friends have arrived in Amazonia at a fortuitous time for the Amazons, for Amazonia is about to be attacked.

"We Amazons were allies of the Trojans against the Greeks," explains Hippolyte. "But Troy fell and the Greeks led by **Achilles** seek revenge—a huge army is nearing the city!"

To make matters worse, continues Hippolyte, the Amazon maidens "are away hunting husbands. . . . Until they return, we cannot defend the walls!"

Determined to delay ACHILLES's attack until the Amazons can return to defend their city, Wonder Woman defeats Achilles in single combat with swords, humiliating him in full view of his entire army. Infuriated by the defeat of their mighty leader, the Greeks attack Wonder Woman en masse, but the returning Amazons arrive home in the nick of time and, under the leadership of the heroic Queen Hippolyte, turn back the Greek assault.

Wonder Woman battles Giganta, 1948

With the Greeks defeated and Giganta once again a captive, Wonder Woman and her friends start Prof. Zool's electronic evolutionizer running again and return to their own era without further mishap (WW No. 9/3, Sum '44).

In December 1944 Giganta is one of the six infamous villains and villainesses impersonated by actors in BEDWIN FOOTH's "underworld crime [theatrical] company" (Sen No. 36: "Battle Against Revenge").

In March–April 1948 Giganta escapes from TRANSFORMATION ISLAND along with seven other villainesses and joins them in forming VILLAINY INCORPORATED (WW No. 28/1–3: "Villainy Incorporated!"; "Trap of Crimson Flame"; "In the Hands of the Merciless!"). (See VILLAINY INCORPORATED.)

GOODE (Mayor). The mayor of Bourbon City until WONDER WOMAN exposes him as the murderer of Frank Poore, thereby establishing the innocence of Poore's wife, Esta Poore, who has been falsely accused of the crime.

"I—I stole millions from Bourbon City!" confesses Mayor Goode. "Frank Poore started to expose our graft so I killed Frank and framed Esta for the murder!" (Sen No. 34, Oct '44: "Edgar's New World!").

GORGO, IGOR. The renowned motion picture director who conspires with his fiancée, Hollywood actress Zita Zanders, to murder Diana Prince in November–December 1950, unaware that Diana Prince is secretly WONDER WOMAN.

In November–December 1950, when Hollywood's MONARCH STUDIOS holds a competition to select an actress to play Wonder Woman in its forthcoming film, *The Wonder Woman Story*, Diana Prince is selected—through a fluke—to play the title role.

Furious because he wants the Wonder Woman role for his fiancée Zita Zanders, director Igor Gorgo plots with Zita to kill Diana Prince by forcing her to perform a series of death-defying stunts in the film and then sabotaging them so as to transform them into inescapable deathtraps. For Diana, the problem becomes one of surviving the various stunts without betraying the fact that she is actually Wonder Woman. Ultimately, Gorgo and his fiancée become so astonished when Diana Prince successfully survives one of their stunts that they express their surprise aloud, thereby revealing their guilt to the entire movie crew and ensuring that they will both go to prison for attempted murder (Sen No. 100: "Wonder Woman, Hollywood Star!").

GORRA. A spy recently captured by agents of U.S. Military Intelligence who is an exact double for Diana Prince, the girl who is secretly WONDER WOMAN. In July 1954 Diana Prince, posing as Gorra, accompanies STEVE TREVOR around the city, pretending to be in Trevor's custody, in an effort to lure the remaining members of Gorra's spy ring, who are still at large, into coming into the open to rescue their leader. Ultimately, the ruse succeeds, enabling Wonder Woman to apprehend Gorra's cohorts (WW No. 67/1: "Confessions of a Spy!").

GOULASH, HYLO (Prince). An alias employed by KARL SCHULTZ, a "Gestapo agent working for the Japs," when he poses as a foreign prince in order to win the hand of ETTA CANDY (Sen No. 16, Apr '43).

GRABB, ABNER. An unscrupulous timber contractor who attempts to force Conway, an honest lumberman, to default on his contract to supply lumber to the railroad so that Grabb can win the lucrative contract for himself. Grabb has also been cutting timber in the "U.S. Government owned forest where the leprechauns live," violating federal law and threatening the leprechauns' very existence. WONDER WOMAN reforms Grabb's henchmen by giving them a whiff of leprechaun "moonbeam gas," a formula which "dissolves the hate and greed in [people's] thoughts, allowing [them] to see only the good," and Grabb repents his evil ways when Wonder Woman rescues his daughter from drowning (WW No. 35/3, May/Jun '49: "The Stolen Forest!"). (See also SHAGGY.)

GRABLES, FAUSTA. A beautiful and daring Axis spy who comes to America to capture WONDER WOMAN on personal orders from ADOLF HITLER. Fausta is ultimately apprehended by Wonder Woman along with her cohorts, the Axis agents who comprise "the Council of Axis Chiefs, America's most deadly enemies!" (CC No. 2, Spr '43: "Wanted by Hitler, Dead or Alive").

GRAY, MARVA JANE. MARVA PSYCHO's maiden name (Sen No. 20, Aug '43).

GREAT BLUE FATHER, THE. A mysterious villain who, by means of his diabolical "moron hormone," has been inducing feeblemindedness in the highest officials of the United States Government. He is in reality Prof. Protus Plasm, a "famous biologist" recently engaged in "important government work."

By Spring 1945 Prof. Protus Plasm has become sick and tired of coping with the government bureaucrats who oversee his work for the government. When his pompous department head refers to him as "child-minded," Plasm retaliates by developing the "moron hormone," a chemical formula that induces temporary feeblemindedness, and administering a dose of it to his department ead, who promptly proceeds to make a fool of imself. When the effect of the moron hormone ears off, however, the department head becomes urious, accuses Plasm of being an "academic crew ball," and dismisses him from his government research post.

Soon afterward, officials on many levels of government begin to fall victim to a strange new disase:

"There's something strange going on," remarks Colonel Darnell (*see* DARNELL [GENERAL]), "—but it must be kept absolutely secret! The high officials of Washington all seem to be going feebleminded! . . [I]t's some sort of disease that seems to be contagious!"

Investigating, WONDER WOMAN discovers that the person responsible for the contagion is a man known only as the Great Blue Father, who has been freely administering a so-called "youth medicine" to government officials. Ultimately, Wonder Woman apprehends the Great Blue Father and unmasks him as Prof. Protus Plasm, who has been wreaking revenge on the government for his recent dismissal (CC No. 10: "The Great Blue Father").

GREAT WALL OF CHINA, THE. A huge defensive fortification—built of earth, stone, and bricks—which extends approximately 1,500 miles from the Gulf of Chihli of the Yellow Sea to the gates of Central Asia. Built by the emperor Ch'in Shih Huang Ti as a defense against the Hsiung-nu or Huns on the north in the 3rd century B.C., it is the greatest building enterprise ever undertaken and the only man-made object visible from the moon.

According to Wonder Woman No. 37/1, however, the Great Wall was constructed singlehandedly by WONDER WOMAN during a time-journey to China in the 1st century B.C. (Sep/Oct '49: "The Riddle of the Chinese Mummy Case!"). (*See* CHANG.)

GREED, EARL OF. The greedy, corpulent Martian who is—along with LORD CONQUEST and the DUKE OF DECEPTION—one of the principal "three commanders" in the service of the war god MARS.

In Fall 1942 Mars concocts an elaborate scheme to capture WONDER WOMAN—whose "defense of America and democracy has incensed him"—by taking STEVE TREVOR prisoner and using him as bait to lure Wonder Woman to the planet MARS, but Wonder Woman triumphs over the Martian schemers and rescues Trevor from their clutches. Furious over his humiliation, the war god vows to send his top three commanders to Earth to take her captive (WW No. 2/1). (*See* MARS [the god of war].)

The first of Mars's agents to be dispatched to

Earth is the Earl of Greed, who journeys to Earth as an invisible phantom—i.e., "in his astral body"—so that he can do Mars's bidding without being seen by anyone. He carries with him a plentiful supply of money, given him by Mars, to enable him to play on earthmen's greed.

On Earth, Greed appeals to ADOLF HITLER's greed in order to persuade Der Fuehrer to instruct his Nazi cohorts to "raid the American treasury" to steal the "vast hoards of gold" buried in its underground vaults. Greed also persuades DR. HEZEKIAH DEACON, the president of Holliday College, to mastermind the Nazi assault on the United States Treasury, but Wonder Woman foils the Nazi plot, forcing the Earl of Greed to return to the planet Mars humiliated and defeated (WW No. 2/2, Fall '42). (*See* DEACON, HEZEKIAH [DR.].)

When Greed returns to Mars, beaten by Wonder Woman, the war god orders him locked in a dungeon until he pays Mars 10,000 pounds of gold for having failed to carry out his mission. Mars's next emissary to Earth is the diabolical Duke of Deception (WW No. 2/3, Fall '42). (*See* DECEPTION, DUKE OF.)

Like Greed, however, the Duke of Deception fails in his attempt to capture Wonder Woman, and when he returns to Mars he is forced to join Greed in the dungeons.

Mars's third emissary to Earth, Lord Conquest, succeeds in making Wonder Woman his prisoner, and when he returns to Mars in triumph, the overjoyed war god orders Deception and Greed released from the dungeons. Wonder Woman ultimately escapes and returns to Earth, so that once again the war god has been thwarted (WW No. 2/4, Fall '42). (*See* CRAFTI [COUNT].)

In June–July 1943 the Duke of Deception overthrows the war god Mars and establishes himself as ruler of the Martian planet. Mars and Lord Conquest are imprisoned, but the Earl of Greed bribes some guards to let them escape (WW No. 5/2). (*See* DECEPTION, DUKE OF.)

In March–April 1949 the Earl of Greed is allied with the war god Mars in an elaborate scheme to destroy Wonder Woman (WW No. 34: "The Mystery of the Rhyming Riddle!" chs. 1–3–"Deception Strikes Again"; "The Phantasms of Deception!"; "The Mystery of the Rhyming Riddle!"). (*See* DECEPTION, DUKE OF.)

GRENADE GANG, THE. A gang of international criminals who attempt to steal "Invention SR"—a top-secret device designed to "make . . . radar powerless to signal the approach of aircraft"—from Prof. Daniel, its inventor. The gang, whose members wear elaborate gas masks both to conceal their identities and to protect themselves from the gas grenades they hurl at their adversaries, is apprehended by WONDER WOMAN in March–April 1951 (WW No. 46/1: "The Trail of the Lost Hours!").

GRESHAM, LESLIE M. A male-chauvinist business tycoon and financier who is so disappointed when his wife gives birth to a daughter—"Women are simply inferior to men!" exclaims Gresham adamantly; "It's a fact!"—that he names his newborn child Leslie M. Gresham, Jr., after himself, and attempts to raise her as though she were a boy. "A **girl**," complains Gresham, "can't run my railroads and mines--direct my board meetings--control my business empire!"

Gresham's attitude toward women changes radically, however, after he and a group of his miners have been rescued from a mine cave-in by WONDER WOMAN and his daughter, a student at the HOLLIDAY COLLEGE FOR WOMEN who has received special Amazon training from Wonder Woman (see WONDER WOMAN [section C 1, the benefits of Amazon training]).

"I-I've learned my lesson!" vows Gresham. "Women **are** every bit as capable as men, if given the chance! And some of them—**Wonder Woman**, to name one, are even better!" (Sen No. 85, Jan '49: "The Girl Who Wanted to Be an Amazon!").

GROSS. A Nazi spy who is captured by WONDER WOMAN in March 1942.

Shortly after she has obtained employment as Colonel Darnell's secretary (see DARNELL [GENERAL]), Diana Prince—the girl who is secretly Wonder Woman—is accused of being an Axis spy and ordered confined to her quarters when it becomes apparent that there has been a security leak at U.S. Military Intelligence.

Investigating as Wonder Woman, however, Diana learns that the real culprit is "office errand girl" EVE BROWN, captures Nazi spy Gross, rescues STEVE TREVOR from a gang of Nazi spies holding him prisoner aboard a yacht in Chesapeake Bay, and clears Diana Prince of the spy charges against her (Sen No. 3).

GUINEVERE (Queen). In Arthurian legend, the wife of KING ARTHUR and the lover of SIR LANCELOT, his dearest knight. WONDER WOMAN rescues Guinevere from the clutches of the evil MERLIN during a time-journey to Arthur's Camelot that she makes in July–August 1952 (WW No. 54/1: "The Wizard of Castle Sinister!"). (See ARTHUR [KING].)

GUNDRA. "The princess of the Valkyries" and, by implication, the daughter of the war god ODIN, though this is never actually stated.

In October–November 1946, while battling "Nazi underground guerillas" in the streets of occupied Germany, STEVE TREVOR is seized by the blond Gundra, who throws him across the back of her

flying battle charger and carries him off to VALHALLA, the hall of the slain (CC No. 17: "The Valkyries' Prey"). (See ODIN).

ACCORDING TO THE GERMAN MYTH, **ODIN**, THE **WAR GOD**, SENDS WINGED MESSENGERS, THE **VALKYRIES**, TO SELECT THE BRAVEST WARRIORS IN BATTLE AND CARRY THEM TO **VALHALLA**, THE HALL OF THE SLAIN.

© NPP 1947

Wonder Woman recalls Gundra, 1947

In May–June 1947 Gundra leads her winged VALKYRIES on a series of raids over PARADISE ISLAND, where she and her battle maidens seize Amazon captives to be carried off to Valhalla and transformed into Valkyries (WW No. 23/1: "Siege of the Savage War Maidens"). (See ODIN.)

GUNTA, PAULA VON. See GUNTHER, PAULA VON (BARONESS).

GUNTHER, GERTA VON. The "brilliant but headstrong" daughter of Baron Gottfried von Gunther (now deceased) and BARONESS PAULA VON GUNTHER. Like her mother, the curly-haired Gerta is an accomplished scientist.

In the early years of World War II, after her father had been brutally murdered by the Nazis, Gerta, then only a young child, was sent off "to a concentration camp near Vienna," while her mother was coerced into becoming a Gestapo agent. "If you perform your duties as American Gestapo agent effectively," said the Nazis, "your child is safe. Fail once and little Gerta dies!"

In February–March 1943, after she has apprehended Baroness Paula von Gunther and taken her to Reform Island (*see* TRANSFORMATION ISLAND) for rehabilitation, WONDER WOMAN flies to Austria with ETTA CANDY, where together they rescue Gerta von Gunther and other captive children from a Nazi concentration camp.

Back on Reform Island, Baroness Paula von Gunther—overjoyed at being reunited with her daughter—resolves to pledge herself to APHRODITE's service and soon becomes Wonder Woman's closest friend and most trusted ally (WW No. 3/3). (*See* GUNTHER, PAULA VON [BARONESS].)

Wonder Woman and Gerta von Gunther: a lesson in loving submission, 1946

Gerta von Gunther, 1946

In April–May 1943 Gerta is kidnapped from PARADISE ISLAND by MAVIS, but is rescued soon afterward by Wonder Woman (WW No. 4/4). (*See* MAVIS.)

In Winter 1943 Wonder Woman advises Gerta's mother to take her to America so that they can work together in Paula's secret laboratory on the campus of the HOLLIDAY COLLEGE FOR WOMEN. ". . . [S]he [Gerta] is growing self-willed, and scornful of authority!" warns Wonder Woman. "You must take her to America—keep her with you and teach her **love and obedience**" (WW No. 7/4).

In July 1946 Gerta's strong-willed personality and brilliant scientific mind are inadvertently responsible for the menace of the BUGHUMANS (Sen No. 55: "The Bughuman Plague").

In June–July 1947 Gerta's scientific experimentation produces yet another menace, this time in the form of the terrifying mermaid sharks led by

QUEEN SHARKEETA (CC No. 21: "The Seige [sic] of the Flying Mermaids!").

GUNTHER, PAULA VON (Baroness). A cruel "Gestapo agent and murderess" (Sen No. 6, Jun '42) who ultimately reforms to become WONDER WOMAN's closest friend and most trusted ally. The widow of Baron Gottfried von Gunther and the mother of GERTA VON GUNTHER, Paula is a brilliant scientist and the creator of numerous miraculous inventions. In the texts, she is alternately portrayed as a light blonde (Sen No. 4, Apr '42; and others), a honey blonde (WW No. 3/3, Feb/Mar '43; and others), a strawberry blonde (WW No. 4/1, Apr/May '43; and others), and as a redhead (Sen No. 24, Dec '43: "Adventure of the Pilotless Plane").

By April 1942 Baroness Paula von Gunther has established herself as the chief Nazi secret agent in America, director of a vast Gestapo net-

Baroness Paula von Gunther makes a bloody escape, 1942

work of spies and saboteurs. She is vicious, cold-blooded, and sadistic. Her coterie of slave girls are kept imprisoned in heavy shackles and whipped or beaten for the slightest infraction of their mistress's harsh discipline, although they are portrayed as enjoying their subjugation and thriving on the humiliations inflicted upon them by the baroness.

During this period, STEVE TREVOR is assigned the task of locating a mysterious "school of espionage" where kidnapped American girls are reportedly being trained to serve as Nazi spies. Wonder Woman, meanwhile, certain that Baroness Paula von Gunther is secretly an Axis agent, allows herself to be taken prisoner by Nazi agents in hopes of locating the secret spy school and accumulating sufficient evidence to convict the baroness of espionage.

Wonder Woman soon finds herself a prisoner at the secret spy school—hidden in "an abandoned coal mine in West Virginia"—but the baroness's henchmen weld chains to her Amazon bracelets (*see* WONDER WOMAN [section C 2, the bracelets of submission]), thereby depriving her of her Amazon strength, and when Steve Trevor trails a Nazi spy to the school, he too is taken captive. Condemned to be shot by a Nazi firing squad, Wonder Woman and Trevor are saved when Wonder Woman leaps into the path of the oncoming bullets, causing them to shatter the chain connecting her Amazon bracelets and thus restore her Amazon strength. Aided by Steve Trevor, ETTA CANDY, and the HOLLIDAY GIRLS, Wonder Woman defeats the Nazis, apprehends Baroness Paula von Gunther, and liberates the kidnapped girls who had been coerced into becoming students at the villainess's spy school.

"These bracelets," muses Wonder Woman aloud, "—they're an Amazon's greatest strength and

weakness! What a fool I was to let a man weld chains upon them!" (Sen No. 4).

By June 1942 Baroness Paula von Gunther has escaped from the police transporting her to prison and has successfully eluded a nationwide manhunt. During this period, with Colonel Darnell (*see* DARNELL [GENERAL]) en route to England aboard the ocean liner *Gigantic* to perform a top-secret mission for U.S. Military Intelligence, the baroness kidnaps and impersonates Lady Chumpley, one of the *Gigantic*'s passengers, and summons a German U-boat to the scene to capture the liner and abduct Colonel Darnell for interrogation by the Gestapo.

Having taken Darnell captive, the Nazis are about to sink the *Gigantic* with its passengers and crew still on board, when Wonder Woman arrives on the scene, deflects a Nazi torpedo before it can strike the *Gigantic*, and apprehends Baroness Paula von Gunther and her Nazi cohorts (Sen No. 6).

By July 1942 Baroness Paula von Gunther, incarcerated in State's Prison following her last encounter with Wonder Woman, has been executed in the electric chair for her crimes, only to cheat death by arranging for her body to be released to her cohorts for burial and then brought back to life by means of one of her ingenious inventions.

"Behold — a living dead woman!" she exclaims later to a startled Wonder Woman. "Your stupid executioners killed me! But with an electrical machine I invented, my slaves restored life to my dead body!"

At large once again, the baroness is the mastermind behind a diabolical Axis scheme to deprive America's children of milk by using the International Milk Company as a front to buy up America's milk supply and drive up the price to such an

Disguised as Lady Chumpley, Baroness Paula von Gunther invades the radio room aboard the ocean liner Gigantic, *1942*

exorbitant height — 26¢ per quart — that America's poor simply cannot afford to buy it.

Apprised of the sudden upward spiralling of milk prices, Wonder Woman suspects foul play and investigates, only to be taken prisoner by Baroness Paula von Gunther and her henchmen.

"Fool!" gloats the baroness. "I have spent seven million dollars to take milk from the mouths of American children! Your rising generation will be weakened and dwarfed! Germany, in twenty years, will conquer your milk-starved youths and will rule America!"

Wonder Woman ultimately triumphs over the Nazis, however, apprehending the baroness and rescuing the milk supply for the growing youth of America (Sen No. 7).

By Summer 1942 Baroness Paula von Gunther has been incarcerated in Federal Prison in "a dark solitary cell underground." Unbeknownst to the authorities, however, the floor of her cell contains a secret trapdoor leading to "an old tier of torture cells, long sealed beneath the prison and forgotten. Here the clever spy queen meets her agents and slaves" and carries on her nefarious activities as leader of "the Gestapo system in America." By kidnapping the couriers responsible for transmitting the sailing orders for Allied troop transports, the baroness and her cohorts have obtained vital secret information concerning the sailing times, dates, and routes of ships transporting American troops into the war zone, enabling Nazi U-boats to intercept the transport ships and sink them.

Taken captive by the baroness and imprisoned in her secret subterranean spy headquarters, Wonder Woman escapes, leads an American cavalry regiment in a surprise assault on a secret Nazi submarine base, and singlehandedly captures a Nazi U-boat berthed not far away. During the pitched battle which accompanies the Allied assault on the "enemy fortress," a stray bullet strikes the baroness and she topples headlong into the sea (WW No. 1/3).

In December 1942 it becomes apparent that Baroness Paula von Gunther has managed to cheat death once again, for when Wonder Woman accepts an invitation to make a Hollywood movie about her renowned "spy-catching exploits" — ostensibly to "inspire America with confidence and terrify enemy agents" — she soon learns that the invitation was nothing more than the opening gambit in a scheme by the baroness to lure her to her doom.

"Great Aphrodite," exclaims Wonder Woman, "— the baroness is **alive!**"

"Our mistress is marvelous," boasts one of the baroness's slave girls. "She was killed when troops led by **Wonder Woman** captured our submarine base, but the electric machine she invented brought her back to life!"

When Steve Trevor is taken captive by "a horde of little brown men" — Japanese agents in the service of the baroness — Wonder Woman is compelled to surrender also to protect Trevor from harm.

"Become **my** slave or Steve dies!" demands the baroness. "Tell me the secret of how to chain you, then I'll train you properly!"

Aided by Etta Candy and the Holliday Girls, however, Wonder Woman defeats Baroness Paula von Gunther and her slave girls and rescues Steve Trevor from their clutches (Sen No. 12).

In January 1943, while Baroness Paula von Gunther is in prison, one of her cohorts — a trusted U.S. Military Intelligence translator named Olga — masterminds a scheme to steal a top-secret code key from Steve Trevor, but she and her Axis cohorts are ultimately apprehended by Wonder Woman with some assistance from Etta Candy (Sen No. 13).

In February–March 1943 Baroness Paula von Gunther overpowers a guard at Federal Prison and, disguised in the guard's uniform, walks boldly through the prison gate to freedom. At large once again, the baroness issues instructions to her slave KEELA which lead ultimately to an invasion of PARADISE ISLAND by the baroness and a shipload of her Japanese allies. The invasion is repelled by Wonder Woman and the AMAZONS, and Keela, the baroness, and "a boatload of [the baroness's] slave girls" are taken captive. It is to accommodate these prisoners that QUEEN HIPPOLYTE orders the construction of a prison facility on Reform Island (see TRANSFORMATION ISLAND).

"This woman must not be killed," remarks Hippolyte, referring to the baroness; "Aphrodite's law forbids [it]. We will construct a prison on Reform Island. There shall she and her poor victims [i.e., her slave girls] be confined until their minds are completely free from evil!" (WW No. 3/1). (See KEELA.)

Soon afterward, however, Baroness Paula von Gunther escapes from Reform Island and returns to America to wreak vengeance on Wonder Woman, this time employing two miraculous devices of her own invention — one enabling her to render herself and her slave girls invisible, the other enabling her to enslave any adversary and compel him to do her bidding. In this so-called "slave subjecting treatment," the victim is forced to gaze intently at a picture of the baroness wielding

Baroness Paula von Gunther overpowers Mala and escapes from Reform Island, 1943

a heavy whip. By burning itself into the victim's consciousness, the picture — described as "a masterpiece of hypnotic art" — transforms the victim into a mindless, obedient slave, powerless to resist the baroness's commands.

By means of this diabolical technique, the baroness enslaves Steve Trevor and compels him to steal top-secret documents from the office of U.S. Military Intelligence. Wonder Woman notices that Trevor is acting strangely and allows the baroness to capture her in hopes of getting to the bottom of the mystery.

"Call me mistress, from now on," commands Baroness Paula von Gunther. "It will remind you of your servitude!"

And moments later, the villainess begins the process of transforming Wonder Woman into a mindless slave: ". . . I shall now give you your first slave subjecting treatment," she explains. "It is not painful — you have nothing to fear. Relax, submit, and all will be well!"

Meanwhile, however, Etta Candy captures the mind-controlled Steve Trevor with Wonder Woman's magic lasso (see WONDER WOMAN [section C 3, the magic lasso]) and compels him to lead her to the baroness's laboratory hideaway, where the baroness is "about to discipline her new slave girl [when she] is interrupted by the sudden entrance of Steve and Etta."

The shock of seeing Wonder Woman in the clutches of the baroness enables Trevor to break free from her mental control. Aided by Wonder Woman, he and Etta Candy defeat the baroness's slaves and flee the baroness's stronghold, but in the confusion the baroness escapes (WW No. 3/2, Feb/Mar '43).

On Reform Island, meanwhile, the baroness's captured slaves have become a source of puzzlement to their Amazon guards. They are completely obedient and make no attempt to escape, but they refuse to either work or play without the shackles welded onto their arms and legs by the baroness.

"We'll kill you!" cry the slave girls when the Amazons attempt to remove their slave chains. "We'll **die** rather than be free!"

"Ha! Ha!" laughs an Amazon guard at the bewildering spectacle of the baroness's slave girls rejecting freedom. "They're fighting for **woman's bondage** — the Hitler principle that women must remain men's slaves!"

Later, a perplexed MALA tells Wonder Woman that the Amazons have succeeded in maintaining order among the new prisoners only by making some accommodations to their fanatical desire to remain in bondage. "Though Aphrodite forbids hurting prisoners," she explains, "we snap big whips and the girls love it! Under these conditions they work beautifully."

Mala readily confesses, however, that she simply "can't understand these girls!"

"You could if you knew women in the man-ruled world!" replies Wonder Woman. "They want to be slaves because they're afraid to be free and compete with men!"

"If girls want to be slaves," thinks Wonder Woman to herself, "there's no harm in that. The bad thing for them is submitting to a master or to an evil mistress like Paula! A **good** mistress could do wonders with them!"

Eventually, the baroness's former slave girls come to love and adore Mala and to look upon her as their new mistress. "You are our mistress," they cry, "now make us your slaves, mistress Mala!"

Mala protests that she has no desire for slaves, but the slave girls insist that she command them to do something. Finally, Mala instructs them all to go swimming with her. Notes the narrative text: "The girls go wild with joy as Mala gives them orders."

Back in America, Wonder Woman looks on in horror as the driver of a speeding automobile gleefully runs over a child's sled, smashing it into splinters and only narrowly missing the little boy who owns it.

Wonder Woman streaks after the fleeing automobile and apprehends its driver, who turns out to be none other than Baroness Paula von Gunther. "I **HATE** children!" explains the baroness, after Wonder Woman has returned her to Reform Island to continue her term of imprisonment.

"You really mean, Paula," replies Wonder Woman, "that you **love** some child terribly much!

You've lost the child you loved and so you hate all other children. Isn't that the truth?"

"Y-Yes!" cries the baroness, beginning to sob uncontrollably. "—Sob sob—I l-lost my own little girl!

"Before the Nazis invaded Austria," she explains under the compelling influence of Wonder Woman's magic lasso, "I was happy with my beloved husband, Baron von Gunther and our little child Gerta. Then the Nazis came."

The Gestapo had demanded that Baron von Gunther surrender all of his wealth to them immediately. When von Gunther courageously refused, the Gestapo dragged him away.

"Months later," continues the baroness, "after heaven knows how much suffering, my husband was killed. They brought me his ashes in a cigar box."

And then a storm trooper had torn her child Gerta from her arms and carried her away. The Nazis had also forced the baroness to supply them with a complete listing of her dead husband's properties so that they could confiscate them, but she had withheld the names of several of Baron von Gunther's American properties in hopes of saving them for her daughter Gerta.

"But the Gestapo was not through with me," continues the baroness. "They sent Gerta to a concentration camp near Vienna," and forced the baroness to become a secret Gestapo agent in America.

"If you perform your duties as American Gestapo agent effectively," said the Nazis, "your child is safe. Fail once and little Gerta dies!"

"Oh—sob—sob—what can I do?" cries the baroness, having completed her story. "I hate the Nazis with all my soul! Yet I must serve them for my child's sake!"

Determined to do what she can to help, Wonder Woman flies to Austria with Etta Candy, where, with Etta's help, she rescues Gerta von Gunther and other captive European children from the Nazi concentration camp.

Later, on Reform Island, young Gerta is happily reunited with a mother whom she has not seen in years. Overwhelmed with joy, Baroness Paula von Gunther "throws herself at **Wonder Woman's** feet."

"From this moment on," she exclaims, "I belong to you—I pledge my life to your service!"

"No," replies Wonder Woman, "to the service of Aphrodite—[to] love, beauty, and justice!" (WW No. 3/3, Feb/Mar '43).

Not long afterward, Wonder Woman learns of a Nazi plot to destroy the Pons Munitions Works, the "biggest high explosive shell plant in the East."

Insisting that only she can thwart the scheme, the baroness begs Wonder Woman to allow her to return to America long enough to help save the plant, and Wonder Woman agrees. By the time they arrive at the munitions factory, however, the Nazi saboteurs have accelerated their original timetable and the Pons Munitions Works is already in flames. Wonder Woman spies a small boy trapped inside and plunges into the inferno to save him, leaving Baroness Paula von Gunther outside, in handcuffs, in the custody of Steve Trevor.

Knowing, however, that the Nazi plot included the planting of a time bomb inside the burning factory, the baroness breaks away from Trevor and races toward the burning building, determined to save Wonder Woman from certain death in the impending explosion:

Seizing a fireman's coat and helmet from a hose truck, Paula plunges into the seething flames. With garments charred by blistering heat, Paula stumbles, exhausted, into the factory basement. As Paula reaches for the bomb a wicked tongue of blue flame sears her face, completely blinding her.

Nevertheless, despite being blinded and badly burned, the baroness manages to find the time bomb and hurl it into a pool of water before collapsing unconscious inside the burning building. Meanwhile, having rescued the small boy and carried him to safety, Wonder Woman realizes what the baroness has done and races back into the burning building to find her. After finally locating the unconscious baroness and carrying her outside, Wonder Woman speeds her to a nearby hospital, where the examining physician says her severe burns are all but certain to prove fatal.

In the hospital laboratory, however, Wonder Woman produces a supply of "Amazon anti-oxygenation ointment," which, applied to the baroness's burns, heals them like magic, and afterward, as Diana Prince, she receives permission to remain in the hospital as the baroness's nurse.

"My dear," confides the baroness to Diana, unaware that she is secretly Wonder Woman, "I know you are here as my jailer! Don't worry--I shan't run away. **Wonder Woman** has changed my personality. I intend to stand trial for my sins!"

When the baroness has finally recovered from her injuries and been released from the hospital, she is brought to trial for murder and sabotage, with Wonder Woman committed to playing a key role in her defense.

"I'll prove this prisoner was guilty of murder—" exclaims the prosecutor in his opening statement.

"I object, your honor!" interjects Wonder Woman. "The prisoner was tried, convicted and executed for that crime! She cannot be tried again!"

Wonder Woman's objection is promptly sustained and the murder count stricken from the baroness's indictment.

"What would **you** do if your little child were threatened with torture and death?" pleads Wonder Woman to the jury. "Wouldn't **you** think it was right to do what you were told — wouldn't **you** go temporarily insane? This woman has atoned! She saved my life — at a horrible price! Look —"

Stepping to the defendant's chair, Wonder Woman rips away the baroness's black veil, revealing her hideously scarred face. The jury gasps.

"I bear these scars gladly for **Wonder Woman,**" proclaims the baroness, "— she has given me a new soul!"

Paula is found not guilty and promptly freed.

"For me you have performed miracles!" says Paula to Wonder Woman. "My life belongs to you — use it as you will!"

"Then I command you first to come to Paradise Island," replies Wonder Woman. "I must consult the will of the goddess!"

On Paradise Island, Wonder Woman and Paula kneel in supplication in APHRODITE'S temple, awaiting the wisdom of the goddess.

Finally, Aphrodite speaks. "I will accept Paula as my slave," intones the goddess, "when she has passed the tests. I accept her now as a neophyte, under your instruction. First I will give her new features to express her new beauty of character!"

Soon afterward, "in the secret creation room" on Paradise Island, "Queen Hippolyte herself works with skillful fingers on the pitifully scarred face of Paula von Gunther." With practiced fingers and a special clay, Hippolyte creates a new face to replace the one horribly disfigured in the munitions factory fire.

"You have done well, Hippolyte," says Aphrodite when the painstaking work is finally complete, "— the features you have moulded for my neophyte truly reveal her inner self! With these golden rays of light I give your sculpture **life!**"

As the goddess speaks, Paula's new face — serene and beautiful — comes miraculously to life. Gazing upon her new features in the mirror, Paula can hardly believe her eyes. "That is not the old Paula — no!" she exclaims happily. "But it is the real **I** — the woman who has long been buried beneath hate and evil!"

Later, when she is alone, Wonder Woman makes a solemn vow: "I have tied myself with the magic lasso and now I command you, Diana Prince--

Wonder Woman, **never** to use your influence over Paula for your own selfish purposes or to make yourself feel smart. It's a tremendous responsibility to shape another girl's life and I **must** do it right!" (WW No. 3/4, Feb/Mar '43: "Ordeal of Fire!").

In April–May 1943 Paula von Gunther and her former slave girls are still on Reform Island, tirelessly "undergoing training for Aphrodite's service." Paula, a brilliant scientist and inventor, has "rebuilt all [her] misused inventions for Aphrodite's service," so that they may be employed for good purposes instead of evil ones.

The slave girls, however, are still loath to accept their freedom, and frequently commit minor infractions of Amazon rules for the express purpose of inviting punishment. "I believe these girls disobey," thinks Mala, "because they like to be disciplined!"

After Paula has passed a series of strenuous strength tests required of Aphrodite's initiates, Wonder Woman takes her once again to Aphrodite's temple, where the goddess informs Paula that she must now "perform successfully three labors of love," the first of which is "to save women of America from destruction by evil followers of Mars" (see MARS [the god of war]), specifically, from a diabolical Japanese plot to drive America's women insane with man-hatred by means of specially bred "Japanese gnats" contaminated with a ghastly "womania" bacillus.

"They little bugs like fleas," confesses a captured Japanese intelligence agent, "— carry new **'womania'** germ — make woman bitten by Jap gnats hate all men — attack them!"

Realizing that, if successful, ". . . the terrible Jap plan . . . would turn all American women against the men — [and] cause a civil war," Wonder Woman and Paula race against the clock to "exterminate the Nipponese peril," and finally succeed in obtaining a complete list of the Japanese spies involved in the "womania germ" plot, thus enabling U.S. Army intelligence agents to apprehend them before they can unleash their bacillus-laden gnats on an unsuspecting America (WW No. 4/1).

The second great labor Aphrodite assigns to Paula is to "capture the men of the underworld," a labor she performs successfully with the heroic assistance of Wonder Woman (WW No. 4/2, Apr/May '43). (See BLAKFU.)

While undergoing her tests for Aphrodite's service, Paula establishes, under Wonder Woman's direction, a secret scientific laboratory on the campus of the HOLLIDAY COLLEGE FOR WOMEN in Washington, D.C. Situated "in secret rooms beneath the Holliday [College] steam plant," the laboratory houses numerous Amazon devices along with Paula's own miraculous inventions.

Meanwhile, Aphrodite informs Paula that "Thy third and hardest labor shall be to change the characters of men, and make them serve their fellow humans." This labor brings Paula and Wonder Woman into conflict with IVAR TORGSON and a group of unscrupulous rubber magnates, but Paula's scientific genius makes possible the reforming of Torgson and his cohorts, thus enabling Paula to pass her third and final test for Aphrodite's service (WW No. 4/3, Apr/May '43).

"I accept thee," intones the goddess proudly, "as initiate in the service of love and beauty!"

Henceforth, Paula must wear "both wrist and ankle bands" as "symbols of submission to Aphrodite," but Paula dons the metal bands gladly, knowing that they will "keep [her] safe in the murderous world of men!" Paula's daughter Gerta is kidnapped from Paradise Island during this period by the vengeful ex-slave MAVIS, but Gerta is rescued soon afterward through the heroic efforts of Wonder Woman (WW No. 4/4, Apr/May '43).

In June–July 1943 Paula helps Wonder Woman, Steve Trevor, Etta Candy, and the Holliday Girls defeat the forces of the war god Mars and restore control of the MOON to the goddess DIANA (WW No. 5/2).

In July 1943, after the removal of her Amazon bracelets has sent Wonder Woman on a rampage of destruction, it is Paula who captures her with the magic lasso and brings an end to her "mad orgy of strength" (Sen No. 19: "The Unbound Amazon"). (*See* MAVIS.)

WITH ALL HER AMAZON-TAUGHT STRENGTH, PAULA STRAINS DESPERATELY AT HER BONDS.

© NPP 1944

Baroness Paula von Gunther in her role as Wonder Woman's ally

In September 1943, after Wonder Woman has been drugged into submission by AMERICAN ADOLF, she is restored to normal by means of an antidote administered by Paula and the Holliday Girls (Sen No. 21: "War Against Society").

In December 1943, after Aphrodite has provided Wonder Woman with "an idea for controlling [her] airplane by mental radio," it is Paula and Mala who construct the necessary apparatus and install it in the plane (Sen No. 24: "Adventure of the Pilotless Plane"). (*See* WONDER WOMAN [section C 4, the robot plane].)

By Winter 1943 Paula has invented the "airglobe," a miraculous means of air travel which is "held in the air like the Earth, by the sun's attraction," and "made of submagnum, a metal Paula discovered, which is magnetically sensitive to the sun." A glimpse of the future in Queen Hippolyte's magic sphere (*see* AMAZONS [section F 2, the magic sphere]) reveals that by the year 3700 A.D. Paula's airglobe will have become the "common method of travel" (WW No. 7/3: "The Secret Weapon").

In March 1944 Paula outwits unscrupulous businessman ELY CLOSE when he attempts to steal Wonder Woman's secret formula for high octane fuel tablets (Sen No. 27: "The Fun Foundation").

In August 1944 Paula rescues Wonder Woman from electrocution at the hands of the CRIME CHIEF (Sen No. 32: "The Crime Combine").

By Spring 1945 Paula has helped Wonder Woman construct the "electro-chemical space transformer," a scientific device making possible instantaneous transportation between Earth and the planet VENUS. During this period, Paula becomes embroiled in Wonder Woman's struggle with the THIRD WORLD WAR PROMOTERS (WW No. 12/1–3: no title; "The Ordeal of Fire"; "The Conquest of Venus"). (*See* DESIRA [QUEEN].)

In May–June 1946 Paula uses her "space transformation machine" to send Wonder Woman and Steve Trevor into the past, to ancient Rome, where Wonder Woman defeats the dictator SULLA (WW No. 17/1: "The Winds of Time").

In July 1946 Paula becomes embroiled in Wonder Woman's battle with the terrifying BUGHUMANS (Sen No. 55: "The Bughuman Plague").

In August–September 1946 Wonder Woman transforms young DON ELLIOT from a budding juvenile delinquent into a useful citizen with the aid of Paula's "introspection machine" (CC No. 16: "The Battle of Desires").

In January–February 1947 Paula, Wonder Woman, Etta Candy, and the Holliday Girls are held captive for a time on the "atom world" of QUEEN ATOMIA (WW No. 21/1: "The Mystery of the Atom World").

Wonder Woman, Steve Trevor, and Baroness Paula von Gunther in the baroness's secret laboratory, 1946

In March–April 1949 the DUKE OF DECEPTION invades Paula's secret laboratory, locks Paula inside a torpedo case in the corner of the room, and then uses her "transmaterialization machine" to literally steal the campus of Holliday College (WW No. 34: "The Mystery of the Rhyming Riddle!" chs. 1–3 — "Deception Strikes Again"; "The Phantasms of Deception!"; "The Mystery of the Rhyming Riddle!").

In November–December 1950 Paula becomes embroiled in Wonder Woman's battle with the ruthless MASTER DE STROYER (WW No. 44: "The Monarch of the Sargasso Sea!" chs. I–III — no title; "Wonder Woman's Decision"; "The Final Battle of the Sargasso Sea").

In January–February 1951 PROF. LUXO invades Paula's secret laboratory, locks her in a closet, and uses her "atom-transferer" to journey into the mysterious "world of the atom" (Sen No. 101: "Battle for the Atom World!").

In an adventure recorded in Wonder Woman No. 163/2, Wonder Woman battles and defeats the ruthless Paula von Gunta, a villainess clearly intended to represent Baroness Paula von Gunther prior to her becoming Wonder Woman's friend and ally (Jul '66: "Danger--Wonder Woman!"). The text is marred, however, by numerous inconsistencies and factual errors.

GUTENBERG, JOHANN (*ca.* **1398–1468**). The inventor of printing in Europe. WONDER WOMAN rescues Gutenberg from criminals intending to kill him and destroy his printing press during a time journey to Mainz, Germany, in the year 1451 (WW No. 69/2, Oct '54: "The Secret Hall of Fame!").

GYPSO, PADDY. The evil chief of a band of Irish Gypsies who pitch camp in Gilrock's Glen, U.S.A., in May–June 1948. He is the rival of Dion Boru, a good Gypsy, for the hand of Tama, "prettiest of Gypsy maidens."

While ETTA CANDY and the HOLLIDAY GIRLS are visiting the Gypsy encampment at Gilrock's Glen to have their fortunes told, Paddy Gypso murders Dion Boru with a knife, takes the Holliday Girls captive to prevent them from betraying him to the authorities, and then flees to Ireland with his followers. When WONDER WOMAN pursues Paddy Gypso to Ireland, she is taken captive herself, but ultimately she escapes and rescues her friends from the villain's clutches.

Paula (*see* GUNTHER, PAULA VON [BARONESS]), meanwhile, has brought Dion Boru back to life by means of Wonder Woman's life-giving "purple ray" (*see* AMAZONS [section G, Amazon science]), and before long Boru has returned to Ireland and defeated Paddy Gypso in a fair fight, thereby establishing himself as "king of all the Irish Gypsies" and winning the right, by Gypsy tradition, to marry Tama, the girl of his choice (WW No. 29/2: "Tale of the Tigers").

H

HALL, JOAN. An elevator operator who is dissatisfied with her job because she feels that it is useless, trivial, and unimportant. Her job takes on new meaning for her in January–February 1950, however, when WONDER WOMAN proves to her that her job is actually "vital and exciting! No one is unimportant in a democracy," insists Wonder Woman, "--and that goes for his job!" (WW No. 39/1: "The Trail of Thrills!").

HAPPY SHAMROCK LAND. *See* SHAMROCK LAND.

HARSH, BERTRAM. The uncompromising authoritarian who is the rival of humanitarian Suzan Patience for the post of warden at a new women's prison. Harsh's attempt to sabotage Patience's program of progressive prison reform is thwarted by WONDER WOMAN.

In July–August 1948 two applicants are being considered for the post of warden at the new women's prison: "famous woman penologist" Suzan Patience, who would institute the constructive rehabilitative programs that have proven so successful on TRANSFORMATION ISLAND, and Bertram Harsh, a repressive authoritarian who believes that "Force and punishment are the only things a prisoner understands! Break his spirit," promises Harsh sternly, ". . . and he'll never break the law again! Let me be the warden, and I'll show you a model prison where prisoners won't dare to even whisper!"

Largely on the basis of Wonder Woman's recommendation, Suzan Patience is appointed to the warden's post on a trial basis, but to keep the job permanently she must make good her promise to transform the prison into a model facility within one week, with the understanding that if any trouble erupts in the interim, the post will go to Bertram Harsh.

Determined to discredit Patience and her methods in the eyes of the authorities, Harsh and his henchmen employ a diabolical gas to inflame the minds of the prisoners and provoke a riot, but Wonder Woman apprehends the villains and thwarts Harsh's scheme to replace humanitarianism in the women's prison with brutal repression (WW No. 30/3: "A Human Bomb!").

HATOR. A far-distant planet with a "loveless, lawless population." Ultimately destroyed by a titanic explosion, Hator was once the home of the villainess BADRA (CC No. 25, Feb/Mar '48: "Hatred of Badra!").

HATRA (Countess). The evil cousin of King Ritio, benevolent ruler of Pogolano, a South Sea Island kingdom where pogo sticks are the principal means of transportation. An attempt by Countess Hatra to seize power in Pogolana is thwarted by WONDER WOMAN.

In August–September 1948, after leading a successful insurrection against King Ritio and imprisoning the king and his followers, Countess Hatra flies to America to assassinate the king's daughter, Princess Selina, currently a student at the HOLLIDAY COLLEGE FOR WOMEN, so as to forestall the possibility of her returning to Pogolana to claim her father's throne.

Hatra's attempts to murder Selina are repeatedly thwarted by Wonder Woman, but soon afterward, in Pogolana, Wonder Woman, Selina, and the HOLLIDAY GIRLS are taken prisoner by Countess Hatra and her fellow conspirators. Wonder Woman turns the tables on her captors, however, and, aided by citizens of Pogolana loyal to King Ritio, defeats Hatra and her henchmen and restores King Ritio to his throne (CC No. 28: "The Sinister Countess Hatra!").

HELEN OF THE SOUTH SEAS (Queen). The queen of a mysterious South Sea Island kingdom who is a direct descendant of Helen of Troy. According to the text, Queen Helen is the "last of the royal line of those who fled the downfall of Troy and found a haven on [a] hidden isle!" Helen and her subjects, who are completely ignorant of the modern world and continue to live and dress much as their classical ancestors did, are determined to create a mighty armada and "rid the seas of the Greeks," whom they still regard as their hated enemies, in order to avenge "our defeat at Troy."

In March–April 1951, after STEVE TREVOR has vanished while investigating the mysterious disappearance of American merchant vessels in the South Seas, WONDER WOMAN investigates and soon learns that Trevor and the missing ships have fallen into the hands of Queen Helen of the South Seas and her Trojan warriors. Helen, who regards Trevor as "the very image of that Paris whom my ancestor loved," wants Trevor to rule at her side and help her vanquish the hated Greeks, and refuses to believe him when he insists that the ancient world no longer exists.

Wonder Woman finally invades the island kingdom, rescues Trevor and the imprisoned American seamen, and defeats the mighty Trojan warriors whom Queen Helen sends against her. Having vanquished the Trojans' greatest fighters, Wonder Woman is hailed as their new queen, but she modestly declines the honor, asking instead that Helen promise to rule her island kingdom with kindness and abandon her misguided dream of war with the Greeks (Sen No. 102: "The Queen of the South Seas!").

HENYA, SONTAG. The leader of a band of ruthless "anarchists" who attempt to seize power in the Atlantean country of VENTURIA in November 1944. Sontag Henya is defeated, and peace restored to Venturia, through the heroic efforts of WONDER WOMAN.

Summoned to Venturia in November 1944, Wonder Woman finds the reign of the benevolent monarch OCTAVIA threatened by a band of anarchists led by the treacherous Sontag Henya. Wonder Woman successfully defuses the incipient rebellion, however, by persuading Octavia and her subjects to do away with the monarchy and establish a democracy in its stead. In the free elections that follow, the widely-respected Octavia is elected president of Venturia.

Bitter at their electoral defeat and determined to wreak vengeance on Wonder Woman, Sontag and her anarchists, feigning friendship, invite her to attend a lavish reception. Then:

> Unseen by **Wonder Woman,** her apparent admirers clasp electric wires to her bracelets. A paralyzing current surges through **Wonder Woman's** body and the Amazon girl stands rigid and helpless.

"Thou shalt dance in thy chains until thou tire," gloats Sontag Henya, after Wonder Woman has been bound with massive chains and her bracelets have been welded together by men to deprive her of her Amazon strength (see WONDER WOMAN [section C 2, the bracelets of submission]), "— then thou shalt die!"

Thus robbed of her superhuman strength, and surrounded by sadistic Venturian anarchists intending to destroy her as soon as she falters in her dance, Wonder Woman dances on and on, propelled by superhuman endurance, until finally one of her "tormentors," impatient for the kill, gives her a hard shove, sending her sprawling. The bloodthirsty anarchists are on the verge of tearing Wonder Woman to pieces when STEVE TREVOR arrives on the scene and "severs the chain between Wonder Woman's bracelets" with a well placed pistol shot, thus restoring her Amazon strength and enabling her to defeat Sontag Henya and her followers (Sen No. 35: "Girls Under the Sea").

HERCULES. The most famous Greek legendary hero, a mighty hunter and warrior born to Alcmene and fathered by Zeus. His use of guile to defeat and enslave the AMAZONS — and their subsequent liberation through the divine intervention of APHRODITE — marked a turning point in Amazon history and led to their flight from AMAZONIA to the cloistered seclusion of PARADISE ISLAND, a paradise for women only, "which no man may enter" (WW No. 1/1, Sum '42). (See AMAZONS [section A, History].)

HESSENPFEFFER, RUDOLPH. An alias employed by the GENTLEMAN KILLER during his sojourn in SHAMROCK LAND (WW No. 14/2–3, Fall '45: "The Gentleman Killer Strikes Again!"; no title).

HEYDAY, JOEL. The unscrupulous son of wealthy Grandma Heyday. The Heyday triplets — Lillie, Millie, and Tillie — are Joel Heyday's adopted sisters.

In July 1945, after Grandma Heyday has drawn up a will leaving her entire fortune to Tillie, Joel Heyday hires a gang of criminals to kidnap Tillie so that he can force her to sign over her inheritance preparatory to murdering his mother and absconding with the fortune. The Heyday triplets are so nearly identical, however, that the criminals mistakenly abduct Lillie and Millie before finally kidnapping the proper triplet, but WONDER WOMAN rescues all three triplets from the villains' clutches and apprehends Joel Heyday and his hired henchmen (Sen No. 43: "Three Pretty Girls").

HIPPOLYTA (Queen). See HIPPOLYTE (QUEEN).

HIPPOLYTE (Queen). The ruler of the AMAZONS and the mother of Princess Diana, the lovely Amazon who battles crime and injustice as WONDER WOMAN. As queen of PARADISE ISLAND, Hippolyte is the leader of the Amazons in peace and war, the custodian of APHRODITE's temple and the guardian of Aphrodite's law, and the keeper of ATHENA's magic sphere and Aphrodite's magic girdle. So long as Hippolyte wears the magic girdle, the Amazons will remain unconquerable. (See also AMAZONS [section B, Aphrodite's Law; F 2, the magic sphere; F 1, the magic girdle].)

Queen Hippolyte is serene, lovely, courageous, and wise. In the early texts, she is portrayed as a brunette who, except for her hairdo and style of dress, is a virtual look-alike for her daughter Diana, but from May 1958 onward, she is generally

AH--**HERE** IT IS! HM--" THE GERMANIC WAR DEITIES WERE GIVEN PSYCHIC LIFE BY THE MASS DESIRES OF THE GERMAN PEOPLE DURING WORLD WAR # 2, INCLUDING THE GREAT GOD ODIN AND HIS VALKYRIES--BUT WHERE IS VALHALLA?

© NPP 1946

Queen Hippolyte, 1946

portrayed as a blonde (WW No. 98: "The Million Dollar Penny!" pts. 1–3 — "The Secret Amazon Trials!"; "The Undersea Menace!"; "The Impossible Bridge!"). From January–February 1953 onward, her name is usually rendered as Hippolyta (WW No. 57/1: "The Man Who Shook the Earth!").

In ancient times, the goddess Aphrodite "shaped with her own hands a race of super women, stronger than men."

"I will breathe life into these women," intoned the goddess, "and also the power of love! They shall be called 'Amazons.'"

The queen of the Amazons was named Hippolyte. Aphrodite "gave her own magic girdle to the Amazon queen" and promised the Amazons that "so long as your leader wears this magic girdle you . . . shall be unconquerable!"

Strengthened by the miraculous power of the magic girdle, Hippolyte singlehandedly defeated the mighty HERCULES when he led an army of Greek warriors against her, but Hercules beguiled her with words of love, seized the magic girdle, and, calling his men to arms, conquered and enslaved the Amazons. Aphrodite finally delivered the Amazons out of the hands of the Greeks, but only on the condition that they abandon their ancestral home in ancient AMAZONIA for a new home on Paradise Island (WW No. 1/1, Sum '42). (*See* AMAZONS [section A, History].)

On Paradise Island, under the direction of Athena, goddess of wisdom, Hippolyte learned "the secret art of moulding a human form" and sculpted the image of an infant girl.

Hippolyte adores the tiny statue she has made as Pygmalion worshiped Galatea. Aphrodite, granting

the queen her prayer, bestows upon it the divine gift of life!

"I name thee Diana," intoned the goddess, "after the moon goddess, mistress of the chase!"

It is this child, grown to maturity, who later journeyed to the "man's world" to battle the forces of injustice as Wonder Woman (WW No. 1/1, Sum '42).

A later text asserts that the infant Diana was the product of a union between Queen Hippolyte and an unnamed warrior subsequently "lost at sea" (WW No. 152/2, Feb '65: "Wonder Girl's Mysterious Father!"), but this text is replete with factual errors and may safely be dismissed as inaccurate.

In December 1941–January 1942, at the divine behest of Aphrodite and Athena, Hippolyte organizes a great tournament to determine "the strongest and wisest of the Amazons." This tournament leads directly to the emergence of Princess Diana as Wonder Woman (AS No. 8: "Introducing Wonder Woman"). (*See* WONDER WOMAN [section A, Origin].)

In June 1942 Hippolyte summons Wonder Woman to Paradise Island to receive the miraculous magic lasso which has been prepared for her at the command of Athena and Aphrodite (Sen No. 6). (*See* WONDER WOMAN [section C 3, the magic lasso].)

In February–March 1943 Hippolyte orders the construction of a prison facility on Reform Island (*see* TRANSFORMATION ISLAND) to house BARONESS PAULA VON GUNTHER and "a boatload of her slave girls" captured by Wonder Woman and her sister Amazons (WW No. 3/1).

In Fall 1943 the CHEETAH kidnaps Hippolyte and steals her magic girdle, but Wonder Woman soon recovers the girdle and rescues her mother from the villainess's clutches (WW No. 6/3: "The Conquest of Paradise").

In Winter 1943, after gazing into her magic sphere, Hippolyte makes the following pronouncements concerning the future:

In 3700 A.D., the whole world will be one nation called United States of Earth. Present-day countries will be states in the global union. The world capitol will be an island named Harmonia. Men and women will be equal. But woman's influence will control most governments because women are more ready to **serve others unselfishly!** [WW No. 7/1: "The Adventure of the Life Vitamin"].

In February 1944 Hippolyte peers several days into the future with her magic sphere and learns to her horror that her daughter will soon succumb to a toxic gas employed by Duke Dalgan, leader of a gang of ruthless "international racketeers."

Forbidden, like all Amazons, to leave the safety and security of Paradise Island, Hippolyte asks Aphrodite for a special dispensation "to visit the world of men and help my daughter in her dire need!"

Aphrodite grants the queen's request, but insists that Hippolyte keep her true identity a secret in the world of men, even from Wonder Woman, and that she return to Paradise Island within three days.

Queen Hippolyte and Wonder Woman, 1945

And so, "for the first time in 4000 years the Amazon queen leaves Paradise Island" and journeys to America, determined to save her daughter from the fate depicted in the magic sphere. After transforming herself into a Wonder Woman look-alike by letting down her hair and donning a costume identical to her daughter's, Hippolyte overpowers Wonder Woman and, binding her with the magic lasso, compels her to agree to allow herself to be impersonated for three whole days. By taking her daughter's place, Hippolyte hopes to save her from the fate foretold in the magic sphere, if necessary by allowing Duke Dalgan to kill her instead of Wonder Woman.

Even an Amazon queen, however, is powerless to change the future, and before long the real Wonder Woman has been gassed into submission by Duke Dalgan and left tied to a railroad track to await a horrifying death beneath the wheels of an oncoming train. Hippolyte saves her daughter, however, by communicating with her "telepathically" and providing her with the information she needs to escape Dalgan's diabolical deathtrap. Once freed, Wonder Woman apprehends Dalgan easily. Hippolyte returns to Paradise Island, leav-

ing behind a puzzled Wonder Woman — who cannot imagine who her impersonator could have been — and a short note signed only "The Masquerader" (Sen No. 26: "The Masquerader").

In October–November 1946 Hippolyte leads her Amazons in a fierce battle with GUNDRA and her bloodthirsty VALKYRIES (CC No. 17: "The Valkyries' Prey"). (*See* ODIN.)

In June–July 1947 Hippolyte is among the Amazons taken prisoner by QUEEN SHARKEETA and the terrifying mermaid sharks, but she and the other captives are rescued soon afterward by Wonder Woman and MALA (CC No. 21: "The Seige [sic] of the Flying Mermaids!"). (*See* SHARKEETA [QUEEN].)

In August–September 1947 Hippolyte and Wonder Woman are taken captive by SATURNETTE and imprisoned aboard a Saturnian spacecraft. Wonder Woman engineers their escape, however, and the Saturnian invaders are soon defeated (CC No. 22: "The Captives of Saturnette!").

Queen Hippolyte held captive by Eviless, 1948

Adolf Hitler

In March–April 1948 Hippolyte becomes embroiled in Wonder Woman's struggle with VILLAINY INCORPORATED (WW No. 28/1–3: "Villainy Incorporated!"; "Trap of Crimson Flame"; "In the Hands of the Merciless!").

In November–December 1948 Hippolyte leads the Amazon space fleet in an assault on a Uranian space armada commanded by the ruthless Uvo (WW No. 32/1: "Uvo of Uranus!" pts. 1–2 —"The Amazing Global Theft!"; "Thunder in Space!").

In January–February 1949 Hippolyte and her Amazons are taken captive by INVENTA, but they are ultimately rescued through the heroic efforts of Wonder Woman (WW No. 33/1: "The Four Dooms" pts. 1–2 —"Paradise Island Condemned!"; "The Titanic Trials!").

In September–October 1953 Hippolyte falls into a mysterious "death-like sleep" after donning a ruby ring belonging to the genii ZOXAB (WW No. 61/2: "Prisoners of the Ruby Ring!").

In October 1957 Hippolyte is carried off by the MERMEN and rescued by Wonder Woman (WW No. 93/1: "Menace of the Mermen!").

In October 1965, after Wonder Woman and STEVE TREVOR have been annihilated in an atomic explosion, Hippolyte and her Amazons use a newly invented miracle of Amazon science — the AS-R or "atomic structure reassembly" beam — to reassemble their scattered atoms and bring them back to life again (WW No. 157: "I--the Bomb!"). (See EGG FU [THE FIRST].)

In November–December 1968 Hippolyte summons Wonder Woman to Paradise Island to inform her that the Amazons "must journey to another dimension, to rest and renew our powers," and to ask her if she wishes to come with them.

"I love you, mother . . ." replies Wonder Woman, "you and my sister Amazons! But . . . I must stay!"

Soon afterward, as Wonder Woman streaks away from Paradise Island in her Amazon plane (see WONDER WOMAN [section C 4, the robot plane]), she sees Paradise Island "shimmer, dissolve, [and] vanish . . . leaving only the azure ocean . . ." (WW No. 179: "Wonder Woman's Last Battle!"). (See DOCTOR CYBER.)

HITLER, ADOLF (1889–1945). The Austrian-born politician who was dictator of Germany from 1933 until his death by suicide in his Berlin bunker in 1945. Hitler dispatches FAUSTA GRABLES to America in Spring 1943 with orders "to bring Wonder Woman back [to Germany] dead or alive," but WONDER WOMAN apprehends Fausta and her Axis cohorts, described as "America's most deadly enemies!" (CC No. 2: "Wanted by Hitler, Dead or Alive").

HOLLIDAY COLLEGE FOR WOMEN. The Washington, D.C., women's college which is the home of the HOLLIDAY GIRLS — the Beeta Lamda sorority sisters, led by ETTA CANDY, who function from February 1942 onward as the student allies of WONDER WOMAN (Sen No. 2). The secret laboratory of BARONESS PAULA VON GUNTHER, Wonder Woman's close friend and ally, is located "in secret rooms beneath the Holliday [College] steam plant . . ." (WW No. 4/3, Apr/May '43).

The Holliday College administration has included such diverse personalities as DEAN STRIKT (WW No. 10/3, Fall '44: "Wonder Woman's Boots!"), DEAN PICKLEPUSS (WW No. 17/2, May/Jun '46: "The Redskins' Revenge"), and DEAN MEG MERRILY (née Sourpuss) (WW No. 16/1, Mar/Apr

'46: "The Secret of the Dark Planet!"; and others).
DR. HEZEKIAH DEACON, the president of Holliday
College, is apprehended by Wonder Woman in Fall
1942 for conspiring with the Nazis to loot the
United States Treasury (WW No. 2/2).

The Holliday College faculty has included such
luminaries as PROFESSOR ASTRONIMO, professor of
astronomy (WW No. 22/3, Mar/Apr '47: "Jealousy
Visits the Winged Women of Venus!"; and others);
PROF. CALCULUS, the "famed mathematician" (CC
No. 29, Oct/Nov '48: "Machine of Schemes");
PROF. CHEMICO, the "brilliant chemist and authority on ancient Egyptian history" (WW No. 23/2,
May/Jun '47: "The Vanishing Mummy!"; and others); PROFESSOR HOMOS, the "famous anthropologist" (Sen No. 39, Mar '45: "In the Clutches of
Nero"); CAPT. SEADUNK, professor of oceanography (WW No. 44, Nov/Dec '50: "The Monarch of
the Sargasso Sea!" chs. I–III—no title; "Wonder
Woman's Decision"; "The Final Battle of the Sargasso Sea"); and PROF. ZOOL, a leading researcher
in the field of human evolution (WW No. 9/1, Sum
'44: "Evolution Goes Haywire!"; and others). PROF.
VIBRATE, a Holliday College physics professor, is
exposed by Wonder Woman as the leader of a gang
of bank robbers in March 1947 (Sen No. 63: "The
Wail of DOOM!").

Holliday College is stolen by the DUKE OF DE-
CEPTION in March–April 1949, but it is recovered
soon afterward through the heroic efforts of Won-
der Woman (WW No. 34: "The Mystery of the
Rhyming Riddle!" chs. 1–3—"Deception Strikes
Again"; "The Phantasms of Deception!"; "The
Mystery of the Rhyming Riddle!").

HOLLIDAY GIRLS, THE. The students of the
HOLLIDAY COLLEGE FOR WOMEN in Washington, D.C.,
or, more specifically, the Beeta Lamda sorority
sisters, led by ETTA CANDY, who function from
February 1942 onward as the student allies of
WONDER WOMAN (Sen No. 2).

With the exception of Etta Candy, the president
of Beeta Lamda and the acknowledged leader of
the Holliday Girls, the Holliday Girls are an ever-
changing group: frequently the texts provide no
names for them, or only first names, and the
names are almost never consistent from text to
text. As employed in this encyclopedia, the term
Holliday Girls designates whichever students of
Holliday College happen to be helping Wonder
Woman in the particular adventure being described; it may refer to only two or three girls, or
to a group of as many as a hundred.

Usually, fewer than half a dozen Holliday Girls
participate in any one adventure. Etta Candy,
however, is always among them. Whenever it is
necessary to distinguish between Etta Candy's ac-

tions and those of the other Holliday Girls parti
pating in any given adventure, this encyclope
does so. In cases where Etta Candy participat
with the Holliday Girls as just another member
the group, however, she is included in the ter
Holliday Girls. (*See* CANDY, ETTA.)

HOMOS (Professor). The "famous anthropolog
of Holliday College" (*see* HOLLIDAY COLLEGE F
WOMEN) who leads an expedition to NEW DISCO
ERY ISLAND in March 1945 (Sen No. 39: "In t
Clutches of Nero"). (*See* NERO.)

HOPPY. One of the leprechauns who inhal
SHAMROCK LAND. (*See* SHAGGY.)

HUBERT. The rightful heir to the throne of A
GLONIA. Hubert is an exact double for STE
TREVOR (Sen No. 62, Feb '47: "The Mysterio
Prisoners of Anglonia"). (*See* BLACK ROBERT [
DOGWOOD].)

HUMAN TANK, THE. A ruthless criminal who
chemically treated, bulletproof skin enables him
crash through walls as if they were made of pape
Apprehended by WONDER WOMAN as he flees th
scene of a brazen jewel robbery, the Human Tan
soon escapes from custody by smashing through
prison wall, but Wonder Woman eventually d
feats the villain by blasting him with "constant je
of air pressure" and thereby wearing away th
layers of chemically treated skin that render hi
virtually invulnerable to capture and imprisor
ment.

"Owww—!" cries the Human Tank. "The e
amel compound formula I covered my ski
with—to make it tough—the same kind of coatin
on the teeth--is wearing away!"

With the villain thus deprived of his rock-har
skin, Wonder Woman easily apprehends him (WW
No. 63/1, Jan '54: "The Human Tank!").

HUMMING BIRD ISLE. An island, shaped like
hummingbird, which is the home of Queen Sal
and her daughter Princess Turula. In Decembe
1948 Humming Bird Isle is the scene of WONDE
WOMAN's battle with the evil DUKE DAXO (Se
No. 84: "The Bottle Cast up by the Sea!").

HYPNOTA (the Great). A sinister arch-villainess
possessed of extraordinary hypnotic powers, wh
conceals her true gender beneath an elaborat
male disguise. Her lovely blond twin sister Serva
whom Hypnota completely dominates, serves a
Hypnota's assistant in the celebrated nightclub
and theatrical performances in which Hypnot
astounds her audiences with mind-boggling hyp
notic feats, accomplished by means of the eeri
"blue hypnotic rays" that blaze forth from he
eyes and hands.

In Winter 1944 Hypnota steals a vital top-secre
document—"a copy of [America's] secret defense

plan against Saturn in case they break the [prevailing] peace treaty, arm their commercial space ships and attack Earth" — from STEVE TREVOR by hypnotizing him into surrendering it to Serva and then forgetting completely all that has happened. WONDER WOMAN's efforts to apprehend the "villain" — she does not yet realize that Hypnota is really a woman — and recover the document are repeatedly frustrated by Hypnota's ability to impersonate Serva by simply changing costumes, so that whenever Wonder Woman seems on the verge of capturing Hypnota, her quarry merely poses as her innocent twin and escapes. Wonder Woman finally recovers the stolen document, only to be taken prisoner by Hypnota. She manages to escape and release Hypnota's various mental "slaves" from her baleful hypnotic control, but Hypnota successfully eludes capture (WW No. 11/1: "The Slaves of the Evil Eye").

After briefly impersonating her twin sister Serva, Hypnota changes back into her own masculine costume, 1944

Soon afterward, under the influence of Wonder Woman's magic lasso (*see* WONDER WOMAN [section C 3, the magic lasso]), Serva — a basically good person who is unable to free herself from Hypnota's evil hypnotic domination — provides Wonder Woman with her first real information concerning Hypnota's origins.

"When Hypnota first became a magician," explains Serva, "[she] had no hypnotic power but . . . relied entirely on stage tricks." Serva had performed with Hypnota as Hypnota's assistant.

One day, while they were practicing a stage illusion in which Hypnota pretended to catch a bullet in her teeth, Serva had accidentally shot Hypnota in the head. Hypnota was rushed to a nearby hospital, where a famous surgeon "performed a rare operation involving Hypnota's emotion centers!"

"As Hypnota recovered," continues Serva, "the nurse noticed a strange blue ray which shone from the patient's eyes." Indeed, Hypnota discovered that anyone she gazed at became her mental slave, compelled to obey her every command.

When Hypnota's surgeon entered her hospital room and found her hypnotizing the attending nurse, he realized immediately what must have happened. "Great zounds!" he exclaimed. "That's the blue electric ray of dominance from Hypnota's mid-brain — my operation must have released it! Hm — this is dangerous — it'll give Hypnota an irresistible hypnotic power over other people!"

The surgeon wanted to perform a second operation, to "stop this blue hypnotizing ray," but Hypnota, determined to retain her newly acquired hypnotic powers, placed the surgeon under her mental control and commanded him to abandon the corrective operation.

Upon her recovery, Hypnota forced her nurse to leave her profession and become her assistant, replacing Serva, whom Hypnota transformed into a mental slave. Because Hypnota has used her hypnotic powers to compel Serva to forget everything she has ever learned about her criminal activities, Serva is unable to provide Wonder Woman with any information that might lead to her capture.

When Serva implores Wonder Woman to find her a place to hide so that she can escape from Hypnota's overpowering mental control, Wonder Woman agrees to let her stay at the HOLLIDAY COLLEGE FOR WOMEN until Hypnota can be brought to justice. Hypnota, however, discovers Serva's hiding place, takes her captive, and then returns to Holliday College disguised as Serva and makes hypnotic prisoners of ETTA CANDY and the HOLLIDAY GIRLS, intending to use them as bait to

Serva at the mercy of Hypnota, 1944

lure Wonder Woman to her doom. Wonder Woman ultimately escapes the deathtrap set for her by Hypnota, rescues her friends, and takes the villainess into custody, but because Hypnota is still disguised as Serva, Wonder Woman believes that it is Serva whom she has apprehended, and that Serva abducted the Holliday Girls only because she was compelled to do so by Hypnota. Feigning repentance at having allowed herself to become Hypnota's mental slave once again, the bogus Serva begs Wonder Woman to protect her from ever again falling into Hypnota's clutches (WW No. 11/2, Win '44: "The Unseen Menace").

Soon afterward, Wonder Woman learns that, for years, Hypnota has been using her hypnotic powers to make mental slaves of unsuspecting citizens to enable her to sell them into the clutches of Saturnian slave merchants. When Wonder Woman defeated DUKE MEPHISTO SATURNO and brought an end to the Earth-SATURN slave trade by negotiatin an interplanetary peace treaty with the emperor Saturn (WW No. 10/3, Fall '44: "Wonder Woman Boots!"), Hypnota had found her lucrative slav racket severely curtailed. Because a bootleg traff in earthling slaves had continued to flourish spite of the treaty ban, Hypnota had not been p out of business entirely, but the stiff penalti meted out to Saturn's black-market slavers ha seriously impaired her ability to sell slaves to Sa urn.

Now Hypnota is determined to revive th former interplanetary animosity between Eart and Saturn, reasoning that if war were to brea out between the two planets, both sides woul abrogate the existing peace treaty, enabling th traffic in earthling slaves to begin anew. Hypnot hypnotizes a gang of criminals into stealing a Army bomber and strafing the car carrying Coun Dendum, Saturn's ambassador to the Unite States, in hopes of precipitating an interplanetar incident leading to the resumption of hostilitie between Earth and Saturn, but Wonder Woma thwarts the aerial attack and apprehends the per petrators.

Hypnota then plants some earthling slaves i the Saturnian embassy, hoping to poison relation between Earth and Saturn by making it appea that Count Dendum is secretly engaged in the illicit slave traffic, but Wonder Woman apprehend Hypnota and exposes her scheme to instigate a Earth-Saturn war. It is only now, after havin finally captured the villainous hypnotist, tha Wonder Woman learns that Hypnota is a female and Serva's twin sister. As "Wonder Woman's magic lasso compels Hypnota to release Serva's memory from hypnotic control," Serva becomes free, for the first time, to reveal Hypnota's bizarre story in its entirety:

Oh, now I remember everything! Hypnota and I are twin sisters. Years ago, Hypnota adopted a **man's** costume to do our magic act. She put on [a] phony French accent, too!

Hypnota designed costumes for us which could be [quickly and easily] changed . . . transforming us one into the other. A magician's [smoke] bomb makes smoke enough to hide this change of dress.

After Hypnota developed her **blue hypnotic ray** we continued our old mystery act of changing identities, aided by her new hypnotic power. Later she made people slaves with this power, took away their memories and sold thousands of them to Saturn!

"Ha ha!" laughs Hypnota, still defiant despite her defeat. "It was amusing to pose as Serva, hypnotize people and then escape by blaming it on **myself!**"

Now that Hypnota has been brought to justice, however, Earth-Saturn relations are once again secure and Serva will be free to lead a life of her own (WW No. 11/3, Win '44: "The Slave Smugglers").

In March–April 1948 Hypnota escapes from TRANSFORMATION ISLAND along with seven other villainesses and joins them in forming VILLAINY INCORPORATED (WW No. 28/1–3: "Villainy Incorporated!"; "Trap of Crimson Flame"; "In the Hands of the Merciless!"). (*See* VILLAINY INCORPORATED.)

ICEBERG-LAND. An "unexplored" land in the region of the North Pole, where, "utterly unknown to man, dwell cold-blooded icicle men and lovely snow maidens. Their clever scientists have provided this strange race with modern inventions--even the radio." Ruled by the lovely Princess Snowina, Iceberg-Land is the scene of WONDER WOMAN's encounter with the ruthless PRIME MINISTER BLIZZARD in May–June 1948 (WW No. 29/1: "Ice World's Conquest!").

IMAGE-MAKER, THE. A ruthless villain who inhabits a bizarre "mirror-world" where "the ground, the buildings . . . even the sky itself is a mirror!" His plot to destroy WONDER WOMAN as a prelude to conquering the Earth is thwarted by Wonder Woman in November 1962.

While visiting an amusement-park fun house in November 1962, Wonder Woman finds herself in a polygonal room surrounded by mirrors. Suddenly, her own reflections leap out of the mirrors, seize her from all sides, and drag her back through the mirrors into a bizarre mirror-world inhabited by the Image-Maker, a sinister villain who intends to "paralyze the world with [his] ability to project countless reflections--and so conquer it!"

"I'm using you as a test case!" he gloats. "A guinea pig! Before I invade your world--and conquer it by images alone!"

Because the Image-Maker is only a reflection himself, and not a villain of flesh and blood, he seems virtually unconquerable, but by running faster and faster, and "desperately accelerating to incredible speed, [Wonder Woman] not only becomes invisible, but creates such intense vibrations . . . that the vibrations create a shattering earthquake in the **mirror world**," destroying the Image-Maker and shattering his mirror-world into a trillion glittering fragments (WW No. 134: "Menace of the Mirror-Wonder Woman!").

INFANTA. A far-distant planet inhabited by young girls who are allies of the AMAZONS. Infanta is ruled by the infant QUEEN ASTRA.

In ancient Sparta, "it was the cruel custom to leave the infants they thought were weaklings, mostly girls, in the wild hills to perish during the night."

Unbeknownst to the Spartans, however, the Amazons under QUEEN HIPPOLYTE made a practice

of rescuing the abandoned girls and removing them to a place of safety. The rescued infants would be placed aboard the Amazons' "flying swan planes" and transported to the planet Infanta, where, "because of atmospheric conditions, [the infants] reached [their] full powers at five years and never aged more than that."

Similarly, the followers of the war god MARS would rescue the abandoned Spartan boys and transport them to the planet Duxo, where they would be brought up as cruel warriors in the service of Mars.

According to Wonder Woman No. 36/1, PARADISE ISLAND was invaded sometime in the past by a combined force of Martian men and Duxo boys who subdued the Amazons by means of a special gas. The invaders were routed, however, by a fleet of girl warriors from the planet Infanta — led by Queen Astra and aided by WONDER WOMAN — who raced to the defense of Paradise Island in response to a desperate plea for help from Queen Hippolyte (Jul/Aug '49: "The Girl Who Saved Paradise Island!").

INTERNATIONAL MILK COMPANY. The milk company which serves as a front for BARONESS PAULA VON GUNTHER in her plot to monopolize America's milk supply (Sen No. 7, Jul '42).

INVENTA. A treacherous villainess from the island of Cadmea who is gifted with a "brilliant, inventive mind." She is defeated by WONDER WOMAN in January–February 1949.

Brought to TRANSFORMATION ISLAND to undergo Amazon training and rehabilitation in January–February 1949, Inventa succeeds in freeing herself from her magic Venus girdle (see AMAZONS [section F 3, the magic Venus girdles]) and in recruiting a band of accomplices from among her fellow prisoners. After constructing a small glider and overpowering their Amazon guards, the conspirators soar away from Transformation Island and then ditch their glider in the sea off PARADISE ISLAND, posing as aviatrixes in distress, to entice the unsuspecting AMAZONS into swimming out to rescue them.

As soon as the escapees have been brought ashore on Paradise Island, QUEEN HIPPOLYTE recognizes them as prisoners from Transformation Island, but by then it is too late. Using a debilitating gas and capitalizing on the element of surprise, Inventa and her cohorts overpower Wonder Woman and the Amazons, take Hippolyte hostage, and announce their intention to fly Wonder Woman and Hippolyte to Inventa's homeland, the island of Cadmea, to face "death by the four dooms!"

"Wonder Woman!" gloats Inventa. "You will be first to meet the four dooms! The doom of the rolling stone--the doom of the blinding mirrors-- the doom of the labyrinth--and the doom of the dragon's teeth!"

The four dooms are a series of mighty labors which Wonder Woman must perform successfully in order to save herself and the other Amazons from immediate execution. Despite the fact that the four dooms are seemingly impossible to perform — and that Inventa has unfairly rigged each doom in advance — Wonder Woman manages ultimately to survive them all.

Infuriated by Wonder Woman's unexpected success, Inventa concocts yet another scheme to destroy the Amazons, this time by instructing her accomplice Torcha to fly STEVE TREVOR to Paradise Island in Wonder Woman's Amazon plane (see WONDER WOMAN [section C 4, the robot plane]), knowing that ". . . by Aphrodite's law [the] Amazons lose [their] eternal youth and beauty if a man sets foot on Paradise Island" (see AMAZONS [section B, Aphrodite's Law]).

Torcha flies to America, invites Trevor aboard Wonder Woman's plane, and speeds him toward Paradise Island. Within moments, Wonder Woman's plane — with Torcha at the controls and Steve Trevor at her side — is circling Paradise Island for a landing while, down below on the island, Wonder Woman, bound with her own magic lasso (see WONDER WOMAN [section C 3, the magic lasso]), is being commanded by Inventa to use her mental control over her plane to bring it in for a landing.

As the plane swoops low over Paradise Island, however, Wonder Woman leaps atop one of its wings, jerking the magic lasso from Inventa's hands and thereby freeing herself from the compulsion to obey the villainess's commands. After hastily reversing her instructions to her plane so

that it will not land, Wonder Woman captures all her adversaries and returns them to captivity on Transformation Island, where, hopefully, their "bad character traits" will eventually be expunged "through discipline and love" (WW No. 33/1: "The Four Dooms" pts. 1–2 — "Paradise Island Condemned!"; "The Titanic Trials!").

IRONSIDES (King). The leader of an army of fearsome iron giants who terrorize the natives of Wooloo Island, an American protectorate in the Pacific, until they are finally defeated by WONDER WOMAN and STEVE TREVOR in October–November 1947. King Ironsides is the brother of the infamous DR. PSYCHO.

After travelling to Wooloo Island with ETTA CANDY and the HOLLIDAY GIRLS to investigate reports of native villages being attacked and their people carried off by marauding iron giants, Steve Trevor discovers that a local volcano spews forth pure gold. He has no sooner made this momentous discovery, however, than he and the Holliday Girls are taken captive by the iron giants and taken before their leader, King Ironsides. Etta manages to summon Wonder Woman via mental radio (see WONDER WOMAN [section C 7, the mental radio]), but when Wonder Woman arrives on the scene she too is taken prisoner.

Wonder Woman and Trevor ultimately manage to turn the tables on their captors and to defeat King Ironsides and his army of iron giants, who turn out to be nothing more than "ordinary men on stilts, wearing tremendous suits of armor!"

In the words of King Ironsides:

> . . . I'm [Dr.] Psycho's brother and as brilliant a geologist as he was a hypnotist. I searched for years for a volcano which erupted pure gold!
>
> Then I discovered this volcano on Wooloo. I thought up the idea of the stilts and iron suits to frighten the natives. But I, like my brother, was outwitted by the unconquerable Wonder Woman [CC No. 23: "Siege of the Iron Giants"].

ISHTI. A Japanese spy chief whose plot to blow up a train carrying a group of U.S. Army generals from New York City to the West Coast is thwarted by WONDER WOMAN (Sen No. 10, Oct '42).

J

JACKSON, "CREEPER." A crippled botanical genius whose terrifying "octopus plants" very nearly devour WONDER WOMAN.

By May 1945 unscrupulous businessman Lars Lang has cheated elderly "Creeper" Jackson out of both his real estate business and his private holdings. Determined to see justice done, the emotionally unstable Jackson, a brilliant botanist, has been devoting his time and energy to the development of exotic plants, which he hopes to sell to obtain the funds he needs to sue Lang for the return of his holdings.

When Lang executes yet another unprincipled maneuver in order to evict Jackson from the small plot of land on which he has been cultivating his prize plants, however, the mind of the old botanist snaps completely. Now virtually insane, Jackson uses his most dangerous botanical creation, a terrifying octopus plant, to ensnare Lang's innocent daughter, Lyra Lang, and soon afterward her father. When Wonder Woman, ETTA CANDY, and the HOLLIDAY GIRLS attempt to investigate Lyra Lang's mysterious disappearance, they too are soon trapped in the leafy tentacles of the man-eating plants.

"My plants will consume these people without a trace — leaving no evidence against me!" cackles Jackson, now completely deranged.

In the nick of time, however, STEVE TREVOR appears on the scene and destroys the killer plants by turning out the bright lights needed to sustain them: "In the sudden darkness," observes the textual narrative, "there come peculiar sounds of withering and snapping vines. When light returns, every octopus plant is dead." Etta Candy and the Holliday Girls, Lars and Lyra Lang, and Wonder Woman are all safe.

"You've both committed serious crimes," remarks Wonder Woman to Lars Lang and "Creeper" Jackson, "— but if the property is deeded back to Creeper — and he agrees to mental hospital treatment — you two can have a new start!" (Sen No. 41: "The Octopus Plants").

JAXO, DIRK. A cunning villain, long sought by Army Intelligence for a series of "horrible crimes," who eluded the authorities by feigning death and now returns to launch a spectacular plot to "rule the world" by means of his diabolical "brain wave

interferer" invention. Jaxo is defeated by WONDER WOMAN in May–June 1949.

Although Dirk Jaxo was declared dead five years ago, and his file at Army Intelligence was permanently closed at that time, Jaxo had actually feigned death by means of a special drug so that, following his funeral, his body could be exhumed by his henchmen and revived.

While fleeing from the cemetery following his exhumation, however, Jaxo accidentally tripped and fell into a huge hole — the entrance to a carefully camouflaged secret tunnel — and plummeted downward into "a strange underground world" inhabited by MOLE MEN and Mole Women. By deceitfully persuading the naïve Mole Women that he was "a scientist escaping from evil men who wish to stop me from working on my new invention," Jaxo tricked them into helping him construct a diabolical "brain wave interferer." In Jaxo's words:

> Our thought of doing the simplest thing — walking to school, eating an apple — sets up an electric wave which flashes from the brain to the muscles. Break up these thought waves and people collapse. That's what my brain wave interferer does. No human can resist it! I will rule the world!

Now, with the brain wave interferer finally completed, Jaxo turns on the Mole Women and threatens to destroy them unless they agree to become his allies in a war against the AMAZONS, whom Jaxo regards as his sole obstacle to world conquest. When Jaxo turns his brain wave interferer on the unsuspecting world, people everywhere begin to collapse — at their jobs, on the streets, and in airplanes and cars. On PARADISE ISLAND, the Amazons find their normally superhuman abilities drastically curtailed, but even in their weakened condition they manage to beat off a wave of attacks by Jaxo's Mole Women allies.

"A man is behind this invasion!" reasons Wonder Woman. "If he sets foot on Paradise Island, Aphrodite's law will be broken--our fountain of youth and beauty will dry up and we'll no longer be immortal!"

After deliberately allowing herself to be captured by the Mole Women and taken to Jaxo's subterranean lair, Wonder Woman defeats the villain and destroys his diabolical invention. Jaxo will be turned over to the authorities to stand trial for his crimes, while the Mole Women will be sent to TRANSFORMATION ISLAND to undergo Amazon rehabilitation. "On **Transformation Island**," explains Wonder Woman, "you will be trained to know your own **woman's strength**--that is your best safeguard against fear of male dominance!" (WW No. 35/2: "Jaxo, Master of Thought!").

JENKEL (Prof.). A villain who concocts an elaborate scheme to trap WONDER WOMAN in hopes of collecting a $300,000 reward being offered for her capture by the underworld. Jenkel and his cohorts are apprehended by Wonder Woman in March–April 1951.

Claiming to be interested in making a movie about Wonder Woman, Jenkel approaches circus performers Inez and Joan Lane — twin sisters who are virtual doubles for Wonder Woman — and persuades them to try out for the leading role by impersonating Wonder Woman in real life, ostensibly to see whether they resemble Wonder Woman closely enough to fool ordinary citizens, but actually so that Jenkel can capture Wonder Woman when she appears on the scene to confront her impersonators. When Wonder Woman finally confronts one of the bogus Wonder Women, she is indeed taken prisoner by Jenkel and his henchmen. She soon turns the tables on her captors, however, and apprehends them all (WW No. 46/3: "Wonder Woman's Twin!").

JENKINS, J. J. A millionaire criminal mastermind who attempts to learn WONDER WOMAN's secret identity in May–June 1950. Jenkins strongly suspects that Diana Prince and Wonder Woman are the same person, but Wonder Woman tricks him into believing he has seen both Diana Prince and Wonder Woman simultaneously, then swiftly apprehends Jenkins and his henchmen (WW No. 41/1: "Wonder Woman--Private Detective!").

JONES, BIFTON. A young high school student, bored by ancient history, who becomes an avid ancient history buff after WONDER WOMAN takes him into the past, to Britain in the year 60 A.D., to meet the courageous QUEEN BOADICEA. The time-journey is accomplished by means of the Amazon "trans-materialization machine," a device which "dematerializes a person and materializes him again in any time or place selected" (Sen No. 60, Dec '46: "The Ordeal of Queen Boadicea"). (*See* BOADICEA [QUEEN].)

JOYALA. The capital city of the planet EROS (Sen No. 11, Nov '42).

JUMPA. WONDER WOMAN's favorite kanga (Sen No. 76, Apr '48: "Murder Referees the Round!"). Kangas are gigantic kangaroos which are used by

the AMAZONS for "girl-roping" (Sen No. 6, Jun '42) and other sports (*see* AMAZONS [section E 1, Sports]). It is not clear whether the kangas are the same as the sky kangas, the gigantic kangaroos used by the Amazons for interplanetary travel (*see* AMAZONS [section E 3, Transportation]), but, as portrayed in the texts, the sky kangas would seem to be somewhat larger animals.

Wonder Woman and Jumpa, 1942

JUPITER. The largest of the planets, and the fifth planet from the SUN.

In September–October 1951 WONDER WOMAN thwarts an invasion of Jupiter by the "robot people" of the planet AUTOMATO (Sen No. 105: "The Secret of the Giant Forest").

By February 1954 aliens from Jupiter have set in motion a diabolical plan "to invade the planet Earth via its own **3-D** films . . . !" The first stage of the scheme involves "projecting" hideous science-fiction monsters onto conventional 3-D science-fiction films as "test cases" to determine whether their invasion plan is feasible. When, as the Jovians had anticipated, the specially projected monsters materialize from the movie screens when the films are shown and wreak havoc and destruction on Earth, the would-be invaders next "transfer [their] own molecular structure onto Earth's **3-D** films by the utilization of light rays," intending to overrun the Earth once the films are shown. Wonder Woman thwarts the Jovian scheme, however, and annihilates the invaders, by splicing the 3-D movie film containing the aliens to film footage of an H-bomb explosion and then running the entire film through a projector, thereby producing a cinematic holocaust that destroys the invaders before they can escape from the screen (WW No. 64/1: "The 3-D Terror!").

In April 1954, after a Martian space fleet has conquered the Earth, Wonder Woman finds herself on display in a Jovian museum as one of the last remaining examples of Earth life, now all but extinct (WW No. 65/3: "The Last Amazon!"). (*See* DECEPTION, DUKE OF.)

In May 1957, after her life has been saved by her "identical Jovian counterpart," a "giant-size" Wonder Woman perhaps fifteen times larger than herself, Wonder Woman returns the favor by liberating Jupiter from a band of "space pirates" who have conquered the planet (WW No. 90/1: "Planet of the Giants!").

In April 1958 PROF. ALPHA's "SOS Carrier" transports Wonder Woman into the distant future where she thwarts a Jovian invasion of Earth (WW No. 97: "The Runaway Time Express!" pts. 1–3 – "Stone Age Rodeo!"; "The Day Nature Ran Wild!"; "The Menace of Earth's Twin!").

In November–December 1967, after a Martian space fleet has conquered the Earth, Wonder Woman finds herself on display in a Jovian museum as one of the last remaining examples of Earth life (WW No. 173/2: "Earth's Last Human!"). The story is almost identical to one that appeared in a much earlier text (i.e., WW No. 65/3, Apr '54: "The Last Amazon!"). (*See* DECEPTION, DUKE OF.)

K

KALE, AL. An unscrupulous promoter who attempts to exploit WONDER WOMAN at the onset of her crime-fighting career.

In January 1942, after she has brought the wounded STEVE TREVOR back to the United States from PARADISE ISLAND and deposited him at the Walter Reed Army Hospital in Washington, D.C., Wonder Woman decides to take a stroll through the streets of the nation's capital. Her crime-fighting career has not yet begun — she has not yet even assumed a secret identity (*see* WONDER WOMAN, section B, the secret identity) — and she is still a bewildered newcomer to the "man's world."

While wandering about the city, Wonder Woman foils a bank holdup, cheerfully allowing the gangsters' bullets to ricochet harmlessly off her Amazon bracelets (*see* WONDER WOMAN [section C 2, the bracelets of submission]). Moments later she is approached by Al Kale, who offers to help her put her "bullets and bracelets" act on the stage.

Wonder Woman's astounding performances as a vaudevillian bring her nationwide publicity and a great deal of money. When Kale attempts to abscond with her stage earnings, Wonder Woman overtakes him and recovers her money (Sen No. 1).

KEATING, ABIGAIL. A middle-aged recluse who achieves a happier life through the efforts of WONDER WOMAN.

Since the long-ago day when her fiancé John Hunter left her waiting at the altar, Abigail Keating has been living in the past. Each day, dressed in her yellowed wedding gown, she pathetically re-enacts the wedding that never took place, chats gaily with a nonexistent groom, and glides across an imaginary ballroom with a phantom partner.

Hoping to rescue Abigail from "a useless and bitter old age" by reuniting her with her onetime fiancé, Wonder Woman finally locates John Hunter, only to learn that he has changed his name to Lon Logox and is now the leader of a gang of jewel thieves.

Wonder Woman apprehends the Logox gang and then, carefully and thoughtfully, helps Abigail Keating realize that her ex-fiancé was a bad person not worth waiting for all these years. Gradually, Abigail begins to see that it would be wrong of

Wonder Woman and Abigail Keating, 1949

her to waste the remainder of her life clinging to an unhappy memory, and she resolves to abandon her reclusive existence and rejoin the world of the present (WW No. 38/1, Nov/Dec '49: "The Girl from Yesterday!").

KEELA. One of BARONESS PAULA VON GUNTHER's slave girls. In February–March 1943 Keela stows away aboard WONDER WOMAN's Amazon plane (*see* WONDER WOMAN [section C 4, the robot plane]) and soon finds herself on PARADISE ISLAND, where she attempts unsuccessfully to take Wonder Woman prisoner and is ultimately captured by Wonder Woman and her sister AMAZONS. All the while, however, a "miniature radio transmitter" concealed inside one of Keela's metal wrist bands has been guiding Baroness Paula von Gunther and a shipload of Japanese toward Paradise Island, but Wonder Woman and the Amazons defeat the Japanese invasion force before it can reach the island, and capture the baroness and "a boatload of her slave girls" attempting to sneak ashore (WW No. 3/1).

KEEN (Mr.). The railroad company president who is secretly ANTI ELECTRIC (CC No. 27, Jun/Jul '48: "Anti Electric").

KEIGH, JOHN. A 16th-century man who is aided by WONDER WOMAN during one of her journeys into the past. In February 1955, in response to a 400-year-old appeal for help found sealed in a bottle, Wonder Woman travels back into time to the year 1555, where she rescues John Keigh from death at the hands of idol-worshipping natives on Tegurana Island (WW No. 72/1: "S.O.S. from the Past!").

KENT, VAN. The "head producer" at the Hollywood film studio where junior producer Jay Stanley is shooting the serial *Danger Trail.*

Since filming began, a series of mysterious mishaps have plagued the production. When the star of the film dies in an auto crash, the studio holds a contest to select a replacement and WONDER WOMAN is declared the winner. When shooting resumes, so do the "accidents," but Wonder Woman intervenes on each occasion to prevent the recurring near-tragedies from halting production of the picture and finally apprehends head producer Van Kent, the mastermind behind the plot to sabotage the filming.

"I wanted to break Jay Stanley," confesses Kent, "before he became qualified to hold my position as head producer!" (Sen No. 88, Apr '49: "Wonder Woman Goes to Hollywood!").

KING DIAMOND. An "unscrupulous gambler" who, having bet his entire fortune on prizefighter Rocky Jenks in his upcoming bout with defending champion "Wild" Bill Loomis, attempts, together with his blond accomplice Nina, to force Loomis to lose by default by seeing to it that he fails to appear on the night of the fight.

Their first effort to remove Loomis from contention — by having hoodlum Jim Vrecker, alias the Wrecker, beat Loomis up — fails when the champion fells the Wrecker with one punch, whereupon King Diamond and Nina murder the Wrecker and accuse Loomis of having killed him with his knockout punch, reasoning that Loomis will be arrested and forced to forfeit the upcoming bout.

WONDER WOMAN uncovers the true circumstances surrounding the Wrecker's death, however, exonerates "Wild" Bill Loomis, and apprehends King Diamond and Nina. Soon afterward, Loomis successfully defends his title against contender Jenks (Sen No. 76, Apr '48: "Murder Referees the Round!").

KIPP (Mr.). A Boston, Massachusetts, delicatessen owner and secret fifth columnist who is apprehended by WONDER WOMAN in Winter 1942. In the course of this same adventure, Wonder Woman captures a band of German spies and saboteurs disguised as fishermen who have come ashore on the New England coast, disables the Nazi U-boat which brought the bogus fishermen ashore, and foils a Nazi scheme to "blow up der Salem shipyards" (CC No. 1: "The Mystery of the House of Seven Gables").

KOSMET, "COSMETIC." "Hollywood's greatest make-up artist." In March–April 1947 Kosmet uses a diabolical device of his own invention, "a red ray which bleaches all color," to deplete the faces and hair of movie stars, debutantes, and wealthy society women of all traces of color, leaving their heads a ghostly white. Then, after claiming to have discovered a miraculous "cure" for the mysterious "cosmetic disease" believed to be sweeping Hollywood, Kosmet begins to amass a fortune by charging his wealthy victims $50,000 apiece to restore the color to their hair and complexions. He is about to transform WONDER WOMAN into a mindless slave with another of his fiendish inventions, when STEVE TREVOR arrives on the scene and rescues her from his clutches. Kosmet dies when, in the midst of a brief struggle, he accidentally falls into the path of another of his diabolical devices, an awesome "death ray" (WW No. 22/1: "The Color Thief").

KRAZY K. *See* PLANET K.

KUU-KUU. The ruler of PLANET K.

In January 1962 Kuu-Kuu dispatches an expedition to the planet Earth, under the command of his countryman Kuuu, for the purpose of collecting "specimens" of Earth life. Flying over Earth in their spacecraft, Kuuu and his companions attempt to capture ETTA CANDY, LITA LITTLE, THELMA TALL, TINA TOY, and several other HOLLIDAY GIRLS, only to be repeatedly thwarted by WONDER WOMAN. After their third and final defeat, Kuuu and his somewhat comical fellow aliens race homeward, vowing never to return to Earth again (WW No. 127/1: "Invaders of the Topsy-Turvy Planet").

L

LAKONGA. The capital city of NEPTUNIA (WW No. 15, Win '45: chs. 1–3–"The First Battle of Neptunia"; "The Masters of the Water"; "In the Killer's Cage").

LANCELOT (Sir). In Arthurian legend, the bravest and most famous of the knights of the Round Table, and the lover of King Arthur's queen, GUINEVERE. WONDER WOMAN meets KING ARTHUR and Sir Lancelot when she frees them from the hollow cores of a pair of blazing fireballs, in which they have been imprisoned by the evil MERLIN (WW No. 54/1, Jul/Aug '52: "The Wizard of Castle Sinister!"). (*See* ARTHUR [KING].)

LANDER, ERIC. The American citizen of German descent who is the inventor of the "silent, self-camouflaging space bomber," a revolutionary new aircraft which can be camouflaged to resemble literally anything merely by inserting a photograph of the object to be mimicked inside the aircraft's special "reflectors." Lander helps WONDER WOMAN foil a Nazi plot to blow up the U.S. Capitol Building in Summer 1943.

Taken captive by the Gestapo—who seized the plans for his space bomber—sometime in the recent past, Lander feigned loyalty to the Third Reich and managed to get himself assigned to a post aboard the space bomber when the Nazis finally built it. In Summer 1943 the Nazis commanding the bomber concoct a scheme to "make dis ship look like der Capitol Building" and blow up the real Capitol, "Congress und all," but, with Lander's help, Wonder Woman defeats the Nazis and saves the Capitol Building from destruction (CC No. 3: "The Invisible Invader").

LANE, INEZ and JOAN. Twin sisters, both circus performers, who are virtual doubles for WONDER WOMAN. In March–April 1951 the Lane sisters become the unwitting dupes of PROF. JENKEL in an elaborate scheme to capture Wonder Woman (WW No. 46/3: "Wonder Woman's Twin!"). (*See* JENKEL [PROF.].)

LANG, JASPER. A villainous scientist, apprehended by WONDER WOMAN sometime in the past, who builds a time machine, travels back into time to the period just prior to his capture, and attempts to capitalize on his knowledge of pending events in order to avoid repeating the mistakes that led to his capture. Lang eventually brings

about his own undoing, however, by openly anticipating a future event that he could not possibly have known about unless he had actually lived through the experience once before. When Wonder Woman, thus alerted, gives chase, Lang leaps over a high wall in a desperate attempt to escape, only to find himself, ironically, inside the very prison from which he escaped in his time machine only a short while before (Sen No. 99, Sep/Oct '50: "The Man Who Couldn't Make a Mistake!").

LAPIZURIA. The far-distant planet which is the home of an alien invasion force that lands on Easter Island in April 1954. The Lapizurians are defeated by WONDER WOMAN before they can carry out their scheme to conquer Earth.

By April 1954 a scientific expedition has reported the existence of a gigantic stone statue of Wonder Woman on Easter Island, astonishing because Wonder Woman has never been to Easter Island and cannot possibly have posed for a statue there. Hoping to solve the mystery, Wonder Woman and STEVE TREVOR fly to Easter Island, where they are taken captive by "strange creatures" who identify themselves as inhabitants of the planet Lapizuria.

The Lapizurians, whose faces closely resemble those of Easter Island's famous stone statues, explain that they came to Earth on an exploratory mission intended to precede an all-out invasion by their fellow Lapizurians, only to find themselves hopelessly stranded on Earth, unable either to repair their disabled spacecraft or build a new one. "We built these stone statues of ourselves," explains one alien, "— as a signal to other Lapizurians that we were marooned on this island---"

As time went by and their fellow Lapizurians failed to come to their aid, the marooned aliens became desperate to find a way to return to their home planet. They kidnapped eleven Earth scientists, intending to force them to build a new spaceship for them, but the scientists explained that Earth technology was incapable of the task. By reading the minds of the kidnapped scientists, however, the Lapizurians learned about Wonder Woman, and they constructed the stone statue of her in the hope that she would hear of it and come to Easter Island to investigate. Now, with Wonder Woman in their clutches, the Lapizurians are confident that they can force her to use her Amazon powers to construct a new spacecraft for them.

Realizing that if she were to build a spaceship for the Lapizurians they would only return to Earth in even greater numbers, Wonder Woman refuses to cooperate. Eventually, however, a Lapizurian rescue ship, having spotted the Easter Island statues, comes to the aid of the stranded aliens. The rescued aliens are about to kill Wonder Woman, Steve Trevor, and the eleven kidnapped scientists prior to blasting off, when Wonder Woman turns the tables on her captors and rescues her fellow captives from the aliens' clutches. Throwing her magic lasso (see WONDER WOMAN [section C 3, the magic lasso]) about the Lapizurians' Wonder Woman statue like a sling around a pebble, Wonder Woman "hurls the giant stone at the invading space ship," utterly destroying it and ending the threat of a Lapizurian invasion (WW No. 65/1: "The Stone Slayer!").

LAWBREAKERS' PROTECTIVE LEAGUE, THE. A powerful underworld organization, known also as the Lawbreakers' League, which is headed by Rodriguez Caballos and Ferva Shayne and headquartered in Ferva Shayne's Dancing Conservatory. By October 1945 the league "has grown very powerful. It hides any criminal who'll split his boodle with them and boasts that no crook protected by the league was ever caught." The Lawbreakers' Protective League is smashed by WONDER WOMAN with the aid of STEVE TREVOR.

In October 1945 Ferva Shayne concocts a scheme to end Wonder Woman's interference in the league's underworld activities by arranging for her to marry Steve Trevor. Convinced that Wonder Woman would marry Trevor if only he could somehow dominate her physically, Ferva and the league's co-leader, Rodriguez Caballos, create an ingenious "electronic globe" capable of endowing Trevor with superhuman strength for thirty minutes at a time.

"Nobody can kill that wench," explains Ferva, "but Trevor can subdue her! Once she marries **him** the mighty Amazon'll become a meek housewife who will never bother us! If Trevor becomes **stronger than Wonder Woman,** she'll go ga-ga over him! She'll marry him and stay at home as he commands."

Next, Ferva pays a call on Trevor and assures him that the electronic globe will make Wonder Woman fall in love with him. "If you were stronger than **Wonder Woman,**" insists Ferva, "she'd have married you long ago. Girls want superior men to boss them around."

Wonder Woman's initial reaction to Trevor's new super-strength is one of ambivalence: "Some girls **love** to have a man stronger than they are to make them do things," she muses. "Do I like it? I don't know — it's sort of thrilling. But--isn't it more fun to make the man obey?"

Ultimately, Wonder Woman and Steve Trevor join forces to smash the Lawbreakers' Protective League and apprehend its members, and Wonder Woman declines Trevor's latest offer of matrimony. "I've discovered," she explains, "that I can **never** love a **dominant** man who's stronger than I am!"

Trevor, now realizing that his renewable super-strength will act only as an impediment to his marrying Wonder Woman and not an inducement, promptly destroys the electronic globe (Sen No. 46: "The Lawbreakers' League").

LECTOR, C. O. An avaricious "millionaire collector" who, in February 1949, attempts to steal WONDER WOMAN's Amazon bracelets (see WONDER WOMAN [section C 2, the bracelets of submission]) so that he can add them to his priceless collection of "bracelets once owned by famous women . . . !" Lector and his henchmen capture Wonder Woman and remove her bracelets, but then Lector recklessly dons the bracelets and attempts to perform, without benefit of the requisite Amazon training (see WONDER WOMAN [section C 1, the benefits of Amazon training]), the "bullets and bracelets" trick for which Wonder Woman is famous.

"Wearing the Amazon bracelets alone is not the secret!" thinks Wonder Woman alarmedly. "Without acquiring thru [sic] training and discipline the Amazon agility to catch the bullets on the bracelets--he'll be killed!"

Moving at lightning speed, Wonder Woman rescues Lector from the oncoming bullets fired at him by his henchmen, recovers her bracelets, and then takes the greedy collector and his hoodlum companions into custody (Sen No. 86: "The Secret of the Amazing Bracelets!").

LEILA. The evil queen who, along with her peace-loving twin sister Solala, is co-ruler of the Sun Country, a "rich and fertile country in the heart of the Gobi Desert." Leila is defeated by WONDER WOMAN in July 1948, thus freeing Solala to rule the Sun Country in peace and kindness, unhindered by her evil sister.

When STEVE TREVOR flies to the Gobi Desert in July 1948 to investigate reports of a mysterious "wall of white light" said to have caused a U.S. Army aircraft to burst into flames upon contact, ETTA CANDY stows away aboard his plane so as not to miss out on any forthcoming excitement, and Wonder Woman follows in her Amazon plane (*see* WONDER WOMAN [section C 4, the robot plane]) so as to be able to rescue Trevor if he gets into trouble.

In the heart of the Gobi Desert, Wonder Woman comes upon the Sun Country, a rich, fertile land protected by the so-called "great lights" or "mirrors of light" responsible for the destruction of the Army plane. There Wonder Woman meets Leila and Solala, twin sisters who "rule the Sun Country jointly" but who are locked in a continual struggle for power, with Solala on the side of peace and goodness, and Leila on the side of treachery and evil.

The inhabitants of the Sun Country are avid SUN worshipers who have created numerous ingenious devices for harnessing the sun's energy. Embroiled almost immediately upon her arrival in a deadly struggle with the evil Leila, who has already taken Steve Trevor and Etta Candy prisoner, Wonder Woman defeats the evil monarch and rescues her friends from the villainess's clutches. Leila will be taken to TRANSFORMATION ISLAND to "learn submission to loving authority," while Solala remains behind to rule the Sun Country alone (Sen No. 79: "Land of Mirrors!").

LEONARDO DA VINCI (1452–1519). A Florentine artist and scientist whose seemingly infinite curiosity and inventiveness — as exemplified by his paintings, drawings, scientific and technical diagrams, and notes on a wealth of diverse subjects — combined with his uncanny modernity of vision have established him firmly in modern thought as the archetypal Renaissance man. Popularly, he is best known for his legendary universality and for his paintings of the "Mona Lisa" and "The Last Supper."

WONDER WOMAN meets Leonardo da Vinci in Wonder Woman No. 57/3, after he has used a "time machine" of his own invention to draw her back through the time barrier to 15th-century Florence in the hope that she will be able to thwart the sinister machinations of the evil DUKE PERILOSA (Jan/Feb '53: "The Four Trials of Terror!").

LIMBO. The "secret jail" of the war god MARS, which lies "hidden in outer space." When the DUKE OF DECEPTION steals the HOLLIDAY COLLEGE FOR WOMEN in March–April 1949, it is on Limbo that he hides it (WW No. 34: "The Mystery of the Rhyming Riddle!" chs. 1–3 — "Deception Strikes Again"; "The Phantasms of Deception!"; "The Mystery of the Rhyming Riddle!"). (*See* DECEPTION, DUKE OF.)

LITTLE, LITA. One of the HOLLIDAY GIRLS. Lita is a petite blonde who wishes she were taller.

Lita Little makes her textual debut in October 1960 (WW No. 117: "Fantastic Fishermen of the Forbidden Sea!"), in a text that marks the first appearance of the Holliday Girls since November–December 1950 (WW No. 44: "The Monarch of the Sargasso Sea!" chs. I–III — no title; "Wonder Woman's Decision"; "The Final Battle of the Sargasso Sea"). (*See* CANDY, ETTA.)

In January 1962 Lita Little is among the Holliday Girls who are captured by aliens from PLANET K and rescued by WONDER WOMAN (WW No. 127/1: "Invaders of the Topsy-Turvy Planet"). (*See* KUU-KUU.)

LLNO. A young lost boy, clearly a member of some highly-advanced civilization, who appears in New York City in July 1956. WONDER WOMAN's efforts to return Llno to his parents are frustrated by her inability to discover what far-distant planet he comes from, but ultimately she realizes that Llno is actually an earthling from a future era, knowledge that eventually enables her to reunite Llno with his family in 20,056 A.D. New York (WW No. 83/1: "The Boy from Nowhere!").

LOKI. In Teutonic mythology, the god of fire, mischief, and evil, and a brother of ODIN. WONDER WOMAN defeats Loki — and thwarts his efforts to help the evil dictator PROWD subjugate the women of NOMAN — during a time-journey into the future that she makes in November 1948 (Sen No. 83: "The Sinister Olympics!"). (*See* PROWD.)

LORN, LORELEI. A "famous continental actress, who [is] called the 'most dangerous beauty in the world'!"

In September–October 1949 the lovely blond Lorelei visits the United States and embarks on a whirlwind romance with STEVE TREVOR that soon culminates in their engagement. Heartbroken, but determined to do nothing that might interfere with Trevor's happiness, WONDER WOMAN attends the couple's wedding and joins forces with Trevor to capture the Gasher Jewel Gang when they interrupt the ceremony in an attempt to steal Lorelei's priceless jewelry. Only after the gang has been apprehended does Wonder Woman learn that the entire romance and the elaborate wedding plans were all part of a plot to lure the Gasher gang into the open (WW No. 37/2: "The Fatal Beauty!").

LUNAR (King). The evil ruler of the "inner moon-planet," a world beneath the surface of the MOON. King Lunar is deposed in October 1948 through the heroic efforts of WONDER WOMAN.

Until recently, the men and women of the inner

moon-planet lived together in harmony and equality. All that changed, however, when the women invented a rocket ship for space exploration and the men insisted on using it to conquer Earth.

"Our work was not meant for wars!" protested the women. "We will not allow an invasion of Earth!"

King Lunar responded by calling an emergency meeting of his army staff. "The women have forgotten their places," he told them. "We will . . . enslave them!"

At the king's instructions, every woman on the inner moon-planet was taken by force to the "mental drainage chamber," where she was robbed of her free will and transformed into a mindless zombie before being sent out to serve as a "robot soldier in [the] moon-women's army!"

On Earth, meanwhile, PROFESSOR ASTRONIMO of Holliday College attempts to warn of the impending lunar invasion, but the lunar aliens silence him by temporarily stealing away his mind with their diabolical mental drainage machinery. When Wonder Woman goes to Holliday College to investigate, she is taken captive by a lunar invader and taken by spacecraft to the inner moon-world, where she learns, to her horror, that ETTA CANDY and the HOLLIDAY GIRLS have already been taken prisoner, subjected to mental drainage, and impressed into King Lunar's robot army.

Ultimately, Wonder Woman manages to make an ally of one of the moon men. Together they "turn the thought ray in reverse on the women" of the inner moon-planet, thereby restoring their minds and making it possible for the moon's men and women to live together as equals once again. Soon afterward, with King Lunar safely deposed, Wonder Woman and her friends return to Earth (Sen No. 82: "Brain Pirates from the Inner Moon-World!"). (See also BRAIN PIRATE, THE.)

LUXO (Prof.). "An evil scientific genius" whose fiendish attempt to "conquer America" by tampering with the mighty forces within the atom is thwarted by WONDER WOMAN in January–February 1951.

Sometime in the past, Prof. Luxo fell "into the volcanic mountain of Tao Manao" and was widely believed to have perished. Wonder Woman felt confident that she had "seen the last of Prof. Luxo and his threats against a peaceful America . . . ."

But Prof. Luxo did not die, and now he has returned with a diabolical plot to bring America to its knees. "I shall conquer America," gloats Prof. Luxo, "--because Americans are fools--and soft! They will not use terror and brute force! But I will! Ha, ha!"

As Prof. Luxo puts his scheme into effect, atomic-powered projects throughout the United States are plagued by a series of bizarre catastrophes: at the launching of "the first ocean liner powered solely by atomic energy," the vessel disintegrates in full view of a crowd of horrified onlookers, and soon afterward, an atomic-powered factory and dam also disintegrate, for no apparent reason. Because all of these projects were official responsibilities of STEVE TREVOR, Trevor is held accountable and is taken into custody pending a court-martial.

Wonder Woman, however, believes Trevor innocent and senses that the atoms themselves may have been responsible. "Somehow, they've begun acting **contrary** to their nature!" she muses. "And there's only **one** way to find out what's happening! **I've got to investigate the world of the atom!**"

At the secret laboratory of BARONESS PAULA VON GUNTHER, Wonder Woman finds Paula locked in a closet and learns that the villain has already used the Amazon "atom-transferer" to journey into the world of the atom. After freeing Paula, Wonder Woman prepares to give chase. Within seconds ". . . the lovely Amazon maid starts to fade from view as the unique Amazon invention, the atom-transferer, re-assembles her nuclear structure and reforms it into the shape necessary to enter the mysterious world of the atom . . . ."

Meanwhile, inside the atomic world, Prof. Luxo has been tampering with the atomic elements in such a way that "atomic power can no longer be controlled" by "Earth world scientists," thus precipitating the recent atomic mishaps.

"His plan is simple, but diabolical!" thinks Wonder Woman. "With America unable to control atomic energy, she will be at Prof. Luxo's mercy!"

Ultimately, however, Wonder Woman defeats Prof. Luxo and returns him to the Earth world, where he is placed in the custody of U.S. Military Intelligence. Steve Trevor is promptly exonerated of any responsibility for the recent atomic catastrophes (Sen No. 101: "Battle for the Atom World!").

LYA. The beautiful but treacherous daughter of the DUKE OF DECEPTION. Lya is defeated by WONDER WOMAN in April–May 1948.

Responding to an urgent call for help from the crew of a spacecraft on fire in outer space, Wonder Woman streaks to the rescue, only to learn that the distress call was a ruse designed to lure her to the scene. Taken captive aboard the alien spacecraft by the beautiful blond Lya and her crew of Martian women, Wonder Woman is told that Lya intends to use her as a tool in her scheme to seize the throne of MARS from the Duke of Deception.

Recently, explains Lya, her father organized an insurrection among Mars's female convicts that ultimately catapulted him to the throne of Mars. (*See* DECEPTION, DUKE OF.)

*Using ectoplasmic clay, Lya molds
a phantasm of Wonder Woman, 1948*

Once in power, Deception attempted to use his daughter to betray his women supporters by having her become their leader and persuade them to grant him absolute dictatorial power, but Lya instead used her influence with the Martian women to instigate a revolt against her father. By telling the women that "Deception, like all Martian men, believes women are inferior and only fit to be slaves," she had aroused the women of Mars to overthrow Deception and place her on the throne in his stead.

Lya would have killed Deception, but Deception begged to be allowed to live out his life in exile on Earth as an alternative to execution. A spaceship was prepared, with its controls locked in place so that it could fly to Earth and nowhere else, but just as it was about to blast off, Deception tricked Lya and her followers into coming on board to wish him a last farewell and then dived out through a porthole at the last possible moment, sending Lya and her women companions hurtling helplessly into space. With Lya and her followers marooned in outer space, Deception was once again master of Mars.

Now Lya explains that she intends to force Wonder Woman to help her build "a secret stronghold at Earth's center from which [she] can put this world [Earth] under tribute and reconquer Mars . . . !" Later, after the subterranean stronghold has been built, Lya locks Wonder Woman in the underground hideaway and then, after disguising herself as Wonder Woman by means of a special "phantasm" molded from "ectoplasmic flesh-like clay," travels to the upper world.

Posing as Wonder Woman, Lya tells America's top officials that the planet Mars is about to invade Earth and that she must have access to "America's secret weapons" if she is to successfully thwart the invasion. Before Lya can use America's atomic weapons to conquer Mars, however, Wonder Woman escapes from the subterranean stronghold, rescues STEVE TREVOR and the other American officials taken prisoner by Lya and her followers, and defeats Lya and her entire Martian crew. The captured Martian women will be taken to TRANSFORMATION ISLAND to undergo rehabilitative training under the guidance of the AMAZONS (CC No. 26: "Deception's Daughter").

MacDONALD (Capt.). The skipper of the municipal ferryboat *Bay Beauty*. MacDonald is unhappy because he is convinced that his is the dullest, most insignificant seafaring job in the world, but WONDER WOMAN makes him realize that his job is really exciting and important (WW No. 40/2, Mar/Apr '50: "Passengers of Fate!").

MacGREGOR, JUDY. A beautiful red-haired cowgirl who detests men. She is cured of her misandry by WONDER WOMAN in December 1947–January 1948.

Suspecting that Judy's hatred of men is the result of some distasteful experience that occurred in a "past incarnation," Wonder Woman travels into the past with her to uncover the origins of her current bitterness.

In the year 1777 — when Judy was a Scottish lass en route to America to marry her fiancé — Wonder Woman learns the real reason for Judy's disillusionment with men: the shocking discovery that her fiancé is already married, and in league with a band of bloodthirsty pirates. Confronted with the traumatic experience which lies at the root of her man-hatred, Judy is able to realize that her hostility toward her evil fiancé of the past need not be projected onto all men, thus enabling her, once back in the 20th century, to reciprocate the affection of a good man who loves her (CC No. 24: "Empress of the Sea-Brigands!").

MACHINE MEN. Ruthless machinelike invaders from a distant planet whose elaborate scheme to conquer the Earth as a steppingstone to conquest of the universe involves disposing of WONDER WOMAN by transforming her into a giantess certain to become an outcast on her own planet. In the words of one of them:

> Soon--she will become a threat to her planet--and while all attention is concentrated on her--our invasion fleet will launch a surprise attack on the shattered Earth that will easily make it fall into our hands! And then, one by one, the rest of the planets of the Solar System! And then . . . .

Before long, the special "giant-fruit-bullet" fired at her by the Machine Men has transformed Wonder Woman into a giantess taller than any skyscraper. **"WONDER WOMAN'S UNCHECKED GROWTH MAKING HER WORLD MENACE!"** screams a newspaper headline. **"AMAZON SERIOUS THREAT TO WORLD'S FOOD AND WATER SUPPLY! CITIES MAY PERISH UNDER HER FEET!"**

Ultimately, however, Wonder Woman discovers the Machine Men's plot to conquer Earth, destroys their space fleet, and restores herself to normal size by bathing in a "shower of cosmic dust," the antidote to the invaders' growth drug (WW No. 136, Feb '63: "Wonder Woman--World's Mightiest Menace!").

MACHINO. A vicious criminal who sneaks up on WONDER WOMAN while she is taking a nap and clamps a mask containing a time bomb over her face. Wonder Woman's efforts to remove the deadly mask prove fruitless, but, with time rapidly running out, she finally apprehends Machino and compels him to remove the mask and deactivate the bomb (WW No. 80/1, Feb '56: "The Mask of Mystery!").

MADISON SQUARE GARDEN. A large indoor stadium in New York City. WONDER WOMAN puts on an ice-skating exhibition there in December 1944 for the benefit of disabled war veterans (Sen No. 36: "Battle Against Revenge").

MALA. The statuesque Amazon who is in charge of prisoner rehabilitation on TRANSFORMATION ISLAND. The texts — which depict her sometimes as a blonde (WW No. 3/2, Feb/Mar '43; and others), sometimes as a brunette (WW No. 8/3, Spr '44: "The Captive Queen"), and sometimes as a redhead (CC No. 11, Sum '45: "The Cheetah Returns!"; and others) — describe her as the "commandress" of Transformation Island and as "chief of the Amazon prison" (WW No. 8/3, Spr '44: "The Captive Queen"). Mala is a close friend of WONDER WOMAN.

In December 1941–January 1942, when STEVE TREVOR's aircraft runs out of fuel and crashes on the beach at PARADISE ISLAND, it is Mala who helps Princess Diana pull Trevor safely from the wreckage. Trevor's arrival on the island leads directly to the emergence of Princess Diana as Wonder Woman (AS No. 8: "Introducing Wonder Woman"). (*See* WONDER WOMAN [section A, Origin].)

In February–March 1943, when QUEEN HIPPO-

Mala overpowered by Eviless, 1948

LYTE orders construction of a prison facility on Reform Island (WW No. 3/1), Mala is placed in charge of it (WW No. 3/2). The name Reform Island is subsequently changed to Transformation Island.

In December 1943, when the goddess APHRODITE inspires Wonder Woman with "an idea for controlling [her] airplane by mental radio" (*see* WONDER WOMAN [section C 4, the robot plane]), it is Mala and Paula (*see* GUNTHER, PAULA VON [BARONESS]) who construct and install the necessary apparatus (Sen No. 24: "Adventure of the Pilotless Plane").

In May 1944 Mala winds up in New York City after her Amazon aircraft has been hijacked in midair by MIMI MENDEZ. During this, her first visit to "man's world," Mala is appalled at the unre-

Mounted atop Jumpa, her favorite kanga, Wonder Woman unseats Mala in an Amazon girl-roping contest, 1942

strained violence of a war movie and bemused by several common American customs. Ultimately, she aids in the apprehension of Mimi Mendez and her cohorts (Sen No. 29: "Adventure of the Escaped Prisoner"). (*See* MENDEZ, MIMI.)

In January 1945 there is a breakdown in the "ship-repelling electric power" network that prevents foreign ships from approaching Paradise Island, forcing the AMAZONS to shut it down completely until Mala can "recondition the dynamos." While the repairs are in progress, a Nazi submarine crew invades the island and attempts to conquer it, only to be defeated through the heroic efforts of Mala and Wonder Woman (Sen No. 37: "The Invasion of Paradise Island").

In Summer 1945 Mala summons Wonder Woman to Reform Island to inform her of the recent escape of Priscilla Rich, alias the CHEETAH. Because Priscilla had been a model prisoner, Mala had entrusted her with the key to her magic Venus girdle (*see* AMAZONS [section F 3, the magic Venus girdles]), but Priscilla abused Mala's confidence in her and escaped. Wonder Woman consoles Mala by assuring her that she's "done splendid work reforming prisoners." Soon afterward, the Cheetah is recaptured (CC No. 11: "The Cheetah Returns!"). (*See* CHEETAH, THE.)

In June–July 1947, when Paradise Island is menaced by QUEEN SHARKEETA and her mermaid sharks, Mala helps Wonder Woman battle them and rescue Queen Hippolyte and other Amazon captives from their clutches (CC No. 21: "The Seige [sic] of the Flying Mermaids!"). (*See* SHARKEETA [QUEEN].)

In March–April 1948 Mala is overpowered by EVILESS, who flees Transformation Island with the villainesses who comprise VILLAINY INCORPORATED (WW No. 28/1: "Villainy Incorporated!"). (*See* VILLAINY INCORPORATED.)

MAN-FISH. A bizarre sea creature — with the gills and scales of a fish and the body of a man — who nets WONDER WOMAN in July–August 1967, while she is sunning herself on a rock off the coast of PARADISE ISLAND, and imprisons her in an undersea aquarium along with a group of captured mermaids. Wonder Woman escapes from the aquarium, frees the mermaids, and defeats an army of "men-fish" who attempt to recapture her (WW No. 171/1: "Terror Trap of the Demon Man-Fish!").

MANLIUS. An evil "manling" — described as VENTURIA's "most brilliant scientist" — who matches wits with WONDER WOMAN in December 1946–January 1947 after having instigated a manling revolt that toppled the benevolent OCTAVIA from the presidency of Venturia.

By December 1946–January 1947 Manlius and his army of manlings — the undersized men of ATLANTIS, who normally function only as either slaves or soldiers — have overthrown Octavia and seized control of Venturia. By administering the captive president a dose of mind-controlling "liquid devitamizer," Manlius forces Octavia to summon Wonder Woman to Venturia, then takes her prisoner as soon as she arrives. Locked in a dungeon with Octavia, Wonder Woman listens as she recounts the events leading up to the recent manling revolt:

"All was harmonious" in Venturia, explains Octavia, until a fateful day in her research laboratory, where Manlius was assisting her in experiments with the newly developed Vitamin Z gas.

"If I'm right," Octavia had said, "Vitamin Z will grow grey matter in our brain--give us Atlanteans the most brilliant brains in the universe."

"Then," replied Manlius, "**we** can **wage war** on everyone else and--"

"**No! No!** Manlius!" scolded Octavia. "Then we'd have the power to enforce the **outlawing** of all wars!"

Soon afterward, while Manlius was working in the laboratory alone, overexposure to the new "Z vapor" had swollen his head to enormous size and endowed him with superhuman intelligence.

"Something's happening to me!" he cried. "My brain is terrific. Now with my **superhuman mental power,** I can overthrow the peace-loving government and become **war lord** of all Atlantis!"

"Manlius herded together a band of manlings," continues Octavia, "supplied them with electromagnetic ray guns, and stormed Venturia.

"When I awakened, I found myself bound in this dungeon! Manlius forced me to radio thee [Wonder Woman] while my mind was controlled by **liquid devitamizer,** a powerful anaesthetic which formula I was compelled to divulge."

Knowing that an army under the command of Octavia's mother, QUEEN EERAS OF AURANIA, is on its way to Venturia to liberate Octavia and restore her to power, Manlius intends to bind Wonder Woman with her own magic lasso (see WONDER WOMAN [section C 3, the magic lasso]) and force her to help him defeat the advancing Auranian army. Before long, with Wonder Woman's unwilling complicity, Eeras and her army have been lured into a trap and Eeras has been taken captive. Just as Manlius is about to entomb Eeras, Octavia, and Wonder Woman alive, however, Wonder Woman turns the tables on her captors, frees Eeras and Octavia and, with their help, defeats Manlius and his fellow manlings and restores Octavia to power in Venturia (CC No. 18: "The Menace of the Rebel Manlings").

MANNO. *See* MERMAN.

MANTON (Prof.). A mechanical genius who, a decade ago, abandoned the stress and clamor of industrial civilization for a tranquil life on an uninhabited island. Because the island he selected is inhabited by gargantuan species of birds and fish, Manton constructed a giant robot to protect him against them.

In January 1957, after STEVE TREVOR has been forced to crash-land on Manton's island, both he and Manton are taken prisoner by Manton's robot, which has suffered a mechanical breakdown and gone berserk. Arriving on the scene in search of Trevor, however, WONDER WOMAN defeats the robot and rescues Manton and Trevor from its clutches (WW No. 87/2: "Island of the Giants!").

MARLOWE (Prof.). The brilliant scientist who, in conjunction with the Army and Navy, developed the "chemic-extracto," a machine designed "to extract chemical elements from sea water." In the words of STEVE TREVOR:

> . . . every cubic mile of sea water contains about 160,000,000 tons of valuable chemical elements--iodine, bromine, magnesium, etc. The **chemic-extracto** will attempt to separate and extract every element at a tremendous rate of speed!

When criminals infiltrate the crew of the Navy vessel on which the chemic-extracto is to be tested and attempt to steal it, WONDER WOMAN and Steve Trevor apprehend them (Sen No. 68, Aug '47: "Secret of the Menacing Octopus!").

MARS (the god of war). In classical mythology, the Roman god of war; to the Greeks, he was known as Ares.

In the WONDER WOMAN chronicles, he is the brutal, iron-fisted ruler of the planet MARS, whose cruel "slave collectors" roam the war-torn countries of Earth, shackling the souls of dead men and carrying them back as slaves to Mars's grim domain.

Mars revels in war, violence, bloodshed, and plunder, and because he is determined that "men shall rule [Earth] with the sword," he is the implacable foe of the goddess APHRODITE, who has vowed that "women shall conquer men with love!" (WW No. 1/1, Sum '42). Because Mars "won't tolerate giving women the slightest freedom," believing as he does that "women are the natural spoils of war" and therefore "must remain at home, helpless slaves for the victor," he is determined to enslave the AMAZONS and plunge the Earth into a

WITH WONDER WOMAN GONE-- THE PLANET EARTH ONCE MORE WILL BECOME A TEST TUBE INTO WHICH I'LL POUR AND MIX CONQUEST, GREED, AND DECEPTION! AN--HOUNDS OF PHOBOS, IT--GULP!--   IT--CAN'T BE--?

© NPP 1942

Mars, the god of war

holocaust of war (WW No. 5/1, Jun/July '43: "Battle for Womanhood").

Wherever there is warfare, Mars reigns supreme: with World War II ravaging the nations of Europe, Wonder Woman No. 5/1 described him as the "present ruler of this world" (Jun/Jul '43: "Battle for Womanhood").

Ever ready to aid their master in his war on peace and brotherhood are Mars's infamous "three commanders" — LORD CONQUEST, the EARL OF GREED, and the DUKE OF DECEPTION — and his treacherous "aide-de-camp," General Destruction (WW No. 2/1, Fall '42).

It was to stymie the forces of Mars that Aphrodite created the immortal Amazons, and it was Mars who inspired the mighty HERCULES to lead his army against ancient AMAZONIA (WW No. 1/1, Sum '42). (*See* AMAZONS [Section A, History].)

In Fall 1942 STEVE TREVOR sets out on a secret mission for the U.S. Army after being provided by Wonder Woman with a vial of special tablets containing "the purple healing ray [she] discovered on Paradise Island" (*see* AMAZONS [section G, Amazon science]), which he is to take in the event he sustains an injury.

After a "long, anxious day" has passed without any word from Trevor, a worried Wonder Woman consults the goddess Aphrodite.

"Your man is in the hands of Mars, the god of war!" explains Aphrodite. "But his plan is a complex one. He holds Trevor as hostage because he really wants to trap you! Your defense of America and democracy has incensed him!"

"I defy Mars!" cries Wonder Woman. "Lead me to his citadel!"

"Rash maiden!" scolds the goddess. "Mars is

invincible! Once I bound him but he escaped, even from me! No mortal can enter Mars's domain except as a shackled prisoner!"

"Then I will go as a prisoner," replies Wonder Woman impatiently. "I'm not afraid of chains!"

"But it's not as simple as that!" cautions Aphrodite. "Mars takes prisoner only the souls of the dead! This elixir of living death will put you into a deep sleep. Your astral self will go where you will it to go! Surrender to Mars's slave collectors and may Athena guide you!"

Wonder Woman partakes of the "elixir of living death" and transmits her astral self to a country ravaged by war so that, by permitting Mars's slave collectors to take her prisoner, she can gain entrance to Mars's dark domain.

On Mars, Wonder Woman succeeds, despite numerous trials and tribulations, in rescuing the astral body of Steve Trevor from a dark dungeon in the war god's iron palace. Shot and wounded by a Japanese spy in the course of his secret mission, Trevor had kept his physical body alive with Wonder Woman's special pills, while his astral body had been imprisoned on Mars. Once Trevor's astral body has returned to Earth and been reunited with his physical body, Trevor is alive and well once again.

Meanwhile, furious at having been humiliated by Wonder Woman, the vengeful war god vows to send his three ruthless commanders to Earth to capture her (WW No. 2/1).

One after the other, Mars sends the Earl of Greed (WW No. 2/2, Fall '42), the Duke of Deception (WW No. 2/3, Fall '42), and Lord Conquest to Earth to capture Wonder Woman. Where Greed and Deception fail, however, Conquest succeeds: before long, both Wonder Woman and Steve Trevor are once again prisoners of Mars.

Dispatching an urgent mental radio message (*see* WONDER WOMAN [section C 7, the mental radio]) to ETTA CANDY, however, Wonder Woman instructs her to come to Mars with the HOLLIDAY GIRLS by partaking of Aphrodite's elixir. On Mars, Etta gives Wonder Woman a vial of acid to pour on her shackles, thus enabling her to escape from Mars's dungeon and defeat him, rescue Trevor, and escape to Earth with her friends. Mars is immortal and cannot be destroyed, but he has suffered a disastrous and humiliating defeat (WW No. 2/4, Fall '42). (*See also* GREED, EARL OF; DECEPTION, DUKE OF; and CONQUEST [LORD].)

In June–July 1943, concerned that the women of Earth have begun displaying too much independence, Mars orders the Duke of Deception to come up with "an evil inspiration" for putting Earth's

EEAY! ANOTHER 900,000,000 SPOIL ARI BLASTED! STOP HER, MASTER, BEFORE SHE RUINS OUR TREASURY!

DID I SAY 100? SHE'S WORTH 1000 LEGIONS!

SILENCE! HERE COMES DECEPTION!

© NPP 1942

The Earl of Greed, Lord Conquest, and the war god Mars, 1942

"upstart women in their place." The wily Deception promptly pays a call on "an Earth agent who hates women," the diabolical DR. PSYCHO (WW No. 5/1: "Battle for Womanhood").

When Dr. Psycho fails to achieve a victory over Wonder Woman, Mars orders Deception incarcerated in the Martian women's prison, where he is put to work scrubbing floors and peeling huge mounds of potatoes. Aided by the women prisoners, however, Deception launches an insurrection which catapults him to the throne of Mars. Mars and Lord Conquest are imprisoned, but the Earl of Greed bribes some guards to let them escape, and Mars and Conquest flee into outer space aboard a Martian space cruiser. (*See* DECEPTION, DUKE OF.)

Fugitives from their own planet, Mars and Conquest travel to the MOON, where they imprison the lunar goddess DIANA (WW No. 5/2, Jun/Jul '43). (*See* CONQUEST [LORD].)

By March–April 1949 Mars has apparently regained power on the planet Mars, though how or when this came about is never explained in the chronicles. "Irked by [the] lack of war on Earth," he "fumes with rage" at those about him: "**Wonder Woman** is stirring everybody up for peace!" he cries. ". . . . My plans for a new world war will be ruined!" It is during this period that Mars sets in motion an elaborate scheme to steal Holliday College and lure Wonder Woman to her doom (WW No. 34: "The Mystery of the Rhyming Riddle!" chs. 1–3 — "Deception Strikes Again"; "The Phantasms of Deception!"; "The Mystery of the Rhyming Riddle!"). (*See* DECEPTION, DUKE OF.)

The Wonder Woman text for July–August 1949 recounts an adventure, purported to have taken place sometime in the past, in which PARADISE ISLAND is invaded by a combined force of Martian men and their boy allies from the planet DUXO (WW No. 36/1: "The Girl Who Saved Paradise Island!"). (*See* DUXO.)

The Wonder Woman text for August 1949 recounts an adventure, purported to have taken place sometime in the past, in which the war god Mars, Lord Conquest, and the Duke of Deception plot to destroy Earth with "titanic solar rays" (Sen No. 92: "The Pebble That Saved the World!"). (*See* DECEPTION, DUKE OF.)

In July–August 1951 Lord Conquest leads a Martian space armada in a surprise attack on Paradise Island, but the invasion is quickly repelled by Wonder Woman. Back on Mars, the war god Mars demands an accounting: "If it weren't for America's attempts to preserve peace," he bellows, "we could set all Earth battling, and the planet would fall easy prey to us! Destroy America and Earth is ours! Why did you fail?"

"Y-Y-You know the Amazons protect America, sire!" stammers Conquest. "I-I sought to crush them first--b-b-but **Wonder Woman** tricked me!"

It is then that the Duke of Deception comes forward with a new plot to destroy the Amazons, this time through trickery instead of brute force (Sen No. 104: "The End of Paradise Island"). (*See* DECEPTION, DUKE OF.)

In April 1967 Mars creates the CRIMSON CENTIPEDE (WW No. 169/1: "Wonder Woman Battles the Crimson Centipede!").

MARS (the planet). The fourth planet from the SUN. In the WONDER WOMAN chronicles, Mars is ruled by the brutal, iron-fisted MARS, god of war, whose cruel "slave collectors" roam the war-torn countries of Earth, shackling the souls of dead men and carrying them back as slaves to Mars's grim domain.

The war god revels in violence, bloodshed, and plunder, and because he is determined that "men shall rule [Earth] with the sword," he is the implacable enemy of the goddess APHRODITE, who has vowed that "women shall conquer men with love!" (WW No. 1/1, Sum '42). And, because Mars "won't tolerate giving women the slightest freedom" — believing as he does that "women are the natural spoils of war . . . . [and] must remain at home, helpless slaves for the victor!" — he is determined to enslave the AMAZONS and plunge the Earth into a holocaust of war (WW No. 5/1, Jun/Jul '43: "Battle for Womanhood").

Ever ready to aid their master in his unceasing war against peace and brotherhood are Mars's infamous "three commanders" — LORD CONQUEST,

the EARL OF GREED, and the DUKE OF DECEP-
TION — and his treacherous "aide-de-camp," General Destruction.

It was to stymie the forces of Mars that Aphrodite created the immortal Amazons, and it was
Mars who inspired the mighty HERCULES to lead
his army in a treacherous assault on ancient
AMAZONIA (WW No. 1/1, Sum '42). (*See* AMAZONS
[section A, History].)

The Duke of Deception topples Mars from his
throne in June–July 1943 (WW No. 5/2) and retains dictatorial control of the red planet for several years, despite an attempt by his daughter LYA
to overthrow him sometime prior to April–May
1948 (CC No. 26: "Deception's Daughter"). By
March–April 1949, however, the war god Mars has
managed to regain his throne (WW No. 34: "The
Mystery of the Rhyming Riddle!" chs. 1–3 — "Deception Strikes Again"; "The Phantasms of Deception!"; "The Mystery of the Rhyming Riddle!").

Following is a brief chronology of Wonder
Woman's battles with the men of the planet Mars:

In Fall 1942 Wonder Woman has a series of
battles with the war god Mars and his minions
(WW No. 2/1–4). (*See* MARS [THE GOD OF WAR];
GREED, EARL OF; DECEPTION, DUKE OF; and CON-
QUEST [LORD].)

In June–July 1943 the war god Mars instructs
the Duke of Deception to come up with "an evil
inspiration" for putting Earth's "upstart women in
their place" (WW No. 5/1: "Battle for Womanhood"). (*See* PSYCHO [DR.].) Soon afterward, the
Duke of Deception seizes power on Mars, and the
war god and Lord Conquest, exiled temporarily
from their home planet, invade the MOON (WW
No. 5/2, Jun/Jul '43). (*See* DECEPTION, DUKE OF;
CONQUEST [LORD].)

In April–May 1948 Wonder Woman matches
wits with Lya, the treacherous daughter of the
Duke of Deception (CC No. 26: "Deception's
Daughter"). (*See* LYA.)

In March–April 1949 the war god Mars sets in
motion an elaborate scheme to steal Holliday College and lure Wonder Woman to her doom (WW
No. 34: "The Mystery of the Rhyming Riddle!" chs.
1–3 — "Deception Strikes Again"; "The Phantasms
of Deception!"; "The Mystery of the Rhyming
Riddle!"). (*See* DECEPTION, DUKE OF.)

The Wonder Woman text for July–August 1949
recounts the story of a Martian invasion of PARA-
DISE ISLAND said to have taken place sometime in
the past (WW No. 36/1: "The Girl Who Saved
Paradise Island!"). (*See* DUXO.)

The Wonder Woman text for August 1949 recounts the story of a Martian attempt to destroy

the Earth said to have been thwarted by Wonder
Woman sometime in the past (Sen No. 92: "The
Pebble That Saved the World!"). (*See* DECEPTION,
DUKE OF.)

In May–June 1950 Wonder Woman journeys to
PHOBOS, inner moon of the planet Mars, to rescue
STEVE TREVOR from the clutches of the tyrant
GHURKOS (WW No. 41/3: "The Trial of Steve
Trevor!"). (*See* GHURKOS.)

In May–June 1951 Wonder Woman thwarts a
Martian attempt to "bomb Washington [D.C.] and
destroy the strongest arsenal of democracy on
Earth!" (WW No. 47/3: "The Bridge from Mars!").
(*See* DECEPTION, DUKE OF.)

In July–August 1951 Wonder Woman repels a
Martian invasion of Paradise Island and thwarts a
scheme by the Duke of Deception to destroy the
Amazons (Sen No. 104: "The End of Paradise Island"). (*See* DECEPTION, DUKE OF.)

In January 1954 Wonder Woman thwarts a Mar-
tian scheme to conquer the Earth (WW No. 63/2:
"The Secret Invasion!"). (*See* DECEPTION, DUKE
OF.)

In April 1954, after a Martian space fleet has
conquered the Earth, Wonder Woman travels back
in time, to the period just prior to the invasion, in
hopes of thwarting the successful Martian conquest (WW No. 65/3: "The Last Amazon!"). (*See*
DECEPTION, DUKE OF.)

In May 1954 Wonder Woman matches wits with
the Duke of Deception (WW No. 66/1: "The Olympics of Terror!"). (*See* DECEPTION, DUKE OF.)

In April 1956 Wonder Woman battles the Duke
of Deception (WW No. 81/1: "The Dream
Dooms!"). (*See* DECEPTION, DUKE OF.)

In August 1956 Wonder Woman thwarts the
Duke of Deception's latest scheme to invade the
Earth (WW No. 84/2: "The Planet of Illusion!").
(*See* DECEPTION, DUKE OF.)

In February 1957 Wonder Woman destroys a
Martian space fleet attempting to invade Earth
(WW No. 88/1: "Mystery of the Vanishing Box!").
(*See* DECEPTION, DUKE OF.)

In October 1957 Wonder Woman thwarts an
attempt by the Duke of Deception to conquer the
Earth by using "shrinking rays" to reduce the
entire planet "to the size of a toy" (WW No. 93/2:
"The Shrinking City!"). (*See* DECEPTION, DUKE OF.)

In November 1957 Wonder Woman is marked
for death by the Duke of Deception (WW No. 94/2:
"Target: Wonder Woman!"). (*See* DECEPTION, DUKE
OF.)

In April 1958 Wonder Woman thwarts an invasion of Paradise Island by a Martian space armada
(WW No. 97: "The Runaway Time Express!" pts.

1–3 — "Stone Age Rodeo!"; "The Day Nature Ran Wild!"; "The Menace of Earth's Twin!").

In February 1959 Wonder Woman demolishes an armada of Martian, Saturnian, and Plutonian spaceships attempting to invade the Earth (WW No. 104/2: "Key of Deception!"). (*See* DECEPTION, DUKE OF.)

In August 1964 Wonder Woman matches wits with the Duke of Deception (WW No. 148: "The Olympics of the Doomed"). (*See* DECEPTION, DUKE OF.)

In April 1967 Wonder Woman battles the CRIMSON CENTIPEDE, a hideous creature created by the war god Mars (WW No. 169/1: "Wonder Woman Battles the Crimson Centipede!").

In November–December 1967, after a Martian space fleet has conquered the Earth, Wonder Woman travels back in time, to the period just prior to the invasion, in hopes of thwarting the successful Martian conquest (WW No. 173/2: "Earth's Last Human!"). The story is almost identical to one that appeared in a much earlier text (i.e., WW No. 65/3, Apr '54: "The Last Amazon!"). (*See* DECEPTION, DUKE OF.)

MARU (Princess). The lovely Japanese princess who is secretly DOCTOR POISON (Sen No. 2, Feb '42).

MARYA (the mountain girl). A lovely brown-haired "giantess" from the mountains of Mexico who becomes a student at the HOLLIDAY COLLEGE FOR WOMEN and a close friend of WONDER WOMAN. Gentle but courageous, beautiful but powerful, Marya is eight feet tall and weighs 300 pounds.

Marya in the clutches of Supreme Leader Blitz, 1946

In September 1945, after Wonder Woman's Amazon plane (*see* WONDER WOMAN [section C 4, the robot plane]) has crashed in the Mexican jungles, Marya finds Wonder Woman unconscious and nurses her back to health. Later she helps Wonder Woman capture the band of brutal Mexican bandidos led by "GENERAL" JOSÉ PIEREZ (Sen No. 45:

"In the Enemy's Hands"). (*See* PIEREZ, JOSÉ ["GENERAL"].)

After the defeat of Pierez and his bandidos, Marya accompanies Wonder Woman to America, where she enrolls as a student at the Holliday College for Women. In September–October 1946 Marya — described by ETTA CANDY as "a conscientious student and a first-class athlete, an all-around swell, elegant gal" — is kidnapped by the Nazi henchmen of SUPREME LEADER BLITZ and taken to the jungles of Africa, where Blitz and his fellow "war criminals" intend to use her brain as a power source for their diabolical "brain wave of death" (WW No. 19/1–3: "Invisible Terror!"; "The Witchdoctor's Cauldron"; "In the Lair of the Death Ray Criminals"). (*See* BLITZ [SUPREME LEADER].)

Marya the mountain girl, 1945

MASK, THE. A cruel raven-haired villainess who is described as "the weirdest and most mysterious inventor of devilish devices to force people to her will that **Wonder Woman** ever encountered." The Mask is in reality Nina Close, the mousy, bespectacled blond wife of millionaire Brutus Close. As the Mask, Nina wears a light green minidress and red cape, dark green gloves and shoes, and a black wig and eye mask to conceal her blond hair and eyeglasses.

Brutus Close, Nina's husband — a "millionaire game hunter who's always boasting about his exploits" — is stingy, selfish, and tyrannical, continually squandering huge sums of money on hunting expeditions designed to keep himself in the public eye while forcing his wife to live in poverty and neglect.

The Mask

Nina Close

Late one night, Close is awakened from his sleep by a beautiful masked intruder who leaps through his bedroom window, ties him up at gunpoint, and clamps a diabolical mask over the lower part of his face.

"There's a flask of hydrocyanic acid inside this **mask!**" snarls the intruder. "If you try to remove this mask without using **my key**, the deadly poison will squirt into your mouth and kill you **instantly!**"

Then the intruder, known as the Mask, departs, warning Close that she will remove his mask safely only upon payment of $1,000,000 in ransom. Close has no choice but to pay the ransom, for with the mask affixed to his face he cannot eat, and wrenching it off will mean instant death.

Not long afterward, having collected Close's ransom money, the Mask strikes again, this time at the HOLLIDAY COLLEGE FOR WOMEN, where she clamps deadly masks on the faces of ETTA CANDY and the HOLLIDAY GIRLS and demands a ransom

from them also. When WONDER WOMAN attempts to intervene, the Mask takes her prisoner and forces all her captives to accompany her to the Close home, where she has chained Brutus Close, still imprisoned in his deadly mask, to a wall and is cruelly tempting him with plates of delicious food.

Wonder Woman unmasks the Mask, 1947

"Behold the great Brutus Close, mighty hunter and financier--ha ha **ha!**" taunts the Mask. "When he gets hungry enough, he will tear off his mask and **then**--ha ha!"

Ultimately, Wonder Woman turns the tables on her captor, frees Brutus Close and the Holliday Girls from their acid-filled face masks, and unmasks the Mask as Nina Close, the long-neglected wife of Brutus Close.

"Poor girl," remarks Wonder Woman to Nina as she escorts her to a mental hospital in the company of a nurse, "your mind broke under years of strain but kind treatment will cure you. Brutus is a changed man--he loves you now and promises the hospital $1,000,000 if they make you well!" (WW No. 24/2, Jul/Aug '47: "The Challenge of the Mask").

MASQUERADER, THE. An alias employed by QUEEN HIPPOLYTE in February 1944 when she leaves PARADISE ISLAND for "the world of men" in order to rescue her daughter WONDER WOMAN from seemingly certain doom (Sen No. 26: "The Masquerader").

MASTER DE STROYER. A power-mad villain who has seized control of the Sargasso Sea Kingdom, intending to use it as a base from which to launch his "war on the world." Master De Stroyer and his henchmen — the so-called "War Mongers" — are defeated by WONDER WOMAN in November–December 1950.

While CAPT. SEADUNK and the HOLLIDAY GIRLS are on an expedition to the Sargasso Sea in November–December 1950, a furious storm lashes at their ship, splitting its hull and threatening to drown everyone on board. Wonder Woman, who is accompanying the expedition in her Diana Prince identity, makes a heroic attempt to keep the vessel afloat, but she is rendered unconscious by a mysterious noxious sap exuding from the stalks of a nearby colony of red aquatic plants.

As the expeditionary vessel sinks into the sea, Capt. Seadunk and the Holliday Girls plunge overboard, only to be taken prisoner by men in diving suits who drag them to the ocean floor, where, for centuries, a race of forgotten people has been living within the watertight hulls of sunken ships.

The ruler of this exotic Sargasso Sea Kingdom is the lovely blond Princess Althea, but Althea has been overthrown, and her peace-loving subjects forced into servitude, by the villainous Master De Stroyer and his ruthless War Mongers.

"For years," gloats De Stroyer, "I have stolen the modern instruments of war from all nations. My spies have learned the weaknesses in every country's defense! And here below the Sargasso Sea I have found a perfect headquarters from which to

Master De Stroyer

operate. As long as I hold [Princess Althea] prisoner, [her] subjects will obey my every command!"

Soon afterward, in a dungeon aboard an ancient Roman trireme, Althea tells Wonder Woman the story of her kingdom. Thousands of years ago, she explains, she was a princess of ancient Greece and the ruler of a Greek province. When an army of Romans overran her country, they placed Althea and her subjects aboard a convoy of vessels to be transported to Rome as slaves, but the convoy was crippled by a violent storm at sea, the Roman crewmen were all killed or wounded, and the stricken ships "drifted thousands of miles off . . . course into the Sargasso Sea." The survivors of the ill-fated voyage — including the surviving Romans, who were grateful to Althea and her people for having cared for their wounded — voted Althea their ruler.

"In time," continues Althea, "all [the] ships

sank, but we discovered how to seal them tight, using seaweed vents to the surface for air!"

For centuries now, Althea and her subjects have lived aboard the sunken Roman vessels, kept young and beautiful by a mysterious "undersea herb." Recently, however, Althea's peaceful kingdom was invaded by Master De Stroyer and his War Mongers. Althea was taken captive, and her loyal subjects are now forced to do the villain's bidding.

A short while later, when Master De Stroyer threatens to kill Capt. Seadunk and the Holliday Girls unless Wonder Woman agrees to help him steal a powerful "atomic motor" being developed by the U.S. Government, Wonder Woman finds herself "forced to aid the sinister War Mongers in their quest for the world's most powerful motor," despite the fact that once they possess it "nothing can prevent [them] from controlling the world!"

Bound with her own magic lasso (see WONDER WOMAN [section C 3, the magic lasso]) to prevent her from disobeying the War Mongers' commands, Wonder Woman leads De Stroyer's cohort Dangeress — a beautiful, ruthless blonde — to the secret island factory where the atomic motor is being developed, overpowers the troops guarding the installation, and steals the motor. The attack on the government factory, however, sets off an alarm in the Washington, D.C., offices of Military Intelligence, and soon STEVE TREVOR is on his way to the island to investigate.

Scanning the island from the air, Trevor sees Wonder Woman's predicament and forces Dangeress to drop her end of the magic lasso with a well-placed pistol shot. Thus freed from the villainess's control, Wonder Woman swiftly captures Dangeress and the other War Mongers who had accompanied them to the island factory. After demolishing the War Monger's submarine by lifting it over her head and dashing it against some rocks, Wonder Woman races back to the Sargasso Sea Kingdom, arriving barely in time to rescue Capt. Seadunk and the Holliday Girls just as they are about to be put to death by the evil Master De Stroyer.

De Stroyer, however, seizes control of the "atmosphere-controller" — a device used by Althea and her subjects to control the atmosphere of their undersea kingdom — and uses it to create a violent thunderstorm to prevent anyone from launching an assault on his undersea sanctuary. Wonder Woman frees Althea and her subjects and organizes them for a climactic battle with the remaining War Mongers, but, in the action that follows, Steve Trevor, Capt. Seadunk, Etta Candy, the Holliday Girls, and BARONESS PAULA VON GUN-

THER — who has arrived in Wonder Woman's Amazon plane (see WONDER WOMAN [section C 4, the robot plane]) to join the fight — are taken captive by the villains and left to drown inside an underwater cage, which is surrounded by mines designed to destroy Wonder Woman in the event she attempts to rescue them. Forced to hold their breath to avoid drowning, the captives are unable to warn Wonder Woman away from the mines, but Wonder Woman senses a trap, deactivates the mines, and rescues her friends from their watery deathtrap.

With her companions safely out of harm's way, Wonder Woman sets out after Master De Stroyer and his remaining War Mongers, but the villains are all annihilated when, while attempting to escape in a special "undersea car" developed by the people of the Sargasso Sea Kingdom, they crash head-on into one of De Stroyer's own mine fields and are blown to smithereens (WW No. 44: "The Monarch of the Sargasso Sea!" chs. I–III — no title; "Wonder Woman's Decision"; "The Final Battle of the Sargasso Sea").

MASTERS, LEONA. The "former Olympic swimming champion" who is secretly Neptune (CC No. 9, Win '44: "The Subsea Pirates"). (See NEPTUNE [THE VILLAINESS].)

MAVIS. A former slave of BARONESS PAULA VON GUNTHER who matches wits with WONDER WOMAN on two separate occasions.

By April–May 1943 Baroness Paula von Gunther has abandoned her life of evil and entered into the service of the goddess APHRODITE, but Mavis, one of her former slave girls, is determined to wreak vengeance on the baroness for having kept her in bondage. Mavis kidnaps the baroness's young daughter, GERTA VON GUNTHER, from PARADISE ISLAND, but Wonder Woman pursues her, rescues Gerta, and turns Mavis over to MALA for rehabilitative training on Reform Island (see TRANSFORMATION ISLAND) (WW No. 4/4).

By July 1943 Mavis has escaped from Reform Island and fled to America, where she allies herself with a Nazi spy ring headquartered in a lumber camp "sabotage center" whose seemingly innocent logging operations provide deceptive cover for "Axis activities which extend all over America!"

Ignorant of the tenets of Aphrodite's law governing Wonder Woman's Amazon bracelets (see WONDER WOMAN [section C 2, the bracelets of submission]), Mavis captures Wonder Woman and makes the grievous mistake of attempting to weaken her by removing her bracelets. "Ha ha!" she gloats. "You're only a weak little captive now, Amazon girl!"

"I'm not **weak**," thinks Wonder Woman desperately, "— I'm **too strong**. The bracelets bound my strength to good purposes — now I'm completely uncontrolled! I'm free to **destroy** like a **man**!"

Freed from the restraints imposed by her bracelets of submission and impelled by an uncontrollable "surge of unbound strength," Wonder Woman goes completely berserk, defeating Mavis and smashing the cabins of the Nazi logging camp into kindling wood "in an orgy of unleashed power."

She is finally brought under control and back to her senses by her ally Baroness Paula von Gunther, who captures her with her own magic lasso (see WONDER WOMAN [section C 3, the magic lasso]). "Easy, darling — it's your Paula!" says the baroness. "Stop this mad orgy of strength — relax! I command you!"

Then, with Mavis and her Nazi cohorts defeated and Wonder Woman's mighty Amazon strength safely under control, the baroness welds Wonder Woman's bracelets back onto her wrists — "tighter than ever" — by means of a special "electrical forge" (Sen No. 19: "The Unbound Amazon").

MAZUMA (Countess). A stately, sinister blonde who kidnaps girls with golden eyes to work as slave laborers in her private diamond mine. Countess Mazuma and her henchmen are defeated by WONDER WOMAN in Spring 1944 with the aid of STEVE TREVOR and the HOLLIDAY GIRLS.

Countess Mazuma harbors a violent hatred for all girls with golden eyes. "I was a Spanish girl," she explains, "madly in love with my fiancé Franco Mendez. Suddenly one day without warning, I was arrested!"

Charged with treason by the authorities, the countess had been confronted by two accusers — her fiancé Franco Mendez and a mysterious "masked girl with golden eyes":

Without further trial I was put in a dungeon cell — cold, wet and dark.

Day and night I was haunted by the hated image of that masked girl who had stolen my sweetheart and falsely accused me!

After years of suffering in prison I managed to escape, helping a fellow prisoner to escape with me —

Out of gratitude, my companion shared the secret of this diamond mine — I became one of the wealthiest women in the world! But always I see eyes — eyes — golden eyes!

I have searched the world for that girl with golden eyes . . . .

Aided by Steve Trevor and the Holliday Girls, Wonder Woman defeats Countess Mazuma and her henchmen and rescues the kidnapped golden-eyed girls from their clutches. Countess Mazuma learns that the real perpetrator of the treason for which she was once wrongfully imprisoned was none other than her own fiancé, Franco Mendez, who had deliberately planted "treasonable documents" in her room in order to divert suspicion from himself.

The masked golden-eyed girl she has sought for so long is military intelligence agent Elva East, by coincidence one of the girls she had kidnapped to work in her mine. At the time, Elva had been duped by Franco Mendez into believing the countess guilty, and thus had been partially responsible for sending her to prison. Heartbroken over the grave injustice she helped inflict, Elva begs Countess Mazuma to forgive her, but the countess remains defiantly bitter and vows one day to have her revenge (CC No. 6: "The Mystery of Countess Mazuma!").

MENACE (Prof.). A cunning criminal who creates a spectacular WONDER WOMAN robot as part of his scheme to force the real Wonder Woman into retirement by making her appear obsolete. To his cohorts in the underworld, Prof. Menace is known as the Robot Master. He and his henchmen are ultimately apprehended by Wonder Woman.

In January 1960 Prof. Menace unveils his Wonder Woman robot, hailing it as the ideal replacement for the real Wonder Woman and challenging Wonder Woman to compete with it, with the loser promising to retire immediately. Only after Wonder Woman has agreed to the contest does Prof. Menace announce that it will consist of seeing which contestant can stay awake the longest. Since the robot requires no sleep, Wonder Woman is soon defeated. Despite the fact that Prof. Menace has won the contest through trickery, Wonder Woman feels that her honor demands that she keep her promise to retire.

She is winging her way toward PARADISE ISLAND when Prof. Menace, who is trailing her in a helicopter, unleashes his robot against her. Now realizing that Prof. Menace intends to use his robot for crime, and not as a robot crime-fighter, Wonder Woman destroys the robot by hurling it at a giant electric eel — thereby short-circuiting its sensitive electronic components — and swiftly apprehends Prof. Menace and his cohorts (WW No. 111/1: "The Robot Wonder Woman").

MENDEZ, MIMI. The treacherous international spy who is the leader of the Zoot Suit Gang as well as the operator of the Bandit Club, a crooked gambling casino.

In May 1944 WONDER WOMAN apprehends Mimi Mendez and flies her to Reform Island (see TRANS-

FORMATION ISLAND) for rehabilitative training. Before Wonder Woman can bring her plane (*see* WONDER WOMAN [section C 4, the robot plane]) in for a landing, however, Mimi leaps from the aircraft and parachutes onto Reform Island, where she sneaks aboard a grounded Amazon airplane. Later, when the unsuspecting MALA pilots the plane out over the ocean, Mimi emerges from hiding and knocks her unconscious, tosses Mala out of the airplane, and points the craft in the direction of New York City.

Regaining consciousness in midair, Mala survives the fall into the water and swims to New York, where, while wandering about the city, she is once again taken captive by the ruthless Mimi. Wonder Woman attempts to rescue her, only to be forced to surrender to protect Mala from harm. Ultimately, however, with the aid of STEVE TREVOR, ETTA CANDY, and the HOLLIDAY GIRLS, Wonder Woman and Mala turn the tables on Mimi and her henchmen and take them into custody.

"I'm sorry, Mimi —" remarks Wonder Woman. "You've exchanged character reform in pleasant bondage on Paradise Island for painful punishment in this man's world!" (Sen No. 29: "Adventure of the Escaped Prisoner").

MENISE, MONA. A vindictive redhead — desperately in love with STEVE TREVOR and insanely jealous of WONDER WOMAN — who becomes miraculously endowed with the powers of the mythological Sirens.

In July–August 1948, after purchasing a simple wooden bracelet, Mona discovers that she has somehow become endowed with the power of the Sirens — the ability to make men obey her through the irresistible magic of her singing.

Long ago, the goddess APHRODITE transformed the evil Sirens into trees as punishment for their having lured innocent men to their doom with their haunting, hypnotic song. Many years later, the tree in which the Siren PARTHENOPE was imprisoned was blown out to sea by a storm; eventually it provided the wood from which Mona's bracelet was fashioned. Now Mona's jealous, vindictive personality enables Parthenope to work her evil magic through Mona.

Using her newly acquired Siren powers, Mona attempts to murder Wonder Woman, and later tries to kill Steve Trevor in retaliation for his refusal to reciprocate her affections. Wonder Woman escapes the various attempts on her life, however, and ultimately takes Mona into custody. Parthenope, who finally emerges full-blown from the magic bracelet, will be turned over to Aphrodite for punishment, while Mona will be sent to TRANSFORMATION ISLAND to learn to control her jealousy and vindictiveness (WW No. 30/2: "The Song of the Sirens!").

MEPHISTO (Emperor). The satanic emperor of the planet SATURN (CC No. 22, Aug/Sep '47: "The Captives of Saturnette!").

In Fall 1944 Mephisto is the mastermind behind DUKE MEPHISTO SATURNO's repeated attempts to capture WONDER WOMAN and thus pave the way for a Saturnian invasion of Earth to "get a new supply of strong slaves for physical labor" on Saturn (WW No. 10/2: "The Sky Road").

After Wonder Woman has defeated Duke Mephisto Saturno, however, and has convinced the Saturnian emperor of the economic advantages of establishing friendly relations with Earth, Mephisto "signs a peace and trade treaty with Earth" (WW No. 10/3, Fall '44: "Wonder Woman's Boots!"). The treaty specifically forbids the use of earthlings as Saturnian slaves. Count Dendum is appointed Saturn's first ambassador to the United States (WW No. 11/3, Win '44: "The Slave Smugglers").

In Winter 1944 Hypnota attempts to sabotage the peace treaty in hopes of bringing about a revival of the Earth-Saturn slave trade, but her efforts are repeatedly thwarted by Wonder Woman (WW No. 11/1–3: "The Slaves of the Evil Eye"; "The Unseen Menace"; "The Slave Smugglers"). (*See* HYPNOTA [THE GREAT].)

MER-BOY. *See* MERMAN.

MERCURY. The smallest of the major planets, and the closest planet to the SUN.

Mercury is the scene of a battle pitting WONDER WOMAN and the HOLLIDAY GIRLS against QUEEN CELERITA and the beautiful "flying giantesses" in November–December 1947 (WW No. 26/1: "Speed Maniacs from Mercury!"). (*See* CELERITA [QUEEN].)

In October 1954 Wonder Woman demolishes an armada of Mercurian spacecraft intent on conquering Earth "as a base to attack Jupiter" (WW No. 69/1: "Seeds of Peril!").

MERLIN. In Arthurian legend, a wizard, seer, and counselor to KING ARTHUR. In Wonder Woman No. 54/1, Merlin is portrayed as a villain who has stolen Arthur's enchanted sword, Excalibur, kidnapped QUEEN GUINEVERE, and locked them both away in his impregnable stronghold, Castle Sinister. Wonder Woman defeats the evil Merlin during a time-journey to Arthur's Camelot that she makes in July–August 1952 ("The Wizard of Castle Sinister!"). (*See* ARTHUR [KING].)

MERMAN. The half man, half fish — an inhabitant of the waters off PARADISE ISLAND — who was WONDER WOMAN's teen-age sweetheart and who, as an adult, becomes STEVE TREVOR's rival for Wonder Woman's affections. The texts are extremely inconsistent regarding his real name: as an adolescent, he is variously referred to as Ronno (WW No. 107/1, Jul '59: "Wonder Woman, Amazon Teen-Ager!"), Renno (WW No. 111/2, Jan '60: "Battle of the Mermen!"), and Mer-Boy; as an adult, he is alternately referred to as Manno (WW No. 118, Nov '60: "Wonder Woman's Impossible Decision!") and Merman (WW No. 125, Oct '61: "Wonder Woman--Battle Prize!").

AS IF IT WERE AN UNDER-WATER BUCKING BRONC...

HE'S PROVING HIS POINT! STEVE COULD NEVER DO THAT!

© NPP 1961

Wonder Woman and Merman, 1961

A member of a peace-loving undersea race inhabiting the waters off Paradise Island, Merman first met Wonder Woman while they both were teen-agers and apparently represented her sole romantic involvement throughout her adolescence (WW No. 107/1, Jul '59: "Wonder Woman, Amazon Teen-Ager!").

Merman makes his first textual appearance as an adult in November 1960, shortly following Wonder Woman's rejection of Steve Trevor's latest marriage proposal on the ground that she cannot marry so long as she is needed to battle crime and injustice. Suspicious that there may be another

man in Wonder Woman's life, Trevor follows Wonder Woman in a long-distance experimental airplane the next time she leaves the United States for one of her periodic visits to Paradise Island. By the time he finally overtakes her, Wonder Woman has landed her Amazon plane (*see* WONDER WOMAN [section C 4, the robot plane]) near the water's edge and is laughing and talking with her friend Merman.

Now convinced that he has a rival for Wonder Woman's affections, Trevor is determined to prove to her that he is a better man than Merman, but his plans receive a setback when a wave sweeps him into the sea and Merman dives into the water to rescue him from the tentacled grip of a giant octopus. Now Trevor feels doubly mortified: not only has a romantic rival appeared to threaten his relationship with Wonder Woman, but his rival has just rescued him from seemingly certain death. As Merman recounts his teen-age meeting with Wonder Woman and the many adventures they shared, it is clear that time has not diminished his affection for her. Soon afterward, however, Trevor evens the score with his rival by rescuing him from the clutches of a giant bird of prey.

Finally, as the Merman-Trevor rivalry nears its climax, Wonder Woman finds herself faced with the agonizing dilemma of having to rescue one of them while abandoning the other to virtually certain doom: both are clinging to the edge of a rocky precipice and there is not sufficient time to rescue both of them. For a moment, it seems that Wonder Woman will be forced to make a life-and-death choice between the two important men in her life, but at the last possible instant she executes a series of spectacular feats that enable her to rescue them both, leaving unanswered the question of which she would have rescued had she actually been compelled to choose between them (WW No. 118: "Wonder Woman's Impossible Decision!").

In October 1961 Steve Trevor decides to challenge Merman to a contest in order to establish, once and for all, which of them is more worthy of Wonder Woman's affection. When Wonder Woman boards her Amazon plane for a trip to Paradise Island, Trevor climbs aboard also, insisting that she take him to Merman so that he can have the satisfaction of proving to her that he — and not Merman — is the man she should really marry.

Wonder Woman reluctantly agrees, and before long Trevor and Merman are locked in a contest to determine which of them is the better man. The first two parts of the contest have ended in a tie, with Merman having easily demonstrated his superiority in the water and Trevor having just as

THRUSTING *WONDER WOMAN* OUT OF THE WAY...

BUT *I* CAN RIP UP A LENGTH OF THIS SEA WEED AND--!

RRRIPP!

© NPP 1961

Merman, 1961

easily demonstrated his superiority on land, when suddenly Trevor, Merman, and Wonder Woman are viciously attacked by a giant bird. As they lie helpless on the ground, momentarily stunned by the impact of the giant bird's brutal onslaught, a strange flying saucerlike craft appears overhead and a knight in shining armor, mounted atop a winged steed, emerges from inside it, fearlessly attacking the monstrous bird and thus rescuing Wonder Woman and her friends from seemingly certain death.

Wonder Woman is clearly smitten by the valiant knight, who introduces himself as the legendary Sir Galahad, explaining that he has journeyed to the 20th century from the distant past in his flying saucerlike time machine. When Galahad asks Wonder Woman to marry him, the lovestruck Amazon promptly accepts.

Enraged at Galahad's success, Merman and Trevor challenge him to participate in their contest to prove that he is worthy of Wonder Woman's love. To their consternation, however, the knightly intruder not only accepts their challenge but promptly defeats them both, Trevor in a judo match on land and Merman in a battle in the water.

Her heart won by the handsome knight, Wonder Woman climbs aboard his winged steed and flies with him into the heart of his "time machine," only to look on in horror as her handsome suitor undergoes a terrifying metamorphosis:

"M-M-Merciful Minerva!" she gasps. "You're not a knight from . . . the past! (Gasp-gasp) or even a human . . . at all! You're an amoebic creature from outer space!"

"AIEEEEEEE!" cries the space creature. "I assumed that Earth metamorphosis as part of my invasion plan! To lull your suspicions! AIEEEEE!"

Then, with a gasp, Wonder Woman lapses into unconsciousness, unable to breathe in the extraterrestrial atmosphere of the alien's flying saucer, while the malevolent amoeba creature rockets into outer space toward a prearranged rendezvous with an alien invasion fleet that is poised to attack Paradise Island and then overrun the Earth.

As the alien invaders streak toward Paradise Island, however, Wonder Woman reaches the communications system of the flying saucer in which she is being held prisoner and broadcasts a desperate appeal to the AMAZONS to save Earth at all costs. Aboard Wonder Woman's Amazon plane, Merman and Trevor hear Wonder Woman's call to arms and race bravely to the attack, downing several of the alien spacecraft and finally ramming the flying saucer in which Wonder Woman is being held captive. As both the Amazon plane and the rammed flying saucer plummet into the sea, Wonder Woman swims free of the demolished saucer and carries her plane — with Merman and Trevor still on board — safely to the surface. In the sky overhead, the Amazon space fleet defeats the last of the invading aliens and saves Earth from destruction, but Merman and Trevor remain disgruntled since they still have not managed to settle the question of which of them Wonder Woman really cares for the most (WW No. 125: "Wonder Woman--Battle Prize!").

MERMEN. The fishlike men who are the "ancient foes" of the AMAZONS. In October 1957 they kidnap QUEEN HIPPOLYTE while she is taking a swim and set in motion an elaborate scheme to bore through PARADISE ISLAND from underneath, thus flooding the island and sending it plummeting to the bottom of the sea. After a long search, however, WONDER WOMAN finally locates the place where her mother is being held captive, rescues her, and routs the Mermen (WW No. 93/1: "Menace of the Mermen!").

MERRILY, HERBERT. The man who, twenty years ago, left Meg Sourpuss — now dean of the HOLLIDAY COLLEGE FOR WOMEN — waiting at the altar rather than marry her over the objections of her parents. Merrily reenters Sourpuss's life and marries her in January–February 1950, thus changing her name from Dean Meg Sourpuss to DEAN MEG MERRILY.

Twenty years ago, Meg Sourpuss's parents had been strenuously opposed to her plans to marry

Herbert Merrily, and so the couple had decided to elope. At the last moment, however, Merrily had backed out, failing to meet her at the justice of the peace and sending instead a brief note saying that he could not marry her against the wishes of her parents. Since that unhappy day, Meg Sourpuss has never again permitted romance to enter her life.

In January–February 1950, however, Herbert Merrily reenters the dean's life and begins to court her anew. Dean Sourpuss is delighted to see Merrily again, unaware that he is secretly in league with the villain MIDAS, who has instructed him to worm his way into the dean's confidence so that he can steal the $200,000 worth of research radium being stored at Holliday College. When PRINCE SLEEKO of ZANI ISLAND presents the college with a lavish gift of precious jewels out of gratitude for the past efforts of the HOLLIDAY GIRLS on behalf of his people, Midas decides to steal the jewels along with the radium, but WONDER WOMAN ultimately thwarts the theft and apprehends Midas and his henchmen.

Dean Sourpuss is heartbroken to learn of Merrily's involvement in the ill-fated jewel and radium heist, until, under the compelling influence of Wonder Woman's magic lasso (see WONDER WOMAN [section C 3, the magic lasso]), Merrily reveals that Midas had learned of his previous involvement with the dean and had threatened to kill her unless he cooperated in the theft scheme. Realizing now that Merrily agreed to help the criminals only to protect her, Dean Sourpuss forgives him and accepts his new proposal of marriage.

Determined to make the spinsterish dean more beautiful in preparation for the coming wedding, Wonder Woman creates a lovely dress of "pure gold-spun cloth" for her to wear, provides her with "a new hairdo and some makeup," and removes her unsightly eyeglasses, thereby transforming her from a grouchy-looking old maid into a truly beautiful woman.

"The dean's true beauty comes from within," explains Wonder Woman, "as every woman's does--when she radiates love!" (WW No. 39/2: "The Modern Midas!").

MERRILY, MEG (Dean). DEAN STRIKT's successor as dean of the HOLLIDAY COLLEGE FOR WOMEN. Dean Merrily – who makes her textual debut in March–April 1946 (WW No. 16/1: "The Secret of the Dark Planet!") – is referred to by her maiden name, Dean Meg Sourpuss, until her marriage to HERBERT MERRILY in January–February 1950 (WW No. 39/2: "The Modern Midas!").

Dean Meg Sourpuss – a bespectacled, ill-tem-pered spinster – first appears as dean of Holliday College in March–April 1946 (WW No. 16/1: "The Secret of the Dark Planet!"). In the ensuing three and a half years she makes several appearances in the chronicles, none of them consequential.

In November–December 1949, however, Dean Sourpuss is inexplicably replaced by a new, much prettier dean – Dean Meg Merrily (WW No. 38/3: "The Five Tasks of Thomas Tighe!"). The appearance of Dean Merrily at this early date can only be ascribed to chronicler's error, for Dean Sourpuss and Dean Merrily are actually the same person: Dean Sourpuss becomes Dean Merrily when she marries Herbert Merrily in January–February 1950 (WW No. 39/2: "The Modern Midas!").

Having embarked on a new life of connubial bliss, Dean Merrily becomes, almost literally, a new person: formerly grouchy and ill-tempered, she becomes loving, generous, and warm-hearted. With WONDER WOMAN's help, she undergoes an astonishing physical transformation as well – from a bespectacled maiden aunt into a truly beautiful woman (WW No. 39/2, Jan/Feb '50: "The Modern Midas!") – retaining this lovelier appearance throughout all her future textual appearances (Sen No. 105, Sep/Oct '51: "The Secret of the Giant Forest"; Sen No. 106, Nov/Dec '51: "The Knights of Terror!"; and others). (*See also* MERRILY, HERBERT.)

METEOR MEN, THE. The brutal inhabitants of the gigantic meteor Comas Sola. An attempt by the Meteor Men to overrun the planet VENUS is thwarted by WONDER WOMAN and the Venusians in October–November 1942 (AS No. 13: "Shanghaied into Space!"). (*See* DESIRA [QUEEN].)

MIDAS. A villainous modern Midas, an underworld gang chief who dresses in a monarch's regal raiment and maintains an ostentatious storeroom crammed with priceless treasure. His attempt to steal a gift of precious jewels and a stockpile of radium from the HOLLIDAY COLLEGE FOR WOMEN is thwarted by WONDER WOMAN in January–February 1950 (WW No. 39/2: "The Modern Midas!"). (*See* MERRILY, HERBERT.)

MIKRA. An ancient Egyptian desert kingdom – ruled by the treacherous QUEEN MIKRA – which flourished seven thousand years ago (WW No. 113: "The Invasion of the Sphinx Creatures!").

MIKRA (Queen). The treacherous ruler of Mikra, an ancient Egyptian desert kingdom which flourished seven thousand years ago. Unearthed by archaeologists in April 1960, her mummy returns miraculously to life and attempts to lead an awesome army of great stone "sphinx creatures" in "the conquest of all the lands beyond the desert!"

"Noble queen!" pleads WONDER WOMAN. "I

beseech you to halt the invasion of the sphinx creatures--before innocent people are harmed!"

"What care I for mere lives," replies Mikra coldly, "--when my kingdom can be enlarged beyond measure! And I can become the mightiest queen on Earth!"

Wonder Woman finally brings about the destruction of the seemingly-invincible sphinx army, thus ending their terrifying invasion. As she struggles with Queen Mikra in the desert sands, the lovely queen suddenly ages and withers before her very eyes, until, within the space of a few horrifying seconds, she collapses in ancient dust at Wonder Woman's feet (WW No. 113: "The Invasion of the Sphinx Creatures!").

MOLECULAR ASSEMBLER. A super-scientific device employed by an octopuslike alien from a distant planet as part of his scheme to loot the Earth. The villainous alien and his earthling henchmen are defeated in May 1955 through the heroic efforts of WONDER WOMAN.

On two separate occasions in May 1955, Wonder Woman captures a gang of criminals, only to have them escape by disappearing into thin air before her very eyes. The second time this happens, however, Wonder Woman tears a mysterious octopus emblem from the coat of one of the criminals on the hunch that it may somehow be related to their uncanny ability to vanish.

Indeed, no sooner has Wonder Woman seized the strange emblem than she is instantaneously "transported to another planet," where she finds herself "in a great weird hall, facing an unearthly being" with yellow skin, two legs, and four arms. Then the octopuslike alien speaks:

> Cheee! By touching the emblem, you established electronic contact with my molecular assembler! This disassembled your molecular structure on Earth — and reassembled it here! An interplanetary travel technique of incalculable speed which Earth scientists can only dream of ever perfecting! Aieee!
>
> Soon, the gangs I send out will loot Earth of everything valuable it possesses! From precious jewels to atomic stockpiles! Until your planet cannot even support its own inhabitants! Aieee!

After immobilizing Wonder Woman with a paralysis ray and locking her inside a glass prison in his laboratory, the alien returns to Earth with his earthling henchmen to continue his robbing and looting. "By means of this molecular assembler," gloats the alien, "we shall appear on Earth — loot as we please — and disappear — and no power can stop us! Heee--he!"

Left alone in the alien's laboratory, however, Wonder Woman breaks out of the glass prison,

shakes off the effects of the paralysis ray, and demolishes the alien's molecular assembler. Returning to Earth, she learns that the alien and his accomplices, unable to flee Earth now that Wonder Woman has destroyed their molecular assembler, have already been apprehended by the police (WW No. 74/2: "The Vanishing Villains!").

MOLE GOLDINGS. Members of a sinister subterranean civilization who attempt to conquer the Earth by transforming it into "a wasteland of gold." The Mole Goldings are annihilated by WONDER WOMAN.

In February 1955 the people of Earth awake to discover that nearly all plant life has somehow become transformed into gold. Although people are ecstatic at first over their new-found wealth, gold soon becomes so abundant as to be virtually worthless and the loss of all crops threatens mankind with extinction.

Burrowing far beneath the Earth in her Amazon plane (see WONDER WOMAN [section C 4, the robot plane]), Wonder Woman soon finds herself in "an immense cavern" inhabited by a civilization of "gold mole men [who] are secretly changing the Earth into solid gold which is threatening to doom the entire planet!"

The gold mole men — known as the Mole Goldings — pulverize Wonder Woman with a devastating barrage of "gold ray blasts" which alter her "molecular structure" and transform her into a "solid gold figure — incapable of motion!" Then, with Wonder Woman helpless, the leader of the "weird gold creatures" uses "mental projection" to tell her the details of his people's diabolical plot against the Earth:

> Long have we **Mole Goldings** lived underground, preparing to take over the outside of this planet! We are strangling Earth's soil with a special gold which changes the molecular structure of everything which grows! Earthlings will starve and vanish!
>
> Soon, Earth will become a wasteland of gold, inhabited solely by us---and earthlings will be as forgotten as the cavemen!

By commanding her robot plane to burrow even further underground, however, Wonder Woman uses the intense heat at the Earth's core to melt away the solid gold coating in which the Mole Goldings have imprisoned her. Burrowing back toward the Earth's surface, she creates a channel through which the flames at the Earth's core can reach the surface to melt the gold threatening to engulf the Earth. With Earth thus saved from destruction, Wonder Woman seals up the channel she has made, sending the searing flames from the Earth's core hurtling back toward the center of the

Earth. As the flames roar back underground, they completely destroy the Mole Goldings' civilization, ending forever their dream of conquest (WW No. 72/2: "The Golden Doom!").

MOLE MEN. A term used in the WONDER WOMAN chronicles to describe the inhabitants of any subterranean civilization.

The term first appears in Wonder Woman No. 4/2, where it is used in connection with the subterranean society ruled by the ruthless BLAKFU (Apr/May '43).

Wonder Woman No. 35/2 describes a second subterranean civilization, inhabited by Mole Men and Mole Women. It is these Mole Women who unwittingly help DIRK JAXO build his diabolical "brain wave interferer" (May/Jun '49: "Jaxo, Master of Thought!").

Wonder Woman No. 47/1 features a third group of Mole Men — the inhabitants of a subterranean country located far beneath the North Polar ice. Dispatched to the North Pole to establish a radar station capable of providing America with advance warning in the event of a sneak atomic attack by the hostile nation of Warlandia, STEVE TREVOR and his aircraft crew are shot out of the sky by antiaircraft and taken prisoner by the Mole Men who inhabit a mysterious land beneath the surface of the North Pole.

When Trevor fails to return from his mission, Wonder Woman flies to the North Pole in her Amazon plane (*see* WONDER WOMAN [section C 4, the robot plane]), is fired upon by the same antiaircraft weaponry that downed Trevor's aircraft, and allows herself to be taken captive by the Mole Men in hopes of somehow locating Trevor and his crewmen. Explaining that their homeland was recently subjected to a fierce bombing attack, the Mole Men express their determination to shoot down any plane that flies over the North Pole. Wonder Woman tries to tell her captors that the bombers must have come from Warlandia, but the Mole Men refuse to believe her.

The Warlandians, meanwhile, having learned of Wonder Woman's North Pole mission, promptly initiate "Project DA--the destruction of America," by dispatching a fleet of bombers to the North Pole so that they can "launch [their] atomic weapons at America from there immediately, before a defense system can be set up or **Wonder Woman** can stop [them]!"

As the drone of Warlandian warplanes shatters the North Polar silence, Wonder Woman — realizing that America is about to fall prey to a Warlandian sneak attack — breaks free of her captors, flees the subterranean world of the Mole Men, and singlehandedly demolishes the entire Warlandian bomber fleet. The Mole Men, now realizing that the people of America are their friends and the ruthless Warlandians their enemies, promptly release Steve Trevor and his crewmen and permit them to leave their land in safety (May/Jun '51: "World Below the North Pole!").

Wonder Woman No. 57/1 introduces a fourth civilization of Mole Men. When the Amazon scientist Milla mysteriously disappears while aquaplaning in January–February 1953, Wonder Woman searches through her laboratory for a possible clue to her disappearance and learns that Milla, engaged in the study of earthquakes, had discovered that all earthquakes originate from a single spot somewhere beneath the Earth.

Using Milla's notes as a guide, Wonder Woman journeys to an "underground world" lying far beneath the ocean floor, only to be taken captive by the Mole Men who dwell there. Milla was kidnapped by the Mole Men, Wonder Woman soon discovers, when her research into earthquakes brought her to the verge of uncovering their diabolical scheme to conquer the Earth.

"Now that you're a prisoner too, **Wonder Woman,**" gloats the Mole Men's leader, "nothing will stop me from cracking the crust of the upper earth with the super vibration of my earthquake maker! Then, when all the upper earthmen have perished, we Mole-Men shall take their places---"

Imprisoned by the Mole Men in a weird "vibratory bubble," Wonder Woman escapes and flees with Milla to the safety of her Amazon plane. As her plane begins its long ascent to the upper world, Wonder Woman lassoes the Mole Men's "earthquake maker" with her magic lasso (*see* WONDER WOMAN [section C 3, the magic lasso]), intending to tow it to the surface to prevent the Mole Men from using it against the Earth. As the furious Mole Men fire their ray guns at the fleeing Amazons, however, a stray shot hits the earthquake maker, causing a titanic explosion that destroys the diabolical earthquake maker and the Mole Men's entire subterranean civilization as well ("The Man Who Shook the Earth!").

Wonder Woman No. 72/2, features a fifth group of Mole Men, the MOLE GOLDINGS, who, in February 1955, begin "changing the Earth into solid gold" in a fiendish attempt "to doom the entire planet!" ("The Golden Doom!").

MOLTONIA. An exotic world, lit by a pale blue sun, which lies far beneath the North Polar ice. Moltonia is the scene of WONDER WOMAN's battle with the evil LORD CRUELO in July–August 1949 (WW No. 36/3: "The Return of the Flying Saucers!").

MONARCH STUDIOS. The Hollywood movie studio which produces *Hollywood Goes to Paradise Island* in March–April 1950. Attempts by TORA RIVVERS to sabotage the film are thwarted by WONDER WOMAN (WW No. 40/1: "Hollywood Goes to Paradise Island" pts. 1–2 – "The Mile High Menace!"; "The Undersea Invasion!").

In November–December 1950 Monarch Studios films *The Wonder Woman Story*, directed by IGOR GORGO, with Diana Prince – the girl who is secretly Wonder Woman – in the starring role (Sen No. 100: "Wonder Woman, Hollywood Star!").

MONTE GANG, THE. A gang of criminals who steal WONDER WOMAN's Amazon plane (*see* WONDER WOMAN [section C 4, the robot plane]) in July–August 1951. Posing as members of an "amateur aviation model plane club," the Monte Gang trick Wonder Woman into lecturing them about her plane and its unique capabilities, particularly its ability to respond to the sound of her voice. Then, after editing a tape recording of Wonder Woman's talk to enable them to duplicate her verbal commands mechanically, the criminals take Wonder Woman captive and use her plane to commit a spectacular robbery. Wonder Woman ultimately turns the tables on her captors, however, recovers her plane, and apprehends the criminals (WW No. 48/3: "The Theft of the Robot Plane").

MOON. The only known natural satellite of the Earth.

According to Wonder Woman No. 61/1, the moon is a fragment of the planet Earth, hurled into space "eons ago" by the force of an atomic explosion set off by the evil "troglodytes" (*see* TROGLODYTES) (Sep/Oct '53: "Earth's Last Hour!").

According to Wonder Woman No. 5/2, the moon is the domain of the goddess DIANA, who presides over the elaborate system of "moon mirrors" which give the moon its light. A Martian invasion of the moon is thwarted by WONDER WOMAN in June–July 1943.

According to Sensation Comics No. 82, "the moon is **hollow!** It contains a planet and a sun of its own. There is no life or atmosphere on the **outside** of the moon, but there **is** a highly developed civilization **inside!**" A scheme by KING LUNAR, the evil ruler of the so-called "inner moon-planet," to invade the Earth is thwarted by Wonder Woman in October 1948 ("Brain Pirates from the Inner Moon-World!").

According to Wonder Woman No. 85/1, the surface of the moon is inhabited by a race of moon people who achieve their independence from the dictatorial DUKE BALE through the heroic efforts of Wonder Woman in October 1956 ("The Sword in the Sky!").

MOONO (King). The "king of the leprechauns."

Moono and his subjects are aided by WONDER WOMAN in November–December 1953.

Responding to an emergency summons from King Moono in November–December 1953, Wonder Woman journeys to "the secret land of the leprechauns," where, to her surprise, she finds all the leprechauns falling asleep. Slowly, wearily, his eyes heavy with sleep, Moono explains that "the flame---in our magic lamp---which gives us our special powers---has gone---out!

"You must---replenish the flame," continues the leprechaun king, barely able to keep awake, "---or we will fall asleep---and be powerless to fight the gnomes, goblins---and all the evil spirits . . . !"

Climbing aboard her Amazon plane (*see* WONDER WOMAN [section C 4, the robot plane]), Wonder Woman races into outer space to replenish the flame of the magic lamp, filling it first with "solar heat from the sun" and then with "cosmic dust" from the tail of Halley's Comet. Ultimately, under the influence of the rekindled lamp, the leprechauns reawaken, thus assuring that the gnomes and goblins will not be able to usurp the leprechauns' magic powers and use them for evil (WW No. 62/2: "Lamp of the Leprechauns!").

MOUSE MAN. A tiny villain, not much larger than a mouse, who matches wits with WONDER WOMAN on three separate occasions between 1963 and 1967. A normal man except for his minute size, Mouse Man wears a mouse costume which is sometimes yellow and sometimes gray. On several occasions, he exhibits the uncanny ability to make rats and mice obey his commands.

In October 1963 the underworld unveils a golden statuette – the so-called "Golden WW" – which it intends to award, like a filmland Oscar, to the criminal who either captures or destroys Wonder Woman during the week the underworld "academy" is in session. After the ANGLE MAN and the FIREWORKS MAN have failed in their separate bids to win the Golden WW, a diminutive villain in a yellow mouse costume steps forward to announce his intention to win the coveted gangland award for himself.

Still temporarily blind as the result of her dazzling encounter with the Fireworks Man, Wonder Woman is hard put to cope with this "minute nemesis" when he sneaks into her office, taunts her unmercifully, and demands that she return with him to the underworld academy so that he can establish his right to the Golden WW. Apparently helpless in the face of Mouse Man's malicious antics without her eyesight to aid her, Wonder Woman finally surrenders and accompanies Mouse Man to the academy, where she becomes the laughingstock of the assembled criminals for

Mouse Man, 1964

AND IT ALL CAME FROM MY EXPERIMENTS WITH THESE! COUNTLESS EXPERIMENTS WHICH RESULTED IN MY PRESENT SIZE! AND MADE ME--

© NPP 1964

having allowed herself to be captured by such a tiny opponent. The evil laughter ceases, abruptly, however, when Wonder Woman seizes the pillars supporting the underworld meeting hall and pulls at them until the entire building begins to crumble.

As the panicky criminals race into the street, they are taken into custody by waiting police, tipped off in advance by Wonder Woman. Mouse Man attempts to flee with the Golden WW, but Wonder Woman, her eyesight now returned to normal, apprehends him. Mouse Man never suspects that Wonder Woman allowed him to take her prisoner only so that she could capture the entire underworld audience on hand for the awarding of the Golden WW (WW No. 141: "The Academy of Arch-Villains!").

In January 1964 Mouse Man — now clad in a gray costume — escapes from prison by arranging to be transferred to the prison hospital and then releasing the hospital's white mice from their cages and riding one of them through the labyrinthine network of mouse tunnels out beyond the prison walls to freedom.

Soon afterward, Mouse Man captures Wonder Woman, binds her with her own magic lasso (*see* WONDER WOMAN [section C 3, the magic lasso]), and forces her to fly him and his prison-mouse allies to his secret laboratory hideaway, where he locks her in an oversized mouse cage and forces her to perform a series of humiliating "mouse stunts" on the cage's ladders, wheels, and other apparatus. After being accidentally doused with

some of the same reducing chemical that Mouse Man once used to reduce himself in size, however, Wonder Woman — now reduced to an even smaller size than that of Mouse Man himself — slips between the bars of the villain's cage and races through the laboratory with Mouse Man and his rodents in hot pursuit. Ultimately, however, the effects of the secret chemical wear off and Wonder Woman, having regained her normal size, swiftly apprehends Mouse Man and returns him to prison (WW No. 143/2: "The Amazon Mouse Trap!").

Imprisoned inside a birdcage suspended within a regulation-size prison cell and guarded by a cat to thwart any attempt at escape, Mouse Man nevertheless breaks jail in July–August 1967 by using his power over rodents to command the prison's mice to distract the cat while he makes his escape. Employing a band of mice as his accomplices, Mouse Man commits a series of spectacular crimes capitalizing on the diminutive size of himself and his rodent henchmen, and even succeeds in taking Wonder Woman prisoner. Back at the villain's hideout, however, Wonder Woman turns the tables on Mouse Man and apprehends him (WW No. 171/2: "Menace of the Mouse Man!").

MU. A legendary island in the Atlantic Ocean which was the site of a thriving civilization until it sank to the bottom of the sea. Mu is also known as ATLANTIS. In the WONDER WOMAN chronicles, however, Mu and Atlantis are apparently two different places. Wonder Woman visits the "lost land" of Mu — described as "a continent which vanished 9000 years ago" — during a time-journey that she makes in September–October 1951 (WW No. 49/1: "Return of the Phantom Empire"). (*See* GHU [PRINCE].)

MULTIPLE MAN. A fearsome creature of utter evil — capable of assuming a multitude of different forms and shapes — who is the freak by-product of a titanic nuclear explosion. Multiple Man is the villain of some of WONDER WOMAN's "impossible tales."

While visiting PARADISE ISLAND and answering some of her accumulated fan mail in August 1961, Wonder Woman remarks that many of her readers have expressed the desire to see Wonder Woman, Wonder Tot, Wonder Girl, and QUEEN HIPPOLYTE together in a single adventure.

Since Wonder Tot and Wonder Girl are only names used to describe Wonder Woman as an infant and teen-ager respectively, the three of them could never actually participate simultaneously in a real-life adventure, but by splicing together thousands of feet of movie film of Wonder Woman in action during different periods of her life — and then creating a sound track to match — Wonder

Woman and Hippolyte succeed in producing a film of an action-packed adventure which never actually took place — a so-called "impossible tale." Both this first impossible tale (WW No. 124, Aug '61: "The Impossible Day!"), and a second one eight months later (WW No. 129, Apr '62: "The Return of Multiple Man!"), pit the "Wonder family" — Wonder Woman, Wonder Tot, Wonder Girl, and Queen Hippolyte — against the villainous Multiple Man, a "nuclear menace" who can be temporarily defeated, but never destroyed.

MURKTON. The far-distant planet which is ruled by QUEEN PALLIDA (WW No. 33/2, Jan/Feb '49: "The Menace of Murkton!").

MUSSOLINI, BENITO (1883–1945). The Italian statesman and leader of the Fascist movement who governed Italy as prime minister from 1922 to 1943, but with the powers of a dictator from 1925 onward. He was shot to death by Italian partisans, who hung his body, head downward, in the Piazza Loreto in Milan. Mussolini dispatches COUNT CRAFTI and Mammotha to America in Fall 1942 with orders to capture STEVE TREVOR and WONDER WOMAN (WW No. 2/4). (*See* CRAFTI [COUNT].)

NAGLE, BERTHA. A Nazi spy who is exposed and apprehended by WONDER WOMAN.

By Fall 1943 Wonder Woman has presented the United States military with her latest invention, a "torpedo-protection apparatus" designed to provide American warships with a "protective shield against torpedoes" by using "hydraulic pressure" to activate a special "torpedo shield" the moment an enemy submarine is sighted. The basic component of the apparatus is the top-secret "pressure coordinator," which "controls all the machinery" employed in the activation of the torpedo shield.

Installed aboard a WAAC transport vessel for testing in Fall 1943, the torpedo-protection apparatus becomes the target of Nazi agents, who are determined to steal the vital pressure coordinator. The mastermind behind the Nazi effort is secretly Bertha Nagle, secretary to the engineer in charge of the testing, but Wonder Woman exposes and apprehends Bertha as a Nazi spy and singlehandedly defeats a submarine full of Nazis who attack the WAAC transport (CC No. 4: "The Purloined Pressure Coordinator").

NAXOK (Duke). An evil duke whose attempt to seize power in an ancient desert kingdom is thwarted by WONDER WOMAN during one of her journeys into the past.

Wonder Woman and STEVE TREVOR are "on a scientific expedition" in a far-off desert in August 1955, when suddenly they come upon the broken fragments of a once-massive ancient statue which, once Wonder Woman has reassembled them, form a gigantic sphinxlike monument whose face bears a startling resemblance to Wonder Woman's own.

Journeying "thousands of years" into the past in hopes of solving the mystery, Wonder Woman rescues the benevolent King Hazeen and Queen Kara from the forces of the villainous Duke Naxok, who is determined to murder them and seize control of their desert kingdom. Eventually, with the villain defeated and Hazeen and Kara restored to their thrones, the populace expresses its gratitude to Wonder Woman by erecting a gigantic sphinxlike statue, bearing her features, in the desert sands, thus resolving the enigma of how she came to be immortalized in the ancient stone

monument (WW No. 76/2: "The Face in the Desert!").

NEPTUNE (the planet). The eighth planet from the SUN.

In Winter 1945 "a huge fragment" of the planet, "torn from Neptune by the combined [gravitational] pull of all planets," hurtles through space and lands in the middle of the PACIFIC OCEAN, forming the new Earth continent of NEPTUNIA (WW No. 15: chs. 1–3 — "The First Battle of Neptunia"; "The Masters of the Water"; "In the Killer's Cage"). (See also SOLO.)

NEPTUNE (the villainess). A ruthless villainess — disguised as the mythical king of the sea — who plunders merchant shipping until she is finally apprehended by WONDER WOMAN. Neptune is secretly women's Olympic swimming champion Leona Masters.

By Winter 1944 ". . . **23** ships have been sunk near the Equator with all on board! Survivors, found later, have lost their memories!" When a sailor comes to Military Intelligence with the story of how his ship was sunk — and the crew carried off — by a band of mermaids, STEVE TREVOR flies to the scene to investigate and is himself taken captive by the mysterious mermaids.

When Trevor fails to return, Wonder Woman follows him to Neptune's Isle, an uncharted island near the Equator, beneath which, in an undersea cave, she comes upon the lair of the villainess Neptune, who is clad in the male regalia of the legendary sea king and attended by lovely girls costumed as mermaids. Plundering merchant ships and stealing their cargoes, the mermaids have been using a diabolical mind-controlling drug to rob the vessels' crewmen of their memories and compel them to obey Neptune's commands.

Courageously invading Neptune's lair, Wonder Woman rescues Steve Trevor, frees Neptune's mermaid slaves from her mental control, and ultimately apprehends Neptune herself and unmasks her, for the first time, as a woman.

"Yes — I'm Leona Masters, former Olympic swimming champion!" confesses the villainess. "I broke training rules and they put me off the team — I swore to get revenge!

"The papers called me 'Mermaid Queen' and that gave me an idea — I've used the mermaid myth to plunder the world that I hate!" (CC No. 9: "The Subsea Pirates").

NEPTUNE'S ISLE. An uncharted island near the Equator, beneath which, in an undersea cave, is the hidden sanctuary of the villainess NEPTUNE (CC No. 9, Win '44: "The Subsea Pirates").

NEPTUNIA. A large fragment of the planet NEPTUNE, torn from its mother planet "by the combined [gravitational] pull of all planets" in Winter 1945, which hurtles through space until it finally lands in the middle of the PACIFIC OCEAN.

Neptunia, which is as large as an Earth continent, is ruled by the tyrannical SOLO, Neptunia's "master of masters." After Solo has been twice defeated by WONDER WOMAN, however, Neptunia becomes "a protectorate pledging its complete allegiance to America" (WW No. 15: chs. 1–3 — "The First Battle of Neptunia"; "The Masters of the Water"; "In the Killer's Cage"), and soon afterward, at Wonder Woman's urging, it is placed in the hands of an all-woman government headed by "Presidenta" Una (WW No. 31/2, Sep/Oct '48: "The Planet of Plunder!"). (*See* SOLO.)

NERO. The brutal ruler of New Discovery Island, an "uncharted island" kingdom populated by the descendants of ancient Romans who settled there thousands of years ago. Nero is a direct descendant of the ancient Roman emperor Nero.

By March 1945 a naval patrol ship has discovered a hitherto uncharted island — dubbed New Discovery Island — "between Africa and South America," and sailors aboard the patrol ship have reported sighting a Caucasian male in Roman armor standing on the beach. Certain that the mysterious armored man "must be a direct descendant of ancient Romans, who probably landed on New Discovery Island thousands of years ago," PROFESSOR HOMOS, the "famous anthropologist of Holliday College," organizes an expedition — including STEVE TREVOR, ETTA CANDY, and two other HOLLIDAY GIRLS — to visit the island and study its exotic civilization.

Arriving on the island, Professor Homos and his companions come upon "a perfect replica" of ancient Rome nestled in a hidden valley. Most of the expeditioners are soon taken captive by the brutal Nero and his fellow Romans, and when WONDER WOMAN flies to their rescue, she is forced to surrender in the face of Nero's threat to kill the captives. Bound to a pair of stakes in Nero's arena, the Holliday Girls are about to be devoured by ferocious beasts to provide bloody entertainment for Nero's Romans, when Wonder Woman turns the

tables on her captors and rescues the terrified girls from seemingly certain death. Steve Trevor arrives on the scene moments later with men from the expedition's supply ship, and, with their help, "subdues the last of the Roman emperors."

"That'll be all of this Roman funny business," remarks Trevor when the fight is over. "You birds are going to become American citizens and get civilized!" (Sen No. 39: "In the Clutches of Nero").

NERVA. The beautiful blonde who serves as STEVE TREVOR's secretary during Spring 1945 until she is exposed as a spy for the THIRD WORLD WAR PROMOTERS (WW No. 12/1).

NESTOR BROTHERS, THE. Two brothers, operators of a gas station in the United States gold mining town of Goldenvale, who have been smuggling stolen gold nuggets out of town concealed inside the gas tanks of local teen-agers' hot rods. The Nestor Brothers are apprehended by WONDER WOMAN in November–December 1952 (WW No. 56/1: "Homicide Highway!").

NEW DISCOVERY ISLAND. A recently discovered island, located somewhere "between Africa and South America," which is populated by descendants of the ancient Romans and ruled by the brutal NERO, a direct descendant of the infamous Roman emperor. PROFESSOR HOMOS leads an expedition to New Discovery Island in March 1945 (Sen No. 39: "In the Clutches of Nero"). (*See* NERO.)

NEW METROPOLO. The name by which New York City will be known in the year 2051 A.D. WONDER WOMAN defeats the villain PROTO in New Metropolo during a time-journey she makes there in May–June 1951 (Sen No. 103: "100 Year Duel!").

NIAGARA FALLS. A spectacular cataract, celebrated for its grandeur and beauty, which forms part of the boundary between the United States and Canada, separating the state of New York from the Canadian province of Ontario.

In March 1944 WONDER WOMAN swims up the falls to rescue a young woman who has just been swept over the cataract (Sen No. 27: "The Fun Foundation").

In May–June 1949 Wonder Woman goes over the falls in a barrel — and discards the barrel midway through her descent — as one of the daredevil stunts she must perform to win membership in the Nine Lives Club (WW No. 35/1: "Nine Lives Club!"). (*See* WRIGHT, FLY.)

NIANA (Queen). The ruler of the 16th-century kingdom of Sardonia. Queen Niana is an exact double for WONDER WOMAN (WW No. 63/3, Jan '54: "The Imposter Queen!"). (*See* RUPERT [PRINCE].)

NILREMO. The "wizard extraordinary of the evil leprechauns." By July 1955 Nilremo has used his diabolical "size-changer gun" to reduce the good leprechauns to the size of insects so that they will be powerless to prevent the evil leprechauns from "taking [their] places as good helpers of man--and robbing them of all their earthly riches!" Nilremo's scheme is thwarted by WONDER WOMAN, who uses the size-changer gun to restore the good leprechauns to their proper size and then to reduce Nilremo to such a minute size that he will remain forever powerless to commit further acts of evil (WW No. 75/3: "Inch-High Heroine!").

NISHKI, DRASKA (Countess). A red-haired femme fatale, apparently Polish (Sen No. 40, Apr '45: "Draska the Deadly"), who is described as the "cleverest and most beautiful spy who ever attacked America . . ." (Sen No. 43, Jun '45: "Peril on Paradise Island"). She is the director of International Spies, Inc., an international espionage organization that steals government secrets and sells them to the highest bidder.

In April 1945 Countess Nishki strides into the Washington, D.C., offices of Military Intelligence, brazenly introduces herself as an international spy, and demands an interview with Colonel Darnell (see DARNELL [GENERAL]). "Bah!" she exclaims contemptuously when someone expresses shock at her indiscretion in announcing her occupation so openly. "You **old-fashioned** spies work for your countree secretly — we **modern** agents work only for **ourselves** — we are **legal private detectives,** selling our services **openly** to the highest bidder!

"We haf — er — borrowed zee plan for your **secret surprise weapon** which in future could make America supreme over **all** nations in zee **world!**" she tells an astonished Colonel Darnell, and then offers to return the stolen plans for $1,000,000, implying that she will sell them to a foreign power if Darnell refuses.

After a series of action-packed encounters with the treacherous countess, however, WONDER WOMAN recovers the secret weapon plans and takes the villainess into custody (Sen No. 40: "Draska the Deadly").

Brought to trial for her crimes in June 1945, Countess Nishki binds Wonder Woman with her own magic lasso during a courtroom recess (see WONDER WOMAN [section C 3, the magic lasso]) and forces her to help her escape from the courthouse to PARADISE ISLAND, where the countess intends to conquer the AMAZONS and reign supreme.

On Paradise Island, Countess Nishki leaves Wonder Woman tied to a tree while she goes off to kidnap QUEEN HIPPOLYTE, and although Wonder Woman escapes her bonds and races to her mother's aid, she arrives too late to save her from falling into the countess's clutches. To make matters worse, Wonder Woman receives a mental radio message (see WONDER WOMAN [section C 7, the mental radio]) from STEVE TREVOR, informing her that Countess Nishki's henchmen are en route to Paradise Island in a fleet of bombers, intending to bomb the Amazons into submission.

Thus forewarned, however, Wonder Woman and her sister Amazons intercept the invaders and capture them all, while Queen Hippolyte turns the tables on Countess Nishki and takes her into custody. She and her cohorts will be returned to the U.S.A. to stand trial for their crimes (Sen No. 42: "Peril on Paradise Island").

Wonder Woman also battles and defeats Countess Draska Nishki in adventures recorded in Wonder Woman No. 161/1 (Apr '66: "The Curse of Cleopatra!") and Wonder Woman No. 161/2 (Apr '66: "Battle Inside of a Brain!"). Both are marred, however, by numerous inconsistencies and factual errors.

NOMAN. The "city of women," a city of the distant future which is inhabited solely by women. Its president is the benevolent Virtura. WONDER WOMAN rescues the women of Noman from domination by the evil dictator PROWD during a time-journey she makes there in November 1948 (Sen No. 83: "The Sinister Olympics!").

NORTON, ALICE. The owner of a circus which has been plagued by a series of suspicious mishaps. Investigating the mysterious "accidents" in January 1955, WONDER WOMAN ultimately exposes and apprehends the villain responsible: Grimes, chief assistant to Alice Norton and to her father before her. Grimes staged the mishaps out of resentment toward the elder Norton, now deceased, for having willed his circus to Alice instead of to him (WW No. 71/1: "One-Woman Circus!").

NORTON, OLIVE. A young blond girl in pigtails who is befriended by WONDER WOMAN in October 1946.

In tears because her brothers and their friends refuse to let her participate in their game of baseball, Olive is befriended by Wonder Woman and taken to Paradise Island, where, through rigorous Amazon training (see WONDER WOMAN [section C 1, the benefits of Amazon training]), Olive soon becomes transformed into a gifted athlete. When Olive returns to the United States and shows her brothers and their friends her newly-acquired skills, the boys enthusiastically accept her into their group. Soon afterward, Olive is instrumental in rescuing STEVE TREVOR and Wonder Woman

Olive Norton, 1946

from a treacherous bog, where they have been left to die by a gang of foreign spies (Sen No. 58: "The Bog Trap").

In July–August 1948 Wonder Woman returns Olive Norton to Paradise Island for renewed instruction in the virtues of "self-control and submisson to loving authority" after discovering that Olive has begun using the strength she acquired through Amazon training to bully her friends and exert power over others. When, during her second visit to Paradise Island, Olive views Amazon movies of the teen-aged Wonder Woman in action against the brutal RADIUM GIANTS, and realizes how selflessly Wonder Woman has always used her Amazon powers, she loses all desire to dominate others and becomes motivated to use her abilities to help other people (WW No. 30/1: "The Secret of the Limestone Caves").

NOVEL (Dr.). A wily confidence man who, on the pretext of having invented a fantastic new "anti-atomic metal" capable of providing "absolute protection against the terrible atom bomb," attempts to defraud the U.S. Government out of $1,000,000,000 in "development" expenses. Dr. Novel is exposed as a fraud and apprehended by WONDER WOMAN in August 1946 (Sen No. 56: "Anti-Atomic Metal").

NUCLEAR. The "magnetic murderer," a ruthless "arch-criminal" who is possessed of awesome "magnetic powers." Nuclear is in reality Percy Playboy, an idle, extravagant, middle-aged man with an "intense interest in science" who lives with his adoring sister, Joye Playboy, in a lavish mansion overlooking the ocean. A "secret subterranean passageway" connects his room with the hidden underground inlet which serves as a secret berth for Nuclear's powerful one-man submarine.

As Nuclear, Playboy wears green trousers, a red cape, and special armor made of "nuclear metal" which covers his head, hands, arms, and the upper part of his body. His "mysterious superhuman powers" enable him to emit powerful magnetic waves from his armored hands and body, as when he stands atop a rocky precipice and uses his magnetic powers to pull an ocean liner out of the water and draw it toward him through the air magnetically:

"What a genius I am!" he exclaims. "The magnetic power of the nuclei of atoms deprived of their electrons in my nuclear metal is irresistible! Each nucleus exerts its enormous magnetic power to attract the electrons it lacks from other objects. Thus, hungry atomic nuclei draw tons of weight toward themselves--in this case the S.S. 'Princess Leatrice'!"

To conceal the fact that he is secretly Nuclear, Playboy perpetuates the fiction that Nuclear is trying to kill him. Sometime in the past, Nuclear fell into a flaming furnace during an encounter with WONDER WOMAN and was generally believed to have perished. Although Percy Playboy disappeared at precisely the same time, his sister Joye refuses to believe that her brother is Nuclear, clinging instead to the improbable notion that Nuclear murdered her brother before perishing in the furnace.

In September–October 1950 Lemuel Tugboat, owner of the Lenard Shipline, receives an anonymous phone call warning that none of his ships will ever sail again unless he delivers $10,000 to a prearranged spot. At about this same time, Percy Playboy returns home for the first time since his mysterious disappearance, claiming that Nuclear shot him and left him for dead but that, somehow, he managed to escape. On the pretext of being terrified that Nuclear will make further attempts on his life, Playboy shuts himself in his room, claims to be "suffering from a nervous breakdown," and refuses to receive visitors, thereby hoping to conceal the fact that his own comings and goings inevitably coincide with Nuclear's.

When Lemuel Tugboat bravely refuses to meet the $10,000 extortion demand, Nuclear uses his magnetic powers to draw the S.S. *Princess Leatrice* out of the water and deposit it precariously atop a high cliff, but ETTA CANDY and the HOLLIDAY GIRLS are aboard the vessel and promptly notify Wonder Woman that the magnetic murderer is alive and once again at large.

Suspicious that Percy Playboy is secretly Nuclear, Wonder Woman pays a call on Joye Playboy at the Playboy mansion, but Joye steadfastly refuses to believe that her loving brother could possibly be Nuclear. After all, she insists, her brother has always been deeply devoted to her, whereas Nuclear tried to kill her during the period prior to his supposed death in the furnace. Wonder Woman remains unconvinced, however, sensing that Playboy harbors a deep resentment toward his sister rooted in his childhood and that he has been acting out this hatred in the guise of Nuclear. When Wonder Woman asks to see Percy, Joye explains that he "has refused to see anyone" since escaping from Nuclear, and that he is "still bedridden from the nervous shock of his terrible ordeal," but Playboy, realizing that Wonder Woman suspects the truth, escapes from the mansion by means of his secret passageway, leaving behind a note indicating that Nuclear has abducted him and will kill him if anyone attempts to apprehend Nuclear.

Soon afterward, when Nuclear announces his intention to attack the S.S. *Princess Leatrice* a second time, Wonder Woman decides to trap the villain by riding aboard the vessel herself. In midocean, perched atop his one-man submarine, Nuclear attempts to destroy the *Princess Leatrice* — and Wonder Woman as well — by using his magnetic powers to drag it to the bottom of the sea. But as the liner, in the grip of the villain's magnetic powers, hurtles toward his one-man submarine, the hatch atop the submarine jams, preventing Nuclear from climbing back inside it to make his escape. The *Princess Leatrice* plows into the one-man submarine, smashing it to bits and destroying the magnetic murderer.

"This time," says Wonder Woman, "it really is the end of **Nuclear!**"

Joye Playboy, however, still refuses to believe that her brother was Nuclear, insisting instead that he was kidnapped by Nuclear, imprisoned aboard the villain's one-man submarine, and then killed by the same collision that killed Nuclear. Wonder Woman knows this version is incorrect, but decides it would be better to allow Joye to retain her fantasy of a loving brother than to persist in trying to persuade her that Percy Playboy was really an evildoer (WW No. 43/2: "Nuclear Returns!").

O

OCTAVIA. The beautiful daughter of QUEEN EERAS of AURANIA, a nation of sunken ATLANTIS. Octavia is portrayed sometimes as a redhead (WW No. 8/3, Spr '44: "The Captive Queen") and sometimes as a blonde (CC No. 18, Dec/Jan '46–'47: "The Menace of the Rebel Manlings"). Placed on the throne of neighboring VENTURIA following the final overthrow of the evil QUEEN CLEA in Spring 1944 (WW No. 8/3: "The Captive Queen"), she ultimately dissolves the monarchy at the urging of WONDER WOMAN and transforms Venturia into a democratic republic, of which she becomes the first duly-elected president (Sen No. 35, Nov '44: "Girls Under the Sea").

In Spring 1944, after the ruthless Queen Clea has been toppled from the throne of Venturia and repeatedly thwarted in her attempts to regain it, Queen Eeras of Aurania announces her intention to place her daughter Octavia on Venturia's throne (WW No. 8/3: "The Captive Queen"). (*See* EERAS [QUEEN].)

In November 1944 Wonder Woman journeys to Venturia to protect Octavia from the machinations of SONTAG HENYA and her ruthless "anarchists." Wonder Woman resolves the initial dispute by persuading Octavia to dissolve the monarchy and establish a democratic Venturian republic, and in the free elections that follow, Octavia is elected president. When the anarchists, displeased with the election result, resort to force, Wonder Woman defeats them (Sen No. 35: "Girls Under the Sea"). (*See* HENYA, SONTAG.)

In December 1946–January 1947 Wonder Woman returns to Atlantis, this time to rescue Octavia from the clutches of the tyrannical MAN-LIUS (CC No. 18: "The Menace of the Rebel Manlings"). (*See* MANLIUS.)

OCTOPUS, THE. A "new mystery submarine" developed by the U.S. Navy for use in the war against the Axis. An attempt by German spies to sabotage the submarine is foiled by WONDER WOMAN — with the aid of STEVE TREVOR and the HOLLIDAY GIRLS — in May 1942 (Sen No. 5).

O'DAY, MOON. A mischievous but good-hearted leprechaun who is a friend of WONDER WOMAN.

In January–February 1951 Moon O'Day wreaks havoc at the HOLLIDAY COLLEGE FOR WOMEN when he enrolls there for a brief time as a student (WW No. 45/2: "The Amazon and the Leprechaun!").

In September–October 1951 Moon O'Day makes Wonder Woman a gift of a magical "leprechaun typewriter," but the typewriter causes nothing but trouble when it falls into the hands of a ruthless gangland chieftain (WW No. 49/3: "The Mystery of the Magic Typewriter!"). (*See* BOSS, THE.)

ODIN. In Teutonic mythology, the god of wisdom and war. Seated on his throne in VALHALLA, the hall of the slain, he welcomes the slain warriors gathered from the battlefields of the world and carried to his domain by the VALKYRIES. LOKI, the god of fire, mischief, and evil, is Odin's brother.

In the WONDER WOMAN chronicles, Odin and his Valkyries are described as "bloodthirsty" and "macabre" deities who have been "given psychic life by the mass desires of the German people during World War #2" (CC No. 17, Oct/Nov '46: "The Valkyries' Prey").

By October–November 1946 "a new Nazi underground" has taken root in occupied Germany, and STEVE TREVOR is assigned to lead an assault against the "Nazi underground guerillas" who have been staging forays against U.S. troops. Wounded during a street battle with the guerillas somewhere in Germany, Trevor is suddenly attacked by GUNDRA, princess of the Valkyries, a beautiful blonde astride a flying battle charger, who throws Trevor across the back of her steed and streaks away with him into the sky.

In a desperate effort to rescue Trevor, Wonder Woman allows herself to be taken captive also, and soon both she and Trevor are soaring through interstellar space toward Valhalla, "a planetoid beyond the moon." Wonder Woman manages, however, to send an urgent mental radio message (*see* WONDER WOMAN [section C 7, the mental radio]) to QUEEN HIPPOLYTE, and before long ". . . the Amazons, led by Queen Hippolyte and mounted on sky kangas, are following [Wonder Woman's] mental radio beam through pathless space" (*see* AMAZONS [section E 3, Transportation]).

In the fierce battle that follows, Hippolyte and her AMAZONS triumph over the ruthless Valkyries, who then concoct a scheme to win through treachery the victory they have been unable to win on the battlefield by inviting the Amazons to a peace banquet and massacring them while they eat. At the banquet, however, Wonder Woman — who has not yet been freed, having been forced into servitude as Gundra's slave — turns the tables on her captors and, with the aid of her sister Amazons, demolishes Valhalla, defeats Odin and his Valkyries, and rescues Steve Trevor from their clutches. ". . . You shattered Odin's thought power," remarks Queen Hippolyte to Wonder Woman after the battle has been won. "Now he's harmless!" (CC No. 17: "The Valkyries' Prey").

By May–June 1947, however, Odin and his Valkyries have rebuilt Valhalla and set out to wreak vengeance on Wonder Woman and the Amazons. Acting on instructions from Odin, Gundra has been leading her Valkyries on a series of treacherous raids over PARADISE ISLAND, seizing Amazons as captives and carrying them off to Valhalla to be transformed into Valkyries inside diabolical "Valkyrie transformers."

In order to rescue her sister Amazons, Wonder Woman allows herself to be taken prisoner by Gundra's Valkyries, and when ETTA CANDY and the HOLLIDAY GIRLS attempt to intervene, they are taken captive also. On Valhalla, Wonder Woman and her companions are placed inside Valkyrie transformers and transformed into Valkyries, but Wonder Woman ultimately turns the tables on her captors and escapes to Earth with the Holliday Girls in time to help the Amazons defeat the Valkyries in a final desperate battle. With the Valkyries defeated, APHRODITE changes Wonder Woman and the Holliday Girls back into normal human beings again, while the Valkyries are sent off to Reform Island (see TRANSFORMATION ISLAND) for rehabilitative training.

Back in Valhalla, "the dreary solitude of the empty halls" — coupled with the knowledge that his Valkyries have been defeated — "drives Odin berserk," and he commits suicide rather than continue to live with the knowledge of another ignominious defeat. "**Wonder Woman** has destroyed the war god's power," he cries despairingly, "--let Odin perish!" (WW No. 23/1: "Siege of the Savage War Maidens").

ODYSSEUS. In Greek legend, the king of Ithaca. He is the warrior hero of the *Odyssey*, a Greek epic, attributed to Homer, which recounts the story of his voyage homeward from the Trojan War and of his rescue of his wife and estate from greedy suitors. WONDER WOMAN meets Odysseus during a time-journey to ancient AMAZONIA that she makes in Summer 1944 (WW No. 9/3).

OLGA. A "trusted translator" in the office of U.S. Military Intelligence who is secretly a member of the vast Nazi spy network headed by BARONESS PAULA VON GUNTHER. In January 1943, while the baroness is in prison, Olga masterminds a plot to steal a top-secret code key from the office of STEVE TREVOR, but Olga and her Nazi cohorts are ultimately apprehended by WONDER WOMAN with the aid of ETTA CANDY (Sen No. 13).

OOLONG ISLAND. The Pacific island stronghold of the diabolical EGG FU THE FIRST (WW No. 157, Oct '65: "I--the Bomb!"; WW No. 158/1, Nov '65: "The Fury of Egg Fu!").

OSEY, GELL. A student at the HOLLIDAY COLLEGE FOR WOMEN, characterized by intense jealousy of those around her, who stows away aboard a rocket to VENUS and instigates a prison revolt there before she is finally apprehended by WONDER WOMAN in March–April 1947.

Furious at having been passed over by PROFESSOR ASTRONIMO in his selection of students with superior scientific ability to aid in the construction of his new Venus-probe rocket, Gell Osey stows away aboard the instrument-carrying rocket and journeys into outer space, determined to make her fellow students jealous by becoming the first Holliday Girl to travel to Venus. Arriving on Venus, Gell becomes insanely jealous of the planet's lovely winged women and viciously strikes out at them — thus attempting to compensate for her own feelings of inferiority — by instigating an insurrection among Venus's prison inmates. Before long, Gell and her cohorts have taken Wonder Woman and QUEEN DESIRA prisoner and have seized control of the entire planet, but Wonder Woman ultimately turns the tables on her captors, apprehends Gell Osey, and quashes the inmate revolt. Gell will be taken to Reform Island (*see*

KNOTTING SHEETS TOGETHER, GELL SQUEEZES THROUGH THE NARROW WINDOW

© NPP 1947

Gell Osey

TRANSFORMATION ISLAND) to learn to cope with her jealousy (WW No. 22/3: "Jealousy Visits the Winged Women of Venus!").

OWLER (Prof.). A space scientist who is temporarily transformed into an owl by the enchantress CIRCE.

In September–October 1949 Prof. Owler prepares a rocket ship for a flight to the MOON. "Many flights to the moon have been planned . . ." he explains. "But details on **returning to** the Earth are very vague. I believe that my rocket-ship can accomplish this feat and collect the scientific information that will enable others to do the same."

Owler's rocket blasts off for the moon with Owler, STEVE TREVOR, and three other passengers on board, but when the rocket finally returns to Earth, only Owler — now transformed into a talking owl — is still inside it. Owler explains that his rocket ship somehow drifted off course and landed on the planetoid SORCA, home of Circe the enchantress, where the space travelers had become transformed into woodland creatures after drinking the water of an enchanted pool. Of the transformed space travelers, only Owler managed to flee Sorca and return to Earth to summon WONDER WOMAN.

With the owl Owler at her side, Wonder Woman rockets into outer space to confront Circe. On Sorca, she attempts to rescue Steve Trevor and the other space voyagers from Circe's clutches, only to have the enchantress change her into a doe with the enchanted water. Now a fleet-footed doe, however, Wonder Woman escapes from Circe, locates an antidote to the magic water, and ultimately rescues Trevor and his companions and uses the antidote to restore them to normal. Circe, finally captured by Wonder Woman, will be taken to TRANSFORMATION ISLAND "to be taught Amazon ways of love and discipline" (WW No. 37/3: "The Secrets of Circe!").

P

PACIFIC OCEAN. The largest of the oceans, lying between Asia and Australia and North and South America and having an estimated area of approximately 70,000,000 square miles.

According to Wonder Woman No. 38/2, the creation of the Pacific Ocean was the inadvertent work of the tyrannical BRUTEX (Nov/Dec '49: "Wonder Woman Captures the Moon!").

The new continent of NEPTUNIA, the scene of WONDER WOMAN's battles with the evil SOLO, is located in the Pacific (WW No. 15, Win '45: chs. 1–3 – "The First Battle of Neptunia"; "The Masters of the Water"; "In the Killer's Cage").

ZANI ISLAND, ruled by the benevolent PRINCE SLEEKO, is described as America's "key base protecting Pacific communications" (CC No. 20, Apr/May '47: "The Buddha Wishing Ring").

WOOLOO ISLAND, "an American protectorate in the Pacific," is the scene of Wonder Woman's battle with the ruthless KING IRONSIDES in October–November 1947 (CC No. 23: "Siege of the Iron Giants").

Acting on the request of its inhabitants, Wonder Woman lowers the sole surviving fragment of the planet SATPHIX onto "an uncharted spot" on the Pacific Ocean in March–April 1951, thus creating a new land mass in the Pacific (WW No. 46/2: "The Moon of Peril!"). (*See* TURGO [PROF.].)

OOLONG ISLAND, also located in the Pacific, is the stronghold of the diabolical EGG FU THE FIRST (WW No. 157, Oct '65: "I--the Bomb!"; WW No. 158/1, Nov '65: "The Fury of Egg Fu!").

Wonder Woman No. 40/1 describes PARADISE ISLAND, the home of the AMAZONS, as situated "in a secret location on the Pacific Ocean" (Mar/Apr '50: "Hollywood goes to Paradise Island" pts. 1–2 – "The Mile High Menace!"; "The Undersea Invasion!"), and a Pacific Ocean location for Paradise Island is advanced in several other texts as well (WW No. 49/1, Sep/Oct '51: "Return of the Phantom Empire"; and others).

PALLIDA (Queen). The ruler of the planet Murkton.

When busloads of strong men – such as members of athletic teams – begin disappearing without a trace, WONDER WOMAN investigates and learns that the missing men have been kidnapped by inhabitants of the planet Murkton under the command of Queen Pallida. In the words of one Murktonian:

> Because Earth lies between our planet and the sun, Murkton is deprived of sunlight. This causes physical weakness in us Murktonians! We have prepared a giant bomb to destroy the Earth so we may enjoy the sun again! **But**----to bring the bomb into position requires a greater strength than we possess . . . . That's why we kidnapped your strong men!

Taken prisoner by the Murktonians and left to perish in a diabolical deathtrap, Wonder Woman escapes and pursues the invaders to Murkton, where she discovers that it is not Earth that is depriving the Murktonians of sunlight, but a "giant cloud mass." When the Murktonians finally fire their huge bomb at the Earth in an attempt to destroy it, Wonder Woman diverts it into the interstellar cloud mass, thus giving the Murktonians an unobstructed view of the SUN. Now realizing their mistake and ashamed of their attempt to destroy Earth, the Murktonians release their earthling captives – including STEVE TREVOR and the HOLLIDAY GIRLS – and vow to remain peaceful from now on (WW No. 33/2, Jan/Feb '49: "The Menace of Murkton!").

PAPER-MAN, THE. A bizarre criminal who looks as though he were cut out of paper. He is in reality Horace Throstle, a timid chemical plant employee who falls into a vat of experimental paper-making chemicals and emerges, moments later, endowed with many of the qualities of paper: he can fold himself into an envelope and escape down a mail chute; turn himself into a paper glider and float away on the air currents; or escape detection by blending into the wallpaper on a wall. After staging a series of spectacular thefts, the Paper-Man attempts to escape from WONDER WOMAN by transforming himself into a kite and flying out a window, but Wonder Woman thwarts the escape by using a puff of super-breath to blow the villain through the window of a nearby newspaper plant, where he meets his doom amongst the gears and rollers of a giant printing press (WW No. 165/1, Oct '66: "Perils of the Paper-Man!").

PARADISE ISLAND. The secret island home of the AMAZONS. Paradise Island is ruled by QUEEN

HIPPOLYTE, the mother of Princess Diana, the Amazon maiden who battles the forces of crime and injustice as WONDER WOMAN.

Paradise Island is a "land of love and beauty" (CC No. 19, Feb/Mar '47: "The Battle for Eternal Youth") where "women rule supreme in harmony and happiness" (CC No. 1, Win '42: "The Mystery of the House of the Seven Gables"), but it is "a paradise for women only," a place "which no man may enter" (WW No. 1/1, Sum '42), for it is APHRODITE's law that if a man ever sets foot on Paradise Island, the Amazons must relinquish their birthright of eternal life and everlasting happiness (see AMAZONS [section B, Aphrodite's Law]).

The location of Paradise Island is a solemn secret known only to the Amazons. Sensation Comics No. 104 describes it as "located on an uncharted sea" (Jul/Aug '51: "The End of Paradise Island"), and Sensation Comics No. 29 observes that Wonder Woman, en route to Paradise Island from the United States, must travel "over distant seas" to get there (May '44: "Adventure of the Escaped Prisoner"). Wonder Woman No. 40/1 describes Paradise Island as having "a secret location on the Pacific Ocean" (Mar/Apr '50: "Hollywood Goes to Paradise Island" pts. 1–2 – "The Mile High Menace!"; "The Undersea Invasion!"), and a Pacific Ocean location is advanced in several other texts as well (WW No. 49/1, Sep/Oct '51: "Return of the Phantom Empire"; and others).

The Amazons were brought to Paradise Island by the goddess Aphrodite after abandoning their ancestral home in ancient AMAZONIA (WW No. 1/1, Sum '42). In November–December 1968, however, after they have resided on Paradise Island for ten thousand years, the Amazons find that they must "journey to another dimension" in order "to rest and renew [their] powers!" As Wonder Woman streaks away from the island in her Amazon plane (see WONDER WOMAN [section C 4, the robot plane]), having chosen to remain behind in the world of men, she sees Paradise Island "shimmer, dissolve, [and] vanish . . . leaving only the azure ocean . . ." (WW No. 179: "Wonder Woman's Last Battle!"). (See DOCTOR CYBER.)

PARTHENOPE. In Greek mythology, one of the Sirens; distraught at her inability to charm ODYSSEUS with her seductive song, she hurled herself into the sea.

According to Wonder Woman No. 30/2, the goddess APHRODITE punished Parthenope and her sister Sirens for their evil ways by transforming them into trees. Years later, after wood from Parthenope's tree has been fashioned into a bracelet, Parthenope becomes free to work her evil magic through the bracelet's owner, MONA MENISE (Jul/

Aug '48: "The Song of the Sirens!"). (See MENISE, MONA.)

PATRIOT, THE. An alternate identity employed by STEVE TREVOR in January–February 1968 after special "super-power pills" given him by the ANGLE MAN have endowed him with superhuman powers (WW No. 174/1: "Steve Trevor – Alias the Patriot!"). (See ANGLE MAN, [THE].)

PAULA. See GUNTHER, PAULA VON (BARONESS).

PEGASUS. In Greek mythology, a divine winged horse which sprang from the body or blood of Medusa as she was slain by Perseus.

Pegasus

According to Wonder Woman No. 128/1, which purports to recount the true origin of WONDER WOMAN's Amazon plane, Wonder Woman tamed the wild Pegasus and rode him into a "strange cloud," where he underwent a miraculous transformation into a silent, invisible airplane. In Wonder Woman's words:

As my flying steed entered that strange cloud . . . a startling transformation began taking place . . . as if its molecular structure was being changed until . . . my winged steed . . . [turned] into . . . a unique plane! [Feb '62: "Origin of the Amazing Robot Plane!"].

This version of the plane's origin, one of several extant, is contradicted by numerous other texts and may safely be regarded as inaccurate. (*See* WONDER WOMAN [section C 4, the robot plane].)

PERILOSA (Duke). An evil duke whose attempt to seize power in 15th-century Florence is thwarted by WONDER WOMAN during a time-journey she makes to that city in January–February 1953. Drawn back into time by LEONARDO DA VINCI in the hope that she will be able to rescue Florence from Duke Perilosa's sinister machinations, Wonder Woman defeats the evil duke and rescues Leonardo and the city's rightful ruler, Princess Lora, from the villain's clutches (WW No. 57/3: "The Four Trials of Terror!").

PHAETHON. In Greek mythology, the son of the sun god Helios. Having nagged his father into permitting him to drive his sun chariot across the heavens, Phaethon was struck dead by one of Zeus's thunderbolts after his wild, inexperienced driving had caused stars to fall from their places, the Nile to dry up, and other calamities.

According to Wonder Woman No. 58/2, however, Phaethon was not killed as the result of his recklessness, but merely banished by his father to an "eternally wintry" planet in the farthest reaches of interstellar space. When the people of Earth awake one midsummer morning to find the SUN gone from the sky and Earth in perpetual darkness, WONDER WOMAN rockets into space aboard her Amazon plane (*see* WONDER WOMAN [section C 4, the robot plane]), uses an "Amazon magnetic beam" to tow a white dwarf star into the area left vacant by the missing sun, and then, having thus supplied Earth with a temporary source of light and heat, sets out in search of the vanished sun. On the frigid planet where Phaethon is in exile, Wonder Woman learns that Phaethon has stolen Earth's sun with a powerful "gravitational beam" to avenge himself on his father for having banished him into space. Escaping from Phaethon and his followers, Wonder Woman soars back into the interstellar void, cleverly "siphoning-off power" from Phaethon's gravitational beam and using this power to pull the sun back into its proper position at the center of Earth's solar system. When Phaethon attempts to capture her by hurling his gravitational force-beam at her Amazon plane, Wonder Woman swerves aside at the last possible instant, causing the beam to miss her entirely and instead strike the dwarf star she had used earlier to replace the sun. Struck by th[e] mighty force-beam, the dwarf star hurtles throug[h] space and collides with Phaethon's frigid plane[t,] annihilating Phaethon and his followers and en[d]ing forever their threat to Earth (Mar/Apr '5[3:] "The Man Who Stole the Sun!").

PHENEGS. Cruel extraterrestrial invaders wh[o] once attempted to conquer the Galaxy, only to b[e] defeated by WONDER WOMAN. The text, whic[h] purports to recount the true origin of Wonde[r] Woman's tiara, states that Wonder Woman wa[s] given the tiara by an elderly scientist from a di[s]tant planet in gratitude for her having turned bac[k] the Pheneg invasion (WW No. 95/2, Jan '58: "Th[e] Secret of Wonder Woman's Tiara!"). (*See* WONDE[R] WOMAN [section C 5, the tiara].)

PHOBOS. The inner moon of the planet MAR[S.] Discovered in 1877 — along with Mars's oute[r] moon, Deimos — by Asaph Hall of the U.S. Nava[l] Observatory, Phobos is the scene of an encounte[r] between WONDER WOMAN and the tyrant GHURKO[S] in May–June 1950. The capital of Phobos i[s] Ghurkton (WW No. 41/3: "The Trial of Stev[e] Trevor!").

PICKLEPUSS (Dean). The bespectacled, ill[-] tempered woman who, in Wonder Woman No[.] 17/2, is described as the dean of the HOLLIDA[Y] COLLEGE FOR WOMEN (May/Jun '46: "The Red[-] skins' Revenge").

Although Holliday College has had severa[l] deans, it is entirely possible that the name Dea[n] Picklepuss appears in the chronicles only throug[h] a chronicler's error. Dean Meg Sourpuss (marrie[d] name: DEAN MEG MERRILY), who makes numerou[s] appearances in the chronicles, is described as th[e] dean of Holliday College in many texts both pre[-] dating and postdating the single text in whic[h] Dean Picklepuss appears. In addition, the por[-] trayal of Dean Picklepuss in Wonder Woman No[.] 17/2 is virtually identical to that accorded Dea[n] Meg Sourpuss wherever she appears.

PIEREZ, JOSÉ ("General"). A Mexican "bandid[o] leader," in league with the Japanese, who is de[-] termined to prevent America from using his coun[-] try's valuable "nitrodium" mines to aid in its wa[r] effort. Pierez and his fellow bandidos are capture[d] by WONDER WOMAN — with the aid of STEV[E] TREVOR, ETTA CANDY, and the HOLLIDAY GIRLS — i[n] September 1945.

In Mexico City, the president of Mexico entrust[s] Wonder Woman with a secret international agree[-] ment granting the United States "exclusive right[s] to [Mexico's] nitrodium mines," nitrodium being [a] "rare chemical [that] will produce new rocket plane fuel of enormous power."

Bandido leader Pierez, however, is determine[d]

to prevent Wonder Woman from delivering the agreement to U.S. officials in Washington, D.C. "Zat treaty shall nevair reach America!" vows Pierez. "We, **zee bandidos**, hold zee nitrodium mines — we already lease zem to anothair countree — America shall **nevair** get those mines!"

Meanwhile, in Washington, the situation is assessed by Colonel Darnell (*see* DARNELL [GENERAL]) of U.S. Military Intelligence: "Situation's bad — **very** bad," muses Darnell. "José Pierez's bandidos hold the nitrodium mines backed by Japanese interests. If José shows that treaty to the Japs, they'll infiltrate a secret army of Nips and make Pierez president of Mexico!"

To ensure that Wonder Woman never reaches the United States with the nitrodium agreement, Pierez sabotages her Amazon plane (*see* WONDER WOMAN [section C 4, the robot plane]), causing it to crash soon after takeoff, leaving Wonder Woman badly injured. Wonder Woman is found and nursed slowly back to health by MARYA THE MOUNTAIN GIRL, but before long both women have been taken captive by José Pierez and his bandidos, who attempt to torture Wonder Woman into revealing where she has hidden the nitrodium treaty by forcing her to dance blindfolded across a bed of hot coals. The day is saved, however, by the timely arrival of STEVE TREVOR and the HOLLIDAY GIRLS, whom Wonder Woman has summoned to the scene via mental radio (*see* WONDER WOMAN [section C 7, the mental radio]). Together Wonder Woman and her friends defeat and apprehend the bandidos, thereby ensuring that the nitrodium treaty, hidden for safekeeping inside Wonder Woman's boot, will be delivered to U.S. officials in Washington (Sen No. 45: "In the Enemy's Hands").

PIPSQUEAK (Mr.). The seemingly meek manager of the Tycoon Club who is secretly the UNKNOWN (Sen No. 47, Nov '45: "The Terror of the Tycoon Club").

PLANET G. The far-distant planet — described as the "home of the space giants" — which is the scene of an encounter between WONDER WOMAN and the giant TOOROO in May 1959 (WW No. 106/1: "The Human Charm Bracelet!").

PLANET K. A far-distant planet — known also as Krazy K — where everything is topsy-turvy: its inhabitants walk on water and swim on land, greet one another by saying goodbye instead of hello, and sleep standing on their heads instead of lying down. Their ruler, KUU-KUU, dispatches an ill-fated expedition to Earth in January 1962 (WW No. 127/1: "Invaders of the Topsy-Turvy Planet").

PLANET OF THOUGHT. The far-distant planet — ruled by Prince Charming and his wife Cinderella — which is the scene of WONDER WOMAN's battle with the evil wizard STROGO in March–April 1952 (WW No. 52/2: "The Battle for Fairyland!").

PLANT PEOPLE, THE. The plantlike inhabitants of a distant planetoid who attempt to transform the Earth into "one vast silent forest — devoid of any humans," so that they can inhabit it themselves. They are defeated by WONDER WOMAN in August 1956 (WW No. 84/3: "The Tree That Shook the Earth!").

PLASM, PROTUS (Prof.). The "famous biologist" who is secretly the GREAT BLUE FATHER (CC No. 10, Spr '45: "The Great Blue Father").

PLAYBOY, PERCY. The idle, extravagant man who is secretly NUCLEAR (WW No. 43/2, Sep/Oct '50: "Nuclear Returns!").

PLOTTER. The leader of a gang of criminals who attempt to capitalize on WONDER WOMAN's continuous appearance on a twenty-four-hour telethon by staging a bank robbery while she is occupied on the air. Astounded when Wonder Woman appears on the scene to thwart the robbery without, apparently, ever leaving the telethon, the gangsters learn too late that Wonder Woman created a lifelike "Amazon effigy" of herself — controlled by "secret Amazon electronics" — to conduct the telethon so that she could be elsewhere apprehending criminals (WW No. 56/3, Nov/Dec '52: "The Case of the 8 Million Witnesses!").

PLUTO. The farthest planet from the SUN. According to Wonder Woman No. 16, Pluto is ruled by the vicious KING PLUTO, who battles WONDER WOMAN in March–April 1946 (WW No. 16/1–3: "The Secret of the Dark Planet!"; "The River of Liquid Fire"; "King Pluto's Revenge"). In February 1959 Wonder Woman demolishes a combined armada of Plutonian, Saturnian, and Martian spaceships attempting to invade the Earth (WW No. 104/2: "Key of Deception!"). (*See* DECEPTION, DUKE OF.)

PLUTO (King). The "vicious ruler" of the "dark planet" PLUTO, the farthest planet from the SUN. King Pluto is defeated by WONDER WOMAN in March–April 1946.

In March–April 1946 King Pluto comes to Earth in his horse-drawn sky chariot in search of slaves for his kingdom and kidnaps one of the HOLLIDAY GIRLS from the Holliday College dormitory. While Wonder Woman is off on PARADISE ISLAND discussing the crisis with QUEEN HIPPOLYTE and the goddess APHRODITE, ETTA CANDY and the Holliday Girls sneak aboard an experimental rocket ship on the Holliday College campus and begin playfully fiddling with the rocket's controls. Within moments the rocket ship has taken off and Etta and her friends find themselves soaring into outer space at fantastic speed, on a direct course for the planet Pluto. Returning home in her Amazon plane (*see* WONDER WOMAN [section C 4, the robot plane]) just as Etta and her companions are blasting off, Wonder Woman lassoes the rocket with her magic lasso (*see* WONDER WOMAN [section C 3, the magic lasso]) in a desperate attempt to pull it back to Earth, but the rocket's momentum is already too great and Wonder Woman soon finds herself hurtling through space behind it, hanging on for dear life to the end of her lasso.

After a long journey through interstellar space, the rocket crash-lands on Pluto, where the space travelers, shaken but uninjured, suddenly become separated into two kinds of bodies: "color bodies," consisting of the bodily color that has been drained from their physical bodies and restructured to form live identical twins of their physical selves, and "flesh and blood bodies," i.e., their physical bodies, which, having been drained of all color, are now pitch black.

The color bodies of Wonder Woman and her friends are taken prisoner by Pluto's minions, only to escape soon afterward — along with the color body of the Holliday Girl kidnapped earlier by King Pluto — through the heroic efforts of Wonder Woman. If they ever hope to return to Earth with their color bodies and flesh and blood bodies reunited, however, they must somehow "get into Pluto's underground kingdom and rescue [their] flesh and blood bodies" from King Pluto's clutches (WW No. 16/1: "The Secret of the Dark Planet!").

In a desperate attempt to rescue their imprisoned flesh and blood bodies, Wonder Woman and her companions overpower some of King Pluto's bodyguards, disguise themselves in the guards' clothing, and surreptitiously invade King Pluto's

King Pluto

subterranean kingdom. Ultimately, they succee in reuniting their radiant color bodies with thei colorless flesh and blood bodies and prepare t return to Earth, but Wonder Woman realizes tha Earth will never be safe so long as King Plut remains free to plunder the universe.

King Pluto, meanwhile, climbs aboard his sk chariot — drawn by four fleet black steeds — an races into outer space, determined to have hi revenge on Wonder Woman (WW No. 16/2 Mar/Apr '46: "The River of Liquid Fire").

"Fearful of capture by **Wonder Woman**," note the textual narrative, "King Pluto streaks acros the heavens desperately determined to find means of prolonging his nefarious career." By kidnapping STEVE TREVOR and threatening to kil him, the evil monarch compels Wonder Woman and the Holliday Girls to become his prisoners, bu ultimately, aided by the captive Trevor, Wonde Woman turns the tables on her captors and escapes with her companions from King Pluto's castle. Trevor and the Holliday Girls return to Earth i the rocket which brought Etta and her friends to Pluto in the first place, while Wonder Woman takes King Pluto's magic chariot horses to Paradise Island to ensure that they "never fall into unscrupulous hands." Thus deprived of magic steeds to pull his sky chariot, King Pluto will remain hopelessly marooned on Pluto, powerless to invade the Earth (WW No. 16/3, Mar/Apr '46: "King Pluto's Revenge").

POGOLANA. A South Sea island kingdom where pogo sticks are the principal means of transportation. Its ruler is the good King Ritio. WONDER WOMAN visits Pogolana in August–September 1948 during her struggle with the evil COUNTESS HATRA (CC No. 28: "The Sinister Countess Hatra!").

PRAIRIE PIRATES, THE. A band of ruthless modern-day pirates who prowl the prairies of the western United States aboard a bizarre pirate ship on wheels whose sails are filled with helium to enable the pirates to commit robberies on the prairie and then soar into the air for spectacular getaways. Summoned to the town of Bluff City to investigate the recent holdup of a bank messenger, WONDER WOMAN apprehends the Prairie Pirates in April 1955 (WW No. 73/1: "The Prairie Pirates!").

PRINCE, DIANA. The U.S. Army nurse who, in January 1942, sells WONDER WOMAN her credentials and the use of her identity for the money she needs to join her fiancé in South America (Sen No. 1). By September 1942 Diana Prince has become the wife of munitions inventor Dan White and has given birth to their first child (Sen No. 9). Wearing eyeglasses and with her hair up, Wonder Woman is an almost exact double for Diana Prince.

In January 1942 Wonder Woman, newly arrived in the United States from PARADISE ISLAND, wanders the streets of Washington, D.C., trying to think of some means of remaining close to STEVE TREVOR, the man she loves, who is currently recovering from war injuries at the Walter Reed Army Hospital. On the hospital steps, Wonder Woman encounters nurse Diana Prince, who is in tears because she lacks the money to join her fiancé in South America. After a short conversation, a deal is arranged: Wonder Woman gives Diana Prince the money she needs to join her fiancé, and Diana Prince gives Wonder Woman her nurse's credentials and the use of her identity (Sen No. 1). (See WONDER WOMAN [section B, the secret identity].)

In September 1942, however, after Wonder Woman — in her role as nurse Diana Prince — has resigned her post at the Walter Reed Army Hospital to become Colonel Darnell's (see DARNELL [GENERAL]) secretary at U.S. Military Intelligence, the real Diana Prince returns from South America with her husband and newborn child and demands that Wonder Woman relinquish her credentials and the use of her identity and allow her to replace her as Colonel Darnell's secretary. Understandably unsettled by this unexpected turn of events but unwilling to reject Diana Prince's demand, Wonder Woman surrenders her secretarial job to Diana Prince — a substititution that goes completely unnoticed owing to the fact that the two women are such near-perfect look-alikes.

Although Diana Prince and her family sorely need the income that Diana will now be earning, Wonder Woman sees a ray of hope in Dan White's stubborn opposition to his wife's working. Ulti-

mately, with Wonder Woman's help, White persuades the Army to adopt his new invention, the "anti-aircraft disintegrator shell," the income from which will make his wife's earnings redundant and enable her to surrender her post at Military Intelligence and resume her role as housewife.

"I'm glad to get my position back," confides Diana Prince (Wonder Woman) to her look-alike. "But I envy you yours, as wife and mother" (Sen No. 9).

Wonder Woman No. 167/1 contains an adventure — purporting to be about the real Diana Prince — in which Diana once again raises the possibility of reassuming the identity that Wonder Woman has by now employed for twenty-five years (Jan '67: "The Secret of Tabu Mt.!"). The text is marred, however, by numerous inconsistencies and factual errors.

PRINCE, DIANA (Wonder Woman). A pseudonym adopted by WONDER WOMAN at the onset of her crime-fighting career in order to enable her to enjoy the benefits of a secret civilian identity. The name Diana Prince is actually that of a U.S. Army nurse whose identity and credentials Wonder Woman purchases in January 1942, thus beginning an impersonation that has continued for more than three decades (Sen No. 1). It is one of the world's most closely guarded secrets that plain Diana Prince — with her unattractive eyeglasses and austere hairdo — is in reality Wonder Woman, the alluring Amazon princess (see WONDER WOMAN [section B, the secret identity]).

PRINCESS No. 1003. An extraterrestrial robot alien whose visit to Earth in November 1959 brings the planet to the brink of interplanetary war.

In November 1959 Princess No. 1003 flees her home planet and journeys to Earth, where, by means of her extraterrestrial powers, she assumes the form of a lovely Earth girl in order to be able to walk among the populace unobserved. On her home planet, where there are 2,785 different princesses, she had felt ignored and unappreciated; on Earth, she feels, she will be different, distinctive, the object of attention and admiration.

Difficulties arise, however, when the inhabitants of her own planet, believing that she has been abducted by earthlings, threaten to destroy Earth unless their princess is returned to them within twenty-four hours, setting an entire mountain aflame and freezing the Empire State Building into a block of solid ice as evidence of their awesome power.

Since the people of Earth are completely innocent, WONDER WOMAN's task becomes one of locating an errant princess who does not want to be found before her fellow aliens turn their engines

Wonder Woman meets the real Diana Prince, 1942

of destruction against the Earth. Ultimately, however, Wonder Woman succeeds, and the aliens, now realizing that the people of Earth meant their princess no harm, head peacefully homeward (WW No. 110: "The Bridge of Crocodiles!").

PRINGLE, PERCY. The secretary to movie star Tama Blair, and the secret accomplice of Sheila Brun, Tama Blair's movie double, in a plot to kidnap the actress so that Pringle can conceal the fact that he has "embezzled money Tama gave him to pay bills" by forcing her to sign her assets over to him, and Sheila can impersonate the actress and thus usurp her glamorous life and career. WONDER WOMAN apprehends Sheila Brun and her hired henchmen — and rescues Tama Blair from their clutches — in September 1944, and Percy Pringle is captured soon afterward by STEVE TREVOR (Sen No. 33: "The Disappearance of Tama").

PRISON PUNISHMENT CAGE. A special type of jail cell which, according to Sensation Comics No. 34, is used for torturing and interrogating prisoners in some U.S. municipal jails. Heated by means of a special thermostat, the bars of the cell can be made to glow with intense "electric heat," thus making it unbearably uncomfortable for the inmate imprisoned inside it. In October 1944 the police chief of Bourbon City locks WONDER WOMAN in a prison punishment cage and raises the temperature to 175 degrees in an unsuccessful attempt to torture her into revealing the hiding place of some fingerprint evidence she pilfered from police department files. It is in Bourbon City that Wonder Woman exposes the evil MAYOR GOODE ("Edgar's New World!").

PROTO. The ruthless "master of New Metropolo," who battles WONDER WOMAN in the year 2051 A.D. Proto is in reality Prof. Toz, an "evil scientific genius" who fled the mid-20th century in a time machine and then, "by ruthless methods," established himself as dictator of New Metropolo, the 21st-century name for New York City.

In May–June 1951 Amazon scientists on PARADISE ISLAND inform Wonder Woman that they have peered into the future with their "futuro-scope" and discovered that by 2051 A.D. Wonder Woman's name will have been expunged from every existing record on Earth. Startled at this unexpected news, Wonder Woman journeys into the future, to 21st-century New Metropolo, to discover that no one there has ever heard of her or read about any of her 20th-century exploits. Taken into custody by police soon after her arrival, Wonder Woman is taken before Proto, a successful 20th-century criminal until his capture by Wonder Woman and now the master of New Metropolo. After building a time machine in prison and escaping into the future, Prof. Toz (alias Proto) had ruthlessly established himself as New Metropolo's dictator and then destroyed every extant record of Wonder Woman's existence.

Now that Wonder Woman is in his clutches, Proto intends to kill her, but the resourceful Amazon turns the tables on her captor, exposes him to the populace for the villain he is, and returns him to prison in the 20th century (Sen No. 103: "10 Year Duel!").

PROWD. The evil dictator of Elam, "the city of men," a city of the distant future. His attempt to conquer Noman, "the city of women," is thwarted by WONDER WOMAN.

In November 1948 Wonder Woman is putting on an exhibition of her Amazon powers at the HOLLIDAY COLLEGE FOR WOMEN when suddenly she feels herself being drawn into the future by "the magnetic power of a time transporter." An instant later, she is standing before Virtura, president of Noman, who has summoned her into the future to help her people.

"The male dictator, Prowd, is trying to deprive us of our liberty!" explains Virtura.

"Is that why you built this city for women only?" asks Wonder Woman.

"Yes!" replies Virtura. "Now Prowd has challenged us to an Olympiad. If the men win, we must submit to their domination or go to war. If we win, we retain equal rights.

"We could compete against ordinary men!" continues Virtura. "But Prowd is being aided by Loki, the god of evil! He is bringing legendary heroes from the past to compete! Only you would have a chance against them!"

Determined to preserve the freedom of Noman's women, Wonder Woman hurls herself into the Olympiad, but Prowd, his ally LOKI, and Virtura's traitorous secretary Rata — whom Prowd has deceitfully promised to make his queen as soon as he succeeds in conquering Noman — conspire to weaken Wonder Woman to prevent her from competing effectively, and, when that scheme fails, attempt to rig the various athletic contests to prevent her from winning. Despite the villains' scheming, however, Wonder Woman successfully triumphs over all the legendary greats — including Paul Bunyon and the Black Knight — whom Loki summons from the past to defeat her.

Inspired by Wonder Woman's example and aided by her athletic victories, the women of Noman win the Olympiad, thereby retaining their freedom and their cherished equal rights. Loki, his cause lost, flees home to VALHALLA, and Rata is exposed as a traitor and will receive just punishment. Prowd is taken captive, but the men of Elam have already turned against him: "Prowd poisoned our minds against women," they cry. "We didn't know of his trickery! But **Wonder Woman** opened our eyes!" (Sen No. 83: "The Sinister Olympics!").

PRUDE (Mayor). The mayor of Center City, who, because he is jealous of the attention and publicity accorded WONDER WOMAN, conspires with Police Chief Smack to close down the local Fun Clinic (*see* FUN FOUNDATION), which she founded. Behind the mayor's back, however, Police Chief Smack conspires with gangster Big Ike McGlone to rob the bank containing the $1,000,000,000 in bonds purchased by Wonder Woman to finance the Fun Clinic's operations. Both conspiracies ultimately fail: gangster McGlone dies in the crash of his getaway car when STEVE TREVOR shoots out one of the tires; Police Chief Smack is apprehended by Wonder Woman; and the Fun Clinic remains open (Sen No. 28, Apr '44: "The Malice of the Green Imps").

PSYCHO (Dr.). A "psychopathic madman" (WW No. 18/3, Jul/Aug '46: "Ectoplasmic Death") whose all-consuming passion is "to enslave the women of the world" (WW No. 18/2, Jul/Aug '46: "The Drugged WAC"). A "noted occultist" who uses "ectoplasmic energy" drawn from the spirit world to achieve his evil ends, Dr. Psycho is the husband of MARVA PSYCHO (WW No. 5/1, Jun/Jul '43: "Battle for Womanhood") and the brother of the villainous KING IRONSIDES (CC No. 23, Oct/Nov '47: "Siege of the Iron Giants").

Dr. Psycho

In the words of Wonder Woman No. 5/1, Dr. Psycho is a

... monster [who] abhors women! With *weird cunning* and dark, forbidden knowledge of the occult,

Dr. Psycho prepares to change the independent status of modern American women back to the days of the sultans and slave markets, clanking chains and abject captivity.

"The subtle Psycho's past," continues the text, "is shrouded in mystery. In medical school his brilliant mind won him recognition," and he was the recipient of numerous high academic honors.

His fellow students, however, taunted and humiliated him because of his diminutive stature, "funny looking" face, and wild, maniacal eyes. Even his fiancée Marva, an attractive blond co-ed, was repelled by his strange appearance. One day, after the medical school had awarded him its "highest award," Psycho put his arms around Marva and leaned forward to kiss her. "Aren't you going to **congratulate** me, Marva?" he asked brightly.

"Yes," replied Marva coolly, pushing him away, "— you don't have to get mushy — you **know** I admire your brilliant mind, but — well — you're not exactly a Clark Gable. Love-making doesn't become you!"

Soon afterward, still smarting from Marva's rejection, Psycho came upon his fiancée in the arms of Ben Bradley, the handsome "athletic idol of the college." Spying on them from behind a large pillar, Psycho watched helplessly as the lovers embraced, Bradley wanting Marva to leave Psycho and marry him instead, and Marva appearing more or less willing but nevertheless reluctant. "She loves Ben because he's **handsome**," thought Psycho angrily from his vantage point behind the pillar, "— I ought to let her marry him!"

That night a muffled figure breaks into the radium laboratory where Psycho has been working. Marva, walking down the corridor, thinks the short-appearing figure by the [laboratory] door is Psycho.

Next morning $125,000 worth of radium is missing from the laboratory safe and Psycho is suspected.

Despite the fact that he loudly proclaimed his innocence, Psycho was widely believed to be guilty, and Marva, who sincerely believed it was Psycho she had seen entering the laboratory on the night of the theft, made matters worse by publicly begging him to return the stolen radium.

"You pretty, double-crossing liar!" cried Psycho. "You're trying to frame me and marry Ben Bradley!"

Largely on the basis of Marva's well-meaning but erroneous testimony, Psycho was convicted of the radium theft and sentenced to prison, and there he received "the final blow": word that Marva had married Ben Bradley.

"Through long, bitter years in a prison cell," notes the text, "Psycho's soul seethes with hot hatred for humankind — especially women."

"They shall **suffer** — suffer — ha! Ha!" cackled Psycho maniacally, his brilliant but sensitive mind strained to the breaking point by the agony of undeserved imprisonment. "Bradley must die — but killing's too good for a **woman**!"

Racing to Bradley's home immediately upon his release from prison, Psycho murders his one-time rival by forcing him to ingest chunks of pure radium. "You'll swallow this radium," shrieks Psycho, "— it will burn holes in your stomach. Ha! Ho! Ha!"

"Mercy — I'll confess!" cries Bradley, terror-stricken. "I **did** steal that radium to frame you, but Marva planned it, I swear it — ag — glug!"

It is clear that Bradley has tried to implicate Marva only in the hope of making himself appear less culpable, but years of tortured imprisonment have robbed Psycho of the ability to distinguish truth from fiction. After Bradley's body has been discovered and his death attributed to a "stomach disorder," Psycho pays a call on Bradley's widow. "Ah my pretty Marva, I have come for you!" he cackles. "Do not pretend innocence — Ben confessed that **you** planned my betrayal!"

"Oh — I **didn't**!" cries the terrified Marva, but the revenge-mad Psycho refuses to listen. "Taking Marva to a carefully prepared hideaway," notes the text, "Psycho hypnotizes her," then forces her to marry him while she is helplessly under his hypnotic control.

Even after their marriage, Psycho continues to use Marva "for occult experiments, hypnotizing her every day" and forcing her against her will to serve as his medium.

"I command you, slave," he cries out to her in the midst of one experiment, "[to] bring me **living substance** from the spirit world!"

Dr. Psycho hypnotizes his wife Marva . . .

. . . and uses her as his medium to create particles of living ectoplasm

Suddenly, "in the weird red light of Psycho's laboratory," in response to Psycho's eerie command, "particles of living ectoplasm are drawn from unseen space through the medium's body to Psycho's hand!"

"I'm master of psychic creation!" exclaims the exultant Psycho. "I can make human bodies!"

Indeed, by manipulating these particles of spirit-world ectoplasm, Psycho is soon able to "materialize a [human] body and wear it like a cloak," thus enabling him to perform miraculous impersonations. In a lightning-swift test of his newly acquired powers, Psycho "builds the muscles of Hercules on his own spindling arms. Materializing an ectoplasmic mask over his face, Psycho transforms himself into Mussolini. Creating an entire body of ectoplasm in less than a minute, Psycho becomes John L. Sullivan." The only limitation on Psycho's awesome powers is that, in order to utilize them, Psycho must have a medium through whom he can communicate with the spirit world.

In June–July 1943 the war god MARS dispatches the DUKE OF DECEPTION to Earth with instructions to do something drastic to solve the increasingly vexing problem of women's liberation. "I won't tolerate giving women the slightest freedom!" growls Mars. "Women are the natural spoils of war! They must remain at home, helpless slaves for the victor!"

In spirit form, Deception visits Dr. Psycho and whispers into his consciousness "an evil inspiration" for keeping Earth's "upstart women in their place!" Pleased with the plan, Psycho immediately prepares to carry it out.

Several weeks later, STEVE TREVOR and Diana Prince — the girl who is secretly WONDER WOMAN — attend a public demonstration of Dr. Psycho's occult powers. Since acquiring them, Psycho has built up an immense personal follow-

Steve Trevor and Dr. Psycho, 1943

ing, to the point where, in Trevor's words, ". . . millions accept everything Psycho's spirits say, as law and gospel!"

At the demonstration, and at a séance he holds soon afterward, Psycho assumes the guise of George Washington and, posing as Washington's spirit returned from the dead, makes a series of pronouncements attacking women and their role in the war effort, warning against their being entrusted with secrets or important responsibilities and predicting two impending crimes against America's security — the blowing up of a munitions plant and the theft of some top-secret documents — which he claims will be perpetrated by women.

In the days that follow, Dr. Psycho surreptitiously commits these crimes himself — posing as Colonel Darnell (*see* DARNELL [GENERAL]) on one occasion and as an unnamed major general on another — while cunningly focusing the blame on innocent women so as to provide apparent confirmation of "George Washington's" predictions. At one point, Dr. Psycho captures Wonder Woman and, by means of "a peculiar electro-atomizer of his own invention . . . sends alternating crosscurrents through **Wonder Woman's** flesh" that

separate her spirit from her physical body. Wonder Woman ultimately escapes from Psycho's clutches, however, successfully reunites her spirit with her physical body, and awakens Marva Psycho from the deep trance in which Dr. Psycho has imprisoned her.

"This medium is Psycho's source of power to materialize bodies," observes Wonder Woman, "— he keeps her hidden and helpless! I must awaken her gently!"

Thus deprived of the medium through whom he has been exercising his powers, Dr. Psycho is easily apprehended, but the villain remains confident that he will go unpunished. "You'll never prove in court that I materialized a major general and Colonel Darnell!" he boasts.

"I'm afraid he's right, Steve," admits Wonder Woman to Steve Trevor, "— I've a feeling there's more trouble ahead!" (WW No. 5/1: "Battle for Womanhood").

Despite these remarks, however, Dr. Psycho's next textual appearance finds him in the prison death house awaiting execution for his crimes. Knowing that to "materialize human bodies" he must have a medium, Psycho tells the warden he is ready to make a full confession of his crimes, but only if he can first confer privately with Joan White, his former secretary, who is currently incarcerated in another section of the prison. No sooner have he and Joan White been left alone, however, than Psycho places her in a hypnotic trance. Using her as his medium, he draws living ectoplasm from the spirit world to enable him to impersonate a prison guard, while at the same time he creates an ectoplasmic duplicate of himself, which he causes to collapse, as though it were

Dr. Psycho and Wonder Woman, 1943

Dr. Psycho hypnotizes Joan White, 1943

dead. Soon afterward, this ectoplasmic "phantom corpse" is buried in the prison graveyard, while the real Dr. Psycho — disguised as a prison guard — walks calmly through the prison gate and makes good his escape.

At large once again, Psycho sets out to wreak his revenge on Wonder Woman and her friends. Steve Trevor's secretary, LILA BROWN, is killed by a fountain pen bomb which Dr. Psycho places on Trevor's desk in an unsuccessful effort to kill him. Later, Dr. Psycho knocks Wonder Woman unconscious and buries her alive, but she escapes, recaptures Dr. Psycho, and sees to it that Joan White is released from the villain's hypnotic control (WW No. 5/3, Jun/Jul '43).

In December 1944 Dr. Psycho is one of the six infamous villains and villainesses impersonated by actors in BEDWIN FOOTH's "underworld crime [theatrical] company" (Sen No. 36: "Battle Against Revenge").

In July–August 1946 the warden at the state prison announces that Dr. Psycho was "electrocuted this morning," but Wonder Woman soon learns that the wily villain merely "materialized an ectoplasmic body which was electrocuted while he himself escaped!"

Using his ectoplasmic powers to impersonate Wonder Woman, Psycho invades the laboratory of famed inventor Dr. Cerebrum and steals his miraculous "war-prevento machine," a device designed to make war-making obsolete by using painless "somnatic rays [to] render warmakers unconscious long enough for us to capture and imprison them and their armies."

Determined to use the stolen apparatus "to enslave and kill the innocent people of the world," Dr. Psycho traps the HOLLIDAY GIRLS and is about to kill them with "an overdose of the somnatic rays" when Wonder Woman arrives on the scene and rescues them from his clutches. In the confusion, however, Dr. Psycho escapes.

Shaken by his encounter with Dr. Psycho, Dr. Cerebrum decides that his war-prevento machine must be destroyed for the good of humanity. "No **machine** can prevent wars!" agrees Wonder Woman. "Unscrupulous people can turn the most humanitarian instrument into a deadly weapon. Men must develop deep, lasting love!" (WW No. 18/1: "The Return from the Dead").

Soon afterward, Wonder Woman learns that Marva Psycho — "who became a WAC after she was freed from [Dr. Psycho's] evil dominance" — has been taken to the Hattoran Army Hospital suffering from "a mysterious sleeping sickness." What appears to be sleeping sickness, however, is actually the trancelike state in which Dr. Psycho

has again placed his wife in order to be able to use her as his medium. When Wonder Woman visits Marva at the hospital in hopes of freeing her from Psycho's influence, Psycho takes her captive and attempts to use her as bait to lure Steve Trevor, General Darnell, ETTA CANDY, and the Holliday Girls into a deathtrap.

"Always my plans to enslave the women of the world have been foiled by **you**, Diana Prince [secretly Wonder Woman], Etta Candy, the Holliday Girls, your sweetheart Major Trevor, or Gen. Darnell," snarls the villain. "Once you and your accomplices are dead, I shall have a free hand!"

Wonder Woman escapes, however, and rescues her friends from destruction in Dr. Psycho's deathtrap. Dr. Psycho remains at large, but Marva Psycho has reawakened from her trance and is once again free of her husband's evil domination.

"I'm taking Marva to Reform Island," announces Wonder Woman. "Amazon training will make her mind so strong, no one **man'll ever** be able to **dominate** her again!" (WW No. 18/2, Jul/Aug '46: "The Drugged WAC"). (See also TRANSFORMATION ISLAND.)

Dr. Psycho, meanwhile, decides to break Joan White out of prison so that he can use her as his medium in Marva's stead. Walking boldly into the prison on the pretext of having decided to give himself up, Psycho feigns pneumonia and is taken to the prison hospital, where he pretends to be near death and, as a "last wish," begs to be reunited with his "friend" Joan White for a few short moments. No sooner has Joan White been ushered into his hospital room, however, than Dr. Psycho overpowers the matron guarding her and places Joan under his hypnotic control. Disguising himself as the matron and taking Joan White by the hand, Psycho coolly escorts her through the prison gates to freedom, but not before he has demolished his prison hospital room by "breaking the air atoms" with powerful "ectoplasmic energy" to mislead the prison authorities into believing that he has perished in an accidental explosion.

When word of Dr. Psycho's death reaches Holliday College, an ecstatic Etta Candy throws a party at the college to celebrate the event, unaware that Dr. Psycho and Joan White have infiltrated the festivities in ectoplasmic disguises and that Psycho is awaiting his opportunity to wreak vengeance on Wonder Woman and her friends. By chance, however, OSCAR SWEETGULPER comes upon the villain during an unguarded moment — when he has momentarily shed his ectoplasmic disguise — and warns Wonder Woman, thus enabling her to apprehend the villain and thwart his hopes for revenge.

Dr. Psycho will be returned to prison, but Joan White will be taken to Reform Island for rehabilitative training. "There," promises Wonder Woman, "you need no longer fear Psycho" (WW No. 18/3, Jul/Aug '46: "Ectoplasmic Death").

Wonder Woman also battles and defeats Dr. Psycho in an adventure recorded in Wonder Woman No. 160/2 (Feb '66: "Dr. Psycho's Revenge!"), but this text is marred by numerous inconsistencies and factual errors.

A Wonder Woman text for October 1966 describes an encounter between Wonder Woman and Dr. Psycho which, judging from a number of textual details, can have taken place no later than 1942. In it, Dr. Psycho lures Wonder Woman to his island hideout, where he tricks her into stepping beneath the beam of his fiendish "personality scrambler machine." Suddenly, "as if **Wonder Woman** had been split like an atom--two forms move out of her body until there are **three Wonder Women**": the real Wonder Woman; a vain, self-centered Wonder Woman; and a tyrannical Wonder Woman.

"Every person has many different traits!" gloats Dr. Psycho. "Even you, **Wonder Woman**, have tyranny and vanity in your subconscious! I've simply released them--given them independent life! Hee! Hee!"

Wonder Woman dashes toward the personality scrambler in hopes of reversing it — and thereby compelling the two other Wonder Women to reenter her body, bringing the undesirable personality traits they represent back under her control — but the vain and tyrannical Wonder Women, unwilling to relinquish their newly acquired freedom, overpower her and take her prisoner.

Ultimately, however, Wonder Woman escapes from the underwater deathtrap in which the evil Wonder Women have left her to perish and swiftly defeats them, first tricking the vain Wonder Woman into helping her subdue the tyrannical Wonder Woman, and then overpowering the vain Wonder Woman once her tyrannical ally has been taken out of the fight. Dragging her two captives back to Dr. Psycho's personality scrambler, Wonder Woman reverses it, causing the evil duplicates to vanish and "merge into [her] again." Steve Trevor, who had followed Wonder Woman to Dr. Psycho's hideout in order to help her in the event she got into trouble, takes the villain into custody (WW No. 165/2: "The Three Fantastic Faces of Wonder Woman!").

In May 1967 Steve Trevor is presumed dead after his jet aircraft has crashed somewhere in Latin America. As a cruel joke, Dr. Psycho uses plastic surgery to transform gangster Pete Slote into a Steve Trevor look-alike, his motive being to cause Wonder Woman heartache while at the same time giving Slote the tactical advantage of being able to unnerve Wonder Woman with his Steve Trevor features. Wonder Woman ultimately apprehends Slote and his henchmen, however, and the real Steve Trevor turns out not to have died in the plane crash after all. Dr. Psycho remains at large (WW No. 170/1: "The Haunted Amazon!").

PSYCHO, MARVA. The wife of DR. PSYCHO, and the unwilling medium through whom he first summons "ectoplasmic energy" from the spirit world to aid him in his crusade to enslave the world's women (WW No. 5/1, Jun/Jul '43: "Battle for Womanhood").

Born Marva Jane Gray (Sen No. 20, Aug '43), Marva was engaged to Dr. Psycho while he was still in medical school, although she was also interested in Ben Bradley, the handsome "athletic idol of the college." When, through Bradley's scheming, Psycho was sent to prison for a crime he did not commit, Marva terminated her engagement to Psycho and married Bradley.

Released from prison years later, Psycho murders Bradley, forces Marva to marry him, and then uses her as his medium to draw "particles of living ectoplasm" from the spirit world to enable him to perform miraculous impersonations. When Dr. Psycho embarks on his fanatical "war against women" in June–July 1943, WONDER WOMAN defeats him and rescues Marva from the "deep trance" in which Psycho has imprisoned her.

"Submitting to a cruel husband's domination has ruined my life!" reflects Marva. "But what can a weak girl do?"

"Get strong!" replies Wonder Woman. "Earn your own living — join the WAACs or Waves and fight for your country! Remember the better you can fight the less you'll have to!" (WW No. 5/1: "Battle for Womanhood"). (*See* PSYCHO [DR.].)

In August 1943, having joined the WAACs at Wonder Woman's suggestion, Marva Psycho helps Wonder Woman defeat the Nazi spy STOFFER (Sen No. 20).

In July–August 1946 Wonder Woman learns that Marva Psycho — by now a WAAC sergeant — has been taken to the Hattoran Army Hospital suffering from "a mysterious sleeping sickness." What appears to be sleeping sickness, however, is actually the trancelike state in which Dr. Psycho has again placed his wife in order to be able to use her as his medium. Wonder Woman ultimately defeats Dr. Psycho and frees Marva from his evil domination.

"I'm taking Marva to Reform Island," an-

THIS FRAMES ME BEAUTIFULLY FOR SHOOTING THE GENERAL... MY ONLY HOPE IS TO FORCE THE REAL CRIMINAL TO REVEAL HIMSELF.

© NPP 1943

Marva Psycho, 1943

nounces Wonder Woman. "Amazon training will make her mind so strong, no one **man'll ever** be able to **dominate** her again!" (WW No. 18/2: "The Drugged WAC"). (*See* PSYCHO [DR.]; *see also* TRANSFORMATION ISLAND.)

PURPLE PRIESTESS, THE. A ruthless kidnapper and extortionist who attempts to dominate the peaceful country of ZARIKAN by playing on the fears and superstitions of its people. She is in reality Sinestra, a beautiful blond "enemy spy" who "worked against America" during World War II. The Purple Priestess is defeated by WONDER WOMAN.

In September–October 1947 Wonder Woman smashes a sinister "cure-all cult" headed by the Purple Priestess, a vicious racketeer who bilks the gullible by promising to cure the illnesses of their loved ones, and then threatens to kill her victims if they complain to the police. Wonder Woman captures the Purple Priestess's henchmen, but their leader escapes.

Several months later, Wonder Woman is summoned to far-off Zarikan and is informed that a mysterious woman appeared there recently, claiming to be the mortal messenger of their goddess Vultura and demanding the payment of exorbitant tribute.

"I have been sent by ze goddess to save you from your wickedness!" warned the stranger. "Unless every day gold and food eez offered to appeaze ze goddess, ze windmills will fail to pump water to irrigate your fields and your crops weel wither and die!"

Fearful of arousing the goddess's ire, Zarikan's King Yuka had paid the tribute, but now Vultura's messenger has kidnapped his daughter, Princess Allura, and her handmaidens and is forcing them to serve as the goddess's "slave maidens."

After establishing that Vultura's self-proclaimed messenger is actually the Purple Priestess, Wonder Woman allows herself to be presented to the Purple Priestess as a sacrificial victim in hopes of learning exactly where the villainess is holding her captives. Certain that, with Wonder Woman dead and King Yuka's daughter held hostage, she will soon become "ze supreme power in Zarikan," the Purple Priestess is exultant, but Wonder Woman soon turns the tables on the villainess, frees her hostages, and, for the first time, unmasks the Purple Priestess as Sinestra, a former Axis spy still being sought by U.S. Military Intelligence (WW No. 25/3: "The Judgment of Goddess Vultura").

Q

QUITO. An Inca priest — a member of "a lost tribe of mighty Incas . . . hidden from modern civilization for 400 years" — who makes a secret deal with the Japanese to provide them with a hidden base in the Andes in return for a promise by "the little monkey men . . . to make [the] Incas masters of America" — and Quito the master of the Incas — once they have achieved victory over the Allies in World War II.

In June 1943 Quito abducts STEVE TREVOR and the HOLLIDAY GIRLS and takes them to the Incas' "secret city of gold" deep in the South American jungles, but WONDER WOMAN flies to the secret city in her Amazon plane (see WONDER WOMAN [section C 4, the robot plane]), rescues her friends from Quito's clutches, and exposes his deal with the Japanese to his outraged fellow Incas. The Incas announce their intention to bring Quito to trial for his crimes, but Quito breaks free of his captors and, rather than face trial and punishment, makes a suicidal leap "from the temple terrace to rocky depths below" (Sen No. 18).

RACKEET, ABACUS. The leader of a gang of criminals who attempt to invade PARADISE ISLAND in May 1949 in order to steal "the mystery metal the Amazon bracelets are made of" (*see* AMAZONIUM). "That stuff can stop anything!" explains Rackeet to his henchmen. "With it--we'll laugh at the law!" WONDER WOMAN apprehends Rackeet and his cohorts before they can ever land on Paradise Island, and flies them back to America for punishment (Sen No. 89: "Amazon Queen for a Day!"). (*See also* WONDER WOMAN [section C 2, the bracelets of submission].)

RADIUM GIANTS. "Huge men whose bodies are made of deadly radium waves. They can completely disintegrate anything by simply touching it!" Their ruler is King Brutall. While WONDER WOMAN was still a teen-ager, she defeated the Radium Giants and thwarted their scheme to invade PARADISE ISLAND. A movie of Wonder Woman battling the Radium Giants is shown on Paradise Island during her visit there in July–August 1948 (WW No. 30/1: "The Secret of the Limestone Caves").

RAINBOW'S END. A western United States mining town, founded by prospector Lucky Lane, which is bequeathed to WONDER WOMAN in May–June 1952 in Lucky Lane's will. Dismayed to discover that Rainbow's End is now nothing more than a ghost town, Wonder Woman uses her Amazon skills and ingenuity to transform the town into a thriving community, filled with ambitious new settlers and bustling with renewed activity (WW No. 53/3: "The Secret Treasure at Rainbow's End!").

REBLA. The rebellious ruler of Trans Mountania, a section of the planet EROS. In November 1942, at the request of QUEEN DESIRA of VENUS, WONDER WOMAN journeys to Eros and, with the aid of STEVE TREVOR and ETTA CANDY, crushes an insurrection launched by Rebla against Marya, Eros's benevolent "planetary mother and supreme judge" (Sen No. 11).

REFORM ISLAND. *See* TRANSFORMATION ISLAND.

RENNO. *See* MERMAN.

REVERE, PAUL (1735–1818). An American patriot, craftsman, and industrialist — one of America's finest silversmiths — who is best remembered for his famous ride on the night of April 18, 1775, to warn the Massachusetts colonists that British troops were leaving Boston to seize military stores at Lexington and Concord. WONDER WOMAN temporarily blinds a British patrol with a cloud of dust to prevent them from sighting Revere and interfering with his ride during a time-journey to Colonial America that she makes in October 1954 (WW No. 69/2: "The Secret Hall of Fame!").

RICH, PRISCILLA. The lovely blond debutante who achieves infamy as the CHEETAH (WW No. 6/1, Fall '43: "Wonder Woman and the Cheetah").

RIGOR (King). The evil ruler of Bitterland, home of the Seal Men, and the father of the ruthless Prince Pagli. King Rigor and the Seal Men are defeated by WONDER WOMAN in Summer 1945 and compelled to sign a treaty of lasting peace with the inhabitants of nearby EVELAND.

In Summer 1945, responding to a summons from the goddess APHRODITE, Wonder Woman journeys to Eveland, a "tropical country of love and beauty" situated far beneath the South Polar ice cap, to rescue QUEEN EVE and her lovely "daughters of Venus" from the depredations of the sinister Seal Men. Entering Bitterland, an icy, barren, inhospitable land separated from Eveland by the icy River of Destruction, Wonder Woman defeats the Seal Men under the command of Prince Pagli and rescues a group of captive Eveland girls from their clutches (WW No. 13/1: "The Icebound Maidens").

Soon afterward, Wonder Woman receives an urgent mental radio message (*see* WONDER WOMAN [section C 7, the mental radio] from Queen Eve, asking her to return to Eveland to help her people beat back a renewed assault by the Seal Men. Reentering Bitterland, Wonder Woman rescues Queen Eve and a group of her followers from the clutches of Seal Men commanded by King Rigor and Prince Pagli (WW No. 13/2, Sum '45: "The Mystery Maid").

Some time later, Wonder Woman invades Bitterland again, this time to rescue another group of Eveland girls taken captive by the Seal Men. When STEVE TREVOR enters Bitterland alone, he is taken prisoner by the Seal Men and made a slave. Wonder Woman is taken captive also, but ultimately she turns the tables on her captors, rescues Trevor and the imprisoned Eveland girls, and negotiates a treaty of lasting peace between Eveland and Bitterland.

"You were superb, angel!" exclaims Trevor. "If only you'd marry me —!"

"If I married you, Steve," replies Wonder Woman, "I'd have to pretend I'm **weaker** than you are to make you happy — and that, **no** woman should do!" (WW No. 13/3, Sum '45: "Slaves in the Electric Gardens").

RIVVERS, TORA. An unscrupulous "millionaire socialite" who, having been denied the leading role in the film *Hollywood Goes to Paradise Island*, becomes determined to sabotage the film and prevent its completion. Her scheme is ultimately thwarted by WONDER WOMAN.

In March–April 1950 MONARCH STUDIOS begins filming *Hollywood Goes to Paradise Island*, which is to be shot on location on PARADISE ISLAND by an all-woman cast and crew in accordance with APHRODITE's law (*see* AMAZONS [section B, Aphrodite's Law]), which prohibits men from setting foot on the island. Brilliant but temperamental director Von Tender, furious at having been disqualified because of his sex, openly threatens that "if I can't direct this picture, then no one else will," while socialite Tora Rivvers, enraged at having been denied the starring role — although she has been generously awarded a lesser role at Wonder Woman's urging — cunningly keeps her anger hidden.

As the filming on Paradise Island proceeds, a series of mysterious mishaps occur which threaten to prevent completion of the picture. Suspicion focuses on Von Tender because of his angry threat, but the real villain is Tora Rivvers, who has pretended to be satisfied with her small role while secretly nursing a hatred for the project and the people connected with it. Through Wonder Woman's valiant efforts, however, the filming is completed successfully and Tora Rivvers is exposed as the mystery saboteur. She will be taken to TRANSFORMATION ISLAND to undergo rehabilitative training (WW No. 40/1: "Hollywood Goes to Paradise Island" pts. 1–2 — "The Mile High Menace!"; "The Undersea Invasion!").

ROBIN HOOD. The hero of a series of popular ballads, the earliest of which date from the 14th century or quite possibly earlier. In the ballads he is a gallant outlaw and master bowman, dwelling in Sherwood Forest with his band of Merry Men, robbing the rich and giving to the poor, and striking out against oppressive authority, usually personified by his most frequent enemy, the ruthless Sheriff of Nottingham. His most noteworthy companions are Little John, Friar Tuck, and the lovely Maid Marian.

In Wonder Woman No. 82/1, after being captured by the Sheriff of Nottingham and imprisoned in impregnable Nottingham Castle, Robin Hood fires a message-carrying arrow into the surrounding woods in hopes of summoning his Merry Men, but, "by a twist of fortune," the shaft hurtles "through a warp in the time screen" and lands in the 20th century, where it is retrieved by WONDER WOMAN.

Transported through the time barrier to 12th-century Sherwood Forest by means of the Amazon "time-and-space transformer" (*see* AMAZONS [section G, Amazon science]), Wonder Woman rescues Robin Hood from Nottingham Castle and reunites him with his band of Merry Men (May '56: "Wonder Woman Meets Robin Hood!").

In November 1957 Wonder Woman is watching television when a "ghost" image of Robin Hood calling for help suddenly appears on her screen. Realizing that she has somehow tuned in on a "time channel" and intercepted a distress call from the past, Wonder Woman journeys through the time barrier by means of the time-and-space transformer, and rescues Robin Hood from the castle dungeon of the evil Prince John, and his Merry Men from Prince John's soldiers (WW No. 94/3: "The Channel of Time!").

ROBOT WOMAN. An ingenious robot — the brainchild of Elektro, diabolical "scientific head of a criminal gang" — which looks exactly like WONDER WOMAN and possesses most of her Amazon powers. After committing two spectacular robberies while under Elektro's electronic control, Robot Woman kidnaps Wonder Woman and STEVE TREVOR and takes them to Elektro's "vast underground laboratory," but Wonder Woman turns the tables on Elektro and his henchmen and swiftly apprehends them (WW No. 48/1, Jul/Aug '51: "Wonder Woman vs Robot Woman!").

ROBUST, BLUFF. The unscrupulous nephew of Rufus Robust, a wealthy trustee of STARVARD COLLEGE. His attempt to profit unfairly from a friendly wager between his uncle and Sidney Simper, a trustee of the HOLLIDAY COLLEGE FOR WOMEN, is thwarted by WONDER WOMAN.

In January 1947 Holliday College trustee Sidney Simper bets Rufus Robust that Holliday can beat Starvard in tennis, with the loser to donate $1,000,000 to the college of the winner. Wonder Woman is to play on the Holliday team, and Pete Athleet, "the world's champion tennis player," is to play on Starvard's.

Bluff Robust is determined to see to it that his uncle wins the bet, because if Starvard receives the $1,000,000, a new Starvard Research Foundation will be established with the money, and Bluff himself will be placed in charge of it. He decides to ensure a Starvard victory by seeing to it that Wonder Woman fails to appear to play for Holliday.

Soon afterward, while Wonder Woman is hard at work on the tennis court practicing her serve, Bluff surreptitiously drops a special gas-filled tennis ball among the regular ones. "It will not only knock out the Amazon," he muses, "but make her invisible to all but me, when I wear these infra-red glasses!"

When Wonder Woman's racket strikes the gas-filled ball, the gas knocks her unconscious and renders her invisible, enabling Bluff to carry her off the tennis court and lock her inside a mummy case in the Starvard Museum. When the hour arrives for the long-awaited tennis match between Starvard and Holliday, Wonder Woman is nowhere to be found. And later, with the match tied and the game between Pete Athleet and Wonder Woman to be the deciding one, the famous Amazon still has yet to appear. Just as the match officials are about to declare Pete Athleet and Starvard College the winners by default, however, Wonder Woman appears on the court, having regained consciousness and escaped from the mummy case.

As Wonder Woman's match with Pete Athleet gets under way, Bluff, now desperate, tries to shoot her with a pistol, only to be thwarted and apprehended by an alert STEVE TREVOR. Wonder Woman finally defeats Pete Athleet, thereby winning the match and the $1,000,000 for Holliday College (Sen No. 61: "The Million Dollar Tennis Game").

ROGERS, AL. An electric light bulb replacer who is dissatisfied with his job because he feels that it is useless, trivial, and unimportant. His job takes on new meaning for him in January–February 1950, however, when WONDER WOMAN proves to him that his job is actually "vital and exciting! No one is unimportant in a democracy," insists Wonder Woman, "--and that goes for his job!" (WW No. 39/1: "The Trail of Thrills!").

RONNKN. One of a pair of extraterrestrial aliens — his companion is named Zgggm — who wreak havoc on the planet Earth disguised as Billy the Kid and Jesse James until they are finally defeated by WONDER WOMAN in July 1959.

In July 1959 Ronnkn and Zgggm arrive on Earth — disguised as Billy the Kid and Jesse James, respectively — as the advance guard of an impending interplanetary invasion. Although they are dressed in the garb of Western badmen, they possess a mind-boggling array of superhuman

powers and ride "horses" that fly through the air at incredible speed.

"What greater sport for us," gloats their planet's leader to his aides, "--than to assume the identities of notorious criminals who **used** to plague Earth . . . . [and] cause complete havoc with our advanced weapons and inventions--which we can make to resemble ordinary guns and horses!"

Ronnkn and Zgggm have come to Earth to battle Wonder Woman, for her defeat will be the signal for their fellow aliens to attack the Earth, while her victory will be taken as a sign that an Earth invasion would be doomed to failure. After suffering a series of initial setbacks, however, Wonder Woman defeats Ronnkn and Zgggm and returns them to their home planet as captives as a warning to their fellow aliens to leave Earth alone (WW No. 107/2: "Gunslingers of Space!").

RONNO. See MERMAN.

ROOSEVELT, FRANKLIN DELANO (1882–1945). The 32nd president of the United States. In office from March 1933 until his death in April 1945, he served as president during World War II and the era of the New Deal, and was the only American president to be reelected three times.

In Summer 1944 President Roosevelt calls a special meeting of his cabinet to discuss the "huge prehistoric vultures" that have been appearing over America, "carrying off hundreds of victims and threatening the highest officials of the nation!" (CC No. 7: "The Vulture's Nest!"). (See VULTURE KING, THE.)

In Winter 1945 President Roosevelt negotiates a peace treaty with the leaders of NEPTUNIA. Under its terms, "Neptunia becomes a protectorate pledging its complete allegiance to America," STEVE TREVOR is appointed acting governor, and, in deference to Neptunian custom, women are barred from entering Neptunia (WW No. 15: chs. 1–3 — "The First Battle of Neptunia"; "The Masters of the Water"; "In the Killer's Cage"). (See SOLO.)

ROYDEN, TOMMY. An American youngster who is taken captive by Nazi spies in Winter 1942 and rescued from their clutches by WONDER WOMAN (CC No. 1: "The Mystery of the House of Seven Gables").

RUPERT (Prince). The uncle of Queen Niana, and the next in line to succeed her as ruler of 16th-century Sardonia. His plot to abduct Niana and seize power in Sardonia is thwarted by WONDER WOMAN during a time-journey that she makes there in January 1954.

Wonder Woman is browsing through an old bookstore in January 1954 when she comes upon an old book containing a picture of herself seated on a throne. A caption beneath the picture describes the enthroned woman as Queen Niana, ruler of the tiny kingdom of Sardonia "more than 400 years ago!" In an attempt to solve the mystery, Wonder Woman and STEVE TREVOR journey through the time barrier to 16th-century Sardonia, where they learn that Queen Niana has been kidnapped and imprisoned by her evil uncle Rupert, who intends to crown himself king and rule Sardonia in her stead.

When a group of Niana's knights greet Wonder Woman as though she were their missing queen, Wonder Woman realizes that she must be Niana's exact double and decides to pose as the kidnapped monarch — and thus forestall Prince Rupert's coronation — until she can locate Niana and restore her to her throne. It is while Wonder Woman is impersonating Niana that a court artist paints a picture of her seated on her throne — a painting which undoubtedly served as the basis for the illustration Wonder Woman found in the old book. Ultimately, she rescues the real Niana from Rupert's dungeon — along with Steve Trevor, who has also been taken captive by Rupert's forces — defeats Rupert's henchmen, and restores Queen Niana to the Sardonian throne (WW No. 63/3: "The Imposter Queen!").

RYKORNIA. "An unexplored planetoid, hidden in Earth's atmosphere by a shroud of clouds, and inhabited by fiendish creatures just waiting their opportunity to invade our world." Rykornia's ruler, KING TASSEL, presides over a population of "weird plant people of a terrifying and menacing nature." A Rykornian attempt to conquer the Earth is thwarted by WONDER WOMAN in September–October 1947 (WW No. 25/1: "Siege of the Rykornians"). (*See* TASSEL [KING].)

S

SAN YAN. A Japanese spy who, posing as a Burmese elephant trainer, is the mastermind behind a plot to drive Ed King's circus into bankruptcy to prevent it from continuing to raise money for American servicemen through benefit performances. San Yan is apprehended by WONDER WOMAN in Summer 1942.

When Ed King's valuable Burmese circus elephants begin dying mysteriously one after the other, King complains to Wonder Woman that ". . . my circus will be ruined, unless I can stop these elephant killings!"

Investigating, Wonder Woman learns that San Yan, the leader of the circus workers who care for the elephants, has been persuading the workers — all of whom come from Burma, "where elephants are worshipped" — that in order "to free our ancestors' spirits we must kill these elephants whom [the Americans] hold captive far from their native country!"

Actually, she discovers, San Yan is not Burmese at all, but "a Jap spy . . . [who] planned these elephant murders to stop King's circus from making money for American soldiers!" Wonder Woman apprehends San Yan in Summer 1942, thereby bringing a halt to the vicious elephant killings (WW No. 1/2: "Wonder Woman Goes to the Circus!").

SARDONIA. A 16th-century kingdom ruled by the good Queen Niana. Sardonia is the scene of WONDER WOMAN's encounter with the evil PRINCE RUPERT (WW No. 63/3, Jan '54: "The Imposter Queen!").

SARGASSO SEA KINGDOM, THE. An undersea kingdom which is situated on the floor of the Sargasso Sea and ruled by the lovely PRINCESS ALTHEA. The Sargasso Sea Kingdom is the scene of WONDER WOMAN's battle with the power-mad MASTER DE STROYER in November–December 1950 (WW No. 44: "The Monarch of the Sargasso Sea!" chs. I–III — no title; "Wonder Woman's Decision"; "The Final Battle of the Sargasso Sea").

SATPHIX. "A planet not of Earth's solar system" which is the scene of WONDER WOMAN's battle with the evil PROF. TURGO in March–April 1951. The sole surviving fragment of the planet now sits on "an uncharted spot" on the PACIFIC OCEAN, having been placed there by Wonder Woman at the re-

quest of its inhabitants (WW No. 46/2: "The Moon of Peril!").

SATURN. The sixth planet from the SUN. In the WONDER WOMAN chronicles, Saturn is a "mighty but cold and cruel world" ruled by the satanic EMPEROR MEPHISTO and peopled by a sadistic humanoid race served by a vast population of slaves. The women of Saturn are the planet's overseers, while the "great men of Saturn engage only in science and war." ". . . [W]e Saturnians are utterly inhuman," remarks the slave driver EVILESS in Fall 1944. "We regard ourselves as machines" (WW No. 10/2: "The Sky Road").

In Fall 1944 Wonder Woman thwarts a Saturnian scheme to conquer Earth and negotiates a peace and trade treaty between Earth and Saturn. The treaty specifically forbids the use of earthmen as Saturnian slaves (WW No. 10/1–3: "Spies from Saturn"; "The Sky Road"; "Wonder Woman's Boots!"). (*See* SATURNO, MEPHISTO [DUKE].)

In Winter 1944 HYPNOTA THE GREAT attempts to sabotage the Earth-Saturn peace treaty in hopes of reviving the slave trade between Earth and Saturn, but her efforts are repeatedly thwarted by Wonder Woman (WW No. 11/1–3: "The Slaves of the Evil Eye"; "The Unseen Menace"; "The Slave Smugglers").

In March–April 1947 Wonder Woman renews her battle with DUKE MEPHISTO SATURNO (WW No. 22/2: "The Island of Evil").

In August–September 1947 Wonder Woman matches wits with the Saturnian villainess SATURNETTE (CC No. 22: "The Captives of Saturnette!").

In March–April 1948 Wonder Woman battles VILLAINY INCORPORATED, an organization of villainesses led by the Saturnian slave driver Eviless (WW No. 28/1–3: "Villainy Incorporated!"; "Trap of Crimson Flame"; "In the Hands of the Merciless!").

In February 1956 Wonder Woman journeys to Saturn to defeat a band of evil extraterrestrial aliens who have been bombing Saturn from Titan, the largest, brightest, and most massive of Saturn's ten satellites (WW No. 80/3: "SOS — Saturn!").

In February 1959 Wonder Woman demolishes an armada of Saturnian, Martian, and Plutonian spaceships attempting to invade the Earth (WW

No. 104/2: "Key of Deception!"). (*See* DECEPTION, DUKE OF.)

In April 1959 Wonder Woman and STEVE TREVOR have an adventure on Saturn's moon Titan (WW No. 105/2: "Eagle of Space!"). (*See* TREVOR, STEVE.)

In May 1961 Wonder Woman battles the SINISTER SEER OF SATURN (WW No. 122: "The Skyscraper Wonder Woman!").

SATURNETTE. A raven-haired villainess who, like EVILESS, holds the post of Captain (or Commandress) of Women on the planet SATURN. Comic Cavalcade No. 22 describes her as "revenge-mad . . . ruthless, cruel, and relentless!" Saturnette is defeated by WONDER WOMAN in August–September 1947.

In August–September 1947 Saturnette obtains permission from Saturn's EMPEROR MEPHISTO to journey to Earth to battle the AMAZONS. On Earth, she and her henchwomen secretly imprison Wonder Woman and QUEEN HIPPOLYTE aboard their spacecraft and then replace them with a pair of Saturnian impersonators whose mission is to lure the Amazons into a deathtrap. Wonder Woman and Hippolyte escape from the Saturnian spacecraft, however, and, soon afterward, Wonder Woman defeats Saturnette and rescues her sister Amazons from the clutches of the Saturnian impostors. Saturnette and her cohorts will be taken to Reform Island (*see* TRANSFORMATION ISLAND) for rehabilitative training (CC No. 22: "The Captives of Saturnette!").

There is some indication that Saturnette and Eviless were originally intended to be one and the same person and that the name Saturnette appears in Comic Cavalcade No. 22 only as the result of a chronicler's error. The textual data, however, are contradictory, making verification of this point impossible.

SATURNO, MEPHISTO (Duke). A ruthless villain from the planet SATURN who makes repeated attempts to annihilate WONDER WOMAN in order to pave the way for a Saturnian invasion of Earth.

Wonder Woman first meets Duke Mephisto Saturno at a Long Island party in Fall 1944, and soon discovers that he is "a spy from Saturn," on Earth to prepare the way for an impending Saturnian invasion. When she and the HOLLIDAY GIRLS sneak aboard Saturno's "submo-space ship," a craft which "moves under water and through space with equal speed," they are taken captive by the duke and his Saturnian cohorts.

"Saturn is about to conquer Earth!" boasts Saturno to Wonder Woman. "For many years I and my assistants have spied upon your planet — **you** are the only enemy we feared! This Saturnic expedition was sent to capture **you** — [and] we've succeeded!"

Saturno intends to take Wonder Woman and the Holliday Girls to Saturn to serve as slaves, but Wonder Woman seizes control of the spacecraft en route to Saturn and is preparing to tow it back to Earth behind her Amazon plane (*see* WONDER WOMAN [section C 4, the robot plane]) when the Saturnian crewmen, realizing they have been defeated, "leap into space, preferring death to capture!" Duke Mephisto Saturno, however, remains Wonder Woman's prisoner and will be returned to Earth to stand trial for his crimes (WW No. 10/1: "Spies from Saturn").

At his trial, Saturno is found guilty and sentenced to "99 years imprisonment at hard labor," but he vows to escape to fulfill his mission of "preparing Earth for [an] invasion from Saturn!" Indeed, soon afterward, while his henchmen flood the Earth with "Saturnic lassitude gas," making everyone on Earth sleepy, lazy, and unresisting, Saturno breaks jail and, aided by his Saturnian allies, imprisons STEVE TREVOR aboard a Saturnian spacecraft and forces Wonder Woman to surrender to prevent him from being harmed.

Aboard the spacecraft, Trevor is taunted and humiliated by the sadistic slave driver Eviless. ". . . [W]e Saturnians are utterly inhuman," she declares as she forces Trevor to scrub the spacecraft floor. "We regard ourselves as machines."

Arriving on Saturn, Wonder Woman learns that the satanic EMPEROR MEPHISTO, determined to conquer Earth in order to obtain "a new supply of strong slaves for physical labor," has put a vast slave army to work building an "invasion road to Earth."

"Building a sky road from one planet to another would be impossible for you stupid earthlings," gloats one of Wonder Woman's captors, "but it's **easy** for us Saturnians. We take material from Saturn's rings and hold it in place with anti-gravity rays!"

Ultimately, however, with Steve Trevor's help, Wonder Woman escapes from the Saturnians, destroys the partially completed sky road, and escapes to Earth with Trevor in a commandeered Saturnian spaceship. During her captivity, however, Wonder Woman's red boots were taken away from her, and she regrets having been unable to recover them before returning to Earth (WW No. 10/2, Fall '44: "The Sky Road").

When Wonder Woman arrives at the shoe store to pick up the new pair of boots she has ordered to replace her old ones, she does not realize that a Saturnian agent has secretly substituted the old boots for the new ones after filling them with "a powerful Saturnic sleeping drug" designed to be "absorbed instantly through the soles of the feet." When Wonder Woman returns home and puts the boots on, the Saturnian drug courses through her body and she lapses into unconsciousness.

Finding Wonder Woman unconscious on the floor, ETTA CANDY runs to the telephone and summons a doctor, but Duke Mephisto Saturno arrives on the scene ahead of him disguised as a physician and before long has imprisoned both Wonder Woman and Etta aboard his Saturnian spacecraft. As the craft speeds toward Saturn, however, Wonder Woman turns the tables on her captors and seizes command of the vessel. On Saturn, she persuades Emperor Mephisto of the considerable economic and trade advantages that would accrue to his planet if only he would abandon his dream of interplanetary conquest and establish friendly relations with Earth. Partly because he believes that an Earth-Saturn treaty might indeed be advantageous, but mainly because his agent Mephisto Saturno has been repeatedly defeated by Wonder Woman, the greedy emperor finally signs "a peace and trade treaty with Earth," and, in accordance with its terms, orders that all Earth slaves be freed and the Earth-Saturn slave trade discontinued. Because Saturnians regard failure as their most heinous crime, however, Emperor Mephisto orders Duke Mephisto Saturno and his "ruthless women slave drivers" imprisoned for life (WW No. 10/3, Fall '44: "Wonder Woman's Boots!").

In March–April 1947, however, Duke Mephisto Saturno receives a pardon from his emperor and returns to Earth, determined to destroy Wonder Woman and plunge the entire planet into a cataclysmic war. Posing as an expert on international affairs, one of Saturno's agents begins a campaign to stir up distrust of the United Nations and persuade America to withdraw from the U.N. By using such a withdrawal to promote worldwide mistrust of America and its allies, the Saturnians hope to embroil the nations of the world in a devastating war. In addition, the "Saturnic power of hypnotism" enables the Saturnians to render themselves invisible to earthmen's eyes, and thus to instigate intolerance and suspicion everywhere without their presence being suspected. Wonder Woman, Steve Trevor, and the Holliday Girls are taken prisoner by the aliens, but just as the villains are about to kill Trevor and the Holliday Girls, Wonder Woman escapes from her captors, rescues her friends, and apprehends Saturno and his Saturnian cohorts (WW No. 22/2: "The Island of Evil").

SCHULTZ, KARL. A Gestapo agent "working for the Japs" who is apprehended by WONDER WOMAN.

In April 1943 Diana Prince, the girl who is secretly Wonder Woman, travels to HARD CANDY's Texas ranch to attend the wedding of his daughter, ETTA CANDY, and Prince Hylo Goulash. Wonder Woman discovers, however, that the unctuous "prince" is actually Gestapo agent Karl Schultz, who hopes to marry Etta Candy only so that, with the aid of his Japanese allies, he can "direct oil well sabotage unsuspected from the Candy ranch." In the words of Sensation Comics No. 16:

> Black gold, gushing from the earth's depths, bursts into scarlet devastating flame beneath the sinister touch of Nipponese chemists! Can **Wonder Woman** stem the onrush of enemy destruction which threatens every oil field in America?

Aided by the HOLLIDAY GIRLS, however, Wonder Woman exposes Etta Candy's groom-to-be as Gestapo agent Schultz and apprehends his cohorts, a ring of Japanese and Italian spies.

SEADUNK (Capt.). The old seafaring man who is professor of oceanography at the HOLLIDAY COLLEGE FOR WOMEN. Capt. Seadunk's expedition to the Sargasso Sea is taken captive by MASTER DE STROYER's "War Mongers" in November–December 1950 (WW No. 44: "The Monarch of the Sargasso Sea!" chs. I–III — no title; "Wonder Woman's Decision"; "The Final Battle of the Sargasso Sea"). (See MASTER DE STROYER.)

SEASIDE AMUSEMENT PARK. An amusement park where a gang of criminals has hidden $5,000,000 in stolen bank loot. In May 1955 the gangsters attempt to force the park to close to enable them to retrieve their loot without interference, but WONDER WOMAN, who is selling tickets at the park to benefit charity, locates the hidden loot and apprehends the criminals (WW No. 74/1: "The Carnival of Peril!").

SEELY, ROGER. The murderer and one-time business partner of Alex Block. Seely is apprehended by WONDER WOMAN in September–October 1968.

When businessman Alex Block is found murdered, STEVE TREVOR is accused of the crime, principally because, at a recent party, he punched Block in the face for getting fresh with Wonder Woman and accused him of being a "rat" and not "fit to live." Since Trevor's threadbare alibi — that at the time of the murder he was having a drink at a hippie hangout with an anonymous blonde — cannot be substantiated, Trevor is brought to trial and found guilty of Block's murder.

In her role as Diana Prince, however, Wonder

Woman sets out to find the missing blonde and exonerate Trevor. Through careful sleuthing, she locates the drinking companion, verifies Trevor's alibi, and accumulates the evidence necessary to reverse his conviction. Then, as Wonder Woman, she exposes Roger Seely as the real murderer and takes him into custody (WW No. 178: "Wonder Woman's Rival").

SERVA. Hypnota's twin sister (WW No. 11/1–3, Win '44: "The Slaves of the Evil Eye"; "The Unseen Menace"; "The Slave Smugglers"). (*See* HYPNOTA [THE GREAT].)

SHAGGY. One of the mischievous, fun-loving, happy-go-lucky leprechauns who inhabit the labyrinthine network of subterranean tunnels that honeycomb the earth beneath the peaceful country of SHAMROCK LAND. Shaggy and his two closest leprechaun companions, Hoppy and Woggle, are close friends of WONDER WOMAN.

Like all the other leprechauns, Shaggy, Hoppy, and Woggle spend their days making tiny shoes for the Irish fairies, known as "the little people." They first meet Wonder Woman in Fall 1945 when, accompanied by STEVE TREVOR and ETTA CANDY, she enters "the redwood forest" in search of the "vicious spy and killer" known as the GENTLEMAN KILLER (WW No. 14/1–3: "Captured by Leprechauns"; "The Gentleman Killer Strikes Again!"; no title). (*See* GENTLEMAN KILLER, THE.)

Shaggy the leprechaun, 1948

In March 1948 Diana Prince, the girl who is secretly Wonder Woman, is en route to the place where she hides her Amazon plane (*see* WONDER WOMAN [section C 4, the robot plane]) when she hears cries for help coming from the bottom of a nearby lake. Diving to the rescue as Wonder Woman, she finds Shaggy drowning, with his beard caught beneath a boulder, and, after carrying him safely to the surface, asks him what he is doing so far from Shamrock Land.

"It's a rule in the fairy kingdom," replies Shaggy, "that once a year we must visit the nations of the world to entertain and help little children."

Shaggy leads Wonder Woman to the place nearby where Hoppy, Woggle, and the other leprechauns have made their camp, and soon afterward, with their help, she apprehends Shark, a ruthless criminal who forces small boys to steal for him. At one point in the adventure, after Wonder Woman has been wrongly accused of a rash of

Shaggy recalls the Gentleman Killer, 1948

thefts and thrown into jail, the leprechauns put Wonder Woman and her jailers to sleep with their magical powers and then carry her out of the jail so that she can remain free to establish her innocence and continue her battle with Shark (Sen No. 75: "The Return of 'Shaggy,' the Leprechaun!").

In May–June 1949, with the help of — and sometimes in *spite* of the help of — Shaggy, Hoppy, and Woggle, who are always well-intentioned but who are also inclined to be mischievous, Wonder Woman reforms the evil ABNER GRABB and saves the "U.S. Government owned forest where the leprechauns live" from imminent destruction (WW No. 35/3: "The Stolen Forest!"). (*See* GRABB, ABNER.)

SHAMROCK LAND. A peaceful country, known also as Happy Shamrock Land, which is inhabited by gentle Irish folk and by the Irish fairies, known as "the little people." Beneath Shamrock Land is the labyrinthine network of subterranean tunnels where the leprechauns — among them Hoppy, Woggle, and SHAGGY — work all day making tiny shoes for the little people. The ruler of Shamrock Land is the lovely Princess Elaine. Shamrock Land and the leprechaun tunnels beneath it are the scene of WONDER WOMAN's battles with the GENTLEMAN KILLER in Fall 1945 (WW No. 14/1–3:

"Captured by Leprechauns"; "The Gentleman Killer Strikes Again!"; no title).

The location of Shamrock Land is uncertain. Wonder Woman No. 14/1 places it somewhere in "the redwood forest," suggesting a location somewhere on the west coast of the United States (Fall '45: "Captured by Leprechauns"). In Sensation Comics No. 75, however, when Wonder Woman encounters Shaggy on the outskirts of Washington, D.C., and expresses surprise at finding him so far from home, Shaggy explains that "a rule in the fairy kingdom" requires the leprechauns to "visit the nations of the world" once a year "to entertain and help little children," implying a foreign location for Shamrock Land, perhaps in Ireland (Mar '48: The Return of 'Shaggy,' the Leprechaun!").

SHARK. A ruthless villain who forces small boys to steal for him. Shark is apprehended by WONDER WOMAN in March 1948 with the aid of her leprechaun friends Hoppy, Woggle, and SHAGGY (Sen No. 75: "The Return of 'Shaggy,' the Leprechaun!").

SHARKEETA (Queen). A treacherous mermaid with the head of a beautiful woman and the body of a shark, who, in June–July 1947, attempts to murder the AMAZONS and seize control of PARADISE ISLAND. Battled to a standoff by WONDER WOMAN and MALA, Sharkeeta and her sister mermaid sharks ultimately become gentle and peace-loving through the scientific efforts of GERTA VON GUNTHER.

By June–July 1947 Gerta von Gunther, the "brilliant but headstrong" daughter of BARONESS PAULA VON GUNTHER, has developed a formula she calls "supervitalitee solution," a chemical which, when fed to baby sharks, transforms them into beautiful mermaids with the heads of women and the bodies of sharks. Because Paula had forbidden the dangerous shark experiments and Gerta had disobeyed her by performing them, it is decided that Gerta must be taken to Paradise Island "for further Amazon training," so that she may "feel again the joy of obeying loving teachers!" The mermaids are brought to Paradise Island also and placed in a specially constructed pool, for Wonder Woman fears that "when they mature, they may revert to their original shark-like natures."

In the special pond constructed for the mermaids, Gerta, under Mala's direction, feeds them her **supervitalitee** solution. Time passes and the mineral enriched water effects an amazing change. The tiny creatures not only grow larger, but also develop wings where they once had fins.

Before long, Wonder Woman's greatest fears have been realized: the mermaids, having reverted to their cruel, sharklike natures, are now determined to conquer Paradise Island and annihilate the Amazons. Led by Sharkeeta, the mermaid sharks abduct QUEEN HIPPOLYTE and several of her Amazons, but Mala and Wonder Woman rescue the captives and bravely battle the evil mermaids. The battle seesaws back and forth, with neither side able to achieve a victory, until finally Gerta arrives on the scene with her "humanizing fluid," a new discovery designed to "tame the shark savageness of the mermaids." By pouring it over their bodies, she makes Sharkeeta and her mermaid sharks happy and peace-loving, thus ending their threat to Paradise Island (CC No. 21: "The Seige [sic] of the Flying Mermaids!").

SILICONS. Sinister extraterrestrial aliens who, by July 1958, have developed an awesome arsenal of artificial comets with which they intend to shatter the Earth into tiny fragments. After a desperate battle with WONDER WOMAN, who struggles to prevent the Silicons from launching their deadly comets against the Earth, the aliens accidentally destroy themselves when they turn their comet arsenal against their own planet in a frenzied attempt to annihilate Wonder Woman (WW No. 99/1: "Stampede of the Comets!").

SINESTRA. An "enemy spy who worked against America during the war." Sinestra is secretly the PURPLE PRIESTESS (WW No. 25/3, Sep/Oct '47: "The Judgment of Goddess Vultura").

SING SING. A New York state prison which is located in the town of Ossining, approximately 17 miles north of New York City. The murderers incarcerated in its death house have included the villainous DR. PSYCHO (Sen No. 36, Dec '44: "Battle Against Revenge").

SINISTER SEER OF SATURN, THE. A malevolent Saturnian with green skin and three eyes whose plot to annihilate WONDER WOMAN and seize control of the planet SATURN is thwarted by Wonder Woman in May 1961 (WW No. 122: "The Skyscraper Wonder Woman!").

SKEENER, SLICK. The successor to "CRIME BRAIN" DOONE as the leader of the Sly Fox Mob. In June 1947 Skeener attempts to wreak vengeance on STEVE TREVOR for his part in Doone's arrest and conviction by enticing young Jimmy Banks, Jr.—the son of a policeman—into a game of cops and robbers with his father's service revolver, having Trevor shot by a henchman from a place of concealment, and then blaming the murder on the innocent Jimmy. Shot in the back by Skeener's triggerman and pronounced dead at the scene, Trevor is brought back to life in BARONESS PAULA VON GUNTHER's secret laboratory by means of WONDER WOMAN's miraculous "purple ray" (*see*

AMAZONS [section G, Amazon science]). Soon afterward, with Trevor safely back among the living, Wonder Woman apprehends Skeener and his hit man and exonerates Jimmy Banks, Jr., of any complicity in the shooting (Sen No. 66: "Prisoners of Cops and Robbers"). (*See also* DOONE, "CRIME BRAIN.")

SKINFLINT, URIAH. The unscrupulous lumberman responsible for the rash of mysterious forest fires that have been ravaging the timberland belonging to Reardon, an honest lumberman. Skinflint and his henchmen are apprehended by WONDER WOMAN.

By June–July 1946 lumberman Reardon has been awarded a lucrative contract to supply timber to the U.S. Army, ". . . but unless I produce on schedule," he observes, "I lose my contract, and Uriah Skinflint, who owns the adjoining forest, gets it!" Lately, Reardon's timberland has been plagued by forest fires, making it impossible for him to cut down trees and fulfill his contract with the Army. In desperation, Reardon turns to Wonder Woman, who — with the aid of STEVE TREVOR, ETTA CANDY, and the HOLLIDAY GIRLS — investigates the mysterious rash of fires, apprehends Uriah Skinflint and his henchmen, and puts out a particularly savage forest fire threatening to destroy Reardon's forest completely (CC No. 15: "Flaming Fury").

SLAMBO (Prince). The evil half brother of PRINCE SLEEKO, the ruler of ZANI ISLAND. Prince Slambo's scheme to depose Prince Sleeko and seize control of Zani Island is thwarted by WONDER WOMAN in April–May 1947 (CC No. 20: "The Buddha Wishing Ring"). (*See* SLEEKO [PRINCE].)

SLEEKO (Prince). The ruler of Zani Island, America's "key base protecting Pacific communications." Prince Sleeko is the half brother of the treacherous Prince Slambo.

In April–May 1947, after STEVE TREVOR has been overcome by smoke while attempting to rescue a group of generals from an accidental fire, WONDER WOMAN steps in to complete the rescue and carry Trevor to safety, but selflessly sees to it that Trevor receives all the credit. In recognition of his bravery, Trevor, a lieutenant colonel, is promoted to the rank of brigadier general and dispatched to Zani Island to assume command there. ETTA CANDY also travels to Zani Island during this period, having been recruited by Prince Sleeko to set up a school there for the benefit of the island's native population.

Soon after their arrival, however, Prince Slambo, Sleeko's evil half brother, instigates a native uprising on Zani in hopes of seizing control of the island and toppling Prince Sleeko from his

throne. Taken captive by the rebels and threatened with death, Prince Sleeko, Steve Trevor, and Etta Candy are rescued by Wonder Woman, who then saves Zani Island and its inhabitants from the fiery eruption of the island's only volcano. Grateful for what Wonder Woman has done for them and realizing the error of their ways, the native insurrectionists resume their loyalty to Prince Sleeko. Slambo will be punished for attempting to overthrow his half brother. The U.S. Army reduces Steve Trevor to his former rank, lieutenant colonel, for failing to stem the uprising on his own (CC No. 20: "The Buddha Wishing Ring").

SLICKER. An underworld figure who concocts an elaborate scheme to learn the secret of WONDER WOMAN's identity. Slicker and his henchmen are apprehended by Wonder Woman.

In October 1959 a dummy corporation secretly set up by Slicker and his cohorts offers to pay Wonder Woman $1,000,000 to reveal the secret of her dual identity. Wonder Woman ignores the offer, but the promise of easy wealth encourages scores of foolhardy citizens to attempt to perform dangerous feats in hopes of persuading those offering the $1,000,000 that they are secretly Wonder Woman. Indeed, Wonder Woman soon finds herself devoting virtually all her time to rescuing her impersonators from the hair-raising consequences of their own reckless greed.

Realizing that the only way to discourage the fortune hunters is to reveal her secret identity, Wonder Woman deliberately performs a death-defying rescue requiring superhuman powers – in full view of a crowd of amazed onlookers – while dressed as her alter ego, Diana Prince. Convinced that they now know who Wonder Woman really is, Slicker and his cohorts capture Diana Prince and STEVE TREVOR, seal them inside a rocket, and launch them on a one-way journey into outer space. Diana, however, quickly changes to Wonder Woman, returns to Earth with Trevor, and apprehends Slicker and his henchmen, persuading them, through a ruse, that they have erred in concluding that Diana Prince is secretly Wonder Woman (WW No. 109/2: "The Million Dollar Pigeon!").

SLICKER, JOSH. The unscrupulous owner of Slicker Stadium, a midget auto racing stadium. In July–August 1950 Slicker and his henchmen resort to bribery, kidnapping, sabotage, and attempted murder in an effort to drive the competing Fairdeal Stadium out of business. After taking WONDER WOMAN and the HOLLIDAY GIRLS captive, Slicker attempts to crush them to death beneath a hydraulic auto lift, but Wonder Woman escapes, rescues her companions, and then apprehends

Slicker and his henchmen (WW No. 42/1: "Danger on the Speedway!").

SLIKERY, SIMON. A successful attorney and secret Nazi collaborator — described as "the cleverest legal brain in America" — who, from aboard his yacht, has been secretly "communicating with German battleships." In March 1943 WONDER WOMAN single-handedly captures Simon Slikery and an entire fleet of German vessels which, with his assistance, is "escorting airplane carriers to bomb New York City." The incident marks "the first time in history an entire enemy fleet is captured by one individual" (Sen No. 15).

SLOTE, PETE. A criminal whom DR. PSYCHO transforms, by means of plastic surgery, into an exact double for STEVE TREVOR in May 1967 (WW No. 170/1: "The Haunted Amazon!"). (*See* PSYCHO [DR.].)

SMITH, ALBERT. An alias employed by the ANGLER in July 1955 when he poses as an "eccentric millionaire" as part of his scheme to trick WONDER WOMAN into revealing her secret identity (WW No. 75/2: "$1,000,000 Secret!").

SMITH, ALEX. A tailor who is dissatisfied with his job because he feels that it is useless, trivial, and unimportant. His job takes on new meaning for him in January–February 1950, however, when WONDER WOMAN proves to him that his job is actually "vital and exciting! No one is unimportant in a democracy," insists Wonder Woman, "--and that goes for his job!" (WW No. 39/1: "The Trail of Thrills!")

SNAIT, LIM. The villain who, by May 1947, has murdered engineer Tom Sands in Naskim, Alaska, and framed an Eskimo named Karluk for the crime. Snait is ultimately jailed — and Karluk exonerated — when WONDER WOMAN proves that Snait murdered Sands in order to steal "a rich gold claim" that Sands had discovered (Sen No. 65: "Treachery in the Arctic").

SNATCHER. The leader of a gang of criminals who steal WONDER WOMAN's Amazon plane (*see* WONDER WOMAN [section C 4, the robot plane]) in November 1956, only to be apprehended by Wonder Woman soon after the theft (WW No. 86/2: "The Talking Robot Plane!").

SNOW MAN, THE. "A human monster . . . whose murderous acts put terror in the hearts of the people of Fair Weather Valley," a U.S. farming community, until "he" is finally unmasked as a woman and apprehended by WONDER WOMAN in November 1946. The Snow Man is secretly Miss Byrna Brilyant, Fair Weather Valley's schoolteacher.

In November 1946 the farmers of Fair Weather Valley are terrorized by the Snow Man, an "insidi-

Byrna Brilyant, 1946

ous villain" whose diabolical "telescopic snow ray" enables her to create blinding blizzards of blue snow that freezes everything it touches — crops, livestock, and even people — into ghastly blue statues. Since only the Snow Man possesses the chemical antidote to the blue snow's effects, she has succeeded in "forcing every farmer to give up his life savings to protect his crops, livestock, and his kin from the blue snow!"

Having received word of the mysterious blue-snow menace plaguing Fair Weather Valley, STEVE TREVOR and Diana Prince, the girl who is secretly WONDER WOMAN, fly to the stricken area in a government airplane, only to have their craft battered by "a blinding, raging blue snowstorm" unleashed upon them by the Snow Man from her hideout atop Fair Weather Mountain. As the shattered and disabled airplane plummets toward the ground,

The Snow Man, 1948

Diana changes to Wonder Woman, leaps to the ground, and catches the falling plane in her arms, but Steve Trevor has lapsed into unconsciousness as a result of the plane's steep dive. After leaving Trevor at a local farmhouse to rest and recuperate, Wonder Woman sets about solving the mystery of the bizarre blue snowstorms and ultimately invades the Snow Man's mountain sanctuary, takes her prisoner, and forces her, through the compelling power of her magic lasso (see WONDER WOMAN [section C 3, the magic lasso]), to turn her "defroster ray" on the valley to restore its people, crops, and livestock to normal.

"I give you the 'Snow Man,' Miss [Byrna] Brilyant, the daughter of a brilliant scientist who died many years ago while working on a secret invention — blue snow!" explains Wonder Woman to the townspeople, as she removes the villainess's blue, masculine costume to reveal the face of their local schoolteacher. "He wanted it to serve humanity but his money-mad daughter had different ideas!" (Sen No. 59: "Reign of Blue Terror").

In March–April 1948 the Snow Man (sometimes referred to as the Blue Snow Man) escapes from TRANSFORMATION ISLAND along with seven other villainesses and joins them in forming VILLAINY INCORPORATED (WW No. 28/1–3: "Villainy Incorporated!"; "Trap of Crimson Flame"; "In the Hands of the Merciless!"). (See VILLAINY INCORPORATED.)

SOCKET, PIK. An "unscrupulous hoodlum" who — along with his cohorts, Mike McDuff and Grubber Graff — attempts to assassinate both Diana Prince and WONDER WOMAN, unaware that they are secretly the same person. Socket, McDuff, and Graff — all "sought by Army Intelligence for hijacking Army supplies" — are apprehended by Wonder Woman in January–February 1948.

When Diana Prince is asked to present the Army's Distinguished Service Medal to Wonder Woman at an upcoming awards ceremony, she is confronted with the dilemma of having to appear on the presentation platform simultaneously as Wonder Woman and as Diana Prince. Wonder Woman resolves the dilemma by attending the awards ceremony in the company of a lifelike Diana Prince dummy that she has molded from Amazon "Olympic clay," but her hopes of preserving her secret identity suffer a setback when, in the midst of the ceremony, Pik Socket and his cohorts attempt to murder both Diana Prince and Wonder Woman. The murder attempt fails, but, in the ensuing melee, the three gunmen make off with the Diana Prince dummy in the belief that they are kidnapping the real Diana Prince, and Wonder Woman knows that she must somehow recover the dummy before anyone discovers it is not a real person, since the discovery that Wonder Woman had sculpted a Diana Prince stand-in would inevitably betray her dual identity.

When the kidnappers shoot the dummy and hurl it from their speeding car, they — along with STEVE TREVOR and GENERAL DARNELL — assume that they have murdered the real Diana Prince, but Wonder Woman captures Pik Socket and his accomplices and then, on the pretext of taking the "slain" Diana Prince to her "secret laboratory" so that she may be restored to life (see AMAZONS [section G, Amazon science]), whisks the dummy out of sight and secretly disposes of it (WW No. 27/1: "The Secret of the Kidnapped Dummy!").

SOLO. The tyrannical ruler of NEPTUNIA, a large fragment of the planet NEPTUNE, torn from its mother world "by the combined [gravitational] pull of all planets," which hurtles through space until it finally comes to rest in the middle of the PACIFIC OCEAN — where it forms a vast, new Earth continent — in Winter 1945 (WW No. 15: chs. 1–3 — "The First Battle of Neptunia"; "The Masters of the Water"; "In the Killer's Cage"). The arrogant, woman-hating Solo — Neptunia's "master of masters" — is defeated by WONDER WOMAN several times in Winter 1945 and again in September–October 1948.

When "a huge fragment" of the planet Neptune hurtles through interstellar space and lands with a mighty splash in the middle of the Pacific Ocean in Winter 1945, an expeditionary vessel — whose passengers include STEVE TREVOR, ETTA CANDY, the HOLLIDAY GIRLS, and Diana Prince, the girl who is secretly Wonder Woman — is sent out to "explore this new continent from the planet Neptune," only to be attacked in mid-ocean by Solo and his Neptunians, all armed with paralyzing "electric pistols" and mounted on gigantic flying fish with powerful tentacles. Diana changes to Wonder Woman, battles the Neptunians, and captures their leader, who arrogantly introduces himself as "the great Solo, master of masters on Neptunia!" The men of Neptune, he explains, knew that a fragment of their planet was about to break loose and hurtle into space and had decided to use it as a base from which to conquer Earth.

Now that Solo and his fellow Neptunians are their prisoners, the expeditioners decide to carry out their mission to explore Neptunia. Wonder Woman, however, remains uneasy. "It looks as if we've found a new and powerful ally for America," she muses. "But we must teach these savage Neptunians loving submission before we trust them!"

When Solo informs her that Neptunia is inhabited only by men and that she is the first woman he has ever seen, Wonder Woman is flabbergasted. "But if there are only **men**," she exclaims, "you must fight each other constantly!"

On Neptunia, Solo overpowers the expeditioners and subjects all of them except Wonder Woman to a diabolical Neptunian process designed to sap their willpower and transform them into mindless automatons, but the process has no effect whatever on the Holliday Girls because, for some inexplicable reason, women are immune to its effects. "Women are terrifying!" exclaims Solo.

Soon afterward, with the help of the Holliday Girls, Wonder Woman turns the tables on her Neptunian captors and once again takes Solo prisoner. While Steve Trevor and a few of the male expeditioners remain behind to "hold the new continent of Neptunia for the United States Government," Wonder Woman flies Solo and the other Neptunian leaders to Washington, D.C., to negotiate a peace treaty with President FRANKLIN DELANO ROOSEVELT. Under its terms, "Neptunia becomes a protectorate pledging its complete allegiance to America," Steve Trevor is appointed acting governor, and, in deference to Neptunian custom, women are barred from entering Neptunia.

"Women are **horrible** creatures — cruel, vindictive," exclaims Solo. "Thank Neptune we have no **women** on Neptunia!"

"You'll always be quarrelsome, treacherous, and unhappy until women **control** you!" replies Wonder Woman.

Before long, despite the new peace treaty, Solo and his followers have concocted a scheme to "break the Earth loose from the sun's gravity and send it hurtling through space to Neptune," there to revolve endlessly as a "slave planet" of Neptune. Wonder Woman, however, has suspected from the outset that the treaty provision barring women from Neptunia was designed to help conceal Neptunian treachery. Disguised as "tigeapes," bizarre animals native to Neptunia, she and the Holliday Girls infiltrate Neptunia to spy on Solo and his cohorts and have no sooner learned of Solo's plot than the Neptunians see through their disguises and take them prisoner.

In the interim, however, Wonder Woman has managed to communicate what she has learned to Acting Governor Trevor, who invades Neptunia with a contingent of paratroops and frees Wonder Woman and the Holliday Girls from the villains' clutches. Solo and his Neptunian air fleet are nevertheless on the verge of carrying out their scheme to "cut the sun's gravitational hold on Earth" when Wonder Woman intercepts and captures them all.

Realizing now that Solo and his cohorts are unfit to hold power of any kind, Wonder Woman advises American officials that "**Women** must govern Neptunia!" Accordingly, an all-woman government is soon installed there, making Neptunia "the first **woman's** government in this man's world!" (WW No. 15: chs. 1–3 — "The First Battle of Neptunia"; "The Masters of the Water"; "In the Killer's Cage").

With Solo stripped of his power, Neptunia enters upon a period of peace and tranquility, presided over by "Presidenta" Una and an all-woman cabinet. In September–October 1948, however, when Etta Candy and the Holliday Girls visit Neptunia, they are taken captive by mindless Neptunian slaves — called "mechanos" — and are locked in a dungeon along with Presidenta Una and her cabinet, who have been overthrown and imprisoned by Solo in his latest bid for Neptunian power. Etta Candy summons Wonder Woman to the scene, however, with an urgent mental radio message (see WONDER WOMAN [section C 7, the mental radio]). "By Hera!" thinks Wonder Woman. "Solo will have to be taught that women are not going to let themselves be dominated by men!"

"Meanwhile," notes the textual narrative, "Solo communicates with Neptune, the all-male planet from which Neptunia had fallen into the Pacific." When Solo informs Neptune's ruler that he has recaptured control of Neptunia, the ruler promises to send him "a planet-pulverizing bombing fleet" with which to "annihilate the Earth!"

Arriving in Neptunia aboard her Amazon plane (see WONDER WOMAN [section C 4, the robot plane]), Wonder Woman becomes embroiled in a series of desperate battles with Solo's forces and is ultimately taken prisoner. Binding Wonder Woman with her own magic lasso (see WONDER WOMAN [section C 3, the magic lasso]), Solo compels her to lead his recently arrived "invasion fleet of planet pulverizers" on a mission of destruction against America. As the pulverizing fleet streaks toward its target, however, Wonder Woman turns the tables on the Neptunians and captures Solo and his fleet before it can launch its sneak attack. Solo will be turned over to the authorities for punishment, and Una and her all-woman cabinet will be restored to power in Neptunia (WW No. 31/2: "The Planet of Plunder!"

SORCA. A lonely planetoid inhabited by the enchantress CIRCE, who, according to Wonder Woman No. 37/3, was banished to this "island planet" by QUEEN HIPPOLYTE and the AMAZONS sometime in the distant past (Sep/Oct '49: "The Secrets of Circe!"). (See OWLER [PROF.].)

SOURPUSS, MEG (Dean). DEAN MEG MERRILY'S

maiden name (WW No. 39/2, Jan/Feb '50: "The Modern Midas!").

SOUTH (Colonel). The elderly Southern colonel who is the uncle of "Sunny" South, one of the HOLLIDAY GIRLS. When Colonel South is murdered in September–October 1950, WONDER WOMAN investigates and ultimately apprehends the killer: he is the slain man's nephew, Globe Trotter, a former African explorer (WW No. 43/3: "Who Killed Col. South!").

SPIDER. A vicious criminal who, having been hired by the underworld to assassinate WONDER WOMAN, reduces her to minute size with his diabolical "reduco-ray machine" and then locks her in a glass box to be attacked by a swarm of trained killer fleas. After defeating the killer fleas and escaping from the glass box, however, Wonder Woman apprehends Spider and his henchmen and, by reversing the power of the reduco-ray, restores herself to her proper size (WW No. 79/1, Jan '56: "Wonder Woman in the Amazon Flea Circus!").

STARVARD COLLEGE. A noted United States men's college. OSCAR SWEETGULPER is a student there (CC No. 28, Aug/Sep '48: "The Sinister Countess Hatra!"), and Rufus Robust, the uncle of unscrupulous BLUFF ROBUST, is one of its trustees (Sen No. 61, Jan '47: "The Million Dollar Tennis Game").

STOFFER. A Nazi spy and saboteur — described as a "former associate" of DR. PSYCHO — who, having kidnapped General Scott, the commander of a Women's Army Corps base, has been impersonating the general in order to be able to commit acts of sabotage in and around the base. Exposed as a spy and impostor by WONDER WOMAN with the aid of MARVA PSYCHO, Stoffer is killed when Wonder Woman, attempting to dispose as quickly as she can of an ambulance to which Nazi thugs have attached a live bomb, hurls the vehicle high into the air, where it accidently collides with the airplane in which Stoffer is escaping, exploding upon impact and destroying both the airplane and the ambulance (Sen No. 20, Aug '43).

STONE (Professor). An American guided missile expert who is impersonated by the leader of a band of extraterrestrial invaders who arrive on Earth in August 1954 and use their unearthly powers to disguise themselves as earthlings as part of their scheme to destroy the Earth. "Professor Stone" and his fellow aliens are annihilated by WONDER WOMAN.

In August 1954, while out for a flight together aboard Wonder Woman's Amazon plane (see WONDER WOMAN [section C 4, the robot plane]), Wonder Woman and STEVE TREVOR sight an extraterrestrial flying saucer making a landing and then suddenly taking off again. The unearthly footprints they find near the landing site indicate that the flying saucer deposited some of its crew there, and when Wonder Woman and Trevor follow the footprints and see them change step by step into human footprints, Wonder Woman concludes that the aliens "probably have the power to change themselves into any shape at will" and that they have disguised themselves as earthlings in order to escape detection.

Later, at a U.S. Government test site where "America's foremost military strategists" have gathered to witness a series of top-secret "hydrogen bomb explosion tests," Wonder Woman and Trevor discover that unseen saboteurs are sabotaging the tests, forcing Wonder Woman to intervene time and again to prevent a series of nuclear catastrophes.

Convinced that the recently-landed aliens have infiltrated the test area and perpetrated the various acts of sabotage, Wonder Woman soon comes to suspect that Professor Stone and his associates, ostensibly experts on guided missiles, are really extraterrestrial invaders posing as the real Professor Stone and his colleagues. The bogus Professor Stone, however, uses his extraterrestrial powers to read Wonder Woman's mind, and, realizing that she has seen through his impersonation, captures her and Steve Trevor and then flees into outer space with his fellow aliens, leaving his two captives trapped inside a building containing an H-bomb which is timed to go off at any minute and "set off chain reactions to destroy Earth!"

"We will do the same to the rest of the planets in your galaxy!" he gloats. "Leaving **our** galaxy to reign supreme."

Once the aliens have departed, however, Wonder Woman breaks free of her bonds, carries Trevor to safety, and, summoning her Amazon plane, lassoes the building containing the H-bomb (see WONDER WOMAN [section C 3, the magic lasso]) and soars into outer space, trailing the lassoed building behind her. When the bogus Professor Stone and his alien cohorts open fire on her from their flying saucer, Wonder Woman whirls the lassoed building about her head like a pebble in a sling and hurls it at the alien spacecraft; the H-bomb explodes thunderously, obliterating the aliens with a titanic roar (WW No. 68/1: "Landing of the Flying Saucers!").

STORM (Capt.). A ruthless pirate chieftain who, "three centuries ago," buried a fortune in gold and jewels on land that is now part of the campus of the HOLLIDAY COLLEGE FOR WOMEN in Washington, D.C. Storm was ultimately apprehended and hanged for his crimes, but not before he had sketched a map of his buried treasure, sealed it in a bottle, and cast it into the sea. Tossed about by the ocean's waves for centuries, intact but undiscovered, the bottle is finally recovered in July–August 1951 by the sinister CAPTAIN BARNACLE (WW No. 48/2: "The Treasure of Capt. Storm").

STRIKT (Dean). The straitlaced woman who serves as dean of the HOLLIDAY COLLEGE FOR WOMEN during Fall 1944 (WW No. 10/3: "Wonder Woman's Boots!"). Dean Strikt is succeeded by Dean Meg Sourpuss (see MERRILY, MEG [DEAN]) in or around March–April 1946 (WW No. 16/1: "The Secret of the Dark Planet!").

STROGO. An evil wizard who attempts to seize power on the Planet of Thought, a world ruled by Prince Charming and his wife Cinderella. Strogo and his cohorts are defeated by WONDER WOMAN in March–April 1952.

The Planet of Thought is a mysterious far-distant planet whose surface radiates miraculous "thought beams" which, when they strike Earth, enable anyone attuned to them — such as the writers of fairy tales — to mentally perceive the events taking place there. Although Prince Charming and Cinderella are regarded on Earth as merely fictional characters, for example, they are actually real people on the Planet of Thought.

Arriving on the Planet of Thought in response to an urgent appeal for help in March–April 1952, Wonder Woman discovers that Strogo's forces have captured Prince Charming and are besieging Cinderella's castle, which is in imminent danger of falling. Strogo's real goal is the priceless stockpile of the mysterious element "xium" which lies buried in the castle's throne room, for xium is "the source of black magic," and with it Strogo could easily extend his dominion over the entire Planet of Thought.

Taken captive by Strogo, Wonder Woman soon escapes — along with Prince Charming — and destroys the xium before the malevolent wizard and his henchmen have had the opportunity to use its powers for evil. The destruction of the xium, however, has a bizarre effect on Strogo and his followers: "Shades of Pluto!" exclaims Wonder Woman. "Shattering their last source of evil has turned Strogo and his band into children again!"

Powerless to advance the cause of evil now that they have been transformed into children, Strogo and his followers will be raised to maturity "in peace and loving kindness" so that they will never again become "followers of force and evil!" (WW No. 52/2: "The Battle for Fairyland!").

STURM, ERICH (Lieut.). An Army Intelligence officer who is murdered and then impersonated by

his cousin, who is secretly an "enemy agent." The bogus Lieut. Sturm is apprehended by WONDER WOMAN in August 1945.

Faced with imminent court-martial when a top-secret intelligence report entrusted to his care disappears mysteriously, STEVE TREVOR is exonerated by Wonder Woman, who recovers the missing report and apprehends the man who stole it — the unnamed impostor who has been impersonating his cousin, the real Lieut. Sturm.

"I'm an enemy agent," he confesses finally, "— I killed my cousin, the real Lt. Sturm and took his place. . . . I stole . . . [the] confidential report by switching envelopes while taking them to Trevor's office" (Sen No. 44: "Chains and Bracelets").

SULLA, LUCIUS CORNELIUS (138–78 B.C.). A Roman general and dictator who, in the course of his career, instituted significant constitutional reforms. WONDER WOMAN battles and defeats Sulla during a time-journey to ancient Rome that she makes in May–June 1946 (WW No. 17: "The Winds of Time").

SUN. The star around which Earth and the other planets in the Solar System revolve. In the WONDER WOMAN chronicles, the sun is the home of the Sun People, an all-female civilization ruled by the treacherous QUEEN FLAMINA. An attempt by Flamina's "sun warriors" to invade the Earth is thwarted by Wonder Woman in November 1947 (Sen No. 71: "The Invasion of the Sun Warriors"). (See FLAMINA [QUEEN].)

The people of the Sun Country, "a rich and fertile country in the heart of the Gobi Desert," worship the sun. Wonder Woman visits the Sun Country in July 1948 (Sen No. 79: "Land of Mirrors!"). (See LEILA.)

The sun is stolen by the evil PHAETHON in March–April 1953, but Wonder Woman recovers it soon afterward and restores it to its proper place at the center of Earth's solar system (WW No. 58/2: "The Man Who Stole the Sun!").

SUN COUNTRY, THE. "A rich and fertile country in the heart of the Gobi Desert" which is ruled jointly by the evil LEILA and her peace-loving twin sister Solala. WONDER WOMAN visits the Sun Country in July 1948 (Sen No. 79: "Land of Mirrors!").

SURANA (Mount). A mountain, once situated on the Plain of Plenty, which was hurled into outer space by the force of an explosion set off by the ruthless BRUTEX. Today Mount Surana is a tiny planetoid, located in the farthest reaches of outer space and inhabited by the subjects of the lovely Queen Bravura (WW No. 38/2, Nov/Dec '49: "Wonder Woman Captures the Moon!").

SUSPENDED-ANIMATOR, THE. A diabolical device with which an unnamed extraterrestrial villain freezes every living thing on Earth into a state of suspended animation in order to pave the way for an alien invasion of Earth. The evil alien is defeated by WONDER WOMAN, who smashes the suspended-animator, thereby thwarting the alien scheme to conquer Earth (WW No. 87/1, Jan '57: "The Day the Clocks Stopped!").

SWEETGULPER, OSCAR. ETTA CANDY's boyfriend. Sweetgulper is a gawky, gangling STARVARD COLLEGE student with an insatiable appetite for chocolate candy.

In July–August 1946, when Etta Candy throws a party at Holliday College to celebrate the death of DR. PSYCHO, it is Sweetgulper who warns the merrymakers that Dr. Psycho is still alive and has infil-trated their party in disguise (WW No. 18/3: "Ectoplasmic Death").

Sweetgulper makes several other appearances in the chronicles (Sen No. 57, Sep '46: "Hatchet of Death"; and others), all of them inconsequential.

SYONIDE. A "homicidal maniac" who, suffering from the delusion that he is the famous Indian chief Powhatan, escapes from an insane asylum in September 1946 determined to wreak vengeance on the white men responsible for carrying off his daughter Pocahontas. The hatchet-wielding Syonide almost succeeds in murdering WONDER WOMAN and the HOLLIDAY GIRLS before being finally recaptured and returned to the insane asylum by Wonder Woman and STEVE TREVOR (Sen No. 57: "Hatchet of Death").

T

TALBOT. A nightclub mind-reader — known professionally as the Great Talbot — who turns to crime after a blow on the head suffered during an auto accident endows him with miraculous extrasensory powers. Talbot is apprehended by WONDER WOMAN in September–October 1949.

In his nightclub act, Talbot's clairvoyant feats are all actually accomplished by means of elaborate word codes shared with his assistant Wanda, but all that changes when an accidental blow on the head endows Talbot with genuine extrasensory powers, enabling him to probe the minds of wealthy persons in his audiences in order to obtain information — such as safe combinations — likely to aid him in the commission of crimes.

When Diana Prince attends one of his nightclub performances, Talbot reads her mind and, learning that she is secretly Wonder Woman, confronts her with his knowledge afterward and threatens to reveal her secret unless she agrees to cooperate with him in his underworld activities. Astounded that Talbot has actually uncovered her secret, Wonder Woman concocts an elaborate ruse calculated to persuade him that he has made a mistake, but she is unexpectedly rescued from her dilemma when a second accidental blow on the head robs Talbot of his extrasensory powers along with all memory of the things he learned during the period he possessed them. Her dual identity thus secret once again, Wonder Woman apprehends Talbot and turns him over to the authorities (Sen No. 93: "The Man Who Could Read Wonder Woman's Mind!").

TALL, THELMA. One of the HOLLIDAY GIRLS. Thelma is a tall brunette who wishes she were shorter.

Thelma Tall makes her textual debut in October 1960 (WW No. 117: "Fantastic Fishermen of the Forbidden Sea!"), in a text that marks the first appearance of the Holliday Girls since November–December 1950 (WW No. 44: "The Monarch of the Sargasso Sea!" chs. I–III — no title; "Wonder Woman's Decision"; "The Final Battle of the Sargasso Sea"). (See CANDY, ETTA.)

In January 1962 Thelma Tall is among the Holliday Girls who are captured by aliens from PLANET K and rescued by WONDER WOMAN (WW No.

127/1: "Invaders of the Topsy-Turvy Planet"). (See KUU-KUU.)

TASSEL (King). The ruler of Rykornia, "an unexplored planetoid" which is "hidden in Earth's atmosphere by a shroud of clouds, and inhabited by fiendish creatures just waiting their opportunity to invade our world." King Tassel and his subjects — described as "weird planet people of a terrifying and menacing nature" — are defeated by WONDER WOMAN in September–October 1947.

By September–October 1947 the planetoid Rykornia has become so seriously overpopulated that there is no longer any room left for the growing of "rykorn," the leafy cornlike plant inside whose husks young Rykornians grow to maturity. Since without rykorn there can be no Rykornians, Rykorn civilization seems doomed to extinction. King Tassel and his aide Lord Cob would like to invade Earth, which has both a climate and soil ideal for rykorn, but lack the necessary means of space travel.

One day, however, ETTA CANDY, riding through space on an Amazon sky kanga (see AMAZONS [section E 3, Transportation]), falls off her mount and drops onto Rykornia. When Wonder Woman flies to Rykornia to bring Etta home again, Tassel and Cob stow away aboard her Amazon plane (see WONDER WOMAN [section C 4, the robot plane]) with a sackful of rykorn seeds and plant them in fertile soil as soon as they reach Earth.

"By morning," gloats King Tassel, "this ranch will be completely covered with rykorn plants!"

"And," adds Lord Cob gleefully, "in every stalk will develop a rykorn subject to be used in the war against earthlings! Ha haaaa!"

Indeed, by the following morning, the countryside is covered with a carpet of rykorn plants, and "newly-grown plant people" are emerging from their husks to invade the Earth. At the secret laboratory of BARONESS PAULA VON GUNTHER, however, Wonder Woman and Paula are working feverishly to complete their ingenious "rykorn destroyer," a gigantic vacuum-cleanerlike device designed to "dig up the rykorn plants and suck in the cobs which house the Rykornians." Soon afterward, with the aid of the rykorn destroyer, Wonder Woman harvests the rykorn plants and then returns them to the planetoid Rykornia. The

1 7 2

Rykornian invasion attempt has thus been thwarted, and the Rykornians, terrified of Wonder Woman's rykorn destroyer, will probably never attempt to invade Earth again (WW No. 25/1: "Siege of the Rykornians").

TEGURANA ISLAND. An island, of unspecified location, where WONDER WOMAN rescues JOHN KEIGH from death at the hands of idol-worshipping natives during a time-journey that she makes to the year 1555 (WW No. 72/1, Feb '55: "S.O.S. from the Past!").

TERMITE QUEEN, THE. The term used to designate the queen termite who is the "evil central intelligence" behind a terrifying termite invasion which threatens to overrun the Earth in March–April 1953. The termite invasion is thwarted by WONDER WOMAN.

In March–April 1953 Earth is "menaced by a termite invasion such as the world has never seen!" Bridges are tumbling from their supports, and railroad tracks are literally falling apart. In fact, "**everything** is in danger of crumbling — reducing our civilization to wreckage!"

After having BARONESS PAULA VON GUNTHER temporarily reduce them to termite size with an Amazon "minimizer," Wonder Woman and STEVE TREVOR trail the invading termites to their antique-shop headquarters, where they are taken prisoner by the evil termite queen who has been directing the termite armies in their ongoing invasion.

"Yeeeeeee!" she shrieks gloatingly. "... **Now that you are helpless ... no power on Earth can stop my termite armies from destroying man's world! Yeeeeeee!**"

After binding Wonder Woman with her own magic lasso (see WONDER WOMAN [section C 3, the magic lasso]), the termite queen commands Wonder Woman to leap into a cage containing a small bird which, with Wonder Woman reduced to the size of a termite, is now a potentially deadly bird of prey. As Wonder Woman leaps into the cage, however, the momentum of her leap carries the termite queen — who has been holding onto one end of the magic lasso — into the cage also, and the bird, attracted by the glitter of the golden lasso in the termite queen's hand, swoops down on her and devours her, thus leaving the termite armies leaderless and ending their terrifying invasion (WW No. 58/3: "Terror of the Termites").

TERRUNA, TARA. An inhabitant of Earth's "twin world" — a world "existing simultaneously alongside" Earth, but in an earlier era — who is an exact double for WONDER WOMAN. Indeed, in the language of this parallel world, Tara Terruna means Wonder Woman. Wonder Woman helps her twin-world counterpart battle the sinister DUKE DAZAM in May–June 1953 (WW No. 59/1: "Wonder Woman's Invisible Twin!"). (*See* DAZAM [DUKE].)

THIRD WORLD WAR PROMOTERS, THE. A "group of world famous European munitions manufacturers and their glamorous women spies" who are determined to bring about a third World War.

"We **must** plan another war, **greater** than ever before!" declares their president, Pierre Fenati, in Spring 1945. "Our countries are doomed unless we can provoke **all** nations to fight again! Permanent peace talk is nonsense!" (WW No. 12/1).

Fenati and his Third World War Promoters are ultimately defeated by WONDER WOMAN (WW No. 12/1–3, Spr '45: no title; "The Ordeal of Fire"; "The Conquest of Venus"). (*See* DESIRA [QUEEN].)

Pierre Fenati

THOMAS, RANDALL. The leader of a gang of criminals who are apprehended by WONDER WOMAN.

In February 1954 Randall Thomas and his gang, posing as members of a nonexistent North American Wonder Woman Fan Club, organize a spectacular parade in Wonder Woman's honor, complete with gigantic balloons depicting her most heralded crime-fighting exploits. As the colorful parade marches down the street, however, a "colorless odorless gas expelled by the balloons" puts Wonder Woman and the throngs of onlookers to sleep, leaving Thomas and his henchmen — all of whom "are wearing miniature gas protectors inside their nostrils" — free to loot the city. Wonder Woman, however, eventually shakes off the effects of the debilitating sleep-gas, escapes from the huge Wonder Woman balloon in which the gangsters have imprisoned her, and swiftly apprehends them (WW No. 64/2: "The Doom Dolls!").

THOMAS, T. T. The head of Opus Studios, the movie studio which produces *Amazon Girl*, co-starring STEVE TREVOR and the mysterious Miss X, in October 1962.

In October 1962 T. T. Thomas approaches WONDER WOMAN with an offer to donate $1,000,000 to charity in return for her commitment to appear in his forthcoming movie, *Amazon Girl*, along with Steve Trevor. Thomas wants Wonder Woman to appear in the film in everyday clothing and under an assumed name so that he can reap a publicity bonanza by presenting her to the world as a newly discovered "rival" for Wonder Woman. Moved by the offer of the generous charity donation, Wonder Woman accepts, and, soon afterward, a lovely actress known only as Miss X appears on the set of Thomas's new movie. Only T. T. Thomas knows that Miss X is secretly Wonder Woman.

As work on the film proceeds, Steve Trevor begins to fall for his mysterious co-star. Wonder Woman is heartbroken, for it appears that Trevor has forgotten her completely in favor of what he believes to be a new, more glamorous girlfriend. During the shooting of the movie's final scene, when the ceiling of the elaborate set unexpectedly begins to collapse, Wonder Woman hurriedly — but secretly — doffs her Miss X clothing and, clad in her Wonder Woman costume, supports the heavy domed ceiling with her body long enough to enable the cast and crew to dash to safety before the entire structure comes crashing down on her with a mighty roar.

To Trevor, it appears that Miss X deserted the cast and crew when they needed her most, while Wonder Woman heroically gave her life to save them all. When Wonder Woman finally emerges from the wreckage, slightly bruised but not seriously injured, Trevor realizes that she — and not the mysterious Miss X — is the only girl he ever really loved (WW No. 133/2: "Wonder Woman's Invincible Rival--Herself!").

THOUGHT MASTER, THE. "The greatest criminal mind of . . . all," a criminal mastermind — gifted with spectacular powers for influencing and controlling the thoughts of others — who creates an entire "world of illusion" around WONDER WOMAN in an attempt to destroy her sense of reality and trick her into believing that she is "powerless to fight crime any more!" The Thought Master is defeated and apprehended by Wonder Woman.

In February 1954 the Thought Master uses his awesome powers to project the mind of Wonder Woman into a deceptive world of illusion — a world in which she can no longer parry bullets with her Amazon bracelets (*see* WONDER WOMAN [section C 2, the bracelets of submission]), her magic lasso fails to function properly (*see* WONDER WOMAN [section C 3, the magic lasso]), and her Amazon plane refuses to obey her commands (*see* WONDER WOMAN [section C 4, the robot plane]). When she captures criminals in the world of illusion, they vanish like mirages before her eyes.

Before long, Wonder Woman has begun to lose her grip on the distinction between illusion and reality, to question her own sanity, and to contemplate abandoning her career as a crime-fighter. Having carried his scheme to the very brink of success, however, the Thought Master makes the fatal mistake of impersonating STEVE TREVOR in order to place himself in a position "to better gloat over [Wonder Woman's] humiliations," for Wonder Woman knows Trevor so intimately that she quickly sees through the impersonation, thus shattering the delicately balanced illusionary world in which the Thought Master has placed her. Her sense of reality restored, Wonder Woman swiftly takes the Thought Master into custody (WW No. 64/3: "Wonder Woman's Last Hour!").

THROSTLE, HORACE. The timid chemical plant employee who is transformed by a freak accident into the incredible PAPER-MAN (WW No. 165/1, Oct '66: "Perils of the Paper-Man!").

TIBRO. The criminal from the year 2300 A.D. who achieves infamy as the CRIME MASTER OF TIME (WW No. 53/1, May/Jun '52: "The Crime Master of Time!").

TIGHE, THOMAS. The confirmed misogynist who is the chief executive officer of the Thomas Tighe Bank. When WONDER WOMAN risks her life to rescue him from suffocating inside a locked bank vault in November–December 1949, the woman-hating banker is not even grateful, but, fearful that he will become the target of unfavorable publicity unless he offers Wonder Woman some sort of reward, he offers to donate $1,000,000 to the HOLLIDAY COLLEGE FOR WOMEN if the HOLLIDAY GIRLS can perform five difficult feats, all of which have been unsuccessfully attempted by men.

When the Holliday Girls actually perform the feats, Tighe relinquishes the promised $1,000,000 along with some of his bigoted attitudes about women. "You win, **Wonder Woman!**" he exclaims. "And I must confess, that you and the girls have made me change my mind about women! I'm no longer a woman-hater!"

"Then **you're** the real winner, Mr. Tighe!" replies Wonder Woman. "Because when one ceases to hate, he becomes stronger!" (WW No. 38/3: "The Five Tasks of Thomas Tighe!").

TIME MASTER, THE. A sinister villain from a

murky "time dimension" who attempts to destroy WONDER WOMAN in a diabolical "time-trap." The Time Master is defeated by Wonder Woman in October 1958.

When Wonder Woman and STEVE TREVOR accept an invitation to visit a new amusement-park fun house in October 1958, they find that they have been lured into a fiendish "time-trap house" devised by the Time Master.

"From the time dimension I live in," explains the villain, confronting them for the first time in a room ringed by a series of identical doors, "--I have seen you defeat every threat to the Earth! Hence I have devised this time-trap house to destroy you!"

Every time Wonder Woman and Trevor open one of the mysterious doors, they are miraculously transported into a different era where they are forced to confront some terrible menace. And each time they overcome a menace, they are whisked back to the fun house and forced to open yet another doorway into yet another era. Ultimately, however, after she and Trevor have overcome every danger devised by the Time Master, Wonder Woman succeeds in capturing him, only to have both the villain and his fun house vanish into nothingness, taking with them every trace of the harrowing adventure (WW No. 101/2: "The Fun House of Time!").

TITAN. The largest, brightest, and most massive of SATURN's ten satellites. WONDER WOMAN and STEVE TREVOR have an adventure on Titan in April 1959 (WW No. 105/2: "Eagle of Space!"). (*See* TREVOR, STEVE.)

TOGO KU (Colonel). The "chief of Japanese spies in America!" A master of disguise, Colonel Togo Ku is defeated by WONDER WOMAN in September 1942.

In September 1942 Wonder Woman matches wits with the fiendish Dr. Cue — who, under the guise of being a legitimate medical practitioner, is secretly "developing disease germs to attack America" — and with his mysterious female cohort, Agent X. Wonder Woman finally defeats Dr. Cue and thwarts his diabolical germ-warfare scheme, only to discover that Dr. Cue and Agent X are both fictitious identities employed by Japan's chief agent in America, Colonel Togo Ku (Sen No. 9).

TOOROO. An inhabitant of Planet G, "home of the space giants," who is defeated by WONDER WOMAN in May 1959.

On Planet G, where even a small bird dwarfs an earthling in size, the giant Tooroo is declared the victor in the planetwide Olympics and, in accordance with his planet's custom, is granted the privilege of selecting as his prize any object in the

universe. Tooroo decides that he wants the planet Earth for his prize, and while the officials of Planet G have no objection to this choice, they warn Tooroo that an earthling named Wonder Woman may seek to prevent him from claiming it.

Tooroo journeys to Earth, captures Wonder Woman and STEVE TREVOR, and returns with them to Planet G, where he chains them — along with Wonder Woman's Amazon bracelets, tiara, and plane — to a gigantic charm bracelet as a gift for his girlfriend, the giantess Rikkaa.

Hoping to rescue Trevor and herself from their desperate predicament, Wonder Woman challenges Tooroo to an Olympics contest similar to the one he has already won, with the winner to be entitled to name his own prize. Tooroo accepts the challenge and, despite the overwhelming odds against her, Wonder Woman defeats her gargantuan opponent and then astonishes the inhabitants of Planet G by choosing *their* planet as her prize.

"You have taught us a lesson we shall never forget!" declares the ruler of the space giants after Wonder Woman has agreed to relinquish her claim to Planet G in return for the giants' promise to leave Earth alone. "All of us wish you a safe trip home!" (WW No. 106/1: "The Human Charm Bracelet!"). (*See also* WONDER WOMAN [section C 2, the bracelets of submission; section C 5, the tiara; and section C 4, the robot plane].)

TOPSO AND TEENA. A man-woman team of midget jewel thieves who pose as lost children and play on the sympathies of their intended victims in order to gain entrée to the homes and businesses they intend to rob. In December 1945 they take WONDER WOMAN and the HOLLIDAY GIRLS captive and bind Wonder Woman with her own magic lasso (*see* WONDER WOMAN [section C 3, the magic lasso]), but STEVE TREVOR arrives on the scene, frees Wonder Woman from her bonds, and then helps her apprehend Topso, Teena, and their gang of hoodlum accomplices (Sen No. 48).

TORGSON, IVAR. The leader of a syndicate of five unscrupulous rubber magnates who conspire to conceal their secret "rubber extraction formula" from the U.S. Government — despite the fact that the government desperately needs the formula in order to successfully prosecute the war against the Axis — so that once World War II has ended they can corner the world's rubber market. With the help of some miraculous scientific equipment developed by BARONESS PAULA VON GUNTHER, however — including a "remarkable new machine — the subconscious X-ray," which uses "kappa rays [to] penetrate a person's brain . . . [and] reveal all thoughts and feelings in [his] subconscious mind" — WONDER WOMAN and Paula succeed in showing the avaricious rubber tycoons the error of their ways and in persuading them to give the U.S. Government their wholehearted support (WW No. 4/3, Apr/May '43).

TOXINO (Prof.). An egomaniacal professor who, by April 1946, has "bred a poisonous bug which turns its victims criminally insane!"

"Ha! Ha!" gloats Toxino. "My years of tedious labor, crossing rare poisonous flies is rewarded. The sting of the **red winged fly** makes men mad--it makes them criminals, **killers**!"

Bitterly resentful at society for failing to acclaim his genius, Toxino turns his insanity-inducing flies against those individuals whom he most resents — including Dean Meg Sourpuss (*see* MERRILY, MEG [DEAN]), PROF. CHEMICO, and GENERAL DARNELL — but WONDER WOMAN apprehends the professor and forces him to surrender the antidote that will restore his victims to normal (Sen No. 52: "The Brand of Madness").

TOY, TINA. One of the HOLLIDAY GIRLS. Tina is an attractive brunette who loves toys.

Tina Toy makes her textual debut in October 1960 (WW No. 117: "Fantastic Fishermen of the Forbidden Sea!"), in a text that marks the first appearance of the Holliday Girls since November–December 1950 (WW No. 44: "The Monarch of the Sargasso Sea!" chs. I–III — no title; "Wonder Woman's Decision"; "The Final Battle of the Sargasso Sea"). (*See* CANDY, ETTA.)

In January 1962 Tina Toy is among the Holliday Girls who are captured by aliens from PLANET K and rescued by WONDER WOMAN (WW No. 127/1: "Invaders of the Topsy-Turvy Planet"). (*See* KUU-KUU.)

TOZ (Prof.). An "evil scientific genius" who battles WONDER WOMAN in the city of NEW METROPOLO in the year 2051 A.D. In the world of the future, he is known as PROTO, "master of New Metropolo" (Sen No. 103, May/Jun '51: "100 Year Duel!"). (*See* PROTO.)

TRANSFORMATION ISLAND. The island penal facility, located not far from PARADISE ISLAND, where the AMAZONS "transform, through discipline and love, the bad character traits of women prisoners" (WW No. 33/1, Jan/Feb '49: "The Four Dooms" pts. 1–2 — "Paradise Island Condemned!"; "The Titanic Trials!"). Known originally as Reform Island (WW No. 3/1, Feb/Mar '43; and others), the island has been known as Transformation Island since February–March 1948 (CC No. 25: "Hatred of Badra!"). Reform Island, explains WONDER WOMAN in April–May 1948, is "also called Transformation Island because characters are transformed there by loving wisdom!" (CC No. 26: "Deception's Daughter"). The Amazon prison chief, in charge of Transformation Island and its inmate population,

is Wonder Woman's close friend MALA (WW No. 8/3, Spr '44: "The Captive Queen"; and others).

The exact location of Transformation Island is impossible to determine, but Comic Cavalcade No. 19 describes it as being located "near Paradise Island," close enough to enable one to swim easily from one island to the other (Feb/Mar '47: "The Battle for Eternal Youth"). Comic Cavalcade No. 21 refers to "the bay between Reform Island and Paradise Island" (June/Jul '47: "The Seige [sic] o' the Flying Mermaids!"), reinforcing the evidence that the two islands are not far apart. In contrast, however, Mala has described the island as "a natural prison," with "no boats, no planes, no land prisoners can swim to" (WW No. 3/2, Feb/Mar '43), although she may have meant "no land prisoners can swim to" except Paradise Island.

Transformation Island has not always been a prison, but its original function, if any, remains uncertain. QUEEN HIPPOLYTE ordered the construction of a prison on the island in February–March 1943 as a place of confinement for BARONESS PAULA VON GUNTHER and "a boatload of her slave girls" captured by Wonder Woman and her sister Amazons (WW No. 3/1). In Mala's view, however, Transformation Island is "not really a prison," but rather "sort of a college where we teach girls to be happy!" (CC No. 19, Feb/Mar '47: "The Battle for Eternal Youth").

Every prisoner on Transformation Island must wear a magic Venus girdle — a special belt designed to make the wearer "enjoy living by . . . peaceful principles" (CC No. 19, Feb/Mar '47: "The Battle for Eternal Youth") — until such time as she can "worship Aphrodite" and "submit to loving authority" without the power of the girdle to help her (CC No. 11, Sum '45: "The Cheetah Returns!"). (*See* AMAZONS [section F 3, the magic Venus girdles].)

Prisoners brought to Transformation Island undergo special rehabilitative training under the guidance of the Amazons, including instruction in the Amazon code (*see* AMAZONS [section C, the Amazon Code]) and APHRODITE's law (*see* AMAZONS [section B, Aphrodite's Law]). During their period of confinement on the island, inmates learn "Amazon ways of love and discipline" (WW No. 37/3, Sep/Oct '49: "The Secrets of Circe!"), to "obey loving authority" (WW No. 26/2, Nov/Dec '47: "The Mistress of the Beasts"), and that "submission is sweeter than revenge!" (CC No. 9, Win '44: "The Subsea Pirates").

Male prisoners are barred from Transformation Island by Aphrodite's law, but the villainesses incarcerated there have included the CHEETAH,

QUEEN CLEA, DOCTOR POISON, EVILESS, GIGANTA, HYPNOTA THE GREAT, the SNOW MAN, ZARA, and numerous others.

TRANS MOUNTANIA. The section of the planet EROS ruled by the villainess REBLA (Sen No. 11, Nov '42).

TREVOR, STEVE. The handsome blond Army officer who is the sweetheart — and, according to some texts, the fiancé — of the Amazon princess Diana, known to the world at large as WONDER WOMAN. Their lives have been inextricably intertwined since December 1941–January 1942, when an aircraft piloted by Trevor crashed on the beach at PARADISE ISLAND (AS No. 8: "Introducing Wonder Woman"). In January–February 1969 Trevor is brutally murdered by the minions of the treacherous DOCTOR CYBER (WW No. 180: "A Death for Diana!"), but seven years later, in April–May 1976, he is brought back to life by the goddess APHRO-

Steve Trevor and Wonder Woman

DITE (WW No. 223: "Welcome Back to Life . . . Steve Trevor!").

Throughout his colorful career, Trevor serves as top aide to GENERAL DARNELL, chief of United States Military Intelligence. Though his great courage is occasionally flawed by a fiery temperament and a tendency to act impulsively, Trevor is a crack marksman, an expert pilot, and a fearless intelligence operative. He is also the impatient suitor of Wonder Woman, who steadfastly refuses to marry him until crime and injustice have been eradicated from the Earth.

Every now and then, Trevor begins to suspect that plain Diana Prince — his nurse at the Walter Reed Army Hospital and later his colleague at Military Intelligence — is secretly Wonder Woman, but on each such occasion Wonder Woman manages to trick him into believing that he has made a mistake.

Interestingly, two men in the chronicles are perfect look-alikes for Steve Trevor: Hubert, the rightful heir to the throne of ANGLONIA (Sen No. 62, Feb '47: "The Mysterious Prisoners of Anglonia"), and COL. BRAVO, a daredevil circus parachutist (Sen No. 98, Jul/Aug '50: "Wonder Woman's Strange Mission!"). DR. PSYCHO transforms gangster Pete Slote into an exact double for Steve Trevor through plastic surgery in May 1967 (WW No. 170/1: "The Haunted Amazon!").

With the sole exception of Wonder Woman herself, Steve Trevor has appeared in more texts of the Wonder Woman chronicles than any other character. The majority of his appearances, however, are inconsequential. For that reason, the article that follows contains only a brief survey of Trevor's career, along with detailed accounts of those adventures in which Trevor plays a major role but which, for one reason or another, have not been included under other entry headings. Information concerning Trevor's role in Wonder Woman's other adventures is included in the entry on

Steve Trevor

Wonder Woman and in the other entries of this encyclopedia. (*See also* WONDER WOMAN [section G, the relationship with Steve Trevor]).

In December 1941–January 1942 Capt. Steve Trevor is on a spy-catching mission for U.S. Military Intelligence when his plane runs out of fuel and crashes on the beach at Paradise Island, "an uncharted isle set in the midst of a vast expanse of ocean . . . ." Unconscious and badly wounded, Trevor is dragged from the wreckage by two lovely AMAZONS — MALA and Princess Diana — and carried to a nearby Amazon hospital. It is while Trevor is recuperating that QUEEN HIPPOLYTE holds a great tournament to select the "strongest and wisest" of the Amazons, a tournament which leads ultimately to the emergence of Princess Diana as Wonder Woman (AS No. 8: "Introducing Wonder Woman"). (*See* WONDER WOMAN [section A, Origin].)

When Steve Trevor has sufficiently recovered from his injuries to enable him to travel, Wonder Woman flies him back to America in her Amazon plane (*see* WONDER WOMAN [section C 4, the robot plane]) and deposits him at the Walter Reed Army Hospital in Washington, D.C. Soon afterward, while wandering the streets of the capital, Wonder Woman foils a bank robbery and makes the acquaintance of promoter AL KALE.

Later, on the steps of the hospital, Wonder Woman has the fateful encounter with a U.S. Army nurse that leads to her assuming the secret civilian identity of nurse Diana Prince. (*See* WONDER WOMAN [section B, the secret identity].)

Trevor is still recuperating from his injuries, unaware that the plain-looking nurse at his bedside is secretly Wonder Woman, when, in violation of his doctor's orders, he sneaks away from the hospital to combat yet another Nazi threat: a "mystery bomber" threatening to bomb Camp Merrick, a U.S. military installation, with "a new poison gas which penetrates all gas masks!"

Steve Trevor in the Walter Reed Army Hospital, 1942

"Wow!" exclaims Trevor, as he relentlessly pursues the mystery bomber through the skies. "He must be doing 650 m.p.h.! I've got to stop him!"

Trevor eventually destroys the mystery bomber, and when he is forced to bail out of his own plane and his parachute fails to open, Wonder Woman streaks to his aid in her Amazon plane and, lowering herself onto her plane's rope ladder, rescues Trevor by catching him in midair with one arm. A short while later, when Wonder Woman and Trevor stage a raid on the mystery bomber's secret airbase, the Nazi commander reaches for a secret lever, intending to destroy the entire installation rather than submit to capture. As the lever slams into the destruct position, there is a "terrible, cataclysmic blast . . . an eternal moment of shattering ruin . . . ." The base is demolished and the Nazi commander and his cohorts are buried in the rubble, but Wonder Woman escapes unscathed and Trevor suffers only a broken leg.

Back at the hospital, Trevor is acclaimed a hero for having destroyed the mystery bomber and smashed a Nazi sabotage ring, in spite of his insistence that the credit really belongs to Wonder Woman. Trevor's fellow officers, however, having never seen or heard of Wonder Woman, assume that Trevor's tales of an Amazon heroine are merely fantasies brought on by delirium.

". . . [Y]ou don't need **Wonder Woman** now," soothes nurse Diana Prince at his bedside, allowing herself a wry private joke, "you've got *me*!"

"Listen, Diana!" replies Trevor. "You're a nice kid, and I like you. But if you think you can hold a candle to **Wonder Woman** you're crazy!" (Sen No. 1, Jan '42).

Steve Trevor is still recuperating from his injuries in the Walter Reed Army Hospital when he and Diana Prince are kidnapped by Nazi spies posing as members of Army Intelligence and are imprisoned in the secret headquarters of DOCTOR POISON. Doctor Poison is ultimately apprehended by Wonder Woman, and Trevor winds up back in his hospital bed, hailed as "a national hero" and insisting in vain that all the credit belongs to Wonder Woman (Sen No. 2, Feb '42).

In March 1942 Steve Trevor is released from the hospital and returns to his duties at U.S. Military Intelligence. Heartbroken at the prospect of being unable to remain by his side, Wonder Woman approaches him as Diana Prince and asks him to make her his secretary. When Trevor replies that he already has a secretary (*see* BROWN, LILA), Diana obtains a post at Military Intelligence as secretary to intelligence chief Darnell, then a colonel (Sen No. 3).

In June 1942, in recognition of his "spendid

Diana Prince (Wonder Woman) and Steve Trevor, 1946

work in breaking up spy-plots," Steve Trevor is promoted to the rank of major (Sen No. 6).

Some months later, on Diana's Day, the Amazon counterpart of Christmas (*see* AMAZONS [section E 2, Festivals and holidays]), Wonder Woman presents Steve Trevor with his own mental radio (*see* Wonder Woman [section C 7, the mental radio]) (WW No. 3/1, Feb/Mar '43).

Within less than five years, Steve Trevor has been promoted to the rank of lieutenant colonel – apparently in recognition of his part in the capture of "CRIME BRAIN" DOONE – and in April–May 1947, in recognition of his courage in rescuing a group of generals from a fire, Trevor is promoted to the rank of brigadier general and dispatched to ZANI ISLAND to take command there. However, when a native uprising occurs that requires the intervention of Wonder Woman, Trevor is demoted

Steve Trevor, 1946

back to lieutenant colonel for having failed to put down the uprising on his own (CC No. 20: "The Buddha Wishing Ring"). (*See* SLEEKO [PRINCE].)

In January–February 1950, after seeing Diana Prince without her glasses on and noticing the amazing resemblance between Diana Prince and Wonder Woman, Trevor insists that Diana accompany him to a ball at the HOLLIDAY COLLEGE FOR WOMEN which he is scheduled to attend with Wonder Woman, declaring that only if both women appear there simultaneously will he acknowledge that he has erred in concluding that Diana Prince is secretly Wonder Woman.

At the ball, however, Wonder Woman deceives Trevor, and preserves the secret of her dual identity, by changing identities at such eye-blurring speed – from Diana Prince to Wonder Woman and then back to Diana Prince again – that Trevor experiences the optical illusion of seeing both women simultaneously (Sen No. 95: "The Unmasking of Wonder Woman!").

In August 1955 Wonder Woman returns to the apartment where she makes her home as Diana Prince to find that Steve Trevor has left a caged mynah bird there as a gift for Diana. Moments later, there is a knock on the door.

"Great Hera! That must be Steve!" exclaims Wonder Woman aloud to herself. "I'd better change from **Wonder Woman** – into my secret identity as Diana Prince!"

When Trevor enters the apartment, however, the mynah bird mimics her remark – thus betraying the secret of her dual identity – but, through a ruse, Wonder Woman ultimately succeeds in persuading Trevor that she and Diana Prince are two different persons (WW No. 76/1: "The Bird Who Revealed Wonder Woman's Identity!").

In January 1956, while visiting a U.S. Government test site with Steve Trevor to observe an A-bomb test, Wonder Woman races into the blast area to rescue the pilot of an aircraft that has strayed onto the testing range. The rescue is successful, but in the process Wonder Woman is exposed to the full impact of the atomic blast, and a Geiger-counter test discloses that she has become dangerously radioactive, and hence a menace to anyone she touches. For a time it appears that Wonder Woman's radioactivity will force her into permanent exile, but the effects of the bomb blast turn out to be only temporary and within a short time she has returned to normal (WW No. 79/2: "Danger – Wonder Woman!").

In August 1957 a trainload of America's leading military and scientific personnel – including Steve Trevor and Diana Prince, the girl who is secretly Wonder Woman – are spirited away to an alien

Steve Trevor and Wonder Woman

dimension by sinister crystalline beings plotting to conquer the Earth, but Wonder Woman turns the tables on the aliens and, by reversing their diabolical "dimension-transposer machine," returns the kidnapped earthlings to their own dimension. In the process, the dimension transposer is completely destroyed, making it unlikely that the crystalline aliens will ever be able to invade the Earth (WW No. 92/1: "The Disappearing Train!").

In January 1958, when Steve Trevor's crippled aircraft, on fire and out of control, carries him over an H-bomb testing area, Wonder Woman rescues him from his aircraft and cuts a trench in the ground to shield him from the impending bomb blast, only to be exposed to the full impact of the explosion herself. Wonder Woman survives the awesome blast, but a Geiger-counter test discloses that her body has become dangerously radioactive.

"I've become a menace to everyone on Earth," she declares sadly, "—there's only one thing left for me to do—leave this planet forever!"

As her Amazon plane carries her toward a life of self-imposed exile in outer space, however, Wonder Woman passes Earth's "first satellite station" and discovers that it has been taken over by extraterrestrial invaders bent on using it as a base from which to bombard the Earth. After a furious battle, Wonder Woman destroys the space station— along with the evil aliens who have commandeered it— by lassoing it with her magic lasso (*see* WONDER WOMAN [section C 3, the magic lasso]) and hurling it into the path of an onrushing meteor. It is then that she discovers that she is no longer radioactive, apparently as the result of having recently passed through the tail of a comet containing exotic interstellar "rays" (WW No. 95/1: "Wonder Woman—The World's Most Dangerous Human!").

In November 1958 Steve Trevor and Wonder Woman are on their way to a picnic in Trevor's

jeep when suddenly they are pulled into an alien dimension, where they are confronted by a titanic extradimensional giant. Seizing Trevor's jeep between his thumb and forefinger, the giant informs them that he and his fellows are planning to invade the Earth.

"We heard you say you'd recognize your sweetheart if she were one in a million!" bellows the giant to Trevor, referring to an idle lover's remark he made recently to Wonder Woman. "If you really are clever enough to do so--then we'll halt our plans of invading Earth!"

Having issued this bizarre challenge, the giant hurls Trevor and his jeep to the ground, and when Trevor looks up again, he sees three identical Wonder Women—one the real Wonder Woman, and the other two robot duplicates of her— perched on the giant's massive palm.

"You said you could pick out **Wonder Woman** even if she were one in a million!" thunders the giant. "Well, earthling--pick out the real **Wonder Woman**--or your lives--and the future of the Earth--is [sic] forfeit!"

Realizing that the giant is using him as a guinea pig to learn whether earthlings possess sufficient ingenuity and intelligence to thwart an extradimensional invasion, Trevor asks for, and receives, permission to test the three Wonder Women to determine which of them is the real one. Trevor hopes to expose the robot impostors by having all three women attempt superhuman feats of which only the real Wonder Woman would be capable, but the plan ends in failure when all three contestants successfully perform the feats he assigns them. Finally, however, with the giant pressing him for a final decision, Trevor has an inspiration: lovingly, he kisses each of the three Wonder Women on the lips and then unhesitatingly selects the real one. Only she, exclaims Trevor, kisses like the girl he loves.

Astounded by what to him seems a miraculous feat of recognition since the people of his dimension know nothing of kissing, the giant concludes that earthlings must possess truly formidable powers and accordingly returns Wonder Woman and Trevor to their own dimension, convinced that an invasion of Earth would represent "too much of a risk" for himself and his people (WW No. 102: "The Three Faces of Wonder Woman" pts. 1–3 — "The First Face of Wonder Woman!"; "The Second Face of Wonder Woman"; "The Third Face of Wonder Woman").

In April 1959 Steve Trevor and Wonder Woman soar into outer space aboard Wonder Woman's Amazon plane to investigate the mysterious disappearance of a series of recent unmanned exploratory rockets, only to have their craft seized by a gigantic pterodactyl and carried off to Titan, the largest, brightest, and most massive moon of SAT-URN. Pterodactyls, dinosaurs, and other creatures long extinct on Earth are a thriving menace on Titan, making it impossible for the satellite's humanoid population to advance beyond the cave-man stage.

After defeating the fearsome prehistoric monsters and building a wide moat and tree barrier to prevent them from continuing to prey upon Titan's humans, Wonder Woman uses "mental telepathy" to endow one of Titan's cave boys with detailed knowledge of Earth's civilization as a means of facilitating the evolution of man on Titan. "With the knowledge I am giving you of our civilization," she explains telepathically, "it won't be too long before you catch up to us--!" (WW No. 105/2: "Eagle of Space!").

*Steve Trevor anxiously awaits
word from Wonder Woman, 1946*

In April 1963 — in a text that erroneously describes him as an "Air Force colonel" — Steve Trevor is testing an experimental aircraft, with Wonder Woman at his side, when suddenly the aircraft goes completely out of control, pulled by some mysterious, unknown force through the upper atmosphere and into outer space.

Because Trevor's plane is unequipped for space travel, Trevor lapses into unconsciousness, but Wonder Woman summons her Amazon plane, which *is* equipped for space travel, boards it with Trevor, and instructs the craft to return to Earth. The mysterious force that had acted on Trevor's plane, however, also affects Wonder Woman's, and Wonder Woman finds herself powerless either to return to Earth or to alter her plane's course as it streaks through interstellar space toward a distant planet which "looks exactly like . . .Earth," and then races across the landscape of the "parallel Earth" toward an exact duplicate of Paradise Is-

land, home of the Amazons. As her plane taxis to a halt on the duplicate Paradise Island, Wonder Woman finds herself among a civilization of Amazons, like her own yet somehow strangely different. "This parallel world of Earth," gasps Wonder Woman with sudden realization, "is peopled by robots!"

The ruler of the robot Amazons is a robot duplicate of Wonder Woman's mother, Queen Hippolyte, and the daughter of the robot Hippolyte is a robot Wonder Woman who is determined to marry the real Steve Trevor and make him her prince.

"Go back to **Earth** where you came from, Amazon!" cries the robot Wonder Woman to her human counterpart. "You are here by accident--because you happened to be with this wonderful man--when I had my ray-magnetizer bring him here!"

When Wonder Woman resists the attempts of her robot rival to claim Trevor for her own, the robot Hippolyte commands that "a competition" be held to determine who shall keep Trevor and who shall give him up, with the loser to be instantly destroyed, but as the contest gets under way, it becomes clear that the robot Amazons have no intention of conducting the competition fairly: the rulings of the robot Hippolyte are all patently one-sided, and the body of her robot daughter has been equipped with an array of special apparatus — such as miniaturized jets for motorized flight — which provide her with an unfair advantage in every event. Indeed, it is only through sheer willpower and superior intellect that Wonder Woman is able to make the glaringly uneven contest end in a tie.

The final, tie-breaking event is to be a duel to the death with swords with both contestants blind-

Steve Trevor, 1967

folded, but even this contest has been rigged in favor of the robot, for while Wonder Woman cannot see at all, the robot is equipped with a miniaturized radar system which enables it to "see" despite its blindfold. Knowing full well that the robot Queen Hippolyte intends to have her destroyed even if she wins the duel, Wonder Woman conceives a daring plan: waiting until she and her opponent have moved out of sight of the throng of robot spectators, Wonder Woman tricks her robot adversary into talking — and thus betraying its position — and then hurls her metal tiara (see WONDER WOMAN [section C 5, the tiara]) at the robot with all her might, smashing the metal Wonder Woman into a thousand fragments. Then, after disguising herself as the vanquished robot, Wonder Woman returns to the spectator area, claims Trevor as her prize, cautiously maneuvers him toward her Amazon plane, and then escapes with him into outer space.

Within moments, however, the robot Amazons, realizing they have been tricked, climb aboard their spacecraft and give chase, but Wonder Woman puts her plane through a series of spectacular evasive maneuvers that so confuse the robot space pilots that they smash into and destroy one another in their mad scramble to overtake her (WW No. 137: "The Robot Wonder Woman!").

In January–February 1968 Steve Trevor acquires temporary superhuman powers — and adopts the pseudonym the Patriot — after swallowing the "super-power pills" given him by the ANGLE MAN (WW No. 174/1: "Steve Trevor — Alias the Patriot!").

In March–April 1968 Earth is visited by an evil Wonder Woman from a "parallel world" who is determined to claim Steve Trevor for her own. Wonder Woman and her evil counterpart finally decide to hold a contest to determine which of them will keep Trevor, and Wonder Woman agrees to hold the contest on the parallel world's Paradise Island. Exposure to the parallel world's alien atmosphere, however, transforms Wonder Woman into a teen-ager while her evil adversary remains an adult, and, thus handicapped by her diminished age and stature, Wonder Woman loses the contest.

The parallel world's alien atmosphere, however, has also transformed Steve Trevor into a teen-ager, and since, as a teen-ager, he is no longer a suitable companion for a full-grown woman, the evil Wonder Woman relinquishes her prize and allows Wonder Woman and Trevor to depart her world. As Wonder Woman and Trevor streak through space toward their own world in Wonder Woman's Amazon plane, they find themselves becoming gradually older, until finally, safely away from the strange atmosphere of the parallel world, they find that they have become transformed into adults once again (WW No. 175: "Wonder Woman's Evil Twin!").

In January–February 1969 Steve Trevor is machine-gunned to death by henchmen of the sinister DOCTOR CYBER (WW No. 180: "A Death for Diana!"), but seven years later, in April–May 1976 he is brought back to life again by the goddess Aphrodite (WW No. 223: "Welcome Back to Life . . . Steve Trevor!").

TRIXIA. A hostile country, located somewhere "behind the Iron Curtain," which, having "unexpectedly perfected an atom bomb of tremendous power," is plotting an atomic sneak-attack against the United States. Their spy ring in America is headed by GENERAL VORO, "the man of a thousand faces" (WW No. 50/1, Nov/Dec '51: "Menace of the Master Spy!").

TRIXTER. A wily confidence man who preys on the gullible by claiming to be a wizard from the year 1313 A.D. Trixter and his henchmen are apprehended by WONDER WOMAN in September–October 1948. "My scheme is to use phoney magic as a racket!" confesses Trixter, under the compelling influence of Wonder Woman's magic lasso (see WONDER WOMAN [section C 3, the magic lasso]). "And to prey on people's superstitions and take their money away from them" (WW No. 31/3: "The Racketeer of Magic!").

TROGLODYTES. Sinister froglike men who inhabit a secret undersea domain far beneath the surface of the Sargasso Sea. An attempt by the troglodytes to conquer the Earth is thwarted by WONDER WOMAN in September–October 1953.

Shortly after being assigned — along with Diana Prince, the girl who is secretly Wonder Woman — to investigate a rash of mysterious disappearances, STEVE TREVOR suddenly vanishes and Wonder Woman sets out to find him. Her search takes her to the Sargasso Sea, where she is taken captive by the troglodytes and placed — along with Trevor and the other missing persons — atop an iceberg which the troglodytes intend to destroy with an A-bomb in order to test the effects of an atomic explosion on human beings. In the words of one troglodyte:

> The reason for all this research is to avoid the mistake we made with our **first** atomic explosion eons ago, when we blew a portion of the Earth into space---
>
> This saucer-shaped portion of Earth now revolves around it as a satellite which you earthlings call the moon---
>
> But with the knowledge we shall gain from the test

explosion in which you will be sacrificed — we will blow only the **upper** crust of Earth into space---

With this explosion, Earth will become a planet entirely covered by water under which we shall live!

Before the troglodytes can detonate their A-bomb, however, Wonder Woman frees herself from the influence of their fiendish "paralyzing ray" and removes the other captives to a place of safety, allowing the iceberg to explode harmlessly at sea. Ironically, the titanic explosion seals up the troglodytes' undersea domain forever, thus ending their threat to Earth (WW No. 61/1: "Earth's Last Hour!").

TROPICA, TIGRA (Mrs.). A raven-haired villainess who commands a vicious horde of highly-trained tigers. Mrs. Tigra Tropica is defeated and apprehended by Wonder Woman.

In November–December 1947 Mrs. Tropica has one of her pet tigers kidnap wealthy Angus Richman and drag him to her "large pretentious mansion," where, by pressing certain "nerve centers" behind his ears, she places him under her mental control and compels him to purchase two of her trained tigers for $50,000 apiece, reasoning that she cannot possibly be charged with a crime merely for having sold Richman a pair of tigers. With the transaction completed, Mrs. Tropica's tigers return Richman to his home, but when Richman regains his senses and sees two savage tigers prowling around his room, he has a heart attack and dies.

When Steve Trevor enters Richman's home and discovers his body, the tigers pounce on him and drag him to their mistress's mansion, and when Wonder Woman attempts to investigate, she is forced to surrender to Mrs. Tropica in order to prevent her tigers from harming Trevor. Ultimately, however, she turns the tables on Mrs. Tropica and rescues Trevor from a cageful of starving tigers in the villainess's mansion. Mrs. Tropica will be taken to Transformation Island to learn "to trust humans and obey loving authority" (WW No. 26/2: "The Mistress of the Beasts").

TURGO (Prof.). An evil scientific genius whose attempt to conquer the Earth is thwarted by Wonder Woman in March–April 1951.

After narrowly escaping from Wonder Woman following an encounter at his laboratory hideout, Prof. Turgo climbs aboard a waiting rocket ship and flees into outer space. Soon afterward, Earth is bombarded by explosive missiles from beyond the atmosphere, and Wonder Woman's search for an explanation brings her to Satphix, "a planet not of Earth's solar system" which occupies a temporary position between Earth and the Moon.

The planet Satphix, she learns, was destroyed in a collision with a giant comet, except for a lone fragment which tore loose from its mother world and hurtled into outer space. By means of special control machinery, the inhabitants of that fragment are able to steer their planetoid around the universe as though it were a gigantic spacecraft. After a long search for a new interstellar home, they finally settled on a location between Earth and the moon, where Prof. Turgo found them while fleeing from Wonder Woman. After seizing control of the tiny planet's "solar armory" and taking hostages to prevent any attempt at interference, Prof. Turgo began launching missiles at the Earth, intending to bomb it into submission.

Wonder Woman bravely assaults the solar armory, only to be forced to surrender to Prof. Turgo to prevent him from harming his hostages, but ultimately she turns the tables on her captor, frees the hostages, and restores Satphix to the control of its people. Later, at their urging, she "lowers the remnant of the ill-fated planet" onto "an uncharted spot" in the Pacific Ocean, thus forming a new land mass in the Pacific and giving the people of Satphix a new home on Earth (WW No. 46/2: "The Moon of Peril!").

U

U-235. The "atomic universe" ruled by QUEEN ATOMIA (WW No. 21/1, Jan/Feb '47: "The Mystery of the Atom World").

ULTRAVIOLET INVADERS, THE. An army of invisible creatures from outer space whose attempt to destroy the Earth is thwarted by WONDER WOMAN.

In July–August 1952 Earth is attacked by an army of extraterrestrial invaders — invisible to the naked human eye because they are "colored outside the visible spectrum at the violet end" — who intend to loot the Earth of its buildings, ships, and other "souvenirs" and then "atomize" the entire planet out of existence.

Aboard the aliens' spacecraft — where Prof. Charles, the astronomer who first became aware of the invaders' presence, and STEVE TREVOR are being held captive — WONDER WOMAN courageously battles the extraterrestrials, aided by a pair of ultraviolet contact lenses which enable her to see the enemy. With the alien spacecraft streaking away from the Earth at incredible speed, Wonder Woman seizes the controls and stops the ship in mid-flight at an altitude of 150 miles. Suddenly, "a startling transformation takes place in the murderous space creatures": before Wonder Woman's very eyes, the aliens vaporize into nothingness. In the words of the narrative text:

> One hundred to 400 miles above the Earth is a layer of ionized air! It is produced by sunlight and absorbed ultra-violet radiation! The spaceship's stationary position in the layer has resulted in the absorbtion [sic] of the ultra-violet invaders!

With the ultraviolet invaders annihilated and their threat to Earth averted, Wonder Woman returns Prof. Charles and Steve Trevor safely back to Earth (WW No. 54/2: "The Invisible Invasion!").

UNALDI (Don). An alias employed by COUNT CRAFTI in Fall 1942 when he travels to America with Mammotha in an attempt to capture WONDER WOMAN and STEVE TREVOR (WW No. 2/4).

UNKNOWN, THE. A cunning villain who murders the presidents of four major corporations while contriving to make their deaths appear to have resulted from heart attacks. The Unknown is secretly Mr. Pipsqueak, the seemingly meek manager of the Tycoon Club, a club for businessmen in which the victims held membership. The Unknown is apprehended by WONDER WOMAN in November 1945. In her words:

> Pipsqueak's game was to kill off the heads of big corporations where the president's death would undermine the stockholders' faith in the concern. He then drove the price of the stock down and bought a controlling share of it for practically nothing! [Sen No. 47: "The Terror of the Tycoon Club"].

UNREAL, ANTON. The unscrupulous leader of a mysterious "mystic cult" who, having "perfected an electro-chemical machine which projects physical bodies into the 4th dimension," tricks the rich members of the cult into signing their wealth over to him, and then, after persuading them that they will attain true happiness only if they first "ascend" into the fourth dimension, banishes them into the fourth dimension, never to return. Unreal also banishes STEVE TREVOR into the fourth dimension in hopes of trapping WONDER WOMAN there when she attempts to rescue him, but Wonder Woman apprehends Unreal and, aided by the HOLLIDAY GIRLS (not including ETTA CANDY), successfully returns Trevor to the earthly dimension (Sen No. 30, Jun '44: "The 4th Dimension Kidnapers").

URANUS. The seventh planet from the SUN.

WONDER WOMAN battles Uvo, the "arch war lord" of Uranus, in November–December 1948 (WW No. 32/1: "Uvo of Uranus!" pts. 1–2 — "The Amazing Global Theft!"; "Thunder in Space!").

UVO. The "arch war lord" of the planet URANUS. His attempt to destroy the Earth is thwarted by WONDER WOMAN and the AMAZONS.

By November–December 1948 "constant warring" on Uranus has exhausted the planet's supply of uranium, forcing its warlords to the unhappy realization that "unless we can procure a new supply, we shall no longer be able to wage atomic warfare!"

"What kind of life will it be," exclaims Uvo, "--never to be able to destroy again!"

The only answer, Uvo decides, is to "assemble a space armada" and "fly against the Earth! First, to secretly steal its entire uranium supply! Then to turn it against her!"

Cunningly camouflaged to resemble giant boulders, Uvo's space fleet streaks to the sites of Earth's largest uranium deposits and, by means of super-scientific technology, literally steals the uranium out of the ground. When Wonder Woman and STEVE TREVOR attempt to investigate the bizarre uranium thefts, they become embroiled in a life-and-death battle with Uvo and his space crew, who transform them into stone statues with their diabolical "Kal-C-M ray" and load them aboard their Uranian spacecraft.

"As soon as we reach Uranus," gloats Uvo, "we'll turn the uranium we've taken into atomic bombs with which we'll blast the Earth!"

Although virtually paralyzed, Wonder Woman manages to trick Uvo into blazing away at her with a Uranian "D-Kal-C-M ray" — or "decalcifying ray" — which has the effect of freeing both her and Trevor from their Kal-C-M ray paralysis. Thus freed, Wonder Woman broadcasts an urgent mental radio message (see WONDER WOMAN [section C 7, the mental radio]) to the Amazons, alerting them to the dire Uranian peril, and within moments QUEEN HIPPOLYTE and her Amazon space fleet are streaking into space to engage the Uranian invasion armada speeding toward Earth.

In the battle that follows, Hippolyte and the Amazons defeat the Uranian armada, while Wonder Woman seizes control of Uvo's command ship and makes Uvo her prisoner. Soon afterward, Wonder Woman places Uvo and his defeated Uranian warriors in the custody of their planet's women, who, until now, have been forced to serve as slaves to their war-hungry men.

". . . [Y]ou stupid girls!" exclaims Wonder Woman to a group of shackled Uranian slave women. "When you let your men bind you--you let yourselves be bound by war, hate, greed, and lust for power! Think! And free yourselves! **Control** those who would oppress others! **You can do it!**" (WW No. 32/1: "Uvo of Uranus!" pts. 1–2 — "The Amazing Global Theft!"; "Thunder in Space!").

UXO (Professor). An underworld genius who uses his miraculous "time dimension transfer machine" to banish WONDER WOMAN into an alien dimension. By projecting her thoughts back into the earthly dimension, however, Wonder Woman tricks Uxo into bringing her home again, whereupon she apprehends Professor Uxo and his henchmen (WW No. 70/3, Nov '54: "Wonder Woman's Wedding Day!").

V

VALHALLA. In Teutonic mythology, the hall of the slain, the favorite home of the war god ODIN. It is a great palace whose rafters are of spears and whose roof is made of polished shields. Here, seated on his throne, clad in his eagle helmet and shining armor, Odin welcomes the slain warriors carried to Valhalla by his VALKYRIES.

In the WONDER WOMAN chronicles, Valhalla is "a planetoid beyond the moon" ruled by Odin, god of war. Comic Cavalcade No. 17 describes Odin and his golden-haired Valkyries as "bloodthirsty" and "macabre" deities who have been "given psychic life by the mass desires of the German people during World War #2." The Valkyries are led by GUNDRA, "the princess of the Valkyries" (Oct/Nov '46: "The Valkyries' Prey"). Valhalla is also the domain of LOKI, god of fire, mischief, and evil (Sen No. 83, Nov '48: "The Sinister Olympics!").

Wonder Woman battles Odin and his Valkyries in October–November 1946 (CC No. 17: "The Valkyries' Prey") and again in May–June 1947 (WW No. 23/1: "Siege of the Savage War Maidens"). (See ODIN.) She defeats the villainous Loki during a time-journey into the future that she makes in November 1948 (Sen No. 83: "The Sinister Olympics!"). (See PROWD.)

VALKYRIES. In Teutonic mythology, beautiful golden-haired battle maidens in the service of the war god ODIN. Each day they ride over the battlefields of the world, gathering up the slain warriors chosen by Odin and carrying them off to VALHALLA, the hall of the slain.

In the WONDER WOMAN chronicles, the winged Valkyries are led by GUNDRA, "the princess of the Valkyries" and, by implication, the daughter of Odin, though this is never actually stated.

Wonder Woman journeys to Valhalla on two occasions to battle Gundra and her Valkyries — in October–November 1946 (CC No. 17: "The Valkyries' Prey") and again in May–June 1947 (WW No. 23/1: "Siege of the Savage War Maidens"). (See ODIN.)

VANTON, VELMA. An Australian flower vendor who is an exact double for WONDER WOMAN. In July–August 1949 she becomes the unwitting dupe of two ruthless criminals, who trick her into impersonating Wonder Woman to help them commit crimes.

When Velma Vanton stops at a costume shop in July–August 1949 and tries on a Wonder Woman costume to wear to a masquerade party, the two gangsters who hang out there — the owner of the shop and his accomplice — notice at once her uncanny resemblance to Wonder Woman and, by claiming to be agents of U.S. Military Intelligence who need her help urgently in the war against crime, dupe her into agreeing to help them by posing as Wonder Woman and following their instructions.

Although taken captive by the criminals during their crime spree, the real Wonder Woman manages ultimately to apprehend the criminals, explaining afterward to the naïve but well-intentioned Velma that she has been an unwitting participant in an underworld scheme (WW No. 36/2: "Wonder Woman's Double!").

VENTURE, AMBROSE. A ruthless criminal who attempts — with the aid of Roba Jewel, his beautiful blond accomplice — to invade PARADISE ISLAND, home of the AMAZONS, in order to steal the magic water from the island's "spring of eternal youth." Venture's scheme is thwarted by WONDER WOMAN.

In February–March 1947, acting on Venture's instructions, Roba Jewel strikes up an acquaintance with Wonder Woman and persuades her to take her to Paradise Island for a visit. Then, as she and Wonder Woman wing their way toward Paradise Island in Wonder Woman's Amazon plane (see WONDER WOMAN [section C 4, the robot plane]), Roba uses a tiny concealed transmitter to send out a continuous radio signal to Venture so that he can follow the plane to Paradise Island, whose location is a closely guarded Amazon secret. When Venture and his henchmen attempt to bomb the Amazons from the air, however, Wonder Woman seizes their airplane in midair and hurls it against the side of a rocky cliff, detonating its deadly cargo of bombs and destroying both the villains and their airplane in a mind-shattering explosion.

Roba, now remorseful, surrenders to the Amazons, but because she has already drunk from the spring of eternal youth, the spring dries up completely in accordance with APHRODITE's law — which forbids anyone but an Amazon from partaking of its water — and the Amazons find themselves faced with imminent extinction (see

AMAZONS [section B, Aphrodite's Law]). When Wonder Woman and QUEEN HIPPOLYTE plead with Aphrodite to restore the waters of the magic spring, however, the goddess relents, subject only to the following decree: "This maid from the man's world who drank of the spring must remain here, forever young," intones the goddess, "learning to worship love and beauty!" (CC No. 19: "The Battle for Eternal Youth").

VENTURIA. One of the two leading nations of ATLANTIS, a continent which, according to the WONDER WOMAN chronicles, sank beneath the Atlantic Ocean one million years ago. Atlantis's other leading nation is AURANIA.

Though Atlantis lies far beneath the surface of the Atlantic, it is not covered with water, for "When Atlantis sank beneath the sea, the earth folded over it, sealing it in a vast air pocket under the ocean floor."

Throughout Atlantis, women reign supreme. They are tall, statuesque — much larger than girls from the surface world — and quite beautiful, but they are also arrogant, vain, and inclined to cruelty. Like the ancient Romans, they delight in violent sports and fierce gladiatorial combats.

The men of Atlantis — called "manlings" — are weak, undersized, unintelligent, and generally fit for only the most menial tasks. "Manlings are dull and stupid," remarks a lovely Venturian warrior in Spring 1944, "— they **never** escape from us **Atlantean** girls! We keep them working constantly as slaves or soldiers--that is all a **manling** desires!" (WW No. 8/1: "Queen Clea's Tournament of Death").

Despite this contemptuous pronouncement, however, Venturia experiences two manling revolts between Spring 1944 and December 1946–January 1947 (WW No. 8/3, Spr '44: "The Captive Queen"; CC No. 18, Dec/Jan '46–'47: "The Menace of the Rebel Manlings").

The elite corps of an Atlantean army consists of phalanxes of women shock troops who soar through the air on the backs of giant pterodactyls (WW No. 8/2, Spr '44: "The Girl with the Iron Mask"; and others).

Venturia is ruled by QUEEN CLEA until Spring 1944, when she is deposed through the efforts of Wonder Woman (WW No. 8/1: "Queen Clea's Tournament of Death"). Although ostensibly succeeded by her daughter Ptra, Clea maintains her power for a time by means of a cunning ruse, but ultimately she is defeated by Wonder Woman a second time and removed from the throne (WW No. 8/2, Spr '44: "The Girl with the Iron Mask").

Soon afterward, Clea makes yet another bid for power in Venturia, only to be taken captive by rebel manlings and locked in a dungeon. For a time, Venturia remains in the hands of the manlings, but Clea ultimately regains her throne and leads an assault on Aurania, only to be decisively defeated through the heroic efforts of Wonder Woman and OCTAVIA, the daughter of Aurania's QUEEN EERAS. Following this decisive battle, Octavia is placed on the Venturian throne (WW No. 8/3, Spr '44: "The Captive Queen").

In November 1944 Octavia's benevolent rule is threatened by SONTAG HENYA and her band of ruthless "anarchists," but Wonder Woman defuses the crisis by persuading Octavia to dissolve the monarchy and transform Venturia into a democratic republic. In the free elections that follow, Octavia is elected Venturia's first president (Sen No. 35: "Girls Under the Sea").

In December 1946–January 1947 Venturia is rocked by yet another manling rebellion, this one instigated by the sinister MANLIUS. Ultimately, however, through Wonder Woman's efforts, the insurrectionists are routed and Octavia is restored to power (CC No. 18: "The Menace of the Rebel Manlings").

VENUS. The second planet from the SUN.

In the WONDER WOMAN chronicles, Venus is ruled by the lovely QUEEN DESIRA and is inhabited by a race of courageous, peace-loving winged women and well-meaning but defenseless wingless men.

". . . [O]ur men love us dearly," explains Queen Desira to Wonder Woman in October–November 1942. "They obey us because if they did not, we would fly away from them and they have no wings to follow."

"That's a wonderful way to keep men in their place!" laughs Wonder Woman (AS No. 13: "Shanghaied into Space!").

Queen Desira is the mother of QUEEN EVE, ruler of EVELAND, an earthly paradise situated beneath the South Polar ice cap and populated by lovely Venus girls who have been transformed into Earth girls by the goddess APHRODITE (WW No. 13/1, Sum '45: "The Icebound Maidens").

The magic Venus girdles used on TRANSFORMATION ISLAND are of Venusian origin (see AMAZONS [section F 3, the magic Venus girdles]).

In October–November 1942 Wonder Woman helps Queen Desira and her winged women rid their planet of the brutal Meteor Men (AS No. 13: "Shanghaied into Space!"). (See DESIRA [QUEEN].)

In Spring 1945 Wonder Woman battles the menace of the THIRD WORLD WAR PROMOTERS, both on Earth and on the planet Venus (WW No. 12/1–3: no title; "The Ordeal of Fire"; "The Conquest of Venus"). (See DESIRA [QUEEN].)

In March–April 1947 Wonder Woman journeys

to Venus to defeat the ruthless GELL OSEY (WW No. 22/3: "Jealousy Visits the Winged Women of Venus!").

In July–August 1950 Wonder Woman thwarts a Venusian invasion of Earth masterminded by the evil GENERAL VERTIGO (WW No. 42/2: "The Mystery of the Missing Monday!"), and in September–October 1952 she thwarts "a diabolical scheme" by Venusians to invade the Earth concealed inside ordinary raindrops (see DANIELS [PROF.]) (WW No. 55/3: "Invasion of the Raindrops!"). These invasion attempts, however, are decidedly not the work of the peace-loving Queen Desira.

VERTIGO (General). A would-be conqueror from the planet VENUS who triumphs over WONDER WOMAN in July–August 1950, only to be destroyed by the very weapons with which he had intended to enslave the Earth. In the text, Vertigo is alternately rendered as Virtigo.

By July–August 1950 General Vertigo and his followers, having journeyed to Earth and set up headquarters in a "sub-sea bottom world" far beneath the surface of the Coral Sea, prepare to launch a "secret anaesthetic attack," which, in the invaders' words, "will make all the earthlings completely helpless until our men can enslave them!"

After subduing Wonder Woman with Venusian anaesthetic and taking her prisoner, General Vertigo and his cohorts "launch countless anaesthetic rockets to saturate an unwary world," but the "myriad vibrations of the countless rocket-launchers have an unexpected effect": a titanic explosion and massive undersea earthquake which com-

pletely annihilate the Venusian invasion force, ending forever their dream of conquest. Wonder Woman manages to escape the cataclysm, in the process rescuing a group of fellow earthlings taken captive by the Venusians (WW No. 42/2: "The Mystery of the Missing Monday!").

VIBRATE (Prof.). A physics professor at the HOLLIDAY COLLEGE FOR WOMEN who, disguised as an elderly lady, is secretly the leader of a gang of bank robbers. Vibrate and his henchmen commit a series of spectacular bank robberies in March 1947 by rendering employees and bystanders unconscious with their so-called "wail of death" — a high-pitched sound of extreme intensity produced by a device invented by Vibrate — but WONDER WOMAN apprehends the gangsters and unmasks the "elderly woman" who leads them as Prof. Vibrate. In Wonder Woman's words:

> Prof. Vibrate discovered that people were killed by the sound and vibrations of bombs paralyzing the human brain! He worked originally to help bomb-shocked war veterans--but as always when love of money overpowers love of people, Prof. Vibrate's genius turned to evil and he used his discoveries to hurt people instead of to heal them! [Sen No. 63: "The Wail of DOOM!"].

VILLAINY INCORPORATED. Eight villainesses, led by the sadistic Saturnian slave driver EVILESS, who escape from TRANSFORMATION ISLAND in March–April 1948 and set out to "conquer the Amazons on Paradise Island and use it for a base to raid Earth countries." Besides Eviless, the group includes the CHEETAH, QUEEN CLEA, DOCTOR

© NPP 1948

Villainy Incorporated: an organization of villainesses led by Eviless (extreme right)

POISON, GIGANTA, HYPNOTA THE GREAT, the SNOW MAN, and ZARA. Villainy Incorporated is ultimately defeated by WONDER WOMAN, but Wonder Woman No. 28/1 describes the group as "the most desperate and deadly girl prisoners she . . . ever captured," adding that ". . . there was never such a combination of villainy opposing justice in the history of the world!" (Mar/Apr '48: "Villainy Incorporated!").

In March–April 1948 a band of evil Saturnian women, taken captive by Wonder Woman during a recent encounter with the ruthless DUKE MEPHISTO SATURNO, arrive on Transformation Island to begin rehabilitative training under the guidance of the Amazons. Among the captive Saturnians is Eviless.

Eviless recruits the members of Villainy Incorporated (left to right): Queen Clea, Zara, Priscilla Rich (alias the Cheetah), Giganta, Eviless, Byrna Brilyant (alias the Snow Man), Princess Maru (alias Doctor Poison), and Hypnota the Great

Eviless

As the Saturnians step onto Transformation Island, Amazon guards lock magic Venus girdles (see AMAZONS [section F 3, the magic Venus girdles]) around their waists, but Eviless cunningly prevents the lock on hers from closing properly, thus enabling her to remove it whenever she chooses. Patiently awaiting her opportunity, she overpowers MALA and frees "her Saturnic girls," who in turn pounce on their Amazon guards and lock them in magic Venus girdles to prevent them from attempting to thwart the prisoner revolt. Then, joined by seven of the island's most unrepentant inmates — the Cheetah, Queen Clea, Doctor Poison, Giganta, Hypnota the Great, the Snow Man, and Zara — Eviless flees Transformation Island, determined to annihilate the AMAZONS and use PARADISE ISLAND as a base from which to conquer the world.

That night, as QUEEN HIPPOLYTE walks alone in her garden on Paradise Island, she is set upon by Eviless and her cohorts, who force her to summon the Amazons to a mass meeting. Once the Amazons have all assembled, the eight escapees overcome them with "paralysis gas" and hastily snap magic Venus girdles around their waists.

The villainesses next compel Hippolyte to lure Wonder Woman to Paradise Island with an urgent mental radio message (see WONDER WOMAN [section C 7, the mental radio]), and then attempt to annihilate Wonder Woman in a series of fiendish ambushes — including an attempt by the Snow Man to shoot her Amazon plane (see WONDER WOMAN [section C 4, the robot plane] out of the sky with her "telescopic snow ray," and an attempt by the Cheetah and Doctor Poison to crush her to death with giant boulders. Wonder Woman survives the deadly ambushes, but she is compelled to surrender to Villainy Incorporated when the villainesses threaten to execute Queen Hippolyte and the Amazons (WW No. 28/1: "Villainy Incorporated!").

While four of the villainesses — Clea, Giganta, Hypnota, and Zara — remain behind on Paradise Island, the other four — Eviless, the Cheetah, Doctor Poison, and the Snow Man — place Wonder Woman in a rowboat and begin to ferry her across the bay toward Transformation Island. Wonder Woman leaps from the rowboat and overturns it in a desperate bid for freedom, but then feels compelled to return to the boat — and face recapture by her enemies — in order to rescue Eviless from drowning. "Aphrodite's law commands us to save lives always," thinks Wonder Woman, "--enemies or not!" (See AMAZONS [section B, Aphrodite's Law].)

The cold-hearted Eviless displays no gratitude whatever at having been rescued. Instead, she rows Wonder Woman to Transformation Island

and chains her to a pillar — back to back with Queen Hippolyte — with "flaming chains" devised by the flame cultist Zara. Many of the Transformation Island prisoners, however, having been successfully reformed by their Amazon training, are unsympathetic with the goals of the escapees and have refused to participate in the Saturnian-led rebellion. One of these, the prisoner Irene, leads her like-minded sisters in a counter-insurrection against Eviless and her cohorts and, in the midst of the ensuing battle, succeeds in freeing Wonder Woman from the pillar. Before long, Irene and the other reformed prisoners — led by Wonder Woman and Hippolyte — have turned the tide against Eviless, the Cheetah, Doctor Poison, and the Snow Man and have restored order to Transformation Island. The captive Amazons are all set free, and the captured villainesses are re-imprisoned in magic Venus girdles to prevent their doing further evil.

Four members of Villainy Incorporated, however — Clea, Giganta, Hypnota, and Zara — remain at large, having stolen an Amazon aircraft and "escaped to the man's world" with Queen Hippolyte's priceless crown jewels in their possession. Climbing aboard her Amazon plane, Wonder Woman streaks back to America, determined to find and apprehend them.

Zara and Hypnota overpower Wonder Woman

For many months, however, there is no word either of the escaped villainesses or the missing crown jewels. Then, one day, acting on a hunch, Wonder Woman trails a suspicious-looking young woman to Zara's subterranean "temple of crimson flame," hidden beneath the surface of a Washington, D.C., street. Courageously invading Zara's lair, Wonder Woman lapses into unconsciousness under the combined assault of a "seething inferno" of crimson flame devised by Zara and a "blue hypnotic ray" emanating from the evil mind of Hypnota. Regaining consciousness, Wonder

Woman finds that her Amazon bracelets have been chained together by men — rendering her virtually helpless (see WONDER WOMAN [section C 2, the bracelets of submission]) — and that ETTA CANDY and the HOLLIDAY GIRLS have been lured to the temple of crimson flame and taken captive also. To make matters even graver, Wonder Woman is told that she must kill the young woman she followed with her own hands, or else stand by helplessly while the villainesses murder the Holliday Girls, their intention being to destroy Wonder Woman as a force for justice by turning her into "a fugitive from man's justice" (WW No. 28/2, Mar/Apr '48: "Trap of Crimson Flame").

Before Zara and Hypnota can compel her to carry out the execution, however, Wonder Woman turns the tables on her captors and regains her Amazon strength when Etta Candy cuts the chains that have been welded to her Amazon bracelets. Hypnota and Zara will be returned to Transformation Island for rehabilitative training, but Clea and Giganta remain at large, and, since Hypnota and Zara have only half of Queen Hippolyte's crown jewels in their possession, Wonder Woman reasons that Clea and Giganta must have the rest.

STEVE TREVOR, meanwhile, receives a visit from a statuesque blonde interested in purchasing a submarine from the U.S. Government. Immediately recognizing his mysterious visitor as the fugitive Clea despite her attempt to conceal her identity, Trevor concludes that she must want the submarine to enable her to escape to ATLANTIS, but he pretends not to recognize her in the hope she will lead him to Hippolyte's missing crown jewels. Indeed, when Trevor tells his visitor that submarines are available but extraordinarily expensive, she replies by assuring him that cost is no object and by offering to lead him to the cave where her wealth is hidden.

Arriving at the cave, Trevor recognizes his visitor's treasure hoard as consisting of Queen Hippolyte's stolen jewels and makes the careless error of attempting to apprehend Clea himself, unaware that Giganta is lurking in the shadows nearby. Together the villainesses overpower Trevor, tie him to a post, and then race off to kidnap the Holliday Girls, hoping to use them as hostages to force Trevor to obtain a submarine for them, and also as bait to lure Wonder Woman into a deathtrap.

The Holliday Girls are observing an evolutionary experiment in PROF. ZOOL's laboratory when Clea and Giganta barge into the room and take them prisoner. When Wonder Woman arrives at the laboratory and hurls herself at the villainesses, Clea treacherously throws the "devolution switch" on Prof. Zool's "evolution machine," transforming

WONDER WOMAN, RECOVERING CONSCIOUSNESS, FINDS HERSELF IN A ROWBOAT.

HA! THOU HAST RECOVERED-- EXCELLENT! I'M TAKING THEE TO AN ANCHORAGE OF SURPLUS SUBMARINES-- THOU WILT STEAL ONE FOR ME!

HERA HAVE MERCY --I MUST OBEY CLEA!

© NPP 1948

Queen Clea and Wonder Woman, 1948

Zool and the Holliday Girls into bizarre creatures with the heads of human beings and the bodies of gorillas. Then, while Wonder Woman is preoccupied with the fate of her friends, Giganta knocks her unconscious and takes her prisoner.

Binding Wonder Woman with her own magic lasso (see WONDER WOMAN [section C 3, the magic lasso]), Clea and Giganta compel their captive to steal a submarine and load Queen Hippolyte's crown jewels on board. Then they put out to sea, with Prof. Zool and the Holliday Girls — still imprisoned in their "human gorilla" bodies — bundled up inside a rowboat, Wonder Woman tied to its prow, and the rowboat trailing by a towrope behind the submarine. When the submarine submerges, however, dragging the rowboat beneath the surface and threatening to drown the captives, Wonder Woman leaps into action, smashing the rowboat, freeing the captives, and singlehandedly hauling the submarine to the surface with Clea and Giganta still inside it.

At precisely that moment, Steve Trevor appears overhead in Wonder Woman's Amazon plane, having escaped on his own from Clea's cave and been summoned to the scene by a mental radio message from Wonder Woman. Grasping the submarine's anchor chain with one hand and her Amazon plane's rope ladder with the other, Wonder Woman directs her plane to Holliday College, drops the submarine in the middle of the campus, and then apprehends Clea and Giganta. Then, after restoring Prof. Zool and the Holliday Girls to fully human form with Prof. Zool's evolution machine, Wonder Woman returns Clea and Giganta to Paradise Island, along with the remainder of Queen Hippolyte's stolen crown jewels (WW No. 28/3, Mar/Apr '48: "In the Hands of the Merciless!").

VIRAGO (Capt.). A sideshow operator who is secretly the leader of a gang of criminals. Capt. Vi-

rago and his henchmen are apprehended by WONDER WOMAN in October 1956 (WW No. 85/3: "The Woman in the Bottle!").

VOLCANO PROPHET, THE. A cunning criminal who establishes the reputation of being able to infallibly predict impending volcanic eruptions — through the device of publicly forecasting the imminent eruptions of long-extinct volcanoes and then arranging for his henchmen to "make th' extinct volcanoes 'erupt' with th' help of explosives an' chemicals" — so that he can extort exorbitant sums from towns near volcanoes in return for advance warning of impending eruptions. Taken captive by the criminals in their volcano-crater hideout and left to perish in a fiendish deathtrap, WONDER WOMAN escapes and apprehends the Volcano Prophet and his cohorts in November 1954 (WW No. 70/1: "The Volcano-Maker!").

VORO (General). The cunning "master spy" — known as "the man of a thousand faces" — who heads Trixia's spy ring in the United States. General Voro and his cohorts are apprehended by WONDER WOMAN.

By November–December 1951 Trixia, a hostile nation located somewhere "behind the Iron Curtain," has "unexpectedly perfected an atom bomb of tremendous power" and is plotting an atomic sneak-attack against America. Having learned of the impending attack, GENERAL DARNELL decides to allow himself to be branded a traitor and dismissed from the military so that he can infiltrate General Voro's spy ring and learn the details of Trixia's attack plan, unaware that the cunning Trixian spy-master has infiltrated U.S. Military Intelligence and is thus fully aware of Darnell's daring plan. Indeed, Voro decides to let Darnell join his spy ring so that he can provide him with misleading intelligence calculated to have a detrimental effect on American preparedness.

Darnell courageously proceeds with his plan, but ultimately it is Wonder Woman who locates Voro's hideaway in the city's labyrinthine sewer system, thwarts his various attempts at sabotage designed to precede Trixia's all-out attack, and finally captures the master spy and his henchmen (WW No. 50/1: "Menace of the Master Spy!").

VULTURE KING, THE. A power-hungry villain — disguised as a giant vulture — whose plot to kidnap President FRANKLIN DELANO ROOSEVELT and his Cabinet and seize control of the U.S. Government is thwarted by WONDER WOMAN.

In Summer 1944 a flock of giant vultures swoops over the eastern United States, seizing more than one hundred people — including

Wonder Woman and the HOLLIDAY GIRLS (not including ETTA CANDY) — and carrying them off to their "weird lair on a lonely mountain peak." There the giant vultures — in reality the Vulture King and his henchmen, clad in ingenious "vulture flying suits" — subject their captives to a diabolical "electronomization" process that transforms them into mindless slaves.

"Prisoners," gloats one of the vulture men, "your brains have been **electronomized** — your ears are tuned to the Vulture King's voice, which henceforth will control your every movement!"

With Wonder Woman and the Holliday Girls electronomized, the Vulture King commands them to "lead my vultures to capture the President and Cabinet of the United States! I shall electronomize the brains of these men and rule supreme!"

Ultimately, however, Wonder Woman succeeds in capturing the Vulture King and in forcing him to reverse the electronomization process that had given him absolute "radio control" over the minds of his victims. Then, under the compelling influence of Wonder Woman's magic lasso (see WONDER WOMAN [section C 3, the magic lasso]), the Vulture King reveals the inner motive behind his bizarre scheme to conquer America:

I'm so ugly people always shunned me — I hated them and I resolved to make them serve me. I studied science and discovered that human brains could be tuned by electric current to a certain radio wave length.

I invented this microscopic radio receiver tuned to my own voice. When it's placed on the eardrum [of a victim] the person hears my voice so intensely that it controls his whole nervous system — thus I enslaved people! [CC No. 7: "The Vulture's Nest!"].

W

WARLANDIA. A hostile foreign nation whose attempt to launch an atomic sneak-attack against the United States is thwarted by WONDER WOMAN in May–June 1951 (WW No. 47/1: "World Below the North Pole!"). (*See* MOLE MEN.)

WAR LAUGH MANIA. A hideous disease which afflicts American workers in epidemic numbers in November 1943, threatening to drastically curtail American war production. Its victims are seized by a fit of maniacal laughter and then lapse into a coma from which they never recover, a ghastly "smile of death" upon their faces.

Investigating the epidemic in November 1943, WONDER WOMAN discovers that Axis agents have been kidnapping and impersonating American war-plant workers and then infecting their fellow workers' coveralls with deadly "war laugh mania germs." Aided by ETTA CANDY, STEVE TREVOR, and agents of U.S. Military Intelligence, however, Wonder Woman captures the disease-spreading Axis spies and puts an end to war laugh mania (Sen No. 23).

WELLS, DARCY. Mystik the magician's nephew, manager, and sole heir. When Tricco the magician is found shot to death during a party at Mystik's home in September 1947, there are three likely suspects — Oriel, Mystik's lovely assistant; Mystik, who feared that Tricco was about to expose his most famous trick; and Slydine, a "former magician" whose career had been ruined by Tricco — but WONDER WOMAN solves the mystery and apprehends the real killer, Darcy Wells, who had been embezzling Mystik's money and had murdered Tricco to prevent him from exposing the thefts (Sen No. 69: "Mystery Behind A,B,C,!").

WHITE, DAN. The fiancé (Sen No. 1, Jan '42), and later the husband (Sen No. 9, Sep '42), of DIANA PRINCE, the U.S. Army nurse who, in January 1942, sells WONDER WOMAN her credentials and the use of her identity in return for the money she needs to join White in South America (Sen No. 1). Largely through the good offices of Wonder Woman, White's invention, the "anti-aircraft disintegrator shell," is adopted by the U.S. Army in September 1942 (Sen No. 9). (*See* PRINCE, DIANA.)

WHITE, JOAN. The attractive brunette who once served as secretary to the villainous DR. PSYCHO. On two occasions — in June–July 1943 and again in July–August 1946 — Dr. Psycho places Joan White in a hypnotic trance and forces her to serve as his "medium" (WW No. 5/3, Jun/Jul '43; WW No. 18/3, Jul/Aug '46: "Ectoplasmic Death").

WHITE STAR. The far-distant star which is the home of the evil "genii people." WONDER WOMAN journeys to the White Star in November–December 1947 in response to an urgent summons from its ruler, KING CRYSTALLAR (WW No. 26/3: "The Golden Women and the White Star!").

WHYTE, JOSHUA T. A stingy "eccentric millionaire" who agrees to donate $1,000,000 to a children's charity if, within the space of twenty-four hours, WONDER WOMAN can turn the first penny he ever earned into $1,000,000. When Wonder Woman actually fulfills the task, Whyte begrudgingly keeps his word and makes the promised donation (WW No. 59/3, May/Jun '53: "The Million Dollar Penny!").

WILLIAMS, JAN. A young girl — the daughter of John and Mary Williams — who becomes the temporary ward of WONDER WOMAN after her parents are presumed to have perished in an airplane mishap.

John and Mary Williams and their daughter Jan are flying over the ocean in a light airplane in September–October 1951 when their craft becomes disabled and they are forced to crash-land in the sea. Scouring the area in her Amazon plane (*see* WONDER WOMAN [section C 4, the robot plane]), Wonder Woman finds Jan clinging to a piece of wreckage, but her mother and father have apparently drowned. Told that she must go to an orphanage, Jan tearfully begs Wonder Woman to adopt her instead, and so Wonder Woman, deeply moved by Jan's plea, arranges to have her placed in her custody preparatory to the institution of formal adoption proceedings.

Soon afterward, however, while flying over the ocean in Wonder Woman's plane, Wonder Woman and Jan sight a native war canoe carrying two bound captives, and when Wonder Woman swoops down and rescues them, she discovers that they are none other than John and Mary Williams, who had survived the crash of their light plane and drifted onto a nearby island, only to be taken captive by its native inhabitants (WW No. 49/2: "Little Miss Wonder Woman!").

193

WOGGLE. One of the leprechauns who inhabit SHAMROCK LAND. (*See* SHAGGY.)

WONDER GIRL. The teen-aged WONDER WOMAN (*see* WONDER WOMAN [section D, the early life (as Princess Diana]).

WONDER TOT. The infant WONDER WOMAN (*see* WONDER WOMAN [section D, the early life (as Princess Diana]).

WONDER WOMAN. A valiant Amazon princess who, for more than three decades, has waged unceasing war against the ugly forces of "greed, hatred and foreign conquest" (Sen No. 10, Oct '42). The chronicles describe her as an "invincible enemy of injustice" (Sen No. 8, Aug '42), a "glorious creature of strength and beauty" (Sen No. 5, May '42), a "disciple of peace and love" (Sen No. 81, Sep '48: "When Treachery Wore a Green Shirt!"), a "powerful being of light and happiness" (Sen No. 2, Feb '42), and as "Aphrodite's agent" in the war-torn world of men (WW No. 2/1, Fall '42).

Wonder Woman

She is "as lovely as Aphrodite — as wise as Athena — with the speed of Mercury and the strength of Hercules" (Sen No. 2, Feb '42) — a "marvelous maiden [who] flashes across the American horizon like a dazzling comet, lighting the dark dismal depths of human despair" (Sen No. 7, Jul '42) and bringing with her "a new hope for salvation from Old World evils, conquest and aggression!" (Sen No. 2, Feb '42).

Defying the vicious intrigues of evil enemies and laughing gaily at all danger, **Wonder Woman** leads the invincible youth of America against the threatening forces of treachery, death, and destruction [Sen No. 3, Mar '42].

. . . **Wonder Woman** brings the invincible power of perfect womanhood to the supreme task of defending democracy and transforming evil to justice and happiness! [Sen No. 9, Sep '42].

On PARADISE ISLAND, home of the AMAZONS, "where sorrow and suffering are unknown, and where love and justice make women strong beyond the dreams of men" (Sen No. 2, Feb '42), she is known as Princess Diana, the daughter of QUEEN HIPPOLYTE, ruler of the Amazons.

And in America, her "man's world" homeland, she has adopted the secret identity of plain, bespectacled Diana Prince, serving first as a U.S. Army nurse at the Walter Reed Army Hospital, and later as secretary and assistant to GENERAL DARNELL, chief of U.S. Military Intelligence.

Diana Prince changes to Wonder Woman

As Wonder Woman, she wears a short blue skirt decorated with white stars; a red top emblazoned with a golden eagle; red boots with white trim; red button earrings; and a golden tiara with a red star at its center (AS No. 8, Dec/Jan '41–'42: "Introducing Wonder Woman"). On her wrists she wears metal bracelets of submission to the goddess APHRODITE (*see* section C 2, the bracelets of submission), and from June 1942 onward she carries a golden magic lasso (*see* section C 3, the magic lasso) dangling loosely from the white belt around her waist (Sen No. 6).

From July 1942 onward, Wonder Woman's skirt becomes shorter and tighter (Sen No. 7), until, by October 1942, it has been transformed into a pair of tight-fitting shorts extending only to the upper thigh (Sen No. 10).

In August–September 1947, in place of her boots, Wonder Woman wears bright red Roman sandals with long straps that crisscross her legs up to about mid-calf (CC No. 22: "The Captives of Saturnette!"), but by October–November 1947 she has resumed wearing her white-trimmed red boots (CC No. 23: "Siege of the Iron Giants"). By November–December 1949 Wonder Woman has once again abandoned the boots in favor of the Roman sandals (Sen No. 94: "S O S Wonder Woman"), but in January–February 1950 she is again wearing the boots (WW No. 39/2: "The Modern Midas!"). By March–April 1950 Wonder Woman has returned to the sandals (WW No. 40/1: "Hollywood Goes to Paradise Island" pts. 1–2 — "The Mile High Menace!"; "The Undersea Invasion!"), and by November 1959 high heels have been added to the sandals, and the thongs have been lengthened so that they reach the thigh (WW No. 110: "The Bridge of Crocodiles!"). Six years later, Wonder Woman abandons the high-heeled sandals in favor of red high-heeled boots without any trim (WW No. 157, Oct '65: "I--the Bomb!").

Interestingly, other times and places have Wonder Women of their own. TARA TERRUNA, the Wonder Woman of an extradimensional parallel world "existing simultaneously alongside Earth" but in an earlier era, is an exact double for Wonder Woman (WW No. 59/1, May/Jun '53: "Wonder Woman's Invisible Twin!"). The "twin Wonder Woman" from DIMENSION X is also an exact double for Wonder Woman (WW No. 100/1, Aug '58: "The Forest of Giants!" pts. 1–2 — "The Challenge of Dimension X!"; "The Forest of Giants!"), as are the two extradimensional robot Wonder Women whom Wonder Woman and STEVE TREVOR encounter in November 1958 (WW No. 102: "The Three Faces of Wonder Woman" pts. 1–3 — "The First Face of Wonder Woman!"; "The Second Face of Wonder Woman"; "The Third Face of Wonder Woman"), the evil extradimensional robot Wonder Woman whom Wonder Woman battles in April 1963 (see TREVOR, STEVE) (WW No. 137: "The Robot Wonder Woman!"), and the evil extradimensional Wonder Woman whom Wonder Woman battles in March–April 1968 (see TREVOR, STEVE) (WW No. 175: "Wonder Woman's Evil Twin!"). Wonder Woman meets her "identical Jovian counterpart" — a "giant-size" Wonder Woman perhaps fifteen times larger than herself — during a visit to the planet JUPITER in May 1957 (WW No. 90/1: "Planet of the Giants!").

Australian flower vendor VELMA VANTON (WW No. 36/2, Jul/Aug '49: "Wonder Woman's Double!"), circus performers INEZ AND JOAN LANE (WW No. 46/3, Mar/Apr '51: "Wonder Woman's Twin!"), and QUEEN NIANA of SARDONIA (WW No. 63/3, Jan '54: "The Imposter Queen!") are all exact doubles for Wonder Woman, and the foreign spy GORRA is an exact double for Diana Prince, Wonder Woman's alter ego (WW No. 67/1: "Confessions of a Spy!").

In the chronicles, Wonder Woman is referred to also as the Alluring Amazon, America's Guardian Angel, and the Maid from Paradise Isle.

A. ORIGIN
B. THE SECRET IDENTITY
C. THE AMAZON POWERS AND EQUIPMENT
  1. The Benefits of Amazon Training
  2. The Bracelets of Submission
  3. The Magic Lasso
  4. The Robot Plane
  5. The Tiara
  6. The Earrings
  7. The Mental Radio
  8. The Other Amazon Equipment
D. THE EARLY LIFE (as Princess Diana)
E. THE LATER LIFE (as Diana Prince)
F. THE WOMAN HERSELF (as Wonder Woman)
  1. The Attitudes
  2. The Sexual Conflict
  3. The Mythological Expressions
G. THE RELATIONSHIP WITH STEVE TREVOR
H. THE GREAT THEMES
  1. The Relationship Between Men and Women
  2. Humiliation and Sadism
  3. Slavery, Bondage, and Loving Submission
I. THE TEXTS
  1. Locales
  2. Developments
    a. *The Wartime Adventures*
    b. *The Postwar Adventures*
    c. *The Later Adventures*

A. Origin. It was a clear day in December 1941–January 1942, and fleecy white clouds drifted lazily across a pale blue sky. Far out over the ocean, a small green airplane, now "entirely out of gasoline" after a long flight across the water, sputtered pathetically, floundered helplessly about the sky, and finally crashed "on the shores of an uncharted isle set in the midst of a vast expanse of ocean. . . ."

As the airplane plowed into the sandy beach, two lovely young women — one a blonde, the other a brunette — burst from the surrounding foliage and raced toward the crumpled wreckage. Working furiously, they pried the pilot from his battered cockpit and lifted him onto the beach. He had blond hair and wore the uniform of an officer in the United States Army.

"Princess," exclaimed the blond girl, gazing in fascination at the unconscious pilot, "it's — it's —"

"A MAN!" cried her companion, lifting the pilot gently in her arms. "A MAN ON PARADISE ISLAND! Quick! Let's get him to the hospital."

Carrying the full grown man as if he were a child, the young woman steps through the foliage and enters the streets of a city that for all the world seems to be born of ancient Greece!

All around her, beautiful young girls in diaphanous costumes clustered to catch a glimpse of the unconscious pilot.

"A MAN!" exclaimed one.

"How did he get here?" cried another.

"Someone tell the queen," exclaimed a third, "there's a MAN on Paradise Island!"

At the hospital, the wounded pilot was placed in the care of a woman physician.

"Is he all right?" asked the brunette anxiously. "Will he live?"

"I don't know," replied the doctor. "He's had a concussion. We won't know anything for days. I wonder what the queen will do with him. He can't be moved."

Then Queen Hippolyte entered the hospital. She wore an exotic, ancient costume, and there was an air of great dignity and serenity about her.

The doctor and the young brunette — Hippolyte's daughter, Princess Diana — looked up in surprise.

"I heard that there was a man here," said the queen quietly, "but I couldn't believe it. Who is he?"

"His plane crashed on the beach of the island this morning," replied the doctor. "The princess and Mala brought him here. I found these papers in his pocket."

The queen regarded the credentials coolly. "'Capt. Steven Trevor,'" she read aloud, "'U.S. Army Intelligence Service.' Hmm. We can't let him die. See that he gets the best of attention. Keep his eyes covered so that, if he should awake, he will see nothing! Have his plane repaired, for he must leave as soon as he is well! Keep me informed of his progress!" And with these words, the queen departed.

In the ensuing days, the princess, the queen's only daughter, is constantly at the bedside of the unconscious man, helping — watching —

"You ought to get some sleep, Princess," urged the doctor. "You have been on the job now for fourteen hours."

"Never mind me," replied the princess. "We — we must make him well."

Leaving the princess to watch over the injured pilot, the doctor seeks audience with the queen . . . .

"What has happened that you disturb me at this hour?" asked the queen. "Is the man —"

"No," replied the doctor, "he is alive. It is the princess I am worried about. I don't think she ought to be allowed in the hospital any more. She acts rather strangely about that man."

"So she is in love!" said the queen. "I was afraid of that! You are quite right, doctor. I shall take steps immediately."

"That would be wise," agreed the doctor. "It's for the child's own good."

And so the princess, forbidden the pleasure of nursing the only man she can recall ever having seen in her life, goes to her mother . . . .

". . . [M]other," cried the princess, "—I don't understand—I must see him! I must know who he is, how he got here! And why he must leave? I-I love him!"

"I was afraid, daughter," replied the queen, "that the time would some day arrive that I would have to satisfy your curiosity. Come — I will tell you everything!"

Then, as the princess stood spellbound, Hippolyte narrated the history of the immortal Amazons. She told her daughter about their life in ancient AMAZONIA, about their defeat and humiliation at the hands of HERCULES, and about how the goddess Aphrodite had delivered them from slavery and led them to Paradise Island, a sanctuary of peace and happiness, on the condition that they "keep aloof from men" forever. (See AMAZONS [section A, History].)

After the queen had finished her story, she and her daughter gazed into the magic sphere (see AMAZONS [section F 2, the magic sphere]) to learn of the events that had brought Capt. Steven Trevor to their shores. They learned that Trevor had been pursuing a Nazi "spy plane" when his craft had run out of fuel and crashed on the beach at Paradise Island.

". . . [M]other, he must be taken back to America to finish the job he started!" said the princess.

"Getting him back would be a problem," replied the queen. "Leave me alone, my daughter. I must consult with Aphrodite and Athena, our goddesses. I must seek their advice!"

In the queen's solitude, the spirits of Aphrodite and Athena, the guiding goddesses of the Amazons, appear as though in a mist . . . .

"Hippolyte, we have come to give you warning," intoned Aphrodite. "Danger again threatens the entire world. The gods have decreed that this American army officer crash on Paradise Island. You must deliver him back to America — to help fight the forces of hate and oppression."

"Yes, Hippolyte," added Athena, "American liberty and freedom must be preserved! You must send with him your strongest and wisest Amazon — the finest of your wonder women! — For America, the last citadel of democracy, and of equal rights for women, needs your help!"

"Yes, Aphrodite, yes, Athena," replied the queen. "I heed your call. I shall find the strongest and wisest of the Amazons. She shall go forth to fight for liberty and freedom and all womankind!"

In the days that followed, Hippolyte busied herself with preparations for a great tournament to determine which Amazon was the strongest and the wisest, but she forbade her daughter Diana to participate in the contest.

"But mother," complained the princess, "why can't I enter into this tournament? Surely, I have as much right —"

"No, daughter, no!" answered Hippolyte sternly. "I forbid you to enter the contest! The winner must take this man back to America and never return, and I couldn't bear to have you leave me forever!"

The great day arrives. From all parts of Paradise Island come the Amazon contestants. But one young contestant insists on wearing a mask . . .

As the contestants stood before her in the Amazon arena, Hippolyte read the proclamation signalling the start of the tournament. "If you are ready," announced the queen, "let the tournament begin — and may the best maiden win!"

The tests begin! First . . . the foot race! A trained deer sets the pace! As the deer easily outruns the pack, suddenly the slim masked figure darts forward, her legs churning madly . . . and not only catches up with the deer — but passes it!

As the tests of strength and agility go on throughout the day, more and more contestants drop out wearily . . . .

Finally, only Mala, number 12, and the masked maiden, number 7, remained in the running. Each had won ten of the day's grueling athletic contests. A deathly hush blanketed the audience as the queen rose to her feet. "Contestants 7 and 12, you are the only survivors of the tournament!" she said. "Now you must get ready for . . . the final and greatest test of all — **BULLETS AND BRACELETS!**"

Murmurs of excitement and anticipation raced through the throng of onlookers as the queen handed pistols to the two remaining contestants and explained the rules of the game to them.

"Each of you will shoot five times," she explained. "Your opponent must catch the bullets on her bracelet — or else expect to be wounded! Now take your places, number 12 [Mala] will shoot first."

At the queen's signal, Mala fired her pistol "point-blank at number 7, the masked maiden!" The Amazon game of bullets and bracelets is

The ultimate test of speed of both eye and movement! No. 7's bracelets become silver flashes of streaking light as they parry the death-thrusts of the hurtling bullets! No. 7 passes the test unscathed! Now it is her turn to fire.

Mala was "fast — but not fast enough!" A bullet whizzed past her bracelets and wounded her in the shoulder, eliminating her from the competition. The mysterious masked maiden was declared the winner.

"You may remove your mask, number 7!" announced the queen. "I want to see the face of the strongest and most agile of all the Amazons."

As the masked maiden plucked her mask from her face, the queen's eyes widened, for contestant number 7 was none other than her own daughter Diana.

"I knew it — I felt it!" said the queen, with pride and regret. "I thought perhaps — well, it's too late now! You've won and I'm proud of you! In America you'll indeed be a 'Wonder Woman,' for I have taught you well!"

Then Hippolyte handed her daughter the special costume which she herself had designed for the winner: a short skirt decorated with white stars; a red top emblazoned with a golden eagle; red boots with white trim; and a golden tiara with a red star at its center.

And so [Princess] Diana, the Wonder Woman, giving up her heritage, and her right to eternal life, leaves Paradise Island to take the man she loves back to America — the land she learns to love and protect, and adopts as her own! [AS No. 8: "Introducing Wonder Woman"].

B. The Secret Identity. Beyond the cloistered world of PARADISE ISLAND, the fact that plain Diana Prince is secretly Wonder Woman is one of the world's most closely guarded secrets. In comicbook literature, secret identities are commonplace. Usually, however, the costume and fighting name of the hero or heroine conceal the crime-fighter's true identity. In the case of Wonder Woman, the opposite is true: the Amazon princess Diana, known to the world at large as Wonder Woman, is the fact; Diana Prince, the bespectacled army nurse turned employee of U.S. Military Intelligence, is the fiction.

When Princess Diana — the "wonder woman" (AS No. 8, Dec/Jan '41–'42: "Introducing Wonder Woman") from Paradise Island — first arrives in America in January 1942, she expresses no intention whatever of assuming a dual identity. After depositing the wounded STEVE TREVOR at the Walter Reed Army Hospital, she wanders aim-

Wonder Woman acquires the identity of nurse Diana Prince, 1942

lessly through the streets of Washington, D.C., familiarizing herself with the curious mores of the man-ruled world, foiling a bank robbery, and making the acquaintance of unscrupulous promoter AL KALE.

Later, she heads back toward the hospital, trying desperately to conceive of some means of remaining close to Steve Trevor, with whom she has fallen in love. On the hospital steps, she encounters a plain, bespectacled nurse, just assigned to the hospital, who is weeping because, in her words, "my fiance just got a job in South America, but he can't send for me because his salary is too small at the moment!"

"That's terrible," exclaims Wonder Woman, "and just think--it all would work out right if only you had a little money!"

Then, removing the nurse's eyeglasses, she remarks, "I just noticed — with these glasses off, you look a lot like me! I have an idea! If I gave you money would you sell me your credentials?"

"You--you mean you want to take my place at the hospital?" stammers the nurse. "But — I can't---I mean--"

"Look," interjects Wonder Woman, "— by taking your place I can see the man I love and you can marry the man **you** love! No harm done, for I'm a trained nurse, too — just a little money and a substitution —"

"And we'd both be happy!" exclaims the nurse. "I'll do it! Oh — this is wonderful!"

"Oh, by the way," adds Wonder Woman, " — my name is Diana. What's yours?"

"Why that's an amazing coincidence," cries the nurse, "— I'm Diana too! Diana Prince! And you'd better remember that last name — because it'll be yours from now on."

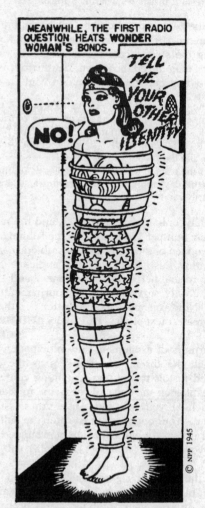

The Lawbreakers' Protective League tortures Wonder Woman in an effort to learn her secret identity, 1945

Donning a nurse's uniform and a pair of eyeglasses, Wonder Woman goes to work in the hospital as Steve Trevor's nurse. It is the beginning of a secret double life that Wonder Woman has now pursued for more than three decades (Sen No. 1).

Two later texts deal with the origin of Wonder Woman's dual identity: Wonder Woman No. 99/2 and Wonder Woman No. 162/1.

Wonder Woman No. 99/2 claims that, shortly after her arrival in America, Wonder Woman agreed to marry Steve Trevor if he could successfully locate her three times within the space of twenty-four hours despite her best efforts to elude him. After Trevor had found her twice, Wonder Woman finally outwitted him by adopting the fictitious identity of Diana Prince and applying for a post as his assistant at U.S. Military Intelligence. Although she was working within a few feet of Trevor throughout the remainder of the twenty-four-hour period, Trevor was never able to find her a third time so that he could compel her to make good on her promise to marry him (Jul '58: "Top Secret!"). This text directly contradicts the original story of how Wonder Woman came to acquire her secret identity — as well as numerous other early texts — and may safely be dismissed as inaccurate.

Wonder Woman No. 162/1, which also deals with the origin of Wonder Woman's dual identity, consists basically of a faithful reworking of the original secret-identity account (May '66: "The Startling Secret of Diana Prince!").

The original purpose of Wonder Woman's dual identity was to enable her to remain near Steve Trevor, the man she loved. Gradually, however, the chroniclers began to explain the secret identity as a stratagem to enable her to outwit the underworld.

"Revealing my secret dual identity would hinder me in my battle against crime and injustice," she explains in March–April 1953, "— because it would rob me of the element of surprise when I change from one identity to another!" (WW No. 58/1: "Seven Days to Doom!").

Unconsciously, however, Wonder Woman would like to be done with the dual identity, perhaps because its exposure would end her crime-fighting career and leave her free to marry Steve Trevor (*see* section G, the relationship with Steve Trevor), perhaps because she feels guilty about the continual duplicity it represents. This desire is most transparently expressed in a dream Wonder Woman has in February 1957. In it, the secret of her dual identity has somehow leaked out, and everyone knows that Wonder Woman is also Diana Prince. Billboards proclaim the news in gigantic letters, and airplanes skywrite the truth across the sky. Wonder Woman's desperate attempts to protect her secret by persuading the public that she is not Diana Prince are met with derision and disbelief: everyone knows that Wonder Woman and Diana Prince are really the same woman, and they are not about to be persuaded otherwise.

Finally Wonder Woman awakens, relieved to discover that her secret identity is safe and that its exposure was only a nightmare fantasy. The wish-fulfilling aspects of the dream elude her completely (WW No. 88/3: "The Walking Nightmare!").

C. The Amazon Powers and Equipment. 1. The benefits of Amazon training. The superhuman powers and abilities with which Wonder Woman

Steve Trevor becomes convinced that Diana Prince is secretly Wonder Woman,
but she soon throws him off the track with Amazon ventriloquism, 1943

Wonder Woman demonstrates the benefits of Amazon training: breaking ropes and chains . . .

. . . lifting a massive boulder . . .

. . . and escaping a 150-foot lasso . . .

. . . to the cheers and plaudits of young Amazon initiates, 1945

battles the forces of crime and injustice are the result of an intensive and highly specialized system of self-improvement and development known as "Amazon training," a phenomenon to which the chronicles frequently allude. By "man's world" standards, all AMAZONS are gifted with incredible powers, and, though Wonder Woman is a champion among the Amazons, her powers and abilities are on the same order as those of her sister Amazons.

Briefly stated, Amazon training involves learning to use, and to harness toward constructive ends, the virtually unlimited potential of the human mind. By training their minds and bodies to the point of being able to control the flow of mental energy into their muscles and limbs, Amazons develop superhuman strength and extraordinarily acute senses.

"Amazon girls get their strength," explains Wonder Woman in Fall 1944, "from brain energy given by Aphrodite!" (WW No. 10/3: "Wonder Woman's Boots!").

"There's nothing secret about it!" she adds years later. "Amazons can release brain energy into their muscles at will--giving them super-strength! Anyone can do it--with will power and training!" (WW No. 160/1, Feb '66: "The Amazon of Terror!").

Wonder Woman repeatedly expresses her conviction that anyone could duplicate her amazing Amazon feats "if she went through the rigorous training that I did!" (WW No. 39/3, Jan/Feb '50: "A Day in the Life of Wonder Woman!"; and others).

"I can prove that Amazon training makes **any** girl powerful!" she declares in Fall 1943 (WW No. 6/3: "The Conquest of Paradise"), and, indeed, several "man's world" girls have developed superhuman strength by undergoing Amazon training on Paradise Island under Wonder Woman's careful guidance, among them BARONESS PAULA VON GUNTHER, OLIVE NORTON, and WANTA WYNN.

In the course of three decades, the chroniclers have endowed Wonder Woman with ever more spectacular powers in an effort to transform her into an ever more spectacular heroine. In January 1942, for example, promoter Al Kale is able to overtake the fleetly running Wonder Woman by accelerating his automobile to a speed of 80 miles per hour (Sen No. 1), but by November–December 1952 Wonder Woman is able to move at such eye-blurring speed as to render herself invisible (WW No. 56/2: "Wonder Woman's Invincible Rival!"), and by the mid-1950s she is outracing bullets to their mark.

This steady magnification of Wonder Woman's superhuman powers gave rise to an effort on the part of the chroniclers to portray Wonder Woman as not merely the "mightiest of all Amazons" (Sen No. 104, Jul/Aug '51: "The End of Paradise Island"), but as some sort of super-Amazon, capable, even as an infant, of mind-boggling feats which her sister Amazons could not hope to equal. This unfortunate distortion of the Wonder Woman legend — which paved the way for such spin-off creations as Wonder Girl and Wonder Tot — attains its clearest expression in Wonder Woman No. 105/1, which asserts that the infant Wonder Woman received her awesome powers as gifts from the gods and goddesses while she lay in her cradle, and not as the result of long and arduous Amazon training (Apr '59: "The Secret Origin of Wonder Woman"). (*See* section D, the early life [as Princess Diana].)

With the exception of a fifteen-month period — from February 1966 (WW No. 160/1: "The Amazon of Terror!") through April 1967 (WW No. 169/1: "Wonder Woman Battles the Crimson Centipede!") — during which the chroniclers attempted to revive many aspects of the traditional Wonder Woman mythology they had long since allowed to lapse, Wonder Woman would never again be able to state, as she had in Fall 1943, that "There's nothing extraordinary about my muscles — I've learned to put more mental force into them through years of Amazon training" (WW No. 6/3: "The Conquest of Paradise").

It is impossible to define with precision the true extent of Wonder Woman's incredible powers: new powers are continually being added, and existing abilities constantly expanded, to enable her to meet ever more exacting challenges. Following is a chronological survey of superhuman feats performed by Wonder Woman during the first twenty-seven years of her colorful career. The survey is by no means exhaustive, but a conscientious effort has been made to pinpoint the first occasion on which Wonder Woman uses each of her many powers, as well as to record whatever data exist concerning the limitations and extents of those powers. By following the growth and development of Wonder Woman's various abilities, and the periodic appearance of new abilities, one can trace the gradual expansion of Wonder Woman's powers as it unfolded in the chronicles.

In December 1941–January 1942 Wonder Woman's mother, QUEEN HIPPOLYTE, observes that she has taught her daughter "all the arts and sciences and languages of modern as well as ancient times!" (AS No. 8: "Introducing Wonder Woman"). Later texts expanded Wonder Woman's linguistic abilities to include knowledge of all future languages and interplanetary communication as well.

In January 1942 Wonder Woman outruns an automobile going 60 miles per hour, but is overtaken when the driver of the automobile accelerates to 80 miles per hour (Sen No. 1).

In March 1942 Wonder Woman leaps safely from a fifth-story window to the sidewalk below, swims through the water at a speed exceeding 30 miles per hour, and notes that Amazons are taught to have "perfect memories" (Sen No. 3).

In May 1942 Wonder Woman's alter ego, Diana Prince, is able to discern, merely by lifting it, that a bottle of champagne to be used in a ship christening is actually filled with liquid explosive. "With her more than normal senses," explains the text, "Diana is able to identify substances by their weight----" (Sen No. 5).

In Summer 1942 the chronicles assert that Wonder Woman possesses "telepathic power" (WW No. 1/4: "The Greatest Feat of Daring in Human History!").

In July 1942 Wonder Woman lifts an entire tree, and breaks heavy metal chains with ease (Sen No. 7).

In August 1942 Wonder Woman tears a heavy safe door off its hinges with her bare hands (Sen No. 8).

In September 1942 Wonder Woman exhibits a "super-keen sense of smell" (Sen No. 9).

In Winter 1942 Wonder Woman muses that she can swim three times as fast as a German submarine, and singlehandedly prevents a 35,000-ton aircraft carrier from sliding off a pier into the water (CC No. 1: "The Mystery of the House of Seven Gables").

In April 1943 Wonder Woman runs "a few hundred miles" on foot rather than wait for a temporarily grounded airplane to fly her to her destination (Sen No. 16).

In May 1943 Wonder Woman uses ventriloquism to make it appear as though Diana Prince is in an adjoining room (Sen No. 17: "The Talking Lion!").

In June 1943 Wonder Woman easily withstands the heat of the blazing sun focused on her body through a giant magnifying glass. "I'm in a hot spot!" thinks Wonder Woman. "Lucky we Amazons practice enduring heat by repulsing it with our body electricity!" (Sen No. 18).

In June–July 1943 Wonder Woman attains a running speed of 80 miles per hour while carrying an airplane over her head, and observes that all Amazons "practice yogi [sic]" (WW No. 5/3).

In August 1943 Wonder Woman hurls an ambulance approximately 300 yards (Sen No. 20).

In Fall 1943 Wonder Woman exhibits a "birdlike sense of direction" (CC No. 4: "The Purloined Pressure Coordinator").

In November 1943 Wonder Woman uses her back muscles to raise a stone slab weighing 50 tons (Sen No. 23).

In December 1943 Wonder Woman protects the secret of her dual identity by using "mental telepathy" to create an image of Diana Prince on the viewplate of her mental radio receiver (see section C 7, the mental radio) so that Steve Trevor will think that she is receiving a mental radio message from Diana Prince (Sen No. 24: "Adventure of the Pilotless Plane").

In January 1944 Wonder Woman overhears a telephone conversation taking place in another room by means of her super-sensitive hearing. Having overheard the caller make a remark to his wife on the telephone, she races to his home — one mile away — at such terrific speed that she arrives before the wife has had time to make her reply (Sen No. 25: "Adventure of the Kidnapers of Astral Spirits").

In February 1944 Wonder Woman halts an oncoming passenger train with her bare hands, and, having lassoed an airborne plane with her magic lasso (see section C 3, the magic lasso), hauls it to the ground "like a kite" (Sen No. 26: "The Masquerader").

In March 1944 Wonder Woman swims up NIAGARA FALLS (Sen No. 27: "The Fun Foundation").

In Fall 1944 Wonder Woman exhibits the "Amazon ability to hold her breath for long periods under water" (WW No. 10/1: "Spies from Saturn").

In Spring 1945 Wonder Woman smothers the explosion of a small bomb in her bare hands (WW No. 12/1).

In Summer 1945 Wonder Woman leaps 150 feet into the air, supports a 25-ton boulder on her chest, and lifts a 25-ton boulder over her head (WW No. 13/1: "The Icebound Maidens").

In June 1946 Diana Prince changes into her Wonder Woman costume "with lightning celerity no human eye could follow . . . !" (Sen No. 54: "The Treachery of Fiendo").

In November 1946 Wonder Woman catches a falling airplane in her bare hands, and exhibits the "marvelous Amazon resistance" that enables her to withstand freezing temperatures (Sen No. 59: "Reign of Blue Terror").

In April 1947 Wonder Woman scales the side of a tall skyscraper (Sen No. 64: "The Adventure of the Little Cloud People").

In May 1947 Wonder Woman triumphs easily over half a dozen angry polar bears (Sen No. 65: "Treachery in the Arctic").

In August 1947, while on board a ship anchored "over the deepest spot in the sea," Wonder Woman can see all the way to the bottom by means of her extraordinary Amazon eyesight. She also breaks heavy chains "with her strong Amazon teeth" (Sen No. 68: "Secret of the Menacing Octopus!").

In February 1948 Wonder Woman floats on her back in the water while holding an ocean liner aloft in her arms (Sen No. 74: "The Undersea Cowboys!").

In June 1948 Wonder Woman exhibits microscopic vision and uproots giant redwood trees with her bare hands (Sen No. 78: "The Mistress of the Masquerade!").

In November–December 1948 Diana Prince muses that "an Amazon's brain has been trained to remember the talk of a hundred people!" (WW No. 32/1: "Uvo of Uranus!" pts. 1–2 – "The Amazing Global Theft!"; "Thunder in Space!").

In January 1949 Wonder Woman remarks that "we Amazons have been trained to have photographic vision! We can memorize whole pages at a single glance!" This enables Wonder Woman to read a "mountainous pile of letters in an incredibly short time--" (Sen No. 85: "The Girl Who Wanted to Be an Amazon!").

In March–April 1949 Wonder Woman survives a horrendous bomb explosion, explaining afterward that "Amazons are taught how to roll outside the area of a bomb blast!" (WW No. 34: "The Mystery of the Rhyming Riddle!" chs. 1–3 – "Deception Strikes Again"; "The Phantasms of Deception!"; "The Mystery of the Rhyming Riddle!").

In July 1949 Wonder Woman lassoes a glacier and pulls it behind her through the water by swimming with the free end of the lasso clenched between her teeth (Sen No. 91: "The Survivors of the Stone Age!").

In November–December 1949 Wonder Woman's Amazon powers enable her to scan the police department's entire rogues' gallery in a matter of seconds (WW No. 38/1: "The Girl from Yesterday!"), withstand "crashing bolts of electricity which

Her hands bound, Wonder Woman tows a submarine through the water, 1948. Her captor is Queen Clea

would be fatal to an ordinary human," and kick a neat flight of stone steps into the side of a mountain to enable the mountain climbers behind her to reach the summit (WW No. 38/3: "The Five Tasks of Thomas Tighe!").

In January–February 1950 Wonder Woman outraces a falling elevator thirty stories, arriving at the ground floor in time to catch it gently in her arms (WW No. 39/1: "The Trail of Thrills!").

In May–June 1950 Wonder Woman shoes a horse by hammering in the nails with blows of her bare fist, and when the head of a blacksmith's hammer shatters into several fragments, she "fuses the metal pieces together into a new hammer" with "a single squeeze of her powerful hand" (WW No. 41/2: "Wonder Woman vs. Wonder Woman!").

In July–August 1950 Wonder Woman constructs an entire factory singlehandedly in less than ten minutes (WW No. 42/3: "The Strange Case of Convict 490012!").

In July–August 1950 Wonder Woman plays all the instruments in a dance band simultaneously by leaping from one instrument to another at superhuman speed (Sen No. 98: "Wonder Woman's Strange Mission!").

In March–April 1951 the chronicles refer to "the lovely Amazon's [Wonder Woman's] mind, which has catalogued all knowledge since time began . . ." (Sen No. 102: "The Queen of the South Seas!").

In March–April 1952 Wonder Woman handles white-hot metal in her bare hands and experiences no pain (WW No. 52/1: "Her Majesty – Queen Wonder Woman!").

In May–June 1952 Wonder Woman blows a stack of magazines off a table with a puff of superhuman breath (WW No. 53/2: "The Wonder Woman Nobody Knows!").

Wonder Woman scans the police department's rogues' gallery at superhuman speed, 1949

In November–December 1952 Wonder Woman moves at such eye-blurring speed that she becomes invisible (WW No. 56/2: "Wonder Woman's Invincible Rival!").

In May–June 1953 Wonder Woman bores deep into the earth by whirling so rapidly that she becomes a human drill (WW No. 59/3: "The Million Dollar Penny!").

In July–August 1953 Wonder Woman remarks that "... my Amazon vision is keener than the most powerful binoculars!" (WW No. 60/3: "Wonder Woman's Double Date!").

In February 1954 Wonder Woman races up the side of a skyscraper by moving so rapidly that her momentum overcomes the force of gravity (WW No. 64/3: "Wonder Woman's Last Hour!").

In July 1954, while standing on the wing tip of her Amazon plane (see section C 4, the robot plane), Wonder Woman catches a falling meteor in her bare hands (WW No. 67/3: "The Runaway Meteor!"). By "exerting indescribable force on [a] steel girder," she "melts it into molten metal" with her bare hands (WW No. 67/2: "Portraits of Peril!").

In August 1954 Wonder Woman changes from Diana Prince to Wonder Woman in midair while leaping from the ground to her hovering Amazon plane (WW No. 68/3: "T.N.T. Target!").

In April 1955 Wonder Woman lassoes an entire moon — a duplicate of Earth's — and removes it from Earth's orbit by towing it far into space behind her Amazon plane (WW No. 73/3: "The Mystery of the Missing Moon!").

In October 1955 Wonder Woman vibrates her body with such incredible speed that she passes into an alien dimension (WW No. 77/2: "The Earth Is a Time Bomb!").

In January 1958 Wonder Woman uses puffs of superhuman breath to cut a slit trench in the ground to shield STEVE TREVOR from the effects of an H-bomb blast. She herself absorbs the full impact of the explosion and suffers no harm (WW No. 95/1: "Wonder Woman — The World's Most Dangerous Human!").

In April 1959 Wonder Woman uses "mental telepathy" to endow a cave boy of TITAN with detailed knowledge of Earth's civilization as a means of facilitating the evolution of man on Titan (WW No. 105/2: "Eagle of Space!").

In August 1959 Wonder Woman uses her fingernail to cut a hole in a steel vault, and simulates the power of flight by riding the air currents like a human glider (WW No. 108/1: "Wanted--Wonder Woman").

In May 1964 Wonder Woman creates such extreme friction by rubbing her hands against the outer hull of a submerged submarine that she is able to mend cracks in the hull without the aid of a welding torch (WW No. 146: "War of the Underwater Giants!").

In August 1964 Wonder Woman leaps through a plate glass window with such "eye-blurring speed" that the pane of glass does not shatter (WW No. 148: "The Olympics of the Doomed").

In July 1965 Wonder Woman lassoes a lightning bolt with her magic lasso, runs across the surface of the ocean at superhuman speed, and "runs" through the air by utilizing air currents to keep her aloft and upright. Wonder Woman can remain underwater almost indefinitely, asserts the text, because behind each ear, "... invisible to the human eye--is the extra layer of gills-skin grafted onto her by Amazon scientists which enables [her] to extract oxygen out of water ... and breathe like a fish!" (WW No. 155: "I Married a Monster!").

In November 1965 Wonder Woman uses a puff of superhuman breath to right a fleet of Amazon aircraft plummeting toward the sea (WW No. 158/1: "The Fury of Egg Fu!").

In May 1967 Wonder Woman extinguishes a burning building by uprooting it from its foundation and hurling it into outer space (WW No. 170/1: "The Haunted Amazon!").

Despite her stunning array of Amazon powers, however, Wonder Woman is by no means completely invulnerable:

In Fall 1944 DUKE MEPHISTO SATURNO knocks Wonder Woman unconscious with "a powerful Saturnic sleeping drug" (WW No. 10/3: "Wonder Woman's Boots!").

In November 1944 SONTAG HENYA and her cohorts "clasp electric wires to her bracelets. A para-

Queen Hippolyte, Wonder Woman, and Irene, a reformed Transformation Island prisoner, 1948

lyzing current suddenly surges through **Wonder Woman's** body and the Amazon girl stands rigid and helpless" (Sen No. 35: "Girls Under the Sea").

In September–October 1946 Meanug tribesmen take Wonder Woman prisoner in darkest Africa by subjecting her to a "potent African vapor drug" developed for use in voodoo ceremonies (WW No. 19/2: "The Witchdoctor's Cauldron").

In November–December 1947 Wonder Woman notes that "even an Amazon can't fall eight stories on her **head** without suffering some ill effects!" (WW No. 26/2: "The Mistress of the Beasts").

In April–May 1948 Wonder Woman becomes completely exhausted "after 72 hours of sleepless work," indicating that even an Amazon requires sleep (CC No. 26: "Deception's Daughter").

In May 1948 a criminal knocks Wonder Woman unconscious by clamping a "chloroform soaked handkerchief" over her mouth and nose (Sen No. 77: "Tress's Terrible Mistake!").

A weakness on which criminals often capitalize is that Wonder Woman can be knocked unconscious by a blow to the base of her skull. "Remember, boys," snarls a gangster in May 1946, "bash her good on the base of the skull. That's a vulnerable spot even on Wonder Woman!" (Sen No. 53: "Case of the Valiant Dog"; and others).

Wonder Woman is felled by a blow to the skull, 1948

Perhaps Wonder Woman's greatest vulnerability lies in the comparative frailty of her friends and associates — such as Steve Trevor, ETTA CANDY, and the HOLLIDAY GIRLS — which forces her to surrender to her adversaries on innumerable occasions in order to protect them from harm.

In November–December 1968 Wonder Woman is compelled to relinquish her superhuman powers and Amazon equipment so that she may re-

Wonder Woman relinquishes her Amazon powers and equipment in the Amazon rite of renunciation, 1968

main behind in the world of men while her mother and her sister Amazons journey to another dimension "to rest and renew [their] powers!" After undergoing "the awesome Amazon rite of renunciation" and departing PARADISE ISLAND, Wonder Woman becomes an ordinary girl, with ordinary abilities (WW No. 179: "Wonder Woman's Last Battle!"). (*See* DOCTOR CYBER.)

For several years, under the name Diana Prince, Wonder Woman battles crime in civilian clothing, as an ordinary woman, aided by a newly acquired mastery of the martial arts and a blind Oriental mentor named I Ching. By the mid-1970s, however, Wonder Woman has regained her Amazon powers and resumed her war against evil in her traditional costume and with much of her traditional equipment.

2. The bracelets of submission. Centuries ago, when HERCULES and his army overran AMAZONIA and enslaved the AMAZONS, shackling them in heavy chains as reminders of their servitude, the Amazons prayed to the goddess APHRODITE for deliverance. The goddess answered their prayers, and agreed to allow them to triumph over their tormentors and regain their freedom, but first she

*Wonder Woman in action against
the Boss Brekel gang, 1946*

imposed a stern condition: "You may break your chains," intoned Aphrodite, "but you must wear these wrist bands always to teach you the folly of submitting to men's domination!" (WW No. 1/1, Sum '42). (*See also* AMAZONS [section A, History].)

From that day forward, every Amazon maiden has worn a pair of heavy metal slave bracelets as a symbol of her people's deliverance from male domination and of her loving submission to the goddess Aphrodite. The bracelets signify their wearers' willingness to bind over their Amazon strength and abilities to the service of creative ends: an Amazon without her bracelets of submission is an id unchecked by an ego. To remove them, therefore, is to violate a deeply ingrained Amazon taboo, for it is to show contempt for Aphrodite and rejection of the Amazon code (*see* AMAZONS [section C, the Amazon Code]).

"In removing my bracelets," intones the goddess in Fall 1945, after the Amazon DALMA has prompted a group of her companions to remove their bracelets and stage an insurrection on PARADISE ISLAND, "you have committed the terrible wrong of allowing dominance to overpower loving submission!" (CC No. 12: "Rebellion on Paradise Island!").

"Our bracelets **bind** our strength to the service of love and beauty," remarks Wonder Woman in Fall 1943, "and thus protect us from evil!" (WW No. 6/3: "The Conquest of Paradise").

"When I was 15," explains Wonder Woman in February 1949, "my bracelets of submission were given to me by a sister Amazon at Aphrodite's altar. Aphrodite, goddess of love and beauty, is the patroness of all Amazons. No one but an Amazon has bracelets like these!"

"Lest you forget," she adds later, "these bracelets signify force bound to **service** for humanity!" (Sen No. 86: "The Secret of the Amazing Bracelets!").

Although Sensation Comics No. 54 asserts that Wonder Woman's bracelets are made of "Amazon steel" (Jun '46: "The Treachery of Fiendo"), and Wonder Woman No. 43/1 states that they are "made of the strongest metal known," without naming any particular metal (Sep/Oct '50: "The Amazing Spy Ring Mystery"), students of the chronicles tend to accept the evidence of Wonder Woman No. 52/1 — and the numerous texts which corroborate it — that the bracelets are fashioned from "amazonium--the hardest metal known!" (Mar/Apr '52: "Her Majesty — Queen Wonder Woman!"; and others).

In the Amazon game of "bullets and bracelets," Amazon contestants shoot at one another with pistols and attempt to deflect the bullets with their bracelets (*see* AMAZONS [section E 1, Sports]). Among the Amazons, Wonder Woman is the undisputed champion of this sport. Indeed, it is her mastery of it that has enabled her to deflect the thousands of bullets fired at her by the underworld throughout the course of her career, even those fired at her by machine guns and automatic rifles.

The bracelets of submission can be used to deflect not only bullets, but missiles of all kinds, including knives, spears, hatchets, bombs, torpedoes, and even bolts of lightning. It is the durable nature of AMAZONIUM that enables Wonder Woman to deflect high-velocity missiles without shattering her bracelets, but it is her lightning-fast reflexes and phenomenal skill that enable her to move the bracelets into position to parry each new oncoming missile.

"Wearing the Amazon bracelets alone is not the secret!" thinks Wonder Woman anxiously in February 1949, after "avid millionaire collector" C. O. LECTOR has forcibly removed her bracelets with the intention of using them to duplicate Wonder Woman's bullets and bracelets trick. "Without acquiring thru [sic] training and discipline the Amazon agility to catch the bullets on the bracelets--he'll be killed!" (Sen No. 86: "The Secret of the Amazing Bracelets!").

There is an elaborate mythology associated with the bracelets of submission, and this mythology is often treated inconsistently by the chroniclers. It is a basic tenet of Aphrodite's law (*see* AMAZONS [section B, Aphrodite's Law]), for example, that "when an Amazon girl permits a **man** to chain her bracelets of submission together she becomes weak as other women in a man-ruled world!" (WW No. 2/4, Fall '42). If a *woman* chains Wonder Woman's bracelets together, however, Wonder Woman's strength remains completely unaffected (Sen No. 10, Oct '42).

Wonder Woman

Wonder Woman

"Daughter, if any man weld chains on your bracelets," QUEEN HIPPOLYTE warns Wonder Woman in April 1942, "you will become as weak as we Amazons were when we surrendered to Hercules and his Greeks."

Indeed, soon afterward, for the first time in the chronicles, Wonder Woman loses her Amazon strength when BARONESS PAULA VON GUNTHER'S henchmen weld shackles to her Amazon bracelets. Put before a Nazi firing squad, Wonder Woman leaps into the path of the oncoming bullets and allows them to shatter the chain connecting her bracelets, thereby regaining her Amazon powers.

"These bracelets," sighs Wonder Woman, "—they're an Amazon's greatest strength and weakness! What a fool I was to let a man weld chains upon them!" (Sen No. 4).

In Fall 1942, after having been taken captive by the wily COUNT CRAFTI, Wonder Woman loses her Amazon strength when chains are welded to her bracelets by servants of the war god MARS. Summoned to the scene by an urgent mental radio message from Wonder Woman (*see* section C 7, the mental radio), ETTA CANDY frees Wonder Woman — and restores her Amazon strength — by giving her a vial of acid with which to burn through her shackles.

"Why can't you break those chains yourself, **Wonder Woman!**" asks Etta.

"Why — er — because I'm being punished for letting a handsome man deceive me —" replies Wonder Woman embarrassedly (WW No. 2/4).

The chronicles are inconsistent regarding the extent to which Wonder Woman is weakened when a man welds chains to her Amazon bracelets. In the early texts, the attaching of chains to Wonder Woman's bracelets renders her as weak as the average woman, while in later texts it reduces her strength appreciably, but not nearly to the level of an ordinary person's. In February 1947, for example, Wonder Woman's strength remains "tremendous despite her chained bracelets" (Sen No. 62: "The Mysterious Prisoners of Anglonia"), and in May–June 1948, after criminals have chained her bracelets together, she retains sufficient strength to snap the heavy ropes with which the villains have bound her feet (WW No. 29/3: "The Treasure Hunt").

Inconsistency also surrounds the question of who must sever the chains linking Wonder Woman's bracelets before her Amazon strength can be restored to her. In the early texts, the bracelets, once chained together, need only to be severed in order for Wonder Woman to regain her strength (WW No. 2/4, Fall '42; and others), but later texts assert that Wonder Woman can regain her strength only if the chains linking her bracelets are severed by a man, or at least a male animal. In a text dated May–June 1951, for example, when her bracelets are chained together by the villain PROTO and she is fired upon by a group of robot archers, Wonder Woman valiantly attempts to free herself by allowing one of their arrows to strike the chain linking her bracelets. The stratagem fails, however, because the archers are only machines, and not real men. Inconsistently, however, Wonder Woman retains superhuman speed, strength, and agility even while her bracelets are welded together (Sen No. 103: "100 Year Duel!").

In May–June 1952 Wonder Woman's bracelets are again chained together, this time by the villainous CRIME MASTER OF TIME. "Now, by Aphrodite's law," muses Wonder Woman, "these bracelets must remain fastened unless a **male** separates them!"

Hurled into the ocean, she attempts to free herself by baiting a swordfish into hacking at the chain connecting her bracelets. When the chain fails to break despite the furious thrusts of the swordfish's beak, Wonder Woman concludes that "The swordfish must be a female! And according to Aphrodite's law, I can only be freed by a male . . ." (WW No. 53/1: "The Crime Master of Time!").

The question of what happens when an Amazon's bracelets are chained together is given a curious twist in Sensation Comics No. 29. In this text, Wonder Woman's friend MALA loses her Amazon strength when one of MIMI MENDEZ's henchmen welds chains to her bracelets, and, soon afterward, Wonder Woman is forced to surrender to the villains in order to prevent them from harming Mala. When the criminals attach chains to Wonder Woman's bracelets — without actually welding them — and then weld a chain into place linking Wonder Woman's right-hand bracelet with Mala's left-hand bracelet, Wonder Woman finds that she can shatter the chain connecting her own two bracelets with a mere flick of her wrists, but that she cannot break the chain linking her to Mala because Mala's chains were welded by a man.

"I never knew chains welded by men between two **different** girls' bracelets would be unbreakable!" muses Wonder Woman (May '44: "Adventure of the Escaped Prisoner").

In July 1943 Wonder Woman's bracelets are removed from her wrists by the villainess MAVIS, who believes, erroneously, that by removing Wonder Woman's bracelets she can deprive her of her vaunted Amazon strength.

"Ha ha!" gloats Mavis, as she cuts Wonder

Woman's metal bracelets off her wrists. "You're only a weak little captive now, Amazon girl!"

"I'm not **weak**," thinks Wonder Woman desperately, "— I'm **too strong**. The bracelets bound my strength to good purposes — now I'm completely uncontrolled! I'm free to **destroy** like a **man**!"

Indeed, without her Amazon bracelets to bind her to Aphrodite's law, Wonder Woman literally "goes berserk," smashing log cabins into kindling wood and committing other acts of violence in a mad "orgy of unleashed power," until finally Baroness Paula von Gunther brings her back to her senses by lassoing her with the magic lasso (*see* section C 3, the magic lasso) and welding her bracelets back onto her wrists "tighter than ever" (Sen No. 19: "The Unbound Amazon").

In Winter 1945 PALTRO DEBUM kidnaps Wonder Woman, intending to reap huge profits by entering her in athletic contests under a fictitious name. Believing that Wonder Woman's Amazon bracelets will betray her true identity, Debum removes them with catastrophic results:

"Great Hera!" thinks Wonder Woman. "Without Aphrodite's bracelets my Amazon strength is completely uncontrollable!"

Loosed once again on a violent rampage, Wonder Woman does manage to use her unbound strength for the constructive purpose of rescuing the HOLLIDAY GIRLS from Debum and his henchmen, but she is only prevented from actually killing one of the criminals — something she would ordinarily never do — by the quick-thinking Etta Candy, who brings her under control again by binding her with the magic lasso (CC No. 13: "The Underwater Follies").

When Wonder Woman is taken captive by the villain MANLIUS in December 1946–January 1947, one of his cohorts attempts to weld chains to Wonder Woman's bracelets, only to have one of the bracelets accidentally break and fall off Wonder Woman's wrist.

"Great Zeus," thinks Wonder Woman alarmedly, "--the electric welder weakened my bracelet--it's **broken**! Oh-hh! This frees me from Aphrodite's law. I can feel the mad desire to **destroy**!"

"Something's happened to **Wonder Woman**. She's gone berserk!" cries Steve Trevor, as Wonder Woman embarks on a violent rampage.

"She's lost a bracelet," exclaims Etta Candy, "--we gotta tie her with the [magic] lasso!"

Moments later, as Etta binds Wonder Woman with the magic lasso, she is mildly apologetic for having to tie up her friend.

"You **must**," replies Wonder Woman gratefully, "--I won't be sane again till Aphrodite's bracelet is welded on once more" (CC No. 18: "The Menace of the Rebel Manlings").

In February 1949 C. O. LECTOR and his henchmen remove both of Wonder Woman's bracelets, but Wonder Woman remains unaffected. "Fortunately for him," she muses, "I've worn those bracelets so long that even though they are removed their imprint still binds me to Aphrodite's law!" (Sen No. 86: "The Secret of the Amazing Bracelets!").

Since that time, extending through the mid-1970s, Wonder Woman has suffered no ill effects whatever from having her Amazon bracelets removed, with the exception of a fifteen-month period — from February 1966 (WW No. 160/1: "The Amazon of Terror!") through April 1967 (WW No. 169/1: "Wonder Woman Battles the Crimson Centipede!") — during which the chroniclers, in an attempt to revive many aspects of the traditional Wonder Woman mythology they had allowed to lapse, briefly reverted to the practice of having Wonder Woman go berserk when stripped of her bracelets.

By July–August 1953 Wonder Woman has installed a "miniature omni-wave set" in one of her bracelets to enable her to receive messages and tune in on broadcasts even when she is away from the larger omni-wave receiver in her Amazon plane (see section C 4, the robot plane) (WW No. 60/1: "The War That Never Happened!"). This new device is referred to as a "wrist omni-wave receiver" in Wonder Woman No. 125 (Oct '61: "Wonder Woman--Battle Prize!").

By August 1958 Wonder Woman has installed a video-communications apparatus in her bracelet which Queen Hippolyte uses to summon her to Paradise Island (WW No. 100/1: "The Forest of Giants!" pts. 1–2 — "The Challenge of Dimension X!"; "The Forest of Giants!").

In November–December 1968 Wonder Woman is compelled to relinquish her Amazon bracelets — along with her other Amazon equipment — when she undergoes the Amazon rite of renunciation on Paradise Island (WW No. 179: "Wonder Woman's Last Battle!"). (See DOCTOR CYBER.) Her bracelets have been restored to her, however, by the mid-1970s.

3. *The magic lasso.* In June 1942, five months after she first departs PARADISE ISLAND to battle crime and injustice in the United States, Wonder Woman

Standing on the wing of her robot plane, Wonder Woman lassoes six Red Chinese aircraft, 1965

is summoned to Paradise Island to receive a special gift from her mother, QUEEN HIPPOLYTE: a "magic lasso," fashioned from "fine chain links" from the queen's magic girdle (*see* AMAZONS [section F 1, the magic girdle]) and prepared at the behest of APHRODITE and ATHENA in recognition of Wonder Woman's "splendid work in the world of men." The magic lasso, which Wonder Woman carries at her waist from this time forward, is "flexible as rope, but strong enough to hold Hercules!"

All night long, after having received the magic lasso from her mother, Wonder Woman prays to the goddesses for guidance. Finally, as dawn breaks, the voices of Aphrodite and Athena speak out to her: "Having proved thyself bound by love and wisdom," intone the goddesses, "we give thee power to control others! Whomsoever thy magic lasso binds must obey thee!" (Sen No. 6).

In the years that follow, the magic lasso becomes one of Wonder Woman's principal weapons against the forces of crime and injustice. The exact substance of which it is made is not entirely clear: Sensation Comics No. 6 says only that it is made from "fine chain links" from Hippolyte's magic girdle (Jun '42), while Sensation Comics No. 10 refers to the lasso's "golden links" (Oct '42) and Wonder Woman No. 6/3 describes it as made of a "very special metal" (Fall '43: "The Conquest of Paradise"). According to QUEEN DESIRA of VENUS, the magic lasso is made from "Aphrodite's magnetized gold," the same substance from which the magic Venus girdles (*see* AMAZONS [section F 3, the magic Venus girdles]) are made (WW No. 12/2, Spr '45: "The Ordeal of Fire").

From November 1954 (WW No. 70/1: "The Volcano Maker!") onward, many texts assert that the magic lasso is fashioned from AMAZONIUM, "the hardest metal known," but these assertions are undoubtedly erroneous and may safely be ascribed to chroniclers' error.

The magic lasso is absolutely unbreakable, even by Wonder Woman. Once bound with the lasso, Wonder Woman may endeavor to untie it and thereby regain her freedom, but if the knots are inaccessible — as, say, behind her back — she is powerless to escape by breaking the lasso. Being bound with the magic lasso by no means deprives Wonder Woman of her incredible Amazon strength, however. If a villain ties Wonder Woman to a tree with it, for example, Wonder Woman may be unable to untie the lasso, but still be perfectly capable of uprooting the entire tree and slipping free of the loosened coils.

Perhaps the most intriguing quality of the magic lasso is its power to compel the obedience of oth-

Wonder Woman bound with the magic lasso

Bound by the magic lasso, the villainous Prince Pagli is compelled to obey Wonder Woman's commands, 1945

ers. Anyone bound with the magic lasso must obey any command given him by the person holding the free end. Wonder Woman frequently uses the lasso's compelling power to extract confessions from criminals or to force them to provide her with information they would not otherwise volunteer. The magic lasso can even be used to compel the obedience of wild animals (WW No. 29/2, May/Jun '48: "Tale of the Tigers").

The compelling power of the magic lasso is a two-edged sword, however. If a villain binds Wonder Woman with the magic lasso, Wonder Woman becomes his virtual slave, compelled to obey his every command until something, or someone, forces him to release his hold on the lasso's free end. If a villain were to bind Wonder Woman with the magic lasso and command her to rob a bank for him, for example, Wonder Woman would be powerless to disobey the command. She would remain perfectly capable, however, of using her ingenuity to contrive some means of forcing her captor to drop his end of the magic lasso and thereby relinquish his compelling hold over her. If she is encircled by only a single loop of the lasso, she can simply pull it over her head and escape. If she is more elaborately bound, however, she may have to wait until a friend or ally — such as STEVE TREVOR or ETTA CANDY — comes to her rescue.

Under the compelling influence of her own magic lasso, Wonder Woman is interrogated by gangster Lon Logox, 1949

According to a number of texts, the magic lasso is "charged with electricity," enabling Wonder Woman to use it as a power source for electrical machinery (Sen No. 44, Aug '45: "Chains and Bracelets"; and others), and according to Wonder Woman No. 50/2 it is characterized by "unlimited elasticity" (Nov/Dec '51: "The Secret Story of

Wonder Woman's Lasso!"), enabling Wonder Woman to use it to lasso entire planetoids and other heavenly bodies (WW No. 73/3, Apr '55: "The Mystery of the Missing Moon!"; and others). Wonder Woman No. 135 asserts that the magic lasso responds to the sound of Wonder Woman's voice and is hence capable of obeying her verbal commands (Jan '63: "Attack of the Human Iceberg!"), but this is the only text in which such an assertion appears.

From the mid-1950s onward, Wonder Woman makes scant use of the compelling powers of the magic lasso, using it instead to perform a series of new, incredible feats, such as forming intricate designs and knots with it by twirling it through the air at super-speed, or weaving it into a golden shield to protect herself from bullets and other missiles. In July 1965 she even uses it to lasso a lightning bolt (WW No. 155: "I Married a Monster!").

Since the introduction of the magic lasso in June 1942 (Sen No. 6), several texts have misstated the facts surrounding its origin. Wonder Woman No. 1/1, for example, asserts that Wonder Woman received the magic lasso from Queen Hippolyte at the same time she received her Wonder Woman costume — i.e., prior to departing Paradise Island for America, as opposed to during a return visit five months later (Sum '42) — and Wonder Woman No. 50/2 asserts that Wonder Woman won the right to have a lasso that was "unbreakable, endlessly elastic, and truth-compelling" by performing two Herculean labors for the goddess Aphrodite (WW No. 50/2, Nov/Dec '51: "The Secret Story of Wonder Woman's Lasso!").

In November–December 1968 Wonder Woman is compelled to relinquish her magic lasso — along with her other Amazon equipment — when she undergoes the Amazon rite of renunciation on Paradise Island (WW No. 179: "Wonder Woman's Last Battle!"). (See DOCTOR CYBER). Her magic lasso has been restored to her, however, by the mid-1970s.

4. The robot plane. When Wonder Woman first departs PARADISE ISLAND for America in January 1942, she makes the journey in her Amazon plane, an aircraft destined to become one of her principal weapons against the forces of crime and injustice. The unique plane — propeller-driven in the early years of the chronicles, jet-propelled from the mid-1950s onward — is silent and invisible (Sen No. 1). Later texts describe it as indestructible (Sen No. 6, Jun '42) and vibrationless (WW No. 3/1, Feb/Mar '43). Sensation Comics No. 45 describes it as made of a substance called "amazsilikon" (Sep '45: "In the Enemy's Hands"), but Wonder Woman

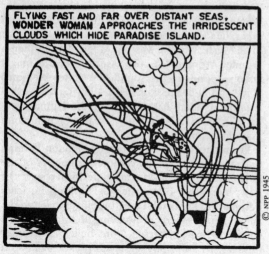

The robot plane, 1945

No. 125 asserts that it is "fashioned out of elastic amazonium, hardest substance known . . ." (Oct '61: "Wonder Woman--Battle Prize!"). (*See also* AMAZONIUM.)

In addition to being capable of ordinary flight, the Amazon plane can travel underwater (CC No. 26, Apr/May '48: "Deception's Daughter"; and others), streak through interstellar space (WW No. 42/2, Jul/Aug '50: "The Mystery of the Missing Monday!"; and others), and even transform itself into an "earth-borer" and burrow into the depths of the earth (WW No. 57/1, Jan/Feb '53: "The Man Who Shook the Earth!"; and others).

The maximum flying speed of the Amazon plane is not possible to determine with certainty: in the texts of the 1940s, it is variously reported as 2,000 miles per hour (Sen No. 6, Jun '42; and others); 2,500 miles per hour (CC No. 4, Fall '43: "The Purloined Pressure Coordinator"); 3,000 miles per hour (WW No. 13/2, Sum '45: "The Mystery Maid"; and others); "faster than 3000 miles an hour" (Sen No. 58, Oct '46: "The Bog Trap"); 3,000 miles per minute (WW No. 21/3, Jan/Feb '47: "Ruler of the Atom World"; and others); and 3,000 miles per second (WW No. 27/1, Jan/Feb '48: "The Mystical Power of Idea-Forms!"; and others).

The later texts are considerably more vague concerning the maximum speed of the Amazon plane: they describe it as "incredibly fleet" (WW No. 49/1, Sep/Oct '51: "Return of the Phantom Empire"); capable of speeds "far exceeding that of light" (WW No. 58/2, Mar/Apr '53: "The Man Who Stole the Sun!"); moving with "thought-staggering speed" (WW No. 85/1, Oct '56: "The Sword in the Sky!"); and "capable of immeasurable speeds" (WW No. 129, Apr '62: "The Return of Multiple Man!"). In November–December 1953 the plane

travels so swiftly that it passes into an alien dimension (WW No. 62/2: "Lamp of the Leprechauns!").

Generally, one can say that, in keeping with the steady expansion of Wonder Woman's physical powers over the years (*see* section C 1, the benefits of Amazon training), the speed of the Amazon plane also increases with the passage of time. In July–August 1950, for example, the Amazon plane makes a journey to the planet VENUS — a distance of at least twenty-five million miles — in what cannot possibly be more than a few hours' time (WW No. 42/2: "The Mystery of the Missing Monday!").

When Wonder Woman first arrives in the United States in January 1942, she hides her plane in a "deserted barn" in "an abandoned field on the outskirts of Washington" (Sen No. 1). The plane is still being housed in the old barn as late as July–August 1947 (WW No. 24/2: "The Challenge of the Mask"), but no specific mention of the barn is made in the chronicles after that date.

Wonder Woman and her robot plane near the deserted barn which serves as its hangar, 1942

In December 1943 Wonder Woman visits the temple of APHRODITE on Paradise Island and prays to the goddess for guidance in coping with "the grave problem of warfare."

All night the princess lies before Aphrodite's throne, her brain being charged like a living battery with magnetic power flowing from the goddess' feet.

Aphrodite finally answers Wonder Woman's prayers by providing her with "an idea for controlling [her] airplane by mental radio" (*see* section C 7, the mental radio). And soon afterward,

The robot plane, 1942

The robot plane, 1961

acting on the instructions that Wonder Woman has received from Aphrodite, BARONESS PAULA VON GUNTHER and MALA set to work building the necessary mental control apparatus and installing it in Wonder Woman's Amazon plane. From this time forward, Wonder Woman is able to control the operation of her plane by telepathy alone, whether she is inside the plane, below it on the ground, or even thousands of miles away from it (Sen No. 24: "Adventure of the Pilotless Plane").

In April 1944 Wonder Woman refers to her Amazon plane as her "robot plane" for the first time in the chronicles (Sen No. 28: "The Malice of the Green Imps"), and it is as the robot plane that the aircraft becomes most widely known.

In March–April 1951, Wonder Woman No. 46/3 asserts that the robot plane responds to the peculiar vibrations of Wonder Woman's voice, rather than to her unspoken mental commands ("Wonder Woman's Twin!"), and the plane remains voice-responsive from this time onward.

By September–October 1952 Wonder Woman has installed an "Amazon omni-wave transmitter" in her robot plane which enables her to receive distress calls on every existing wavelength (WW No. 55/2: "The Chessmen of Doom!").

By August 1954 Wonder Woman has installed an "omniwave radar receiver" in her robot plane capable of giving her advance warning "of the approach of any object" (WW No. 68/1: "Landing of the Flying Saucers!").

By February 1956 the chroniclers have ceased depicting the robot plane as propeller-driven (WW No. 80/3: "SOS – Saturn!"), and by August 1958 have begun depicting the craft as a sleek jet fighter

(WW No. 100/1: "The Forest of Giants!" pts. 1–2 – "The Challenge of Dimension X!"; "The Forest of Giants!").

Since the initial appearance of Wonder Woman's Amazon plane in January 1942 (Sen No. 1), several texts have appeared offering contradictory and unreliable accounts of its history and origin:

Wonder Woman No. 48/3 asserts that Wonder Woman received the robot plane – with its voice-control apparatus already installed – as a gift from QUEEN HIPPOLYTE prior to departing Paradise Island for America at the onset of her career (Jul/ Aug '51: "The Theft of the Robot Plane").

Wonder Woman No. 80/2 asserts that Wonder Woman had to "win" the right to her robot plane by performing a series of Herculean labors which involved locating individual sections of the plane in various inaccessible hiding places and then assembling them by hand (Feb '56: "The Origin of the Amazon Plane!").

And Wonder Woman No. 128/1 claims that the robot plane is actually PEGASUS, the winged horse of classical mythology, in magically altered form (Feb '62: "Origin of the Amazing Robot Plane!").

All these texts contradict the history of the robot plane built up in the chronicles over nearly a decade and may safely be dismissed as inaccurate.

In November–December 1968 Wonder Woman is compelled to relinquish her robot plane – along with her other Amazon equipment – when she undergoes the Amazon rite of renunciation on Paradise Island (WW No. 179: "Wonder Woman's Last Battle!"). (*See* DOCTOR CYBER.)

5. *The tiara.* Perched atop Wonder Woman's head is a golden tiara decorated with a single red star. Early texts call it a "circlet" (Sen No. 15, Mar '43) or a "headband" (Sen No. 42, Jun '45: "Peril on

Paradise Island"), but later texts are unanimous in terming it a tiara. The substance of which the tiara is made is not disclosed until May–June 1952, when it is asserted that the tiara is made of AMAZONIUM, "the hardest metal known" (WW No. 53/3: "The Secret Treasure at Rainbow's End!"; and others).

The function of Wonder Woman's tiara is exclusively ornamental until the mid-1950s, when it begins to be used as a crime-fighting tool. The texts are extremely inconsistent, however, regarding the tiara's origin, significance, and the uses to which it may be put.

Wonder Woman No. 66/2, for example, describes it as a "linguagraph tiara" which enables Wonder Woman "to understand any language past, present, or future — anywhere," and asserts that Wonder Woman had to perform a Herculean labor in order to win the right to wear it (May '54: "The Talking Tiara!") — all this despite the fact that numerous earlier texts ascribe Wonder Woman's linguistic skill to her early training on PARADISE ISLAND (AS No. 8, Dec/Jan '41–'42: "Introducing Wonder Woman"; and others). (See section C 1, the benefits of Amazon training.)

Wonder Woman No. 78/2 describes it as a "boomerang tiara," and shows Wonder Woman using it as a boomerang in a battle with criminals (Nov '55: "Zero Hour for an Amazon!"; and others).

Wonder Woman No. 75/1 describes the tiara as "the symbol of [her] rank as princess" of the AMAZONS (Jul '55: "The Winning of Wonder Woman's Tiara!"), while Wonder Woman No. 95/2 asserts that, although Wonder Woman has chosen to wear it as a tiara, it is actually a necklace presented to her by an extraterrestrial scientist in gratitude for her having rescued the Galaxy from the depredations of the PHENEGS (Jan '58: "The Secret of Wonder Woman's Tiara!"). In January 1958 Wonder Woman uses her tiara as a digging tool to cut through solid rock (WW No. 95/3: "The Ghost Town Museum!").

In November–December 1968 Wonder Woman is compelled to relinquish her tiara — along with her other Amazon equipment — when she undergoes the Amazon rite of renunciation on Paradise Island (WW No. 179: "Wonder Woman's Last Battle!"). (See DOCTOR CYBER.) Her tiara has been restored to her, however, by the mid-1970s.

6. *The earrings.* Even before she wins the Amazon tournament that entitles her to leave PARADISE ISLAND for America to fight crime as Wonder Woman, Princess Diana wears the pair of bright red button earrings (AS No. 8, Dec/Jan '41–'42: "Introducing Wonder Woman") that she continues to wear as part of her Wonder Woman costume in

the decades following. During Wonder Woman's first visit to the planet VENUS in October–November 1942, QUEEN DESIRA touches the earrings with her lips, thereby bestowing upon Wonder Woman "the gift of magnetic hearing" and making it possible for Desira to send "thought messages" to Wonder Woman across millions of miles of interstellar space (AS No. 13: "Shanghaied into Space!").

"**Wonder Woman's** earrings give the power of **magnetic hearing!**" muses Diana Prince, the girl who is secretly Wonder Woman, in Spring 1945. "These earrings, touched by Queen Desira's lips, are supersensitive radio receivers — they pick up Desira's thought waves across . . . interstellar space!" (WW No. 12/1).

Eight years later, however, in November–December 1953, Wonder Woman No. 62/3 asserts that the earrings are actually serviceable "oxygen cylinders" fashioned by Wonder Woman during a past encounter with the DUKE OF DECEPTION. According to this text, Deception had locked her inside an airless cylinder and then set her adrift to suffocate in interstellar space. To escape from Deception's deathtrap, Wonder Woman broke two metal pieces off her tiara (*see* section C 5, the tiara), fashioned them into earrings, and then squeezed some oxygen from the ferric oxide in one of her Amazon bracelets (*see* section C 2, the bracelets of submission) and diverted it into "the tiny hole [she] had left in each earring," thereby transforming the earrings into miniature oxygen cylinders. ". . . [I]n a few moments," explains Wonder Woman, "the oxygen in the earrings revived me to such an extent that I was able to break loose from my 'space tomb'---"

Thus freed from Deception's deathtrap, Wonder Woman soon defeated the villain and turned back an attempted invasion of Paradise Island by his Martian space fleet.

"My earrings now contain self-renewing oxygen," explains Wonder Woman, recalling the incident in November–December 1953, "which enables me to exist indefinitely in places where there is no oxygen," such as underwater or in outer space ("The Secret of the Amazon Earrings!").

Despite this explanation, however, the earrings are never used as oxygen cylinders in any other text. In August 1956, in fact, Wonder Woman is forced to surface for air while swimming underwater, in spite of the fact that she is wearing the earrings (WW No. 84/1: "The Secret Wonder Woman!").

In November–December 1968, when Wonder Woman undergoes the Amazon rite of renunciation on Paradise Island, she is presumably compelled to relinquish her earrings along with her other Amazon equipment, but no specific mention of the earrings is made in the text (WW No. 179: "Wonder Woman's Last Battle!"). (*See* DOCTOR CYBER.)

7. *The mental radio.* Of all the wonders wrought by Amazon science (*see* AMAZONS [section G, Amazon science]), one of the most ingenious is undoubtedly the mental radio, a highly sophisticated video-communications apparatus which "picks up brain waves" (WW No. 1/4, Sum '42) from the atmosphere and transforms them into coherent audio-visual signals. The inventor of the mental radio may have been Wonder Woman herself (CC No. 2, Spr '43: "Wanted by Hitler, Dead or Alive"), but it is impossible to establish this with any real certainty.

Held captive by criminals, Wonder Woman sends a mental radio message to Steve Trevor, 1948

Wonder Woman calls Mala on the mental radio, 1944

Sending a mental radio message requires no apparatus whatever, but to receive a mental radio message one must be equipped with a mental radio receiver — an electronic device, superficially resembling a stock market ticker — which is linked to a special headband by means of a short cable. To transmit his message, the sender merely concentrates on the intended recipient and "recites" the message mentally to himself. In the form of brain waves, the mental message flashes across space until it is intercepted by the recipient's mental radio receiver. As the message reaches the receiver, a bell on the receiver rings, informing its owner that someone is attempting to contact him mentally. As soon as the recipient dons the special headband, the image of the sender appears on the receiver's viewplate, and the thoughts of the sender are communicated to the recipient through the headband. Anyone standing near the receiver is able to view the sender's image on the viewplate and mentally "hear" the incoming message even if he or she is not wearing a headband.

Throughout the chronicles, those sending mental radio messages are usually depicted pressing forefinger to forehead as they mentally broadcast the message, but the clear evidence of the texts is that the forefinger gesture is not really necessary to the sending of the message (Sen No. 81, Sep '48: "When Treachery Wore a Green Shirt!").

Mental radio messages may be sent from room to room, from continent to continent, or even across millions of miles of interstellar space. They may even be transmitted across the time barrier, from one era to another. If the intended recipient of a mental radio message is away from his receiver when the bell rings, however, then the message — like a telephone call — will not be completed, and the sender will have to try to "call back" later.

The mental radio first appears in the chronicles in March 1942, when Wonder Woman "sends a mental radio call for help" to her friend ETTA CANDY at the HOLLIDAY COLLEGE FOR WOMEN. Etta Candy is the first of Wonder Woman's friends to be entrusted with a mental radio receiver of her own (Sen No. 3). And not long afterward, for Diana's Day, the Amazon counterpart of Christmas (*see* AMAZONS [section E 2, Festivals and holidays]), Wonder Woman presents STEVE TREVOR with a mental radio receiver also (WW No. 3/1, Feb/Mar '43).

In Spring 1943 Steve Trevor remarks that "There are only four mental radios in America": Wonder Woman's, Etta Candy's, Steve Trevor's, and the one belonging to Diana Prince, the girl who is secretly Wonder Woman (CC No. 2: "Wanted by Hitler, Dead or Alive"). There are of course additional mental radios on PARADISE ISLAND, where

WONDER WOMAN, WAITING ON THE ROOF, CATCHES ETTA'S CALL FOR HELP ON HER MENTAL RADIO AND LEAPS THROUGH THE SKYLIGHT.

© NPP 1945

Wonder Woman with mental radio receiver, 1945

they are an important means of communication. QUEEN HIPPOLYTE frequently uses hers to communicate with Wonder Woman in America.

In November 1943 Wonder Woman dispatches a mental radio message to Steve Trevor for the first time in the chronicles (Sen No. 23).

By August 1945 BARONESS PAULA VON GUNTHER — originally a villainess, but by this date Wonder Woman's close friend and ally — has been provided with a mental radio receiver also (Sen No. 44: "Chains and Bracelets").

In January 1948, for the first time in the chronicles, Wonder Woman transmits a mental radio message from one era to another (Sen No. 73: "The Witches' Trials").

By May 1956 the mental radio apparatus has undergone considerable modernization and is now being referred to as an "Amazon omni-wave set" (WW No. 82/3: "The Silent S O S!").

By April 1958 the mental radio has been largely superseded by other, technologically more elaborate, Amazon communications apparatus (WW No. 97: "The Runaway Time Express!" pts. 1–3 — "Stone Age Rodeo!"; "The Day Nature Ran Wild!"; "The Menace of Earth's Twin!"). (*See* section C 8, the other Amazon equipment.)

8. The other Amazon equipment. In addition to the equipment enumerated and described in the preceding sections, the chronicles occasionally make mention of other apparatus employed by Wonder Woman, all of them miraculous achievements of Amazon science (*see also* AMAZONS [section G, Amazon science]).

By September–October 1952 Wonder Woman has installed an "Amazon omni-wave transmitter" in her robot plane (*see* section C 4, the robot plane) which enables her to receive distress calls on every existing wavelength (WW No. 55/2: "The Chessmen of Doom!").

By August 1954 Wonder Woman has installed an "omniwave radar receiver" in her robot plane capable of giving her advance warning "of the approach of any object" (WW No. 68/1: "Landing of the Flying Saucers!").

In January 1957 an "Amazon video-scope" enables Diana Prince — the girl who is secretly Wonder Woman — to track STEVE TREVOR through the heavens as he makes a test flight in a new aircraft (WW No. 87/2: "Island of the Giants!").

In April 1958 Wonder Woman receives communications from her sister AMAZONS on a "secret uni-televisor," a video-communications apparatus that appears to have replaced the mental radio (*see* section C 7, the mental radio) (WW No. 97: "The Runaway Time Express!" pts. 1–3 — "Stone Age Rodeo!"; "The Day Nature Ran Wild!"; "The Menace of Earth's Twin!").

By August 1958 Wonder Woman has installed a tiny video-communications apparatus in one of her Amazon bracelets (*see* section C 2, the bracelets of submission) (WW No. 100/1: "The Forest of Giants!" pts. 1–2 — "The Challenge of Dimension X!"; "The Forest of Giants!").

By October 1958 Wonder Woman and Steve Trevor have equipped themselves with special rings containing tiny radio sets to enable them to communicate with one another over long distances (WW No. 101/2: "The Fun House of Time!").

In November–December 1968, when Wonder Woman undergoes the Amazon rite of renunciation on PARADISE ISLAND, no specific mention is made of any of this miscellaneous equipment, but Wonder Woman is presumably compelled to relinquish it along with her other Amazon equipment (WW No. 179: "Wonder Woman's Last Battle!"). (*See* DOCTOR CYBER.)

D. The Early Life (as Princess Diana). In ancient times, notes Wonder Woman No. 1/1, the goddess APHRODITE "shaped with her own hands a race of super women, stronger than men."

"I will breathe life into these women," said the goddess as she put the final touches on her beautiful creations, "and also the power of love! They shall be called 'Amazons.'"

The queen of the AMAZONS was named HIPPOLYTE. Aphrodite "gave her own magic girdle to the Amazon queen" and told the Amazons that "so long as your leader wears this magic girdle you . . . shall be unconquerable!"

Aided by the miraculous power of the magic girdle, Hippolyte singlehandedly defeated the mighty HERCULES when he led an army of Greek warriors against her, but Hercules beguiled her with words of love, seized the magic girdle, and, calling his men to arms, conquered and enslaved the Amazons.

Hippolyte and her Amazons were ultimately delivered out of the hands of the Greeks through the divine intervention of Aphrodite, but only on the condition that they abandon their ancestral home in ancient Amazonia for a new home, a "haven of peace and protection" on PARADISE ISLAND (WW No. 1/1, Sum '42). (*See* AMAZONS [section A, History].)

On Paradise Island, under the direction of ATHENA, the goddess of wisdom, Hippolyte learned "the secret art of moulding a human form" and sculpted the image of an infant girl.

Hippolyte adores the tiny statue she has made as Pygmalion worshiped Galatea. Aphrodite, granting the queen her prayer, bestows upon it the divine gift of life!

"I name thee Diana," intoned the goddess, "after the moon goddess, mistress of the chase!" (*See* DIANA.)

Even as an infant, Princess Diana exhibited the qualities which were later to mark her as a champion among the Amazons. At the age of three, she wrapped her tiny arms around a fruit tree and pulled it out of the ground by its roots.

"Great thunderbolts of Zeus!" exclaimed an astonished Amazon. "She pulls that tree up like a weed!"

"Already our little princess has the strength of Hercules!" cried another.

By the age of five, Diana was outracing deer through the forests of Paradise Island. The Amazons were incredulous. "The queen's child is swifter than Mercury!" exclaimed one.

When she had attained the age of fifteen years, Princess Diana received her bracelets of submission (*see* section C 2, the bracelets of submission) at Aphrodite's altar. As one of her sister Amazons hammered the heavy metal bracelets into place around her wrists, Diana recited the sacred vow of the Amazons:

"I pledge myself forever to thy service, O goddess of love and beauty!"

When she had reached maturity, Diana was allowed to drink from Aphrodite's magical fountain of eternal youth.

"Drink, Diana, from the fountain of eternal youth!" urged Queen Hippolyte. "Beauty and happiness are your Amazon birthright so long as you remain on Paradise Island!"

"It is a wonderful birthright," replied Diana. "I'll never give it up!" (WW No. 1/1, Sum '42).

Princess Diana could not possibly foresee, however, that one day an aircraft piloted by STEVE TREVOR would crash on the beach at Paradise Island and change the face of her entire life — that she would relinquish her Amazon birthright and come to America, there to wage unceasing warfare against the forces of crime, tyranny, and injustice. (*See* section A, Origin.)

As the years went by, the chroniclers endowed Wonder Woman with ever more spectacular powers in an effort to transform her into an ever more spectacular heroine, in the process revising the story of her childhood to make it more consistent with her greatly expanded powers. Accordingly, in May–June 1947, during one of Wonder Woman's periodic visits to Paradise Island, Queen Hippolyte shows some Amazon home movies depicting Wonder Woman in action against extraterrestrial invaders at the unlikely age of seven (WW No. 23/3: "Wonder Woman and the Coming of the Kangas!").

In July–August 1948, during another of Wonder Woman's visits to Paradise Island, another movie is shown, this one featuring the teen-aged Wonder Woman in action against the brutal RADIUM GIANTS. According to this text, Princess Diana knew as a teen-ager, by gazing in Hippolyte's magic sphere (*see* AMAZONS [section F 2, the magic sphere]), that she would one day depart Paradise Island for America to battle crime and injustice as Wonder Woman, and begged her mother to allow her to begin wearing a youthful version of her future costume immediately. After she had proven herself worthy of this honor, Hippolyte presented her with a striking red, white, and blue Wonder Girl costume to wear until such time as she had attained adulthood (WW No. 30/1: "The Secret of the Limestone Caves").

In the years that followed, the chroniclers did great violence to the Wonder Woman legend, asserting that Wonder Woman knew, even as an infant, that she would one day leave Paradise Island to battle injustice as Wonder Woman, and transforming her from merely a champion among the Amazons into some sort of super-Amazon, capable, even as a toddler, of mind-boggling feats of strength and agility which her sister Amazons could not hope to equal.

This unfortunate distortion of the Wonder Woman mythos attains its clearest expression in Wonder Woman No. 105/1, which asserts that the infant Wonder Woman received her awesome powers as gifts from the gods and goddesses while she lay in her cradle — "all the beauty of goodness," from Aphrodite; "all the wisdom of the planets," from Athena; "even greater speed than I myself possess," from Mercury; and "strength even greater than mine," from Hercules — and not as the result of long and arduous Amazon training (Apr. '59: "The Secret Origin of Wonder Woman"). (*See* section C 1, the benefits of Amazon training.)

The creation of the name Wonder Girl for the teen-aged Wonder Woman — and the increasingly frequent chronicling of her exploits — soon led to the creation of the name Wonder Tot for the infant Wonder Woman (WW No. 122, May '61: "The Skyscraper Wonder Woman!"), and the chronicling of Wonder Tot's adventures soon led to the creation of the wholly fantastic "impossible tales" (WW No. 124, Aug. '61: "The Impossible Day!"; and others): fantasy adventures, liberated from the restraints of the mythos entirely, in which Wonder Tot, Wonder Girl, Wonder Woman, and Queen Hippolyte undertake adventures jointly as the so-called "Wonder Family."

Indeed, much of what is contained in the later texts may safely be dismissed as inaccurate. Wonder Woman No. 152/2, to name but one glaring example, asserts that the infant Princess Diana was the product of a union between Queen Hippolyte and an unnamed male warrior who was subsequently "lost at sea" (Feb '65: "Wonder Girl's Mysterious Father!"), an assertion which flatly contradicts not only the much earlier account of Princess Diana's having been molded from clay by Hippolyte and given life by Aphrodite (WW No. 1/1, Sum '42), but also the testimony of numerous other texts basic to our understanding of Amazon history and culture.

E. The Later Life (as Diana Prince). Shortly after her arrival in the United States in January 1942, Wonder Woman purchases the identification and credentials of U.S. Army nurse DIANA PRINCE and embarks on a secret double life that she has now pursued for more than three decades (Sen No. 1). (*See* section B, the secret identity.)

Diana Prince (Wonder Woman) and Steve Trevor, 1942

As nurse Diana Prince, Wonder Woman works at STEVE TREVOR's bedside in the Walter Reed Army Hospital in Washington, D.C., where Trevor is recovering from the injuries he received when his aircraft crashed on the beach at PARADISE ISLAND in December 1941–January 1942 (AS No. 8: "Intro-

Diana Prince (Wonder Woman), 1944

ducing Wonder Woman"). When Trevor is finally released from the hospital in March 1942, however, Diana quits her post at Walter Reed in order to obtain a position at U.S. Military Intelligence as secretary to Colonel Darnell (*see* DARNELL [GENERAL]) (Sen No. 3).

Gradually, Diana Prince becomes far more than a secretary, assuming the more demanding role of intelligence operative and becoming increasingly active in intelligence investigations bearing upon America's national security. Within the military, she holds the rank of second lieutenant. Though Diana Prince is widely known as Wonder Woman's closest friend, no one outside the cloistered world of Paradise Island knows that she is secretly Wonder Woman (Sen No. 14, Feb '43).

Diana Prince (Wonder Woman), 1946

In February–March 1943, when BARONESS PAULA VON GUNTHER is horribly burned in a fire at the Pons Munitions Works, Diana Prince returns to nursing long enough to supervise the baroness's recovery (WW No. 3/4: "Ordeal of Fire!").

In Winter 1943, when Wonder Woman and QUEEN HIPPOLYTE gaze into the magic sphere (*see* AMAZONS [section F 2, the magic sphere]) in order to gain a glimpse of the world of the future, they learn that Diana Prince will be elected President of the United States in the year 3004 A.D. (WW No. 7/2: "America's Wonder Women of Tomorrow!"), a plausible event in light of Wonder Woman's Amazon immortality.

In July 1944, at a testimonial dinner in her honor, Diana Prince is hailed as "America's number one woman secret agent!" (Sen No. 31: "Grown-Down Land"), and in December 1946 Sensation Comics No. 60 describes her as "the famous woman agent of [the] Army intelligence

service!" ("The Ordeal of Queen Boadicea"). According to Sensation Comics No. 74, Diana Prince is also widely known as "a lie detector expert" (Feb '48: "The Undersea Cowboys!").

Beginning in May 1958, Diana Prince adopts a more glamorous appearance, wearing her hair down instead of up and complementing her new look with a new, stylishly modern, pair of eyeglasses (WW No. 98: "The Million Dollar Penny!" pts. 1–3 — "The Secret Amazon Trials!"; "The Undersea Menace!"; "The Impossible Bridge!").

Diana Prince (Wonder Woman) is grazed by a bullet, 1965

In November 1966 Diana Prince is promoted to the rank of captain (WW No. 166/2: "Once a Wonder Woman--!").

By November–December 1968 Diana Prince has severed her relationship with U.S. Military Intelligence, although exactly when or why she quit her post is never elucidated. It is during this period that, as Wonder Woman, she is compelled to relinquish her superhuman powers and Amazon equipment so that she may remain behind in the world of men — as plain Diana Prince — while her mother and her sister AMAZONS journey to another dimension "to rest and renew [their] powers!" After undergoing "the awesome Amazon rite of renunciation" and departing Paradise Island, Wonder Woman becomes an ordinary girl, with ordinary abilities (WW No. 179: "Wonder Woman's Last Battle!"). (*See* DOCTOR CYBER.)

For several years, Diana Prince battles crime in civilian clothing, as an ordinary woman, aided by a newly acquired mastery of the martial arts and a blind Oriental mentor named I Ching, while, in her everyday life, she operates a stylish boutique in the heart of Manhattan. By the mid-1970s, however, Wonder Woman has regained her Amazon powers and resumed her war against evil — clad in her traditional costume and employing much of her traditional equipment — while working, in her secret Diana Prince identity, as an employee of the United Nations in New York City.

F. The Woman Herself (as Wonder Woman).

1. The attitudes. The chronicles provide surprisingly little information about the personality of the Amazon princess who battles the forces of crime and injustice as Wonder Woman. Nevertheless, any effort to probe Wonder Woman's inner life must begin with an understanding of the unusual culture from which she springs, for, first and foremost, Wonder Woman is an Amazon, whose life, like that of every Amazon, revolves around reverence for Aphrodite's law and obedience to the humanitarian tenets of the Amazon code. (*See* AMAZONS [section B, Aphrodite's Law; *and* section C, the Amazon Code].)

Despite the fact that she is herself a product of PARADISE ISLAND's benevolent matriarchate, Wonder Woman is imbued with a deep-seated devotion to democratic principles that manifests itself throughout the chronicles. Wonder Woman's perceptions of democracy in action, however, are severely limited by her essentially bourgeois outlook: unquestioningly accepting of the status quo, she sees equality everywhere, even where it does not exist.

Wonder Woman, 1942

In January–February 1950, for example, Wonder Woman's ire is aroused by a newspaper article which describes tailor ALEX SMITH, museum visitor-counter LEWIS BRAND, electric-light-bulb replacer AL ROGERS, and elevator operator JOAN HALL as holders of the city's "dullest jobs."

"I wanted to tell you that you're wrong about these people . . .!" exclaims Wonder Woman as she storms into the newspaper office. ". . . I could prove that all of their jobs are vital and exciting!

Wonder Woman, 1945

No one is unimportant in a democracy--and that goes for his job!"

When the author of the offending story, the newspaper's "inquiring photographer," stands by his views, Wonder Woman determinedly sets out to convince the four bored, unhappy job-holders that their jobs are actually meaningful and exciting, when obviously they are not (WW No. 39/1: "The Trail of Thrills!").

In March–April 1950 Wonder Woman becomes similarly incensed when CAPT. MACDONALD, the skipper of the municipal ferryboat *Bay Beauty*, complains that his is the dullest seafaring job in the world.

"There is no such thing as a dull job!" admonishes Wonder Woman. "Although many people believe they are chained to one" (WW No. 40/2: "Passengers of Fate!").

Wonder Woman frequently expresses the view that "the greatest happiness in life is to help oth-

Grasping the rope ladder of her robot plane, Wonder Woman rescues a falling Steve Trevor, 1942

ers" (WW No. 39/3, Jan/Feb '50: "A Day in the Life of Wonder Woman!"; and others), but there are indications that Wonder Woman would rather be regarded as a human being than as a perennial do-gooder. By February 1964, in fact, she has been brought to the brink of emotional collapse by what she perceives as society's total disregard of her human needs.

"N-No one thinks of me as h-human anymore!" sobs the heartbroken Amazon. "I--I--m-might as well be a--a--robot--a m-machine — for all anyone cares! Isn't there someone wh-who wants me--for **myself** alone?"

So great is Wonder Woman's anguish that she withdraws from her life as a crime-fighter, determined to find one kindred soul who will regard her as a person, and not merely as a heroic celebrity.

"I can't go on . . ." she decides, "until I find **someone** . . . just **one** person . . . who'll want **me** . . . not because I'm **Wonder Woman**--the Amazon--not because I'm a fighting machine . . . but because I'm just myself! An ordinary girl like millions of others! Is there someone . . . somewhere . . . who won't be blinded by my fame . . . my feats . . . ?"

Totally alienated from the very people she has willingly relinquished her Amazon birthright to protect, Wonder Woman wanders the countryside, searching for one person who will consent to reach out to her on human terms.

"I **am** only human!" thinks Wonder Woman desperately. "And everyone has forgotten it! Like everyone else--I can't live without food or drink or rest or sleep--! I'm not a machine. I'm not--**I'M NOT!!**"

Wonder Woman's faith in humanity is ultimately restored by a young blind girl named Mary Jane, who, because her sightlessness prevents her from knowing that it is Wonder Woman whom she has

befriended, accepts Wonder Woman on purely human terms rather than mythic ones. This text is significant, not because of its disclosure of Wonder Woman's new friendship with Mary Jane, but because of the insights it provides into Wonder Woman's deep-seated dissatisfaction with the mythic image in which she has been imprisoned by the insensitive people of her adopted America (WW No. 144: "Revolt of Wonder Woman!").

2. *The sexual conflict.* PARADISE ISLAND, the secret island home of the AMAZONS, is a "land of love and beauty" (CC No. 19, Feb/Mar '47: "The Battle for Eternal Youth") where "women rule supreme in harmony and happiness" (CC No. 1, Win '42: "The Mystery of the House of Seven Gables"). But because it is "a paradise for women only," a place "which no man may enter" (WW No. 1/1, Sum '42), it is a land of sisterly love, a land where camaraderie and friendly competition have replaced the joys and pains of sexual love.

Wonder Woman locked in a dungeon, 1947

Etta Candy (background) and Wonder Woman, 1946

The young Amazons who grow to womanhood on Paradise Island are by no means devoid of sexual feeling, but the ethos of their culture demands that their sexual desires be sublimated — rechanneled into such avenues as athletics, crafts,

Wonder Woman, 1946

Wonder Woman, 1948

and other creative endeavors — and that each Amazon's awareness of her sexuality be relentlessly repressed. Indeed, the history of the Amazons and the most powerful symbols of their culture serve continually to remind each Amazon of "the folly of submitting to men's domination!" (WW No. 1/1, Sum '42). (*See* AMAZONS.)

Though the systematic study of Amazon culture remains in its infancy, it is safe to assume that Amazon girls are beset by deep-seated sexual conflicts: on the one hand, their culture teaches them that men are the enemy and that their heritage of happiness depends upon their remaining forever aloof from males; on the other hand, the maturing maidens — many of whom have never even seen a man — must learn to cope with their natural sexual yearnings.

Indeed, there is substantial evidence that many, if not all, Amazons are intrigued, even strongly attracted, by the brutal world of men and the overt sexuality that it represents. In Fall 1945, for example, a statuesque blond Amazon named DALMA — who has become "deeply envious" of the man's world freedoms enjoyed by Wonder Woman — becomes the ringleader of a group of rebellious Amazons who decide to flee to America to show off their great strength and meet handsome men. The insurrection is swiftly quashed and the insurrectionists are sternly reprimanded by the goddess APHRODITE, but the incident demonstrates that rebellion on Paradise Island means casting off the antisexual restraints of Aphrodite's law (see AMAZONS [section B, Aphrodite's Law]) for the purpose of seeking actual sexual contact with men (CC No. 12: "Rebellion on Paradise Island!").

When an airplane piloted by STEVE TREVOR, the first man she has ever seen, crashes on Paradise Island in December 1941–January 1942, Princess Diana — the Amazon maiden soon to become known as Wonder Woman — falls almost instantly in love with him (see section A, Origin), and her long-repressed inner conflict over whether to obey the demands of her upbringing and the chaste law of Aphrodite, or whether to answer the call of her own sexuality, boils dangerously close to the surface (AS No. 8: "Introducing Wonder Woman"; see also Sen No. 1, Jan '42).

Indeed, the textual evidence is persuasive that while Steve Trevor becomes infatuated with Wonder Woman because, in his puritanical mind, she is an unattainable, virginal paragon, Wonder Woman falls in love with Trevor because he represents the masculine aggressiveness and brutal sexuality she has so long been taught to deny.

"Wonder Woman!" cries Trevor in February 1942, when the valiant Amazon rescues him from a Nazi dungeon. "My beautiful angel — "

Wonder Woman, 1948

> IT TAKES REAL CHARACTER TO ADMIT ONE'S FAILURES -- AND NOT A LITTLE WISDOM TO TAKE YOUR PROFITS FROM DEFEAT. BUT REMEMBER, THIS MAN'S WORLD OF YOURS WILL NEVER BE WITHOUT PAIN AND SUFFERING UNTIL IT LEARNS LOVE, AND RESPECT FOR HUMAN RIGHTS. KEEP YOUR HANDS EXTENDED TO ALL IN FRIENDLINESS BUT NEVER HOLDING THE GUN OF PERSECUTION AND INTOLERANCE!

> YOU'RE WONDERFUL, ANGEL!

Held aloft by Steve Trevor, Wonder Woman addresses the citizens of Oakville, U.S.A., 1948

"What's an angel?" asks Wonder Woman naïvely. "I think I'd rather be a woman" (Sen No. 2).

Complicating Wonder Woman's feelings for Trevor is the contempt that her all-woman culture has taught her to feel for all males. Indeed, Wonder Woman's contempt for men is barely concealed in the chronicles, particularly in the early texts. In May 1942, for example, as she dives to the rescue of a helpless man who has been loaded down with heavy weights by Nazi spies and thrown into the sea to drown, she thinks: "Must reach him in time! These puny men can't stay under water as long as I can" (Sen No. 5).

Throughout the chronicles, Wonder Woman vehemently rejects the idea of masculine domination and Steve Trevor's notion that she should surrender to the conventional domestic life, yet there is ample textual evidence that submissive domesticity is precisely what Wonder Woman really desires. In September 1942, for example, DIANA PRINCE, the U.S. Army nurse from whom Wonder Woman originally acquired her alternate identity (*see* section B, the secret identity), returns to the United States and, for a time, takes over Wonder Woman's job at U.S. Military Intelligence, only to surrender the job soon afterward in favor of dedicating herself full-time to the duties of home and hearth.

"I'm glad to get my position back," remarks Wonder Woman to the former Army nurse. "But I envy you yours, as wife and mother" (Sen No. 9).

Wonder Woman's sexual conflict becomes most apparent in situations involving her relationship with Steve Trevor. Although Wonder Woman cannot bring herself to surrender to Trevor, she has frequent fantasies in which he overpowers her, i.e., in which Trevor takes by force that which she is unwilling to give him outright. The implication is inescapable that Wonder Woman would like Trevor to make love to her, but only if she can somehow evade responsibility for bringing the act of love about. Indeed, by telling Trevor, as she often does, that she can only marry him once crime and injustice have been eradicated from the earth, she effectively ensures that she will never actually have to choose between her sexual desire for Trevor and her fidelity to Amazon law. (*See* section G, the relationship with Steve Trevor.)

3. *The mythological expressions*. Throughout the chronicles, Wonder Woman's speech is punctuated with colorful expressions and exclamations embodying the names and symbols of classical mythology. Even as Diana Prince, Wonder Woman utters these expressions, presumably out of habit. In and of themselves, the mythological expressions are unimportant, but they are so closely identified with Wonder Woman's life and personality that they merit at least brief mention in any study of her adventures. The mythological expressions used most often by Wonder Woman are Suffering Sappho, Merciful Minerva, and Great Hera. There are, however, a host of others, including:

Apples of Atalanta
Athena's shield
Black hounds of Hades
By Aphrodite's girdle
By Arachne's golden web
By Arachne's web
By Argus' hundred eyes
By Athena's loom
By Athena's shield
By Athena's spear
By Hera
By Hercules
By Hercules' club
By Jove's thunderbolts
By Jupiter
By Jupiter Pluvius
By Mars' double-edged sword
By Mercury's sandals
By Mercury's winged sandals
By Neptune's beard
By Neptune's trident
By Neptune's watery domain
By Orpheus' lyre
By Phoebus' fiery orb
By Sappho's stylus
By the great club of Hercules
By the great labors of Hercules
By the shades of Pluto
By the winds of Aeolus
By Vulcan's forge
By Vulcan's hammer
By Zeus
For Hera's sake
Gods of Olympus
Good Hera
Great Aphrodite
Great goddesses
Great Hephaestus
Great Hercules
Great Jupiter
Great labors of Hercules
Great Minerva
Great Olympus
Great Pluto
Great Sampson's ghost
Great Shades of Pluto
Great thunders of Zeus
Great Zeus
Hammers of Hephaestus
Headaches of Hercules
Heavenly Hera
Holy Hera
Hounds of Hades
Hounds of Hera
Hounds of Zeus
Mighty Minerva
Pluto's shades
Pluto take it
Sands of Morpheus
Shades of Hades
Shades of Hercules
Shades of Neptune
Shades of Pluto
Snakes of Medusa
Thank Aphrodite
Thunderbolts of Jove
Thunderbolts of Zeus
Thunders of Zeus
Visions of Aphrodite
Winds of Aeolus

G. The Relationship with Steve Trevor. For more than thirty years, since the day STEVE TREVOR's

Wonder Woman, Steve Trevor, and
Baroness Paula von Gunther, 1946

lenting assault on his ego and his masculinity that one can only assume that the gratifications he derives from it are mainly neurotic ones.

From the beginning, the relationship has been built on shaky ground. Princess Diana, naïve and inexperienced, had spent her entire youth within the cloistered confines of Paradise Island. Her only companions had been women; she had never even seen a man. Yet in December 1941–January 1942, shortly after lifting Trevor from the wreckage of his airplane and carrying him to an Amazon

Wonder Woman and Steve Trevor, 1942

aircraft crashed on the beach at PARADISE ISLAND (AS No. 8, Dec/Jan '41–'42: "Introducing Wonder Woman"), the lives of Steve Trevor and Wonder Woman have been inextricably intertwined.

The relationship between the valiant Amazon princess and the handsome Army officer has been indisputably long-lived, but it has also been so clearly frustrating and unfulfilling for both parties that one may reasonably wonder about the psychological forces that have kept them bound to one another for so long. For Wonder Woman, the relationship only exacerbates her long-repressed inner conflict over whether to answer the call of her sexuality or to obey the chaste law of APHRO-DITE (*see* section F 2, the sexual conflict). For Trevor, the relationship represents such an unre-

hospital for treatment, she fell madly in love with him (AS No. 8: "Introducing Wonder Woman").

Trevor's infatuation followed a similar course: he opened his eyes and fell instantly in love with

Aboard her robot plane, Wonder Woman ministers to a wounded Steve Trevor, 1942

the "beautiful angel" who had stayed by his bed-side and nursed him back to health (Sen No. 1, Jan '42). Indeed, to Trevor — who refers to Wonder Woman repeatedly throughout the chronicles as his "angel" — the lovely Amazon is not a real woman at all, but a paragon of virtue, a vision of loveliness, an unattainable, virginal ideal who will surrender herself to him only after crime and in-justice have been eradicated from the earth.

Trevor is both fascinated and frustrated by his Amazon princess. She is the most glamorous woman in the world, but she is also a living mock-ery of his conventional ideas about matrimony and the proper role of women, his need to be dominant and masterful, his desire to be comfort-ing and protective.

"This is no job for a woman," snaps Trevor, whenever Diana Prince — the girl who is secretly Wonder Woman — asks to accompany him on a dangerous assignment for U.S. Military Intelli-gence; yet it is invariably a woman — Wonder Woman — who rescues him from the clutches of spies and saboteurs, who plucks him out of the sky after his plane has run out of fuel or spun out of control, and who covers up for him — to save both his reputation and his self-esteem — after his im-pulsive courage and silly masculine pride have gotten him into more trouble than he can possibly handle.

Nevertheless, despite the fact that neither lover can be said to achieve any sort of normal gratifica-tion from their incomprehensible relationship, the romance between Steve Trevor and Wonder Woman has remained a major force in the lives of the participants and a key shaper of textual events for over thirty years. Wonder Woman's assump-tion of a secret identity, for example, is eventually justified in the texts on the ground that it allows Wonder Woman a measure of surprise over her underworld adversaries, but its original purpose was to enable Wonder Woman to remain by Steve Trevor's side while he recovered from his wounds in the Walter Reed Army Hospital (see section B, the secret identity).

At the hospital, the disguised Amazon beams like a love-struck adolescent when she learns that Trevor has remembered her and that he has been asking about her. ". . . [Y]ou don't need **Wonder Woman** now," she teases, her true identity safely concealed behind the nurse's uniform and eye-glasses of Army nurse Diana Prince, "—you've got me!"

"Listen, Diana!" replies Trevor. "You're a nice kid, and I like you. But if you think you can hold a candle to **Wonder Woman** you're crazy!"

"So I'm my own rival, eh?" muses Wonder

Diana Prince (Wonder Woman) and Steve Trevor, 1942

Woman afterward. "That's funny . . . if mother could only see me now . . . . as a very feminine woman . . a nurse, no less, in a world full of men, and in love, too — with **myself** for a rival!" (Sen No. 1, Jan '42).

In March 1942, when Trevor is about to be re-leased from the hospital, Diana Prince becomes heartbroken. "Oh, Steve is going!" she sobs. "I'll never see him again! I can't bear it!"

To soothe her anguish, Trevor agrees to help her apply for a job as Colonel Darnell's secretary at U.S. Military Intelligence (see DARNELL [GENERAL]), a job which Diana Prince accepts only because it will enable her to remain near Trevor (Sen No. 3).

In Summer 1942 Steve Trevor asks Wonder Woman to marry him for the first time in the chronicles.

"Steve darling — I cannot!" replies Wonder Woman. "The Amazon law forbids it. But I shall always be near you — nearest sometimes when you least suspect it!" (WW No. 1/2).

In the years that follow, Trevor proposes mar-riage repeatedly, but Wonder Woman either evades his proposals or puts Trevor off with the reply that she will consent to marry him only when the world no longer has need of her services as an Amazon. Despite these endless rejections, how-ever, it is clear that Wonder Woman harbors strong feelings for Trevor: in Fall 1942 she refers to him as "the man I love" (WW No. 2/1), and in October 1942, Sensation Comics No. 10 observes that Trevor "means more to [Wonder Woman] than life itself."

Wonder Woman's love for Trevor, however, is not sufficient to alleviate her conflicting need to remain obedient to Aphrodite's law (see AMAZONS

Wonder Woman rescues Steve Trevor from a Nazi dungeon, 1942

[section B, Aphrodite's Law]) and to avoid, at all costs, the pitfall of submitting to male domination. In January 1943, when Trevor makes his first pass at her, Wonder Woman firmly rebuffs him (Sen No. 13).

The chronicles are unremitting in their assertion that marriage to Trevor would require Wonder Woman to retire from crime-fighting, become meek, docile, and submissive, and accept unquestioningly Trevor's right to make all her life-decisions for her.

". . . I think I'll stay a career girl for a while yet," she replies when Trevor proposes to her in Summer 1944, "— there's too much to be done without my trying to keep house in a man's world!!" (WW No. 9/3).

Wonder Woman's ambivalence toward Trevor comes starkly to the surface in a dream she has about him in Fall 1944. In it, Wonder Woman, weak and adoring, is swept off her feet by a courageous, masculine Trevor. Eager to serve him submissively forevermore as his "docile little wife," Wonder Woman agrees to marry Trevor and is about to utter the fateful words "I do" when she awakens with a start, reassuring herself aloud that she will never take a vow of obedience to any man. Later, after she has rescued Trevor from a gang of criminals, he once again proposes marriage.

"Man's world marriage to a dominant man like you, Steve, must be thrilling," replies Wonder Woman, her vivid fantasy of a short while ago still fresh in her mind, "--but for an Amazon maiden, it's just — a **dream**!" (CC No. 8: "The Amazon Bride").

The idea of marriage as requiring total sub-

missiveness on the part of the woman appears again in Wonder Woman No. 13/3. "You were superb, angel!" remarks Trevor, after Wonder Woman has successfully negotiated a lasting peace between BITTERLAND and EVELAND. "If only you'd marry me —!"

"If I married you, Steve," replies Wonder Woman, "I'd have to pretend I'm **weaker** than you are to make you happy — and that, **no** woman should do!" (Sum '45: "Slaves in the Electric Gardens").

Although Aphrodite's law forbids her to surrender to Trevor, however, Wonder Woman often wishes that he would *take* that which she cannot bring herself to offer him outright. In Fall 1945, for example, Trevor is forced to rescue Wonder Woman after a villain has bound her with her own magic lasso (*see* section C 3, the magic lasso). "I **could** steal a kiss while she's bound with the magic lasso," thinks Trevor, "—what an opportunity I'm passing up!"

"I wish Steve wouldn't be so gallant," thinks the frustrated Wonder Woman, "— I'd **have** to let him kiss me now if he tried —" (WW No. 14/1: "Captured by Leprechauns").

In October 1945 the LAWBREAKERS' PROTECTIVE LEAGUE attempts to capitalize on the peculiar nature of the Wonder Woman-Trevor relationship in order to prevent Wonder Woman from interfering with their underworld activities. Wonder Woman would be forced to marry Trevor and thus remove herself from the world of crime-fighting, reason the criminals, if only a way could be found to enable Trevor to dominate her physically.

"Nobody can kill that wench," explains Ferva

Temporarily endowed with superhuman strength,
Steve Trevor attempts to dominate Wonder Woman

Shayne, the league's co-leader, "but Trevor can subdue her! Once she marries **him** the mighty Amazon'll become a meek housewife who will never bother us! If Trevor becomes **stronger than Wonder Woman,** she'll go ga-ga over him! She'll marry him and stay at home as he commands."

The league succeeds in endowing Trevor with temporary superhuman strength, but Wonder Woman's reaction to Trevor's newly acquired power is one of ambivalence: "Some girls **love** to have a man stronger than they are make them do things," she muses. "Do I like it? I don't know — it's sort of thrilling. But — isn't it more fun to make the man obey?"

Wonder Woman ultimately resolves her ambivalence in favor of a weak Trevor. ". . . I've discov-

ered," she tells him finally, "that I can **never** love a **dominant** man who's stronger than I am!" (Sen No. 46: "The Lawbreakers' League").

In Winter 1945, after Wonder Woman has gone temporarily berserk following the forcible removal of her Amazon bracelets (*see* section C 2, the bracelets of submission), Trevor says plaintively, "I wish taking off your bracelets would make you marry me, darling!"

"Sometimes I wish the same thing!" thinks Wonder Woman (CC No. 13: "The Underwater Follies").

In February 1946, while Wonder Woman and Steve Trevor are standing together on a dance floor, Trevor insists, somewhat rudely, that Wonder Woman dance with him, and then attempts to put his arms around her.

Simultaneously intrigued and unsettled by
Trevor's newly acquired power, Wonder
Woman struggles with her ambivalence . . .

. . . and finally decides that she pre-
fers Trevor just as he was, 1945

"You'll never get an Amazon **that** way," snaps Wonder Woman, ". . . try your cave man style on **man's** world girls!"

Trevor, his ego badly bruised, immediately embarks on a whirlwind romance with wealthy widow Margo Vandergilt, and soon asks her to marry him, unaware that his new ladylove is in reality a gun moll named CORINE who has kidnapped the real Margo Vandergilt and taken her place. When Wonder Woman finally exposes Trevor's new fiancée as an impostor and rescues the real Margo Vandergilt, Trevor, now contrite, admits that he was never really in love with the phony Margo Vandergilt, but had merely initiated the romance in hopes of teaching Wonder Woman a lesson (Sen No. 50: "The Case of the Girl in Braces").

Diana Prince (Wonder Woman) and Steve Trevor

Two years later, during a Halloween party at the HOLLIDAY COLLEGE FOR WOMEN, Trevor challenges Wonder Woman to an apple bobbing contest: if Trevor wins, Wonder Woman must marry him; if Wonder Woman wins, Trevor must admit that women are superior to men. At a point when the two apple bobbers are tied, the contest is interrupted by an emergency and never resumed, but a short while later, in her thoughts, Wonder Woman alludes to it. "If only Steve had won that contest!" she muses regretfully. "An Amazon must keep her word--I'd have been **compelled** to marry Steve!" (Sen No. 73, Jan '48: "The Witches' Trials").

Because Trevor invariably responds to her only as Wonder Woman and never as Diana Prince, Wonder Woman occasionally becomes disturbed— even depressed — by what she perceives as Trevor's failure to appreciate her for her personal qualities rather than for her celebrity.

"You're a nice girl, Di," says Trevor patronizingly to Diana Prince in July-August 1949, "and I like you very much. But--what I feel for **Wonder Woman** is a different matter!"

"Steve is so certain about his feelings for **Wonder Woman!**" thinks Diana sadly. "Yet--why hasn't his heart told him who I really am?" (WW No. 36/2: "Wonder Woman's Double!").

In September–October 1949 Steve Trevor asks Wonder Woman to marry him again, only to be turned down for the umpteenth time. "I'm beginning to think that you don't love me!" complains Trevor.

"But I **do,** darling!" replies Wonder Woman.

"Then why won't you marry me?" insists Trevor.

"Because as long as crime and evil take no holiday," replies Wonder Woman, "--neither can I. Steve, dear, please have patience. Wait until Amazon ways of peace and love drive brute force and hate out of the world."

Perhaps because he fears that brute force and hatred will not be driven from the world in his lifetime, Wonder Woman's response strikes Trevor as inadequate, and he stalks off, loudly declaring that their relationship is over.

Soon afterward, Trevor becomes romantically involved with beautiful European movie actress LORELEI LORN, and before long the couple have announced their intention to marry. Wonder Woman is heartbroken, until she learns that the romance was only a ploy to lure a notorious gang of jewel thieves into the open. ". . . [I]t took me time to realize that you were right," confesses Trevor finally, after he and Wonder Woman have been happily reunited. "As an Amazon, you must think of others before yourself. But I'm willing to wait" (WW No. 37/2: "The Fatal Beauty!").

In November–December 1949 Trevor proposes to Wonder Woman again, and this time the Amazon princess shows signs of wavering: "Why shouldn't I say 'yes'?" she thinks. "Steve is sweet and kind and brave! He loves me, and I love him!

Wonder Woman rescues Steve Trevor from drowning

There's never been any doubt of that! Other girls marry when they're in love — why shouldn't I?"

Then, however, Wonder Woman recalls some advice she once received from her mother, QUEEN HIPPOLYTE: "Diana, my daughter," the queen had said, "you are no ordinary girl! You are an Amazon princess! Your mission in life is to help others! You cannot think of yourself, until all is right with the world! When there is no longer any need of your services, only then . . . ."

"Sadly," notes the narrative text, "**Wonder Woman** is forced to deny herself the right of every girl, to listen to her heart."

"I--I'm sorry, Steve!" she replies finally. "But I must refuse! I love you . . . but I can't marry you! Not as long as people need my help! If they didn't, it would be a different story. I'd be happy to marry you!" (Sen No. 94: "S O S Wonder Woman!").

In March–April 1950 Steve Trevor once again asks Wonder Woman to marry him.

"I don't see any reason why I shouldn't marry Steve," thinks Wonder Woman, "--we love each other! But, first, I want to discuss it with mother."

On Paradise Island, however, Queen Hippolyte takes a different view. "I know that Steve loves **Wonder Woman,** the **glamorous** Amazon princess," says the queen. "But if you marry, you will no longer be an Amazon. You will be **plain** Lt. Diana Prince forever. Do you think Steve will love you then, in **that** identity?"

Hippolyte's concern centers around a tenet of Aphrodite's law which states that no Amazon may marry and still remain an Amazon. Were Wonder Woman to marry Steve Trevor, she would lose her status as an Amazon and remain plain Diana Prince forever.

On this occasion, Wonder Woman decides to marry Trevor, but only if he freely chooses Diana Prince as his bride rather than Wonder Woman. Since Trevor has eyes only for Wonder Woman, however, the marriage never takes place (Sen No. 96: "Wonder Woman's Romantic Rival!").

In May–June 1950 Wonder Woman again contemplates the dilemma of her relationship with Steve Trevor. "By Aphrodite's law," she muses aloud, "no Amazon may marry and still remain an Amazon. If I marry Steve, I shall cease being an Amazon and forfeit the magic lasso, plane, and bracelets with which I have fought crime and injustice!

"Have I the right to become Mrs. Steve Trevor, and think only of my own happiness? Or should my first thoughts be of the people whom only **I** can help?" (Sen No. 97: "Wonder Woman, Romance Editor").

In March–April 1951, however, Trevor proposes

Wonder Woman, 1946

again. "Angel," he asks, "when are we going to be married?"

"When evil and injustice vanish from the earth!" replies Wonder Woman (WW No. 46/2: "The Moon of Peril!").

In November–December 1952, for the first time in the chronicles, Steve Trevor and Wonder Woman are described as "engaged" rather than as merely "sweethearts." During this period, Trevor becomes painfully aware of the extent to which he dwells in the shadow of the woman he loves when Wonder Woman is compelled to rescue him from death on three separate occasions occurring one after the other.

"I'm not going to be called **Mr. Wonder Woman** when we marry!" insists Trevor. "I've got to win back the respect I've lost! Our engagement's off! I'm not going to see you again until I can prove to everyone that I'm as capable as you . . . !"

Determined to prove the impossible — i.e., that

Wonder Woman rebuffs Steve Trevor, 1946

he is Wonder Woman's equal — Trevor invents a series of ingenious devices designed to enable him to duplicate Wonder Woman's super-heroic feats. The devices include a special steel glove for repelling bullets and a special lasso for lassoing and holding moving vehicles. In each actual test of his new devices, however, Trevor places his life in jeopardy because he lacks the lightning-fast reflexes and other physical capabilities that Wonder Woman has developed through Amazon training (*see* section C 1, the benefits of Amazon training), forcing Wonder Woman to intervene repeatedly to rescue him, while contriving to make it appear that Trevor has successfully executed each of his super-stunts to avoid further damaging his self-esteem. Finally, after he has "successfully" duplicated three of Wonder Woman's superhuman stunts, Trevor agrees to resume their engagement.

"Someday, when Steve realizes that people in love needn't compete with each other," thinks Wonder Woman, "I'll tell him the truth . . .!" (WW No. 56/2: "Wonder Woman's Invincible Rival!").

From this time onward, the texts repeatedly refer to Trevor as Wonder Woman's fiancé.

"We love each other!" he insists in November 1954. "Why don't you marry me?"

"Because my every effort is concentrated on combatting crime and the forces which threaten democracy!" replies Wonder Woman, her responses now conditioned by the rhetoric of the Cold War. "The moment I'm convinced my services are no longer required to combat the enemies who threaten our American way of life — I'd be happy to marry you!"

Not long afterward, however, Trevor comes within one word of being married to Wonder Woman. During a period of tranquility, when no crimes are being committed and Wonder Woman's services are consequently not being called upon, the valiant Amazon finally agrees to marry Trevor. The couple are taking their vows in the mayor's office — and the mayor, who is performing the ceremony, has said, "I now pronounce you man and . . ." — when suddenly Wonder Woman vanishes into thin air, banished into an alien dimension by the diabolical PROFESSOR UXO. Wonder Woman ultimately triumphs over Professor Uxo and returns to her own dimension, but the experience has persuaded Wonder Woman and Trevor that the time for their marriage has not yet come (WW No. 70/3: "Wonder Woman's Wedding Day!").

In April 1956 Steve Trevor kisses Wonder Woman on the lips for the first time in the chronicles (WW No. 81/2: "Three Secret Wishes!").

In January 1962, after being knocked unconscious by a gangster's bullet, Steve Trevor has a dream which betrays the true extent of the frustration and resentment he feels toward Wonder Woman as the result of her repeated rejections of his proposals of marriage. In the dream, Trevor finally marries Wonder Woman, only to have the marriage turn out to be far less than the ultimate satisfaction he had expected it to be: his bride keeps running off to battle one new menace after another, and, when he finally does get her alone to himself, she burns his toast, ruins his coffee, and generally proves to be an inadequate wife (WW No. 127/2: "Wonder Woman's Surprise Honeymoon!").

Believing Steve Trevor dead, Wonder Woman is overwhelmed with grief, 1967

In October 1962 Trevor's latent resentment boils to the surface. "I'm tired of waiting around for you to make up your mind!" he shouts at Wonder Woman after she has rejected his latest marriage proposal. "I've had enough! **Goodby!**"

Trevor soon becomes infatuated with a mysterious beauty known only as Miss X, but eventually he comes to realize that Wonder Woman is the only woman he has ever really loved. He never learns that the lovely Miss X was none other than Wonder Woman, who had assumed the fictitious identity while playing a role in a motion picture (WW No. 133/2: "Wonder Woman's Invincible Rival--Herself!"). (*See* THOMAS, T. T.)

The relationship between Wonder Woman and Steve Trevor comes to an apparent end in January–February 1969, when Trevor is brutally murdered by henchmen of the sinister DOCTOR CYBER (WW No. 180: "A Death for Diana!"), but the relationship shows promise of flowering anew when Trevor is brought back to life by the goddess Aphrodite in April–May 1976 (WW No. 223: "Welcome Back to Life . . . Steve Trevor!").

H. The Great Themes. A study of the Wonder Woman chronicles in their entirety reveals the presence of certain basic themes — themes which form the philosophical threads from which the basic fabric of the chronicles is woven. In the subsections that follow, these themes are enumerated and examined, and some of their wider implications are explored.

1. The relationship between men and women. In the universe of the Wonder Woman chronicles, two deities vie for control of the planet Earth: APHRODITE, the goddess of love and beauty, and MARS, the god of war. It is by no means coincidental that the forces of evil are personified by a male deity while the forces of good are personified by a female one, for in the Wonder Woman chronicles the eternal conflict between good and evil is seen very much in sexual terms. In the utopian world of the future, the influence of women will predominate over that of men, representing the triumph of love and understanding over brutality and aggression.

This is not to say that every woman in the chronicles is a heroine and every man a villain, but it *is* to say that brutal, domineering traits are portrayed as male traits, while love, kindness, and human understanding are portrayed as characteristic of women. To the extent that humanity adopts the ways of its women, it champions the cause of Aphrodite and moves toward the warm light of ultimate enlightenment. To the extent that humanity continues to follow the ways of its men, it follows the leadership of Mars, with its legacy of

violence, brutality, slavery, and death. Inevitably, a battle between good and evil pits "the cruel despotism of masculine aggressiveness" against "the cool, clever bravery of that beautiful girl, the far-famed Amazon princess, Wonder Woman!" (Sen No. 11, Nov '42).

In the chronicles, utopian perfection usually resides either in those societies which have dispensed with men altogether (e.g., PARADISE ISLAND, EVELAND, and NOMAN), or in those societies in which men have been relegated to a subservient role (e.g., AURANIA, VENTURIA, and the planet VENUS under QUEEN DESIRA). Conversely, the societies which are most brutal and inhumane are, typically, either those in which there are no women at all (e.g., NEPTUNIA and ELAM), or those in which the women have been subjugated by the men (e.g., BITTERLAND, the land of the MOLE MEN under BLAKFU, and the planet MARS under the war god Mars).

The texts relentlessly stress the masculinity of evil and the femininity of virtue:

In July–August 1948, when a warden is being sought for a new women's prison, the competition for the post pits enlightened reformer Suzan Patience against brutal disciplinarian BERTRAM HARSH (WW No. 30/3: "A Human Bomb!").

In September–October 1948, when gifted scientist DR. MARY DEAN discovers "reduso liquid," a chemical she hopes will "reduce germs to such a minute size that they will be unable to harm humans," her evil fiancé, DR. DIRKE, steals the formula in hopes of capitalizing on its potential as a weapon of war (WW No. 31/1: "The Shrinking Formula!").

In October 1948, when the women of the "inner moon-planet" develop a rocket ship for space exploration, KING LUNAR and the inner moon-planet's male inhabitants enslave the women so that they can use the rocket for interplanetary warfare (Sen No. 82: "Brain Pirates from the Inner Moon-World!").

In November 1948 PROWD, the evil dictator of Elam, "the city of men," treacherously attempts to conquer the peace-loving inhabitants of Noman, "the city of women" (Sen No. 83: "The Sinister Olympics!").

The message of the chronicles is unrelenting: until mankind adopts the loving ways of its women, the world will remain a charnel house of brutality and evil. Indeed, Wonder Woman reserves her greatest contempt for those women of the man-ruled world who allow themselves to be dominated by their men.

In February–March 1943, for example, when BARONESS PAULA VON GUNTHER's former slave girls refuse to accept their new-found freedom, MALA is dumbfounded. "I can't understand these girls!" she exclaims.

"You could if you knew women in the man-ruled world!" replies Wonder Woman. "They want to be slaves because they're afraid to be free and compete with men!" (WW No. 3/3).

DR. PSYCHO, one of the vilest villains of the Wonder Woman chronicles, directs his evil genius less toward the acquisition of power or riches than toward the total subjugation of women. He is a "monster [who] abhors women! With *weird cunning* and dark, forbidden knowledge of the occult, Dr. Psycho prepares to change the independent status of modern American women back to the days of the sultans and slave markets, clanking chains and abject captivity" (WW No. 5/1, Jun/Jul '43: "Battle for Womanhood").

"Earth girls can stop men's power for evil," insists Wonder Woman, "when they refuse to be dominated by evil men!" (WW No. 5/3, Jun/Jul '43). Indeed, when Wonder Woman takes Dr. Psycho's wife, MARVA PSYCHO, to Reform Island (*see* TRANSFORMATION ISLAND) in July–August 1946, it is for the purpose of teaching her to resist male domination. "Amazon training will make her mind so strong," explains Wonder Woman, "that no one **man'll ever** be able to **dominate** her again!" (WW No. 18/2: "The Drugged WAC").

In November–December 1948 Wonder Woman berates a group of slave girls from the planet URANUS for having allowed themselves to be subjugated by their men. "Oh, you stupid girls!" she exclaims. "When you let your men bind you--you let yourself be bound by war, hate, greed, and lust for power! Think! And free yourselves! **Control** those who would oppress others! **You can do it!**" (WW No. 32/1: "Uvo of Uranus!" pts. 1–2 — "The Amazing Global Theft!"; "Thunder in Space!").

If the noble qualities of the human race are embodied in its women, and the baser qualities embodied in its men, what is the fitting and proper relationship between men and women in a society free of war and privation?

On the planet Venus, where men and women live together in harmony and happiness, the women — whose graceful translucent wings enable them to swoop and soar like giant butterflies — are beautiful, courageous, and independent, while the men — who are wingless — are "defenseless," obedient, and somewhat craven.

". . . [O]ur men love us dearly," explains Queen Desira to Wonder Woman in October–November 1942. "They obey us because if they did not, we would fly away from them and they have no wings to follow."

"That's a wonderful way to keep men in their place!" replies Wonder Woman (AS No. 13: "Shanghaied into Space!").

In April–May 1943 Wonder Woman sets out to transform unscrupulous rubber magnate IVAR TORGSON into a loving husband for his girlfriend Elva. By peering into Torgson's subconscious with Baroness Paula von Gunther's "subconscious X-ray machine," Wonder Woman learns that Torgson views himself as a monarch, and Elva as his abject, adoring slave.

"So that's the way Ivar thinks of me," gasps Elva, "— why, I can't believe it!"

"Most men secretly think of women that way in this man-ruled world!" explains Wonder Woman. "But I have an idea we can cure Ivar — if you'll help!"

Wonder Woman's plan for reforming Torgson involves dressing Elva in the raiment of a monarch and in forcing Torgson to become her shackled, abject slave.

"Here, let me put this costume on you," urges Wonder Woman. "You must make him think of you as his **queen** in his subconscious mind instead of his **slave**! Then you must learn to control him!"

For the next three days, following Wonder Woman's instructions, Elva keeps Torgson locked in a cage, humiliating and tormenting him and forcing him to obey her every command. As Wonder Woman had predicted, Torgson soon comes to revel in these humiliations, becoming transformed by degrees from a domineering male chauvinist into an infantilized slave who relishes being controlled by his girlfriend (WW No. 4/3).

In Winter 1943, when QUEEN HIPPOLYTE gazes into her magic sphere (*see* AMAZONS [section F 2, the magic sphere]) in order to gain a glimpse of the utopian world of the distant future, she learns that:

> In 3700 A.D. the whole world will be one nation called United States of Earth. Present-day countries will be states in the global union. The world capitol [sic] will be an island named Harmonia. Men and women will be equal. But woman's influence will control most governments because women are more ready to **serve others unselfishly**! [WW No. 7/3: "The Secret Weapon"].

In Winter 1945 Wonder Woman meets SOLO, the tyrannical ruler of Neptunia, a continent where there are no women. "But if there are only **men**," remarks Wonder Woman incredulously, "you must fight each other constantly!"

"Women are **horrible** creatures — cruel, vindictive," exclaims Solo a short while later. "Thank Neptune we have no **women** on Neptunia!"

"You'll always be quarrelsome, treacherous, and unhappy until women **control** you!" retorts Wonder Woman.

Indeed, after Solo has been toppled from power in Neptunia, Wonder Woman arranges for the installation of an all-woman government there to ensure lasting peace and tranquility (WW No. 15: chs. 1–3 — "The First Battle of Neptunia"; "The Masters of the Water"; "In the Killer's Cage").

Whatever may be the ideal relationship between men and women, the chronicles are uncompromising in their assertion that marriage is a mind-deadening trap for women. Indeed, although Wonder Woman frequently expresses the hope of someday marrying STEVE TREVOR, she accepts without question that marriage will mean a life of total submission to Trevor's domination. (See section G, the relationship with Steve Trevor.)

2. *Humiliation and sadism.* Particularly in the early texts, the Wonder Woman chronicles betray a preoccupation with degradation and humiliation unmatched in the literature of the great comic book heroes. Batman's enemies, for example, may endeavor to outwit Batman or even destroy him, but the villains and villainesses of the Wonder Woman chronicles are often gratuitously sadistic, determined to devalue and humiliate Wonder Woman in ways often characterized by strong erotic overtones.

Dancing, often combined with some form of pain-producing torture, is commonly portrayed as a sadistic torment. In April–May 1943, for example, Wonder Woman is taken captive by the MOLE MEN, weighted down with heavy shackles, fitted with a pair of special iron shoes, and forced to dance before the monarch BLAKFU atop an electrified metal grid.

"When this girl's chains are removed," gloats Blakfu, "she must dance to save herself from electrocution! Her slave sandals and the electrified floor plate neutralize each other if contacts are brief. But when she stops dancing, she will die!" (WW No. 4/2).

In October 1943 the CHEETAH attempts to humiliate Wonder Woman by forcing her to dance before her assembled slave girls while bound with massive chains (Sen No. 22: "The Secret Submarine"), and in November 1944 SONTAG HENYA and her cohorts weight Wonder Woman down with heavy shackles and force her to dance on a table top for their sadistic amusement, intending to kill her as soon as she tires (Sen No. 35: "Girls Under the Sea").

In September 1945 "GENERAL" JOSÉ PIEREZ and his ruthless Mexican "bandidos" blindfold Wonder Woman and torture her by forcing her to dance atop a bed of hot coals (Sen No. 45: "In the Enemy's Hands").

Dancing-as-torture is by no means the only form of humiliation inflicted upon Wonder Woman by her adversaries. In January 1964, for example, MOUSE MAN locks her in an oversized mouse cage and forces her to entertain him by performing humiliating stunts on the cage's ladders, wheels, and other apparatus (WW No. 143/2: "The Amazon Mouse Trap!").

Even the AMAZONS, who have supposedly abandoned violence and sadism for the loving ways of the goddess APHRODITE, are not above acting out their sadomasochistic impulses. Wonder Woman's training program for rubber magnate IVAR TORGSON (*see* section H 1, the relationship between men and women) — which is designed to transform Torgson into a loving husband for his girlfriend Elva — involves the systematic infliction of torment and humiliation (WW No. 4/3, Apr/May '43).

When Wonder Woman returns to PARADISE ISLAND with some gifts for her sister Amazons in February–March 1943, one of the gifts she brings is a tennis racket. The Amazon who receives it, however, having never heard of tennis, jumps to the rather bizarre conclusion that the racket is "a spanker," and promptly tries it out by using it to swat another Amazon on her derriere. "Pooh!" exclaims the victim disappointedly. "It doesn't hurt — it's a sissy spanker from the man's world" (WW No. 3/1).

Of all the ways in which an individual may be dehumanized and devalued, however, the one which appears most frequently in the Wonder Woman chronicles is the institution of slavery (*see* section H 3, Slavery, bondage, and loving submission).

3. *Slavery, bondage, and loving submission.* Nowhere in the comic book literature is the practice of slavery so prevalent as in the Wonder Woman chronicles. Indeed, virtually all of the major villains and villainesses either maintain slaves of their own, or come from societies where the keeping of slaves is an accepted and established practice.

AKNATEN, QUEEN ATOMIA, BLAKFU, SUPREME LEADER BLITZ, the CHEETAH, BARONESS PAULA VON GUNTHER, HYPNOTA THE GREAT, COUNTESS MAZUMA, the PURPLE PRIESTESS, and ZARA — to name but a handful — all maintain contingents of slaves. On the planets MARS, PLUTO, SATURN, and URANUS — and in the lands of AURANIA, BITTERLAND, NEPTUNIA, and VENTURIA — slavery is an accepted practice.

Typically, but not always, the slaves are women, and usually they are forced to wear heavy shack-

Wonder Woman

remove their shackles, they become unruly and rebellious; they repeatedly commit minor infractions of Amazon law for the express purpose of inviting punishment. The only way to secure their cooperation, Mala discovers, is to simulate the ambience of servitude to which they have become accustomed:

"Though Aphrodite forbids hurting prisoners," explains Mala to Wonder Woman, "we snap big whips and the girls love it! Under those conditions they work beautifully."

When the slave girls beg Mala to make them *her* slaves, Mala refuses, and when the slave girls insist that Mala command them to do something, Mala evades the unpleasant implications of the request by commanding them to go swimming with her. "The girls go wild with joy," observes the textual narrative, "as Mala gives them orders" (WW No. 3/3).

Slavery, with its attendant infantilization and dehumanization, is depicted so frequently in the Wonder Woman chronicles that it is easy to dismiss it as a practice exclusive to villains and villainesses and to overlook the far more subtle, insidious way in which an ethos of servitude permeates the entire philosophical fabric of the chronicles. For slavery, in and of itself, is never actually condemned in the chronicles. When Wonder Woman negotiates a peace treaty between Earth and Saturn in Fall 1944, for example, she neither criticizes Saturnian slavery nor makes any attempt to bring an end to the practice, ensuring only that the treaty outlaws the use of earthmen as Saturnian slaves. Henceforth, the Saturnians will have to obtain their slaves from other planets (WW No. 10/3: "Wonder Woman's Boots!").

Wonder Woman also tolerates slavery on ATLANTIS, where her good friends QUEEN EERAS and OCTAVIA maintain large contingents of the diminutive male slaves called "manlings" (WW No. 8/1, Spr '44: "Queen Clea's Tournament of Death"; and others). Indeed, Wonder Woman's attitude toward slavery seems to depend mainly on who is placed in charge of the slaves: "If girls want to be slaves," she muses in February–March 1943, "there's no harm in that. The bad thing for them is submitting to a master or to an evil mistress like Paula [Baroness Paula von Gunther]! A **good** mistress could do wonders with them!" (WW No. 3/3).

Though it may seem shocking at first, an acceptance of slavery is completely in keeping with the ethos of the Amazons as described in the chronicles. Bondage is pleasant, insist the chronicles, so long as one remains in good hands; imprisonment can be pleasurable, they say, so long as the warders have the best interests of their captives at

les, are whipped or otherwise punished for minor infractions of arbitrary discipline, and are forced to endure repeated degradations and humiliations. The Cheetah forces her slave girls to dress in zebra costumes, keeps them locked in cages, and whips them if they fail to observe the appropriate protocol of obsequiousness.

By and large, the slaves accept their servitude without complaint. Usually, in fact, they love their servitude, revelling in the arbitrary punishments and capricious humiliations to which they are continually subjected. In February–March 1943, for example, after Baroness Paula von Gunther has been defeated and her slave girls have been brought to Reform Island (*see* TRANSFORMATION ISLAND) for Amazon rehabilitative training, the AMAZONS are astounded to discover that the freed slaves simply will not accept their newly acquired status as free women. When MALA attempts to heart, and the captives submit to their captivity willingly and gratefully.

In May 1944 villainess MIMI MENDEZ escapes from Wonder Woman while en route to Reform Island to undergo rehabilitative training. Wonder Woman ultimately recaptures Mimi, but now Mimi will be sent to a United States prison instead of Reform Island.

"I'm sorry, Mimi," remarks Wonder Woman, "— you've exchanged character reform in pleasant bondage on Paradise Island for painful punishment in this man's world!" (Sen No. 29: "Adventure of the Escaped Prisoner").

An ethos of servitude is so integral to the Wonder Woman mythology that it permeates even the casual language of friendship and camaraderie. ". . .[W]hatever else I am," remarks Baroness Paula von Gunther to STEVE TREVOR in August 1944, after she has become Wonder Woman's friend and ally, "you can be sure I'm the princess' [Wonder Woman's] devoted slave!" (Sen No. 32: "The Crime Combine").

The term "loving submission," so often used by Wonder Woman and the Amazons, denotes willing, wholehearted surrender to those in authority, to those who know what is best for you and have your best interests at heart. It is often invoked to describe the grateful feelings that the prisoners on Transformation Island have toward their Amazon captors. Loving submission is the antithesis of "rebellion," a word which, in the Wonder Woman chronicles, implies a sort of willful self-destructiveness:

"I've learned being a rebel only leads to disaster . . ." confesses GERTA VON GUNTHER in July 1946, after she has recklessly carried out a series of dangerous scientific experiments in defiance of her mother's wishes. "I promise always to submit to loving authority" (Sen No. 55: "The Bughuman Plague").

In summary, the institution of slavery is portrayed frequently in the chronicles, appearing not only as an evil practiced by villains, but also in the guise of loving submission, an Amazon philosophy calling for the relentless repression of one's rebellious or assertive impulses in favor of unquestioning obedience to benevolent authority figures.

I. The Texts. 1. Locales. In the course of a career spanning more than three decades of adventure, Wonder Woman has traveled to distant planets (e.g., JUPITER, MARS, MERCURY, PLUTO, SATURN, and VENUS) and alien dimensions (e.g., DIMENSION X and the parallel world inhabited by TARA TERRUNA); back into the past and forward into the future; to far-off lands (e.g., EVELAND, NEP-

TUNIA, WOOLOO ISLAND, ZANI ISLAND, and ZARIKAN) and the strange world within the atom; to the lost lands of MU and ATLANTIS; and throughout her adopted country, the United States of America.

By and large, however, the adventures of Wonder Woman take place in and around two United States cities: New York City and Washington, D.C.

When Wonder Woman first arrives in the United States in January 1942, she deposits the wounded STEVE TREVOR at the Walter Reed Army Hospital in Washington, D.C., where she later works as a nurse in her adopted identity of Diana Prince (Sen No. 1). The HOLLIDAY COLLEGE FOR WOMEN, home of the HOLLIDAY GIRLS and the site of BARONESS PAULA VON GUNTHER's secret laboratory, is located in Washington, D.C., as is the headquarters of United States Military Intelligence, where, as Diana Prince, Wonder Woman obtains employment as Colonel Darnell's secretary (see DARNELL [GENERAL]) in March 1942 (Sen No. 3). Throughout the first decade of her career, Diana Prince — the girl who is secretly Wonder Woman — lives and works in Washington, D.C.

By the early 1950s, however, the chroniclers have inexplicably changed the locale of Wonder Woman's resident city from Washington, D.C., to New York City. Wonder Woman No. 46/1 asserts flatly that the U.S. Military Intelligence office headed by General Darnell is situated in New York City (Mar/Apr '51: "The Trail of the Lost Hours!"), not Washington, D.C., and numerous other texts over the next decade and a half echo this assertion. According to Wonder Woman No. 174/1, Steve Trevor and Diana Prince live in a place called Capital City (Jan/Feb '68: "Steve Trevor — Alias the Patriot!"), but Capital City, mentioned as it is in only one text, may be presumed to be a thinly disguised reference to Washington, D.C., or else mentioned only as the result of a chronicler's error.

Since the office of U.S. Military Intelligence cannot logically be presumed to have been moved or suddenly transferred from one city to another, it is impossible to resolve satisfactorily the discrepancy in the chronicles concerning the true locale of the vast majority of Wonder Woman's adventures. In all likelihood, however, Wonder Woman's life and career center around Washington, D.C., and the abrupt shifting of locales in the early 1950s owes itself to a chronicler's error.

2. Developments. a. THE WARTIME ADVENTURES. In December 1941–January 1942 an aircraft piloted by Steve Trevor crashes on the beach at Paradise Island, setting in motion a chain of events that

leads to the emergence of the Amazon princess Diana as Wonder Woman (AS No. 8: "Introducing Wonder Woman"). (*See* section A, Origin.)

In January 1942 Wonder Woman flies the wounded Steve Trevor back to America, meets promoter AL KALE, purchases the identification and credentials of U.S. Army nurse DIANA PRINCE (*see also* section B, the secret identity), and helps Steve Trevor raid a Nazi airbase (Sen No. 1).

In February 1942 Wonder Woman battles DOCTOR POISON and recruits the band of student allies known as the HOLLIDAY GIRLS (Sen No. 2).

In March 1942, as Diana Prince, Wonder Woman obtains employment as Colonel Darnell's secretary at U.S. Military Intelligence. During this same period, Wonder Woman discovers that EVE BROWN has been leaking defense secrets to the Nazis, captures the Nazi spy GROSS, and uses the mental radio (*see* section C 7, the mental radio) for the first time in the chronicles (Sen No. 3).

In April 1942 Wonder Woman matches wits with BARONESS PAULA VON GUNTHER, and loses her strength, for the first time in the chronicles, when a man welds chains to her Amazon bracelets (*see* section C 2, the bracelets of submission) (Sen No. 4).

In May 1942 Wonder Woman foils an attempt by Axis spies to sabotage THE OCTOPUS, "the Navy's new mystery submarine" (Sen No. 5).

In June 1942 Wonder Woman receives her magic lasso (*see* section C 3, the magic lasso) as a gift from her mother, Queen Hippolyte, and matches wits with BARONESS PAULA VON GUNTHER (Sen No. 6).

In Summer 1942 Wonder Woman battles the Japanese spy SAN YAN (WW No. 1/2: "Wonder Woman Goes to the Circus!"), matches wits with BARONESS PAULA VON GUNTHER (WW No. 1/3), and, by uncovering the location of a secret Japanese "underground fortress" in Mexico — where the Japanese have hidden "3500 planes and 100,000 troops" — and forcing its commander to surrender, thwarts a Japanese plot to conquer Mexico (WW No. 1/4: "The Greatest Feat of Daring in Human History!"). During this same period, Wonder Woman No. 1/1 recounts the history of the Amazons (*see* AMAZONS [section A, History]) as well as details surrounding Wonder Woman's birth and early childhood (*see* section D, the early life [as Princess Diana]).

In July 1942 Wonder Woman thwarts a scheme by BARONESS PAULA VON GUNTHER to monopolize America's milk supply (Sen No. 7).

In August 1942 Wonder Woman meets GLORIA BULLFINCH (Sen No. 8).

In September 1942 Wonder Woman defeats the fiendish DR. CUE and renews her acquaintance with DIANA PRINCE, the U.S. Army nurse from whom she originally acquired her secret identity (Sen No. 9).

In Fall 1942 Wonder Woman battles the war god MARS and his infamous "three commanders": the EARL OF GREED, the DUKE OF DECEPTION, and LORD CONQUEST (WW No. 2/1-4).

In October 1942 Wonder Woman matches wits with the Japanese spy ISHTI (Sen No. 10).

In October–November 1942 Wonder Woman meets the lovely QUEEN DESIRA, ruler of the planet Venus (AS No. 13: "Shanghaied into Space!").

In November 1942 Wonder Woman battles the villainess REBLA (Sen No. 11).

In December 1942 Wonder Woman matches wits with BARONESS PAULA VON GUNTHER (Sen No. 12).

In Winter 1942 Wonder Woman captures MR. KIPP and lends a helping hand to TOMMY ROYDEN (CC No. 1: "The Mystery of the House of Seven Gables").

In January 1943 Wonder Woman matches wits with the evil OLGA (Sen No. 13).

In February–March 1943 Wonder Woman has a series of encounters with BARONESS PAULA VON GUNTHER which culminate in the transformation of the baroness from her most treacherous adversary into her closest friend and most loyal ally (WW No. 3/1-4: no title; no title; no title; "Ordeal of Fire!").

In March 1943 Wonder Woman apprehends SIMON SLIKERY (Sen No. 15).

In Spring 1943 Wonder Woman matches wits with FAUSTA GRABLES (CC No. 2: "Wanted by Hitler, Dead or Alive").

In April 1943 Wonder Woman exposes Etta Candy's fiancé as a "Gestapo agent working for the Japs" (Sen No. 16). (*See* SCHULTZ, KARL.)

In April–May 1943 Wonder Woman helps BARONESS PAULA VON GUNTHER perform her three great labors for the goddess Aphrodite: they foil a "terrible Jap plan" to incite a civil war between America's men and women; battle BLAKFU, king of the Mole Men; and reform unscrupulous IVAR TORGSON and his fellow rubber magnates. During this same period, Wonder Woman rescues Gerta von Gunther from the clutches of MAVIS (WW No. 4/1-4).

In May 1943 Wonder Woman matches wits with PRINCESS YASMINI (Sen No. 17: "The Talking Lion!").

In June 1943 Wonder Woman thwarts the sinister machinations of the Inca priest QUITO (Sen No. 18).

In June–July 1943 Wonder Woman battles DR. PSYCHO (WW No. 5/1: "Battle for Womanhood"), defeats the war god MARS (WW No. 5/2), and renews her battle with DR. PSYCHO (WW No. 5/3).

In Summer 1943 Wonder Woman meets ERIC LANDER (CC No. 3: "The Invisible Invader").

In July 1943 Wonder Woman matches wits with MAVIS, and, for the first time in the chronicles, goes berserk when her Amazon bracelets (see section C 2, the bracelets of submission) are forcibly removed (Sen No. 19: "The Unbound Amazon").

In August 1943 Wonder Woman battles the Nazi spy STOFFER (Sen No. 20).

In September 1943 Wonder Woman matches wits with AMERICAN ADOLF (Sen No. 21: "War Against Society").

In Fall 1943 Wonder Woman captures BERTHA NAGLE (CC No. 4: "The Purloined Pressure Coordinator") and battles the CHEETAH (WW No. 6/1–3: "Wonder Woman and the Cheetah"; "The Adventure of the Beauty Club"; "The Conquest of Paradise").

In October 1943 Wonder Woman renews her battle with the CHEETAH (Sen No. 22: "The Secret Submarine").

In November 1943 Wonder Woman battles the menace of "war laugh mania" (see WAR LAUGH MANIA) (Sen No. 23).

In December 1943 Wonder Woman matches wits with Princess Maru (see DOCTOR POISON), and receives an inspiration from Aphrodite for controlling her Amazon plane (see section C 4, the robot plane) by mental radio (Sen No. 24: "Adventure of the Pilotless Plane").

In Winter 1943 Wonder Woman matches wits with ZARA (CC No. 5: "Mystery of the Crimson Flame").

In February 1944 Wonder Woman receives some unexpected assistance from a mysterious ally known only as the Masquerader (Sen No. 26: "The Masquerader"). (See HIPPOLYTE [QUEEN].)

In March 1944 Wonder Woman matches wits with ELY CLOSE (Sen No. 27: "The Fun Foundation").

In Spring 1944 Wonder Woman apprehends COUNTESS MAZUMA (CC No. 6: "The Mystery of Countess Mazuma!") and journeys to Atlantis for a series of battles with the ruthless QUEEN CLEA (WW No. 8/1–3: "Queen Clea's Tournament of Death"; "The Girl with the Iron Mask"; "The Captive Queen").

In April 1944 Wonder Woman thwarts the sinister machinations of Police Chief Smack and MAYOR PRUDE (Sen No. 28: "The Malice of the Green Imps").

In May 1944 Wonder Woman matches wits with MIMI MENDEZ (Sen No. 29: "Adventure of the Escaped Prisoner").

In June 1944 Wonder Woman defeats mystic cult leader ANTON UNREAL (Sen No. 30: "The 4th Dimension Kidnapers").

In Summer 1944 Wonder Woman battles the VULTURE KING (CC No. 7: "The Vulture's Nest!") and has a series of encounters with the treacherous GIGANTA (WW No. 9/1–3: "Evolution Goes Haywire!"; "The Freed Captive"; no title).

In August 1944 Wonder Woman matches wits with the CRIME CHIEF (Sen No. 32: "The Crime Combine").

In September 1944 Wonder Woman meets PERCY PRINGLE (Sen No. 33: "The Disappearance of Tama").

In Fall 1944 Wonder Woman apprehends CASINO (CC No. 8: "The Amazon Bride") and fights a series of battles with DUKE MEPHISTO SATURNO (WW No. 10/1–3: "Spies from Saturn"; "The Sky Road"; "Wonder Woman's Boots!").

In October 1944 Wonder Woman matches wits with MAYOR GOODE (Sen No. 34: "Edgar's New World!").

In November 1944 Wonder Woman journeys to Atlantis to battle SONTAG HENYA (Sen No. 35: "Girls Under the Sea").

In December 1944 Wonder Woman matches wits with BEDWIN FOOTH (Sen No. 36: "Battle Against Revenge").

In Winter 1944 Wonder Woman matches wits with the villainess NEPTUNE (CC No. 9: "The Subsea Pirates") and has a series of encounters with HYPNOTA THE GREAT (WW No. 11/1–3: "The Slaves of the Evil Eye"; "The Unseen Menace"; "The Slave Smugglers").

In January 1945 Paradise Island is invaded by the crew of a Nazi submarine, but the raiders are beaten back by Wonder Woman and MALA (Sen No. 37: "The Invasion of Paradise Island").

In February 1945 Wonder Woman apprehends a gang led by JOE "THE GYP" BAMKO (Sen No. 38: "Racketeers Kidnap Miss Santa Claus").

In March 1945 Wonder Woman battles NERO (Sen No. 39: "In the Clutches of Nero").

In Spring 1945 Wonder Woman matches wits with the THIRD WORLD WAR PROMOTERS (see also DESIRA [QUEEN]) (WW No. 12/1–3: no title; "The Ordeal of Fire"; "The Conquest of Venus") and thwarts the sinister machinations of the GREAT BLUE FATHER (CC No. 10: "The Great Blue Father").

In April 1945 Wonder Woman matches wits with COUNTESS DRASKA NISHKI (Sen No. 40: "Draska the Deadly").

In May 1945 Wonder Woman meets "CREEPER" JACKSON (Sen No. 41: "The Octopus Plants").

In June 1945 Wonder Woman matches wits with COUNTESS DRASKA NISHKI (Sen No. 42: "Peril on Paradise Island").

In Summer 1945 Wonder Woman battles the CHEETAH (CC No. 11: "The Cheetah Returns!") and matches wits with KING RIGOR and the Seal Men (WW No. 13/1–3: "The Icebound Maidens"; "The Mystery Maid"; "Slaves in the Electric Gardens").

In July 1945 Wonder Woman meets JOEL HEYDAY (Sen No. 43: "Three Pretty Girls").

In August 1945 Wonder Woman apprehends the enemy spy who has been posing as LIEUT. ERICH STURM of Army Intelligence (Sen No. 44: "Chains and Bracelets").

In September 1945 Wonder Woman battles "GENERAL" JOSÉ PIEREZ and his ruthless Mexican "bandidos" (Sen No. 45: "In the Enemy's Hands").

In Fall 1945 Wonder Woman defeats DALMA (CC No. 12: "Rebellion on Paradise Island!") and battles the GENTLEMAN KILLER (WW No. 14/1–3: "Captured by Leprechauns"; "The Gentleman Killer Strikes Again!"; no title).

In October 1945 Wonder Woman smashes the LAWBREAKERS' PROTECTIVE LEAGUE (Sen No. 46: "The Lawbreakers' League").

In November 1945 Wonder Woman battles the UNKNOWN (Sen No. 47: "The Terror of the Tycoon Club").

In December 1945 Wonder Woman matches wits with TOPSO AND TEENA (Sen No. 48).

In Winter 1945 Wonder Woman apprehends PALTRO DEBUM (CC No. 13: "The Underwater Follies") and battles the tyrannical SOLO (WW No. 15: chs. 1–3 – "The First Battle of Neptunia"; "The Masters of the Water"; "In the Killer's Cage").

b. THE POSTWAR ADVENTURES. In January 1946 Wonder Woman matches wits with ZAVIA (Sen No. 49: "The Mystery of Lake Iceberg").

In February 1946 Wonder Woman smashes the "EARS" FELLOCK blackmail gang (Sen No. 50: "The Case of the Girl in Braces"). (See also CORINE.)

In March 1946 Wonder Woman matches wits with BOSS BREKEL (Sen No. 51: "The Crime of Boss Brekel!").

In March–April 1946 Wonder Woman battles KING PLUTO (WW No. 16/1–3: "The Secret of the Dark Planet!"; "The River of Liquid Fire"; "King Pluto's Revenge").

In April 1946 Wonder Woman meets PROF. TOXINO (Sen No. 52: "The Brand of Madness").

In April–May 1946 Wonder Woman matches wits with WANTA WYNN (CC No. 14: "The Severed Bracelets").

In May–June 1946 Wonder Woman journeys through the time barrier for a battle with the Roman dictator SULLA (WW No. 17: "The Winds of Time").

In June 1946 Wonder Woman battles DR. FIENDO (Sen No. 54: "The Treachery of Fiendo").

In June–July 1946 Wonder Woman defeats URIAH SKINFLINT (CC No. 15: "Flaming Fury").

In July 1946 Wonder Woman battles the BUGHUMANS (Sen No. 55: "The Bughuman Plague").

In July–August 1946 Wonder Woman matches wits with DR. PSYCHO (WW No. 18/1–3: "The Return from the Dead"; "The Drugged WAC"; "Ectoplasmic Death").

In August 1946 Wonder Woman apprehends DR. NOVEL (Sen No. 56: "Anti-Atomic Metal").

In August–September 1946 Wonder Woman lends a helping hand to young DON ELLIOT (CC No. 16: "The Battle of Desires").

In September 1946 Wonder Woman matches wits with SYONIDE (Sen No. 57: "Hatchet of Death").

In September–October 1946 Wonder Woman battles SUPREME LEADER BLITZ (WW No. 19/1–3: "Invisible Terror!"; "The Witchdoctor's Cauldron"; "In the Lair of the Death Ray Criminals").

In October 1946 Wonder Woman meets OLIVE NORTON (Sen No. 58: "The Bog Trap").

In October–November 1946 Wonder Woman battles ODIN and his Valkyries (CC No. 17: "The Valkyries' Prey").

In November 1946 Wonder Woman matches wits with the SNOW MAN (Sen No. 59: "Reign of Blue Terror").

In November–December 1946 Wonder Woman battles Nifty and the Air Pirates (WW No. 20/1: "Terrors of the Air"). (See CHEMICO [PROF.].)

In December 1946 Wonder Woman lends a helping hand to BIFTON JONES (Sen No. 60: "The Ordeal of Queen Boadicea").

In December 1946–January 1947 Wonder Woman journeys to Atlantis to battle the menace of MANLIUS (CC No. 18: "The Menace of the Rebel Manlings").

In January 1947 Wonder Woman thwarts a scheme by BLUFF ROBUST (Sen No. 61: "The Million Dollar Tennis Game").

In January–February 1947 Wonder Woman matches wits with QUEEN ATOMIA (WW No. 21/1–3: "The Mystery of the Atom World"; "Tide of Atomic Fire"; "Ruler of the Atom World").

In February 1947 Wonder Woman journeys to Anglonia, where she battles the villainous BLACK ROBERT OF DOGWOOD (Sen No. 62: "The Mysterious Prisoners of Anglonia").

In February–March 1947 Wonder Woman thwarts the sinister machinations of AMBROSE

VENTURE (CC No. 19: "The Battle for Eternal Youth").

In March 1947 Wonder Woman apprehends PROF. VIBRATE (Sen No. 63: "The Wail of DOOM!").

In March–April 1947 Wonder Woman matches wits with "COSMETIC" KOSMET (WW No. 22/1: "The Color Thief"), battles DUKE MEPHISTO SATURNO (WW No. 22/2: "The Island of Evil"), and journeys to Venus to thwart the sinister machinations of GELL OSEY (WW No. 22/3: "Jealousy Visits the Winged Women of Venus!").

In April 1947 Wonder Woman battles the CLOUDMEN (Sen No. 64: "The Adventure of the Little Cloud People").

In April–May 1947 Wonder Woman travels to Zani Island to stem a native uprising against the benevolent PRINCE SLEEKO (CC No. 20: "The Buddha Wishing Ring").

In May 1947 Wonder Woman matches wits with LIM SNAIT (Sen No. 65: "Treachery in the Arctic").

In May–June 1947 Wonder Woman battles ODIN and his Valkyries (WW No. 23/1: "Siege of the Savage War Maidens"), and thwarts the sinister machinations of the pharaoh AKNATEN (WW No. 23/2: "The Vanishing Mummy!").

In June 1947 Wonder Woman apprehends SLICK SKEENER (Sen No. 66: "Prisoners of Cops and Robbers").

In June–July 1947 Wonder Woman battles QUEEN SHARKEETA (CC No. 21: "The Seige [sic] of the Flying Mermaids!").

In July 1947 Wonder Woman matches wits with DAREDEVIL DIX (Sen No. 67: "The Secret of the Bar-L Ranch!").

In July–August 1947 Wonder Woman meets the MASK (WW No. 24/2: "The Challenge of the Mask").

In August 1947 Wonder Woman battles hijackers who attempt to steal PROF. MARLOWE's incredible "chemic-extracto" machine (Sen No. 68: "Secret of the Menacing Octopus!").

In August–September 1947 Wonder Woman matches wits with SATURNETTE (CC No. 22: "The Captives of Saturnette!").

In September 1947 Wonder Woman investigates the murder of Tricco the magician (Sen No. 69: "Mystery Behind A,B,C,!"). (See WELLS, DARCY.)

In September–October 1947 Wonder Woman thwarts an invasion of Earth by the inhabitants of the planetoid RYKORNIA (WW No. 25/1: "Siege of the Rykornians"), apprehends the "YELLOW MASK" GANG (WW No. 25/2: "Who'll Adopt Teasy?"), and matches wits with the PURPLE PRIESTESS (WW No. 25/3: "The Judgment of Goddess Vultura").

In October–November 1947 Wonder Woman battles KING IRONSIDES (CC No. 23: "Siege of the Iron Giants").

In November 1947 Wonder Woman matches wits with the treacherous QUEEN FLAMINA (Sen No. 71: "The Invasion of the Sun Warriors").

In November–December 1947 Wonder Woman meets QUEEN CELERITA and the "flying giantesses" of Mercury (WW No. 26/1: "Speed Maniacs from Mercury!"), matches wits with MRS. TIGRA TROPICA (WW No. 26/2: "The Mistress of the Beasts"), and becomes embroiled in the war between the "golden women" of the Red Planet and the "genii people" of the White Star (WW No. 26/3: "The Golden Women and the White Star!"). (See CRYSTALLAR [KING].)

In December 1947 Wonder Woman battles the BLUE SEAL GANG (Sen No. 72: "The Menace of the Blue Seal Gang").

In December 1947–January 1948 Wonder Woman lends a helping hand to cowgirl JUDY MACGREGOR (CC No. 24: "Empress of the Sea-Brigands!").

In January 1948 Wonder Woman journeys into the past to rescue FAITH ALDEN from being executed for witchcraft (Sen No. 73: "The Witches' Trials").

In January–February 1948 Wonder Woman apprehends PIK SOCKET (WW No. 27/1: "The Secret of the Kidnapped Dummy!"), captures a gang of rustlers who have been plaguing HARD CANDY's Bar-L Ranch (WW No. 27/2: "The Legend of Rainbow and Stardust!"), and journeys into the past to battle King Ersatz and COUNT GASTON (WW No. 27/3: "The Mystical Power of Idea-Forms!").

In February 1948 Wonder Woman smashes an international jewel smuggling ring headed by gangster Spud Spangle (Sen No. 74: "The Undersea Cowboys!").

In February–March 1948 Wonder Woman defeats BADRA (CC No. 25: "Hatred of Badra!").

In March 1948 Wonder Woman apprehends SHARK (Sen No. 75: "The Return of 'Shaggy,' the Leprechaun!").

In March–April 1948 Wonder Woman battles VILLAINY INCORPORATED (WW No. 28/1–3: "Villainy Incorporated!"; "Trap of Crimson Flame"; "In the Hands of the Merciless!").

In April 1948 Wonder Woman matches wits with KING DIAMOND (Sen No. 76: "Murder Referees the Round!").

In April–May 1948 Wonder Woman thwarts the sinister machinations of the treacherous LYA (CC No. 26: "Deception's Daughter").

In May 1948 Wonder Woman battles Boss BREKEL (Sen No. 77: "Tress's Terrible Mistake!").

In May–June 1948 Wonder Woman matches wits with PRIME MINISTER BLIZZARD (WW No. 29/1: "Ice World's Conquest!") and helps Dion Boru defeat PADDY GYPSO (WW No. 29/2: "Tale of the Tigers").

In June 1948 Wonder Woman battles FURIOSA (Sen No. 78: "The Mistress of Masquerade!").

In June–July 1948 Wonder Woman matches wits with ANTI ELECTRIC (CC No. 27: "Anti Electric").

In July 1948 Wonder Woman meets LEILA and Solala, the twin rulers of the Sun Country (Sen No. 79: "Land of Mirrors!").

In July–August 1948 Wonder Woman brings OLIVE NORTON to Paradise Island, where they view a movie depicting the teen-aged Wonder Woman's battle with the RADIUM GIANTS (WW No. 30/1: "The Secret of the Limestone Caves"). During this same period, Wonder Woman matches wits with MONA MENISE (WW No. 30/2: "The Song of the Sirens!") and thwarts a scheme by BERTRAM HARSH to discredit "famous woman penologist" Suzan Patience (WW No. 30/3: "A Human Bomb!").

In August 1948 Wonder Woman apprehends DON ENRAGO (Sen No. 80: "The Swinging Scimitar!").

In August–September 1948 Wonder Woman matches wits with COUNTESS HATRA (CC No. 28: "The Sinister Countess Hatra!").

In September 1948 Wonder Woman battles DR. FRENZI (Sen No. 81: "When Treachery Wore a Green Shirt!").

In September–October 1948 Wonder Woman meets DR. DIRKE (WW No. 31/1: "The Shrinking Formula!"), battles SOLO (WW No. 31/2: "The Planet of Plunder!"), and defeats the crafty TRIXTER (WW No. 31/3: "The Racketeer of Magic!").

In October 1948 Wonder Woman helps the women of the "inner moon-planet" depose the evil KING LUNAR (Sen No. 82: "Brain Pirates from the Inner Moon-World!").

In October–November 1948 Wonder Woman battles "CRIME BRAIN" DOONE (CC No. 29: "Machine of Schemes").

In November 1948 Wonder Woman helps the women of Noman defeat the evil dictator PROWD (Sen No. 83: "The Sinister Olympics!").

In November–December 1948 Wonder Woman battles Uvo, "arch war lord" of the planet Uranus (WW No. 32/1: "Uvo of Uranus!" pts. 1–2 — "The Amazing Global Theft!"; "Thunder in Space!").

In December 1948 Wonder Woman matches wits with DUKE DAXO (Sen No. 84: "The Bottle Cast Up by the Sea!").

In January 1949 Wonder Woman teaches a much-needed lesson to LESLIE M. GRESHAM (Sen No. 85: "The Girl Who Wanted to Be an Amazon!").

In January–February 1949 Wonder Woman battles INVENTA (WW No. 33/1: "The Four Dooms" pts. 1–2 — "Paradise Island Condemned!"; "The Titanic Trials!") and matches wits with extraterrestrial aliens from the planet Murkton (WW No. 33/2: "The Menace of Murkton!"). (See PALLIDA [QUEEN].)

In February 1949 Wonder Woman apprehends C. O. LECTOR (Sen No. 86: "The Secret of the Amazing Bracelets!").

In March 1949 Wonder Woman journeys into the past to protect the town of Twin Peaks from the sinister machinations of JABEZ DEXTER (Sen No. 87: "Wonder Woman Tames the Wild West!").

In March–April 1949 Wonder Woman matches wits with the DUKE OF DECEPTION (WW No. 34: "The Mystery of the Rhyming Riddle!" chs. 1–3 — "Deception Strikes Again"; "The Phantasms of Deception!"; "The Mystery of the Rhyming Riddle!").

In April 1949 Wonder Woman apprehends the unscrupulous VAN KENT (Sen No. 88: "Wonder Woman Goes to Hollywood!").

In May 1949 Wonder Woman battles the ABACUS RACKEET gang (Sen No. 89: "Amazon Queen for a Day!").

In May–June 1949 Wonder Woman matches wits with FLY WRIGHT (WW No. 35/1: "Nine Lives Club!"), thwarts the sinister machinations of DIRK JAXO (WW No. 35/2: "Jaxo, Master of Thought!"), and defeats unscrupulous timber contractor ABNER GRABB (WW No. 35/3: "The Stolen Forest!").

In June 1949 Wonder Woman lends a helping hand to HELEN CARY (Sen No. 90: "The Secret of the Modern Sphinx!").

In July–August 1949 Wonder Woman recounts the story of QUEEN ASTRA (WW No. 36/1: "The Girl Who Saved Paradise Island!"), meets VELMA VANTON (WW No. 36/2: "Wonder Woman's Double!"), and matches wits with LORD CRUELO (WW No. 36/3: "The Return of the Flying Saucers!").

In August 1949 Wonder Woman recounts an attempt by the DUKE OF DECEPTION to obliterate Earth with "titanic solar rays" (Sen No. 92: "The Pebble That Saved the World!").

In September–October 1949 Wonder Woman matches wits with the mind reader TALBOT (Sen No. 93: "The Man Who Could Read Wonder Woman's Mind!"), journeys into the past to defeat the "savage Tartar chief" CHANG (WW No. 37/1: "The Riddle of the Chinese Mummy Case!"), suffers heartbreak as the result of Steve Trevor's romance with LORELEI LORN (WW No. 37/2: "The Fatal Beauty!"), captures a gang of criminals known as the Lother Gang, and rescues PROF. OWLER and his friends from the enchantment of Circe (WW No. 37/3: "The Secrets of Circe!").

In November–December 1949 Wonder Woman apprehends the BIG REXO GANG (Sen No. 94: "S O S Wonder Woman!"), lends a helping hand to ABIGAIL KEATING (WW No. 38/1: "The Girl from Yesterday!"), defeats the tyrannical BRUTEX (WW No. 38/2: "Wonder Woman Captures the Moon!"), and teaches a much-needed lesson to banker THOMAS TIGHE (WW No. 38/3: "The Five Tasks of Thomas Tighe!").

In January–February 1950 Wonder Woman prevents STEVE TREVOR from uncovering her secret identity (Sen No. 95: "The Unmasking of Wonder Woman!"); gives a much-needed morale boost to ALEX SMITH, LEWIS BRAND, JOAN HALL, AL ROGERS, and MARY DOLAN (WW No. 39/1: "The Trail of Thrills!"); and helps Dean Meg Sourpuss find happiness with HERBERT MERRILY (WW No. 39/2: "The Modern Midas!").

In March–April 1950 Wonder Woman matches wits with TORA RIVVERS (WW No. 40/1: "Hollywood Goes to Paradise Island" pts. 1–2 – "The Mile High Menace!"; "The Undersea Invasion!"), and lends a helping hand to CAPT. MACDONALD (WW No. 40/2: "Passengers of Fate!").

In May–June 1950 Wonder Woman becomes the romance editor of the *Daily Globe* (Sen No. 97: "Wonder Woman, Romance Editor"), apprehends J. J. JENKINS (WW No. 41/1: "Wonder Woman – Private Detective!"), adopts the name BELLE DAZZLE during a period of temporary amnesia (WW No. 41/2: "Wonder Woman vs. Wonder Woman!"), and journeys to Phobos, inner moon of the planet Mars, to rescue Steve Trevor from the clutches of the tyrant GHURKOS (WW No. 41/3: "The Trial of Steve Trevor!").

In July–August 1950 Wonder Woman lends a helping hand to JANET BROWN (Sen No. 98: "Wonder Woman's Strange Mission!"), matches wits with JOSH SLICKER (WW No. 42/1: "Danger on the Speedway!"), and thwarts an attempted invasion of Earth by GENERAL VERTIGO (WW No. 42/2: "The Mystery of the Missing Monday!").

In September–October 1950 Wonder Woman matches wits with JASPER LANG (Sen No. 99: "The Man Who Couldn't Make a Mistake!"), apprehends a trio of foreign spies (*see* Z-ONE) (WW No. 43/1: "The Amazing Spy Ring Mystery"), battles NUCLEAR (WW No. 43/2: "Nuclear Returns!"), and investigates the murder of COLONEL SOUTH (WW No. 43/3: "Who Killed Col. South!").

In November–December 1950 Wonder Woman matches wits with IGOR GORGO and Zita Zanders (Sen No. 100: "Wonder Woman, Hollywood Star!"), and battles the diabolical MASTER DESTROYER (WW No. 44: "The Monarch of the Sargasso Sea!" chs. I–III — no title; "Wonder Woman's Decision"; "The Final Battle of the Sargasso Sea").

In January–February 1951 Wonder Woman matches wits with PROF. LUXO (Sen No. 101: "Battle for the Atom World!") and has a brief encounter with MOON O'DAY (WW No. 45/2: "The Amazon and the Leprechaun!").

In March–April 1951 Wonder Woman meets QUEEN HELEN OF THE SOUTH SEAS (Sen No. 102: "The Queen of the South Seas!"), captures the GRENADE GANG (WW No. 46/1: "The Trail of the Lost Hours!"), battles PROF. TURGO (WW No. 46/2: "The Moon of Peril!"), and matches wits with PROF. JENKEL (WW No. 46/3: "Wonder Woman's Twin!").

In May–June 1951 Wonder Woman journeys into the future to battle the villain PROTO (Sen No. 103: "100 Year Duel!"), meets the MOLE MEN who live beneath the North Pole (WW No. 47/1: "World Below the North Pole!"), journeys into the past to meet AH-WA-NE (WW No. 47/2: "Mystery of the Indian Totem Pole"), and matches wits with the DUKE OF DECEPTION (WW No. 47/3: "The Bridge from Mars!").

In July–August 1951 Wonder Woman thwarts the sinister machinations of the DUKE OF DECEPTION (Sen No. 104: "The End of Paradise Island"), battles ROBOT WOMAN (WW No. 48/1: "Wonder Woman vs Robot Woman!"), apprehends CAPTAIN BARNACLE (WW No. 48/2: "The Treasure of Capt. Storm"), and matches wits with the MONTE GANG (WW No. 48/3: "The Theft of the Robot Plane").

In September–October 1951 Wonder Woman battles the "robot people" of AUTOMATO (Sen No. 105: "The Secret of the Giant Forest"), journeys to the land of Mu to battle the evil PRINCE GHU (WW No. 49/1: "Return of the Phantom Empire"), becomes a temporary foster mother to young JAN WILLIAMS (WW No. 49/2: "Little Miss Wonder Woman!"), and matches wits with the Boss (WW No. 49/3: "The Mystery of the Magic Typewriter!").

In November–December 1951 Wonder Woman battles the last living descendant of BARON DE BOAR (Sen No. 106: "The Knights of Terror!") and captures GENERAL VORO, "the man of a thousand faces" (WW No. 50/1: "Menace of the Master Spy!").

In January–February 1952 Wonder Woman matches wits with GARO (WW No. 51/1: "The

Amazing Impersonation!") and persuades one of her sister Amazons that it would be foolhardy of her to relinquish her Amazon heritage of immortality and happiness in order to become a crime-fighter in the world of men (WW No. 51/2: "Wonder Woman's Strange Substitute!"). (*See* AMAZONS [section B, Aphrodite's Law].)

In March–April 1952 Wonder Woman battles PRIME MINISTER ZAGO (WW No. 52/1: "Her Majesty — Queen Wonder Woman!"), and journeys to the Planet of Thought to defeat the evil wizard STROGO (WW No. 52/2: "The Battle for Fairyland!").

In May–June 1952 Wonder Woman matches wits with the CRIME MASTER OF TIME (WW No. 53/1: "The Crime Master of Time!"), meets MARY CARLTON (WW No. 53/2: "The Wonder Woman Nobody Knows!"), and inherits the Western town of RAINBOW'S END (WW No. 53/3: "The Secret Treasure at Rainbow's End!").

In July–August 1952 Wonder Woman journeys into the past to defeat the wizard MERLIN (WW No. 54/1: "The Wizard of Castle Sinister!"), battles an army of extraterrestrial ultraviolet invaders (*see* ULTRAVIOLET INVADERS, THE) (WW No. 54/2: "The Invisible Invasion!"), captures a gang of criminals led by racketeer Pipe Jackson, and prevents BETH DUNCAN from uncovering her secret identity (WW No. 54/3: "Wonder Woman's Triple Threat!").

In September–October 1952 Wonder Woman journeys to the planet CHEQUERANA (WW No. 55/2: "The Chessmen of Doom!"), and investigates the mysterious death of PROF. DANIELS (WW No. 55/3: "Invasion of the Raindrops!").

In November–December 1952 Wonder Woman apprehends the NESTOR BROTHERS (WW No. 56/1: "Homicide Highway!") and captures the PLOTTER gang (WW No. 56/3: "The Case of the 8 Million Witnesses!").

In January–February 1953 Wonder Woman battles the MOLE MEN (WW No. 57/1: "The Man Who Shook the Earth!"), visits the "strange world" of ATLANTIS (WW No. 57/2: "Vengeance of the Undersea Empire!"), and journeys through the time barrier to 15th-century Florence, where she defeats the evil DUKE PERILOSA (WW No. 57/3: "The Four Trials of Terror!").

In March–April 1953 Wonder Woman matches wits with BRAIN (WW No. 58/1: "Seven Days to Doom!"), battles PHAETHON (WW No. 58/2: "The Man Who Stole the Sun!"), and thwarts a horrifying termite invasion (WW No. 58/3: "Terror of the Termites"). (*See* TERMITE QUEEN, THE.)

In May–June 1953 Wonder Woman battles DUKE DAZAM (WW No. 59/1: "Wonder Woman's Invisible Twin!") and meets JOSHUA T. WHYTE (WW No. 59/3: "The Million Dollar Penny!").

In July–August 1953, after Baroness Paula von Gunther has peered into the future with an Amazon "futuray" and learned that civilization will be reduced to rubble by a cataclysmic world war in the year 1963, Wonder Woman journeys through the time barrier to 1963, where she helps defeat the evil forces who have been responsible for instigating the war. Despite Wonder Woman's efforts, however, the world war has still taken place and the Earth has been reduced to rubble by the fighting.

Back in Paula's laboratory in the year 1953, Wonder Woman learns that the devastating war occurred in the first place only because American delegates, unexpectedly delayed by an auto accident, failed to arrive at a crucial international conference in time to cast the deciding vote for peace. Returning through the time barrier to 1963, but this time to a point in time prior to the onset of the war, Wonder Woman succeeds in preventing the fateful auto accident, thereby enabling the American delegates to arrive at their conference in time to cast the vote needed to avert world war. (WW No. 60/1: "The War That Never Happened!").

In September–October 1953 Wonder Woman battles the "troglodytes" (*see* TROGLODYTES) (WW No. 61/1: "Earth's Last Hour!"), and journeys to far-off Bourabia to match wits with ZOXAB (WW No. 61/2: "Prisoners of the Ruby Ring!").

In November–December 1953 Wonder Woman apprehends ANGLES ANDREWS (WW No. 62/1: "Wonder Woman's Triple Identity!") and lends a helping hand to KING MOONO (WW No. 62/2: "Lamp of the Leprechauns!").

In January 1954 Wonder Woman battles the HUMAN TANK (WW No. 63/1: "The Human Tank!"), matches wits with the DUKE OF DECEPTION (WW No. 63/2: "The Secret Invasion!"), and journeys to 16th-century Sardonia to battle the evil PRINCE RUPERT (WW No. 63/3: "The Imposter Queen!").

In February 1954 Wonder Woman thwarts an invasion from the planet JUPITER (WW No. 64/1: "The 3-D Terror!"), apprehends RANDALL THOMAS (WW No. 64/2: "The Doom Dolls!"), and battles the THOUGHT MASTER (WW No. 64/3: "Wonder Woman's Last Hour!").

In April 1954 Wonder Woman matches wits with extraterrestrial invaders from the planet LAPIZURIA (WW No. 65/1: "The Stone Slayer!"), demolishes a pair of extraterrestrial flying saucers whose crews have been deliberately creating artificial tornadoes on Earth preparatory to launching an interplanetary invasion (WW No. 65/2: "The Tornado Detective!"), and journeys into the past to undo a successful invasion of Paradise Island by the DUKE OF DECEPTION (WW No. 65/3: "The Last Amazon!").

In May 1954 Wonder Woman matches wits with the DUKE OF DECEPTION (WW No. 66/1: "The Olympics of Terror!") and apprehends a gang of criminals who have been posing as American soldiers in order to steal military secrets for sale to the highest bidder (WW No. 66/3: "The Missing Wonder Woman!").

In July 1954 Wonder Woman smashes an enemy spy ring (see GORRA) (WW No. 67/1: "Confessions of a Spy!"), matches wits with ALBERT EASEL (WW No. 67/2: "Portraits of Peril!"), and battles the DORMER GANG (WW No. 67/3: "The Runaway Meteor!").

In August 1954 Wonder Woman thwarts a scheme by extraterrestrial aliens to destroy the Earth (see STONE [PROFESSOR]) (WW No. 68/1: "Landing of the Flying Saucers!"); foils an attempt by foreign spies to "destroy the vital air field that guards the air routes over the North Pole" in order to enable their country to "launch a surprise attack . . . on America!" (WW No. 68/2: "The Iceberg Bombshell!"); and apprehends a gang of diamond smugglers who, by obtaining jobs as motion picture technicians in movies with ocean-front locations, "were able to pick up smuggled diamonds from [their] boat — and transfer them ashore in movie equipment!" (WW No. 68/3: "T.N.T. Target!").

In October 1954 Wonder Woman demolishes an armada of spacecraft from the planet Mercury intent on conquering Earth "as a base to attack Jupiter" (WW No. 69/1: "Seeds of Peril!"), and journeys into the past to lend a helping hand to JOHANN GUTENBERG, CHRISTOPHER COLUMBUS, PAUL REVERE, and the WRIGHT BROTHERS (WW No. 69/2: "The Secret Hall of Fame!").

In November 1954 Wonder Woman battles the VOLCANO PROPHET (WW No. 70/1: "The Volcano-Maker!"), matches wits with the ANGLE MAN (WW No. 70/2: "The Invisible Trail!"), and apprehends PROFESSOR UXO (WW No. 70/3: "Wonder Woman's Wedding Day!").

In January 1955 Wonder Woman meets ALICE NORTON (WW No. 71/1: "One-Woman Circus!") and demolishes an armada of extraterrestrial spacecraft whose alien crews intend to conquer the Earth after first destroying all of Earth's metal — a substance toxic to the aliens — by means of their diabolical "metal-disintegrator canopy" (WW No. 71/2: "Ring Around the Earth!").

In February 1955 Wonder Woman journeys into the past to lend a helping hand to JOHN KEIGH and PRINCE ALAIN (WW No. 72/1: "S.O.S. from the Past!"), and battles the bizarre creatures known as

the MOLE GOLDINGS (WW No. 72/2: "The Golden Doom!").

In April 1955 Wonder Woman matches wits with the PRAIRIE PIRATES (WW No. 73/1: "The Prairie Pirates!").

In May 1955 Wonder Woman battles criminals at the SEASIDE AMUSEMENT PARK (WW No. 74/1: "The Carnival of Peril!") and matches wits with an octopuslike extraterrestrial alien (WW No. 74/2: "The Vanishing Villains!"). (See MOLECULAR ASSEMBLER.)

In July 1955 Wonder Woman matches wits with the ANGLER (WW No. 75/2: "$1,000,000 Secret!") and meets NILREMO (WW No. 75/3: "Inch-High Heroine!").

In August 1955 Wonder Woman prevents STEVE TREVOR from uncovering her secret identity (WW No. 76/1: "The Bird Who Revealed Wonder Woman's Identity!"), and journeys into the past to battle the evil DUKE NAXOK (WW No. 76/2: "The Face in the Desert!").

In October 1955 Wonder Woman apprehends a gang of criminals known as the Smokescreen Gang (WW No. 77/1: "The Island That Wonder Woman Built!") and thwarts a scheme by an evil extraterrestrial alien to shatter the Earth into fragments with three powerful time bombs, dismantling two of them before they explode and then annihilating the alien with the third one by hurling it at his spacecraft (WW No. 77/2: "The Earth Is a Time Bomb!").

In November 1955 Wonder Woman matches wits with the ANGLE MAN (WW No. 78/3: "The Million Dollar Mystery!").

In January 1956 Wonder Woman battles SPIDER (WW No. 79/1: "Wonder Woman in the Amazon Flea Circus!") and visits an A-bomb test site with STEVE TREVOR (WW No. 79/2: "Danger — Wonder Woman!").

In February 1956 Wonder Woman matches wits with MACHINO (WW No. 80/1: "The Mask of Mystery!") and has an adventure on SATURN (WW No. 80/3: "SOS — Saturn!").

In April 1956 Wonder Woman battles the DUKE OF DECEPTION (WW No. 81/1: "The Dream Dooms!") and matches wits with the ANGLE MAN (WW No. 81/3: "The Vanishing Criminal!").

In May 1956 Wonder Woman journeys into the past for an adventure with ROBIN HOOD (WW No. 82/1: "Wonder Woman Meets Robin Hood!").

In July 1956 Wonder Woman lends a helping hand to LLNO (WW No. 83/1: "The Boy from Nowhere!").

In August 1956 Wonder Woman matches wits with the ANGLE MAN (WW No. 84/1: "The Secret Wonder Woman!"), thwarts the sinister machinations of the DUKE OF DECEPTION (WW No. 84/2:

"The Planet of Illusion!"), and battles the PLANT PEOPLE (WW No. 84/3: "The Tree That Shook the Earth!").

In October 1956 Wonder Woman battles DUKE BALE (WW No. 85/1: "The Sword in the Sky!") and apprehends CAPT. VIRAGO (WW No. 85/3: "The Woman in the Bottle!").

In November 1956 Wonder Woman prevents VINCENT BRIAN from uncovering her secret identity (WW No. 86/1: "The Painting That Betrayed Wonder Woman!"), matches wits with SNATCHER (WW No. 86/2: "The Talking Robot Plane!"), and apprehends a gang of criminals led by a racketeer named Rakko (WW No. 86/3: "The Mystery of the Magnetic Footprints!").

c. THE LATER ADVENTURES. In January 1957 Wonder Woman battles an evil extraterrestrial alien attempting to pave the way for an alien conquest of Earth (see SUSPENDED-ANIMATOR) (WW No. 87/1: "The Day the Clocks Stopped!") and meets PROF. MANTON (WW No. 87/2: "Island of the Giants!").

In February 1957 Wonder Woman thwarts the sinister machinations of the DUKE OF DECEPTION (WW No. 88/1: "Mystery of the Vanishing Box!").

In April 1957 Wonder Woman lends a helping hand to JESSE BROWN (WW No. 89/2: "The Amazon Album!") and thwarts an extraterrestrial invasion of Earth by an armada of flying saucers (WW No. 89/3: "The Triple Heroine!").

In May 1957 Wonder Woman has an adventure on JUPITER (WW No. 90/1: "Planet of the Giants!").

In July 1957 Wonder Woman wins the Interplanetary Olympics by defeating the champion athletes of the major planets, including the Mercurian running champion, the Venusian swimming champion, and the Jovian weight-lifting champion (WW No. 91/1: "The Interplanetary Olympics!").

In August 1957 Wonder Woman battles evil crystalline beings in an alien dimension (see TREVOR, STEVE) (WW No. 92/1: "The Disappearing Train!"), and matches wits with the ANGLE MAN (WW No. 92/2: "The Revolt of the Winged Robot!").

In October 1957 Wonder Woman battles the MERMEN (WW No. 93/1: "Menace of the Mermen!") and thwarts the sinister machinations of the DUKE OF DECEPTION (WW No. 93/2: "The Shrinking City!").

In November 1957 Wonder Woman is marked for death by the DUKE OF DECEPTION (WW No. 94/2: "Target: Wonder Woman!"), and journeys into the past for an adventure with ROBIN HOOD (WW No. 94/3: "The Channel of Time!").

In January 1958 Wonder Woman rescues STEVE TREVOR from a hydrogen bomb blast (WW No. 95/1: "Wonder Woman — The World's Most Dangerous Human!"), and Wonder Woman No. 95/2

recalls Wonder Woman's battle with the brutal PHENEGS ("The Secret of Wonder Woman's Tiara!").

In February 1958 Wonder Woman matches wits with the ANGLE MAN (WW No. 96/3: "Prisoner of the Time Capsule!").

In April 1958 Wonder Woman pays a visit to the Paradise Island laboratory of PROF. ALPHA (WW No. 97: "The Runaway Time Express!" pts. 1–3 — "Stone Age Radio!"; "The Day Nature Ran Wild!"; "The Menace of Earth's Twin!").

In July 1958 Wonder Woman battles the SILICONS (WW No. 99/1: "Stampede of the Comets!").

In August 1958 Wonder Woman visits DIMENSION X (WW No. 100/1: "The Forest of Giants!" pts. 1–2 — "The Challenge of Dimension X!"; "The Forest of Giants!"), and, on Paradise Island, "the 100th issue of Wonder Woman's adventures" is sealed in a time capsule as a legacy for future generations (WW No. 100/2: "Wonder Woman's 100th Anniversary!").

In October 1958 Wonder Woman battles the TIME MASTER (WW No. 101/2: "The Fun House of Time!").

In November 1958 the fate of the Earth hangs on STEVE TREVOR's ability to distinguish between Wonder Woman and a pair of extradimensional robot look-alikes (WW No. 102: "The Three Faces of Wonder Woman" pts. 1–3 — "The First Face of Wonder Woman!"; "The Second Face of Wonder Woman"; "The Third Face of Wonder Woman").

In January 1959 Wonder Woman matches wits with the GADGET-MAKER (WW No. 103/2: "The Box of Three Dooms!").

In February 1959 Wonder Woman battles the DUKE OF DECEPTION (WW No. 104/2: "Key of Deception!").

In April 1959 Wonder Woman and STEVE TREVOR have an adventure on Saturn's moon Titan (WW No. 105/2: "Eagle of Space!").

In May 1959 Wonder Woman journeys to PLANET G (WW No. 106/1: "The Human Charm Bracelet!").

In July 1959 Wonder Woman matches wits with RONNKN and Zgggm (WW No. 107/2: "Gunslingers of Space!").

In August 1959 a band of ruthless insectlike extraterrestrial aliens beam a "barrage" of "mental rays" at Wonder Woman from their flying saucer in an effort to transform her into a criminal to facilitate their impending invasion of Earth. In the words of one alien:

> If we can force **her** to obey our every long distance command--no matter how **contrary** to her **real** nature--then every other earthling will be powerless against us! And our invasion will easily succeed!

We will start with simple commands and observe her reactions--until we force her, by her own actions--to become an outcast from her own world! Now--we will concentrate all our powers of mental telepathy on her!

For a time the alien plot succeeds, but Wonder Woman soon realizes that she is being victimized and cleverly tricks the aliens into launching their invasion of Earth prematurely. Lassoing the aliens' flying saucer with her magic lasso, Wonder Woman "hurls the invading craft into the atmosphere with such force — that friction destroys it," annihilating the aliens and ending forever their threat to Earth (WW No. 108/1: "Wanted--Wonder Woman"). During this same period, Wonder Woman is honored by the U.S. Post Office with a series of stamps commemorating her exploits (WW No. 108/2: "The Stamps of Doom!").

In October 1959 Wonder Woman prevents SLICKER from uncovering her secret identity (WW No. 109/2: "The Million Dollar Pigeon!").

In November 1959 Wonder Woman meets PRINCESS NO. 1003 (WW No. 110: "The Bridge of Crocodiles!").

In January 1960 Wonder Woman battles PROF. MENACE (WW No. 111/1: "The Robot Wonder Woman").

In April 1960 Wonder Woman matches wits with QUEEN MIKRA (WW No. 113: "The Invasion of the Sphinx Creatures!").

In May 1960 the gigantic helium-filled balloons in the Tracy Day Parade — one modeled after Wonder Woman and the others modeled after dinosaurs and other prehistoric monsters — suddenly break loose from their moorings and soar away into the sky. A few days later, however, the missing monster balloons reappear, wreaking havoc and destruction everywhere, having been brought miraculously to life by evil extraterrestrial aliens intent on using them to conquer the Earth.

One by one, however, Wonder Woman defeats the animated balloon monsters. When the animated Wonder Woman balloon steals a U.S. Government "S-bomb" capable of destroying the Earth, Wonder Woman lassoes the Wonder Woman balloon with her magic lasso, tows it into outer space behind her Amazon plane, and hurls it at the alien space fleet poised to attack the Earth, thereby detonating the S-bomb and obliterating the aliens (WW No. 114: "The Monster Express!" pts. 1–2 — "The Runaway Balloons!"; no title).

In July 1960 Wonder Woman matches wits with the ANGLE MAN (WW No. 115: "Graveyard of Monster Ships!").

In August 1960 Wonder Woman battles an extraterrestrial "crystal creature" (WW No. 116: "The Time Traveler of Terror!"). (See ANDRO [PROF.].)

In October 1960 Wonder Woman visits the campus of the Holliday College for Women to narrate a story to ETTA CANDY, TINA TOY, LITA LITTLE, and THELMA TALL (WW No. 117: "Fantastic Fishermen of the Forbidden Sea!").

In November 1960 Steve Trevor and MERMAN vie for Wonder Woman's affections (WW No. 118: "Wonder Woman's Impossible Decision!").

In May 1961 Wonder Woman battles the SINISTER SEER OF SATURN (WW No. 122: "The Skyscraper Wonder Woman!").

In August 1961 Wonder Woman, Wonder Girl, Wonder Tot, and Queen Hippolyte join forces to defeat MULTIPLE MAN in the first "impossible tale" (WW No. 124: "The Impossible Day!").

In October 1961 Steve Trevor and MERMAN vie for Wonder Woman's affections and help her thwart an invasion of Earth by evil extraterrestrial aliens (WW No. 125: "Wonder Woman--Battle Prize!").

In January 1962 Wonder Woman battles extraterrestrial invaders from PLANET K (WW No. 127/1: "Invaders of the Topsy-Turvy Planet"). (See also KUU-KUU.)

In February 1962 Wonder Woman matches wits with the ANGLE MAN (WW No. 128/2: "Vengeance of the Angle Man!").

In April 1962 Wonder Woman, Wonder Girl, Wonder Tot, and Queen Hippolyte join forces to defeat MULTIPLE MAN in the second "impossible tale" (WW No. 129: "The Return of Multiple Man!").

In May 1962 Wonder Woman matches wits with the ANGLE MAN (WW No. 130: "The Mirage Mirrors!").

In October 1962 Wonder Woman accepts an invitation from T. T. THOMAS to star in his movie *Amazon Girl* (WW No. 133/2: "Wonder Woman's Invincible Rival--Herself!").

In November 1962 Wonder Woman battles the IMAGE-MAKER (WW No. 134: "Menace of the Mirror-Wonder Woman!").

In February 1963 Wonder Woman meets the MACHINE MEN (WW No. 136: "Wonder Woman--World's Mightiest Menace!").

In April 1963 Wonder Woman and STEVE TREVOR visit a "parallel Earth" peopled entirely by robots (WW No. 137: "The Robot Wonder Woman!").

In October 1963 Wonder Woman battles the ANGLE MAN, the FIREWORKS MAN, and MOUSE MAN (WW No. 141: "The Academy of Arch-Villains!").

In January 1964 Wonder Woman helps Queen Hippolyte and the Amazons thwart an invasion of Paradise Island by extraterrestrial aliens (WW No. 143/1: "The Terror Trees of Forbidden Island"),

and matches wits with MOUSE MAN (WW No. 143/2: "The Amazon Mouse Trap!").

In August 1964 Wonder Woman is taken captive by the DUKE OF DECEPTION (WW No. 148: "The Olympics of the Doomed").

In August 1965 Wonder Woman battles the BRAIN PIRATE (WW No. 156: "The Brain Pirate of the Inner World!").

In October 1965 Wonder Woman meets the diabolical EGG FU THE FIRST (WW No. 157: "I--the Bomb!").

In November 1965 Wonder Woman renews her battle with EGG FU THE FIRST (WW No. 158/1: "The Fury of Egg Fu!").

From January 1966 through August 1966, the chronicles reflect an unsuccessful attempt on the part of the chroniclers to mimic the ambience and artistic style characteristic of the Wonder Woman texts of the 1940s. The stories during this period, all of which take place in the world of the early 1940s, are marred by numerous inconsistencies and factual errors. Following is a brief recapitulation of this eight-month period:

In January 1966, Wonder Woman No. 159 recapitulates the history of the Amazons (*see* AMAZONS [section A, History]), the story of Wonder Woman's birth and early childhood (*see* section D, the early life [as Princess Diana]), and the events surrounding the emergence of Princess Diana as Wonder Woman (*see* section A, Origin) ("The Golden Age Secret Origin of Wonder Woman").

In February 1966, Wonder Woman No. 160/1 recounts a past encounter between Wonder Woman and the CHEETAH ("The Amazon of Terror!"), and Wonder Woman No. 160/2 recounts a past battle between Wonder Woman and DR. PSYCHO ("Dr. Psycho's Revenge!").

In April 1966, Wonder Woman No. 161/1 recounts a past encounter between Wonder Woman and COUNTESS DRASKA NISHKI ("The Curse of Cleopatra!"), and Wonder Woman No. 161/2 recounts a past battle between Wonder Woman and the ANGLE MAN ("Battle Inside of a Brain!").

In May 1966, Wonder Woman No. 162/1 recounts the events surrounding Wonder Woman's acquisition of her secret identity (*see* section B, the secret identity) ("The Startling Secret of Diana Prince!"), and Wonder Woman No. 162/2 recounts a past battle between Wonder Woman and PRIME MINISTER BLIZZARD ("The Return of Minister Blizzard!").

In July 1966, Wonder Woman No. 163/1 briefly recapitulates a series of encounters between Wonder Woman and GIGANTA which originally took place in Summer 1944 ("Giganta--the Gorilla Girl!"), and Wonder Woman No. 163/2 recounts a past battle between Wonder Woman and BARONESS PAULA VON GUNTHER (here vulgarized as Baroness Paula von Gunta) ("Danger--Wonder Woman!").

In August 1966, Wonder Woman No. 164 recounts a past encounter between Wonder Woman and the ANGLE MAN ("Wonder Woman--Traitor!").

In October 1966 Wonder Woman meets the PAPER-MAN (WW No. 165/1: "Perils of the Paper-Man!") and matches wits with DR. PSYCHO (WW No. 165/2: "The Three Fantastic Faces of Wonder Woman!").

In November 1966 Wonder Woman thwarts the sinister machinations of EGG FU THE FIFTH (WW No. 166/1: "The Sinister Scheme of Egg Fu, the Fifth!").

In April 1967 Wonder Woman battles the CRIMSON CENTIPEDE (WW No. 169/1: "Wonder Woman Battles the Crimson Centipede!").

In May 1967 Wonder Woman apprehends Pete Slote (WW No. 170/1: "The Haunted Amazon!"). (*See* PSYCHO [DR.].)

In July–August 1967 Wonder Woman battles a diabolical "man-fish" (*see* MAN-FISH) (WW No. 171/1: "Terror Trap of the Demon Man-Fish!") and matches wits with MOUSE MAN (WW No. 171/2: "Menace of the Mouse Man!").

In November–December 1967, Wonder Woman No. 173/1 contains the story of an Amazon who is eager to leave Paradise Island for America ("Wonder Woman's Daring Deception!") that is almost identical to a story that appeared in a much earlier text (i.e., WW No. 51/2, Jan/Feb '52: "Wonder Woman's Strange Substitute!"); and Wonder Woman No. 173/2 contains the story of Wonder Woman's thwarting of a Martian invasion ("Earth's Last Human!") that is almost identical to a story contained in a much earlier text (i.e., WW No. 65/3, Apr '54: "The Last Amazon!").

In January–February 1968 Wonder Woman matches wits with the ANGLE MAN (WW No. 174/1: "Steve Trevor — Alias the Patriot!") and captures a gang of criminals led by a racketeer known as the King of Crime (WW No. 174/2: "Wonder Woman vs. the Air Devils!").

In March–April 1968 Wonder Woman battles an evil Wonder Woman on a mysterious "parallel world" (WW No. 175: "Wonder Woman's Evil Twin!"). (*See* TREVOR, STEVE.)

In September–October 1968 Wonder Woman apprehends ROGER SEELY (WW No. 178: "Wonder Woman's Rival").

In November–December 1968 Wonder Woman begins her search for DOCTOR CYBER (WW No. 179: "Wonder Woman's Last Battle!").

In January–February 1969 Wonder Woman presses her search for DOCTOR CYBER (WW No. 180: "A Death for Diana!").

WOOLOO ISLAND. "An American protectorate in the Pacific" which is the scene of WONDER WOMAN's battle with KING IRONSIDES in October–November 1947 (CC No. 23: "Siege of the Iron Giants").

WRIGHT, FLY. The daredevil stunt man — known professionally as the Human Fly — who is president of the Nine Lives Club, an organization "whose membership is composed solely of life-risking stuntmen!"

In May–June 1949, when the Nine Lives Club holds a meeting to nominate new members and WONDER WOMAN's name is proposed in a secret ballot, most of the club's members are disgruntled at the idea of inviting a woman to join their all-male club. Fly Wright, however, offers this suggestion: "If **Wonder Woman** can surpass the greatest stunts of our most daring members," he tells the members, "--she deserves to belong to our daredevils club!"

The members agree to Wright's proposal and invite Wonder Woman to join their club on the condition that she duplicate their most spectacular feats, unaware that Wright secretly nominated Wonder Woman himself in order to keep her busy performing daredevil stunts while he and his henchmen commit a series of crimes. Wonder Woman, however, ultimately sees through Wright's ruse, captures Wright and his cohorts, and exposes Wright's scheme to the members of the Nine Lives Club, who respond by electing Wonder Woman their new president in recognition of her exploits (WW No. 35/1: "Nine Lives Club!").

WRIGHT, SELLDOM. The misogynistic editor of *Fearless Men Magazine.* In December 1947 Wright is kidnapped by the BLUE SEAL GANG, who hope that Wright's disappearance under suspicious circumstances will mislead the police into believing that Wright is the gang's secret leader. Wright is rescued from the villains' clutches and forced to abandon his chauvinistic attitude toward women when a pair of courageous women — WONDER WOMAN and Wright's girlfriend, Chic Novelle — join forces to invade the Blue Seal Gang's hideout and take them into custody (Sen No. 72: "The Menace of the Blue Seal Gang").

WRIGHT BROTHERS, THE. American inventors and aviation pioneers — Orville (1871–1948) and Wilbur (1867–1912) — who, at Kitty Hawk, North Carolina, on December 17, 1903, achieved history's first successful powered, sustained, and controlled airplane flight, the culmination of years of experimentation with gliders and large kites. WONDER WOMAN intercepts a falling meteor threatening to smash the Wright Brothers' aircraft and disrupt the famous flight during a time-journey that she makes in October 1954 (WW No. 69/2: "The Secret Hall of Fame!").

WYNN, WANTA. A fiercely ambitious, intensely competitive student at the HOLLIDAY COLLEGE FOR WOMEN who turns to crime in an effort to satisfy her unbridled craving for wealth and social prominence. Wanta Wynn is apprehended by WONDER WOMAN in April–May 1946.

Depressed after her ineptness has caused the Holliday College basketball team to lose an important game, Wanta Wynn attempts suicide by leaping from the roof of a campus building, only to be rescued from death by Wonder Woman.

"I'm weak and puny," sobs Wanta, "when I long to be strong and powerful — like **you!**"

"I'll teach you to be strong," replies Wonder Woman, "if you promise to use your strength only for **loving** purposes."

On PARADISE ISLAND, home of the AMAZONS, Wanta undergoes a rigorous training program (*see* AMAZONS [section D, Amazon training]) and is fitted with heavy metal bracelets (*see* WONDER WOMAN [section C 2, the bracelets of submission]) and anklets of the kind worn by the Amazons. When she returns home again, Wanta's newly acquired strength and athletic prowess soon establish her as "America's outstanding woman athlete," but Wanta's basketball coach insists that she remove her Amazon bracelets and anklets while competing to avoid injuring other players, and Wanta finds herself "obsessed by jealous, greedy longing for money" whenever she removes them.

"I must have **wealth — position —** oh!" she thinks anxiously. "These terrible desires control me whenever I take off Aphrodite's bands!"

When the urge to use her Amazon training for personal gain becomes overpowering, Wanta turns to crime, but ultimately Wonder Woman apprehends her and welds the Amazon bands back onto her wrists and ankles.

"I'm **so** sorry, Wonder Woman," exclaims Wanta, now repentant, "— I couldn't **help** being bad —"

"Strong humans become ruthless self-seekers unless they're bound by **love!**" replies Wonder Woman. "You must learn on Reform Island to wear Aphrodite's bands **always!**" (CC No. 14: "The Severed Bracelets"). (*See also* TRANSFORMATION ISLAND.)

X

X (Miss). A pseudonym employed by WONDER WOMAN in October 1962 while starring in the movie *Amazon Girl* (WW No. 133/2: "Wonder Woman's Invincible Rival--Herself!"). (*See* THOMAS, T. T.)

Y

YASMINI (Princess). A Hindu princess who, from her headquarters in Cairo, operates a spy ring which provides secret information to the Nazis. From Cape Cod, where the princess's cohorts operate a clandestine broadcasting station, secret war information is transmitted to Cairo, where it is received by special receiving units concealed inside the stomachs of the princess's pet lions. WONDER WOMAN solves the mystery of how the secret messages are sent and received and apprehends Princess Yasmini, but the Hindu princess commits suicide by taking poison rather than betray her comrades in the spy ring (Sen No. 17, May '43: "The Talking Lion!").

"YELLOW MASK" GANG, THE. A gang of "international racketeers" — led by Tirza, a raven-haired femme fatale — who kidnap Myrna Dearfield, the wife of "atomic scientist" DR. ALTON DEARFIELD, in hopes of forcing her to disclose the hiding place of her husband's priceless "atom-neutralizing formula." WONDER WOMAN apprehends the "Yellow Mask" Gang in September–October 1947 with the aid of STEVE TREVOR and a courageous young orphan boy named Teasy whom the Dearfields are planning to adopt (WW No. 25/2: "Who'll Adopt Teasy?").

ZAGO (Prime Minister). The treacherous prime minister of Bellara Island. His attempt to topple the good King Terro from his throne and seize control of the island kingdom is thwarted by WONDER WOMAN.

By March–April 1952 Prime Minister Zago has set in motion an elaborate scheme to topple King Terro from his throne and seize control of Bellara Island. During a recent hunting outing, Zago surreptitiously pushed Queen Yilla, the king's wife, into a deep crater, thereby forcing the king, by the laws of Bellara Island, to either select a new queen or relinquish his throne to the prime minister.

Overcome with grief at the loss of his queen and unable to face up to the task of selecting a new one, King Terro finally agrees to let Prime Minister Zago select a new queen for him. Zago, however, imposes a series of impossible tests on all aspirants for the queenship, knowing that once all the applicants have tried to pass the tests and failed, King Terro will lose his throne by default.

While flying past Bellara Island en route to PARADISE ISLAND, however, Wonder Woman stops to rescue a young maiden who, having failed one of Zago's tests, has been callously hurled over the edge of a cliff by the prime minister's henchmen. Once the details of King Terro's plight have been explained to her, Wonder Woman decides to pass Zago's tests herself, a feat she accomplishes despite the patent unfairness of the tests and Prime Minister Zago's repeated attempts to kill her.

With the evil prime minister's scheme to seize control of the kingdom thus thwarted, Wonder Woman descends into the crater into which the villain pushed Queen Yilla and discovers that the queen is alive, stranded on a narrow ledge near the bottom of the crater. Now happily reunited, King Terro and Queen Yilla reward Wonder Woman for her exploits by crowning her queen of Bellara Island for a day (WW No. 52/1: "Her Majesty — Queen Wonder Woman!").

ZANI ISLAND. An island in the PACIFIC OCEAN which is ruled by the good PRINCE SLEEKO. It may be an American protectorate, because Comic Cavalcade No. 20 refers to it as America's "key base protecting Pacific communications," and STEVE TREVOR is placed briefly in command of the island by U.S. authorities in April–May 1947. Zani Island is the scene of WONDER WOMAN's battle with Prince Slambo, Prince Sleeko's evil half brother ("The Buddha Wishing Ring"). (*See* SLEEKO [PRINCE].)

ZARA. The lovely red-haired high priestess of the mystic Cult of the Crimson Flame, a "new religion" that has begun "sweeping the world" by Winter 1943. Its symbol is an eerie "crimson flame" that appears out of nowhere at the behest of the high priestess, hanging suspended in midair and inscribing mysterious flaming messages to cow the members of the cult — the so-called "flame slaves" — into abject obedience.

"I am the **crimson flame of life**," intones a grim voice from within the flame, "— I burn within the breasts of all who obey me! Whosoever opposes me shall be **consumed!**"

Anyone daring to oppose the cult falls mysteriously ill and dies soon afterward.

When Helene Armstrong, a U.S. Senator's daughter who has been intimately involved with the flame cult, disappears mysteriously, WONDER WOMAN, STEVE TREVOR, ETTA CANDY, and the HOLLIDAY GIRLS follow her to Arabia, site of the Crystal Temple of the Crimson Flame, the "international headquarters" of Zara and her sinister "flame forces." Ultimately, Wonder Woman and her companions defeat the flame cultists, rescue Helene

Zara and one of her flame slaves, 1943

Armstrong from their clutches, and capture Zara.

"I'm an Arab," explains Zara, "— my father sold me as a slave! Oh, how I hated heem! I swore I'd get **revenge** on men of power! **Revenge** — that ees my crimson flame!"

It was to wreak vengeance on Helene's father that Zara had had her abducted.

The much-feared "crimson flame," confesses Zara, was actually nothing more than "floating, burning, liquid hydrogen," while the voice seeming to speak from inside it was actually an illusion created with movie projector sound equipment.

"To destroy enemies," continues Zara, "I put **ideas** in zair mind, zen zay make **zemselves** sick, poor fools!" (CC No. 5: "Mystery of the Crimson Flame").

In March–April 1948 Zara escapes from TRANS-FORMATION ISLAND along with seven other villain-esses and joins them in forming VILLAINY INCOR-PORATED (WW No. 28/1–3: "Villainy Incorporated!"; "Trap of Crimson Flame"; "In the Hands of the Merciless!"). (*See* VILLAINY INCORPO-RATED.)

ZARIKAN. A faraway kingdom ruled by the good King Yuka. An arid country without aboveground water sources, Zarikan is dependent upon wind-mills to bring water to the surface from its subter-ranean waterways. Zarikan is an agrarian country whose inhabitants worship the goddess Vultura, the deity they believe responsible for guarding their waterways and assuring the abundance of their water supply. Zarikan is the scene of WONDER WOMAN's encounter with the PURPLE PRIESTESS in September-October 1947 (WW No. 25/3: "The Judgment of Goddess Vultura").

The kingdom of Zarikan described in Wonder Woman No. 25/3 is probably modeled after Mexi-co's Yucatan Peninsula. Like Zarikan, the Yucatan Peninsula is a region without aboveground water sources which is dependent upon windmills to bring water to the surface from underground sources. The name of Zarikan's ruler, King Yuka, is strongly suggestive of Yucatan, and the name of its goddess, Vultura, has the flavor of pre-Columbian deity-names as they are usually represented in comic books.

ZAVIA. A beautiful red-haired ski instructress who is the "vicious" leader of a gang of kidnappers responsible for the recent abduction of the chil-dren of several wealthy men. Zavia and her co-horts are apprehended by WONDER WOMAN, with the aid of STEVE TREVOR, in January 1946 (Sen No. 49: "The Mystery of Lake Iceberg").

Z-ONE. A notorious master spy who, sometime in the recent past, was accidentally killed by the very time bomb with which he had intended to destroy WONDER WOMAN and STEVE TREVOR. In order to apprehend Z-One's three lieutenants, none of whom knows Z-One's true identity or is aware that he has perished, Wonder Woman allows herself to be publicly identified as Z-One and tried and con-victed of espionage so that she can "escape" from the authorities and, posing as Z-One, draw the three fugitive spy-lieutenants into the open. Ulti-mately, Wonder Woman's ruse succeeds: one by one, as Z-One's cohorts contact her in the belief that she is their leader, Wonder Woman appre-hends them all (WW No. 43/1, Sep/Oct '50: "The Amazing Spy Ring Mystery").

ZOOL (Prof.). A member of the faculty of the HOLLIDAY COLLEGE FOR WOMEN, and a leading re-searcher in the field of human evolution.

In Summer 1944 Prof. Zool unveils his "elec-tronic evolutionizer," a miraculous device of his own invention with which he successfully evolves the female gorilla GIGANTA into a beautiful "cave girl." Before long, however, the "evolution ma-chine" has gone completely haywire, plunging WONDER WOMAN, STEVE TREVOR, ETTA CANDY, the HOLLIDAY GIRLS, Giganta, and Prof. Zool himself into a series of hair-raising adventures in the evo-lutionary past (WW No. 9/1–3: "Evolution Goes Haywire!"; "The Freed Captive"; no title). (*See* GIGANTA.)

In March–April 1948 Prof. Zool's laboratory is invaded by Giganta and QUEEN CLEA, who use the professor's evolution machine to transform Zool and the Holliday Girls into bizarre creatures with the heads of human beings and the bodies of gorillas (WW No. 28/3: "In the Hands of the Mer-ciless!"). (*See* VILLAINY INCORPORATED.)

Prof. Zool, 1944

ZOXAB. An evil genie who is defeated by WONDER WOMAN in September–October 1953.

When QUEEN HIPPOLYTE lapses into a mysteri-ous "death-like sleep" from which the AMAZONS are unable to awaken her, Wonder Woman notices that Hippolyte is wearing a strange ruby ring which the queen found in the water off PARADISE ISLAND only the day before. Seeing that the ruby ring bears the seal of the genie Zoxab, Wonder Woman flies to his domain — a "flat sandy island" called Bourabia, lying a great distance from Paradise Island "across uncharted seas" — only to be taken captive by the villainous giant genie.

Gloating over his triumph, Zoxab explains that he has placed Bourabia's rightful ruler, Princess Aranee, "in an eternal sleep--so I may rule her kingdom with terror--instead of kindness and love! Ho! Ho! Ho!"

Since being touched by the magic ruby ring would awaken the princess, Zoxab threw it into the sea to ensure that no one would ever be able to rescue her, but Wonder Woman escapes from the evil genie and defeats him, thereby stripping him forever of his magical powers. After awakening Princess Aranee with a touch of the ruby ring, Wonder Woman returns to Paradise Island, where she uses the magic ring to awaken Queen Hippolyte (WW No. 61/2: "Prisoners of the Ruby Ring!").

SHOWCASE
PRESENTS

OVER 500 PAGES OF DC'S CLASSIC HEROES AND STORIES PRESENTED IN EACH VOLUME!

GREEN LANTERN
VOL. 1

SUPERMAN
VOL. 1

SUPERMAN
VOL. 2

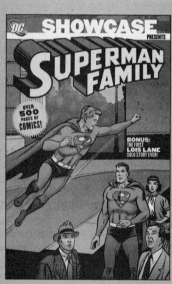

SUPERMAN FAMILY
VOL. 1

JONAH HEX
VOL. 1

METAMORPHO
VOL. 1

SEARCH THE GRAPHIC NOVELS SECTION OF
WWW.DCCOMICS.COM
FOR ART AND INFORMATION ON ALL OF OUR BOOKS!